MICROECONOMICS

Seventh Edition

William Boyes
Arizona State University

Michael Melvin
Arizona State University

Houghton Mifflin Company   BOSTON   NEW YORK

To Melissa, Katie, and Lindsey —W. B.

To Bettina, Jason, Jeremy, and Anna —M. M.

Vice President, Executive Publisher: George Hoffman
Senior Sponsoring Editor: Ann West
Senior Marketing Manager: Mike Schenk
Marketing Coordinator: Erin Lane
Senior Development Editor: Amy Whitaker
Editorial Assistant: Diane Akerman
Senior Project Editor: Tamela Ambush
Editorial Assistant: Joanna Carter
Art and Design Manager: Gary Crespo
Cover Design Manager: Anne S. Katzeff
Senior Photo Editor: Jennifer Meyer Dare
Composition Buyer: Chuck Dutton

Cover image © Ralph Mercer: photo-illustrator, ralphmercer.com

Printed in the U.S.A.

Library of Congress Control Number: 2006938375

Instructor's exam copy
ISBN-10: 0-618-83326-9
ISBN-13: 978-0-618-83326-9

For orders, use student text ISBNs:
ISBN-10: 0-618-76126-8
ISBN-13: 978-0-618-76126-5

1 2 3 4 5 6 7 8 9 —DOW— 11 10 09 08 07

Contents

chapter 5

The Public Sector 98

part two PRODUCT MARKET BASICS

chapter 6

Elasticity: Demand and Supply 120

appendix to chapter 6
Calculating Elasticity   138

chapter 7
Consumer Choice   140

appendix to chapter 7
Indifference Analysis   162

part four   RESOURCE MARKETS

part six   ISSUES IN INTERNATIONAL TRADE AND FINANCE

Suggested Outlines for One-Term Courses

Macroeconomic Emphasis	Microeconomic Emphasis	Balanced Micro-Macro
1. Economics: The World Around You	1. Economics: The World Around You	1. Economics: The World Around You
2. Choice, Opportunity Costs, and Specialization	2. Choice, Opportunity Costs, and Specialization	2. Choice, Opportunity Costs, and Specialization
3. Markets, Demand and Supply, and the Price System	3. Markets, Demand and Supply, and the Price System	3. Markets, Demand and Supply, and the Price System
4. The Market System and the Private Sector	4. The Market System and the Private Sector	4. The Market System and the Private Sector
5. The Public Sector	5. The Public Sector	5. The Public Sector
6. National Income Accounting	20. Elasticity: Demand and Supply	6. National Income Accounting
7. An Introduction to the Foreign Exchange Market and the Balance of Payments	21. Consumer Choice	7. An Introduction to the Foreign Exchange Market and the Balance of Payments.
8. Unemployment and Inflation	22. Supply: The Costs of Doing Business	8. Unemployment and Inflation
9. Macroeconomic Equilibrium: Aggregate Demand and Supply	23. Profit Maximization	9. Macroeconomic Equilibrium: Aggregate Demand and Supply
10. Aggregate Expenditures	24. Perfect Competition	12. Fiscal Policy
11. Income and Expenditures Equilibrium	25. Monopoly	13. Money and Banking
12. Fiscal Policy	26. Monopolistic Competition and Oligopoly	14. Monetary Policy
13. Money and Banking	27. Antitrust and Regulation	20. Elasticity: Demand and Supply
14. Monetary Policy	28. Government and Market Failure	21. Consumer Choice
15. Macroeconomic Policy: Trade-offs, Expectations, Credibility, and Sources of Business Cycles	29. Resource Markets	22. Supply: The Costs of Doing Business
16. Macroeconomic Viewpoints: New Keynesian, Monetarist, and New Classical	30. The Labor Market	23. Profit Maximization
17. Economic Growth	31. Financial Markets: Institutions and Recent Events	29. Resource Markets
18. Development Economics	32. The Land Market and Natural Resources	34. Income Distribution, Poverty, and Government Policy
19. Globalization	33. Aging, Social Security, and Health Care	35. World Trade Equilibrium
35. World Trade Equilibrium	34. Income Distribution, Poverty, and Government Policy	
36. International Trade Restrictions	35. World Trade Equilibrium	
37. Exchange Rates and Financial Links Between Countries	36. International Trade Restrictions	

Preface

In the first edition of *Microeconomics*, we integrated a global perspective with traditional economic principles to give students a framework to understand the globally developing economic world. Events since then have made this approach even more imperative. In the 1990s, the Soviet Union disintegrated and newly independent nations emerged. Much of Latin America was turning toward free markets and away from government controls. But by 2005, several of these nations were turning away from free markets. Hugo Chavez and Eva Morales were guiding Venezuela and Bolivia away from free markets and toward government-run and -controlled economies. Alexander Putin was driving Russia toward more government control. Other events were making the world seem very small: North Korea was testing nuclear weapons, Somalia was embroiled in a civil war, terrorism was prevalent in nations around the world, and much of Africa remained mired in poverty. Students and instructors have embraced the idea that the economies of countries are interrelated and that this should be made clear in the study of economics. *Microeconomics* gives students the tools they need to make connections between the economic principles they learn and the now-global world they live in.

In this edition, we continue to refine and improve the text as a teaching and learning instrument while expanding its international base by updating and adding examples related to global economics.

Changes in the Seventh Edition

The seventh edition of *Microeconomics* has been thoroughly updated and refined. A detailed account of all the additions, deletions, and modifications can be found in the Transition Guide in the *Instructor's Resource Manual* at the Boyes/Melvin Online Teaching Center.

Revised Microeconomic Coverage

The principal objective of the microeconomic material is to enable students to see the forest while wandering around in the trees; to learn the fundamentals while seeing their applicability to current events. The chapter on elasticity has been significantly revised in order to focus on important concepts and applications. Calculations of arc and point elasticities and a greater emphasis on applications of elasticity have been assigned to

an appendix. The discussion of regulation has been expanded to include intellectual property rights. Financial markets have been incorporated into the chapter on capital markets so that both physical and financial capital are discussed.

Successful Features Retained from the Sixth Edition

In addition to the considerable updating and revising we've done for the seventh edition, there are several features preserved from the previous edition that we think instructors will find interesting.

Enhanced Student Relevance

With all of the demands on today's students, it's no wonder that they resist spending time on a subject unless they see how the material relates to them and how they will benefit from mastering it. We incorporate features throughout the text that show economics as the relevant and necessary subject we know it to be.

Real-World Examples Students are rarely intrigued by unknown manufacturers or service companies. Our text talks about people and firms that students recognize. We describe business decisions made by McDonald's and Wal-Mart, and by the local video store or café. We discuss standards of living around the world, comparing the poverty of sub-Saharan Africa to the wealth of the industrial nations. We discuss the policies of George W. Bush and other world leaders. We talk about political, environmental, and other social issues. These examples grab students' interest. Reviewers have repeatedly praised the use of novel examples to convey economic concepts.

Economic Insight Boxes These brief boxes use contemporary material from current periodicals and journals to illustrate or extend the discussion in the chapter. By reserving interesting but more technical sidelights for boxes, we lessen the likelihood that students will be confused or distracted by issues that are not critical to understanding the chapter. By including excerpts from articles, we help students move from theory to real-world examples. And by including plenty of contemporary issues, we guarantee that students will see how economics relates to their own lives.

Economically Speaking Boxes The objective of the principles course is to teach students how to translate to the real world the predictions that come out of economic models, and to translate real-world events into an economic model in order to analyze and understand what lies behind the events. The Economically Speaking boxes present students with examples of this kind of analysis. Students read an article that appears on the left-hand page of a two-page spread at the end of each chapter. The commentary on the right-hand page shows how the facts and events in the article translate into a specific economic model or idea, thereby demonstrating the relevance of the theory. Nearly two-thirds of the articles and commentaries are new to the seventh edition, and cover such current events as U.S. trade with China, the record U.S. trade deficit, drug wars in Mexico, illegal immigration, Venezuela's redistribution of wealth, high gasoline prices, and budget deficits in the European Union.

Global Business Insight Boxes These boxes link business events and developments around the world to the economic concepts discussed in the main text of the chapters. A map is used to highlight the area of the world under discussion and to provide a geographic context for the economic issues examined. Topics include such basic micro- and macroeconomic issues as global competition, resource pricing, and foreign exchange.

An Effective and Proven System of Teaching and Learning Aids

This text is designed to make teaching easier by enhancing student learning. Tested pedagogy motivates students, emphasizes clarity, reinforces relationships, simplifies review, and fosters critical thinking. And, as we have discovered from reviewer and user feedback, this pedagogy works.

In-Text Referencing System Sections are numbered for easy reference and to reinforce hierarchies of ideas. Numbered section heads serve as an outline of the chapter, allowing instructors flexibility in assigning reading, and making it easy for students to find topics to review. Each item in the key terms list and summary at the end of the chapter refers students back to the appropriate section number.

The section numbering system appears throughout the Boyes/Melvin ancillary package; the *Test Banks, Study Guides,* and *Instructor's Resource Manual* are all organized according to the same system.

Fundamental Questions These questions help to organize the chapter and highlight those issues that are critical to understanding. Each fundamental question also appears in the margin next to the related text discussion and, with brief answers, in the chapter summaries. A fuller discussion of and answer to each of these questions may be found in the *Study Guides*

that are available as supplements to this text. The fundamental questions also serve as one of several criteria used to categorize questions in the *Test Banks.*

Preview This motivating lead-in sets the stage for the chapter. Much more so than a road map, it helps students identify real-world issues that relate to the concepts that will be presented.

Recaps Briefly listing the main points covered, a recap appears at the end of each major section within a chapter. Students are able to quickly review what they have just read before going on to the next section.

Summary The summary at the end of each chapter is organized along two dimensions. The primary organizational device is the list of fundamental questions. A brief synopsis of the discussion that helps students to answer those questions is arranged by section below each of the questions. Students are encouraged to create their own links among topics as they keep in mind the connections between the big picture and the details that make it up.

Comments Found in the text margins, these comments highlight especially important concepts, point out common mistakes, and warn students of common pitfalls. They alert students to parts of the discussion that they should read with particular care.

Key Terms Key terms appear in bold type in the text. They also appear with their definition in the margin and are listed at the end of the chapter for easy review. All key terms are included in the Glossary at the end of the text.

Friendly Appearance

Microeconomics can be intimidating; this is why we've tried to keep *Microeconomics* looking friendly and inviting. The one-column design and ample white space in this text provide an accessible backdrop. More than 150 figures rely on well-developed pedagogy and consistent use of color to reinforce understanding. Striking colors were chosen to enhance readability and provide visual interest. Specific curves were assigned specific colors, and families of curves were assigned related colors.

Annotations on the art point out areas of particular concern or importance. Students can see exactly which part of a graph illustrates a shortage or a surplus, a change in consumption, or a consumer surplus. Tables that provide data from which graphs are plotted are paired with their graphs. Where appropriate, color is used to show correlations between the art and the table, and captions clearly explain what is shown in the figures and link them to the text discussion.

The color photographs not only provide visual images but make the text appealing. These vibrant photos tell stories as well as illustrate concepts, and lengthy captions explain what is in the photos, again drawing connections between the images and the text discussion.

Thoroughly International Coverage

Students understand that they live in a global economy; they can hardly shop, watch the news, or read a newspaper without stumbling upon this basic fact. International examples are presented in every chapter but are not merely added on, as is the case with many other texts. We introduce international effects on demand and supply in Chapter 3 incorporating the international sector into the economic models and applications wherever appropriate thereafter. Because the international content is incorporated from the beginning, students develop a far more realistic picture of the national economy; as a result, they don't have to alter their thinking to allow for international factors later on. The three chapters that focus on international topics at the end of the text allow those instructors who desire to delve much more deeply into international issues to do so.

The global applicability of economics is emphasized by *using traditional economic concepts to explain international economic events and using international events to illustrate economic concepts that have traditionally been illustrated with domestic examples.* Instructors need not know the international institutions in order to introduce international examples, since the topics through which they are addressed are familiar; for example, price ceilings, price discrimination, expenditures on resources, marginal productivity theory, and others.

Unique international elements of microeconomic coverage in the text include:

- The introduction of exchange rates as a determinant of demand and supply in Chapter 3
- Extensive analyses of the effects of trade barriers, tariffs, and quotas
- An examination of strategic trade
- An examination of dumping as a special case of price discrimination
- The identification of problems faced by multinational firms
- A comparison of behavior, results, and institutions among nations with respect to consumption, production, firm size, government policies toward business, labor markets, health care, income distribution, environmental policy, and other issues

Modern Microeconomic Organization and Content

Instructors often face a quandary when teaching microeconomic material. They want students to understand the basic theories of economics and the powerful intuition that thinking like an economist can provide, but they also want to enlist students' attention with real-life, current issues. In the seventh edition of *Microeconomics,* theory is never far away from applications. Students can see why environmental issues such as pollution and the razing of rain forests occur and can learn about the costs and benefits of various proposed solutions to these problems. Students can see why incomes are unequal within a country and among countries and can learn about the costs and benefits of attempting to reduce inequality. Students can see why collusion occurs among competing firms and what the costs and benefits are of minimizing such behavior through antitrust action or regulation.

Part Two presents basic concepts such as elasticity, consumer behavior, and costs of production. Parts Three and Four both begin with overview chapters (Chapter 9 on profit maximization and Chapter 15 on resource markets). These overviews give students a chance to look at the big picture before delving into details they often find confusing. Chapter 9, for instance, gives students an intuitive overview of market structures before they explore each type of structure in more detail in succeeding chapters. Chapter 9 lightens the load that the more detailed chapters have to bear, easing students into the market-structure material. Traditional topics are covered in the separate market structure chapters, Chapters 10 to 12, but the coverage is also modern, including such topics as strategic behavior, price discrimination, nonprice competition, and the economics of information. Having fought their way first through the cost curves and then the market structures, students often complain that they do not see the relevance of that material to real-world situations. The intuitive overview chapter alleviates some of that frustration.

A Complete Teaching and Learning Package

In today's market no book is complete without a full complement of ancillaries. Those instructors who face huge lecture classes find good PowerPoint slides and a large variety of reliable test questions to be critical instructional tools. Those who teach online in distance or hybrid courses need reliable course management systems with built-in assignments and resource materials. Other instructors want plenty of options available to their students for review, application, and remediation. All of these needs are addressed in the Boyes/Melvin supplements package. And to foster the development of consistent teaching and study strategies, the ancillaries pick up pedagogical features of the text—like the fundamental questions—wherever appropriate.

Support for Instructors

Instructor's Resource Manual (IRM)

Patricia Diane Nipper has produced a manual that will streamline preparation for both new and experienced faculty. Preliminary sections cover class administration, alternative syllabi, and an introduction to the use of cooperative learning in teaching the principles of economics.

The *IRM* also contains a detailed chapter-by-chapter review of all the changes made in the seventh edition. This Transition Guide should help instructors more easily move from the use of the sixth edition to this new edition.

Each chapter of the *IRM* contains an Overview that describes the content and unique features of the chapter and the Objectives that students will need to master in order to succeed with later chapters; the chapter's fundamental questions and key terms; a lecture outline with teaching strategies—general techniques and guidelines, essay topics, and other hints to enliven classes; opportunities for discussion; answers to every end-of-chapter exercise; answers to *Study Guide* homework questions; and active learning exercises.

Testing Materials

Printed Test Banks   Four separate Test Banks for *Macroeconomics* and *Microeconomics* revised and edited by Chin-Chyuan Tai of Averett University, are available with the seventh edition of *Economics*, including new Alternate Micro and Macro Test Banks that can be used to vary questions in different semesters. In all, more than 8,000 test items, approximately 30 percent of which are new to this edition, provide a wealth of material for classroom testing. Features include:

- Multiple choice, true/false, and essay questions in every chapter
- Questions new to this edition marked for easy identification
- An increased number of analytical, applied, and graphical questions
- The identification of all test items according to topic, question type (factual, interpretive, or applied), level of difficulty, and applicable fundamental question

HM Testing CD-ROM   HM Testing—powered by *Diploma*™—is available to help instructors quickly create tests from the more than 8,000 test bank items included in the four printed test banks. Questions can be chosen according to a variety of selection criteria, including random selection. The program prints graphs as well as the text part of each question. Instructors can scramble the answer choices, edit questions, add their own questions to the pool, and customize their exams in various other ways. HM Testing provides a complete testing solution, including classroom administration and online testing features in addition to test generation. This program is available for Windows and Macintosh users.

Online Teaching Center

The Boyes/Melvin seventh edition Online Teaching Center provides a rich store of teaching resources for instructors. Instructors will need a username and password (available from their Houghton Mifflin sales representative) to get onto the password-protected parts of the site. The Online Teaching Center includes a variety of support materials to help you organize, plan, and deliver your lectures, assign and grade homework, and stay up-to-date with current economics news. Here you'll find a thoroughly updated set of **multimedia PowerPoint** slides covering key points in each chapter, with graphs, charts, and photos. Solutions to end-of-chapter exercises, discussion questions, a supplementary set of problems (with solutions) paralleling those offered at the end of each chapter are also found here. Timely *Economic News You Can Use* news links prepared by John Min from Northern Virginia Community College are updated continuously throughout the week to provide current economic news that you can use in the classroom to illustrate key economic principles. Also included on the instructor site are multiple-choice questions customized for Classroom Response Systems (CRS) for reviewing key content in the student text.

Course Management Systems (CMS)

Eduspace and Other CMS   The Eduspace® (powered by Blackboard®) online learning tool pairs the widely recognized resources of Blackboard with quality, text-specific content. Inside the Boyes/Melvin, *Microeconomics*, Seventh Edition Eduspace course, instructors will find a set of homework assignments and quizzes for each chapter. The homework is based on the end-of-chapter exercises from the text, adapted for automatic grading. Chapter quizzes provide a quick way to gauge student understanding of their reading. Instructors can also create their own tests from pools of questions corresponding to each chapter and section of the seventh-edition textbook.

Within the "Learn on Your Own" section of their Eduspace course, students can choose from a variety of resources aimed at helping them review, apply, and practice. **Interactive Tutorials** based on each chapter's content, audio (MP3) files of chapter summaries and quizzes, Flashcards, and links to **Smarthinking® Online Tutoring Service** and the Online Study Center provide a wealth of review and remediation options. Smarthinking gives students access to trained, qualified "e-structors" from wherever students are, whenever they need help. Students may interact live online with an experienced Smarthinking "e-structor" during peak study hours or send an email question at other times which will be answered within 24 hours. Smarthinking provides state-of-the-art communication tools, such as chat technology and virtual white-boards designed for easy rendering of economic formulas and graphs.

In addition, a **multimedia ebook** is available inside the Eduspace course for quick access to text content and links to relevant tutorials, Associated Press Interactives, and review activities. For instructors who use other course management systems (such as Blackboard and WebCT®) to manage their online or distance courses, much of the text-specific content included in Eduspace is available in course cartridge form.

Aplia Online Learning Platform Founded in 2000 by economist and professor Paul Romer in an effort to improve his own economics courses at Stanford, Aplia is the leading online learning platform for economics. Houghton Mifflin has partnered with Aplia to provide a rich online experience that gets students involved and gives instructors the tools and support they need. The integrated Aplia courses offered for Boyes/Melvin include math review/tutorials, news analyses, and online homework assignments correlated to the relevant Boyes/ Melvin text. In addition, a digital version of the text is embedded in the course, to make it easy for students to access the text when completing assignments. Instructors should consult their Houghton Mifflin sales representative for more information on how to use Aplia with this text.

Support for Students

Study Guides

Janet L. Wolcutt and James E. Clark of the Center for Economic Education at Wichita State University have revised the *Macroeconomics* and *Microeconomics Study Guides* to give students the practice they need to master this course. Initially received by students and instructors with great enthusiasm, the guides maintain their warm and lively style to keep students on the right track. Each chapter includes:

- Fundamental questions, answered in one or several paragraphs and the list of Key Terms.
- A Quick Check Quiz, organized by section, so any wrong answers send the student directly to the relevant material in the text.
- Practice Questions and Problems, also organized by section, include a variety of question types to test understanding of concepts and skills.
- Thinking About and Applying . . . uses newspaper headlines or other real-life applications to test students' ability to reason in economic terms.
- A Homework page at the end of each chapter with five questions that can be answered on the sheet and turned in for grading.
- Sample tests consisting of 25 to 50 questions similar to *Test Bank* questions to help students determine whether they are prepared for exams.
- Answers to all questions except the Homework questions. Students are referred back to the relevant sections in the main text for each question.

Online Study Center

The Online Study Center lets students continue their learning at their own pace with ACE practice quizzes, chapter summaries, Internet exercises, and chapter and full-text glossaries, among other resources.

"Your Guide to an 'A'" New copies of Boyes/ Melvin, *Microeconomics*, Seventh Edition come packaged with a passkey providing access to a set of online premium resources which focus on helping students improve their grade. "Your Guide to an 'A'" material includes ACE+ self-test quizzes, Flashcards, crossword puzzles and games, and audio (MP3) chapter summaries and quizzes. **Interactive tutorials** provide an opportunity for students to review concepts and models for each text chapter and to test themselves on what they have learned. In each tutorial, students are guided through a series of interactive lessons that allow them to change data and immediately see how curves shift. The simulation component of the software includes over 70 years of data on more than 20 key economic indicators, allowing students to plot data, compare various measurement instruments, and print out the results in table or graph form.

Acknowledgments

Writing a text of this scope is a challenge that requires the expertise and efforts of many. We are grateful to our friends and colleagues who have so generously given their time, creativity, and insight to help us create a text that best meets the needs of today's students.

We'd especially like to thank the many reviewers of *Microeconomics* listed on the following pages, and in particular, the members of the Boyes/Melvin Advisory Board, who weighed in on key issues throughout the development of the seventh edition. Their comments have proved invaluable in revising this text. Unsolicited feedback from current users has also been greatly appreciated.

We would also like to thank James E. Clark and Janet L. Wolcutt of Wichita State University for their continued contributions to the *Study Guides* and Patricia Diane Nipper of Southside Virginia Community College for her work on the seventh and previous editions of the *Instructor's Resource Manual*. Thanks also to Chin-Chyuan Tai of Averett University for his intensive work on the *Test Banks* and for his attention to the accuracy of the text. We want to thank the many people at Houghton Mifflin Company who devoted countless hours to making this text the best it could be, including Amy Whitaker, Paula Kmetz, Charline Lake, Tamela Ambush, Ann Schroeder, Brett Pasinella, and Joanne Butler. We are grateful for their enthusiasm, expertise, and energy. Our editor, Ann West, deserves special recognition for her role in directing the project, contributing to content, and structural ideas. We thoroughly enjoy working with her.

Finally, we wish to thank our families and friends. The inspiration they provided through the conception and development of this book cannot be measured but certainly was essential.

Our students at Arizona State University continue to help us improve the text through each edition; their many questions have given us invaluable insight into how best to present this intriguing subject. It is our hope that this textbook will bring a clear understanding of economic thought to many other students as well. We welcome any feedback for improvements.

W. B.   M. M.

Reviewers

Boyes/Melvin Advisory Board

1

Economics: The World Around You

? **Fundamental Questions**

1. Why study economics?

2. What is economics?

3. What is the economic way of thinking?

Americans today are more educated than ever before. According to the 2000 Census, 30.7 percent of Americans aged 25 and older hold a college (bachelor's or associate's) degree, whereas 20 years ago, only 19 percent of Americans held a similar degree. Nearly 15.5 million Americans (5 percent of the population) are currently attending college, and over 50 percent of Americans aged 18 to 22 are currently enrolled in a degree program.

Why is the rate of college attendance so high? College has not gotten any cheaper—indeed, the direct expenses associated with college have risen much more rapidly than average income. Perhaps it is because college is more valuable today than it was in the past. In the 1990s, technological change and increased international trade placed a premium on a college education; more and more jobs required

the skills acquired in college. As a result, the wage disparity between college-educated and non-college-educated workers rose fairly rapidly in the 1990s. Those with a college degree could expect to make about 45 percent more than those without a college degree. Since 2001, however, this differential has actually declined. Outsourcing of skilled jobs to China and India may be part of the explanation, and a large supply of college workers may have kept wages from rising. The number of college-trained workers in the United States has grown by 32 percent over the past 10 years, compared with only an 8 percent rise for all other education levels. Still, even though the differential has been declining, college-educated people earn nearly twice as much as people without college degrees over their lifetimes.

Why are you attending college? Perhaps you've never really given it a great deal of thought—your family always just assumed that college was a necessary step after high school; perhaps you analyzed the situation and decided that college was better than the alternatives. Whichever approach you took, you were practicing economics. You were examining alternatives and making choices. This is what economics is about. ▦

1. Why study economics?

1. Why Study Economics?

Why are you studying economics? Is it because you are required to, because you have an interest in it, because you are looking for a well-paying job, or because you want to do something to help others? All of these are valid reasons. The college degree is important to your future living standards; economics is a fascinating subject, as you will see; an economics degree can lead to a good job; and understanding economics can help policymakers, charities, and individuals design better ways to help the unfortunate.

1.a. The Value of a Degree

What is the difference between a high school diploma and a medical degree? About $3.2 million (U.S.), says the U.S. Census Bureau. Someone whose education does not go beyond high school and who works full-time can expect to earn about $1.2 million between the ages of 25 and 64. Graduating from college and earning an advanced degree translate into much higher lifetime earnings: an estimated $4.4 million for doctors, lawyers, and others with professional degrees; $2.5 million for those with a master's degree; and $2.1 million for college graduates.

Putting money into a four-year college education turns out to be a better financial investment than putting the same money into the stock market. The rate of return on the money spent to earn a bachelor's degree is 12 percent per year, compared with the long-run average annual return on stocks of 7 percent. Despite the high return on investment, just 30 percent of the American adults have a college degree. In comparison, more than 50 percent of Americans invest in the stock market, according to the American Shareholders Association.

In the 1970s, when the information age was young, kids from poorer, less educated families were catching up to kids from more affluent families when it came to earning college degrees. But now the gap between rich and poor is widening. Students in the poorest quarter of the population have an 8.6 percent chance of getting a college degree, whereas students in the top quarter have a 74.9 percent chance. The difference between being college-educated and not extends to more than just income. Divorce rates for college grads are plummeting, but they are not for everyone else. The divorce rate for high school grads is now twice as high as that of college grads. High school grads are twice as likely to smoke as college grads, they are much less likely to exercise, and they are likely to live shorter and less healthy lives.

Once you choose to go to college, how do you choose what to study? A bachelor's degree in economics prepares you for a career in any number of occupations—in business, finance, banking, the nonprofit sector, journalism, international relations, education, or government. Graduates find positions at investment banking companies and public utilities, in real estate and international relations, in government and private organizations. An economics degree is also excellent preparation for graduate study—in law, finance, business, economics, government, public administration, environmental studies, health-care administration, labor relations, urban planning, diplomacy, and other fields.

1.b. What Is Economics?

Economists are concerned with why the world is what it is. The Soviet Union collapsed, setting countries throughout eastern Europe and Asia free, because of economics. The nations of Latin America are struggling with progress and development because of economics. It is estimated that somewhere between 11 and 20 million people live in the United States illegally, and they do so because of economics. General Motors loses $4 billion and millions of workers worry that their jobs and pension plans may disappear because of economics. In fact, every issue in the news today concerns economics. It is a broad, fascinating field of study that deals with every aspect of life.

Economics is often counterintuitive. In fact, economics is probably best defined as the study of unintended consequences. When you study economics, you learn that there are costs to everything—"there is no free lunch." This is the logic of economics that those who have not studied economics may fail to understand.

Your study of economics will be interesting and challenging. It will challenge some beliefs that you now hold. It will also help you build skills that will be of value to you in your life and in whatever occupation you choose.

Why do the citizens of different countries have different standards of living? Why is the difference between rich and poor much greater in emerging nations than it is in the industrial nations? Answers to questions like these emerge in your study of economics. In this photo, a shantytown is shown next to new, modern apartment buildings and other structures in the Philippines.

2. The Definition of Economics _____

What is economics? It is the study of how scarce resources are allocated among unlimited wants. People have unlimited wants—they always want more goods and services than they have or can purchase with their incomes; they want more time; they want more love or support or health. Whether they are wealthy or poor, what they have is never enough. Since people do not have everything they want, they have to make choices. The choices they make and the manner in which these choices are made explain much of why the real world is what it is.

2.a. Scarcity

Scarcity is the foundation of economics—without it, there would be no need to study allocation. Everyone would have everything that he or she wants. **Scarcity** of something means that there is not enough of that item to satisfy everyone who wants it. Any item that costs something is scarce. If it were not scarce, it would be free, and you could have as much as you wanted without paying for it. Anything with a price on it is called an **economic good**. An economic good refers to *goods and services*—where goods are physical products, such as books or food, and services are nonphysical products, such as haircuts or golf lessons.

2.a.1. Free Goods, Economic Bads, and Resources

If there is enough of an item to satisfy wants, even at a zero price, the item is said to be a **free good**. It is difficult to think of examples of free goods. At one time people referred to air as free, but with air pollution control devices and other costly activities directed toward the maintenance of air quality standards, "clean" air, at least, is not a free good.

An **economic bad** is anything that you would pay to get rid of. It is not so hard to think of examples of bads: pollution, garbage, and disease fit the description.

Some goods are used to produce other goods. For instance, to make chocolate chip cookies, we need flour, sugar, chocolate chips, butter, our own labor, and an oven. To distinguish between the ingredients of a good and the good itself, we call the ingredients **resources**. (Resources are also called **factors of production** and **inputs**; the terms are interchangeable.) The ingredients of the cookies are the resources, and the cookies are the goods.

Economists have classified resources into three categories: land, labor, and capital.

1. **Land** includes all natural resources, such as minerals, timber, and water, as well as the land itself.

2. **Labor** refers to the physical and intellectual services of people, including the training, education, and abilities of the individuals in a society.

3. **Capital** refers to products such as machinery and equipment that are used in production. You will often hear the term *capital* used to describe the financial backing for some project or the stocks and bonds used to finance some business. This common usage is not incorrect, but it should be distinguished from the physical entity—the machinery and equipment and the buildings, warehouses, and factories. Thus we refer to stocks and bonds as *financial capital* and to the physical entity as capital.

People obtain income by selling their resources or the use of their resources. Owners of land receive *rent*; people who provide labor services are paid *wages*; and owners of capital receive *interest*.

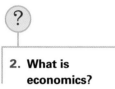

2. What is economics?

scarcity: the shortage that exists when less of something is available than is wanted at a zero price

economic good: any item that is scarce

free good: a good for which there is no scarcity

economic bad: any item for which we would pay to have less

resources, factors of production, or **inputs:** goods used to produce other goods, i.e., land, labor, and capital

land: all natural resources, such as minerals, timber, and water, as well as the land itself

labor: the physical and intellectual services of people, including the training, education, and abilities of the individuals in a society

capital: products such as machinery and equipment that are used in production

The income that resource owners acquire from selling the use of their resources provides them with the ability to buy goods and services. And producers use the money received from selling their goods to pay for the resource services.

2.b. Choices

Scarcity means that people have to make choices. People don't have everything they want, and they do not have the time or the money to purchase everything they want. When people choose some things, they have to give up, or forgo, other things. *Economics is the study of how people choose to use their scarce resources to attempt to satisfy their unlimited wants.*

2.c. Rational Self-Interest

rational self-interest: the means by which people choose the options that give them the greatest amount of satisfaction

Rational self-interest is the term that economists use to describe how people make choices. It means that people will make the choices that, at the time and with the information they have at their disposal, will give them the greatest amount of satisfaction.

You chose to attend college, although many in your age group chose not to attend. All of you made rational choices based on what you perceived was in your best interest. How could it be in your best interest to do one thing and in another person's best interest to do exactly the opposite? Each person has unique goals and attitudes and faces different costs. Although your weighing of the alternatives came down on the side of attending college, other people weighed similar alternatives and came down on the side of not attending college. Both decisions were rational because in both cases the individual compared alternatives and selected the option that the *individual* thought was in his or her best interest.

It is important to note that rational self-interest depends on the information at hand and the individual's perception of what is in his or her best interest. People will make different choices even when they have the same information. Even though the probability of death in an accident is nearly 20 percent less if seat belts are worn, many people choose not to use them. Are these people rational? The answer is yes. Perhaps they do not want their clothes wrinkled, or perhaps seat belts are just too inconvenient, or perhaps they think the odds of getting in an accident are just too small to worry about. Whatever the reason, these people are choosing the option that at the time gives them the greatest satisfaction. *This is rational self-interest.* Economists sometimes use the term *bounded rationality* to emphasize the point that people do not have perfect knowledge or perfect insight. In this book we simply use the term *rational* to refer to the comparison of costs and benefits.

Economists think that most of the time most human beings are weighing alternatives, looking at costs and benefits, and making decisions in a way that they believe makes them better off. This is not to say that economists look upon human beings as androids who lack feelings and are only able to carry out complex calculations like a computer. Rather, economists believe that people's feelings and attitudes enter into their comparisons of alternatives and help determine how people decide that something is in their best interest.

Human beings are self-interested, *not selfish.* People do contribute to charitable organizations and help others; people do make individual sacrifices because those sacrifices benefit their families or people that they care about; soldiers do risk their lives to defend their country. All these acts are made in the name of rational self-interest.

RECAP	1. Scarcity exists when people want more of an item than exists at a zero price.
	2. Goods are produced with resources (also called factors of production and inputs). Economists have classified resources into three categories: land, labor, and capital.
	3. Choices have to be made because of scarcity. People cannot have or do everything that they desire all the time.
	4. People make choices in a manner known as rational self-interest; people make the choices that at the time and with the information they have at their disposal will give them the greatest satisfaction.

(?)

3. What is the economic way of thinking?

3. The Economic Approach

Economists often refer to the "economic approach" or to "economic thinking." By this, they mean that the principles of scarcity and rational self-interest are used in a specific way to search out answers to questions about the real world.

3.a. Positive and Normative Analysis

positive analysis: analysis of what is

normative analysis: analysis of what ought to be

In applying the principles of economics to questions about the real world, it is important to avoid imposing your opinions or value judgments on others. Analysis that does not impose the value judgments of one individual on the decisions of others is called **positive analysis**. If you demonstrate that unemployment in the automobile industry in the United States rises when people purchase cars produced in other countries instead of cars produced in the United States, you are undertaking positive analysis.

However, if you claim that there ought to be a law to stop people from buying foreign-made cars, you are imposing your value judgments on the decisions and desires of others. That is not positive analysis. It is, instead, **normative analysis**. *Normative means "what ought to be"; positive means "what is."* If you demonstrate that the probability of death in an automobile accident is 20 percent higher if seat belts are not worn, you are using positive analysis. If you argue that there should be a law requiring seat belts to be worn, you are using normative analysis.

Conclusions based on opinion or value judgments do not advance one's understanding of events.

3.b. Common Mistakes

Why are so many items sold for $2.99 rather than $3? Most people attribute this practice to ignorance on the part of others: "People look at the first number and round to it—they see $2.99 but think $2." Although this reasoning may be correct, no one admits to such behavior when asked. A common error in the attempt to understand human behavior is to argue that other people do not understand something or are stupid. Instead of relying on rational self-interest to explain human behavior, ignorance or stupidity is called on.

fallacy of composition: the mistaken assumption that what applies in the case of one applies to the case of many

Another common mistake in economic analysis, called the **fallacy of composition**, is the error of attributing what applies in the case of one to the case of many. If one person in a theater realizes that a fire has broken out and races to the exit, that one person is better off. If we assume that a thousand people in a crowded theater would be better off if they all behaved exactly like the single individual, we would be committing the mistake known as the fallacy of composition. For example, you reach an intersection just as the light switches to yellow. You reason that you can make it into the intersection before the light turns red. However, others reason the same way. Many people enter the intersection with the yellow light; it turns red, and traffic in the intersection is congested. The traffic going the other way can't move. You correctly reasoned that you alone could enter the intersection on the yellow light and then move on through. But it would be a fallacy of composition to assume that many drivers could enter the intersection and pass on through before the intersection is congested.

association as causation: the mistaken assumption that because two events seem to occur together, one causes the other

The mistaken interpretation of **association as causation** occurs when unrelated or coincidental events that occur at about the same time are believed to have a cause-and-effect relationship. For example, the result of the football Super Bowl game is sometimes said to predict how the stock market will perform. According to this "theory," if the NFC team wins, the stock market will rise in the new year, but if the AFC team wins, the market will fall. This bit of folklore is a clear example of confusion between causation and association. Simply because two events seem to occur together does not mean that one causes the other. Clearly, a football game cannot cause the stock market to rise or fall. For another example, on Gobbler's Knob, Punxsutawney, Pennsylvania, at 7:27 A.M. on February 2, Punxsutawney Phil saw his shadow. Six more weeks of winter followed. However, whether the sun was or was not hidden behind a cloud at 7:27 A.M. on February 2 had nothing to do with causing a shortened or extended winter. Groundhog Day is the celebration of the mistake of attributing association as causation.

3.c. Microeconomics and Macroeconomics

Economics is the study of how people choose to allocate their scarce resources among their unlimited wants and involves the application of certain principles—scarcity, choice, and rational self-interest—in a consistent manner. The study of economics is usually separated into two general areas, microeconomics and macroeconomics. **Microeconomics** is the study of economics at the level of the individual economic entity: the individual firm, the individual consumer, and the individual worker. In **macroeconomics**, rather than analyzing the behavior of an individual consumer, we look at the sum of the behaviors of all consumers together, which is called the consumer sector, or household sector. Similarly, instead of examining the behavior of an individual firm, in macroeconomics we examine the sum of the behaviors of all firms, called the business sector.

microeconomics: the study of economics at the level of the individual

macroeconomics: the study of the economy as a whole

RECAP

1. The objective of economics is to understand why the real world is the way it is.

2. Positive analysis refers to what is, while normative analysis refers to what ought to be.

3. Assuming that others are ignorant, the fallacy of composition, and interpreting association as causation are three commonly made errors in economic analysis.

4. The study of economics is typically divided into two parts, macroeconomics and microeconomics.

Summary

1. Why study economics?

- The study of economics may be the road to a better job and will add skills that have value to you in your life and in your occupation. *§1*

- Economics is interesting; it might be called the study of unintended consequences. *§1.b*

2. What is economics?

- The resources that go into the production of goods are land, labor, and capital. *§2.a*

- Economics is the study of how people choose to allocate scarce resources to satisfy their unlimited wants. *§2.b*

- Scarcity is universal; it applies to anything people would like more of than is available at a zero price. Because of scarcity, choices must be made, and these choices are made in a way that is in the decision-maker's rational self-interest. *§2.a, 2.b, 2.c*
- People make choices that, at the time and with the information at hand, will give them the greatest satisfaction. *§2.c*

3. What is the economic way of thinking?
- Positive analysis is analysis of what is; normative analysis is analysis of what ought to be. *§3.a*
- Assuming that others are ignorant, the fallacy of composition, and interpreting association as causation are three commonly made errors in economic analysis. *§3.b*
- The study of economics is typically divided into two parts, macroeconomics and microeconomics. *§3.c*

Key Terms

scarcity *§2.a*

economic good *§2.a*

free good *§2.a*

economic bad *§2.a*

resources *§2.a*

factors of production *§2.a*

inputs *§2.a*

land *§2.a*

labor *§2.a*

capital *§2.a*

rational self-interest *§2.c*

positive analysis *§3.a*

normative analysis *§3.a*

fallacy of composition *§3.b*

association as causation *§3.b*

microeconomics *§3.c*

macroeconomics *§3.c*

Exercises

1. Which of the following are economic goods? Explain why each is or is not an economic good.
   a. Steaks
   b. Houses
   c. Cars
   d. Garbage
   e. T-shirts

2. Many people go to a medical doctor every time they are ill; others never visit a doctor. Explain how human behavior could include such opposite behaviors.

3. Erin has purchased a $35 ticket to a Dave Matthews concert. She is invited to a sendoff party for a friend who is moving to another part of the country. The party is scheduled for the same day as the concert. If she had known about the party before she bought the concert ticket, she would have chosen to attend the party. Will Erin choose to attend the concert? Explain.

4. It is well documented in scientific research that smoking is harmful to health. Smokers have higher incidences of coronary disease, cancer, and other catastrophic illnesses. Knowing this, about 30 percent of young people begin smoking, and about 25 percent of the U.S. population smokes. Are the people who choose to smoke irrational? What do you think of the argument that we should ban smoking in order to protect these people from themselves?

5. Indicate whether each of the following statements is true or false. If the statement is false, change it to make it true.
   a. Positive analysis imposes the value judgments of one individual on the decisions of others.
   b. Rational self-interest is the same thing as selfishness.
   c. An economic good is scarce if it has a positive price.
   d. An economic bad is an item that has a positive price.
   e. A resource is an ingredient used to make factors of production.

6. Are the following statements normative or positive? If a statement is normative, change it to a positive statement.
   a. The government should provide free tuition to all college students.
   b. An effective way to increase the skills of the work force is to provide free tuition to all college students.
   c. The government must provide job training if we are to compete with other countries.

7. In the *New York Times Magazine* in 1970, Milton Friedman, a Nobel Prize–winning economist, argued that "the social responsibility of business is to increase profits." How would Friedman's argument fit with the basic economic model that people behave in ways that they believe are in their best self-interest?

8. Use economics to explain why men's and women's restrooms tend to be located near each other in airports and other public buildings.

9. Use economics to explain why diamonds are more expensive than water, when water is necessary for survival and diamonds are not.

10. Use economics to explain why people leave tips (a) at a restaurant they visit often and (b) at a restaurant they visit only once.

11. Use economics to explain why people contribute to charities.

12. Use economics to explain this statement: "Increasing the speed limit has, to some degree, compromised highway safety on interstate roads but enhanced safety on noninterstate roads."

Take the ACE Practice Test for this chapter to review the important concepts and get immediate feedback with answers.

college.hmco.com/economics/students/

Choice of Major, Years of College Influence Student Debt

AScribe Newswire
October 16, 2002

While a college degree and debt are becoming synonymous, it's degree choices that might be affecting how high that debt will be.

More than half of U.S. college majors graduate students with debts higher than lenders recommend, according to a study co-authored by a former Wichita State University accounting professor.

"In the U.S., educational loans are driven at least partially by choice of major, race and the amount of time necessary to complete a degree," says Steven Harrast, an assistant professor in the W. Frank Barton School of Business' School of Accountancy at the time of this study. He conducted the study with a former colleague, Gary Donhardt from the University of Memphis, and presented the findings this summer at a conference in Vienna, Austria.

To analyze the amount of debt a student could handle at graduation, Harrast and Donhardt figured it's necessary to analyze salary and debt by major.

Previous studies into student debt have typically ignored the differences that a choice of major can make.

They found 56 percent of all majors are graduating students with debts that exceed lender recommendations. Lenders usually recommend that less than 8 percent of an individual's gross income should be spent on student loan repayments.

Harrast and Donhardt found those getting engineering, nursing, special education or other technology-related degrees are generally within lender-recommended debt levels and have higher salaries at graduation.

Some majors don't lend themselves well to paying off loans, Harrast says. Individuals getting degrees in the arts, liberal arts and social sciences find themselves with a lot more excess debt when compared to their salaries. The worst off were art history majors, who had debt levels that nearly triple lender recommendations. . . .

Debt among new college graduates and the rate of defaults on student loans is growing. In Texas, for example, the average indebtedness of college borrowers almost tripled in one decade from 1989–99. Default claims on student loans have reached into the billions.

"The cost of higher education is increasing at about three times the rate of inflation," Harrast says. "And often the cost of education increases when the economy is doing poorly because tax revenues decrease and funding for universities is therefore decreased. And we increase tuition, like we do now, to compensate for the loss in state revenues. Pell grants [a federal program] haven't kept pace so where's the money coming from? Well, students are borrowing. Pell grants used to pay a much larger portion of education. They pay only a small fraction now. If a family doesn't have resources to pay for an education, you've got to find it somewhere and most students have had to borrow."

According to Harrast's presentation, 64 percent of students borrowed money from the federal government during 1999–2000. And even those who seem to have the resources are borrowing: Forty-four percent of students from families earning $100,000 or more borrowed money for their education.

"A degree should further someone's situation in life, and it can't do that if you graduate with a ton of debt and end up in bankruptcy over credit card debt," Harrast says. "Then who can say you were better or worse off?"

Harrast says this study wasn't meant to discourage anyone from pursuing a field they are interested in.

"What we want to let people know is that if they choose a low-paying area of study, they need to make sure they minimize their debt when going through school so they don't have that burden once they get out."

Source: Copyright 2002 AScribe Inc.

Economics is the study of human behavior, so it ought to be able to explain why people would take on such huge debts in order to go to college. Moreover, it should explain why people choose the majors they do when it is so clear which fields provide the greatest future incomes.

Economists argue that decisions are the result of comparing costs and benefits. In this article, two major decisions are discussed, going to college and selecting a major. The first decision compares the future income and quality of living that a college degree will offer with the costs of obtaining that college degree. What is the cost of the degree? It is the expense of college—what many students take out loans to pay. It is also the forgone income—that is, the income that you would have earned had you not gone to college. Someone who takes four or five years to complete college has paid tuition, purchased books and materials, and paid for room and board over those years. Those costs range from a bare minimum of $20,000 to well over $100,000. You may have worked part-time while you were attending college, but if you had not been attending college, you could have worked full-time. The difference for the years of college would have been about $50,000. Thus, the cost of college could have been $150,000 or more.

The article notes that the amount of debt a student should have at the end of college depends on the major chosen. If you choose to be an art history major, you should not take out much debt, and you should hurry through school. Why does it matter if one is pre-med or an art history major? The major you choose will influence your future income. A medical doctor earns on average about $4.5 million more than an art history major during his or her lifetime. Clearly the medical doctor is able to pay off more debt and live better than the art history major.

Selecting a major involves a comparison of costs and benefits. As we just mentioned, different majors mean different amounts of future income. If the choice of major were only a matter of comparisons of future income, there would be fewer art history majors and more medical doctors. But income is not the only thing that enters into one's benefit calculations. Interest in the subject, living styles, amount of leisure time, and other aspects of life enter into one's choice of a college major.

Working with Graphs

According to the old saying, one picture is worth a thousand words. If that maxim is correct, and, in addition, if producing a thousand words takes more time and effort than producing one picture, it is no wonder that economists rely so extensively on pictures. The pictures that economists use to explain concepts are called *graphs.* The purpose of this appendix is to explain how graphs are constructed and how to interpret them.

1. Reading Graphs

The three kinds of graphs used by economists are shown in Figures 1, 2, and 3. Figure 1 is a *line graph.* It is the most commonly used type of graph in economics. Figure 2 is a *bar graph.* It is probably used more often in popular magazines than any other kind of graph. Figure 3 is a *pie graph,* or *pie chart.* Although it is less popular than bar and line graphs, it appears often enough that you need to be familiar with it.

1.a. Relationships Between Variables

Figure 1 is a line graph showing the ratio of the median income of people who have completed four or more years of college to the median income of those who have completed just four years of high school. The line shows the value of a college education in terms of the additional income earned relative to the income earned without a college degree on a year-to-year basis. You can see that the premium for completing college rose from the mid-1970s until 2001 and has declined slightly since.

Figure 2 is a bar graph indicating the unemployment rate by educational attainment. The blue refers to high school dropouts, the red refers to those with four years of high school, and the green refers to those with four or more years of college. One set of bars is presented for males and one set for females. The bars are arranged in order, with the highest incidence of unemployment depicted first, the next highest second, and the lowest third. This arrangement is made only for ease in reading and interpretation. The bars could be arranged in any order. The graph illustrates that unemployment strikes those with less education more than it does those with more education.

Figure 3 is a pie chart showing the percentage of the U.S. population completing various numbers of years of schooling. Unlike line and bar graphs, a pie chart is not actually a picture of a relationship between two variables. Instead, the pie represents the whole, 100 percent of the U.S. population, and the pieces of the pie represent parts of the whole—the percentage of the population completing one to four years

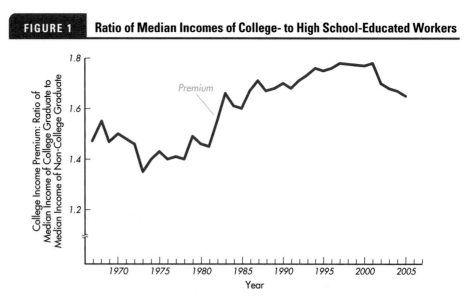

Figure 1 is a line graph showing the ratio of the median income of people who have completed four or more years of college to the median income of those who have completed four years of high school. The line shows the income premium for educational attainment, or the value of a college education in terms of income, from year to year. The rise in the line since about 1979 shows that the premium for completing college has risen. *Source:* U.S. Statistical Abstract, 2005. *U.S. Census Bureau: www.census.gov.*

FIGURE 2   **Unemployment and Education**

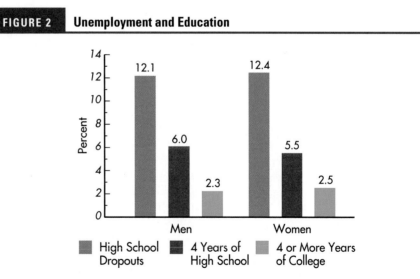

Figure 2 is a bar graph indicating the unemployment rate by educational attainment. The blue refers to high school dropouts, the red refers to those with four years of high school, and the green refers to those with four or more years of college. One set of bars is presented for males and one set for females. The bars are arranged in order, with the highest incidence of unemployment shown first, the next highest second, and the lowest third. This arrangement is made only for ease in reading and interpretation. The bars could be arranged in any order.
Source: U.S. Census Bureau: *www.census.gov/population.*

FIGURE 3   Educational Attainment

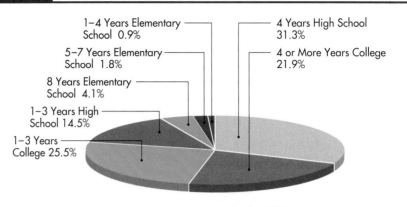

1–4 Years Elementary School 0.9%

5–7 Years Elementary School 1.8%

8 Years Elementary School 4.1%

1–3 Years High School 14.5%

1–3 Years College 25.5%

4 Years High School 31.3%

4 or More Years College 21.9%

Total = 100%

Figure 3 is a pie chart showing the percentage of the U.S. population completing various years of schooling. Unlike line and bar graphs, a pie chart is not actually a picture of a relationship between two variables. Instead, the pie represents the whole, 100 percent of the U.S. population in this case, and the pieces of the pie represent parts of the whole—the percentage of the population completing one to four years of elementary school only, five to seven years of elementary school, and so on, up to four or more years of college.
Source: U.S. Census Bureau, Sept. 15, 2005; *www.census.gov/population.*

of elementary school only, five to seven years of elementary school, and so on, up to four or more years of college.

Because a pie chart does not show the relationship between variables, it is not as useful for explaining economic concepts as line and bar graphs. Line graphs are used more often than bar graphs to explain economic concepts.

1.b. Independent and Dependent Variables

independent variable: a variable whose value does not depend on the values of other variables

dependent variable: a variable whose value depends on the value of the independent variable

direct, or positive, relationship: the relationship that exists when the values of related variables move in the same direction

inverse, or negative, relationship: the relationship that exists when the values of related variables move in opposite directions

Most line and bar graphs involve just two variables, an **independent variable** and a **dependent variable**. An independent variable is one whose value does not depend on the values of other variables; a dependent variable, on the other hand, is one whose value does depend on the values of other variables. The value of the dependent variable is determined after the value of the independent variable is determined.

In Figure 2, the *independent* variable is the educational status of the man or woman, and the *dependent* variable is the incidence of unemployment (the percentage of the group that is unemployed). The incidence of unemployment depends on the educational attainment of the man or woman.

1.c. Direct and Inverse Relationships

If the value of the dependent variable increases as the value of the independent variable increases, the relationship between the two types of variables is called a **direct**, or **positive**, **relationship**. If the value of the dependent variable decreases as the value of the independent variable increases, the relationship between the two types of variables is called an **inverse**, or **negative**, **relationship**.

In Figure 2, unemployment and educational attainment are inversely, or negatively, related: As people acquire more education, they become less likely to be unemployed.

2. Constructing a Graph ⎯⎯⎯⎯⎯⎯⎯

Let's now construct a graph. We will begin with a consideration of the horizontal and vertical axes, or lines, and then we will put the axes together. We are going to construct a *straight-line curve.* This sounds contradictory, but it is common terminology. Economists often refer to the demand or supply *curve,* and that curve may be a straight line.

2.a. The Axes

It is important to understand how the *axes* (the horizontal and vertical lines) are used and what they measure. Let's begin with the horizontal axis, the line running across the page. Notice in Figure 4(a) that the line is divided into equal segments. Each point on the line represents a quantity, or the value of the variable being measured. For example, each segment could represent one year or 10,000 pounds of diamonds or some other value. Whatever is measured, the value increases from left to right, beginning with negative values, going on to zero, which is called the *origin,* and then moving on to positive numbers.

  A number line in the vertical direction can be constructed as well, and this is also shown in Figure 4(a). Zero is the origin, and the numbers increase from bottom to

---

FIGURE 4 **The Axes, the Coordinate System, and the Positive Quadrant**

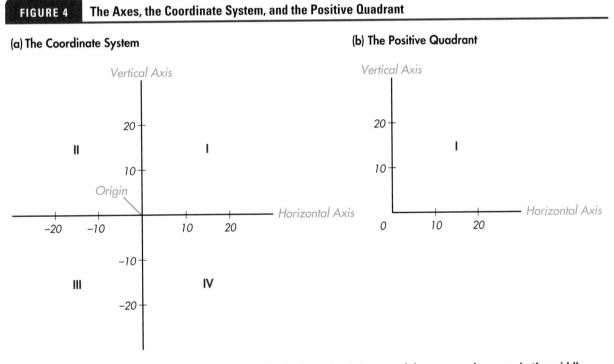

(a) The Coordinate System

(b) The Positive Quadrant

Figure 4(a) shows the vertical and horizontal axes. The horizontal axis has an origin, measured as zero, in the middle. Negative numbers are to the left of zero, and positive numbers are to the right. The vertical axis also has an origin in the middle. Positive numbers are above the origin, and negative numbers are below. The horizontal and vertical axes together show the entire coordinate system. Positive numbers are in quadrant I, negative numbers in quadrant III, and combinations of negative and positive numbers in quadrants II and IV.

  Figure 4(b) shows only the positive quadrant. Because most economic data are positive, often only the upper right quadrant, the positive quadrant, of the coordinate system is used.

---

top. Like the horizontal axis, the vertical axis is divided into equal segments; the distance between 0 and 10 is the same as the distance between 0 and –10, the distance between 10 and 20, and so on.

In most cases, the variable measured along the horizontal axis is the independent variable. This isn't always true in economics, however. Economists often measure the independent variable on the vertical axis. Do not assume that the variable on the horizontal axis is independent and the variable on the vertical axis is dependent.

Putting the horizontal and vertical lines together lets us express relationships between two variables graphically. The axes cross, or intersect, at their origins, as shown in Figure 4(a). From the common origin, movements to the right and up, in the area—called a quadrant—marked I, are combinations of positive numbers; movements to the left and down, in quadrant III, are combinations of negative numbers; movements to the right and down, in quadrant IV, are negative values on the vertical axis and positive values on the horizontal axis; and movements to the left and up, in quadrant II, are positive values on the vertical axis and negative values on the horizontal axis.

Economic data are typically positive numbers: the unemployment rate, the inflation rate, the price of something, the quantity of something produced or sold, and so on. Because economic data are usually positive numbers, the only part of the coordinate system that usually comes into play in economics is the upper right portion, quadrant I. That is why economists may simply sketch a vertical line down to the origin and then extend a horizontal line out to the right, as shown in Figure 4(b). Once in a while, economic data are negative—for instance, profit is negative when costs exceed revenues. When data are negative, quadrants II, III, and IV of the coordinate system may be used.

2.b. Constructing a Graph from a Table

Now that you are familiar with the axes—that is, the coordinate system—you are ready to construct a graph using the data in the table in Figure 5. The table lists a series of possible price levels for a T-shirt and the corresponding number of T-shirts that people choose to purchase. The data are only hypothetical; they are not drawn from actual cases.

The information given in the table is graphed in Figure 5. We begin by marking off and labeling the axes. The vertical axis is the list of possible price levels. We begin at zero and move up the axis in equal increments of $10. The horizontal axis is the number of T-shirts sold. We begin at zero and move out the axis in equal increments of 1,000 T-shirts. According to the information presented in the table, if the price is higher than $100, no one buys a T-shirt. The combination of $100 and 0 T-shirts is point A on the graph. To plot this point, find the quantity zero on the horizontal axis (it is at the origin), and then move up the vertical axis from zero to a price level of $100. (Note that we have measured the units in the table and on the graph in thousands.) At a price of $90, there are 1,000 T-shirts purchased. To plot the combination of $90 and 1,000 T-shirts, find 1,000 units on the horizontal axis and then measure up from there to a price of $90. This is point B. Point C represents a price of $80 and 2,000 T-shirts. Point D represents a price of $70 and 3,000 T-shirts. Each combination of price and T-shirts purchased listed in the table is plotted in Figure 5.

The final step in constructing a line graph is to connect the points that are plotted. When the points are connected, the straight line slanting downward from left to right in Figure 5 is obtained. It shows the relationship between the price of T-shirts and the number of T-shirts purchased.

FIGURE 5   **Constructing a Line Graph**

Point	Price per T-shirt	Number of T-shirts
A	$100	0
B	90	1,000
C	80	2,000
D	70	3,000
E	60	4,000
F	50	5,000
G	40	6,000
H	30	7,000
I	20	8,000
J	10	9,000
K	0	10,000

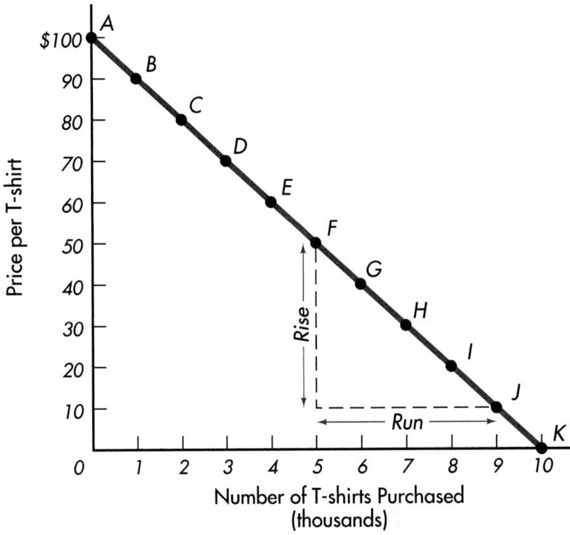

The information given in the table is plotted or graphed. The vertical axis measures price per T-shirt. The horizontal axis measures the number of T-shirts in thousands. We begin at zero in each case and then go up (if the vertical axis) or out (if the horizontal axis) in equal amounts. The vertical axis goes from $0 to $10 to $20 and so on, while the horizontal axis goes from 0 to 1,000 to 2,000 and so on. Each point is plotted. For instance, point A is a price of $100 and a number of T-shirts of 0. This is found by going to 0 on the horizontal axis and then up to $100 on the vertical axis. Point B is a price of $90 and a number of 1,000. Once the points are plotted, a line connecting the points is drawn.

2.c. Interpreting Points on a Graph

Let's use Figure 5 to demonstrate how points on a graph may be interpreted. Suppose the current price of a T-shirt is $30. Are you able to tell how many T-shirts are being purchased at this price? By tracing that price level from the vertical axis over to the curve and then down to the horizontal axis, you find that 7,000 T-shirts are being purchased. You can also find what happens to the number purchased if the price falls from $30 to $10. By tracing from the price of $10 horizontally to the curve and then down to the horizontal axis, you discover that 9,000 T-shirts are purchased. Thus, according to the graph, a decrease in the price from $30 to $10 results in 2,000 more T-shirts being purchased.

2.d. Shifts of Curves

Graphs can be used to illustrate the effects of a change in a variable that is not represented on the graph. For instance, the curve drawn in Figure 5 shows the relationship between the price of T-shirts and the number of T-shirts purchased. When this curve was drawn, the only two variables that were allowed to change were the price and the number of T-shirts. However, it is likely that people's incomes determine their reaction to the price of T-shirts as well. An increase in income would enable people to purchase more T-shirts. Thus, at every price, more T-shirts would be purchased. How would this be represented? As an outward shift of the curve, from points A, B, C, and so on to A', B', C', and so on, as shown in Figure 6.

Following the shift of the curve, we can see that more T-shirts are purchased at each price than was the case prior to the income increase. For instance, at a price of $20, the increased income allows 10,000 T-shirts to be purchased rather than 8,000. The

FIGURE 6   **Shift of Curve**

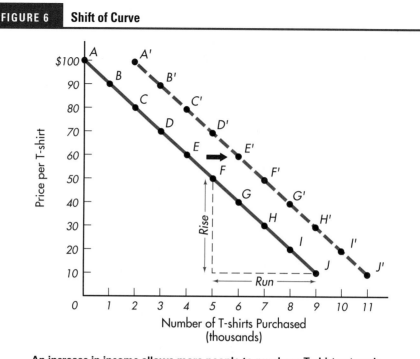

An increase in income allows more people to purchase T-shirts at each price. At a price of $80, for instance, 4,000 T-shirts are purchased instead of 2,000.

important point to note is that if some variable that influences the relationship shown in a curve or line graph changes, then *the entire curve or line changes—that is, it shifts.*

3. Slopes

A curve may represent an inverse, or negative, relationship or a direct, or positive, relationship. The slope of the curve reveals the kind of relationship that exists between two variables.

3.a. Positive and Negative Slopes

slope: the steepness of a curve, measured as the ratio of the rise to the run

The **slope** of a curve is its steepness, the rate at which the value of a variable measured on the vertical axis changes with respect to a given change in the value of the variable measured on the horizontal axis. If the value of a variable measured on one axis goes up when the value of the variable measured on the other axis goes down, the variables have an inverse (or negative) relationship. If the values of the variables rise or fall together, the variables have a direct (or positive) relationship. Inverse relationships are represented by curves that run downward from left to right; direct relationships, by curves that run upward from left to right.

Slope is calculated by measuring the amount by which the variable on the vertical axis changes and dividing that figure by the amount by which the variable on the horizontal axis changes. The vertical change is called the *rise,* and the horizontal change is called the *run.* Slope is referred to as the *rise over the run:*

$$\text{Slope} = \frac{\text{rise}}{\text{run}}$$

The slope of any inverse relationship is negative. The slope of any direct relationship is positive.

Let's calculate the slope of the curve in Figure 5. Price (P) is measured on the vertical axis, and quantity of T-shirts purchased (Q) is measured on the horizontal axis. The rise is the change in price (ΔP), the change in the value of the variable measured on the vertical axis. The run is the change in quantity of T-shirts purchased (ΔQ), the change in the value of the variable measured on the horizontal axis. (The symbol Δ means "change in"—it is the Greek letter delta—so ΔP means "change in P" and ΔQ means "change in Q.") Remember that slope equals the rise over the run. Thus, the equation for the slope of the straight-line curve running downward from left to right in Figure 5 is

$$\frac{\Delta P}{\Delta Q}$$

As the price (P) declines, the number of T-shirts purchased (Q) increases. The rise is negative, and the run is positive. Thus, the slope is a negative value.

The slope is the same anywhere along a straight line. Thus, it does not matter where we calculate the changes along the vertical and horizontal axes. For instance, from 0 to 10,000 on the horizontal axis—a run of 10,000—the vertical change, the rise, is a negative $100 (from $100 down to $0). Thus, the rise over the run is $-100/10,000$, or $-.01$. Similarly, from 5,000 to 9,000 in the horizontal direction, the corresponding rise is $50 to $10, so that the rise over the run is $-40/4,000$ or $-.01$.

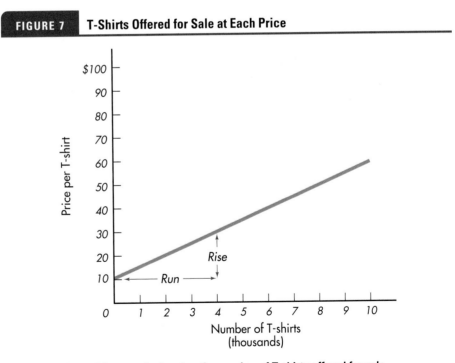

FIGURE 7   **T-Shirts Offered for Sale at Each Price**

Figure 7 is a graph showing the number of T-shirts offered for sale at various prices. The line shows that as price rises so does the number of T-shirts offered for sale. At a price of $10, no shirts are offered. At a price of $20, 2,000 shirts are offered for sale. At a price of $30, 4,000 shirts are offered for sale, and so on. The rise over the run is 20/4,000 = .005.

Remember that direct, or positive, relationships between variables are represented by lines that run upward from left to right. Figure 7 is a graph showing the number of T-shirts that producers offer for sale at various price levels. The curve represents the relationship between the two variables number of T-shirts offered for sale and price. It shows that as price rises, so does the number of T-shirts offered for sale. The slope of the curve is positive. The change in the rise (the vertical direction) that comes with an increase in the run (the horizontal direction) is positive. Because the graph is a straight line, you can measure the rise and run using any two points along the curve and the slope will be the same. We find the slope by calculating the rise that accompanies the run. Moving from 0 to 4,000 T-shirts gives us a run of 4,000. Looking at the curve, we see that the corresponding rise is $20. Thus, the rise over the run is 20/4,000, or .005.

Summary

- There are three commonly used types of graphs: the line graph, the bar graph, and the pie chart. *§1.a*

- An independent variable is a variable whose value does not depend on the values of other variables. The values of a dependent variable do depend on the values of other variables. *§1.b*

- A direct, or positive, relationship occurs when the value of the dependent variable increases as the value of the independent variable increases. An indirect, or negative, relationship occurs when the value of the dependent variable decreases as the value of the independent variable increases. *§1.c*

- Most economic data are positive numbers, and so only the upper right quadrant of the coordinate system is often used in economics. *§2.a*

- A curve shifts when a variable that affects the dependent variable and is not measured on the axes changes. *§2.d*

- The slope of a curve is the rise over the run: the change in the variable measured on the vertical axis over the corresponding change in the variable measured on the horizontal axis. *§3.a*

- The slope of a straight-line curve is the same at all points along the curve. *§3.a*

Key Terms

independent variable *§1.b*

dependent variable *§1.b*

direct, or positive, relationship *§1.c*

inverse, or negative, relationship *§1.c*

slope *§3.a*

Exercises

1. On the right are two sets of figures: the total quantity of Mexican pesos (new pesos) in circulation (the total amount of Mexican money available) and the peso price of a dollar (how many pesos are needed to purchase one dollar). Values are given for the years 1987 through 2005 for each variable.
   a. Plot each variable by measuring time (years) on the horizontal axis and, in the first graph, pesos in circulation on the vertical axis and, in the second graph, peso price of a dollar on the vertical axis.
   b. Plot the combinations of variables by measuring pesos in circulation on the horizontal axis and peso prices of a dollar on the vertical axis.
   c. In each of the graphs in parts a and b, what are the dependent and independent variables?

   d. In each of the graphs in parts a and b, indicate whether the relationship between the dependent and independent variables is direct or inverse.

2. Plot the data listed on the right:
   a. Use price as the vertical axis and quantity as the horizontal axis and plot the first two columns.
   b. Show what quantity is sold when the price is $550.
   c. Directly below the graph in part a, plot the data in columns 2 and 3. Use total revenue as the vertical axis and quantity as the horizontal axis.
   d. What is total revenue when the price is $550? Will total revenue increase or decrease when the price is lowered?

Year	Pesos in Circulation (billions)	Peso Price of a Dollar
1987	13,000	1.3782
1988	22,000	2.2731
1989	29,000	2.4615
1990	47,000	2.8126
1991	106,000	3.0184
1992	122,000	3.0949
1993	144,000	3.1156
1994	145,000	3.3751
1995	151,000,	6.4194
1996	206,000	7.5994
1997	276,000	8.5850
1998	332,000	9.9680
1999	371,000	9.4270
2000	499,000	9.6420
2001	705,000	9.2850
2002	794,000	9.5270
2003	864,000	10.9000
2004	963,000	11.4000
2005	1,147,000	10.4750

Price	Quantity Sold	Total Revenue
$1,000	200	200,000
900	400	360,000
800	600	480,000
700	800	560,000
600	1,000	600,000
500	1,200	600,000
400	1,400	560,000
300	1,600	480,000
200	1,800	360,000
100	2,000	200,000

2

Choice, Opportunity Costs, and Specialization

 Fundamental Questions

1. **What are opportunity costs? Are they part of the economic way of thinking?**

2. **What is a production possibilities curve?**

3. **Why does specialization occur?**

4. **What are the benefits of trade?**

In the previous chapter, we learned that scarcity forces people to make choices. A *choice* means that you select one thing instead of selecting others. What you don't select is the cost of the choice you make. The old saying that "there is no free lunch" means that every choice requires that something be given up or sacrificed. This chapter explains how costs affect the behavior of individuals, firms, and societies as a whole. ■

1. Opportunity Costs

A choice is simply a comparison of alternatives: to attend class or not to attend class, to purchase a double latte mocha with whipped cream or to buy four iTunes, to purchase a new car or to keep the old one. When one option is chosen, the

1. What are opportunity costs? Are they part of the economic way of thinking?

opportunity costs: the highest-valued alternative that must be forgone when a choice is made

benefits of the alternatives are forgone. When you choose to purchase the double latte mocha for $4, you don't have that $4 to spend on anything else. *Economists refer to the forgone opportunities or forgone benefits of the next best alternative as* **opportunity costs**, or just costs. Opportunity costs are the highest-valued alternative that must be forgone when a choice is made. If you would have bought four iTunes if you had not purchased the latte, then we say the opportunity cost of the latte is the benefit you don't enjoy from the iTunes.

The concept of cost is often more than the dollars and cents that you shell out at the cash register. Buying used books saves money but often increases frustration and may affect your grades. The book might be missing pages, unreadable in spots, or out of date. The full cost of the book is the price you paid for the used copy plus the frustration of having an incomplete book. An attorney in Scottsdale, Arizona, is paid $125 an hour to write contracts. The attorney loves Ralph Lauren dress shirts and knows that these can be purchased for $100 at Nordstrom in Scottsdale or, when they are available, for $50 at the outlet mall in Casa Grande. He likes to purchase just one or two shirts at a time and usually buys the shirts at Nordstrom, taking 15 minutes out of his lunch time to go to the store. Is this smart? Well, he figures he could spend two hours driving to Casa Grande and back and save $50 per shirt. But this also means that he is not writing contracts and charging $125 per hour during those two hours. The real cost of the $50 saved on a single shirt in Casa Grande includes the $250 that the attorney would be giving up in income.

The concept of opportunity cost is very important. Every human activity responds to costs in one way or another. When the cost of something falls, it becomes more attractive to us. For instance, when the cost of text messaging phone service dropped, more of us signed up for the service. Conversely, when the cost of something rises, we tend to use less of it. When photo radar machines were placed on the freeways in Phoenix, Arizona, the cost of speeding went up because the likelihood of getting caught speeding dramatically increased. As a result, the amount of speeding dropped precipitously. Average speeds went from 78 to 65 virtually overnight.

It is important to recognize that costs can be more than just the money shelled out at the cash register. Costs include the values of the things that are given up. Suppose your professor invites you to a luncheon to hear John Stossel (a commentator on ABC television) speak. He is really good and the lunch is paid for by the professor, so you go. Is the lunch free? No, because you had to give up your time to go; you chose not to do other things. The activity you would have enjoyed most is the opportunity cost of the lunch.

1.a. Tradeoffs

tradeoff: the giving up of one good or activity in order to obtain some other good or activity

Life is a continuous sequence of decisions, and every single decision involves choosing one thing over another or trading off something for something else. A **tradeoff** means a sacrifice—giving up one good or activity in order to obtain some other good or activity. Each term you must decide whether to register for college or not. You could work full-time and not attend college, attend college and not work, or work part-time and attend college. The time you devote to college will decrease as you devote more time to work. You trade off hours spent at work for hours spent in college; in other words, you compare the benefits you think you will get from going to college this term with the costs of college this term.

1.b. The Production Possibilities Curve

Tradeoffs can be illustrated in a graph known as the **production possibilities curve** (**PPC**). The production possibilities curve shows all possible combinations of quantities of goods and services that can be produced when the existing resources are used *fully and efficiently*. Figure 1 shows a production possibilities curve (based on information in the table in Figure 1) for the production of defense goods and services and nondefense goods and services by a nation. Defense goods and services in-

?

2. What is a production possibilities curve?

production possibilities curve (PPC): a graphical representation showing all possible combinations of quantities of goods and services that can be produced using the existing resources fully and efficiently

FIGURE 1 | **The Production Possibilities Curve**

Point	Defense Goods and Services (millions of units)	Nondefense Goods and Services (millions of units)
A_1	200	0
B_1	175	75
C_1	130	125
D_1	70	150
E_1	0	160
F_1	130	25
G_1	200	75

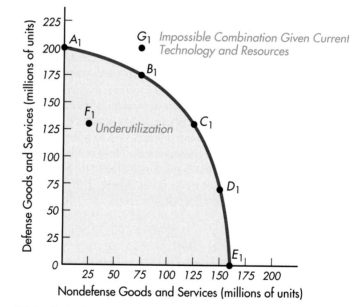

With a limited amount of resources, only certain combinations of defense and nondefense goods and services can be produced. The maximum amounts that can be produced, given various tradeoffs, are represented by points A_1 through E_1. Point F_1 lies inside the curve and represents the underutilization of resources. More of one type of goods could be produced without producing less of the other, or more of both types could be produced. Point G_1 represents an impossible combination. There are insufficient resources to produce quantities lying beyond the curve.

clude guns, ships, bombs, personnel, and so forth that are used for national defense. Nondefense goods and services include education, housing, health care, and food that are not used for national defense. All societies allocate their scarce resources in order to produce some combination of defense and nondefense goods and services. Because resources are scarce, a nation cannot produce as much of everything as it wants. When it produces more health care, it cannot produce as much education or automobiles; when it devotes more of its resources to the military area, fewer resources are available to devote to health care.

In Figure 1, units of defense goods and services are measured on the vertical axis, and units of nondefense goods and services are measured on the horizontal axis. If all resources are allocated to producing defense goods and services, then 200 million units can be produced, but there will be no production of nondefense goods and services. The combination of 200 million units of defense goods and services and 0 units of nondefense goods and services is point A_1, a point on the vertical axis. At 175 million units of defense goods and services, 75 million units of nondefense goods and services can be produced (point B_1). Point C_1 represents 125 million units of nondefense goods and services and 130 million units of defense goods. Point D_1 represents 150 million units of nondefense goods and services and 70 million units of defense goods and services. Point E_1, a point on the horizontal axis, shows the combination of no production of defense goods and services and 160 million units of nondefense goods and services.

1.b.1. Points Inside the Production Possibilities Curve
Suppose a nation produces 130 million units of defense goods and services and 25 million units of nondefense goods and services. That combination, Point F_1 in Figure 1, lies inside the production possibilities curve. A point lying inside the production possibilities curve indicates that resources are not being fully or efficiently used. If the existing work force is employed only 20 hours per week, it is not being fully used. If two workers are used when one would be sufficient—say, two people in each Domino's Pizza delivery car—then resources are not being used efficiently. If there are resources available for use, society can move from point F_1 to a point on the PPC, such as point C_1. The move would gain 100 million units of nondefense goods and services with no loss of defense goods and services.

In France, the unemployment rate of labor is higher than 10 percent. This would be represented as a point inside France's PPC, such as F_1. Should this rate fall to 7 percent, more goods and services would be produced. This would be represented as a move out from a point such as F_1 to a point on the PPC, such as point C_1.

1.b.2. Points Outside the Production Possibilities Curve
Point G_1 in Figure 1 represents the production of 200 million units of defense goods and services and 75 million units of nondefense goods and services. Point G_1, however, represents the use of more resources than are available—it lies outside the production possibilities curve. Unless more resources can be obtained and/or the quality of resources improved (for example, through technological change) so that the nation can produce more with the same quantity of resources, there is no way that the society can currently produce 200 million units of defense goods and 75 million units of nondefense goods.

1.b.3. Shifts of the Production Possibilities Curve
If a nation obtains more resources or if the existing resources become more efficient, then the PPC shifts outward. Suppose a country discovers new sources of oil within its borders and is able to greatly increase its production of oil. Greater oil supplies would enable the country to increase production of all types of goods and services.

Figure 2 shows the production possibilities curve before (PPC_1) and after (PPC_2) the discovery of oil. PPC_1 is based on the data given in the table in Figure 1. PPC_2 is based on the data given in the table in Figure 2, which shows the increase in production of goods and services that results from the increase in oil supplies. The first combination of goods and services on PPC_2, point A_2, is 220 million units of defense goods and 0 units of nondefense goods. The second point, B_2, is a combination of 200 million units of defense goods and 75 million units of nondefense goods. C_2 through F_2 are the combinations shown in the table in Figure 2. Connecting these points yields the bowed-out curve PPC_2. Because of the availability of new supplies of oil, the nation is able to increase production of all goods, as shown by the *shift* from PPC_1 to PPC_2. A comparison of the two curves shows that more goods and services for both defense and nondefense are possible along PPC_2 than along PPC_1.

FIGURE 2   A Shift of the Production Possibilities Curve

Combination	Defense Goods and Services (millions of units)	Nondefense Goods and Services (millions of units)
A_2	220	0
B_2	200	75
C_2	175	125
D_2	130	150
E_2	70	160
F_2	0	165

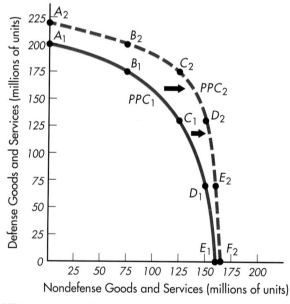

Whenever everything else is not constant, the curve shifts. In this case, an increase in the quantity of a resource enables the society to produce more of both types of goods. The curve shifts out, away from the origin.

The outward shift of the PPC can be the result of an increase in the quantity of resources, but it also can occur because the quality of resources improves. Economists call an increase in the quality of resources an increase in the productivity of resources. Consider a technological breakthrough that improves the speed with which data are transmitted. Following this breakthrough, it might require fewer people and machines to do the same amount of work, and it might take less time to produce the same quantity and quality of goods. Each quality improvement in resources is illustrated as an outward shift of the PPC.

RECAP

1. Opportunity costs are the benefits that are forgone as a result of a choice. When you choose one thing, you must give up—forgo—others.

2. The production possibilities curve (PPC) illustrates the concept of opportunity cost. Each point on the PPC means that every other point is a forgone opportunity.

3. The production possibilities curve represents all combinations of goods and services that can be produced using limited resources efficiently to their full capabilities.

4. Points inside the production possibilities curve represent the underutilization, unemployment, or inefficient use of resources—more goods and services could be produced by using the limited resources more fully or efficiently.

5. Points outside the production possibilities curve represent combinations of goods and services that are unattainable given the limitation of resources.

6. If more resources are obtained or a technological change or innovation occurs, the PPC shifts out.

2. Specialization and Trade

The PPC illustrates the idea of scarcity—there are limits, and combinations outside of the curve are not attainable. The PPC also illustrates the idea of costs—no matter which combination of goods and services a society chooses to produce, other combinations of goods and services are sacrificed. And, the PPC illustrates the idea that choices have to be made—it is not possible to satisfy unlimited wants.

2.a. Marginal Opportunity Cost

As the production of some types of goods is increased, some other types of goods and services cannot be produced. According to the table and graph in Figure 1, we see that moving from point A_1 to point B_1 on the PPC means increasing nondefense production from 0 to 75 million units and decreasing defense production from 200 million to 175 million units. Thus, the marginal cost of 75 million units of nondefense is 25 million units of defense. The incremental amount of defense given up with each increase in the production of nondefense goods is known as the **marginal cost** or **marginal opportunity cost**. *Marginal* means "change" or "incremental," so marginal cost is the incremental amount of one good or service that must be given up to obtain one additional unit of another good or service.

Each move along the PPC means giving up some defense goods to get some more nondefense goods. Each additional nondefense good produced requires giving up an

marginal cost or **marginal opportunity cost:** the amount of one good or service that must be given up to obtain one additional unit of another good or service, no matter how many units are being produced

increasing number of defense goods. The marginal cost increases with each successive increase of nondefense production. In other words, it gets more and more costly to produce nondefense goods.

Marginal cost increases as the output of nondefense goods increases because of specialization. The first resources transferred from defense to nondefense production are those that are least specialized in the production of defense goods. Switching these resources is less costly (less has to be given up) than switching the specialists. Shifting an accountant who can do accounting in either defense- or nondefense-related industries equally well would not cause a big change in defense production. However, shifting a rocket scientist, who is not very useful in producing nondefense goods, would make a big difference.

2.b. Specialize Where Opportunity Costs Are Lowest

If we have a choice, we should devote our time and efforts to those activities that cost the least. In other words, we should specialize in those activities that require us to give up the smallest amount of other things. A plumber does plumbing and leaves teaching to the teachers. The teacher teaches and leaves electrical work to the electrician. A country such as Grenada specializes in spice production and leaves manufacturing to other countries.

2.b.1. Trade

If we focus on one thing, how do we get the other things that we want? The answer is that we trade or exchange goods and services. The teacher teaches, earns a salary, and hires a plumber to fix the sinks. This is called voluntary trade or voluntary exchange. The teacher is trading money to the plumber for the plumber's services. The teacher is trading her time to the students and getting money in return.

By specializing in the activities in which opportunity costs are lowest and then trading, everyone will end up with more than if everyone tried to produce everything. This is the **gains from trade**. Consider two students, Josh and Elena, who are taking the same math and economics classes and are considering working together. They are deciding whether to specialize and trade or not.

If Josh and Elena both devote all their time and effort to doing the math homework, each can do 10 math problems. If they spend all their time and effort on economics, Josh is able to complete 5 economics problems, while Elena can do 10 economics problems

	Elena		Josh	
	Math	*Econ*	*Math*	*Econ*
All resources devoted:				
To Economics	0	10	0	5
To Math	10	0	10	0

Since Elena is better at economics and just as good at math, why should she want to work with Josh? The answer depends on relative costs. What does it cost Elena to do 1 math problem? She has to not do 1 economics problem. So, it costs her 1 economics problem to do 1 math problem. Josh can do 2 math problems in the time he can complete just 1 economics problem. So, it costs Josh just $1/2$ economics problem to do 1 math problem. Josh is *relatively* better at doing math—he can do it for

3. Why does specialization occur?

Individuals, firms, and nations select the option with the lowest opportunity costs.

4. What are the benefits of trade?

gains from trade: the difference between what can be produced and consumed without specialization and trade and with specialization and trade

lower costs than can Elena. Who is relatively better at economics? It costs Josh 2 math problems to do 1 economics problem, and it costs Elena 1 math problem to do 1 economics problem. So Elena is relatively more efficient at doing economics.

If Elena specializes in economics and Josh in math, and then they trade, they will both be better off. To see this, let's begin where there is no trade and Josh and Elena each spend half their time and effort on math and half on economics. By spending half her time on economics problems, Elena can do 5, whereas Josh can only do 2.5 by spending half his time on economics problems. They each can do 5 math problems if they devote half their time to math.

	Elena		Josh	
	Math	*Econ*	*Math*	*Econ*
All resources devoted:				
To Economics	0	10	0	5
To Math	10	0	10	0
No Specialization	5	5	5	2.5

Now, let's assume that they specialize according to comparative advantage and then trade at a rate of 1 math problem for 1 economics problem. Elena produces 10 economics problems. To get 5 math problems, she needs to trade 5 economics problems. She ends up the same as if she did not specialize. Josh, on the other hand, specializes by producing 10 math problems. He can get 5 economics problems for his 5 math problems, and he ends up 2.5 economics problems better than if he had not traded.

	Elena		Josh	
	Math	*Econ*	*Math*	*Econ*
Specialization and trade at ratio of 1:1	5	5	5	5

Notice that there are gains from trade. There are 2.5 more completed economics problems as a result of specialization and trade. In this case, the gains all went to Josh because the trading price, 1 to 1, was the same as Elena's personal opportunity cost ratio. Let's now change the trading price so that Elena gets the gains. Let's assume that they specialize and trade at a ratio of 2 math problems for 1 economics problem, Josh's personal opportunity cost ratio. In this case, Elena trades 2.5 economics problems to get 5 math problems. She is the one who gains this time:

	Elena		Josh	
	Math	*Econ*	*Math*	*Econ*
Specialization and trade at ratio of 2:1	5	7.5	5	2.5

In each of the two examples, just one party gained. This is because the trades took place first at Elena's opportunity cost ratio and then at Josh's opportunity cost ratio. In reality, people won't trade voluntarily unless they gain. Elena and Josh would work out how many economics problems to trade for a math problem so that they both gained something.

Specialization and trade enable individuals, firms, and nations to acquire combinations of goods that lie beyond their own resource capabilities. Voluntary, free trade results in more being created—more income being generated, that is—and higher standards of living are being created because everything is produced at the lowest possible cost.

Imagine your world without trade. A good start would be to put yourself in the place of Tom Hanks's character in the movie *Cast Away*. If you've seen the movie, you can remember the scene where he was able to rub two sticks together to create fire. From then on, he had some light at night and some means for cooking food. But until you got the fire going, you would go to bed in the dark and wake up in a small, drafty tent-house that you had built yourself. You would put on clothes made from items that you had found. You might be able to create some tea or coffee from something you had grown and eat something that you had caught or raised, but you would spend all your waking hours just trying to survive. Not having a world like that illustrates what your gains from trade are.

2.c. Comparative Advantage

We have seen that the choice of which area or activity to specialize in is made on the basis of opportunity costs. Economists refer to the ability of one person or nation to do something with a lower opportunity cost than another as **comparative advantage**. In the example, Elena had a comparative advantage in economics and Josh in math.

Comparative advantage applies to every case of trade or exchange. This sometimes seems counterintuitive. Shouldn't countries that have lots of natural resources and a skilled labor force do everything themselves? The answer is no. Even though the United States has many more natural resources and a much larger

comparative advantage: the ability to produce a good or service at a lower opportunity cost than someone else

Mexico has a comparative advantage in low-skilled, low-wage workers relative to the United States. Free trade means that Mexico should specialize in those activities requiring low-skilled, low-wage workers. However, Mexico's government has intervened in the country's economy to such an extent that resources cannot flow to where their value is highest. As a result, many of the labor resources have to leave Mexico in order to be able to earn a living.

Part One Introduction to the Price System

and better-educated population than Grenada, Grenada has a comparative advantage in producing spices. The United States could produce more of everything than Grenada, but the opportunity cost of producing spices is higher in the United States than it is in Grenada. Both Grenada and the United States gain by having Grenada specialize in spice production and trade with the United States.

If you go around the world and look at what goods and services are traded, you can usually identify the comparative advantage. Some trade occurs simply because a country has more of something. Saudi Arabia trades oil because it has more than anyone else. But countries don't have to have more of something for there to be gains from trade. They simply have to do something at a lower cost than another country. For instance, most developing nations have a comparative advantage in activities that use unskilled labor. Unskilled labor is much less expensive in Mexico, China, India, Pakistan, Bangladesh, and many other countries than in the United States. So gains from trade occur when these countries do things that use unskilled labor and then trade with the United States for foodstuffs or high-technology goods. The United States is sending many unskilled speaking jobs, such as telephone call agents, to India because Indians speak English and their wages are low.

Trade is not based solely on wage differences. Most trade in the world occurs between industrial or developed nations rather than between a developed and a less-developed nation. Each of the nations has comparative advantages in some goods and services. Germany might have a comparative advantage in engineering automobiles, Denmark in producing Havarti cheese, France in wine, Switzerland in banking, and so on. Each country gains by specializing according to comparative advantage and then trading.

Individuals specialize in the activity in which their opportunity costs are lowest.

2.d. Private Property Rights

Each of us will specialize in some activity, earn income, and then trade our output (or income) for other goods and services that we want. Specialization and trade ensure that we are better off than we would be if we did everything ourselves. *Specialization according to comparative advantage followed by trade allows everyone to acquire more of the goods they want.* But, for trade to occur, we must have confidence that we own what we create, and that what we own cannot be taken away. **Private property rights** are necessary for trade to occur. If I order a pizza to be delivered by Papa John's to my house, but anyone can come over and eat it when it arrives, I won't have an incentive to order any pizzas. If I can live in a house, but I can't own it, I have no incentive to take care of it. Private property rights refer to the right of ownership, and it requires a legal system of laws and courts and police to ensure ownership. If someone steals my car, someone will be penalized, since stealing a car is against the law. And that if someone mugs me, takes my wallet, and leaves me bleeding on the sidewalk, that is theft of person and property and is also against the law. I have ownership rights to my body, to my assets, and to the things I have bought.

private property rights: the right of ownership

If no one owns something, no one has the incentive to take care of it. Consider the fish in the ocean. No owns the fish, and hence, no one has the incentive to protect them, raise them, and ensure that future generations of fish exist. Someone has to own an item for someone to care for it. Also, it is *private* property rights that count, not *public* property rights. If no one owns something, no one takes care of it. But equally, if everyone owns something, no one has an incentive to take care of it. In the former Soviet Union, the government owned virtually everything. No one had an incentive to take care of anything. As a result, housing was decrepit and dingy, industries were inefficient and run down, chemicals were dumped in the rivers and on the land, the air was polluted, and, in general, standards of living were very low.

Summary

1. What are opportunity costs? Are they part of the economic way of thinking?

- Opportunity costs are the forgone opportunities of the next best alternative. Choice means both gaining something and giving up something. When you choose one option, you forgo all others. The benefits of the next best alternative are the opportunity costs of your choice. *§1*

2. What is a production possibilities curve?

- A production possibilities curve represents the tradeoffs involved in the allocation of scarce resources. It shows the maximum quantity of goods and services that can be produced using limited resources to the fullest extent possible. *§1.b*

3. Why does specialization occur?

- Comparative advantage accounts for specialization. We specialize in the activities in which we have the lowest opportunity costs, that is, in which we have a comparative advantage. *§2.c*

4. What are the benefits of trade?

- Voluntary trade enables people to get more than they could get by doing everything themselves. The amount they get by specializing and trading is called gains from trade. *§2.b*
- Specialization and trade enable those involved to acquire more than they could if they did not specialize and engage in trade. *§2.c*
- Private property rights are necessary for voluntary trade to occur. Private property rights refer to the legal system that ensures that people own their persons and their property. Others cannot steal that property or harm that person. *§2.d*

Key Terms

opportunity costs *§1*

tradeoff *§1.a*

production possibilities curve (PPC) *§1.b*

marginal cost *§2.a*

marginal opportunity cost *§2.a*

gains from trade *§2.b*

comparative advantage *§2.c*

private property rights *§2.d*

Exercises

1. In most political campaigns, candidates promise more than they can deliver. In the United States, both Democrats and Republicans promise better health care, a better environment, only minor reductions in defense, better education, and an improved system of roads, bridges, sewer systems, water systems, and so on. What economic concept do candidates ignore?

2. Janine is an accountant who makes $30,000 a year. Robert is a college student who makes $8,000 a year. All other things being equal, who is more likely to stand in a long line to get a concert ticket? Explain.

3. In 2006, President George W. Bush and Congress enacted a budget that included increases in spending for the war in Iraq, national defense, welfare programs, education, and many other programs. The budget expenditures exceeded the revenues. The argument was that "we need these things," and therefore there is no limit to what the government should provide. Is there a limit? What concept is ignored by those politicians who claim that there is no limit to what the government should provide?

4. The following numbers measure the tradeoff between grades and income:

Total Hours	Hours Studying	GPA	Hours Working	Income
60	60	4.0	0	$0
60	40	3.0	20	$100
60	30	2.0	30	$150
60	10	1.0	50	$250
60	0	0.0	60	$300

a. Calculate the opportunity cost of an increase in the number of hours spent studying in order to earn a 3.0 grade point average (GPA) rather than a 2.0 GPA.
b. Is the opportunity cost the same for a move from a 0.0 GPA to a 1.0 GPA as it is for a move from a 1.0 GPA to a 2.0 GPA?
c. What is the opportunity cost of an increase in income from $100 to $150?

5. Suppose a second individual has the following tradeoffs between income and grades:

Total Hours	Hours Studying	GPA	Hours Working	Income
60	50	4.0	10	$60
60	40	3.0	20	$120
60	20	2.0	40	$240
60	10	1.0	50	$300
60	0	0.0	60	$360

a. Define comparative advantage.
b. Does either individual (the one in exercise 4 or the one in exercise 5) have a comparative advantage in both activities?
c. Who should specialize in studying and who should specialize in working?

6. A doctor earns $250,000 per year, while a professor earns $40,000. They play tennis against each other each Saturday morning, each giving up a morning of relaxing, reading the paper, and playing with their children. They could each decide to work a few extra hours on Saturday and earn more income. But they choose to play tennis or to relax around the house. Are their opportunity costs of playing tennis different?

7. Plot the PPC of a nation given by the following data.

Combination	Health Care	All Other Goods
A	0	100
B	25	90
C	50	70
D	75	40
E	100	0

a. Calculate the marginal opportunity cost of each combination.
b. What is the opportunity cost of combination C?
c. Suppose a second nation has the following data. Plot the PPC, and then determine which nation has the comparative advantage in which activity. Show whether the two nations can gain from specialization and trade.

Combination	Health Care	All Other Goods
A	0	50
B	20	40
C	40	25
D	60	5
E	65	0

8. A doctor earns $200 per hour, a plumber $40 per hour, and a professor $20 per hour. Everything else the same, which one will devote more hours to negotiating the price of a new car? Explain.

9. Perhaps you've heard of the old saying, "There is no such thing as a free lunch." What does it mean? If someone invites you to a lunch and offers to pay for it, is it free to you?

10. You have waited 30 minutes in a line for the Star Tours ride at Disneyland. You see a sign that says, "From this point on, your wait is 45 minutes." You must decide whether to remain in the line or to move elsewhere. On what basis do you make the decision? Do the 30 minutes you've already stood in line come into play?

11. A university is deciding between two meal plans. One plan charges a fixed fee of $600 per semester and allows students to eat as much as they want. The other plan charges a fee based on the quantity of food consumed. Under which plan will students eat the most?

12. Evaluate this statement: "You are a natural athlete, an attractive person who learns easily and communicates well. Clearly, you can do everything better than your friends and acquaintances. As a result, the term *special-ization* has no meaning for you. Specialization would cost you rather than benefit you."

13. During China's Cultural Revolution in the late 1960s and early 1970s, highly educated people were forced to move to farms and work in the fields. Some were common laborers for eight or more years. What does this policy say about specialization and the PPC? Would you predict that the policy would lead to an increase in output?

14. In elementary school and through middle school, most students have the same teacher throughout the day and for the entire school year. Then, beginning in high school, different subjects are taught by different teachers. In college, the same subject is often taught at different levels—freshman, sophomore, junior-senior, or graduate—by different faculty. Is education taking advantage of specialization only from high school on? Comment on the differences between elementary school and college and the use of specialization.

15. The top officials in the federal government and high-ranking officers of large corporations often have chauffeurs to drive them around the city or from meeting to meeting. Is this simply one of the perquisites of their position, or is the use of chauffeurs justifiable on the basis of comparative advantage?

16. In Botswana, Zimbabwe, and South Africa, individuals can own and farm elephants. In other African countries, the elephants are put on large reserves. Explain why the elephant population in Botswana, Zimbabwe, and South Africa has risen, whereas that in the rest of Africa has fallen.

Take the ACE Practice Test for this chapter to review the important concepts and get immediate feedback with answers.

college.hmco.com/economics/students/

Venezuela's Chavez Urges Cooperation from Ranchers amid Land Reform

Associated Press Worldstream
September 23, 2005

Venezuelan President Hugo Chavez has urged large land owners to cooperate with his government as it pushes ahead with a land reform despite concerns over property rights.

Speaking to government supporters organized into cooperatives, Chavez said: "Whoever doesn't want to cooperate, well, we will apply full weight of the law . . . we are moving forward on the path to socialism."

Business leaders accuse authorities of illegally seizing lands without giving farmers and ranchers an opportunity to prove ownership. Under a 2001 law, the government can seize lands if they are declared idle or if legitimate ownership cannot be proved as far back as 1847.

Land owners have complained that officials of Venezuela's National Lands Institute have unfairly seized their property, but Chavez responded by telling them "to stop squealing."

Authorities have declared at least 21 cattle ranches state property, because they were allegedly "idle" or those who claimed ownership couldn't prove it.

Chavez's administration has helped poor farmers to start to work the lands.

"It's about opening small spaces for socialism," Chavez told supporters inside a packed auditorium. "We are preparing for a period of post-capitalism."

In recent months, government officials accompanied by troops have arrived at dozens of ranches or opened investigations into others across the country.

The president was granting government loans totaling 2.7 billion bolivars (US$1.3 million, [euro]1.06 million) to poor Venezuelans who will be raising cattle and growing crops such as coffee.

Chavez, a close ally of Cuban leader Fidel Castro, says he is leading this oil-rich South American nation toward "21st-century socialism" as part of a "revolution" to help improve living conditions for the poor.

Government opponents claim Chavez is steering Venezuela, the world's fifth largest oil exporter, toward Cuba-style communism.

Business leader Rafael Alfonzo urged Venezuelans who support Chavez's policies "to wake up," and warned that poverty-stricken citizens would remain poor if private property rights are not respected.

Chavez "wants to establish a regime in which the state is the only property owner, and you will be . . . eating only what the government wants you to eat," Alfonzo told the local Globovision television channel.

"I'm talking to businessmen, house wives, shop owners and politicians, wake up! If you don't do it now, it will be too late," added Alfonzo.

Chavez fiercely criticized capitalism, saying it only leads to "misery for the majority" and will eventually endanger the survival of the human race.

Chavez, former paratroop commander, has rejected allegations that he is becoming authoritarian. He claims that his political movement is "deeply democratic" and that Venezuelans will keep him in power through elections until 2013.

Christopher Toothaker

There is a story that goes something like this:

Everybody, Somebody, Anybody, and Nobody were faced with an important task. Everybody was sure that Somebody would do it. Anybody could have done it, but Nobody did it. Somebody got angry about that because it was Everybody's job. Everybody thought Anybody could do it. But Nobody realized that Everybody wouldn't do it. The end result was that Everybody blamed Somebody when Nobody did what Anybody could have.

The story points out that if you own something, you have an incentive to take care of it. When no one owns something or when everyone owns something, no one has an incentive to take care of it. That is what private property rights are all about: They ensure individual ownership. When all housing in China's major cities was owned by the government, the houses and apartments were not taken care of. Similarly, in the projects of the large cities in the eastern United States, where apartments are owned by the government, no one has an incentive to ensure that the housing is cared for. But, as soon as China allowed some private ownership of apartments, the improvements were amazing—clean hallways, lighted hallways, and improvements in the buildings. When the projects are sold to private owners, the apartments are improved and cared for.

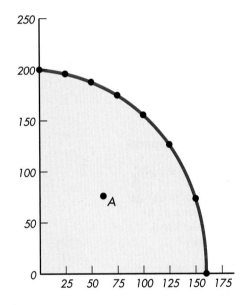

The PPC shows combinations of two goods, services, or activities that people can devote their resources to producing. Points along the curve are all possible combinations of two goods that can be produced using an individual's resources fully and efficiently. If you can own what you create, you have an incentive to produce somewhere along the PPC. But, if you don't own what you create, why should you worry about whether you are using resources efficiently or fully? You will operate at a point inside the PPC, such as point A. You will produce less than you are capable of producing.

Not only will you produce less, but you will not have an incentive to specialize and trade. Since you don't own what you create, you don't care whether what you produce is in accordance with comparative advantage. There is nothing to trade because you own nothing. This is the situation toward which Venezuela is being driven by Hugo Chavez. According to the article, Chavez's administration has helped poor farmers start to work the lands.

"'It's about opening small spaces for socialism,' Chavez told supporters inside a packed auditorium." The problem is not that the poor farmers have no place to work, it is that they own nothing. Over 75 percent of the population in most Latin American nations do not hold title to the property on which their houses rest or the fields in which they labor. Without ownership, the poor farmers have no incentive to improve the property. It is no different for the large rich landowners—when they do not own their property, they have no incentive to take care of it. The direction in which Chavez is taking Venezuela is the direction in which Castro took Cuba, Mao took China, and Lenin, Stalin, and others took Russia. The result is a shrinking PPC and a reduction in standards of living.

chapter

3

Markets, Demand and Supply, and the Price System

Fundamental Questions

1. How do we decide who gets the scarce goods and resources?

2. What is demand?

3. What is supply?

4. How is price determined by demand and supply?

5. What causes price to change?

6. What happens when price is not allowed to change with market forces?

People (and firms and nations) can get more if they specialize in certain activities and then trade with one another to acquire the goods and services that they desire than they can if they do everything themselves. This is what we described in the previous chapter as gains from trade. But how does everyone get together to trade? Who decides who specializes in what, and who determines who gets what?

In many countries, it is the government that decides who gets what and what is produced. In India until the mid-1990s, in the Soviet Union from 1917 until 1989, and in Cuba, Cameroon, and other African nations today, a few government officials dictate what is produced, by whom it is produced, where it is produced, what price it sells at, and who may buy it. China is mixed; it is undergoing a move away from government officials deciding everything, but there are still some areas of the economy where officials do specify what, how, for whom, and at what price something is produced.

In most developed or industrial nations, it is not government officials who dictate what, how, for whom, and at what price things are produced. When you walk into your local Starbucks to get a tall coffee, do you wonder who told the people working there to work there or who told the coffee growers to send their coffee beans to this particular Starbucks, or who told the bakery to provide this Starbucks with croissants? Probably not. Most of us take all these things for granted. Yet, it is a remarkable phenomenon—we get what we want, when we want it, and where we want it. How does this work? It is the market process; no one dictates what is produced, how it is produced, the price at which it sells, or who buys it. All this occurs through the self-interested behavior of individuals interacting in a market.

In this chapter we discuss the allocation of goods and services—how it is determined what is produced and who gets what. ■

?

1. How do we decide who gets the scarce goods and resources?

1. Allocation Systems

An allocation system is the process of determining who gets the goods and services and who doesn't. There are many different allocation systems that we might use. One is to have someone, say the government, determine who gets what, as in Cuba or Cameroon. Another is to have a first-come, first-served system, where those who arrive first get the goods and services. A third is to have a lottery, with the lucky winners getting the goods and services. A fourth is the market, where those with the incomes are able to buy the goods and services. Which is best? Take the following quiz, and then we'll discuss allocation systems some more.

Allocation Quiz

I. At a sightseeing point reachable only after a strenuous hike, a firm has established a stand where bottled water is sold. The water, carried in by the employees of the firm, is sold to thirsty hikers in six-ounce bottles. The price is $1 per bottle. Typically only 100 bottles of the water are sold each day. On a particularly hot day, however, 200 hikers each want to buy at least one bottle of water. Indicate what you think of each of the following means of distributing the water to the hikers by responding to each allocation approach with one of the following five responses:
   a. Agree completely
   b. Agree with slight reservation
   c. Disagree
   d. Strongly disagree
   e. Totally unacceptable

   1. Increasing the price until the quantity of bottles of water that hikers are willing and able to purchase exactly equals the number of bottles available for sale
   2. Selling the water for $1 per bottle on a first-come, first-served basis
   3. Having the local authority (government) buy the water for $1 per bottle and distribute it according to its own judgment
   4. Selling the water for $1 per bottle following a random selection procedure or lottery

II. A physician has been providing medical services at a fee of $100 per patient and typically sees 30 patients per day. One day the flu bug has been so vicious that the number of patients attempting to visit the physician exceeds 60. Indicate what you think of each of the following means of distributing the physician's services to the sick patients by responding with one of the following five answers:

a. Agree completely
b. Agree with slight reservation
c. Disagree
d. Strongly disagree
e. Totally unacceptable

1. Raising the price until the number of patients the doctor sees is exactly equal to the number of patients who are willing and able to pay the doctor's fee
2. Selling the services for $100 per patient on a first-come, first-served basis
3. Having the local authority (government) pay the physician $100 per patient and choose who is to receive the services according to its own judgment
4. Selling the physician's services for $100 per patient following a random selection procedure or lottery.

1.a. Fairness

How did you respond to the four questions in each scenario? If you are like most people, you believe that the price on the bottles of water ought to be raised and that the first patients showing up at the doctor's office ought to get service. Very few believe that the price or the market ought to be used to allocate important items like health care. Most claim that the price system is not fair. Yet none of the allocation approaches is "fair" if fairness means that everyone gets what he or she wants. In every case, someone gets the good or service and someone does not. This is what scarcity is all about—there is not enough to go around. With the market system, it is those without income or wealth who must do without. Is this fair? No. Under the first-come, first-served system, it is those who arrive later who do without. This isn't fair either, since those who are slow, old, disabled, or otherwise not first to arrive won't get the goods and services. Under the government scheme, it is those who are not in favor or those who do not match up with the government's rules who do without. In the former Soviet Union, Cuba, Cameroon, and other government-run countries, it is the government officials who get most of the goods and services, through what we call corruption, graft, and bribes. And, with a random procedure, it is those who do not have the lucky ticket or the correct number who are left out.

None of these allocation systems is fair in the sense that no one gets left out. Scarcity means that someone gets left out. Only if your measure of fair is equal opportunity is the lottery system fair. When everything is allocated by lottery, everyone has an equal chance of winning.

1.b. Incentives

Since each allocation mechanism is unfair, how do we decide which to use? One way might be by the incentives that each creates. Do the incentives lead to behavior that will improve things, increase supplies, and raise standards of living?

With the first-come, first-served allocation scheme, the incentive is to be first. You have no reason to improve the quality of your products or to increase the value of your resources. There is no incentive to increase the amounts of goods and services supplied. Why would anyone produce when all everyone wants is to be first? As a result, with a first-come, first-served allocation system, growth will not occur, and standards of living will not rise. A society based solely on first-come, first-served would die a quick death.

A government scheme provides an incentive either to be a member of government and thus help determine the allocation rules or to do exactly what the government orders you to do. There are no incentives to improve production and efficiency or to increase the quantities supplied, and thus there is no reason for the economy to grow. This type of system is a failure, as evidenced by the Soviet Union, Mao Tse-Tung's China, Cuba, and socialist systems in Latin America and Africa and in virtually every poor country in the world.

The random allocation provides no incentives at all—you simply hope that manna from heaven falls on you.

With the market system, the incentive is to acquire purchasing ability—to obtain income and wealth. This means that you must provide goods that have high value to others and provide resources that have high value to producers—to enhance your worth as an employee by acquiring education or training, and to enhance the value of the resources you own.

The market system also provides incentives for quantities of scarce goods to increase. In the case of the water stand in Scenario I, if the price of the water increases and the owner of the water stand is earning significant profits, others may carry or truck water to the top of the hill and sell it to thirsty hikers; the amount of water available thus increases. In the case of the doctor in Scenario II, other doctors may think that opening an office near the first might be a way to earn more; the amount of physician services available increases. Since the market system creates the incentive for the amount supplied to increase, economies grow and expand, and standards of living improve. The market system also ensures that resources are allocated to where they are most highly valued. If the price of an item rises, consumers may switch to another item, or another good or service, that can serve about the same purpose. When consumers switch, production of the alternative good rises, and thus the resources used in its production must increase as well. As a result, resources are reallocated from lower-valued uses to higher-valued uses.

1.c. The PPC and the Market

Figure 1 shows a production possibilities curve. The curve represents the maximum quantity of goods and services that can be produced using resources fully and efficiently. A country, alone, can produce any combination along the curve or inside the curve. Which combination will it produce: A, B, C, or some other; and who will decide? The answer is that in a market system, buyers and sellers determine what is produced, how much is produced and sold, and how the goods and services are allocated. In other words, the market defines where on the PPC a society will locate.

When the Mazda Miata was introduced in the United States in 1990, the little sports roadster was an especially desired production in southern California. As shown in Figure 2, the suggested retail price was $13,996, the price at which it was selling in Detroit. In Los Angeles, the purchase price was nearly $25,000. Several entrepreneurs recognized the profit potential in the $10,000 price differential and sent hundreds of students to Detroit to pick up Miatas and drive them back to Los Angeles. Within a reasonably short time, the price differential between Detroit and Los Angeles was reduced. The increased sales in Detroit drove the price there up, while the increased number of Miatas being sold in Los Angeles reduced the price there. The price differential continued to decline until it was less than the cost of shipping the cars from Detroit to Los Angeles. This story of the Mazda Miata illustrates how markets work to allocate scarce goods, services, and resources. A product is purchased where its price is low and sold where its price is high. As a result, resources devoted to that product flow to where they have the highest value. The same type of

FIGURE 1   Production Possibilities Curve

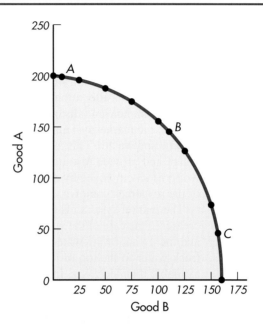

The PPC shows all possible combinations of two goods that can be produced, given that resources are fully and efficiently used. The exact point on the curve where a country produces depends on consumers—what they are willing and able to purchase.

FIGURE 2   Arbitrage

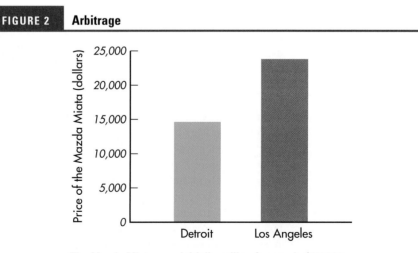

The Mazda Miata was initially selling for nearly $25,000 in Los Angeles and $14,000 in Detroit. People purchased the car in Detroit and sold it in Los Angeles, thereby driving the prices closer together.

situation occurred with the introduction of the Mini Cooper in 2001. The car was selling for much more in California than in New York and Chicago, so people purchased the car in Chicago or New York and had the cars shipped to California.

Suppose an electronics firm is inefficient, its employees are surly, and its products are not displayed well. To attempt to earn a profit, the firm charges more than the efficiently run firm down the street. Where do customers go? Obviously, they seek out the best deal and go to the more efficient firm. The more efficient store has to get more supplies, hire more employees, acquire more space, and so on. The inefficient store lays off employees, sells used equipment, and gets rid of its inventory. The resources thus go from where they were not as highly valued to where they are most highly valued.

Why does the market process work? For a very simple reason: People are looking for the best deal—the highest-quality products at the lowest prices. So when an opportunity for a "best deal" arises, people respond to it by purchasing where the price is low and selling where the price is high.

RECAP

1. Scarce goods and resources can be allocated in many different ways. Four common approaches are first-come-first-serve, prices, government, and random.

2. No allocation mechanism is fair in the sense that everyone gets everything they want. This would defy the idea of scarcity. Some people will get the goods and resources and others will not.

3. The incentives each allocation system creates is a fundamental reason that markets are selected to do the allocation. Only a market system creates the incentives that lead to increasing standards of living.

2. Markets and Money

The market process refers to the way that scarce goods and services are allocated through the individual actions of buyers and sellers. The price adjusts to the actions of buyers and sellers so as to ensure that resources are used where they have the highest value—the price of the Miata in L.A. declines as more Miata's end up in L.A. The price measures the opportunity cost—how much has to be given up in order to get something else. If you pay a dollar for a cup of coffee, then the opportunity cost of that coffee is everything else that dollar could have been used to buy. In most cases, when you buy something you exchange money for that something. There are cases where you actually exchange one good for another—you might mow someone's lawn in exchange for them taking care of your house while you are on vacation. Every market exchange is not necessarily a monetary exchange.

2.a. Market Definition

The supermarket, the stock market, and the market for foreign exchange are similar in that goods and services are exchanged. They are all markets. A market may be a specific location, such as the supermarket, or it may be the exchange of particular goods or services at many different locations, such as the foreign exchange market. A **market** makes possible the exchange of goods and services. A market may be a formally organized exchange, such as the New York Stock Exchange, or it may be loosely organized, like the market for used bicycles or automobiles. A market may be confined to one location, as in the case of a supermarket, or it may encompass a city, a state, a country, or the entire world.

market: a place or service that enables buyers and sellers to exchange goods and services

A market arises when buyers and sellers exchange a well-defined good or service. In this case of a supermarket, buyers purchase groceries and household items. The market occurs in a building at a specific location.

2.b. Barter and Money Exchanges

The purpose of markets is to facilitate the exchange of goods and services between buyers and sellers. In some cases, money changes hands; in others, only goods and services are exchanged. The exchange of goods and services directly, without money, is called **barter**. Barter occurs when a plumber fixes a leaky pipe for a lawyer in exchange for the lawyer's work on a will or when a Chinese citizen provides fresh vegetables to a U.S. visitor in exchange for a pack of U.S. cigarettes.

Most markets involve money because goods and services can be exchanged more easily with money than without it. When IBM purchases microchips from Yakamoto

barter: the direct exchange of goods and services without the use of money

A market arises when buyers and sellers exchange a well-defined good or service. In this case, shoppers at a market can examine the day's assortment and make their choices. The flower market does not occur at a specific location nor in a fixed building.

double coincidence of wants: the situation that exists when A has what B wants and B has what A wants

of Japan, IBM and Yakamoto don't exchange goods directly. Neither firm may have what the other wants. Barter requires a **double coincidence of wants:** IBM must have what Yakamoto wants, and Yakamoto must have what IBM wants. The difficulty of finding a double coincidence of wants for barter transactions is typically very high. Using money makes trading easier. To obtain the microchips, all IBM has to do is provide dollars to Yakamoto. Yakamoto is willing to accept the money, since it can spend that money to obtain the goods that it wants.

RECAP

1. A market is not necessarily a specific location or store. Instead, the term *market* refers to buyers and sellers communicating with each other regarding the quality and quantity of a well-defined product, what buyers are willing and able to pay for a product, and what sellers must receive in order to produce and sell a good or service.

2. Barter refers to exchanges made without the use of money.

3. Money makes it easier and less expensive to exchange goods and services.

3. Demand

2. What is demand?

A market is demand and supply—buyers and sellers. To understand how a price level is determined and why a price rises or falls, it is necessary to know how demand and supply function. We begin by considering demand alone, then supply, and then we put the two together. Before we begin, we discuss some economic terminology that is often confusing.

demand: the amount of a product that people are willing and able to purchase at each possible price during a given period of time, everything else held constant

quantity demanded: the amount of a product that people are willing and able to purchase at a specific price

Economists distinguish between the terms **demand** and **quantity demanded**. When they refer to the *quantity demanded,* they are talking about the amount of a product that people are willing and able to purchase at a *specific* price. When they refer to *demand,* they are talking about the amount that people would be willing and able to purchase at *every possible* price. Demand is the quantities demanded at every price. Thus, the statement that "the demand for U.S. white wine rose following an increase in the price of French white wine" means that at each price for U.S. white wine, more people were willing and able to purchase U.S. white wine. And the statement that "the quantity demanded of white wine fell as the price of white wine rose" means that people were willing and able to purchase less white wine because the price of the wine rose.

3.a. The Law of Demand

law of demand: the quantity of a well-defined good or service that people are willing and able to purchase during a particular period of time decreases as the price of that good or service rises and increases as the price falls, everything else held constant

Consumers and merchants know that if you lower the price of a good or service without altering its quality or quantity, people will beat a path to your doorway. This simple truth is referred to as the **law of demand**.

According to the law of demand, people purchase more of something when the price of that item falls. More formally, the law of demand states that the quantity of some item that people are willing and able to purchase during a particular period of time decreases as the price rises, and vice versa.

The more formal definition of the law of demand can be broken down into five phrases:

1. The quantity of a well-defined good or service that
2. people are willing and able to purchase
3. during a particular period of time
4. decreases as the price of that good or service rises and increases as the price falls,
5. everything else held constant.

The first phrase ensures that we are referring to the same item, that we are not mixing different goods. A watch is a commodity that is defined and distinguished from other goods by several characteristics: quality, color, and design of the watch face, to name a few. The law of demand applies to a well-defined good, in this case, a watch. If one of the characteristics should change, the good would no longer be well defined—in fact, it would be a different good. A Rolex watch is different from a Timex watch; Polo brand golf shirts are different goods from generic brand golf shirts; Mercedes-Benz automobiles are different goods from Saturn automobiles.

The second phrase indicates that not only must people *want* to purchase some good, but they must be *able* to purchase that good in order for their wants to be counted as part of demand. For example, Sue would love to buy a membership in the Paradise Valley Country Club, but because the membership costs $35,000, she is not able to purchase the membership. Though she is willing, she is not able. At a price of $5,000, however, she is willing and able to purchase the membership.

The third phrase points out that the demand for any good is defined for a specific period of time. Without reference to a time period, a demand relationship would not make any sense. For instance, the statement that "at a price of $3 per Happy Meal, 13 million Happy Meals are demanded" provides no useful information. Are the 13 million meals sold in one week or one year? Think of demand as a rate of purchase at each possible price over a period of time—2 per month, 1 per day, and so on.

The fourth phrase points out that price and quantity demanded move in opposite directions; that is, as the price rises, the quantity demanded falls, and as the price falls, the quantity demanded rises.

Demand is a measure of the relationship between the price and quantity demanded of a particular good or service when the determinants of demand do not change. The **determinants of demand** are income, tastes, prices of related goods and services, expectations, and the number of buyers. If any one of these items changes, demand changes. The final phrase, everything else held constant, ensures that the determinants of demand do not change.

determinants of demand: factors other than the price of the good that influence demand—income, tastes, prices of related goods and services, expectations, and number of buyers

3.b. The Demand Schedule

demand schedule: a table or list of prices and the corresponding quantities demanded for a particular good or service

A **demand schedule** is a table or list of prices and the corresponding quantities demanded for a particular good or service. Consider the demand for DVD rentals. You can rent them at a supermarket such as Safeway, from Blockbuster, or through an online service such as Netflix. The table in Figure 3 is a demand schedule for DVDs. It shows the number of DVDs that a consumer named Bob would be willing and able to rent at each price during a year, everything else held constant. As the price of the DVD gets higher relative to the prices of other goods, Bob would be willing and able to rent fewer DVDs.

At a price of $5 per DVD, Bob indicates that he will rent only 10 DVDs during the year. At a price of $4, Bob tells us that he will rent 20 DVDs during the year. As the price drops from $5 to $4 to $3 to $2 and to $1, Bob is willing and able to rent more DVDs. At a price of $1, Bob would rent 50 DVDs during the year.

3.c. The Demand Curve

demand curve: a graph of a demand schedule that measures price on the vertical axis and quantity demanded on the horizontal axis

A **demand curve** is a graph of the demand schedule. The demand curve shown in Figure 3 is plotted from the information given in the demand schedule. Price is measured on the vertical axis, and quantity per unit of time on the horizontal axis. The demand curve slopes downward because of the inverse relationship between the rental price of the DVDs and the quantity that an individual is willing and able to purchase or rent. Point *A* in Figure 3 corresponds to combination *A* in the table: a price of $5 and 10 DVDs demanded. Similarly, points *B, C, D,* and *E* in Figure 3

FIGURE 3 Bob's Demand Schedule and Demand Curve for DVDs

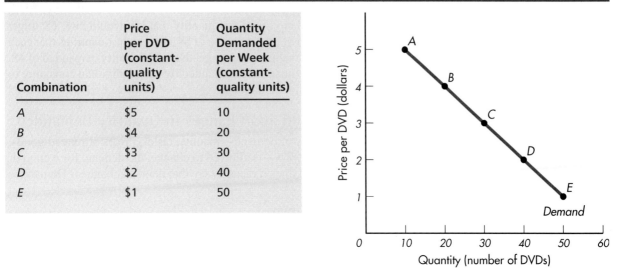

Combination	Price per DVD (constant-quality units)	Quantity Demanded per Week (constant-quality units)
A	$5	10
B	$4	20
C	$3	30
D	$2	40
E	$1	50

The number of DVDs that Bob is willing and able to rent at each price during the week is listed in the table, or demand schedule. The demand curve is derived from the combinations given in the demand schedule. The price-quantity combination of $5 per DVD and 10 DVDs is point *A*. The combination of $4 per DVD and 20 DVDs is point *B*. Each combination is plotted, and the points are connected to form the demand curve.

represent the corresponding combinations in the table. The line connecting these points is Bob's demand curve for DVDs.

All demand curves slope down because of the law of demand: As price falls, quantity demanded increases. The demand curves for bread, electricity, automobiles, colleges, labor services, health care, and any other good or service you can think of slope down. You might be saying to yourself, "That's not true. When the price of some rock concerts goes up, more people want to attend the concert. As the ticket price goes up, going to the concert becomes more prestigious, and the quantity demanded actually rises." To avoid confusion in such circumstances, we say "everything else held constant." With this statement, we are assuming that tastes don't change and that, therefore, the goods *cannot* become more prestigious as the price changes. Similarly, we do not allow the quality or the brand name of a product to change as we define the demand schedule or demand curve. We concentrate on the one quality or the one brand; so when we say that the price of a good has risen, we are talking about a good that is identical at all prices.

When speaking of the demand curve or demand schedule, we are using constant-quality units. The quality of a good does not change as the price changes along a demand curve.

3.d. From Individual Demand Curves to a Market Curve

Bob's demand curve for DVDs is plotted in Figure 3. Unless Bob is the only person who rents DVDs, his demand curve is not the total, or market demand, curve. Market demand is the sum of all individual demands. To derive the market demand curve, then, the individual demand curves of all consumers in the market must be added together. The table in Figure 4 lists the demand schedules of three individuals, Bob, Maria, and Liu. If these three were the only consumers in the market, then the market demand would be the sum of their individual demands, shown as the last column of the table.

Bob's, Maria's, and Liu's demand schedules are plotted as individual demand curves in Figure 4(a). In Figure 4(b), their individual demand curves have been added together to obtain the market demand curve for DVDs. (Notice that we add in a horizontal direction—that is, we add the quantities at each price, not the prices at each quantity.) At a price of $5, we add the quantity that Bob would buy, 10, to the quantity that Maria would buy, 5, to the quantity that Liu would buy, 15, to get the market quantity demanded of 30. At a price of $4, we add the quantities that each of the consumers is willing and able to buy to get the total quantity demanded of 48. At all prices, then, we add the quantities demanded by each individual consumer to get the total, or market quantity, demanded.

3.e. Changes in Demand and Changes in Quantity Demanded

When one of the determinants of demand—income, tastes, prices of related goods, expectations, or number of buyers—is allowed to change, the demand for a good or service changes as well. What does it mean to say that demand changes? Demand is

FIGURE 4   **The Market Demand Schedule and Curve for DVDs**

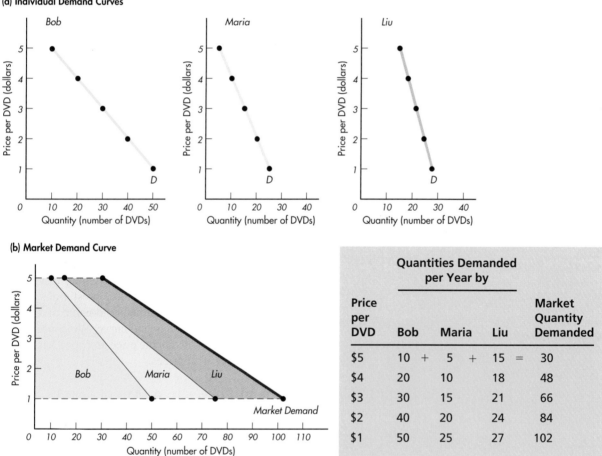

(a) Individual Demand Curves

(b) Market Demand Curve

Price per DVD	Quantities Demanded per Year by			Market Quantity Demanded
	Bob	Maria	Liu	
$5	10 +	5 +	15 =	30
$4	20	10	18	48
$3	30	15	21	66
$2	40	20	24	84
$1	50	25	27	102

The market is defined to consist of three individuals: Bob, Maria, and Liu. Their demand schedules are listed in the table and plotted as the individual demand curves shown in Figure 4(a). By adding the quantities that each demands at every price, we obtain the market demand curve shown in Figure 4(b). At a price of $1, we add Bob's quantity demanded of 50 to Maria's quantity demanded of 25 to Liu's quantity demanded of 27 to obtain the market quantity demanded of 102. At a price of $2, we add Bob's 40 to Maria's 20 to Liu's 24 to obtain the market quantity demanded of 84. To obtain the market demand curve, for every price we sum the quantities demanded by each market participant.

the entire demand schedule, or demand curve. When we say that demand changes, we are referring to a change in the quantities demanded at each and every price.

For example, if Bob's income rises, then his demand for DVDs rises. At each and every price, the number of DVDs that Bob is willing and able to buy each week rises. This increase is shown in the last column of the table in Figure 5. A change in demand is represented by a shift of the demand curve, as shown in Figure 5(a). The shift to the right, from D_1 to D_2, indicates that Bob is willing and able to purchase more DVDs at every price.

When the price of a good or service is the only factor that changes, the quantity demanded changes, but the demand curve does not shift. Instead, as the price of the DVD rental is decreased (increased), everything else held constant, the quantity that people are willing and able to purchase increases (decreases). This change is merely a movement from one point on the demand curve to another point on the same demand curve, not a shift of the demand curve. *Change in the quantity demanded* is the phrase that economists use to describe the change in the quantities of a particular good or service that people are willing and able to purchase as the price of that good or service changes. A change in the quantity demanded, from point A to point B on the demand curve, is shown in Figure 5(b).

The demand curve shifts when income, tastes, prices of related goods, expectations, or the number of buyers changes. Let's consider how each of these determinants of demand affects the demand curve.

FIGURE 5   A Change in Demand and a Change in the Quantity Demanded

According to the table, Bob's demand for DVDs has increased by 5 DVDs at each price. In Figure 5(a), this change is shown as a shift of the demand curve from D_1 to D_2. Figure 5(b) shows a change in the quantity demanded. The change is an increase in the quantity that consumers are willing and able to purchase at a lower price. It is shown as a movement along the demand curve from point A to point B.

Price per DVD	Quantities Demanded per Week	
	Before	After
$5	10	15
$4	20	25
$3	30	35
$2	40	45
$1	50	55

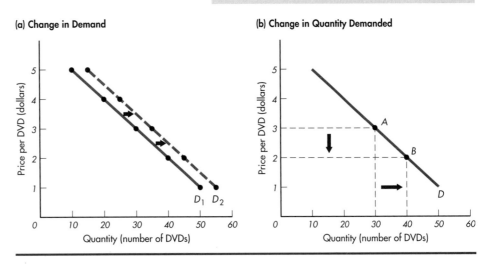

(a) Change in Demand

(b) Change in Quantity Demanded

3.e.1. Income   The demand for any good or service depends on income. For most goods and services, the higher someone's income is, everything else the same, the more that person can purchase at any given price. These are called **normal goods**. The increase in Bob's income causes his demand to increase. This change is shown in Figure 5(a) by the shift to the right from the curve labeled D_1 to the curve labeled D_2. Increased income means a greater ability to purchase goods and services. At every price, more DVDs are demanded along curve D_2 than along curve D_1.

For some goods and services, however, the amount demanded declines as income rises, everything else the same. The reason could be that these are goods or services that people use only when their incomes are declining—such as bankruptcy services. In addition, people might not like the good or service as well as they like a more expensive good or service, so when their income rises, they purchase the more expensive items. These types of items are called **inferior goods**.

3.e.2. Tastes   The demand for any good or service depends on individuals' tastes and preferences. When the iPod came out in 2000, it became an instant success. The Sony Walkman lost market share and essentially disappeared. Tastes changed toward the more mobile iPod and, more important, toward the more powerful iPod. Thousands of songs could be stored on an iPod, while the Walkman was constrained by the size of the CD.

3.e.3. Prices of Related Goods and Services   Goods and services may be related in two ways. **Substitute goods** can be used in place of each other, so that as the cost of one rises, everything else the same, people will buy more of the other. Bread and crackers, BMWs and Acuras, DVD rentals and theater movies, universities and community colleges, electricity and natural gas are, more or less, pairs of substitutes. As the price of movie theater tickets rises, everything else held constant, the demand for DVDs will rise; the demand curve for DVDs will shift to the right.

Complementary goods are goods that are used together, and so as the price of one rises, everything else the same, consumers buy less of it but also buy less of the complementary good. Bread and margarine, beer and peanuts, cameras and film, shoes and socks, CDs and CD players, iPods and iTunes are examples of pairs of complementary goods. As the price of DVD players rises, people tend to purchase fewer DVD players, but they also demand fewer DVD rentals. The demand curve for a complementary good shifts to the left when the price of the related good increases.

3.e.4. Expectations   Expectations about future events can have an effect on demand today. People make purchases today because they expect their income level to be a certain amount in the future, or because they expect the price of certain items to be higher in the future. You might buy running shoes today if you expect the price of those shoes to be higher tomorrow. You might buy your airline ticket home now rather than wait until semester break if you expect the price to be higher next month.

3.e.5. Number of Buyers   Market demand consists of the sum of the demands of all individuals. The more individuals there are with income to spend, the greater the market demand is likely to be. For example, the populations of Florida and Arizona are much larger during the winter than they are during the summer. The demand for any particular good or service in Arizona and Florida rises (the demand curve shifts to the right) during the winter and falls (the demand curve shifts to the left) during the summer.

---

normal goods: goods for which demand increases as income increases

inferior goods: goods for which demand decreases as income increases

substitute goods: goods that can be used in place of each other; as the price of one rises, the demand for the other rises

complementary goods: goods that are used together; as the price of one rises, the demand for the other falls

1. According to the law of demand, as the price of any good or service rises (falls), the quantity demanded of that good or service falls (rises), during a specific period of time, everything else held constant.

2. A demand schedule is a listing of the quantity demanded at each price.

3. The demand curve is a downward-sloping line plotted using the values in the demand schedule.

4. Market demand is the sum of all individual demands.

5. Demand changes when one of the determinants of demand changes. A demand change is a shift of the demand curve.

6. The determinants of demand are income, tastes, prices of related goods and services, expectations, and number of buyers

7. The quantity demanded changes when the price of the good or service changes. This is a change from one point on the demand curve to another point on the same demand curve.

4. Supply

3. What is supply?

Why do students get discounts at movie theaters? Demand *and* supply. Why do restaurants offer early bird specials? Demand *and* supply. Why is the price of hotel accommodations in Phoenix higher in the winter than in the summer? Demand *and* supply. Why is the price of beef higher in Japan than in the United States? Demand *and* supply. Both demand and supply determine price; neither demand nor supply alone determines price. We now discuss supply.

4.a. The Law of Supply

supply: the amount of a good or service that producers are willing and able to offer for sale at each possible price during a period of time, everything else held constant

quantity supplied: the amount that sellers are willing and able to offer at a given price during a particular period of time, everything else held constant

law of supply: the quantity of a well-defined good or service that producers are willing and able to offer for sale during a particular period of time increases as the price of the good or service increases and decreases as the price decreases, everything else held constant

Just as demand is the relation between the price and the quantity demanded of a good or service, supply is the relation between the price and the quantity supplied. **Supply** is the amount of the good or service that producers are willing and able to offer for sale at each possible price during a period of time, everything else held constant. **Quantity supplied** is the amount of the good or service that producers are willing and able to offer for sale at a *specific* price during a period of time, everything else held constant. According to the **law of supply**, as the price of a good or service rises, the quantity supplied rises, and vice versa.

The formal statement of the law of supply consists of five phrases:

1. The quantity of a well-defined good or service that

2. producers are willing and able to offer for sale

3. during a particular period of time

4. increases as the price of the good or service increases and decreases as the price decreases,

5. everything else held constant.

The first phrase is the same as the first phrase in the law of demand. The second phrase indicates that producers must not only *want* to offer the product for sale but be *able* to offer the product. The third phrase points out that the quantities producers will offer for sale depend on the period of time being considered. The fourth

determinants of supply: factors other than the price of the good that influence supply—prices of resources, technology and productivity, expectations of producers, number of producers, and the prices of related goods and services

supply schedule: a table or list of prices and the corresponding quantities supplied of a particular good or service

supply curve: a graph of a supply schedule that measures price on the vertical axis and quantity supplied on the horizontal axis

phrase points out that more will be supplied at higher than at lower prices. The final phrase ensures that the **determinants of supply** do not change. The determinants of supply are those factors other than the price of the good or service that influence the willingness and ability of producers to offer their goods and services for sale—the prices of resources used to produce the product, technology and productivity, expectations of producers, the number of producers in the market, and the prices of related goods and services. If any one of these should change, supply changes.

4.b. The Supply Schedule and Supply Curve

A **supply schedule** is a table or list of the prices and the corresponding quantities supplied of a good or service. The table in Figure 6 presents a single firm's supply schedule for DVDs. The schedule lists the quantities that the firm is willing and able to supply at each price, everything else held constant. As the price increases, the firm is willing and able to offer more DVDs.

A **supply curve** is a graph of the supply schedule. Figure 6 shows NetRents's supply curve for DVDs. The price and quantity combinations given in the supply schedule correspond to the points on the curve. For instance, combination A in the table corresponds to point A on the curve; combination B in the table corresponds to point B on the curve, and so on for each price-quantity combination.

The supply curve slopes upward. This means that a supplier is willing and able to offer more for sale at higher prices than it is at lower prices. This should make sense—if prices rise, everything else held constant, the supplier will earn more profits. Higher profits create the incentive for the supplier to offer more for sale.

4.c. From Individual Supply Curves to the Market Supply

To derive market supply, the quantities that each producer supplies at each price are added together, just as the quantities demanded by each consumer are added together to get market demand. The table in Figure 7 lists the supply schedules of three firms that rent DVDs: NetRents, MGA, and Blockmaster. The supply schedule of

---

FIGURE 6   **NetRent's Supply Schedule and Supply Curve for DVDs**

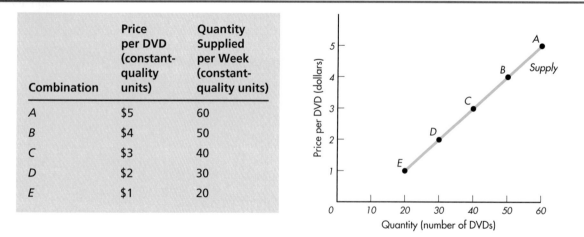

Combination	Price per DVD (constant-quality units)	Quantity Supplied per Week (constant-quality units)
A	$5	60
B	$4	50
C	$3	40
D	$2	30
E	$1	20

The quantity that NetRent is willing and able to offer for sale at each price is listed in the supply schedule and shown on the supply curve. At point A, the price is $5 per DVD and the quantity supplied is 60 DVDs. The combination of $4 per DVD and 50 DVDs is point B. Each price-quantity combination is plotted, and the points are connected to form the supply curve.

FIGURE 7   The Market Supply Schedule and Curve for DVDs

Price per DVD	Quantities Supplied per Year by			Market Quantity Supplied
	NetRent	MGA	Blockmaster	
$5	60 +	30 +	12 =	102
$4	50	25	9	84
$3	40	20	6	66
$2	30	15	3	48
$1	20	10	0	30

(a) Individual Supply Curves

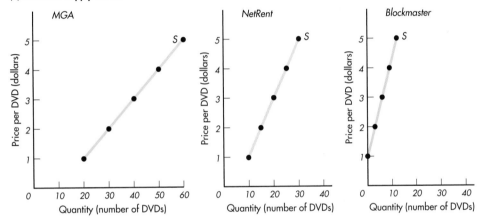

(b) Market Supply Curve

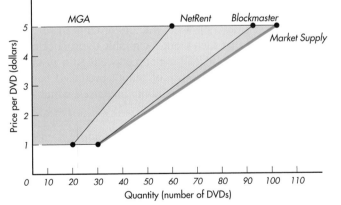

The market supply is derived by summing the quantities that each producer is willing and able to offer for sale at each price. In this example, there are three producers: NetRent, MGA, and Blockmaster. The supply schedules of each are listed in the table and plotted as the individual supply curves shown in Figure 7(a). By adding the quantities supplied at each price, we obtain the market supply curve shown in Figure 7(b). For instance, at a price of $5, NetRent offers 60 units, MGA 30 units, and Blockmaster 12 units, for a market supply quantity of 102. The market supply curve reflects the quantities that each producer is able and willing to supply at each price.

each is plotted in Figure 7(a). Then in Figure 7(b) the individual supply curves have been added together to obtain the market supply curve. At a price of $5, the quantity supplied by NetRents is 60, the quantity supplied by MGA is 30, and the quantity supplied by Blockmaster is 12. This means a total quantity supplied in the market of 102. At a price of $4, the quantities supplied are 50, 25, and 9, for a total market quantity supplied of 84. The market supply schedule is the last column in the table. The graph of the price and quantity combinations listed in this column is the market supply curve. The market supply curve slopes up because each of the individual supply curves has a positive slope. The market supply curve tells us that the quantity supplied in the market increases as the price rises.

4.d. Changes in Supply and Changes in Quantity Supplied

A change in the quantity supplied is a movement along the supply curve. A change in the supply is a shift of the supply curve.

When we draw the supply curve, we allow only the price and quantity supplied of the good or service that we are discussing to change. Everything else that might affect supply is assumed not to change. If any of the determinants of supply—the prices of resources used to produce the product, technology and productivity, expectations of producers, the number of producers in the market, and the prices of related goods and services—changes, the supply schedule changes and the supply curve shifts.

4.d.1. Prices of Resources
If labor costs rise, higher prices will be necessary to induce each store to offer as many DVDs as it did before the cost of the resource rose. The higher cost of resources causes a decrease in supply, meaning a leftward shift of the supply curve, from S_1 to S_2 in Figure 8(a). In 2006, U.S. first-class mail rose from $.36 to $.39 for the first ounce, which meant that the cost of shipping the DVDs rose. This caused the rental companies to offer fewer rentals at each price. Compare point B on curve S_2 with point A on curve S_1. Both points correspond to a price of $3, but along curve S_1, sellers are willing to offer 66 DVDs, whereas curve S_2 indicates that sellers will offer only 57 DVDs.

4.d.2. Technology and Productivity
If resources are used more efficiently in the production of a good or service, more of that good or service can be produced for the same cost, or the original quantity can be produced for a lower cost. As a result, the supply curve shifts to the right, as in Figure 8(b).

The move from horse-drawn plows to tractors or from mainframe computers to personal computers meant that each worker was able to produce more. The increase in output produced by each unit of a resource is called a *productivity increase*. **Productivity** is defined as the quantity of output produced per unit of resource. Improvements in technology cause productivity increases, which lead to an increase in supply.

productivity: the quantity of output produced per unit of resource

4.d.3. Expectations of Suppliers
Sellers may choose to alter the quantity offered for sale today because of a change in expectations regarding the determinants of supply. A supply curve illustrates the quantities that suppliers are willing and able to supply at every possible price. If suppliers expect that something is going to occur to resource supplies or the cost of resources, then they may alter the quantities that they are willing and able to supply at every possible price. The key point is that the supply curve will shift if producers expect something to occur that will alter their anticipated profits at every possible price, not just a change in one price. For instance, the expectation that demand will decline in the future does not lead to a shift of the supply curve; it leads instead to a decline in quantity supplied, because the new demand curve (the expected lower demand) would intersect the supply curve at a lower price and a smaller output level.

FIGURE 8   A Shift of the Supply Curve

(a) Decrease in Supply

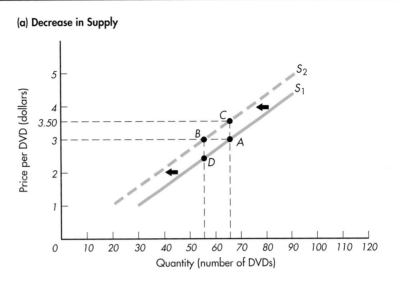

(b) Increase in Supply

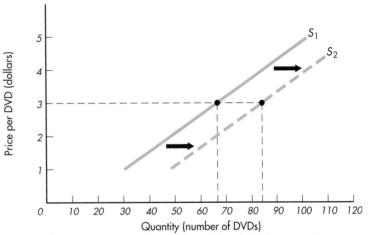

Figure 8(a) shows a decrease in supply and the shift of the supply curve to the left, from S_1 to S_2. The decrease is caused by a change in one of the determinants of DVD supply—an increase in the price of labor. Because of the increased price of labor, producers are willing and able to offer fewer DVDs for rent at each price than they were before the price of labor rose. Supply curve S_2 shows that at a price of $3 per DVD, suppliers will offer 57 DVDs. That is 9 units less than the 66 DVDs at $3 per DVD indicated by supply curve S_1. Conversely, to offer a given quantity, producers must receive a higher price per DVD than they previously were getting: $3.50 per DVD for 66 DVDs (on supply curve S_2) instead of $3 per DVD (on supply curve S_1).

Figure 8(b) shows an increase in supply. A technological improvement or an increase in productivity causes the supply curve to shift to the right, from S_1 to S_2. At each price, a higher quantity is offered for sale. At a price of $3, 66 units were offered, but with the shift of the supply curve, the quantity of units for sale at $3 apiece increases to 84. Conversely, producers can reduce prices for a given quantity—for example, charging $2 per DVD for 66 units.

4.d.4. Number of Suppliers When more people decide to supply a good or service, the market supply increases. More is offered for sale at each and every price, causing a rightward shift of the supply curve.

4.d.5. Prices of Related Goods or Services The opportunity cost of producing and selling any good or service is the forgone opportunity to produce any other good or service. If the price of an alternative good changes, then the opportunity cost of producing a particular good changes. This could cause the supply curve to change. For instance, if McDonald's can offer hamburgers or salads with equal ease, an increase in the price of salads could lead the manager to offer more salads and fewer hamburgers. The supply curve of salads would shift to the right, and the supply curve of hamburgers would shift to the left.

A *change in supply* occurs when the quantity supplied at each and every price changes or there is a shift in the supply curve—like the shift from S_1 to S_2 in Figure 9(a). A change in one of the determinants of supply brings about a change in supply.

When only the price changes, a greater or smaller quantity is supplied. This is shown as a movement along the supply curve, not as a shift of the curve. A change in price is said to cause a *change in the quantity supplied.* An increase in quantity supplied is shown in the move from point A to point B on the supply curve of Figure 9(b).

FIGURE 9 **A Change in Supply and a Change in the Quantity Supplied**

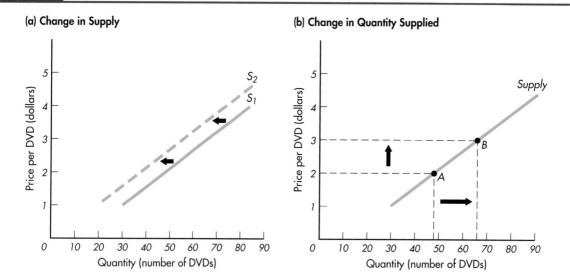

(a) Change in Supply

(b) Change in Quantity Supplied

In Figure 9(a), the quantities that producers are willing and able to offer for sale at every price decrease, causing a leftward shift of the supply curve from S_1 to S_2. In Figure 9(b), the quantities that producers are willing and able to offer for sale increase, because of an increase in the price of the good, causing a movement along the supply curve from point A to point B.

RECAP

1. According to the law of supply, the quantity supplied of any good or service is directly related to the price of the good or service during a specific period of time, everything else held constant.

2. Market supply is found by adding together the quantities supplied at each price by every producer in the market.

Part One Introduction to the Price System

3. Supply changes if the prices of relevant resources change, if technology or productivity changes, if producers' expectations change, if the number of producers changes, or if the prices of related goods and services change.

4. Changes in supply are reflected in shifts of the supply curve. Changes in the quantity supplied are reflected in movements along the supply curve.

4. How is price determined by demand and supply?

equilibrium: the price and quantity at which quantity demanded and quantity supplied are equal

5. Equilibrium: Putting Demand and Supply Together

The demand curve shows the quantity of a good or service that buyers are willing and able to purchase at each price. The supply curve shows the quantity that producers are willing and able to offer for sale at each price. Only where the two curves intersect is the quantity supplied equal to the quantity demanded. This intersection is the point of **equilibrium**.

5.a. Determination of Equilibrium

Figure 10 brings together the market demand and market supply curves for DVD rentals. The supply and demand schedules are listed in the table, and the curves are plotted in the graph in Figure 10. Notice that the curves intersect at only one point, labeled *e,* a price of $3 and a quantity of 66. The intersection point is the equilibrium price, the only price at which the quantity demanded and quantity supplied are the same. You can see that at any other price, the quantity demanded and quantity supplied are not the same. This is called **disequilibrium**.

disequilibrium: prices at which quantity demanded and quantity supplied are not equal at a particular price

Whenever the price is greater than the equilibrium price, a **surplus** arises. For example, at $4, the quantity of DVDs demanded is 48, and the quantity supplied is 84. Thus, at $4 per DVD, there is a surplus of 36 DVDs—that is, 36 DVDs are not rented. Conversely, whenever the price is below the equilibrium price, the quantity demanded is greater than the quantity supplied and there is a **shortage**. For instance, if the price is $2 per DVD, consumers will want and be able to pay for more DVDs than are available. As shown in the table in Figure 10, the quantity demanded at a price of $2 is 84, but the quantity supplied is only 48. There is a shortage of 36 DVDs at the price of $2.

surplus: a quantity supplied that is larger than the quantity demanded at a given price; it occurs whenever the price is greater than the equilibrium price

shortage: a quantity supplied that is smaller than the quantity demanded at a given price; it occurs whenever the price is less than the equilibrium price

Neither a surplus nor a shortage will exist for long if the price of the product is free to change. Suppliers who are stuck with DVDs sitting on the shelves getting brittle and out of style will lower the price and reduce the quantities they are offering for rent in order to eliminate a surplus. Conversely, suppliers whose shelves are empty while consumers are demanding DVDs will acquire more DVDs and raise the rental price to eliminate a shortage. Surpluses lead to decreases in the price and the quantity supplied and increases in the quantity demanded. Shortages lead to increases in the price and the quantity supplied and decreases in the quantity demanded.

Note that a shortage is not the same thing as scarcity.

A shortage exists only when the quantity that people are willing and able to purchase at a particular price is more than the quantity supplied *at that price*. Scarcity occurs when more is wanted at a zero price than is available.

5.b. Changes in the Equilibrium Price: Demand Shifts

Equilibrium is the combination of price and quantity at which the quantities demanded and supplied are the same. Once an equilibrium is achieved, there is no incentive for suppliers or consumers to move away from it. An equilibrium price changes only when demand and/or supply changes—that is, when the determinants of demand or the determinants of supply change.

FIGURE 10   Equilibrium

Price per DVD	Quantity Demanded per Week	Quantity Supplied per Week	Status
$5	30	102	Surplus of 72
$4	48	84	Surplus of 36
$3	66	66	Equilibrium
$2	84	48	Shortage of 36
$1	102	30	Shortage of 72

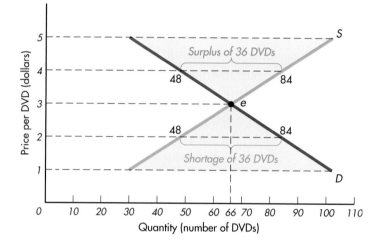

Equilibrium is established at the point where the quantity that suppliers are willing and able to offer for sale is the same as the quantity that buyers are willing and able to purchase. Here, equilibrium occurs at the price of $3 per DVD and the quantity of 66 DVDs. It is shown as point *e*, at the intersection of the demand and supply curves. At prices above $3, the quantity supplied is greater than the quantity demanded, and the result is a surplus. At prices below $3, the quantity supplied is less than the quantity demanded, and the result is a shortage. The area shaded tan shows all prices at which there is a surplus—where quantity supplied is greater than the quantity demanded. The surplus is measured in a horizontal direction at each price. The area shaded blue represents all prices at which a shortage exists—where the quantity demanded is greater than the quantity supplied. The shortage is measured in a horizontal direction at each price.

Let's consider a change in demand and what it means for the equilibrium price. Suppose that experiments on rats show that watching DVDs causes brain damage. As a result, a large segment of the human population decides not to rent DVDs. Stores find that the demand for DVDs has decreased, as shown in Figure 11 by a leftward shift of the demand curve, from curve D_1 to curve D_2.

Once the demand curve has shifted, the original equilibrium price of $3 per DVD at point e_1 is no longer equilibrium. At a price of $3, the quantity supplied is still 66, but the quantity demanded has declined to 48 (look at the demand curve D_2 at a price of $3). There is, therefore, a surplus of 18 DVDs at the price of $3.

?

5. What causes price to change?

FIGURE 11 **The Effects of a Shift of the Demand Curve**

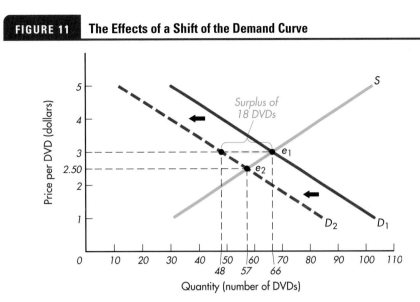

The initial equilibrium price ($3 per DVD) and quantity (66 DVDs) are established at point e_1, where the initial demand and supply curves intersect. A change in the tastes for DVDs causes demand to decrease, and the demand curve shifts to the left. At $3 per DVD, the initial quantity supplied, 66 DVDs, is now greater than the quantity demanded, 48 DVDs. The surplus of 18 units causes producers to reduce production and lower the price. The market reaches a new equilibrium, at point e_2, $2.50 per DVD and 57 DVDs.

With a surplus comes downward pressure on the price. This downward pressure occurs because producers acquire fewer DVDs to offer for rent and reduce the rental price in an attempt to rent the DVDs that are sitting on the shelves. Suppliers continue reducing the price and the quantity available until consumers rent all copies of the DVDs that the sellers have available, or until a new equilibrium is established. That new equilibrium occurs at point e_2 with a price of $2.50 and a quantity of 57.

The decrease in demand is represented by the leftward shift of the demand curve. A decrease in demand results in a lower equilibrium price and a lower equilibrium quantity as long as there is no change in supply. Conversely, an increase in demand would be represented as a rightward shift of the demand curve and would result in a higher equilibrium price and a higher equilibrium quantity as long as there is no change in supply.

5.c. Changes in the Equilibrium Price: Supply Shifts

The equilibrium price and quantity may be altered by a change in supply as well. If the price of relevant resources, technology and productivity, the expectations of suppliers, the number of suppliers, or the prices of related products change, supply changes.

Let's consider an example. The U.S. mail is a key ingredient in sending and receiving DVDs. When delivery costs rise, such as from $.36 to $.39 for the basic letter-sized envelope, the cost of supplying the DVDs increases. This is represented by a leftward shift of the supply curve in Figure 12.

The leftward shift of the supply curve, from curve S_1 to curve S_2, leads to a new equilibrium price and quantity. At the original equilibrium price of $3 at point e_1, 66 DVDs are supplied. After the shift in the supply curve, 48 DVDs are offered for rent at a price of $3 apiece, and there is a shortage of 18 DVDs. The shortage puts

FIGURE 12 The Effects of a Shift of the Supply Curve

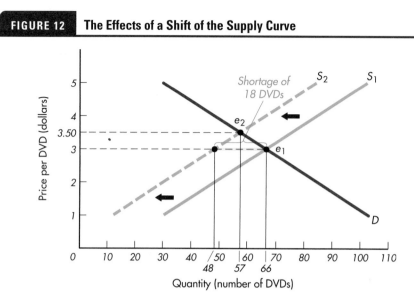

The initial equilibrium price and quantity are $3 and 66 units, at point e_1. When the delivery cost increases, suppliers are willing and able to offer fewer DVDs for rent at each price. The result is a leftward (upward) shift of the supply curve, from S_1 to S_2. At the old price of $3, the quantity demanded is still 66, but the quantity supplied falls to 48. The shortage is 18 DVDs. The shortage causes suppliers to acquire more DVDs to offer for rent and to raise the rental price. The new equilibrium, e_2, the intersection between curves S_2 and D, is $3.50 per DVD and 57 DVDs.

upward pressure on price. As the price rises, consumers decrease the quantities that they are willing and able to rent, and suppliers increase the quantities that they are willing and able to supply. Eventually, a new equilibrium price and quantity is established at $3.50 and 57 DVDs at point e_2.

The decrease in supply is represented by the leftward shift of the supply curve. A decrease in supply with no change in demand results in a higher price and a lower quantity. Conversely, an increase in supply would be represented as a rightward shift of the supply curve. An increase in supply with no change in demand would result in a lower price and a higher quantity.

5.d. International Effects

exchange rate: the rate at which monies of different countries are exchanged

As pointed out in the Global Business Insight "The Foreign Exchange Market," an **exchange rate**, the rate at which monies of different countries are exchanged, can be thought of as the price of one country's money in terms of another country's money. If the exchange rate changes, then the foreign price of a good produced in the United States will change. To illustrate this, let's consider an example using Levi's blue jeans sold to both U.S. and Japanese customers. The Japanese currency is the yen (¥). In March 2006, it took 116 yen to purchase one dollar. Suppose that a pair of Levi's blue jeans is priced at $20 in the United States. That dollar price in terms of yen is ¥2,320. The exchange rate between the yen and the dollar means that ¥2,320 converts to $20; ¥2,320 = $20 × ¥116/$. In July of 1999, the exchange rate was ¥124 per dollar. If the U.S. price of the blue jeans was $20, in Japan, the yen value of the blue jeans would have been $20 × ¥124/$ = ¥2,480. The blue jeans were less expensive in Japan in 2006 than they had been in 1999 because of the

Global Business Insight

The Foreign Exchange Market

Americans buy Toyotas and Nissans from Japan, while U.S. computer companies sell pocket calculators to businesses in Mexico. Some Americans open bank accounts in Switzerland, while U.S. real estate companies sell property to citizens in England. These transactions require the acquisition of a foreign currency. An English business that wants to buy property in the United States will have to exchange pounds sterling for dollars. A U.S. car distributor that imports Toyotas will have to exchange dollars for yen in order to pay the Toyota manufacturer.

The exchange of currency and the determination of the value of national currencies occur in the foreign exchange market. This is not a tightly organized market operating in a building in New York. Usually, the term *foreign exchange market* refers to the trading that occurs among large international banks. Such trading is global and is done largely through telephone and computer communication systems. If, for example, a foreign exchange trader at First Chicago Bank calls a trader at Bank of Tokyo to buy $1 million worth of Japanese yen, that is a foreign exchange market transaction. Banks buy and sell currencies according to the needs and demands of their customers. Business firms and individuals largely rely on banks to buy and sell foreign exchange for them.

The price of one currency expressed in terms of another currency is called a *foreign exchange rate,* or just *exchange rate.* You can think of an exchange rate as the

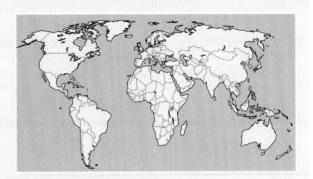

number of dollars it costs to purchase one unit of another country's currency. For instance, how many dollars does it take to purchase one unit of Japan's currency, the yen? One yen (¥) costs about $.008, or eight-tenths of a cent. The list that follows shows the number of U.S. dollars it took to purchase one unit of several different nations' currencies in March 2006.

Number of U.S. Dollars Needed to Purchase One . . .	
Australian dollar	.7409
Canadian dollar	.88
Mexican peso	.009
Euro	1.2
Japanese yen	.00847
Korean won	.001
Swiss franc	.769
United Kingdom pound	1.7492

exchange-rate change, even though the U.S. price of blue jeans did not change. The Japanese demand for U.S. blue jeans would have risen from July 1999 to January 2006 simply because of the exchange-rate change, as long as everything else remained the same. Thus, changes in exchange rates can affect the demand for goods.

Many firms purchase supplies from other nations, or even locate factories and produce in other nations. Events in other parts of the world can influence their costs and thus the amounts they are willing to supply. Nike purchases its shoes from manufacturers in other parts of the world, particularly Asia. Suppose the manufacturing costs in Malaysia are 78 ringgit. In 1997, the exchange rate was .3150 U.S. dollar to the ringgit, so that manufacturing costs in terms of dollars were $24.57 (.3150 × 78). In March 2006, the exchange rate had changed to .28 U.S. dollar to the ringgit. With the same manufacturing costs of 78 ringgit, the dollar costs had fallen to $21.84 (.28 × 78). Thus, the costs to Nike have fallen over the years simply because of the exchange-rate change. Everything else the same, this would mean that the supply curve of Nike shoes had shifted to the right.

6. **What happens when price is not allowed to change with market forces?**

5.e. Equilibrium in Reality

We have examined a hypothetical (imaginary) market for DVD rentals in order to represent what goes on in real markets. We have established that the price of a good or service is defined by an equilibrium between demand and supply. We noted that an equilibrium could be disturbed by a change in demand, a change in supply, or simultaneous changes in demand and supply. The important point of this discussion is to demonstrate that when they are not in equilibrium, the price and the quantities demanded and/or supplied change until equilibrium is established. The market is always attempting to reach equilibrium.

Looking at last year's sweaters piled up on the sale racks, waiting over an hour for a table at a restaurant, or hearing that 5 or 6 percent of people who are willing and able to work are unemployed may make you wonder whether equilibrium is ever established. In fact, it is not uncommon to observe situations in which quantities demanded and quantities supplied are not equal. But this observation does not cast doubt on the usefulness of the equilibrium concept. Even if not all markets clear, or reach equilibrium, all the time, we can be reasonably assured that market forces are operating so that the market is moving toward an equilibrium. When you see the store having a sale, you know that the market is moving toward equilibrium. When you hear that the price of something is rising because so many people are buying it, you know that the market is moving toward equilibrium. Sometimes the market is not allowed to move toward equilibrium, as discussed in the following section.

price floor: a situation in which the price is not allowed to decrease below a certain level

5.e.1. Price Ceilings and Price Floors   A **price floor** is a situation in which the price is not allowed to decrease below a certain level. Consider Figure 13, representing the market for sugar. The equilibrium price of sugar is $.10 a pound, but because the government has set a price floor of $.20 a pound, as shown by the solid yellow line, the price is not allowed to move to its equilibrium level. A surplus of

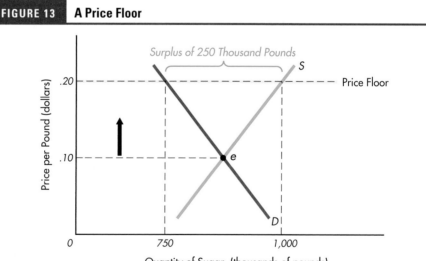

FIGURE 13   **A Price Floor**

The equilibrium price of sugar is $.10 a pound, but because the government has set a price floor of $.20 a pound, as shown by the solid yellow line, the price is not allowed to move to its equilibrium level. A surplus of 250,000 pounds of sugar results from the price floor. Sugar growers produce 1 million pounds of sugar, and consumers purchase 750,000 pounds of sugar.

250,000 pounds of sugar results from the price floor. Sugar growers produce 1 million pounds of sugar, and consumers purchase 750,000 pounds of sugar.

We saw previously that whenever the price is above the equilibrium price, a surplus arises and begins to force the price to decline. The price floor interferes with the functioning of the market; a surplus exists because the government will not allow the price to drop. The sugar surplus builds up as each week, more sugar is produced than is consumed.

What would occur if the government had set the price floor at $.09 a pound? Since at $.09 a pound, a shortage of sugar would result, the price would rise. A price floor keeps the price only from falling, not from rising. So the price rises to its equilibrium level of $.10. Only if the price floor is set above the equilibrium price is it an effective price floor.

price ceiling: a situation in which the price is not allowed to rise above a certain level

A **price ceiling** is the situation in which a price is not allowed to rise to its equilibrium level. Los Angeles, San Francisco, and New York are among over 125 U.S. cities that have some type of *rent controls.* The New York City rent control law places a ceiling on the rents that landlords can charge for apartments. Figure 14 is a demand and supply graph representing the market for apartments in New York. The equilibrium price is $3,000 a month. The government has set a price of $1,500 a month as the maximum that can be charged. The price ceiling is shown by the solid yellow line. At the rent control price of $1,500 per month, 3,000 apartments are available, but consumers want 6,000 apartments. There is a shortage of 3,000 apartments.

The shortage means that not everyone who is willing and able to rent an apartment will be able to. Since the price is not allowed to ration the apartments, something else will have to. It may be that those who are willing and able to stand in line the longest get the apartments. Perhaps bribing an important official might be the way to get an apartment. Perhaps relatives of officials or important citizens will get the apartments. Whenever a price ceiling exists, a shortage results, and some rationing device other than price will arise.

FIGURE 14 **Rent Controls**

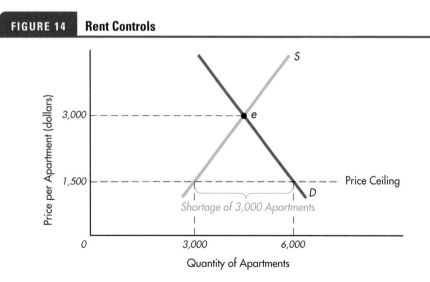

A demand and supply graph representing the market for apartments in New York City is shown. The equilibrium price is $3,000 a month. The government has set a price of $1,500 a month. The government's price ceiling is shown by the solid yellow line. At the government's price, 3,000 apartments are available but consumers want 6,000. There is a shortage of 3,000 apartments.

Had the government set the rent control price at $4,000 per month, the price ceiling would not have had an effect. Since the equilibrium is $3,000 a month, the price would not have risen to $4,000. Only if the price ceiling is below the equilibrium price will it be an effective price ceiling.

Price ceilings are not uncommon in the United States or in other economies. China had a severe housing shortage for 30 years because the price of housing was kept below equilibrium. Faced with unhappy citizens and realizing the cause of the shortage, officials began to lift the restrictions on housing prices in 1985. The shortage has diminished. In the former Soviet Union, prices for all goods and services were defined by the government. For most consumer items, the price was set below equilibrium, and shortages existed. The long lines of people waiting to purchase food or clothing were the result of the price ceilings on all goods and services. In the United States, price ceilings on all goods and services have been imposed at times. During the First and Second World Wars and during the Nixon administration of the early 1970s, wage and price controls were imposed. These were price ceilings on all goods and services. As a result of the ceilings, people were unable to purchase many of the products they desired. The Organization of Petroleum Exporting Countries (OPEC) restricted the quantity of oil in the early 1970s and drove its price up considerably. The U.S. government responded by placing a price ceiling on gasoline. The result was long lines at gas stations because of shortages of gasoline.

Price floors are quite common in economies as well. The agricultural policies of most of the developed nations are founded on price floors—the government guarantees that the price of an agricultural product will not fall below some level. Price floors result in surpluses, and this has been the case with agricultural products as well. The surpluses in agricultural products in the United States have resulted in cases where dairy farmers dumped milk in the river, where grain was given to other nations at taxpayer expense, and where citrus ranchers picked and then discarded thousands of tons of citrus, all to reduce huge surpluses.

When price ceiling or price floors do not allow a market to reach equilibrium, shortages or surpluses will result. Since the price is not allowed to allocate the goods or services, another allocation mechanism will – first-come-first-served, government, or lottery.

5.f. Watch the Price of Eggs

During the 1990s, country after country turned from government-run economies to market economies. In Latin America, in eastern Europe and Russia, and in India, former socialist or dictatorial nations sought to free their stagnant and collapsing economies from government control and allow people the economic freedom that would lead to greater prosperity. Even in the government-run nation of China, reforms were implemented that moved the economy toward a market-based economy. In these countries, government price controls were lifted, and prices were allowed to move toward equilibrium. The leaders of the reforms were told by their economic advisers, "Watch the price of eggs. If the price rises and more eggs are offered for sale, and then the price falls, it is a sign that markets are working." Within hours or a few days of the lifting of price controls, markets arose in which eggs, other produce, and some clothing items appeared. Shortages disappeared. Prices shot upward, but then began to decline. Why? What was occurring?

Why did the advisers focus on eggs and not the heavy industries like shipbuilding, oil refining, or power generation? They focused on eggs because the market for eggs would be the quickest to emerge. Once they were free to do so, local farmers would bring their eggs to the city to sell. As the price of eggs rose, more eggs would

FIGURE 15   **Ending Price Controls**

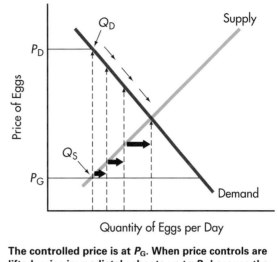

The controlled price is at P_G. When price controls are lifted, price immediately shoots up to P_D because the quantity supplied does not immediately change. As the quantity supplied rises, the price falls. Both quantity and price move toward equilibrium.

be brought to market. Items such as ships, airplanes, tractors, etc., would not increase in supply nearly as rapidly as would eggs.

The market for eggs is depicted in Figure 15. The government-controlled price is P_G. The price ceiling causes a shortage, as the quantity demanded is larger than the quantity supplied. When the price ceiling is lifted, the price immediately shoots up to P_D. This high price leads to increasing quantities of eggs being supplied. In the figure, quantities increase along the supply curve and the price drops down the demand curve. Quite rapidly, the price drops to the equilibrium.

This adjustment process took much more time in the heavy industries. Once the price controls on items like gasoline, electricity, or industrial products were lifted, the price shot up, but the quantities supplied could not increase for quite some time. It might take several years for new suppliers to begin offering gasoline, electricity or ships, airplanes and tractors. Because the quantity of heavy industrial products would take months or years to increase, the price would remain high. To the citizens, it seemed as if the markets were not working because the higher price did not bring forth increased quantities supplied.

Years, not days, were necessary for a complete transition from government-run to market-based economies in those countries where heavy industry was a large part of the economy.[1] In countries that were primarily agricultural, the transition occurred much more rapidly.

---

[1] The video *Commanding Heights*, based on the book of the same name by Daniel Yergin and Joseph Stanislaus, provides a vivid portrayal of the transition from government to market economies during the 1990s.

1. Equilibrium occurs when the quantity demanded and the quantity supplied are equal: It is the price-quantity combination where the demand and supply curves intersect.

2. A price that is above the equilibrium price creates a surplus. Producers are willing and able to offer more for sale than buyers are willing and able to purchase.

3. A price that is below the equilibrium price leads to a shortage, because buyers are willing and able to purchase more than producers are willing and able to offer for sale.

4. When demand changes, price and quantity change in the same direction—both rise as demand increases, and both fall as demand decreases.

5. When supply changes, price and quantity change, but not in the same direction. When supply increases, price falls and quantity rises. When supply decreases, price rises and quantity falls.

6. When both demand and supply change, the direction of the change in price and quantity depends on the relative sizes of the changes of demand and supply.

7. The exchange rate is a determinant of demand when a good is sold in both the United States and other countries. It is also a determinant of supply because it affects the costs of producing goods.

8. A price floor is a situation in which a price is set above the equilibrium price. This creates a surplus.

9. A price ceiling is a case in which a price is set below the equilibrium price. This creates a shortage.

10. When a price ceiling is lifted, the market will adjust. The speed of adjustment of the quantity supplied and prices depends on how rapidly resources can be altered, goods and services produced, and supplies brought to market.

Summary

1. What is a market?

- A market is where buyers and sellers trade a well-defined good or service. *§2*

2. What is demand?

- Demand is the quantities that buyers are willing and able to buy at alternative prices. *§3*

- The quantity demanded is a specific amount at one price. *§3*

- The law of demand states that as the price of a well-defined commodity rises (falls), the quantity demanded during a given period of time will fall (rise), everything else held constant. *§3.a*

- Demand will change when one of the determinants of demand changes, that is, when income, tastes, prices of related goods and services, expectations, or number of buyers changes. A demand change is illustrated as a shift of the demand curve. *§3.e*

3. What is supply?

- Supply is the quantities that sellers will offer for sale at alternative prices. *§4.a*

- The quantity supplied is the amount that sellers offer for sale at one price. *§4.a*

- The law of supply states that as the price of a well-defined commodity rises (falls), the quantity supplied during a given period of time will rise (fall), everything else held constant. *§4.a*

- Supply changes when one of the determinants of supply changes, that is, when prices of resources, technology and productivity, expectations of producers, the number of producers, or the prices of related goods or services change. A supply change is illustrated as a shift of the supply curve. *§4.d*

4. How is price determined by demand and supply?

- Together, demand and supply determine the equilibrium price and quantity. *§5*

5. What causes price to change?

- A price that is above equilibrium creates a surplus, which leads to a lower price. A price that is below equilibrium creates a shortage, which leads to a higher price. *§5.a*
- A change in demand or a change in supply (a shift of either curve) will cause the equilibrium price and quantity to change. *§5.b, 5.c*
- The exchange rate affects the price of foreign-produced goods and services because both demand and supply are affected by the rate at which the different currencies are exchanged. *§5.d*

6. What happens when price is not allowed to change with market forces?

- Markets are not always in equilibrium, but when not, surpluses or shortages arise and force the price to move them toward equilibrium. *§5.e*
- A price floor is a situation in which a price is not allowed to decrease below a certain level—it is set above the equilibrium price. This creates a surplus. A price ceiling is a case in which a price is not allowed to rise—it is set below the equilibrium price. This creates a shortage. *§5.e*

Key Terms

market *§2.a*	normal goods *§3.e.1*	supply curve *§4.b*
barter *§2.b*	inferior goods *§3.e.1*	productivity *§4.d.2*
double coincidence of wants *§2.b*	substitute goods *§3.e.3*	equilibrium *§5*
demand *§3*	complementary goods *§3.e.3*	disequilibrium *§5.a*
quantity demanded *§3*	supply *§4.a*	surplus *§5.a*
law of demand *§3.a*	quantity supplied *§4.a*	shortage *§5.a*
determinants of demand *§3.a*	law of supply *§4.a*	exchange rate *§5.d*
demand schedule *§3.b*	determinants of supply *§4.a*	price floor *§5.e.1*
demand curve *§3.c*	supply schedule *§4.b*	price ceiling *§5.e.1*

Exercises

1. Illustrate each of the following events using a demand and supply diagram for bananas.
   a. Reports surface that imported bananas are infected with a deadly virus.
   b. Consumers' incomes drop.
   c. The price of bananas rises.
   d. The price of oranges falls.
   e. Consumers expect the price of bananas to decrease in the future.

2. Answer true or false, and if the statement is false, change it to make it true. Illustrate your answers on a demand and supply graph.
   a. An increase in demand is represented by a movement up the demand curve.
   b. An increase in supply is represented by a movement up the supply curve.
   c. An increase in demand without any changes in supply will cause the price to rise.
   d. An increase in supply without any changes in demand will cause the price to rise.

3. Using the following schedule, define the equilibrium price and quantity. Describe the situation at a price of $10. What will occur? Describe the situation at a price of $2. What will occur?

Price	Quantity Demanded	Quantity Supplied
$1	500	100
$2	400	120
$3	350	150
$4	320	200
$5	300	300
$6	275	410
$7	260	500
$8	230	650
$9	200	800
$10	150	975

4. Suppose the government imposed a minimum price of $7 in the schedule of exercise 3. What would occur? Illustrate.

5. In exercise 3, indicate what the price would have to be to represent an effective price ceiling. Point out the surplus or shortage that results. Illustrate a price floor and provide an example of a price floor.

6. A common feature of skiing is waiting in lift lines. Does the existence of lift lines mean that the price is not working to allocate the scarce resource? If so, what should be done about it?

7. Why don't we observe barter systems as often as we observe the use of currency?

8. A severe drought in California has resulted in a nearly 30 percent reduction in the quantity of citrus grown and produced in California. Explain what effect this event might have on the Florida citrus market.

9. The prices of the Ralph Lauren Polo line of clothing are considerably higher than those of comparable-quality lines. Yet, this line sells more than a J. C. Penney brand line of clothing. Does this violate the law of demand?

10. In December, the price of Christmas trees rises and the quantity of trees sold rises. Is this a violation of the law of demand?

11. In recent years, the price of artificial Christmas trees has fallen while the quality has risen. What impact has this event had on the price of cut Christmas trees?

12. Many restaurants don't take reservations. You simply arrive and wait your turn. If you arrive at 7:30 in the evening, you have at least an hour wait. Notwithstanding that fact, a few people arrive, speak quietly with the maitre d', hand him some money, and are promptly seated. At some restaurants that do take reservations, there is a month wait for a Saturday evening, three weeks for a Friday evening, two weeks for Tuesday through Thursday, and virtually no wait for Sunday or Monday evening. How do you explain these events using demand and supply?

13. Evaluate the following statement: "The demand for U.S. oranges has increased because the quantity of U.S. oranges demanded in Japan has risen."

14. In December 1992, the federal government began requiring that all foods display information about fat content and other ingredients on food packages. The displays had to be verified by independent laboratories. The price of an evaluation of a food product could run as much as $20,000. What impact do you think this law had on the market for meat?

15. Draw a PPC. Which combination shown by the PPC will be produced? How is this combination determined? Does the combination that is produced depend on how goods and services are allocated?

Take the ACE Practice Test for this chapter to review the important concepts and get immediate feedback with answers.

college.hmco.com/economics/students/

Gas Price Controls Mean Long Lines

The Baltimore Sun
September 12, 2005

WASHINGTON—When Rudyard Kipling said it was a great virtue "if you can keep your head when all about you are losing theirs and blaming it on you," he was not thinking of Sen. Maria Cantwell, a Democrat from Washington. This week, as gasoline prices remained above $3 a gallon, she proposed giving the president the power to tell retailers what they can charge at the pump.

A lot of people grew anxious seeing long lines forming the week before last, as motorists rushed to fill their tanks in the aftermath of Hurricane Katrina. But Ms. Cantwell apparently enjoyed the sight well enough that she'd like to make those lines a permanent feature of the landscape. If so, she has the right approach. The government does many things badly, but one thing it knows how to do is create shortages through the vigorous use of price controls.

That's what it did in the oil market in 1979–80, under President Jimmy Carter. He was replaced by Ronald Reagan, who lifted price caps on gas and thus not only banished shortages but brought about an era of low prices.

Ms. Cantwell thinks oil companies have manipulated the energy market to gouge consumers, though she is awaiting evidence to support that theory. "I just don't have the document to prove it," she declared. Her suspicions were roused when she noticed that prices climbed in Seattle—though most of its oil comes from Alaska, which was not hit by a hurricane.

Maybe no one has told Ms. Cantwell that oil trades in an international market, and that when companies and consumers in the South can't get fuel from their usual sources, they will buy it from other ones, even if they have to go as far as Prudhoe Bay.

If prices rose in Dallas and didn't rise in Seattle, oil producers would have a big incentive to ship all their supplies to Texas—leaving Washingtonians to pay nothing for nothing. When a freeze damages Florida's orange juice crop, does Ms. Cantwell think only Floridians feel the pain?

Sen. Byron Dorgan, a Democrat from North Dakota, meanwhile, was outraged by the thought of giant oil companies making money merely for supplying the nation's energy needs. He claimed they will reap $80 billion in "windfall profits" and wants the government to confiscate a large share of that sum through a special federal tax.

But the prospect of occasional "windfall" profits is one reason corporations are willing to risk their money drilling wells that may turn out to be drier than Alan Greenspan's reading list. Take them away, and investors may decide they'd rather speculate in real estate.

It's hard to see why oil companies shouldn't make a lot of money when the commodity they provide is suddenly in short supply. After all, they are vulnerable to weak profits or even losses during times of glut. Back when Americans were enjoying abundant cheap gasoline, the joke was that the surest way to make a small fortune in the oil industry was to start with a large fortune.

Oil companies are also subject to the whims of nature. No one is holding a charity fundraiser for the business people whose rigs and refineries were smashed by Katrina. No one will come to their aid if prices drop by half.

Besides, high prices serve two essential functions: encouraging production and fostering conservation. Spurred by the lure of windfall profits, oil companies will move heaven and earth to get more gasoline to consumers. Shocked by the tab when they fill up a 5,600-pound SUV, motorists will look for opportunities to leave the Suburban at home. They may even commit a sin not covered by the Ten Commandments: Coveting their neighbor's Prius.

Controlling prices, by contrast, would have exactly the opposite effect: telling consumers they should waste fuel to their hearts' content and telling producers to leave the black stuff in the ground. When events in the world conspire to make oil dear, there is nothing to be gained from masking that fact. We can ignore reality, but reality won't ignore us.

Steve Chapman

Dictating the retail price that companies can sell gasoline at is nothing more than a price ceiling. In the figure below left, the ceiling price of P_m is less than the equilibrium price P_1. This price ceiling creates a shortage: At the controlled price P_m, the quantity of gasoline demanded is Q_d, while the quantity supplied is only Q_s. The difference, $Q_d - Q_s$, is the quantity of gasoline that consumers would be willing and able to buy but can't because there is none available. What does a shortage in gasoline look like? It is long lines at gas pumps. It is people stranded because they have run out of gas.

How is this shortage resolved? Since price cannot be used to resolve the shortage, something else will. Common replacements for price are first-come, first-served and corruption.

First-come, first-served is what we typically see. Long lines form at gas stations. People "top off" their tanks, driving into a station whenever they see an opening in order to keep their gas tanks full. One result is many more people at pumps than would otherwise be the case. Another is that some gas stations close because they can't obtain supplies.

Crude oil, the main source of gasoline, is traded in a global market. If prices rise in one part of the world but are not allowed to rise in others, the crude oil will be shipped to where its return is highest. As the article notes, "If prices rose in Dallas and didn't rise in Seattle, oil producers would have a big incentive to ship all their supplies to Texas—leaving Washingtonians to pay nothing for nothing. When a freeze damages Florida's orange juice crop, does Ms. Cantwell think only Floridians feel the pain?" If the United States limited gasoline prices to $2 per gallon and other parts of the world allowed the price to rise to $4 per gallon, the oil would be shipped to where it could be refined and a profit made from selling gasoline. In short, price ceilings lead to shortages. Even if the oil was not shipped around the world, why would anyone invest millions of dollars in drilling for oil when they would not make a profit? As the commentary notes, controlling prices tells producers to leave the black stuff in the ground. Refineries would be shut down, and no new spending on oil wells and facilities would occur. Over time, the supply of gasoline would decline even further, shown as the move from S_1 to S_2 in the figure below on the right. This would create larger shortages.

In the Soviet Union, China, Cuba, India, and other nations that imposed price controls on many goods and services for a long period of time, first-come, first-served allocation was replaced with graft and corruption. If you bribed the right official, you could get some bread or milk. If you paid off the manager, you could find other items that you needed. Corruption leads to a collapse of civilization—standards of living decline.

As noted in the chapter, allocation schemes other than price do not create incentives for improvement and increases in standards of living. What incentive does the first-come, first-served system create? Just to be first. All you do is stand in lines. Nothing more is produced, and no alternatives to gasoline are ever discovered. In contrast, if price is not controlled, it rises to equilibrium, the quantity supplied rises, and the quantity demanded falls. The higher price brings out entrepreneurs seeking profits. These entrepreneurs will discover more efficient ways to transport people and alternative energy sources to oil and gasoline.

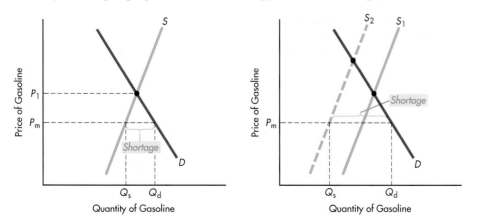

The Market System and the Private Sector

Fundamental Questions

1. In a market system, who decides what goods and services are produced and how they are produced, and who obtains the goods and services that are produced?

2. What is a household, and what is household income and spending?

3. What is a business firm, and what is business spending?

4. How does the international sector affect the economy?

5. How do the three private sectors—households, businesses, and the international sector—interact in the economy?

You decide to buy a new Toyota, so you go to a Toyota dealer and exchange money for the car. The Toyota dealer has rented land and buildings and hired workers in order to make cars available to you and other members of the public. The employees earn incomes paid by the Toyota dealer and then use those incomes to buy food from the grocery store. This transaction generates revenue for the grocery store, which hires workers and pays them incomes that they then use to buy groceries and Toyotas. Your expenditure for the Toyota is part of a circular flow. Revenue is received by the Toyota dealer, which pays its employees, who, in turn, buy goods and services.

Of course, the story is complicated by the fact that your Toyota may have been manufactured in Japan and then shipped to the United States before it was sold by the local Toyota dealer. Your purchase of the Toyota creates revenue for both

the local dealer and the manufacturer, which pays autoworkers to assemble the cars. When you buy your Toyota, you pay a sales tax, which the government uses to support its expenditures on police, fire protection, national defense, the legal system, and other services. In short, many people in different areas of the economy are involved in what seems to be a single transaction.

We begin this chapter by examining the interaction of buyers and sellers in a market system. We then look at the main sectors of an economy—households, firms, and the international sector—to determine how they interact. In this chapter, we focus on the private sector, leaving our discussion of government until Chapter 5. ■

?

1. In a market system, who decides what goods and services are produced and how they are produced, and who obtains the goods and services that are produced?

1. The Market System

As we learned in Chapter 2, the production possibilities curve represents all possible combinations of goods and services that a society can produce if its resources are used fully and efficiently. Which combination, that is, which point on the PPC, will society choose? In a price or market system, the answer is given by demand and supply. Consumers demonstrate what they are willing and able to pay for by buying different goods and services. If a business is to succeed, it must supply what people want at a price that people can afford. In this sense, consumers reign supreme—this is called consumer sovereignty.

1.a. Consumer Sovereignty

In recent years, time-starved Americans have spent about as much time eating out as they have eating at home. In the 1950s and 1960s, this trend was just beginning. Consumers wanted more and more restaurants and fast-food outlets. As a result, McDonald's, Wendy's, Big Boy, White Castle, Pizza Hut, Godfather's Pizza, and other fast-food outlets flourished. The trend toward eating away from home reached fever pitch in the late 1970s, when the average number of meals per person eaten out (excluding brown-bag lunches and other meals prepared at home but eaten elsewhere) exceeded one per day.

In the 1980s, people wanted fast food but didn't want to go get it. By emphasizing delivery, Domino's Pizza and a few other fast-food outlets became very successful. In the 1990s, the takeout taxi business—where restaurant food is delivered to homes—grew 10 percent per year, and it remains very popular today. However, the star of this story is not Domino's, Pizza Hut, or other restaurants. It is the consumer. In a market system, if consumers are willing and able to pay for more restaurant meals, more restaurants appear. If consumers are willing and able to pay for food delivered to their homes, food is delivered to their homes.

Why does the consumer have such power? The name of the game for business is profit, and the only way a business can make a profit is by satisfying consumer wants. Consumers, not politicians or business firms, ultimately determine what is to be produced. A firm that produces something that no consumers want will not remain in business very long. **Consumer sovereignty**—the authority of consumers to determine what is produced through their purchases of goods and services—dictates what goods and services will be produced. Supermarkets and grocery stores are responding to consumers as well, by putting fast-food restaurants, like Pizza Hut and Taco Bell, inside their stores.

consumer sovereignty: the authority of consumers to determine what is produced through their purchases of goods and services

1.b. Profit and the Allocation of Resources

When a good or service seems to have the potential to generate a profit, some entrepreneur will put together the resources needed to offer that good or service for sale. If the potential profit turns into a loss, the entrepreneur may stop buying resources and turn to some other occupation or project. The resources used in the losing operation will then be available for use in an activity where they are more highly valued.

To illustrate how resources get allocated in the market system, let's look at the market for fast food. Figure 1 shows a change in demand for meals eaten in restaurants each month. The initial demand curve, D_1, and supply curve, S, are shown in Figure 1(a). With these demand and supply curves, the equilibrium price (P_1) is $8, and the equilibrium quantity (Q_1) is 100 units (meals). At this price-quantity combination, the number of meals demanded equals the number of meals sold; equilibrium is reached, so we say that the market clears (there is no shortage or surplus).

The second part of the figure shows what happened when consumer tastes changed, and people preferred to have food delivered to their homes. This change in tastes caused the demand for restaurant meals to decline; it is represented by a leftward shift of the demand curve, from D_1 to D_2, in Figure 1(b). The demand curve shifted to the left because fewer in-restaurant meals were demanded at each price. Consumer tastes, not the price of in-restaurant meals, changed first. (A price change would have led to a change in the quantity demanded and would be represented by a move *along* demand curve D_1.) The change in tastes caused a change in demand and a leftward shift of the demand curve. The shift from D_1 to D_2 created a new equilibrium point. The equilibrium price (P_2) decreased to $6, and the equilibrium quantity (Q_2) decreased to 80 units (meals).

FIGURE 1   A Demand Change in the Market for in-Restaurant Food

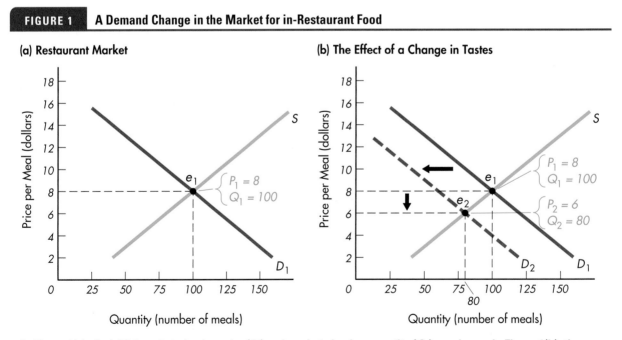

(a) Restaurant Market

(b) The Effect of a Change in Tastes

In Figure 1(a), the initial market-clearing price (P_1) and market-clearing quantity (Q_1) are shown. In Figure 1(b), the market-clearing price and quantity change from P_1 and Q_1 to P_2 and Q_2 as the demand curve shifts to the left because of a change in tastes. The result of decreased demand is a lower price and a lower quantity produced.

FIGURE 2 | A Demand Change in the Market for Delivered Food

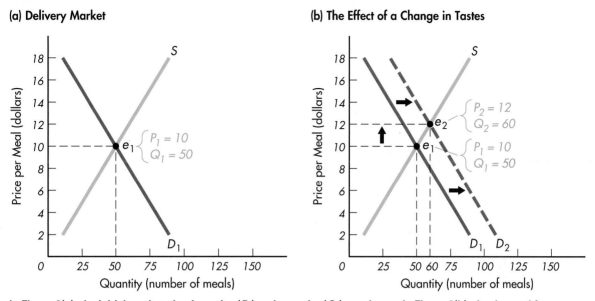

(a) Delivery Market

(b) The Effect of a Change in Tastes

In Figure 2(a), the initial market-clearing price (P_1) and quantity (Q_1) are shown. In Figure 2(b), the demand for delivered food increases, thus driving up the market-clearing price (P_2) and quantity (Q_2) as the demand curve shifts to the right, from D_1 to D_2.

While the market for in-restaurant food was changing, so was the market for delivered food. People substituted meals delivered to their homes for meals eaten in restaurants. Figure 2(a) shows the original demand for food delivered to the home. Figure 2(b) shows a rightward shift of the demand curve, from D_1 to D_2, representing increased demand for home delivery. This demand change resulted in a higher market-clearing price for food delivered to the home, from $10 to $12.

The changing profit potential of the two markets induced existing firms to switch from in-restaurant service to home delivery and for new firms to offer delivery from the start. Domino's Pizza, which is a delivery-only firm, grew from a one-store operation to become the second largest pizza chain in the United States. Pizza Hut, which at first did not offer home delivery, had to play catch-up; by 1992, about two-thirds of Pizza Hut's more than 5,000 restaurants were delivering pizza.

As the market-clearing price of in-restaurant fast food fell (from $8 to $6 in Figure 1[b]), the quantity of in-restaurant meals sold also declined (from 100 to 80) because the decreased demand, lower price, and resulting lower profit induced some firms to decrease production. In the delivery business, the opposite occurred. As the market-clearing price rose (from $10 to $12 in Figure 2[b]), the number of meals delivered also rose (from 50 to 60). The increased demand, higher price, and resulting higher profit induced firms to increase production.

Why did the production of delivered foods increase while the production of meals at restaurants decreased? Not because of a government decree. Not because of the desires of the business sector, especially the owners of restaurants. The consumer—*consumer sovereignty*—made all this happen. Businesses that failed to respond to consumer desires and failed to provide the desired good at the lowest price failed to survive.

1.c. The Flow of Resources

After demand shifted to home-delivered food, the resources that had been used in the restaurants were available for use elsewhere. A few former waiters, waitresses, and cooks were able to get jobs in the delivery firms. Some of the equipment used in eat-in restaurants—ovens, pots, and pans—was purchased by the delivery firms; and some of the ingredients that previously would have gone to the eat-in restaurants were bought by the delivery firms. A few former employees of the eat-in restaurants became employed at department stores, at local pubs, and at hotels. Some of the equipment was sold as scrap; other equipment was sold to other restaurants. In other words, the resources moved from an activity where their value was relatively low to an activity where they were more highly valued. No one commanded the resources to move. They moved because they could earn more in some other activity.

This same story applies in case after case after case. The Sony Walkman was replaced by Apple's iPod, and the iPod will be replaced by another device. Fixed-line telephones were replaced by mobile phones. Desktop computers replaced mainframe computers. The process of new products and new firms replacing existing products and firms is called *creative destruction*. This is what the market process is all about—creating new ideas, new products, and new ways of doing things, and replacing the obsolete, costly, and inefficient. Every year *Forbes* magazine publishes a list of the 100 largest companies in terms of sales. In 1987, *Forbes* compared that year's list to the 100 largest firms in 1917. Only 39 of the 1917 group remained in 1987. Of the 39 that remained in business, 18 had managed to stay in the top 100. Of the 18 that stayed in the top 100, only 2 had performed better than the market average—Kodak and GE. Kodak has since fallen, and GE is a totally different company from what it was in 1917. This seems an amazing change, but the pace of change has only quickened since 1987. Fewer than 25 percent of today's major corporations will continue to exist in 25 years.

Firms produce the goods and services and use the resources that enable them to generate the highest profits. If one firm does this better than others, then that firm earns a greater profit than others. Seeing that success, other firms copy or mimic the first firm. If a firm cannot be as profitable as the others, it will eventually go out of business or move to another line of business where it can be successful. In the process of firms always seeking to lower their costs and make higher profits, society finds that the goods and services that buyers want are produced in the least costly manner. Not only do consumers get the goods and services that they want and will pay for, but they get these products at the lowest possible price.

1.d. The Determination of Income

Consumer demands dictate *what* is produced, and the search for profit defines *how* goods and services are produced. *For whom* are the goods and services produced, that is, who gets the goods and services? As we discussed in Chapter 3, in a price or market system, those who have the ability to pay for the products get the products. Your income determines your ability to pay, but where does income come from? A person's income is obtained by selling the services of the resources that person owns.

In reality, households own all resources. Everyone owns his or her own labor; some households also own land, and many also own firms or portions of firms. When a household owns shares of stock, it owns a portion of the firm whose shares it owns. Many households own shares of stock either as direct investments or as part of their retirement fund. The firm you or your parents work for might provide a

401(k) or some other retirement plan. A portion of these plans typically own shares of stock. All firms, whether private firms or firms traded through stock markets, are owned by households in some way. Thus, if a firm acquires equipment, buildings, land, and natural resources, it is actually households that ultimately own those things. If a firm were taken apart and its parts sold off, households would end up with the money.

Typically we think of our income as what we are paid for our labor services. But you may also receive income from the shares of stock that you own (dividends and appreciation) and the various savings accounts that you own (interest). You may receive rent from being a landlord or from allowing a firm to use the services of your land. You may get profits from a business that you started.

Buyers and sellers of goods and services and resource owners are linked together in an economy. For every dollar someone spends, someone else receives a dollar as income. In the remainder of this chapter, we learn more about the linkages among the sectors of the economy. We classify the buyers and the resource owners into the household sector; the sellers or business firms are the business sector; households and firms in other countries, who may also be buyers and sellers of this country's goods and services, are the international sector. These three sectors—households, business firms, and the international sector—constitute the **private sector** of the economy. In this chapter we focus on the interaction among the components of the private sector. In the next chapter, we focus on the **public sector**, government, and examine its role in the economy.

private sector: households, businesses, and the international sector

public sector: the government

RECAP

1. In a market system, consumers are sovereign and decide by means of their purchases what goods and services will be produced.

2. In a market system, firms decide how to produce the goods and services that consumers want. In order to earn maximum profits, firms use the least-cost combinations of resources.

3. Income and prices determine who gets what in a market system. Income is determined by the ownership of resources.

(?)

2. What is a household, and what is household income and spending?

household: one or more persons who occupy a unit of housing

2. Households

A **household** consists of one or more persons who occupy a unit of housing. The unit of housing may be a house, an apartment, or even a single room, as long as it constitutes separate living quarters. A household may consist of related family members, like a father, mother, and children, or it may comprise unrelated individuals, like three college students sharing an apartment. The person in whose name the house or apartment is owned or rented is called the *householder*.

2.a. Number of Households and Household Income

There are more than 104 million households in the United States. The breakdown of households by age of householder is shown in Figure 3. Householders between 35 and 44 years old make up the largest number of households. Householders between 45 and 54 years old have the largest median income. The *median* is the middle value—half of the households in an age group have an income higher than

FIGURE 3

Age of Householder, Number of Households, and Median Household Income in the United States

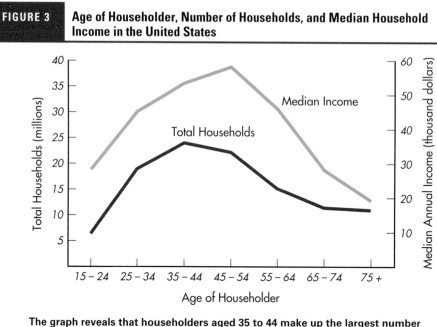

The graph reveals that householders aged 35 to 44 make up the largest number of households, and householders aged 45 to 54 earn the highest median annual income. *Source:* U.S. Department of Commerce, Statistical Abstract of the United States, 2005.

the median, and half have an income lower than the median. Figure 3 shows that households in which the householder is between 45 and 54 years old have a median income of about $58,217, substantially higher than the median incomes of other age groups. Typically, workers in this age group are at the peak of their earning power. Younger households are gaining experience and training; older households include retired workers.

The size distribution of households in the United States is shown in Figure 4. As seen in the figure, 33 percent of all households are two-person households. The

FIGURE 4   **Size Distribution of Households in the United States**

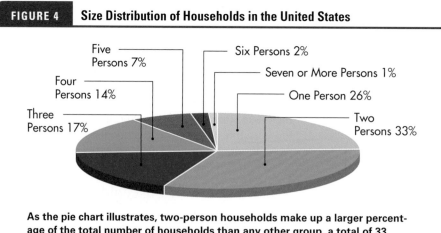

As the pie chart illustrates, two-person households make up a larger percentage of the total number of households than any other group, a total of 33 percent. Large households with seven or more persons are becoming a rarity, accounting for only 1 percent of the total number of households. *Source:* U.S. Department of Commerce, Statistical Abstract of the United States, 2005.

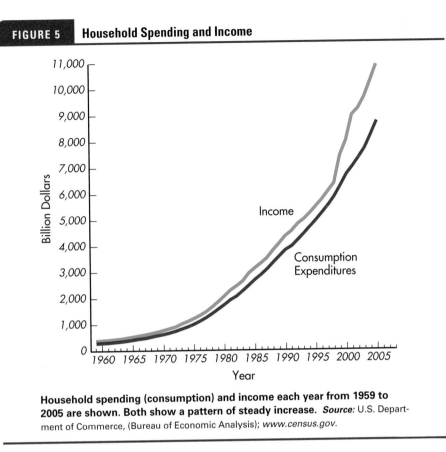

FIGURE 5 **Household Spending and Income**

Household spending (consumption) and income each year from 1959 to 2005 are shown. Both show a pattern of steady increase. *Source:* U.S. Department of Commerce, (Bureau of Economic Analysis); *www.census.gov.*

stereotypical household of husband, wife, and two children accounts for only 14 percent of all households. There are relatively few large households. Of the more than 104 million households in the country, only 1 percent have seven or more persons.

In the United States, the average number of people per household is 2.2. Worldwide, average household size in high-income countries (those with average per capita incomes over $9,000 per year) is close to that in the United States; the average household in middle- and low-income countries is more than twice as large.

2.b. Household Spending

consumption: household spending

Household spending is called **consumption**. Householders consume housing, transportation, food, entertainment, and other goods and services. Household spending (also called *consumer spending*) per year in the United States is shown in Figure 5, along with household income. The pattern is one of steady increase. Spending by the household sector is the largest component of total spending in the economy—rising to over $9 trillion in 2005.

RECAP

1. A household consists of one or more persons who occupy a unit of housing.
2. An apartment or house is rented or owned by a householder.
3. As a group, householders between the ages of 45 and 54 have the highest median incomes.
4. Household spending is called *consumption.*

---

business firm: a business organization controlled by a single management

sole proprietorship: a business owned by one person who receives all the profits and is responsible for all the debts incurred by the business

partnership: a business with two or more owners who share the firm's profits and losses

corporation: a legal entity owned by shareholders whose liability for the firm's losses is limited to the value of the stock they own

multinational business: a firm that owns and operates producing units in foreign countries

3. Business Firms

A **business firm** is a business organization controlled by a single management. The firm's business may be conducted at more than one location. The terms *company*, *enterprise*, and *business* are used interchangeably with *firm*.

3.a. Forms of Business Organizations

Firms are organized as sole proprietorships, partnerships, or corporations. A **sole proprietorship** is a business owned by one person. This type of firm may be a one-person operation or a large enterprise with many employees. In either case, the owner receives all the profits and is responsible for all the debts incurred by the business.

A **partnership** is a business owned by two or more partners who share both the profits of the business and responsibility for the firm's losses. The partners can be individuals, estates, or other businesses.

A **corporation** is a business whose identity in the eyes of the law is distinct from the identity of its owners. State law allows the formation of corporations. A corporation is an economic entity that, like a person, can own property and borrow money in its own name. The owners of a corporation are shareholders. If a corporation cannot pay its debts, creditors cannot seek payment from the shareholders' personal wealth. The corporation itself is responsible for all its actions. The shareholders' liability is limited to the value of the stock they own.

Many firms are global in their operations, even though they may have been founded and may be owned by residents of a single country. Firms typically first enter the international market by selling products to foreign countries. As revenues from these sales increase, the firms realize advantages by locating subsidiaries in foreign countries. A **multinational business** is a firm that owns and operates producing units in foreign countries. The best-known U.S. corporations are multinational firms. Ford, IBM, PepsiCo, and McDonald's all own operating units in many different countries. Ford Motor Company, for instance, is the parent firm of sales organizations and assembly plants located around the world. As transportation and communication technologies progress, multinational business activity undoubtedly will grow.

3.b. Business Statistics

In the United States, there are far more sole proprietorships than there are partnerships or corporations. The great majority of sole proprietorships are small businesses, with revenues under $25,000 a year. Similarly, over half of all partnerships also have revenues under $25,000 a year, but only 23 percent of the corporations are in this category.

The 68 percent of sole proprietorships that earn less than $25,000 a year account for only about 9 percent of the revenue earned by proprietorships. The 0.4 percent of proprietorships with revenue of $1 million or more account for about 19 percent. The figures for partnerships and corporations are even more striking. The 58 percent of partnerships with the smallest revenue account for only 0.4 percent of the total revenue earned by partnerships. At the other extreme, the 5 percent of partnerships with the largest revenue account for 88 percent of total partnership revenue. The 23 percent of corporations in the smallest range account for less than 0.1 percent of total corporate revenue, while the 18 percent of corporations in the largest range account for 94 percent of corporate revenue.

FIGURE 6 **The World's Ten Largest Public Companies**

Rank	Firm (country)	Sales (million dollars)
1	Exxon Mobil (U.S.)	$339,938
2	Wal-Mart Stores (U.S.)	315,654
3	Royal Dutch Shell (Netherlands)	306,731
4	BP (U.K.)	267,600
5	General Motors (U.S.)	192,604
6	Chevron (U.S.)	189,481
7	DaimlerChrysler (Germany/U.S.)	186,106
8	Toyota Motor (Japan)	185,805
9	Ford Motor (U.S.)	177,210
10	ConocoPhillips (U.S.)	166,683

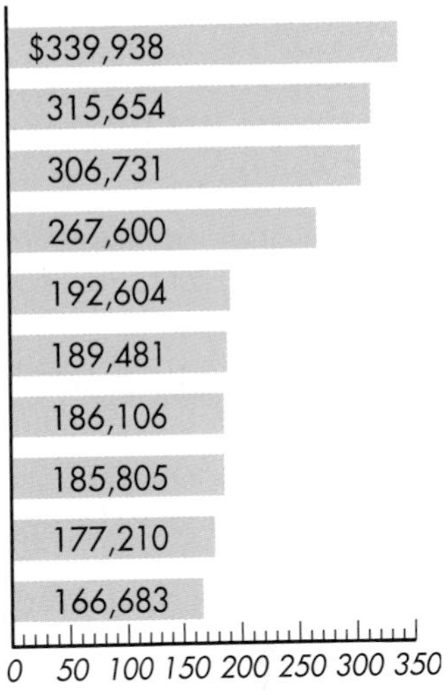

Sales (million dollars)

As shown in the chart, large firms are not just a U.S. phenomenon. *Source:* Fortune Global 500, © 2003 Time Inc. All rights reserved.

Thus, big business is important in the United States. There are many small firms, but large firms and corporations account for the greatest share of business revenue. Although there are only about one-third as many corporations as sole proprietorships, corporations have more than 15 times the revenue of sole proprietorships.

3.c. Firms Around the World

Big business is a dominant force in the United States. Many people believe that because the United States is the world's largest economy, U.S. firms are the largest in the world. Figure 6 shows that this is not true. Of the ten largest corporations in the world (measured by sales), four are foreign. Big business is not just a U.S. phenomenon.

3.d. Entrepreneurial Ability

The emphasis on bigness should not hide the fact that many new firms are started each year. Businesses are typically begun as small sole proprietorships. Many of them are forced to go out of business within a year or two. Businesses survive in the long run only if they provide a good or service that people want enough to yield a profit for the entrepreneur. Although there are fabulous success stories, the failure rate among new firms is high. Thorough research of the market and careful planning play a large part in determining whether a new business succeeds, but so can luck, as the Economic Insight "The Successful Entrepreneur" confirms.

That many new businesses fail is a fact of economic life. In the U.S. economy, anyone with an idea and sufficient resources is free to open a business. However, if buyers do not respond to the new offering, the business will fail. Only firms that satisfy this "market test" survive. Entrepreneurs thus try to ensure that as wants change, goods and services are produced to satisfy those wants.

The Successful Entrepreneur (Sometimes It's Better to Be Lucky Than Good)

Entrepreneurs do not always develop an abstract idea into reality when starting a new firm. Sometimes people stumble onto a good thing by accident and then are clever enough and willing to take the necessary risk to turn their lucky find into a commercial success.

In 1875, a Philadelphia pharmacist on his honeymoon tasted tea made from an innkeeper's old family recipe. The tea, made from 16 wild roots and berries, was so delicious that the pharmacist asked the innkeeper's wife for the recipe. When he returned to his pharmacy, he created a solid concentrate of the drink that could be sold for home consumption.

The pharmacist was Charles Hires, a devout Quaker, who intended to sell "Hires Herb Tea" to hard-drinking Pennsylvania coal miners as a nonalcoholic alternative to beer and whiskey. A friend of Hires suggested that miners would not drink anything called "tea" and recommended that he call his drink "root beer."

The initial response to Hires Root Beer was so enthusiastic that Hires soon began nationwide distribution. The yellow box of root beer extract became a familiar sight in homes and drugstore fountains across the United States. By 1895, Hires, who started with a $3,000 loan, was operating a business valued at half a million dollars (a lot of money in 1895) and bottling ready-to-drink root beer across the country.

Hires, of course, is not the only entrepreneur who was clever enough to turn a lucky discovery into a business success. In 1894, in Battle Creek, Michigan, a sanitarium handyman named Will Kellogg was helping his older brother prepare wheat meal to serve to patients in the sanitarium's dining room. The two men would boil wheat dough and then run it through rollers to produce thin sheets of meal. One day they left a batch of the dough out overnight. The next day, when the dough was run through the rollers, it broke up into flakes instead of forming a sheet.

By letting the dough stand overnight, the Kelloggs had allowed moisture to be distributed evenly to each individual wheat berry. When the dough went through the rollers, the berries formed separate flakes instead of binding together. The Kelloggs toasted the wheat flakes and served them to the patients. They were an immediate success. In fact, the brothers had to start a mail-order flaked-cereal business because patients wanted flaked cereal for their households.

Kellogg saw the market potential of the discovery and started his own cereal company (his brother refused to join him in the business). He was a great promoter who used innovations like four-color magazine ads and free-sample promotions. In New York City, he offered a free box of corn flakes to every woman who winked at her grocer on a specified day. The promotion was considered risqué, but Kellogg's sales in New York increased from two railroad cars of cereal a month to one car a day.

Will Kellogg, a poorly paid sanitarium worker in his mid-forties, became a daring entrepreneur after his mistake with wheat flour led to the discovery of a way to produce flaked cereal. He became one of the richest men in America because of his entrepreneurial ability.

Source: *Entrepreneurs* by Joseph and Suzy Fucini. Hall and Company, 1985.

3.e. Business Spending

investment: spending on capital goods to be used in producing goods and services

Investment is the expenditures by business firms for capital goods—machines, tools, and buildings—that will be used to produce goods and services. The economic meaning of *investment* is different from the everyday meaning, "a financial transaction such as buying bonds or stocks." In economics, the term *investment* refers to business spending for capital goods.

Investment spending in 2005 was $2,100 billion, an amount equal to roughly one-fourth of consumption, or household spending. Investment spending between 1959 and 2005 is shown in Figure 7. Compare Figures 5 and 7 and notice the different patterns of spending. Investment increases unevenly, actually falling at times and then rising very rapidly. Even though investment spending is much smaller than consumption, business expenditures are an important factor in determining the

FIGURE 7   U.S. Investment Spending

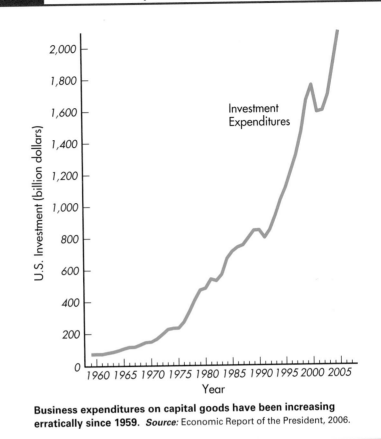

Business expenditures on capital goods have been increasing erratically since 1959. *Source:* Economic Report of the President, 2006.

economic health of the nation. For instance, investment spending declined from 1999 to 2002, causing the U.S. and world economies to grow very slowly or even decline.

RECAP

1. Business firms may be organized as sole proprietorships, partnerships, or corporations.

2. Large corporations account for the largest fraction of total business revenue.

3. Many new firms are started each year, but the failure rate is high.

4. Business investment spending fluctuates widely over time.

?

4. The International Sector

4. How does the international sector affect the economy?

Today, foreign buyers and sellers have a significant effect on economic conditions in the United States, and developments in the rest of the world often influence U.S. buyers and sellers. We saw in Chapter 3, for instance, how exchange-rate changes can affect the demand for U.S. goods and services.

FIGURE 8 **World Economic Development**

The colors on the map identify low-income, middle-income, and high-income economies. Countries have been placed in each group on the basis of GNP per capita and, in some instances, other distinguishing economic characteristics.
Source: World Bank, *http://nebula.worldbank.org/website/GNIwdi/viewer.htm.*

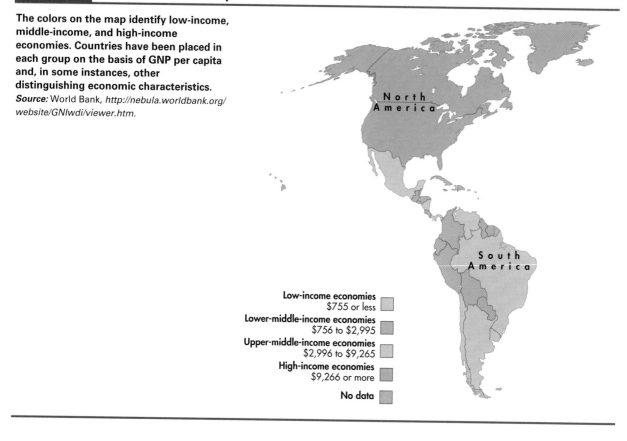

Low-income economies
$755 or less

Lower-middle-income economies
$756 to $2,995

Upper-middle-income economies
$2,996 to $9,265

High-income economies
$9,266 or more

No data

4.a. Types of Countries

The nations of the world may be divided into two categories: industrial countries and developing countries. Developing countries greatly outnumber industrial countries (see Figure 8). The World Bank (an international organization that makes loans to developing countries) groups countries according to per capita income (income per person). Low-income economies are those with per capita incomes of $755 or less. Middle-income economies have per capita annual incomes of $756 to $9,265. High-income economies—oil exporters and industrial market economies—are distinguished from the middle-income economies and have per capita incomes of greater than $9,266. Some countries are not members of the World Bank and so are not categorized, and information about a few small countries is so limited that the World Bank is unable to classify them.

It is readily apparent from Figure 8 that low-income economies are heavily concentrated in Africa and Asia. Countries in these regions have a low profile in U.S. trade, although they may receive aid from the United States. U.S. trade is concentrated with its neighbors Canada and Mexico, along with the major industrial powers. Nations in each group present different economic challenges to the United States.

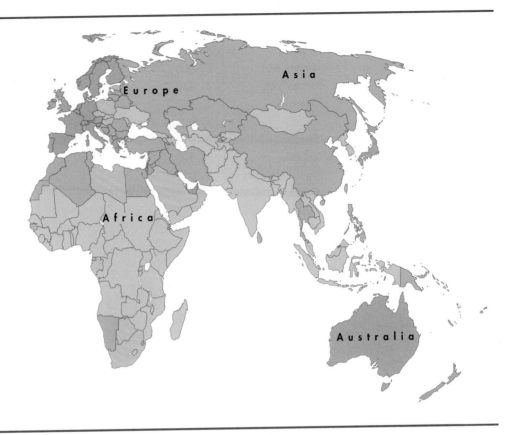

4.a.1. The Industrial Countries The World Bank uses per capita income to classify 23 countries as "industrial market economies." They are listed in the bar chart in Figure 9. The 23 countries listed in Figure 9 are among the wealthiest countries in the world. Not appearing on the list are the high-income oil-exporting nations like Libya, Saudi Arabia, Kuwait, and the United Arab Emirates. The World Bank considers those countries to be "still developing."

The economies of the industrial nations are highly interdependent. As conditions change in one country, business firms and individuals may shift large sums of money between countries. As funds flow from one country to another, economic conditions in one country spread to other countries. As a result, the industrial countries, particularly the major economic powers like the United States, Germany, and Japan, are forced to pay close attention to each other's economic policies.

4.a.2. The Developing Countries The developing countries provide a different set of issues for the United States from that posed by the industrial countries. In the 1980s, the debts of the developing countries to the developed nations reached tremendous heights. For instance, at the end of 1989, Brazil owed foreign creditors $111.3 billion, Mexico owed $95.6 billion, and Argentina owed $64.7 billion. In each case, the amounts owed were more than several times those countries' annual sales of goods and services to the rest of the world. The United States had to arrange loans at special terms and establish special trade arrangements in order for those countries to be able to buy U.S. goods.

FIGURE 9 | The Industrial Market Economies

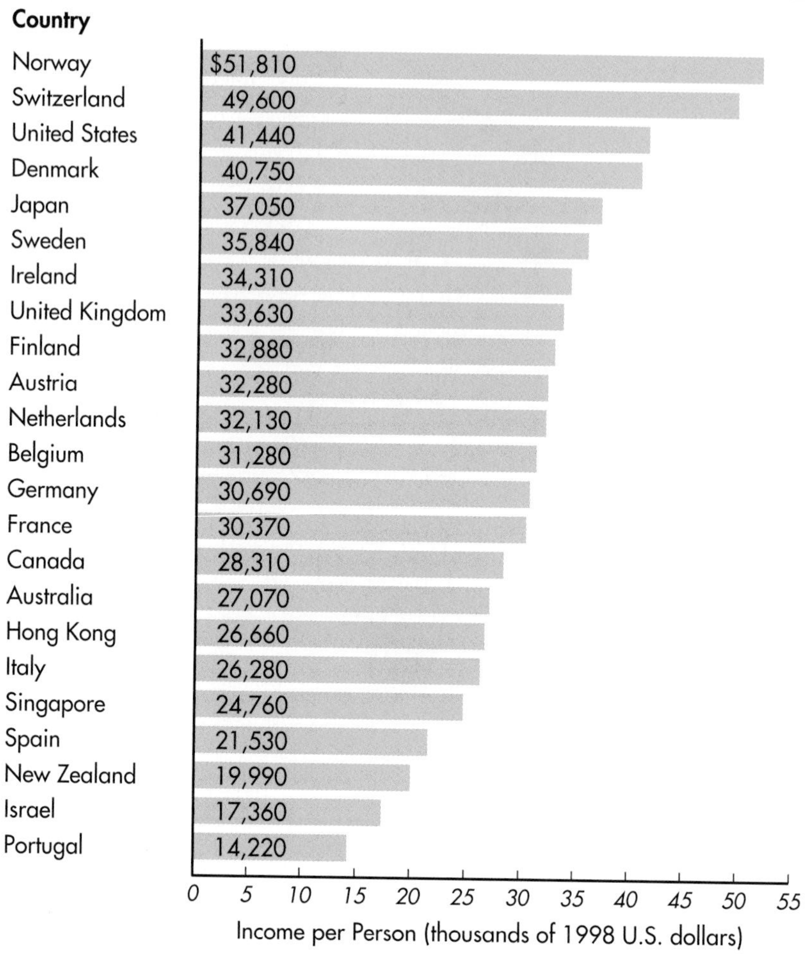

Country

Country	Income
Norway	$51,810
Switzerland	49,600
United States	41,440
Denmark	40,750
Japan	37,050
Sweden	35,840
Ireland	34,310
United Kingdom	33,630
Finland	32,880
Austria	32,280
Netherlands	32,130
Belgium	31,280
Germany	30,690
France	30,370
Canada	28,310
Australia	27,070
Hong Kong	26,660
Italy	26,280
Singapore	24,760
Spain	21,530
New Zealand	19,990
Israel	17,360
Portugal	14,220

Income per Person (thousands of 1998 U.S. dollars)

The bar chart lists some of the wealthiest countries in the world. *Source:* World Bank, World Development Report, 2006; *http://devdata.worldbank.org/data_query.*

The United States tends to buy, or *import,* primary products such as agricultural produce and minerals from the developing countries. Products that a country buys from another country are called **imports**. The United States tends to sell, or *export,* manufactured goods to developing countries. Products that a country sells to another country are called **exports**. In addition, the United States is the largest producer and exporter of grains and other agricultural output in the world. The efficiency of U.S. farming relative to farming in much of the rest of the world gives the United States a comparative advantage in many agricultural products.

imports: products that a country buys from other countries

exports: products that a country sells to other countries

4.b. International-Sector Spending

Economic activity of the United States with the rest of the world includes U.S. spending on foreign goods and foreign spending on U.S. goods. Figure 10 shows how U.S. exports and imports are spread over different countries. Notice that two countries, Canada and Japan, account for roughly one-third of U.S. exports and more

"The best and brightest are leaving." Statements like this are heard in many nations throughout the world. The best trained and most innovative people in many countries find their opportunities greater in the United States. As a result, they leave their countries to gain citizenship in the United States. But it is not easy for people to move from one country to another. The flow of goods and services among nations—international trade—occurs more readily than does the flow of workers.

| FIGURE 10 | Direction of U.S. Trade |

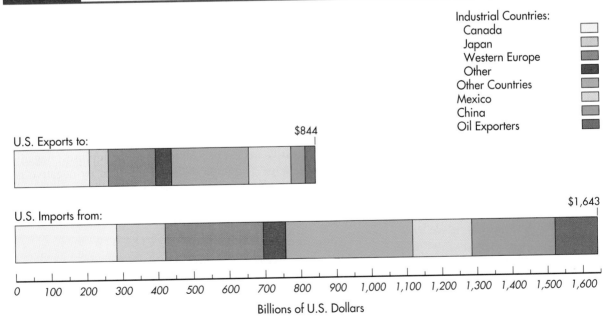

Industrial Countries:
Canada
Japan
Western Europe
Other
Other Countries
Mexico
China
Oil Exporters

U.S. Exports to: $844

U.S. Imports from: $1,643

Billions of U.S. Dollars

This chart shows that a trade deficit exists for the United States, since U.S. imports greatly exceed U.S. exports. The chart also shows that trade with western Europe, Japan, and Canada accounts for about half of U.S. trade. Mexico and China are large trading partners as well. *Source:* Economic Report of the President, 2006; *www.census.gov/foreign_trade.*

FIGURE 11   **U.S. Net Exports**

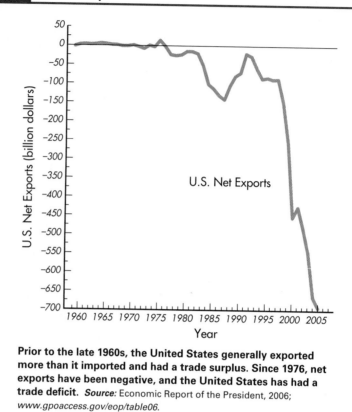

Prior to the late 1960s, the United States generally exported more than it imported and had a trade surplus. Since 1976, net exports have been negative, and the United States has had a trade deficit. *Source:* Economic Report of the President, 2006; *www.gpoaccess.gov/eop/table06.*

than one-third of U.S. imports. Trade with the industrial countries is approximately twice as large as trade with the developing countries, and U.S. trade with eastern Europe is trivial.

When exports exceed imports, a **trade surplus** exists. When imports exceed exports, a **trade deficit** exists. Figure 11 shows that the United States is importing much more than it exports.

The term **net exports** refers to the difference between the value of exports and the value of imports: Net exports equals exports minus imports. Figure 11 traces U.S. net exports over time. Positive net exports represent trade surpluses; negative net exports represent trade deficits. The trade deficits (indicated by negative net exports) starting in the 1980s were unprecedented. Reasons for this pattern of international trade are discussed in later chapters.

trade surplus: the situation that exists when imports are less than exports

trade deficit: the situation that exists when imports exceed exports

net exports: the difference between the value of exports and the value of imports

RECAP

1. The majority of U.S. trade is with the industrial market economies.

2. Exports are products sold to foreign countries; imports are products bought from foreign countries.

3. Exports minus imports equal net exports.

4. Positive net exports signal a trade surplus; negative net exports signal a trade deficit.

5. Linking the Sectors

?

5. How do the three private sectors— households, businesses, and the international sector—interact in the economy?

Now that we have an idea of the size and structure of each of the private sectors— households, businesses, and international—let's discuss how the sectors interact.

5.a. Households and Firms

Households own all the basic resources, or factors of production, in the economy. Household members own land and provide labor, and they are the entrepreneurs, stockholders, proprietors, and partners who own business firms.

Households and businesses interact with each other by means of buying and selling. Businesses employ the services of resources in order to produce goods and services. Business firms pay households for their resource services.

Households sell their resource services to businesses in exchange for money payments. The flow of resource services from households to businesses is shown by the blue-green line at the bottom of Figure 12. The flow of money payments from firms to households is shown by the gold line at the bottom of Figure 12. Households use the money payments to buy goods and services from firms. These money payments

---

FIGURE 12   **The Circular Flow: Households and Firms**

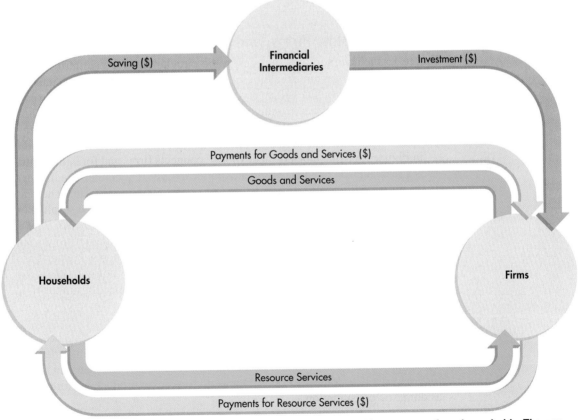

The diagram indicates that income is equal to the value of output. Firms hire resources from households. The payments for these resources represent household income. Households spend their income for goods and services produced by the firms. Household spending represents revenue for firms. Households save some of their income. This income reenters the circular flow as investment spending. Financial intermediaries like banks take in the saving of households and then lend this money to business firms for investment spending.

Chapter 4 The Market System and the Private Sector

are the firms' revenues. The flow of money payments from households to firms is shown by the gold line at the top of the diagram. The flow of goods and services from firms to households is shown by the blue-green line at the top of Figure 12. There is, therefore, a flow of money and of goods and services from one sector to the other. The payments made by one sector are the receipts taken in by the other sector. Money, goods, and services flow from households to firms and back to households in a circular flow.

Households do not spend all of the money that they receive. They save some fraction of their income. In Figure 12, we see that household saving is deposited in **financial intermediaries** like banks, credit unions, and saving and loan firms. A financial intermediary accepts deposits from savers and makes loans to borrowers. The money that is saved by the households reenters the economy in the form of investment spending as business firms borrow for expansion of their productive capacity.

The **circular flow diagram** represented in Figure 12 indicates that income is equal to the value of output. Money flows to the household sector are the sum of the payments to the resource owners, including the payments to entrepreneurs. Money flows to firms are the revenue that firms receive when they sell the goods and services that they produce. Revenue minus the costs of land, labor, and capital is profit. Profit represents the payment to entrepreneurs and other owners of corporations, partnerships, and sole proprietorships. In this simple economy, household income is equal to business revenue—the value of goods and services produced.

financial intermediaries: institutions that accept deposits from savers and make loans to borrowers

circular flow diagram: a model showing the flow of output and income from one sector of the economy to another

5.b. Households, Firms, and the International Sector

Figure 13 includes foreign countries in the circular flow. To simplify the circular flow diagram, let's assume that households are not directly engaged in international trade and that only business firms are buying and selling goods and services across international borders. This assumption is not far from the truth for the industrial countries and for many developing countries. We typically buy a foreign-made product from a local business firm rather than directly from the foreign producer.

In Figure 13, a line labeled "net exports" connects firms and foreign countries, as does a line labeled "payments for net exports." Notice that neither line has an arrow indicating the direction of flow as do the other lines in the diagram. The reason is that net exports of the home country may be either positive (a trade surplus) or negative (a trade deficit). When net exports are positive, there is a net flow of goods from the firms of the home country to foreign countries and a net flow of money from foreign countries to the firms of the home country. When net exports are negative, the opposite occurs. A trade deficit involves net flows of goods from foreign countries to the firms of the home country and net money flows from the domestic firms to the foreign countries. If exports and imports are equal, net exports are zero because the value of exports is offset by the value of imports.

Figure 13 shows the circular flow linking the private sectors of the economy. This model is a simplified view of the world, but it highlights the important interrelationships. The value of output equals income, as always; but spending may be for foreign as well as domestic goods. Domestic firms may produce for foreign as well as domestic consumption.

RECAP

1. The circular flow diagram illustrates how the main sectors of the economy fit together.
2. The circular flow diagram shows that the value of output is equal to income.

FIGURE 13 The Circular Flow: Households, Firms, and Foreign Countries

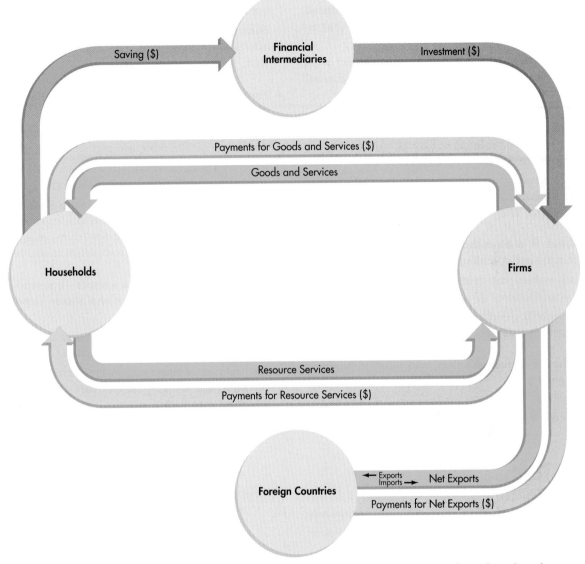

The diagram assumes that households are not directly engaged in international trade. The flow of goods and services between countries is represented by the line labeled "net exports." Neither the net exports line nor the line labeled "payments for net exports" has an arrow indicating the direction of the flow because the flow can go from the home country to foreign countries or vice versa. When the domestic economy has positive net exports (a trade surplus), goods and services flow out of the domestic firms toward foreign countries and money payments flow from the foreign countries to the domestic firms. With negative net exports (a trade deficit), the reverse is true.

Summary

1. In a market system, who decides what goods and services are produced and how they are produced, and who obtains the goods and services that are produced?

- In a market system, consumers are sovereign and decide by means of their purchases what goods and services will be produced. §1.a

- In a market system, firms decide how to produce the goods and services that consumers want. In order to earn maximum profits, firms use the least-cost combinations of resources. §1.c

- Income and prices determine who gets what in a market system. Income is determined by the ownership of resources. §1.d

2. What is a household, and what is household income and spending?

- A household consists of one or more persons who occupy a unit of housing. §2

- Household spending is called *consumption* and is the largest component of spending in the economy. §2.b

3. What is a business firm, and what is business spending?

- A business firm is a business organization controlled by a single management. §3

- Businesses may be organized as sole proprietorships, partnerships, or corporations. §3.a

- Business investment spending—the expenditure by business firms for capital goods—fluctuates a great deal over time. §3.e

4. How does the international sector affect the economy?

- The international trade of the United States occurs predominantly with the other industrial economies. §4.a

- Exports are products sold to the rest of the world. Imports are products bought from the rest of the world. §4.a.2

- Exports minus imports equal net exports. Positive net exports mean that exports are greater than imports and a trade surplus exists. Negative net exports mean that imports exceed exports and a trade deficit exists. §4.b

5. How do the three private sectors—households, businesses, and the international sector—interact in the economy?

- The resources combined to produce goods and services are also known as factors of production. §5.a

- The total value of output produced by the factors of production is equal to the income received by the owners of the factors of production. §5.a

Key Terms

consumer sovereignty §1.a	sole proprietorship §3.a	exports §4.a.2
private sector §1.d	partnership §3.a	trade surplus §4.b
public sector §1.d	corporation §3.a	trade deficit §4.b
household §2	multinational business §3.a	net exports §4.b
consumption §2.b	investment §3.e	financial intermediaries §5.a
business firm §3	imports §4.a.2	circular flow diagram §5.a

Exercises

1. What is consumer sovereignty? What does it have to do with determining what goods and services are produced? Who determines how goods and services are produced? Who receives the goods and services in a market system?

2. Is a family a household? Is a household a family?

3. What is the median value of the following series? 4, 6, 8, 3, 9, 10, 10, 1, 5, 7, 12

4. Which sector (households, business, or international) spends the most? Which sector spends the least? Which

sector, because of its volatility, has an importance greater than is warranted by its size?

5. What does it mean if net exports are negative?

6. Why does the value of output always equal the income received by the resources that produced the output?

7. Total spending in the economy is equal to consumption plus investment plus government spending plus net exports. If households want to save and thus do not use all of their income for consumption, what will happen to total spending? Because total spending in the economy is equal to total income and output, what will happen to the output of goods and services if households want to save more?

8. People sometimes argue that imports should be limited by government policy. Suppose a government quota on the quantity of imports causes net exports to rise. Using the circular flow diagram as a guide, explain why total expenditures and national output may rise after the quota is imposed. Who is likely to benefit from the quota? Who will be hurt?

9. Draw the circular flow diagram linking households, business firms, and the international sector. Use the diagram to explain the effects of a decision by the household sector to increase saving.

10. Suppose there are three countries in the world. Country A exports $11 million worth of goods to country B and $5 million worth of goods to country C; country B exports $3 million worth of goods to country A and $6 million worth of goods to country C; and country C exports $4 million worth of goods to country A and $1 million worth of goods to country B.
    a. What are the net exports of countries A, B, and C?
    b. Which country is running a trade deficit? A trade surplus?

11. Over time, there has been a shift away from outdoor drive-in movie theaters to indoor movie theaters. Use supply and demand curves to illustrate and explain how consumers can bring about such a change when their tastes change.

12. Figure 3 indicates that the youngest and the oldest households have the lowest household incomes. Why should middle-aged households have higher incomes than the youngest and oldest?

13. The chapter provides data indicating that there are many more sole proprietorships than corporations or partnerships. Why are there so many sole proprietorships? Why is the revenue of the average sole proprietorship less than that of the typical corporation?

14. List the four sectors of the economy along with the type of spending associated with each sector. Order the types of spending in terms of magnitude and give an example of each kind of spending.

15. The circular flow diagram of Figure 13 excludes the government sector. Draw a new version of the figure that includes this sector, with government spending and taxes added to the diagram. Label your new figure, and be sure to include arrows to illustrate the direction of flows.

ACE
Practice Test

Take the ACE Practice Test for this chapter to review the important concepts and get immediate feedback with answers.

college.hmco.com/economics/students/

Report: Ramsey Friend Sold Information to *National Enquirer*

Associated Press
November 28, 2002

A confidant of John and Patsy Ramsey said she sold handwriting samples and interrogation transcripts from their daughter's murder investigation to a supermarket tabloid for $40,000.

Susan Bennett, 51, of Hickory, N.C., told the Rocky Mountain News she sold the material to the *National Enquirer* because she believed that its publication would prove the Ramseys' innocence.

It was used in the tabloid's Dec. 3 edition in a 31-page story headlined: "JonBenet Secret Video Evidence: New Clues Expose Mom & Dad!," on newsstands Friday. Ramsey attorney L. Lin Wood said the couple feels betrayed that a friend would sell information. Wood said tabloids have cast suspicion on the parents throughout six years of reporting on the unsolved case.

"It's horribly naive to believe that the tabloids are going to fairly and accurately report on any issue or piece of evidence as it pertains to John and Patsy Ramsey," Wood said.

Wood said the information sold to the *Enquirer* was part of a discovery order in a federal libel lawsuit brought against the Ramseys by Chris Wolf, who the Ramseys called a suspect in a book they wrote about the murder.

Wood said Wolf's lawyer, Darnay Hoffman of New York, denied providing Bennett with the material. Hoffman was unavailable for comment.

Bennett, befriended by the former Boulder couple through her advocacy of their innocence, said she sold a transcript from an April 1997 police interrogation of the Ramseys, videotapes of a June 1998 police interrogation and handwriting samples from Patsy Ramsey.

"People make it sound as though I turned on the Ramseys," Bennett said. "I still believe 100 percent they are innocent."

JonBenet Ramsey was found beaten and strangled in the family's Boulder home on Dec. 26, 1996. No arrests have been made, but JonBenet's parents have remained under suspicion.

David Perel, editor of the *National Enquirer,* did not confirm the source of the information in his publication. He said the *Enquirer* is planning to publish a book about the case next year.

Wood said Bennett does not face legal action, but said he will investigate to see if she obtained the information in violation of a court order, and if the source of that information can be prosecuted for it.

"John and Patsy will no longer communicate with Ms. Bennett and will not share any information with her," Wood said.

The Ramseys previously sued American Media, publisher of the *National Enquirer,* over a story about their son, Burke, and won a settlement.

Source: The Associated Press State & Local Wire.

While standing in line at the grocery store, you notice the headlines on the tabloid, "Aliens Take Body of Britney Spears and Exchange It with Roseanne," and you wonder how anyone could pay for these ridiculous papers. Some people not only wonder about that but think that these tabloids are invading citizens' privacy. As the article notes, "It is terribly naive" to think that the tabloids will be fair or will try to provide a balanced viewpoint. Why, then, do these papers exist? Who determines whether these newspapers and magazines are appropriate, and who defines whether what they report is accurate or fair?

In a market system, it is consumers who determine whether these magazines and newspapers exist. If the producers of the newspapers and magazines cannot cover their costs with their revenues from sales and advertisements, then the producers will change what they do. They will either alter their coverage or presentation of stories or get out of the business altogether.

In a market system, products are provided if they result in a profit to producers. This means that the customer must be willing and able to pay for them. If stories about baseball are of no interest to readers, then consumers will not purchase magazines that focus on baseball. As a result, magazines will have to alter what they present in order to attempt to retain their sales. *Sports Illustrated* would have to have stories about other sports, swimsuits, and other topics instead of baseball.

If people did not want to read tabloids and were unwilling to purchase them, then the tabloids would not exist. Only if people are willing and able to pay a price sufficient for the newspaper publishers to make a profit will the newspapers be published. No one is forcing anyone to read the tabloids.

Suppose that the market for tabloids is represented in the demand and supply diagram shown below. Suppose that for some reason, perhaps the tragedy of JonBenet Ramsey's death, the willingness to purchase tabloids decreases. This is illustrated by an inward shift of the demand curve, from D_1 to D_2. The prices ob tabloids will decline, from P_1 to P_2. In addition, fewer tabloids will be purchased—the quantity sold falls from Q_1 to Q_2.

A decline in sales of the tabloids is not necessarily a good or a bad thing. All it really is, is a change in tastes and preferences and a shift of the demand curve. For some reason, people are not willing and able to purchase as many of the tabloids as they did before. There is no "good" or "bad" to this fact. It is simply a positive statement.

The lesson here is that the consumer does reign supreme in a market system. No profit-maximizing firm will ignore customer desires. Firms may try new cost-reducing approaches or revenue-enhancing techniques, but whether the tabloids are published depends on whether customers are willing and able to buy them.

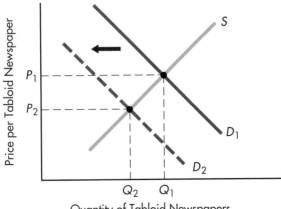

chapter 5

The Public Sector

Fundamental Questions

1. How does the government interact with the other sectors of the economy?

2. What is the economic role of government?

3. Why is the public sector such a large part of a market economy?

4. What does the government do?

5. How do the sizes of public sectors in various countries compare?

From conception to death, we are affected by the activities of the government. Many mothers receive prenatal care through government programs. We are born in hospitals that are subsidized or run by the government. We are delivered by doctors who received training in subsidized colleges. Our births are recorded on certificates filed with the government. Ninety percent of us attend public schools. Many of us live in housing that is directly subsidized by the government or have mortgages that are insured by the government. Most of us at one time or another put savings into accounts that are insured by the government. Virtually all of us, at some time in our lives, receive money from the government—from student loan programs, unemployment compensation, disability insurance, social security, or Medicare. Twenty percent of the work force is employed by the government. The prices of wheat, corn, sugar, and dairy products are controlled or strongly influenced by the government. The prices we pay for cigarettes,

alcohol, automobiles, utilities, water, gas, and a multitude of other goods are directly or indirectly influenced by the government. We travel on public roads and on publicly subsidized or controlled airlines, airports, trains, and ships. Our legal structure provides a framework in which we all live and act; the national defense ensures our rights of citizenship and protects our private property. By law, the government is responsible for employment and the general health of the economy.

According to virtually any measure, government in the United States has been a growth industry since 1930. The number of people employed by the local, state, and federal governments combined grew from 3 million in 1930 to over 19 million today; there are now more people employed in government than in manufacturing. Annual expenditures by the federal government rose from $3 billion in 1930 to approximately $705 billion today, and total government (federal, state, and local) expenditures now equal about $2.2 trillion annually. In 1929, government spending constituted less than 2.5 percent of total spending in the economy. Today, it is around 20 percent. The number of rules and regulations created by the government is so large that it is measured by the number of telephone-book-sized pages needed just to list them, and that number is more than 67,000. The cost of all federal rules and regulations is estimated to be somewhere between $4,000 and $17,000 per U.S. household each year, and the number of federal employees required to police these rules is about 125,000.

There is no doubt that the government (often referred to as the *public sector*) is a major player in the U.S. economy. But in the last few chapters, we have been learning about the market system and how well it works. If the market system works so well, why is the public sector such a large part of the economy? In this chapter, we discuss the public sector and the role that government plays in a market economy. ▩

1. The Circular Flow

?

1. **How does the government interact with the other sectors of the economy?**

Government in the United States exists at the federal, state, and local levels. Local government includes county, regional, and municipal units. Economic discussions tend to focus on the federal government because national economic policy is set at that level. Nevertheless, each level affects us through its taxing and spending decisions and its laws regulating behavior.

To illustrate how the government sector affects the economy, let's add government to the circular flow model presented in the previous chapter. Government at the federal, state, and local levels interacts with both households and firms. Because the government employs factors of production to produce government services, households receive payments from the government in exchange for the services of these factors of production. The flow of resource services from households to government is illustrated by the blue-green line flowing from households to government in Figure 1. The flow of money from government to households is shown by the gold line flowing from government to households. We assume that government, like a household, does not trade directly with foreign countries but obtains foreign goods from domestic firms that do trade with the rest of the world.

Households pay taxes to support the provision of government services, such as national defense, education, and police and fire protection. In a sense, then, the household sector is purchasing goods and services from the government as well as from private businesses. The flow of tax payments from households and businesses

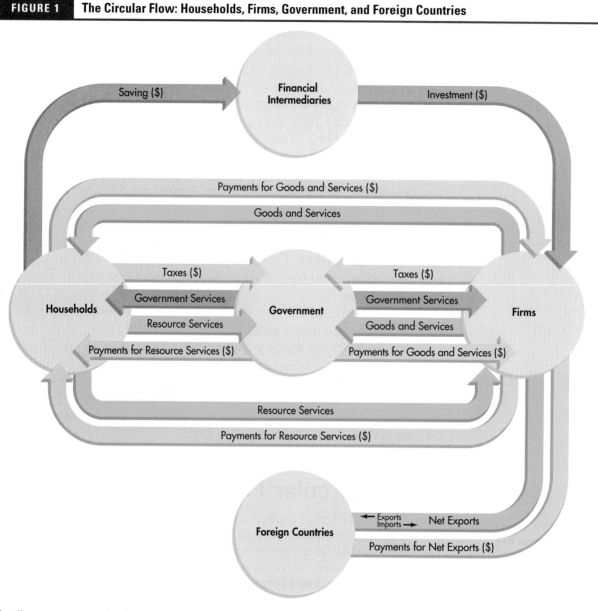

The diagram assumes that households and government are not directly engaged in international trade. Domestic firms trade with firms in foreign countries. The government sector buys resource services from households and goods and services from firms. This government spending represents income for the households and revenue for the firms. The government uses the resource services and goods and services to provide government services for households and firms. Households and firms pay taxes to the government to finance government expenditures.

to government is illustrated by the gold lines flowing from households and businesses to government, and the flow of government services to households and businesses is illustrated by the purple lines flowing from government to households and businesses.

The addition of government brings significant changes to the model. Households have an additional place to sell their resources for income, and businesses have an additional market for the goods and services that they produce. The value of *private* production no longer equals the value of household income. Households receive income from government in exchange for providing resource services to government. The total value of output in the economy is equal to the total income received, but government is included as both a source of income and a producer of services.

2. The Role of Government in the Market System

2. What is the economic role of government?

We have learned that consumers use their limited incomes to buy the goods and services that give them the greatest satisfaction, that resource owners offer the services of their resources to the highest bidder, and that firms produce the goods and services and use the resources that enable them to generate the highest profits. In other words, everyone—consumers, firms, and resource suppliers—attempts to get the most benefits for the least cost.

This apparently narrow, self-interested behavior is converted by the market into a social outcome in which no one can be made better off without making someone else worse off. Any resource allocation that could make someone better off while making no one any worse off would increase efficiency. When all such allocations have been realized, so that the *only* way to make one person better off would be to harm someone else, then we have realized the best allocation that society can achieve. As Adam Smith noted in 1776, self-interested individuals, wholly unaware of the effects of their actions, act as if driven by an *invisible hand* to produce the greatest social good.

2.a. Government as the Guardian of Efficiency

economic efficiency: a situation in which no one in society can be made better off without making someone else worse off

technical efficiency: producing at a point on the PPC

Economic efficiency is the name given to the events described by Adam Smith. Efficiency can mean many things to many different people. Even within economics there are different definitions of efficiency. We have already talked about the production possibilities curve and efficiency; operating at a point on the PPC is called *productive* or **technical efficiency**. A firm is said to be operating efficiently when it produces a given quantity and quality of goods at the lowest possible cost. Consumers are said to be efficient when they are getting the greatest bang for the buck, using their scarce resources to get the greatest benefits. *Economic efficiency* encompasses all of these definitions of efficiency. When *one person cannot be made better off without harming someone else,* then we say that economic efficiency prevails.

Somewhat amazingly, economic efficiency occurs in a market system simply through the self-interested individual actions of participants in that system. Efficiency is not the result of some despot controlling the economy and telling people what they can and cannot do. The market system results in efficiency because people own resources and goods and will exchange their goods or resources for others only if the exchange makes them better off. The higher profits go, the more income is earned by people with entrepreneurial ability. In order to earn profits, entrepreneurs have to provide, at the lowest possible cost, the goods and services that consumers want and are able to buy. This means that the least-cost combination of resources is used by each firm, but it also means that resources are employed in their most highly valued uses. Any reallocation of resources results in a situation that is worse—some resources will not be used where they are most highly valued, and some consumers will be less satisfied with the goods and services that they can purchase.

As we saw in the beginning of this chapter, the government plays a significant role in the U.S. economy; governmental influence is even larger in other market economies and is especially large in a socialist economy like Cuba. If the actions of individuals in the market system result in the best social outcome, why does the government play such a large role?

There are two justifications given for the government's role in a market economy beyond ensuring private property rights. One is based on cases in which the market may not always result in economic efficiency. The second is based on the idea that people who do not like the market outcome use the government to change the outcome. Sections 2.b through 2.f are brief discussions of some situations in which the market system may fail to achieve economic efficiency. Section 2.g is a brief discussion of situations in which people manipulate the market outcome.

?

3. **Why is the public sector such a large part of a market economy?**

2.b. Information and the Price System

As you learned in Chapters 3 and 4, a market is a place or service that allows buyers and sellers to exchange information on what they know about a product, what buyers are willing and able to pay for a product, and what sellers want to receive in order to produce and sell a product. A market price is a signal indicating when more or less of a good is desired. When the market price rises, buyers know that the quantity demanded at the prior equilibrium price exceeded the quantity supplied.

A market price is only as good an indicator as the information that exists in the market. It takes time for people to gather information about a product. It takes time to go to a market and purchase an item. It takes time for producers to learn what people want and bring together the resources necessary to produce that product. Thus, people are not likely to be perfectly informed, nor will everyone have the same information. This means that not all markets will adjust instantaneously, or even at the same speed, to a change in demand or supply. It also means that some people may pay higher prices for a product than others pay. Some people may be swindled by a sharp operator, and some firms may fail to collect debts that are owed to them.

market imperfection: a lack of efficiency that results from imperfect information in the marketplace

When information is not perfect, **market imperfections** may occur. As a result of market imperfections, least-cost combinations of resources may not be used, or resources may not be used where they have the highest value. People have often argued that in these cases, the government should step in with rules and regulations concerning the amount of information that must be provided. The government requires, for example, that specific information be provided on the labels of food products, that warning labels be placed on cigarettes and alcohol products, and that statements about the condition of a used car be made available to buyers. The government also declares certain actions by firms or consumers to be fraudulent or illegal. It also tests and licenses pharmaceuticals and members of many professions—medical doctors, lawyers, beauticians, barbers, nurses, and others.

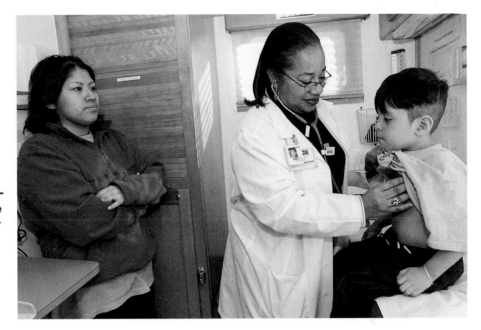

Government plays an active role in regulating some professions. Physicians and other health professionals are licensed by the government with the intent to ensure that health-care providers are properly trained.

2.c. Externalities

The market system works efficiently only if the market price reflects the full costs and benefits of producing and consuming a particular good or service. Recall that people make decisions on the basis of their opportunity costs and that the market price is a measure of what must be forgone in order to acquire some good or service. If the market price does not reflect the full costs, then decisions cannot reflect opportunity costs. For instance, when you drive, you don't pay for all of the pollution created by your car. When you have a loud, late-night party, you don't pay for the disruption you impose on your neighbors. When firms dump wastes or radioactive by-products freely, they don't pay the costs. When homeowners allow their properties to become rundown, they reduce the value of neighboring properties, but they don't pay for this loss of value. Not all such side effects of actions are negative. When people in society are educated, it costs less to produce signs, ballots, tax forms, and other information tools. Literacy enables a democracy to function effectively, and higher education may stimulate scientific discoveries that improve the welfare of society. When you acquire an education, however, you do not get a check for the amount of the savings that your education will create for society. All these side effects—some negative, some positive—that are not included in the market price are called **externalities**.

externalities: the costs or benefits of a transaction that are borne by someone who is not directly involved in the transaction

Externalities are the costs or benefits of a market activity that are borne by someone who is not a direct party to the market transaction. When you drive, you pay only for gasoline and car maintenance. You don't pay for the noise and pollutants that your car emits. You also don't pay for the added congestion and delays that you impose on other drivers. Thus, the *market* price of driving understates the *full* cost to society of driving; as a result, people drive more frequently than they would if they had to pay the full cost.

The government is often called upon to intervene in the market to resolve externality problems. Government agencies, such as the Environmental Protection Agency, are established to set and enforce standards, such as those for air quality, and taxes are imposed to obtain funds to pay for external costs or subsidize external benefits. Thus, the government provides education to society at below-market prices because the positive externality of education benefits everyone.

2.d. Public Goods

The market system works efficiently only if the benefits derived from consuming a particular good or service are available only to the consumer who buys that good or service. When you buy a pizza, only you receive the benefits of eating that pizza. What would happen if you weren't allowed to enjoy that pizza all by yourself? Suppose your neighbors had the right to come to your home when you had a pizza delivered and share your pizza. How often would you buy a pizza? There is no way to exclude others from enjoying the benefits of some of the goods you purchase. These types of goods are called **public goods**, and they create a problem for the market system.

public good: a good whose consumption by one person does not diminish the quantity or quality available for others

National defense is a public good. You could buy a missile to protect your house, but your neighbors, as well as you, would benefit from the protection it provided. A pizza, however, is not a public good. If you pay for it, only you get to enjoy the benefits. Thus, you have an incentive to purchase pizza. You don't have that incentive to purchase public goods. If you and I both benefit from the public good, who will buy it? I'd prefer that you buy it so that I can receive its benefits at no cost. Conversely, you'd prefer that I buy it. The result may be that no one will buy it.

Fire protection provides a good example of the problem that occurs with public goods. Suppose that, as a homeowner, you have the choice of subscribing to fire protection services from a private firm or having no fire protection. If you subscribe and your house catches fire, the fire engines will arrive as soon as possible, and your house may be saved. If you do not subscribe, your house will burn. Do you choose to subscribe? You might say to yourself that as long as your neighbors subscribe, you need not do so. The fact that your neighbors subscribe means that fires in their houses won't cause a fire in yours, and you do not expect a fire to begin in your house. If many people made similar decisions, fire protection services would not be available because not enough people would subscribe to make the services profitable.

private property right: the right of ownership

The problem with a public good is the communal nature of the good. No one has a **private property right** to a public good. If you buy a car, you must pay the seller an acceptable price. Once this price is paid, the car is all yours, and no one else can use it without your permission. The car is your private property, and you make the decisions about its use. In other words, you have the private property right to the car. Public goods are available to all because no one individual owns them or has property rights to them.

free ride: the enjoyment of the benefits of a good by a producer or consumer without having to pay for the good

When goods are public, people have an incentive to try to obtain a **free ride**—to enjoy the benefits of a good without paying for the good. Your neighbors would free-ride on your purchases of pizza if you didn't have the private property right to the pizza. People who enjoy public radio and public television stations without donating money to them are getting free rides from those people who do donate to them. People who benefit from the provision of a good whether they pay for it or not have an incentive not to pay for it.

Typically, in the absence of private property rights to a good, people call on the government to claim ownership and provide the good. For instance, governments act as owners of police departments and specify how police services are used. The Global Business Insight "Government Creates a Market for Fishing Rights" provides one example of government specifying private property rights.

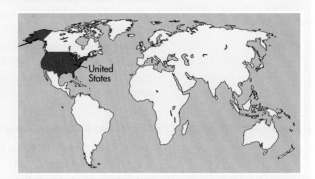

Global Business Insight

Government Creates a Market for Fishing Rights

There is no practical way to establish ownership rights for ocean fish stocks. Traditionally, fish have been free for the taking—a common resource. Theory teaches that such underpricing leads to overconsumption. In the halibut fisheries off Alaska, fishing fleets caught so many halibut that the survival of the stock was threatened. No single fishing boat had an incentive to harvest fewer fish, since the impact on its own future catch would be minimal and others would only increase their take. This is an example of what is known as "the tragedy of the commons."

Countries claim fishing rights to the ocean water off their shores to a certain distance. But this just limits the problem to overfishing by domestic boats. The example of the Alaskan halibut fishery is valuable for all nations to consider.

Officials tried limiting the length of the fishing season. But this effort only encouraged new capital investment, such as larger and faster boats with more effective (and expensive) fishing equipment. In order to control the number of fish caught, the season was shortened from four months to as little as two days in some areas by the early 1990s. Most of the halibut caught had to be frozen rather than marketed fresh, and halibut caught out of season had to be discarded.

In late 1992, the federal government proposed a new approach: assigning each fisherman a permit to catch a certain number of fish. The total number of fish for which permits are issued reflects scientific estimates of the number of fish that can be caught without endangering the survival of the species. Also, the permits are transferable—they can be bought and sold. By making the permits transferable, the system in effect creates a market where one did not exist previously. The proposed system encourages the most profitable and efficient boats to operate at full capacity by buying permits from less successful boats, ensuring a fishing fleet that uses labor and equipment efficiently. Moreover, the transferable permits system establishes a market price for the opportunity to fish—a price that better reflects the true social cost of using this common resource.

Today, the fishing season for halibut is 245 days. This results in much greater availability of fresh rather than frozen fish. Consumers receive a higher-quality product, and the survival of the halibut is protected.

Sources: *Economic Report of the President, 1993*, p. 207; www.lobsterconservation.com/halibutfq/.

2.e. Monopoly

If only one firm produces a good that is desired by consumers, then that firm might produce a smaller amount of the good in order to charge a higher price. In this case, resources might not be used in their most highly valued manner, and consumers might not be able to purchase the goods they desire. A situation in which there is only one producer of a good is called a **monopoly**. The existence of a monopoly can imply a lack of economic efficiency. The government is often called upon to regulate the behavior of firms that are monopolies, or even to run the monopolies as government enterprises. The government also encourages competition through antitrust laws that limit the ability of firms to engage in anticompetitive practices.

monopoly: a situation in which there is only one producer of a good

2.f. Business Cycles

People are made better off by economic growth. Economic growth increases the number of jobs and draws people out of poverty and into the mainstream of economic progress. Economic stagnation, on the other hand, throws the relatively poor

business cycles:
fluctuations in the economy between growth and stagnation

out of their jobs and into poverty. These fluctuations in the economy are called **business cycles**. People call on the government to protect them against the periods of economic ill health and to minimize the damaging effects of business cycles. Government agencies are established to control the money supply and other important parts of the economy, and government-financed programs are implemented to offset some of the losses that result during bad economic times. The U.S. Congress requires that the government promote economic growth and minimize unemployment. History has shown that this is easier said than done.

2.g. The Public Choice Theory of Government

The efficiency justification for government intervention in the economy, discussed in sections 2.b through 2.f, implies that the government is a cohesive organization that functions in much the same way that a benevolent dictator would. This organization intervenes in the market system only to correct the ills created by the market. Not all economists agree with this view of government. Many claim that the government is not a benevolent dictator looking out for the best interests of society, but is instead merely a collection of individuals who respond to the same economic impulses that we all do—that is, the desire to satisfy our own interests.

Economic efficiency does not mean that everyone is as well off as he or she desires to be. It merely means that someone or some group cannot be made better off without harming some other person or group of people. People always have an incentive to attempt to make themselves better off. If their attempts result in the transfer of benefits to themselves and away from others, however, economic efficiency has not increased. Moreover, the resources devoted to enacting the transfer of benefits are not productive; they do not create new income and benefits, but merely transfer existing income and benefits. Such activity is called **rent seeking**. Rent seeking refers to cases in which people devote resources to attempting to create income transfers to themselves. Rent seeking includes the expenditures on lobbyists in Congress, the time and expense that health-care professionals devote to fighting nationalized health care, the time and expense that farmers devote to improving their subsidies, and millions of other examples.

rent seeking: the use of resources simply to transfer wealth from one group to another without increasing production or total wealth

A group of economists, referred to as **public choice** economists, argue that government intervention in the economy is more the result of rent seeking than of market failure. The study of public choice focuses on how government actions result from the self-interested behaviors of voters and politicians. Whereas the efficiency justification for government actions argues that the government steps in only in cases where the market does not work, public choice theory says that the government may be brought into the market system whenever someone or some group can benefit, even if efficiency is not served.

public choice: the study of how government actions result from the self-interested behaviors of voters and politicians

According to the public choice economists, price ceilings or price floors may be enacted for political gain rather than because of market failure; government spending or taxing policies may be enacted not to resolve a market failure, but instead to implement an income redistribution from one group to another; government agencies such as the Food and Drug Administration may exist not to improve the functioning of the market, but to provide a wealth transfer from one group to another. Each such instance of manipulation leads to a larger role for government in a market economy. Moreover, government employees have the incentive to increase their role and importance in the economy and thereby transfer income or other benefits to themselves.

The government sector is far from a trivial part of the market system. Whether the government's role is one of improving economic efficiency or the result of rent seeking is a topic for debate, and in later chapters we discuss this debate in more detail. For now, it is satisfactory just to recognize how important the public sector is in the market system and what the possible reasons for its prevalence are.

?

4. What does the government do?

3. Overview of the U.S. Government

When Americans think of government policies, rules, and regulations, they typically think of Washington, D.C., because their economic lives are regulated and shaped more by policies made there than by policies made at the local and state levels. Who actually is involved in economic policymaking? Important government institutions that shape U.S. economic policy are listed in Table 1. This list is far from complete, but it includes the agencies with the broadest powers and greatest influence.

Economic policy involves macroeconomic issues like government spending and control of the money supply and microeconomic issues aimed at providing public goods like police and military protection, correcting externalities like pollution, and maintaining a competitive economy.

3.a. Microeconomic Policy

Government provides public goods to avoid the free-rider problem that would occur if private firms provided the goods.

One reason for government's microeconomic role is the free-rider problem associated with the provision of public goods. If an army makes all citizens safer, then all citizens should pay for it. But even if one person does not pay taxes, the army still protects this citizen from foreign attack. To minimize free riding, the government collects mandatory taxes to finance the provision of public goods. Congress and the president determine the level of public goods needed and how to finance them.

Government taxes or subsidizes some activities that create externalities.

Microeconomic policy also deals with externalities. Activities that cause air or water pollution impose costs on everyone. For instance, a steel mill may generate air pollutants that have a negative effect on the surrounding population. A microeconomic function of government is to internalize the externality—that is, to force the steelmaker to bear the full cost to society of producing steel. In addition to assuming the costs of hiring land, labor, and capital, the mill should bear the costs associated with polluting the air. Congress and the president determine which externalities to address and the best way of taxing or subsidizing each activity in order to ensure that the amount of the good produced and its price reflect the true value to society.

TABLE 1	U.S. Government Economic Policymakers and Related Agencies

Institution	Role
Fiscal policymakers	
President	Provides leadership in formulating fiscal policy
Congress	Sets government spending and taxes and passes laws related to economic conduct
Monetary policymaker	
Federal Reserve	Controls the money supply and credit conditions
Related agencies	
Council of Economic Advisers	Monitors the economy and advises the president
Office of Management and Budget	Prepares and analyzes the federal budget
Treasury Department	Administers the financial affairs of the federal government
Commerce Department	Administers federal policy regulating industry
Justice Department	Enforces the legal setting of business
Comptroller of the Currency	Oversees national banks
International Trade Commission	Investigates unfair international trade practices
Federal Trade Commission	Administers laws related to fair business practices and competition

Government regulates industries where free market competition may not exist and polices other industries to promote competition.

Another of government's microeconomic roles is to promote competition. Laws that restrict the ability of business firms to engage in practices that limit competition exist and are monitored by the Justice Department and the Federal Trade Commission. Some firms, such as public utilities, are monopolies and face no competition. The government defines the output, prices, and profits of many monopolies. In some cases, the monopolies are government-run enterprises.

3.b. Macroeconomic Policy

The focus of the government's macroeconomic policy is monetary and fiscal policy. **Monetary policy** is policy directed toward the control of money and credit. The major player in this policy arena is the Federal Reserve, commonly called "the Fed." The **Federal Reserve** is the central bank of the United States. It serves as a banker for the U.S. government and regulates the U.S. money supply.

monetary policy: policy directed toward the control of money and credit

Federal Reserve: the central bank of the United States

The Federal Reserve System is run by a seven-member Board of Governors. The most important member of the board is the chairman, who is appointed by the president for a term of four years. The board meets regularly (from 10 to 12 times a year) with a group of high-level officials to review the current economic situation and set policy for the growth of U.S. money and credit. The Federal Reserve exercises a great deal of influence on U.S. economic policy.

fiscal policy: policy directed toward government spending and taxation

Government has the responsibility of minimizing the damage from business cycles.

Fiscal policy, the other area of macroeconomic policy, is policy directed toward government spending and taxation. In the United States, fiscal policy is determined by laws that are passed by Congress and signed by the president. The relative roles of the legislative and executive branches in shaping fiscal policy vary with the political climate, but usually it is the president who initiates major policy changes.

Presidents rely on key advisers for fiscal policy information. These advisers include Cabinet officers such as the secretary of the Treasury and the secretary of state, and also the director of the Office of Management and Budget. In addition, the president has a Council of Economic Advisers made up of three economists—usually a chair, a macroeconomist, and a microeconomist—who, together with their staff, monitor and interpret economic developments for the president. The degree of influence wielded by these advisers depends on their personal relationship with the president.

3.c. Government Spending

Federal, state, and local government spending for goods and services is shown in Figure 2. Except during times of war in the 1940s and 1950s, federal expenditures were roughly similar in size to state and local expenditures until 1970. Since 1970, state and local spending has been growing more rapidly than federal spending.

Spending on goods and services by all levels of government combined is larger than investment spending but much smaller than consumption. In 2004, combined government spending was about $2,184 billion, investment spending was about $1,922 billion, and consumption was about $11,728 billion.

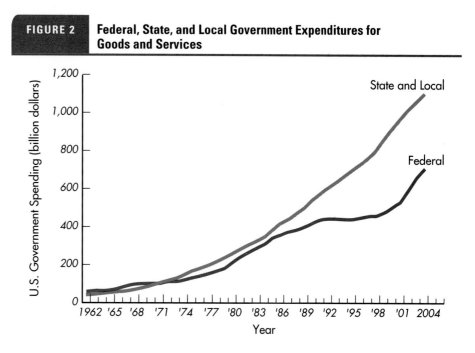

| **FIGURE 2** | **Federal, State, and Local Government Expenditures for Goods and Services** |

In the 1950s and early 1960s, federal government spending was above state and local government spending. In 1970, state and local expenditures rose above federal spending and have remained higher ever since.

Source: Data are from the *Economic Report of the President, 2005.*

transfer payment:
income transferred by the government from a citizen who is earning income to another citizen

In addition to purchasing goods and services, government also serves as an intermediary, taking money from some taxpayers and transferring this income to others. Such **transfer payments** are a part of total government expenditures, so the total government budget is much larger than the expenditures for goods and services reported in Figure 2. In 2004, total expenditures of federal, state, and local government for goods and services were about $2,184 billion. In this same year, transfer payments made by all levels of government were about $1,406 billion.

The magnitude of federal government spending relative to federal government revenue from taxes has become an important issue in recent years. Figure 3 shows that the federal budget was roughly balanced until the early 1970s. The budget is a measure of spending and revenue. A balanced budget occurs when federal spending is approximately equal to federal revenue. This was the case through the 1950s and 1960s.

budget surplus: the excess that results when government spending is less than tax revenue

budget deficit: the shortage that results when government spending is greater than tax revenue

If federal government spending is less than tax revenue, a **budget surplus** exists. By the early 1980s, federal government spending was much larger than revenue, so a large **budget deficit** existed. The federal budget deficit grew very rapidly to about $290 billion by the early 1990s before beginning to drop and turning to surplus by 1998. After four years of surpluses, a deficit was again realized in 2002. When spending is greater than revenue, the excess spending must be covered by borrowing, and this borrowing can have effects on investment and consumption, and also on economic relationships with other countries.

FIGURE 3   U.S. Federal Budget Deficits

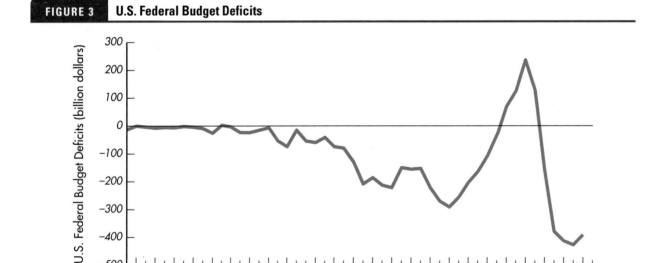

The budget deficit is equal to the excess of government spending over tax revenue. If taxes are greater than government spending, a budget surplus (shown as a positive number) exists.
Source: Data are from the Economic Report of the President, 2005.

---

1. The microeconomic functions of government include correcting externalities, redistributing income from high-income groups to lower-income groups, enforcing a competitive economy, and providing public goods.

2. Macroeconomic policy attempts to control the economy through monetary and fiscal policy.

3. The Federal Reserve conducts monetary policy. Congress and the president formulate fiscal policy.

4. Government spending is larger than investment spending but much smaller than consumption spending.

5. When government spending exceeds tax revenue, a budget deficit exists. When government spending is less than tax revenue, a budget surplus exists.

4. Government in Other Economies

5. How do the sizes of public sectors in various countries compare?

centrally planned economy: an economic system in which the government determines what goods and services are produced and the prices at which they are sold

The government plays a role in every economy, and in most the public sector is a much larger part of the economy than it is in the United States. In some economies, referred to as **centrally planned**, or nonmarket, economies, the public sector is the principal component of the economy. There are significant differences between the market system and a centrally planned system. In market economies, people can own businesses, be private owners of land, start new businesses, and purchase what they want as long as they can pay the price. They may see their jobs disappear as business conditions worsen, but they are free to take business risks and to reap the rewards if taking these risks pays off. Under centrally planned systems, people are not free to own property other than a house, a car, and personal belongings. They are not free to start a business. They work as employees of the state. Their jobs are guaranteed regardless of whether their employer is making the right or wrong decisions and regardless of how much effort they expend on the job. Even if they have money in their pockets, they may not be able to buy many of the things they want. Money prices are often not used to ration goods and services, so people may spend much of their time standing in lines to buy the products that are available on the shelves of government stores. Waiting in line is a result of charging a money price lower than equilibrium and imposing a quantity limit on how much a person can buy. The time costs, along with the money price required to buy goods, will ration the limited supply.

The Soviet Union implemented a centrally planned economy in the 1920s, following its October 1917 revolution. During, and especially following, World War II, the Soviet system expanded into eastern Europe, China, North Korea, and Vietnam. At the peak of Soviet influence, about one-third of the world's population lived in countries that could generally be described as having centrally planned economic systems. The 1980s and 1990s ushered in a new world order, however. The Soviet Union's economy failed, ultimately leading to the fall of the Communist governments in eastern Europe, the disintegration of the Soviet Union, the end of the Cold War, and the reunification of West and East Germany.

4.a. Overview of Major Market Economies

Figure 4 shows the size of government and the type of economy for several countries. The United States is representative of nations that are market economies with

FIGURE 4   The Economic System

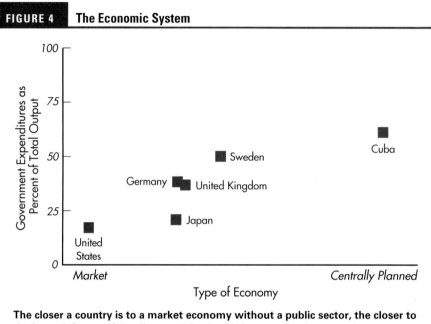

The closer a country is to a market economy without a public sector, the closer to the lower left area of the diagram it is placed. Conversely, the more the country is a centrally planned economy, the closer to the upper-right area of the diagram it is placed.

relatively small public sectors. Cuba is representative of nations where the economy is primarily centrally planned. Germany and Japan are market economies, but the public sector plays a larger role in these countries than it does in the United States.

When one thinks of the richest countries in the world, the countries that come to mind are all market economies. The incentives for efficient production provided by markets create the high incomes enjoyed by residents of these countries. Yet it is important to realize that these countries are not all alike. Some have larger roles for government activity than others.

For instance, the role of the public sector in the United Kingdom is significant, but it is not exceptional by European standards. Great Britain is an island economy with a land area slightly greater than that of the state of Minnesota and a population of just over 59 million persons. The resource base of the economy is quite limited, and the British economy is tied very closely to other economies. Government spending is about 40 percent of total output in the United Kingdom.

In Germany, the public sector owns few businesses, but it intervenes a great deal to foster social programs. For instance, the government regulates business hours, supports minimum prices for brand-name articles, imposes rent controls, regulates the hiring and firing of employees, regulates vacations, and has passed a series of other laws protecting workers and renters. State expenditures are about 40 percent of total output. The unification of the East and West German economies and the resulting merger of two different economic systems led to additional government intervention.

Japan is a capitalist economy whose postwar rate of economic growth is the highest among the major industrialized countries. Japan is a small country with adequate labor but generally limited supplies of natural resources and land. Like Great Britain, Japan is an island economy. With a population of approximately 127 million and a land area slightly smaller than that of the state of California, Japan is densely populated. The public sector appears on the surface to have a relatively small role in the

In Germany, the telephone company, Deutsche Telekom, is owned by private stockholders as well as the German government. When Telekom was "privatized" a few years ago, the government sold shares of stock to the public but retained a big share for itself. Such government involvement in seemingly private enterprise occurs in many industrial as well as developing countries.

Japanese economy: Government spending is only about 20 percent of total output. But this statistic understates the reality. The public sector plays a very important role through the Japanese industrial families known as *keiretsu*. The government wields its influence on the keiretsu through various ministries. For example, the Ministry of International Trade and Industry (MITI) is responsible for international trade, domestic production, and domestic industrial structure. The MITI guides and influences economic decisions by promoting key sectors of the economy and carefully phasing out other, low-productivity sectors. The MITI uses government funds for research and development and to provide assistance for organizational change, such as mergers. Economic planning has not been an important element in the Japanese economy. Japan has had a planning agency since the late 1940s and has assembled numerous plans, but the plans are neither binding nor involuntarily implemented.

The Swedish economic system and its performance are of interest because Sweden is viewed as a system that has been able, over an extended period of time, to sustain economic progress through the efficiency of the market while at the same time ensuring that incomes are equally distributed. Sweden is a relatively small but highly industrialized country. It has a total area of roughly 450,000 square kilometers (somewhat larger than the state of California) and a population of about 8.9 million. Foreign trade is of vital importance to Sweden, accounting for more than 80 percent of its total output. The Swedish economy looks like a market economy in the production of goods and services, but the government accounts for nearly 50 percent of total purchases in Sweden.

RECAP

1. No economy is purely private. The public sector plays a role in every economy.
2. A market economy relies on prices and individual actions to solve economic problems. In centrally planned economies, the government decides what is produced, how it is produced, and who gets what.

Summary

1. How does the government interact with the other sectors of the economy?

- The circular flow diagram illustrates the interaction among all sectors of the economy—households, businesses, the international sector, and the public sector. *§1*

2. What is the economic role of government?

- The market system promotes economic efficiency. Economic efficiency means that one person in an economy cannot be made better off without harming someone else. *§2.a*

- The market system does not result in economic efficiency when there are market imperfections, externalities, or public goods. Market imperfections occur when information is imperfect. *§2.b–2.f*

3. Why is the public sector such a large part of a market economy?

- Two general reasons are given for the government's participation in the economy: The government may act to resolve the inefficiencies that occur in a market system, or the government's actions may be the result of rent seeking. *§2.b–2.g*

- Economic efficiency means that some people cannot be made better off without others being made worse off. Some people do not like the result of the market outcome and want to alter it. In such cases, resources are devoted to creating a transfer of income. This is called rent seeking. *§2.g*

4. What does the government do?

- The government carries out microeconomic and macroeconomic activities. The microeconomic activities include resolving market imperfections, externalities, and public goods problems. The macroeconomic activities are directed toward monetary and fiscal policies and minimizing the disruptions caused by business cycles. *§3*

- Governments often provide public goods and services such as fire protection, police protection, and national defense. Governments place limits on what firms and consumers can do in certain types of situations. Governments tax externalities or otherwise attempt to make prices reflect the full cost of production and consumption. *§3.a*

- Governments carry out monetary and fiscal policies to attempt to control business cycles. In the United States, monetary policy is the province of the Federal Reserve, and fiscal policy is up to Congress and the president. *§3.b*

5. How do the sizes of public sectors in various countries compare?

- Market systems rely on the decisions of individuals. Centrally planned systems rely on the government to answer economic questions for all individuals. *§4*

- The size and influence of the public sector ranges from the market economies of the United States and Canada to the centrally planned economy of Cuba. *§4.a*

Key Terms

economic efficiency *§2.a*	free ride *§2.d*	Federal Reserve *§3.b*
technical efficiency *§2.a*	monopoly *§2.e*	fiscal policy *§3.b*
market imperfection *§2.b*	business cycles *§2.f*	transfer payment *§3.c*
externalities *§2.c*	rent seeking *§2.g*	budget surplus *§3.c*
public goods *§2.d*	public choice *§2.g*	budget deficit *§3.c*
private property right *§2.d*	monetary policy *§3.b*	centrally planned economy *§4*

Exercises

1. Illustrate productive or technical efficiency using a production possibilities curve. Can you illustrate economic efficiency? Are you able to show the exact point where economic efficiency would occur?

2. Why would an externality be referred to as a market failure? Explain how your driving on a highway imposes costs on other drivers. Why is this an externality? How might the externality be resolved or internalized?

3. What is the difference between a compact disk recording of a rock concert and a radio broadcast of that rock concert? Why would you spend $12 on the CD but refuse to provide any support to the radio station?

4. "The American buffalo disappeared because they were not privately owned." Evaluate this statement.

5. Which of the following U.S. economic policies are the responsibility of the Federal Reserve? of Congress and the president?
   a. An increase in the rate of growth of the money supply
   b. A decrease in the rate of interest
   c. An increase in taxes on the richest 2 percent of Americans
   d. A reduction in taxes on the middle class
   e. An increase in the rate of growth of spending on health care

6. "The Department of Justice plans to file a lawsuit against major airlines, claiming that they violated price-fixing laws by sharing plans for fare changes through a computer system, officials said Friday." Is this a microeconomic or macroeconomic policy?

7. People sometimes argue that imports should be limited by government policy. Suppose a government quota on the quantity of imports causes net exports to rise. Using the circular flow diagram as a guide, explain why total expenditures and national output may rise after the quota is imposed. Who is likely to benefit from the quota? Who will be hurt? Explain why the government would become involved in the economy through its imposition of quotas.

8. Most highways are "free" ways: There is no toll charge for using them. What problem does free access create? How would you solve this?

9. In February 2003 the City of London imposed a £5 (British pounds; this is equal to about $8) per day fee for driving in central London between the hours of 7 A.M. and 6:30 P.M. Monday through Friday. The goal is to reduce traffic congestion in the central city. Respond to the following criticisms of the London policy:
   a. The rate charged (£5 per day) can't be the equilibrium price, as surely traffic is heavier at certain times of day than at other times and the equilibrium price should fluctuate with the varying demand for the scarce road space. Charging a constant price seems inefficient, as it will create a shortage of road space at some times and a surplus at other times.
   b. The toll charged is unfair. Only rich people will now drive in London, and the poor will have to ride buses or take the subway.
   c. Instead of charging a toll for all drivers, a better plan would be to regulate who is allowed to drive. All

personal vehicles should be banned, and only taxis, buses, delivery trucks, and emergency vehicles should be permitted.

10. The Global Business Insight in this chapter discussed creating a market for fishing rights to ensure that overfishing and depletion of fish do not occur. What other areas are subject to a "tragedy of the commons" where a lack of private property rights creates overutilization? Give three examples. How could one "create a market" for these activities to help decrease the overutilization?

11. Explain why the suggested government action may or may not make sense in each of the following scenarios.
   a. People purchase a DVD player with a guarantee provided by its maker, only to find that within a year the company has gone out of business. Consumers demand that the government provide the guarantee.
   b. Korean microchip producers are selling microchips at a price that is below the cost of making the microchips in the United States. The U.S. government must impose taxes on the Korean microchips imported into the United States.
   c. The economy has slowed down, unemployment has risen, and interest rates are high. The government should provide jobs and force interest rates down.
   d. Fully 15 percent of all U.S. citizens are without health insurance. The government must provide health care for all Americans.
   e. The rising value of the dollar is making it nearly impossible for U.S. manufacturers to sell their products to other nations. The government must decrease the value of the dollar.
   f. The rich are getting richer at a faster rate than the poor are getting richer. The government must increase the tax rate on the rich to equalize the income distribution.
   g. The AIDS epidemic has created such a state of emergency in health care that the only solution is to give some pharmaceutical firm a monopoly on any drugs or solutions discovered for HIV or AIDS.

12. Many nations of eastern Europe are undergoing a transition from a centrally planned to a market economic system. An important step in the process is to define private property rights in countries where they did not exist before. What does this mean? Why is it necessary to have private property rights?

13. Using the circular flow diagram, illustrate the effects of imposing an increase in taxes on the household sector.

14. Using the circular flow diagram, explain how the government can continually run budget deficits—that is, spend more than it receives in tax revenue.

15. Suppose you believe that government is the problem, not the solution. How would you explain the rapid growth of government during the past few decades?

16. The government intervenes in the private sector by imposing laws that ban smoking in all publicly used buildings. As a result, smoking is illegal in bars, restaurants, hotels, dance clubs, and other establishments. Is such a ban justified by economics?

17. In reference to exercise 16, we could say that before a ban is imposed, the owners of businesses owned the private property right to the air in their establishments. As owners of this valuable asset, they would ensure that it is used to earn them the greatest return. Thus, if their customers desired a nonsmoking environment, then they would provide it. How then does the ban on smoking improve things? Doesn't it merely transfer ownership of the air from the business owners to the nonsmokers?

Take the ACE Practice Test for this chapter to review the important concepts and get immediate feedback with answers.

college.hmco.com/economics/students/

A Big "Nein" to Deutsche Telekom; Telecommunications: Germany Still Doesn't Have a Completely Open Market

Los Angeles Times
July 26, 2000

Deutsche Telekom has become crazed over spending the loose change in its pockets. A few weeks ago, the company was reported to be considering an acquisition of Sprint. This week, Deutsche Telekom announced that it was buying VoiceStream Wireless for a deal valued at $50.5 billion.

This deal makes no sense financially: VoiceStream had a net loss last year of $455 million on revenue of $475 million. To acquire VoiceStream's 2.3 million wireless subscribers, Deutsche Telekom will pay more than $20,000 per subscriber. A return of 10% on this investment over 10 years would require a yearly profit of more than $3,200 per wireless customer. This is impossible, particularly for VoiceStream, which has losses nearly as large as its revenues. Wishful thinking, hopes for the future and faith are fine for religion, but are no way to run a business, as Deutsche Telekom soon will learn if this deal goes through. But if the Germans want to throw away their money, let them.

There are policy reasons, however, to oppose this acquisition because Deutsche Telekom is, in effect, a subsidiary of the German government and is actively expanding and acquiring other telecommunication firms in Germany and around the globe. These acquisitions are being done in the name of globalization, but that is simply a politically correct term for the colonialism and imperialism of the past.

Many countries have claimed to privatize the former government monopolization of telecommunications. Yet much of the stock of the "privatized" telecommunication firms is owned by the government. In the case of Germany, more than half of the stock of Deutsche Telekom is owned by the government. This is partial privatization.

One problem with partial privatization is that it is in the best interests of the government to maximize the value of the stock of the partially owned telecommunications company. This means that the partially privatized company is treated favorably by the government. Another problem is that governments are reluctant to sell their remaining ownership and totally privatize, since such a massive sale would decrease the value of all the shares on the open market. Thus, governments are motivated to manipulate the value of such stocks. The stock of Deutsche Telekom thus is overvalued, since much of it is held by the German government and is not on the open market. It is this overvalued stock that will fund the proposed acquisition of VoiceStream.

Even partial privatization is to be preferred to the old system of complete government ownership and control of telecommunications. Yet the solution to the evils of partial privatization is total privatization, such as what happened with British Telecom. But France, Germany, Japan and Sweden are dragging their feet in achieving complete privatization of their former government monopolies of telecommunications. In the meantime, they should not be allowed market entry into countries that are completely privatized.

Partial privatization is not consistent with open markets and competition. Until Germany completely privatizes Deutsche Telekom, the company should not be allowed to have dominant ownership of any telecommunications firm in the United States—even if it [is] about to lose its lederhosen in this deal.

A. Michael Noll

Source: *Los Angels Times,* July 26, 2000, p. 9. Copyright 2000 Times Mirror Company.

This chapter indicated that there is a legitimate role for government in a market economy. In particular, government is justified in being involved in the production of products when market imperfections like externalities are involved. However, in many countries, government has operated firms that could be better operated by private business. As a result, in recent years there has been a trend toward the *privatization* of such firms. The privatization of government-owned enterprises is generally intended to increase efficiency by giving the activity being privatized the same incentives that private business firms receive. The outcome of such privatization is expected to minimize the costs of production for a given level and quality of output.

The article indicates that the German telephone company, Deutsche Telekom, has been *partially* privatized, but that the German government still owns more than half of the company's stock. So private ownership does not exist in the usual sense of the term. This policy of partial privatization has been followed in many countries where privatization is politically controversial. Why should the government retain ownership of a substantial portion of a seemingly private firm? Politics is the short answer. Those who have benefited from government control of the firm usually have an interest in maintaining government control, and if the government owns more than half of the firm's outstanding stock, then the government exercises majority control of the firm. Perhaps labor unions fear that private ownership will mean fewer jobs at lower wages. In the case of Deutsche Telekom, some services may have been provided at less than their true cost of production, and those households and/or firms that received service at a subsidized rate may fear that privatization may end their subsidy. Such groups provide political support for less than full privatization.

Privatization is likely to continue around the world as more and more governments seek to minimize their role in the economy and allow private business to respond to free market incentives in the production of goods. This article reminds us that partial privatization, where government retains some ownership of formerly government-operated enterprises, is not without controversy. The partially privatized firm may not have to compete with other firms on an equal basis; it may be given favorable treatment by the government that increases its market value beyond that of a fully privatized firm.

This outcome is not a certainty, however, as the shares that are sold to the public may be worth less in a partially privatized firm than in a fully privatized firm if the public believes that the government involvement will reduce the efficiency of the firm and hinder its ability to earn profits. The author assumes that the German government's ownership of more than half of Deutsche Telekom has increased the value of the outstanding stock held by the public beyond the value that a fully privatized firm would have. Although that may or may not be true in this case, it certainly will not be a general rule that will always occur. After all, how many people believe that government can do a better job of running a business than private citizens—managers and employees—who will be compensated on the basis of the firm's performance and profitability?

Fundamental Questions

chapter

6

Elasticity: Demand and Supply

et's begin by trying to gain some perspective on what we have been doing and what we will be doing in the next few chapters. In the first five chapters of this book, we defined economics, opportunity costs, and the "economic way of thinking." The economic way of thinking is to recognize that people are self-interested and as a result do those things that they expect will make them happiest. We say that people compare the costs and benefits of some activity, but it is the incremental, the additional costs and benefits, the change in costs and benefits, or what economists call the marginal costs and marginal benefits that are important. It is the next minute, the next day, the next dollar, the next month's income that matter in people's decisions.

Economists describe behavior by saying that people compare marginal benefits and marginal costs. If the marginal benefits of some activity are larger than the

1. **How do we measure how much consumers alter their purchases in response to a price change?**

2. **Why are measurements of elasticity important?**

3. **What determines whether consumers alter their purchases a little or a lot in response to a price change?**

4. **How do we measure how much changes in income, changes in the price of related goods, or changes in advertising expenditures affect consumer purchases?**

5. **How do we measure how much sellers respond to a price change?**

marginal costs, then people do that activity. If the marginal benefits are less than the marginal costs, then people do not do that activity. One of the things people do is trade or exchange. But, as we discovered, they trade only if they believe that the trade will make them better off. This is what the gains from trade are all about; all parties to a trade can gain and have to think they will gain, or else they will not trade.

The interaction of traders—of buyers and sellers—is represented by a market, that is, by demand and supply. Within a market, demand and supply determine the market price—the price at which buyers and sellers agree to trade.

In Chapters 1, 2, and 3, we examined how markets work to allocate scarce goods, services, and resources. We need to do more, however, if we are to understand why the world is what it is. We have to have a more in-depth understanding of demand and supply. We begin that process here. In this and the following chapter, we examine demand. We delve into the incentives and motivations of consumers. We examine how consumers behave when the price of a good or service changes, when income changes, or, in general, when marginal benefits or marginal costs change. After examining consumer behavior in more detail, we turn to supply. Suppliers are firms of one type or another, so to understand supply, we have to examine how firms behave. We look at sales, revenue, costs, and profits and see what firms do to try to be successful. Businesses often say that they must "know their customer" if they are to succeed. By this they mean that they must know everything they can about demand. What they need to know is what we discuss in this chapter. ▪

1. The Price Elasticity of Demand ____

? 1. How do we measure how much consumers alter their purchases in response to a price change?

The manager of a local movie theater raised the price from $9.50 to $10 per movie in order to pay for a new sound system that he had installed. He knew that the higher price would lower ticket sales, but he expected to more than make this up with the higher ticket price. He found that not only had ticket sales declined, but his revenue had fallen as well. Where had the manager gone wrong? The error he made was not knowing what the price elasticity of demand was.

The day after hurricane Katrina struck the Gulf Coast and New Orleans in August 2005, gasoline prices rose from about $2 to $3 per gallon as gasoline supplies declined by nearly 25 percent. However, once the damage from the hurricane was repaired and supplies were replenished, prices remained high. It took several weeks for gas prices to begin to drop, and then they declined very slowly. Why did gas prices rise so rapidly and decline so slowly? Was it because of unethical or illegal behavior on the part of the gas companies, or was it the result of some market force? The answer requires an understanding of the price elasticity of the demand for gasoline.

1.a. The Definition of Price Elasticity

The price elasticity of demand is a measure of the magnitude by which consumers alter the quantity of some product that they purchase in response to a change in the price of that product. The more price-elastic demand is, the more responsive consumers are to a price change—that is, the more they will adjust their purchases of a product when the price of that product changes. Conversely, the less price-elastic demand is, the less responsive consumers are to a price change.

price elasticity of demand: the percentage change in the quantity demanded of a product divided by the percentage change in the price of that product

The **price elasticity of demand,** e_d, is the percentage change in the quantity demanded of a product divided by the percentage change in the price of that product:

$$e_d = \frac{\%\Delta Q^D}{\%\Delta P}$$

For instance, if the quantity of DVDs that are rented falls by 3 percent whenever the price of a DVD rental rises by 1 percent, the price elasticity of demand for DVD rentals is -3.

Demand can be elastic, unit-elastic, or inelastic. Price elasticity will be a number that lies between 0 and negative infinity.

- When price elasticity is between zero and -1, we say that demand is *inelastic*.
- When price elasticity is between -1 and $-\infty$, we say that demand is *elastic*.
- When price elasticity is -1, we say that demand is *unit-elastic*.

1.b. Demand Curve Shapes and Elasticity

perfectly elastic demand curve: a horizontal demand curve indicating that consumers can and will purchase all they want at one price

A **perfectly elastic demand curve** is a horizontal line that shows that consumers are willing and able to purchase any quantity at the single prevailing price but will switch to another seller at the flip of a switch. In Figure 1(a), a perfectly elastic demand curve represents the demand for the wheat harvested by a single farmer in Canada. The Canadian farmer is only one small producer of wheat, and because he is just one among many, he is unable to charge a price that differs from the price of wheat in the rest of the world. If this farmer's wheat is even slightly more expensive than wheat elsewhere, consumers will buy the wheat produced by other farmers in Canada and the rest of the world and leave this now slightly higher priced farmer without any business.

perfectly inelastic demand curve: a vertical demand curve indicating that there is no change in the quantity demanded as the price changes

A **perfectly inelastic demand curve** is a vertical line, illustrating the idea that consumers cannot or will not change the quantity of a good they purchase when the price of the product is changed. Perhaps insulin to a diabetic is a reasonably vivid example of a good whose demand is perfectly inelastic. Of course, this behavior holds only over a certain price range. Eventually, the price would get so high that even a diabetic would be forced to decrease the quantity demanded. Figure 1(b) shows a perfectly inelastic demand curve.

In between the two extreme shapes of demand curves are the demand curves for most products. Figure 1(c) shows two downward-sloping straight-line demand curves, D_1 and D_2. The first demand curve, the steeper one, D_1, represents a more inelastic demand. The flatter curve, D_2, is more elastic. So we could use D_1 to represent the monthly demand for gasoline; it says that even if the price rises by quite a bit, the quantity of gasoline demanded declines by only a small amount. We could use the more elastic demand curve, D_2, to represent the demand for gasoline at a single station; it would say that as the price of gasoline at the corner Shell station increases, consumers decide to go to the Chevron station down the street instead of buying at the now more expensive Shell station.

1.b.1 Price Elasticity Along a Straight-Line Demand Curve
While we describe an entire demand curve as being more or less elastic than some other curve, we also note that the price elasticity of demand changes as we move up or down a straight-line demand curve. The price elasticity becomes more inelastic as we move down the curve. When we say that an entire demand curve is more elastic than another, such as D_2 compared to D_1, we are just saying that at every single price, D_2 is more elastic than D_1.

FIGURE 1   The Price Elasticity of Demand

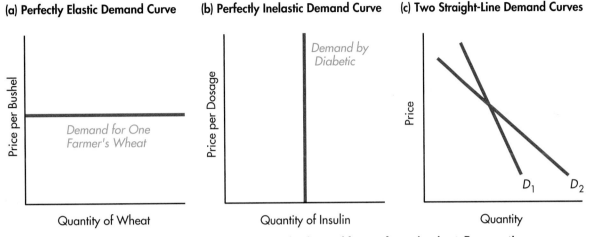

(a) Perfectly Elastic Demand Curve   **(b) Perfectly Inelastic Demand Curve**   **(c) Two Straight-Line Demand Curves**

Figure 1(a), a perfectly elastic demand curve, represents the demand for one farmer's wheat. Because there are so many other suppliers, buyers purchase wheat from the least expensive source. If this farmer's wheat is priced ever so slightly above other farmers' wheat, buyers will switch to another source. Also, because this farmer is just one small producer in a huge market, he can sell everything he wants at the market price. Figure 1(b), a perfectly inelastic demand curve, represents the demand for insulin by a diabetic. A certain quantity is necessary to satisfy the need regardless of the price. Figure 1(c) shows two straight-line demand curves, D_1 and D_2. These demand curves are neither perfectly elastic nor perfectly inelastic.

The terms elastic *and* inelastic *refer to a price range, not to the entire demand curve.*

All downward-sloping straight-line demand curves are divided into three parts by the price elasticity of demand: the *elastic region,* the *unit-elastic point,* and the *inelastic region.* The demand is elastic from the top of the curve to the unit-elastic point. At all prices below the unit-elastic point, demand is inelastic.

?

2. Why are measurements of elasticity important?

1.c. The Price Elasticity of Demand Is Defined in Percentage Terms

Elasticities are ratios of percentages. The price elasticity of demand is the *percentage* change in the quantity demanded divided by the *percentage* change in the price. By measuring the price elasticity of demand in terms of percentage changes, economists are able to compare the way consumers respond to changes in the prices of different products. For instance, the change in sales caused by a 1 percent increase in the price of gasoline (measured in gallons) can be compared to the change in sales caused by a 1 percent change in the price of a Big Gulp. Percentage changes ensure that we are comparing apples to apples, not apples to oranges. What sense could be made of a comparison between the effects on quantity demanded of a $1 rise in the price of college tuition, from $10,000 to $10,001, and a $1 rise in the price of a Big Mac, from $2 to $3? But, the consumer's reaction to a 1 percent change in tuition could be compared to the consumer's reaction to a 1 percent change in the price of a Big Mac.

Demand is price-elastic at the top of the curve and inelastic at the bottom.

In section 1.b, it is pointed out that the price elasticity changes along a straight-line demand curve. This is because elasticities are measured in percentage terms. Along a straight-line demand curve, equal dollar changes in price mean equal unit changes in quantity. For instance, if price changes by $1 in Figure 2, quantity demanded changes by 20 units; if price changes from $1 to $2, quantity demanded falls from 200 to 180; if price changes from $2 to $3, quantity demanded falls from 180

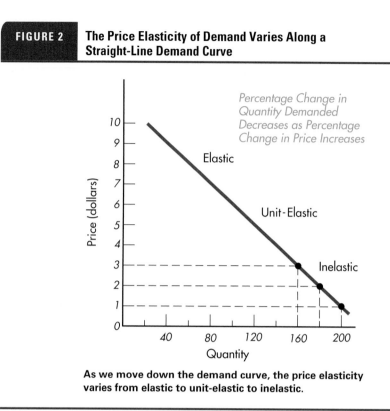

Percentage Change in Quantity Demanded Decreases as Percentage Change in Price Increases

Elastic

Unit-Elastic

Inelastic

Price (dollars)

Quantity

As we move down the demand curve, the price elasticity varies from elastic to unit-elastic to inelastic.

to 160; and so on. Each $1 change in price means a 20-unit change in quantity demanded. But those same amounts (constant amounts of $1 and 20 units) do not translate into constant percentage changes.

A $1 change at the top of the demand curve is a significantly different percentage change from a $1 change at the bottom of the demand curve. A $1 change from $10 is a 10 percent change, but a $1 change from $2 is a 50 percent change. Thus, as we move down the demand curve from higher to lower prices, a given dollar change becomes a larger and larger percentage change in price. The opposite is true of quantity changes. As we move downward along the demand curve, the same change in quantity becomes a smaller and smaller percentage change. A 10-unit change from 20 is a 50 percent change, while a 10-unit change from 200 is a 5 percent change. As we move down the straight-line demand curve, the percentage change in quantity demanded declines and the percentage change in price increases.

1.d. Determinants of the Price Elasticity of Demand

The degree to which the demand is price-inelastic or price-elastic depends on the following factors, which differ among products and among consumers:

- How many substitutes there are
- How well a substitute can replace the good or service under consideration
- The importance of the product in the consumer's total budget
- The time period under consideration

The more substitutes there are for a product, the greater the price elasticity of demand. If you can buy something else when the price of an item goes up and be just as well off, then your demand is elastic. For instance, whether you buy gasoline at one station or another might depend on which one of them charges a penny more a

?

3. What determines whether consumers alter their purchases a little or a lot in response to a price change?

gallon; if so, your demand for gas at a single station is very elastic. In contrast, diabetics have no substitute for insulin, so their demand for insulin is inelastic.

The greater the portion of the consumer's budget that a good constitutes, the more elastic is the demand for the good. Because a new car and an overseas vacation are quite expensive, even a small percentage change in their prices can represent a significant portion of a household's income. As a result, a 1 percent increase in price may cause many households to delay the purchase of a car or a vacation. Coffee, on the other hand, accounts for such a small portion of a household's total weekly expenditures that a large percentage increase in the price of coffee will probably have little effect on the quantity of coffee purchased. The demand for vacations is most likely quite a bit more elastic than the demand for coffee.

The longer the time period under consideration, the more elastic is the demand for any product. The demand for most goods and services will have a lower price elasticity over a shorter time period and will be more price-elastic over a longer span of time. For instance, the demand for gasoline is very inelastic over a period of a month. No good substitutes are available in so brief a period. Over a 10-year period, however, the demand for gasoline is much more elastic. The additional time allows consumers to alter their behavior to make better use of gasoline and to find substitutes for gasoline.

RECAP

1. The price elasticity of demand is a measure of the degree to which consumers will alter the quantities of a product that they purchase in response to changes in the price of that product. The price elasticity of demand is the percentage change in the quantity demanded divided by the corresponding percentage change in the price.

2. When the price elasticity of demand lies between -1 and $-\infty$, demand is said to be *elastic*. When the price elasticity of demand is equal to -1, demand is said to be *unit-elastic*. When the price elasticity of demand lies between -1 and 0, demand is said to be *inelastic*.

3. The price elasticity of demand depends on how readily and easily consumers can switch their purchases from one product to another.

4. Everything else held constant, the greater the number of close substitutes, the greater the price elasticity of demand.

5. Everything else held constant, the greater the proportion of a householder's budget that a good constitutes, the greater is the householder's price elasticity of demand for that good.

6. Everything else held constant, the longer the time period under consideration, the greater is the price elasticity of demand.

2. The Use of Price Elasticity of Demand

The price elasticity of demand tells us whether total revenue will rise or fall following a change in the price of a good or service. If demand is elastic, a price increase will decrease revenue, and a price decrease will increase revenue. If demand is inelastic, the opposite occurs: a price increase will increase revenue, and a price decrease will decrease revenue.

2.a. Total Revenue and Price Elasticity of Demand

Total Revenue (*TR*):
$TR = P \times Q$

Total Revenue (*TR*) equals the price of a product multiplied by the quantity sold: $TR = P \times Q$. If P rises by 10 percent and Q falls by more than 10 percent, then total revenue declines as a result of the price rise. If P rises by 10 percent and Q falls by less than 10 percent, then total revenue rises as a result of the price rise. And if P increases by 10 percent and Q falls by 10 percent, total revenue does not change as the price changes. Thus, total revenue increases as price is increased if demand is inelastic, decreases as price is increased if demand is elastic, and does not change as price is increased if demand is unit-elastic.

Recall the case of the movie theater manager who thought that raising price would increase revenue. For the manager to have been correct, the demand for movie tickets would have to have been inelastic. If the price elasticity of the demand for movies at the theater was -0.2, then a price increase of 10 percent would reduce ticket sales by only 2 percent, and total revenue would rise. But if the price elasticity of demand was -1.1, then the 10 percent increase in price would cause ticket sales to fall by 11 percent, and total revenue would decline.

The price elasticity of the demand for gasoline is only -0.2, meaning that if price is increased by 1 percent, the quantity of gasoline demanded will decline by only 0.2 percent, or a 10 percent increase in price will cause quantity demanded to decline by only 2 percent. Since price goes up 10 percent and sales go down by 2 percent, total revenue rises. Why, since its total revenue will rise as price rises, would a gas station ever want to lower the price of gasoline? The reason is that the demand for gasoline at a single gas station, Joe's Texaco, is elastic. In this case, a 10 percent increase in the price of Joe's gasoline relative to the price at all other stations will cause sales at his station to decline by more than 10 percent. If Joe has a price that is higher than that of other stations, he will lose sales and revenue.

This relationship between price elasticity of demand and total revenue helps explain other oddities we observe in the real world. Ads and marquees proudly proclaim that "Kids stay free" or that "Senior discounts apply," and it is well known that airlines sell vacation travelers tickets for significantly less than the business traveler pays. When demand is elastic, a price decrease causes total revenue to increase; and when demand is inelastic, a price increase causes total revenue to rise. So if different groups of customers have different price elasticities of demand for the same product, and if the groups are easily identifiable and can be kept from trading with each other, then the seller of the product can increase total revenue by charging each group a different price. Charging different prices to different customers for the same product is called **price discrimination.** Price discrimination occurs when senior citizens purchase movie tickets at a lower price than younger citizens or when business travelers pay more for airline tickets than vacation travelers do.

Senior citizens are frequently offered movie tickets at lower prices than younger people. The reason for the discount is that, on average, older people are more inclined than younger people to respond to a change in the price of admission to a movie. Older people have more times when they can see a movie—more substitutes—so that their demand is more elastic than the demand by the rest of the population. Since their demand is elastic, the movie theater can raise revenue by lowering the price to them. But, at the same time, since the rest of the population's demand is less elastic, other people do not get the lower price; revenue will not increase if the price they pay is reduced.

Airline discounts are constructed on the basis of the price elasticity of demand as well. Vacationers know their schedules well in advance and can take advantage of the least expensive means of travel. Business travelers are more constrained. They often do not know their schedules days in advance, and they usually want to travel on Monday through Friday. The airlines recognize that the demand for air travel by

Price discrimination: charging different customers different prices for the same product

vacationers is much more elastic than the demand by business travelers. As a result, airlines offer discounts to travelers who purchase tickets well in advance and stay over a Saturday night. Another example of the relationship between price elasticity and prices is discussed in the Global Business Insight box.

Global Business Insight

Dumping

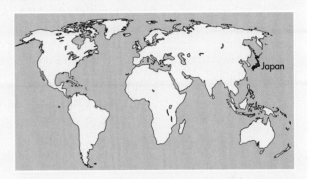

Dumping occurs when an identical good is sold to foreign buyers for a lower price than that charged to domestic buyers. Dumping is a controversial issue. Producers in a country facing foreign competitors are likely to appeal to their domestic government for protection from the foreign goods that are being dumped in their market. Typically, the appeal for government assistance is based on the argument that the dumping firms are practicing *predatory dumping*—dumping that is intended to drive rival firms out of business. A successful predator firm raises prices after its rivals are driven from the market.

Canadian electronics manufacturers might accuse Japanese firms of dumping if the Japanese firms were selling electronics in Canada for less than they charged in Japan. The Canadian manufacturers might appeal to the Canadian government, asserting that the Japanese firms were engaged in predatory dumping to drive the Canadian firms out of business and warning that if they do so, the Japanese firms will then raise the price of electronics products in Canada without fear of competition by the domestic Canadian firms. Claims of predatory dumping are often emotional and stir up the nationalistic sympathy of the rest of the domestic economy.

The U.S. government frequently responds to charges of dumping brought against foreign firms by U.S. industry. The government has pursued claims of predatory dumping against South African manufacturers of steel plate; German, Italian, and French winemakers; Japanese manufacturers of semiconductors; Singapore manufacturers of typewriters; Korean shipbuilders; Chinese motorbike producers; and many other manufacturers.

One famous case involved Sony Corporation of Japan. Sony was selling Japanese-made TV sets in the United States for $180 while charging buyers in Japan $333 for the same model. The U.S. television producers claimed that Sony was dumping TV sets in the U.S. market and seriously damaging U.S. television manufacturers. (Although U.S. producers disliked the low price of Japanese competitors, U.S. consumers benefited.) The U.S. government threatened to place high tariffs on Japanese television sets entering the United States unless Japan raised the price of Japanese televisions sold in the United States. The threat worked, and the price of Japanese TVs exported to the United States increased.

Charges of predatory dumping make good news stories, but are they really that newsworthy? Often the different prices are different because the demands in the two countries have different price elasticities. If the demand for televisions in Japan is more elastic than the demand for televisions in the United States, then the seller of televisions would make more revenue by having a higher price in the United States than in Japan. This would not constitute dumping but instead would be merely a response to the different price elasticities.

RECAP

1. If demand is price-elastic, revenue and price changes move in the opposite direction. An increase in price causes a decrease in revenue, and a decrease in price causes an increase in revenue.

2. If demand is price-inelastic, revenue and price move in the same direction.

3. If demand is unit-elastic, revenue does not change as price changes.

3. Other Demand Elasticities _____

A price change leads to a movement along the demand curve. When something that affects demand, other than price, changes, the demand curve shifts. How far the demand curve shifts is measured by elasticity—the elasticity of the variable whose value changes. As we saw in Chapter 3, "Markets, Demand and Supply, and the Price System," demand is determined by income, prices of related goods, expectations, tastes, number of buyers, and international effects. A change in any one of these "determinants of demand" will cause the demand curve to shift, and a measure of elasticity exists for each. The *income elasticity of demand* measures the percentage change in demand caused by a given percentage change in income, the *cross-price elasticity of demand* measures the percentage change in demand caused by a given percentage change in the price of a related good, the *advertising elasticity of demand* measures the percentage change in demand caused by a given percentage change in advertising expenditures (change in tastes), and so on. Each elasticity is calculated by dividing the percentage change in demand by the percentage change in the variable under consideration.

3.a. The Cross-Price Elasticity of Demand

cross-price elasticity of demand: the percentage change in the demand for one good divided by the percentage change in the price of a related good, everything else held constant

The **cross-price elasticity of demand** measures the degree to which goods are substitutes or complements (for a discussion of substitutes and complements, see Chapter 3). The cross-price elasticity of demand is defined as the percentage change in the demand for one good divided by the percentage change in the price of a related good, everything else held constant:

$$\text{Cross-price elasticity of demand} = \frac{\text{percentage change in demand for good j}}{\text{percentage change in the price of good k}}$$

When the cross-price elasticity of demand is positive, the goods are substitutes, and when the cross-price elasticity of demand is negative, the goods are complements. If a 1 percent *increase* in the price of a movie ticket leads to a 5 percent *increase* in the quantity of movies that are downloaded off the Internet, movies at the theater and downloaded movies are substitutes. If a 1 percent *rise* in the price of a movie ticket leads to a 5 percent *drop* in the quantity of popcorn consumed, movies and popcorn are complements.

3.b. The Income Elasticity of Demand

income elasticity of demand: the percentage change in the demand for a good divided by the percentage change in income, everything else held constant

The income elasticity of demand measures the magnitude of consumer responsiveness to income changes. The **income elasticity of demand** is defined as the percentage change in the demand for a product divided by the percentage change in income, everything else held constant:

$$\text{Income elasticity of demand} = \frac{\text{percentage change in demand for good j}}{\text{percentage change in income}}$$

normal goods: goods for which the income elasticity of demand is positive

Goods whose income elasticity of demand is greater than zero are **normal goods.** Products that are often called necessities have lower income elasticities than products known as luxuries. Gas, electricity, health-oriented drugs, and physicians' services might be considered necessities. Their income elasticities are about 0.4 or 0.5. On the other hand, people tend to view dental services, automobiles, and private education as luxury goods. Their elasticities are 1.5 to 2.0.

As incomes rise, people tend to purchase luxury items rather than basic, less expensive items. In this photo, women display new lines of mobile phones having the ability to take pictures and send them electronically to others. The quantity of mobile phones purchased as income rises is positive; the income elasticity of demand for mobile phones is positive. Not only is it positive, but it is larger than 1, indicating that as income rises by 10 percent, the quantity of phones purchased rises by more than 10 percent.

inferior goods: goods for which the income elasticity of demand is negative

luxury goods: goods for which the income elasticity of demand is a large positive number

When the income elasticity of demand for a good is negative, the good is called an **inferior good.** Some people claim that potatoes, rice, and beans are inferior goods because people who have very low levels of income eat large quantities of these goods but give up those items and begin eating fruit, fish, and higher-quality meats as their incomes rise. Smoking seems to be an inferior good—as income rises, people smoke less.

Clean air, on the other hand, is a **luxury good.** As incomes rise, people are willing to pay to have cleaner air. Air pollution is a problem throughout the world, but air pollution in the poorest nations is much worse than that in the wealthiest nations. Air pollution in India, much of Africa, and China is so bad that associated health problems are epidemic. Isn't it logical that if these nations improved their air, they would improve the condition of their populations considerably, which would contribute to economic growth? It does seem logical, but the problem is that because they have little income, these nations would have to forgo other important things in order to devote resources to cleaning the air. And taking resources away from other areas of the economy, such as health care, could lead to more serious health problems than are caused by the pollution. It turns out that a nation will not begin devoting resources to cleaning its air until its per capita income is above $15,000 per year, and a nation with over $15,000 in income per year per person is considered to be a rich nation. The greater a nation's per capita income, the more likely it is that it can reduce air pollution. Air pollution *reduction* is a luxury good.

RECAP

1. The cross-price elasticity of demand is the percentage change in the demand for one product divided by the percentage change in the price of a related product, everything else held constant. If the cross-price elasticity of demand is positive, the goods are substitutes. If the cross-price elasticity of demand is negative, the goods are complements.

2. The income elasticity of demand is the percentage change in the demand for one product divided by the percentage change in income, everything else held

constant. If the income elasticity of a good is greater than zero, the good is called a *normal good*. If the income elasticity of a good is negative, the good is called an *inferior good*. If the income elasticity of a good is a high positive number, the good is called a *luxury good*.

3. Elasticities can be calculated for any determinant of demand. Although income and related goods elasticities were calculated in the text, other elasticities, such as international development, service, quality, and expectations elasticities, could have been calculated.

4. The Price Elasticity of Supply

5. How do we measure how much sellers respond to a price change?

The price elasticity of supply is a measure of how sellers adjust the quantity of a good or service that they offer for sale when the price of that good changes. The **price elasticity of supply** is the percentage change in the quantity supplied of a good or service divided by the percentage change in the price of that good or service, everything else held constant. The price elasticity of supply is usually a positive number because the quantity supplied typically rises when the price rises. Supply is said to be elastic over a price range if the price elasticity of supply is greater than 1 over that price range. It is said to be inelastic over a price range if the price elasticity of supply is less than 1 over that price range.

4.a. Price Elasticity of Supply and the Shape of the Supply Curve

price elasticity of supply: the percentage change in the quantity supplied divided by the percentage change in price, everything else held constant

The price elasticity of supply is either zero or a positive number. A zero price elasticity of supply means that the quantity supplied will not vary as the price varies. A positive price elasticity of supply means that as the price of an item rises, the quantity supplied rises. The price elasticity of supply is zero for goods whose quantities cannot change. This is illustrated in Figure 3(a), where supply is a vertical line. Land surface, Monet paintings, Beethoven symphonies, and the Beatles' songs are all fixed in quantity. Because Monet, Beethoven, and John Lennon are dead, no matter what happens to price, the quantity of their products cannot change.

Figure 3(b) shows a perfectly elastic supply curve, a horizontal line. There are some goods for which the quantity supplied at the current price can be whatever anyone wants given sufficient time. The production of food, for instance, has increased tremendously during the past century, while the price has remained about the same. For most goods, the supply curve lies between the perfectly inelastic and perfectly elastic extremes. In Figure 3(c), two supply curves are drawn illustrating different shapes that the supply curve might have. The steeper curve, S_1, is more inelastic than curve S_2. Just as the elasticity changes along a straight-line demand curve, it also changes along a straight-line supply curve. However, the steeper curve is less elastic at every price compared to the flatter curve.

4.b. The Long and Short Runs

short run: a period of time short enough that the quantities of at least one of the resources used cannot be varied

The shape of the supply curve depends primarily on the length of time being considered. Economists view time in terms of two distinct periods, the short run and the long run. The **short run** is a period of time long enough for existing firms to change the quantity of output they produce by changing the quantities of *some* of the resources used to produce their output, but not long enough for the firms to change the quantities of *all* of those resources. In the short run, firms are not able to build new factories or retrain workers, and new firms are unable to open up shop and begin to

FIGURE 3   The Price Elasticity of Supply

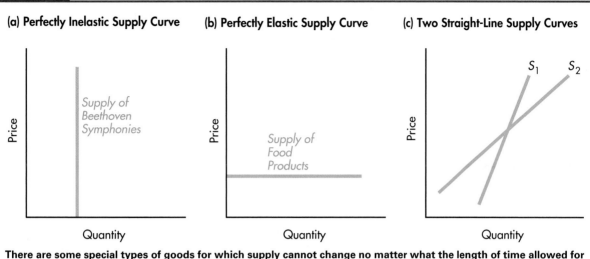

(a) Perfectly Inelastic Supply Curve   **(b) Perfectly Elastic Supply Curve**   **(c) Two Straight-Line Supply Curves**

There are some special types of goods for which supply cannot change no matter what the length of time allowed for change. For such goods, the price elasticity of supply is zero and the supply curve is vertical, as shown in Figure 3(a). Figure 3(b) is a perfectly elastic supply curve, a horizontal line. A perfectly elastic supply curve says that the quantity supplied at the given price is unlimited; a small—infinitesimal—price change would lead to an infinite change in quantity supplied. For most goods, the supply curve lies between the perfectly inelastic and perfectly elastic extremes. In Figure 3(c), two supply curves are drawn. Curve S_1 is less elastic than curve S_2.

long run: a period of time long enough that the quantities of all resources can be varied

supply goods and services. The **long run** is a period of time long enough for existing firms to change the quantities of all the resources they use and for new firms to begin producing the product. So the actual or chronological time for the short and the long run varies from industry to industry. The long run for oil refining may be as long as seven to eight years; for personal computers, perhaps a year; for basket making, probably no longer than a day or two.

Usually, the greater the time period allowed, the more readily firms will increase their quantities supplied in response to a price increase. Thus, supply curves applicable to shorter periods of time tend to be more inelastic than supply curves that apply to longer periods of time. A baker who can switch from producing cupcakes to producing muffins within a day has large price elasticities of supply for cupcakes and for muffins; a small increase in the price of muffins relative to that of cupcakes will cause the bakery to significantly increase the quantity of muffins baked and reduce the quantity of cupcakes baked. An automobile manufacturing plant that requires several months or years to switch from constructing one type of car to another, however, will have a relatively inelastic supply.

In Figure 3(c), supply curve S_1 represents a shorter-run supply curve. For a given price change, the quantity supplied would change by a small amount, shown by moving along S_1. Curve S_2 represents a longer-run supply curve.

4.c. Interaction of Price Elasticities of Demand and Supply

It takes both demand and supply to determine the equilibrium price and quantity in a market. Similarly, it takes both the price elasticity of demand and the price elasticity of supply to determine the full effect of a price change. If the price elasticity of supply of an item is large and the demand for it is price-inelastic, then the firm can raise the price without losing revenue. In this case, the firm can pass on cost increases to the consumer; that is, it can increase the price enough to pay the increased costs. Conversely, if the price elasticity of supply is small and the price elasticity of demand is large, then the firm is unable to raise the price because the consumer will switch to another firm or product. This means that the firm has to keep the price the same.

Consider how this relationship between the price elasticities of demand and supply affects tax policy. It does not matter who writes the check, whether it is the individual or the firm; who really pays the tax depends on price elasticities. Suppose a good that is going to be taxed has a demand that is price-inelastic and a supply that is price-elastic. If the tax is levied on the firm, meaning that it is the firm that has to actually write the check to the government, the firm simply raises its price. It is the consumer who pays the tax because the consumer pays a price that is high enough to include the new tax. But, if the price elasticity of demand is large and supply is price-inelastic, then it is the firm that pays the tax. The firm will have to keep its price the same and absorb the tax increase in order to induce customers to keep purchasing the good.

incidence: a measure of who pays a tax

What we have been discussing is called **incidence**—a measure of who actually pays for a cost increase or a tax. Regardless of whether it is the firm or the consumer who writes the check to the government, the tax incidence depends on the price elasticities of demand and supply. Consider cigarettes, for example. If smokers will buy the same quantity of cigarettes even if the price rises by 20 percent, then an 8 percent tax levied on cigarettes will not affect sales. Firms will not need to reduce their price to keep sales the same. In this case, the smoker bears the incidence of the tax—that is, pays the tax.

In general, the more elastic the demand and the less elastic the supply, everything else held constant, the more the incidence of a tax falls on businesses and the less it falls on consumers.

RECAP

1. The price elasticity of supply is the percentage change in the quantity supplied of one product divided by the percentage change in the price of that product, everything else held constant. The price elasticity of supply increases as the time period under consideration increases.

2. The long run is a period of time just long enough that the quantities of all resources used can be varied. The short run is a period of time just short enough that the quantity of at least some of the resources used cannot be varied.

3. The interaction of demand and supply determines the price and quantity produced and sold; the relative size of demand and supply price elasticities determines how the market reacts to changes. For instance, the size of supply relative to demand price elasticities determines the incidence of a tax.

Summary

1. How do we measure how much consumers alter their purchases in response to a price change?

- The price elasticity of demand is a measure of the responsiveness of consumers to changes in price. It is defined as the percentage change in the quantity demanded of a good divided by the percentage change in the price of the good. *§1.a*

- The price elasticity of demand is always a negative number because price and quantity demanded are inversely related. *§1.a*

- A straight-line demand curve is separated into three parts by the price elasticity of demand. Demand is price-elastic at the top of the curve; as you move down the curve, it becomes unit elastic and then price-inelastic. *§1.b.1*

2. Why are measurements of elasticity important?

- Comparing the price elasticity of demand for various products and services allows economists to see how consumers respond to price changes. In other words, it can tell us how big a difference price makes in a particular purchasing decision. *§1.c*

3. What determines whether consumers alter their purchases a little or a lot in response to a price change?

- Everything else held constant, the greater the number of close substitutes, the greater the price elasticity of demand. *§1.d*
- Everything else held constant, the greater the proportion of a household's budget that a good constitutes, the greater the household's elasticity of demand for that good. *§1.d*
- Everything else held constant, the longer the time period under consideration, the greater the price elasticity of demand. *§1.d*

4. How do we measure how much changes in income, changes in the prices of related goods, or changes in advertising expenditures affect consumer purchases?

- Elasticities can be calculated for any variable that affects demand—the determinants of demand—such as income, prices of related goods, advertising, and others. *§3*

- The cross-price elasticity of demand is defined as the percentage change in the demand for one good divided by the percentage change in the price of a related good, everything else held constant. *§3.a*
- When the cross-price elasticity is positive, the goods are substitutes. When it is negative, the goods are complements. *§3.a*
- The income elasticity of demand is defined as the percentage change in the demand for a good divided by the percentage change in income, everything else held constant. *§3.b*

5. How do we measure how much sellers respond to a price change?

- The price elasticity of supply is defined as the percentage change in the quantity supplied of a good divided by the percentage change in the price of that good, everything else held constant. *§4*
- The short run is a period of time short enough that the quantities of at least some of the resources used in production cannot be varied. The long run is a period of time just long enough that the quantities of all resources used can be varied. *§4.b*
- In general, the more elastic the demand and the less elastic the supply, everything else held constant, the more the incidence of a tax or the incidence of a cost increase falls on businesses and the less it falls on consumers. *§4.c*

Key Terms

price elasticity of demand *§1.a*

perfectly elastic demand curve *§1.b*

perfectly inelastic demand curve *§1.b*

total revenue (*TR*) *§2.a*

price discrimination *§2.a*

cross-price elasticity of demand *§3.a*

income elasticity of demand *§3.b*

normal goods *§3.b*

inferior goods *§3.b*

luxury goods *§3.b*

price elasticity of supply *§4*

short run *§4.b*

long run *§4.b*

incidence *§4.c*

Exercises

Use the following hypothetical demand schedule for movies to do exercises 1–4.

Quantity Demanded	Price	Elasticity
100	$ 5	
80	$10	
60	$15	
40	$20	
20	$25	
10	$30	

1. a. Determine the price elasticity of demand at each quantity demanded using the formula: Percentage change in quantity demanded = $(Q_2 - Q_1)/Q_1$ divided by percentage change in price = $(P_2 - P_1)/P_1$.
   b. Redo exercise 1a using price changes of $10 rather than $5.
   c. Plot the price and quantity data given in the demand schedule. Indicate the price elasticity value at each quantity demanded. Explain why the elasticity value gets smaller as you move down the demand curve.

2. Plot the total revenue curve directly below the demand curve plotted in exercise 1, measuring total revenue on the vertical axis and quantity on the horizontal axis.

3. What would a 10 percent increase in the price of movie tickets mean for the revenue of a movie theater if the price elasticity of demand was 0.1, 0.5, 1.0, and 5.0?

4. Using the demand curve plotted in exercise 1, illustrate what would occur if the income elasticity of demand was 0.05 and income rose by 10 percent. If the income elasticity of demand was 3.0 and income rose by 10 percent, what would occur?

5. Pick a good whose demand is price elastic. List 5 substitutes and 5 complements. Which is easier to come up with, the list of substitutes or the list of complements? Explain.

6. Are the following pairs of goods substitutes or complements? Indicate whether their cross-price elasticities are negative or positive.
   a. Bread and butter
   b. Bread and potatoes
   c. Socks and shoes
   d. Tennis rackets and golf clubs
   e. Bicycles and automobiles
   f. Foreign investments and domestic investments
   g. Cars made in Japan and cars made in the United States

7. Suppose the price elasticity of demand for movies by teenagers is 0.2 and that by adults is 2.0. What policy would the movie theater implement to increase total revenue? Make up some data to illustrate your answer.

8. Explain how consumers will react to a job loss. What will be the first goods they will do without? What is the income elasticity of demand for those goods?

9. Explain why senior citizens can obtain special discounts at movie theaters, drugstores, and other businesses.

10. Calculate the income elasticity of demand from the following data (use the midpoint or average given in the appendix):

Income	Quantity Demanded
$15,000	20,000
$20,000	30,000

   a. Explain why the value is a positive number.
   b. Explain what would happen to a demand curve as income changes if the income elasticity was 2.0. Compare that outcome to the situation that would occur if the income elasticity of demand was 0.2.

11. The poor tend to have a price elasticity of demand for movie tickets that is greater than 1. Why don't you see signs offering "poor people discounts" similar to the signs offering "senior citizen discounts"?

12. Suppose a tax is imposed on a product that has a completely inelastic supply curve. Who pays the tax?

13. Explain why a 40 percent across-the-board tax on businesses might not benefit consumers.

14. The price elasticity of the demand for gasoline is −0.02. The price elasticity of demand for gasoline at Joe's 66 station is −1.2. Explain what might account for the different elasticities.

15. The cross-price elasticity of the demand for cell phones and DVDs is 1.2. Explain. The cross-price elasticity of the demand for the iPod and DVDs is −1.4. Explain.

ACE

Take the ACE Practice Test for this chapter to review the important concepts and get immediate feedback with answers.

college.hmco.com/economics/students/

Higher Gas Prices Make Future Murky for Big SUVs: Impact of Rising Fuel Costs Could Be Bigger in Canada Than U.S.

Edmonton Journal
February 25, 2003

Fuel isn't the only liquid flowing at gasoline stations these days. It's joined by the teardrops of sport utility vehicle owners filling their tanks and paying some of the highest prices ever in Canada.

Sales of SUVs—the big, heavily marketed vehicles loved by many and scorned by others as gas guzzlers owned by fad-conscious drivers—rose significantly in the Canadian new vehicle market in 2002.

And this year, gasoline prices across the country have surpassed the 80-cents-a-litre mark and in some places are approaching 90 cents.

Industry experts generally agree that amid a public perception of SUVs as being environmentally unfriendly, their fuel economy has dramatically improved over the past few years. But the big vehicles—part of the light-truck segment, with car-like features—are still more expensive to fuel than a compact or mid-sized sedan.

That has analysts wondering if the two market trends of higher SUV sales and higher pump prices are destined to collide in a country where fuel economy is considered more important than it is in the United States. . . .

Higher gasoline prices in Canada haven't driven consumers away from the dozens of SUV models available. According to DesRosiers Automotive Consultants Inc., SUV sales rose 17.7 per cent in 2002, to nearly 270,000. . . .

But small cars still sold well in a country that embraces vehicles with better fuel economy. The top six sedans sold in Canada last year were all compact cars, led by the Honda Civic; the family-oriented Dodge Caravan led all vehicle sales, including the light-truck minivan segment.

"There comes a point in time where people say, 'I can't afford to spend that extra money on fuel every day if I'm commuting,'" says Jim Miller, vice-president of communications for Honda Canada. Honda boasted the top-selling sedan in Canada last year—the Civic—while its CR-V compact SUV placed eighth among all light trucks, a category that includes minivans and pickups.

"Is it 80 cents a litre? Is it 90 cents a litre? When do we hit that magic break point that changes people's buying habits?" Miller asks rhetorically. . . .

In the United States, gasoline prices—while vulnerable to price swings based on potential shortages amid war tension in the oil-rich Middle East—are generally lower. Plus, Americans have more disposable income and tend to use more of their available cash for bigger vehicles, favouring style and performance over economical concerns.

Environmental activists are pushing for the wider use of vehicles with cleaner, hybrid or fuel cell engines through new U.S. standards and under Canada's Kyoto commitments to reduce air pollution. But industry observers say those alternative engines are decades away from being used in the mass production of consumer vehicles.

Still, an anti-SUV movement is rising. American TV ads have suggested that owners of gas-guzzling SUVs are indirectly assisting terrorists who obtain financing in oil-exporting Middle East countries.

And a group of Christian ministers launched a "What Would Jesus Drive?" campaign, urging SUV owners to consider whether they could switch to more fuel-efficient vehicles to preserve the planet. . . .

Steve Erwin

A fter September 11, 2001, some of the U.S. public and some of the media started a campaign against the sport utility vehicle, or SUV. As the article states, American TV ads have suggested that owners of gas-guzzling SUVs are indirectly assisting terrorists who obtain financing in oil-exporting Middle East countries, and a group of Christian ministers launched a "What Would Jesus Drive?" campaign, urging SUV owners to consider whether they could switch to more fuel-efficient vehicles to preserve the planet. However, while these campaigns may have changed some consumers' tastes, the real effect on consumers' demand for SUVs has come from the increased gas prices.

A question someone might ask is, why have higher gas prices affected purchases of SUVs rather than purchases of gasoline? It is the price of gasoline that has risen, not the price of SUVs. The answer is that in the short run, the demand for gasoline is very inelastic and the cross-price elasticity of gasoline and SUVs is negative. The demand for gasoline is price-inelastic in the short run because there are no close substitutes. When the price increases, people don't have many alternatives to driving; they do not reduce their consumption very much. In the long run, if the price of gasoline should remain high, substitutes would become available. In fact, the article notes that people are finding more fuel-efficient means of transportation.

The cross-price elasticity is calculated by dividing the percentage change in the demand for SUVs by the percentage change in the price of gasoline. Gasoline prices in the United States rose from $1.30 per gallon in January 2003 to $1.90 per gallon in March 2003, a 46 percent increase. This increase has "hurt sales of SUVs," according to the article. If so, the percentage change in SUV sales would be a negative amount, perhaps 10 percent. Dividing 0.10 by 0.46 gives −0.217; the cross-price elasticity is negative, indicating that the two products are complements.

An interesting aspect of the market for SUVs, according to the article, is that in 2002, SUV sales increased even as gas prices increased. This means that there was little relationship between the SUV purchase and gasoline prices when gasoline prices were low. But as the price of gasoline rose, the cross-price elasticity rose enough that the gas prices affected sales of SUVs.

In 2005, when gasoline prices rose and remained high, sales of SUVs dropped precipitously. Once consumers saw the gasoline price increase as remaining high, they began altering their car purchases.

Calculating Elasticity

arc elasticity: price elasticity of demand measured over a range of prices and quantities along the demand curve

Elasticity can be calculated in one of two ways, the point elasticity and the arc elasticity. The **arc elasticity** is calculated in the following way:

$$\frac{(Q_2 - Q_1)/[(Q_2 + Q_1)/2]}{(P_2 - P_1)/[(P_2 + P_1)/2]}$$

Using the formula, calculate the elasticity when at a price of $6 per ticket, the average moviegoer demands 2 tickets per month, and at a price of $4 per ticket, the average moviegoer purchases 6 tickets per month. The *change* in quantity demanded is $(Q_2 - Q_1) = 6 - 2 = 4$. The *percentage change* is the change divided by the base. The base is the average, or midpoint between the two quantities, the sum of the two quantities divided by 2: $(Q_1 + Q_2)/2$. With 4 as the base, the change in quantity demanded divided by the base is $4/4 = 1$.

The change in price is $-$2$, from $6 to $4, and the average price is $(P_1 + P_2)/2 = 5. The change in price divided by the base is $-$2/$5 = -0.40$. Dividing the percentage change in quantity demanded by the percentage change in price gives us the price elasticity of demand:

$$1/(-2/5) = -5/2 = -2.5$$

According to these calculations, demand is elastic over the price range $4 to $6.

point elasticity: price elasticity of demand measured at a single point on the demand curve

Another formula used to calculate elasticity, known as the **point elasticity,** is

$$\frac{(Q_2 - Q_1)/(Q_1)}{(P_2 - P_1)/(P_1)}$$

The difference between the two formulas is the base. In the point elasticity formula, the initial price and quantity are used as the base rather than the average over the entire price and quantity range. For example, using the same information that at a price of $6 per ticket, the average moviegoer demands 2 tickets per month, and at a price of $4 per ticket, the average moviegoer purchases 6 tickets per month, the *change* in quantity demanded is $(Q_2 - Q_1) = 4$. The *relative change* is the change divided by the base. The base is Q_1. With $Q_1 = 2$ as the base, the relative change in quantity is $4/2$. The change in price is $-$2$, from $6 to $4, and the relative change in price is $-$2$ divided by the base, which is the initial price $P_1 = 6. To get the price elasticity of demand, we divide the relative change in quantity demanded, $4/2$, by the relative change in price, $-2/6$:

$$\text{Elasticity } e_d = (4/2)/(-2/6) = -6$$

Using the point formula, the demand is price-elastic. The point formula applies to just one point, the initial price, so we say that the price elasticity of demand at $P_1 = \$6$ is elastic.

Key Terms

arc elasticity   point elasticity

7

Consumer Choice

Fundamental Questions

1. How do consumers decide what to buy?

2. Why does the demand curve slope down?

3. What are behavioral economics and neuroeconomics?

In previous chapters, we learned that demand measures the quantity of a good or service that people are willing and able to buy at various prices. In the previous chapter, we also learned how the consumer's reaction to price changes, and changes to the consumer's income affect demand. In this chapter, we go behind the scenes of demand. We examine how and why consumers make choices and what factors influence their choices. We even look briefly into their brains—what parts of the brain they use to make decisions and how that makes a difference in their behavior. ■

1. Decisions

Do we go to college or get a job? Do we get married or remain single? Do we live in the dorm, a house, or an apartment? "Decisions, decisions, decisions! Don't we ever get a break from the pressure of making choices?" Not unless

scarcity disappears will we be freed from having to make choices. Although scarcity and choice are pervasive, how people make decisions is a question that has eluded scientific explanation. Some decisions seem to be based on feelings, or to come from the heart, while others seem more calculated. Some are quick and impulsive, while others take months or years of research. Is it the appeal of the book cover that makes you decide to buy one book rather than another? Does a television commercial affect your decision? The answers to these questions depend on your values, on your personality, on where you were raised, on how others might react to your decision, and on many other factors.

Although the important factors in a decision may vary from person to person, everyone makes decisions in much the same way. People tend to compare the perceived costs and benefits of alternatives and select those that they believe will give them the greatest relative benefits.

1.a. Utility

How is success measured in the game of life? It is measured not in the way the bumper sticker says, "The one with the most toys at the end wins," but by happiness. The word *happiness* is used very generally here. It implies that whatever an individual's goals are—peace, serenity, religious devotion, self-esteem, or the well-being of others—the more one has of what one desires, the better off one is. **Utility** is the term that economists and philosophers have used to capture this general concept of happiness. You are nourished by a good meal, entertained by a concert, proud of a fine car, and comforted by a nice home and warm clothing. Whatever feelings are described by *nourishment, entertainment, pride,* and *comfort* are captured in the term *utility.*

People make choices that give them the greatest utility; they maximize their utility. The utility you derive from experiencing some activity or consuming some good depends on your tastes and preferences. You may love opera and intensely dislike country and western music. You may have difficulty understanding how anyone can eat tripe, but you love hot chilies. We shall have little to say about why some people prefer country and western music and others classical music, although the issue is interesting; we simply assume that tastes and preferences are given and use those given tastes and preferences to describe the process of decision making.

> **utility:** a measure of the satisfaction received from possessing or consuming goods and services

> *Individuals behave so as to maximize their utility.*

1.b. Diminishing Marginal Utility

Utility is used to show why the law of demand is referred to as a law. To illustrate how utility maximization can be useful, we must create a hypothetical world in which we can measure the satisfaction that people receive from consuming goods and services. Suppose that a consumer named Gabrielle can listen to as much country and western music as she wishes during the course of the day. The utility, expressed as *utils,* that Gabrielle associates with each hour of listening is presented in Table 1.

Several important concepts associated with consumer choice can be observed in Table 1. First, each *additional* hour of music yields Gabrielle less satisfaction (fewer utils) than the previous hour. According to Table 1, the first hour yields 200 utils, the second yields another 98, the third another 50, the fourth another 10, and the fifth none. Each additional hour of music, until the fifth hour, adds to total utility, but Gabrielle enjoys each additional hour just a little bit less than she enjoyed the prior hour. This relationship is called **diminishing marginal utility.**

> **diminishing marginal utility:** the principle that the more of a good that one obtains in a specific period of time, the less is the additional utility yielded by an additional unit of that good

TABLE 1	The Utility of Listening to Country and Western Music

Hours of Listening per Day	Utility of Each Additional Hour of Listening (marginal utility)	Total Utility
1	200	200
2	98	298
3	50	348
4	10	358
5	0	358
6	−70	288
7	−200	88

marginal utility: the extra utility derived from consuming one more unit of a good or service

Marginal utility is the change in total utility that occurs because one more unit of the good is consumed or acquired:

$$\text{Marginal utility} = \frac{\text{change in total utility}}{\text{change in quantity}}$$

According to the principle of diminishing marginal utility, the more of a good or service that someone consumes during a particular period of time, the less satisfaction another unit of that good or service provides that individual. Imagine yourself sitting down to a plate piled high with cake. The first piece is delicious, and the second tastes good, but not as good as the first. The fourth piece doesn't taste very good at all, and the sixth piece nearly makes you sick. Instead of satisfaction, the sixth

disutility: dissatisfaction

piece of cake yields dissatisfaction, or **disutility.**

total utility: a measure of the total satisfaction derived from consuming a quantity of some good or service

Notice that we are speaking of diminishing *marginal* utility, not diminishing *total* utility. **Total utility,** the measure of the total satisfaction derived from consuming a quantity of some good or service, climbs until dissatisfaction sets in. For Gabrielle, total utility rises from 200 to 298 to 348 and reaches 358 with the fourth hour of music. From the fifth hour on, total utility declines. Marginal utility, however, is the additional utility gained from listening to another hour of music, and it declines from the first hour on.

To illustrate the relation between marginal and total utility, we have plotted the total utility data from Table 1 in Figure 1(a). The total utility curve rises as quantity rises until the fifth hour of listening. After five hours, the total utility curve declines. The reason total utility rises at first is that for the first four hours, each additional hour provides a little more utility. The marginal utility of the first hour is 200; the marginal utility of the second hour is 98; that of the third, 50; that of the fourth, 10; and that of the fifth, zero. By the fifth hour, total utility is 200 + 98 + 50 + 10 + 0 = 358.

We have plotted marginal utility in Figure 1(b), directly below the total utility curve of Figure 1(a). Marginal utility declines with each successive unit, reaches zero, and then turns negative. As long as marginal utility is positive, total utility rises. When marginal utility becomes negative, total utility declines. Marginal utility is zero at the point where total utility is at its maximum (unit 5 in this case). Marginal utility is the slope of the total utility curve.

1.c. Diminishing Marginal Utility and Time

The concept of diminishing marginal utility makes sense only if we define the *period of time* during which consumption is occurring. If Gabrielle listened to the music over

FIGURE 1 **Total and Marginal Utility**

Figure 1(a) shows the total utility obtained from listening to country and western music. Total utility reaches a maximum and then declines as additional listening becomes distasteful. For the first hour, the marginal and total utilities are the same. For the second hour, the marginal utility is the additional utility provided by the second unit. The total utility is the sum of the marginal utilities of the first and second units. The second unit provides less utility than the first unit, the third less than the second, and so on, in accordance with the law of diminishing marginal utility. But total utility, the sum of marginal utilities, rises as long as marginal utility is positive. Figure 1(b) shows marginal utility. When marginal utility is zero, total utility is at its maximum. When marginal utility is negative, total utility declines.

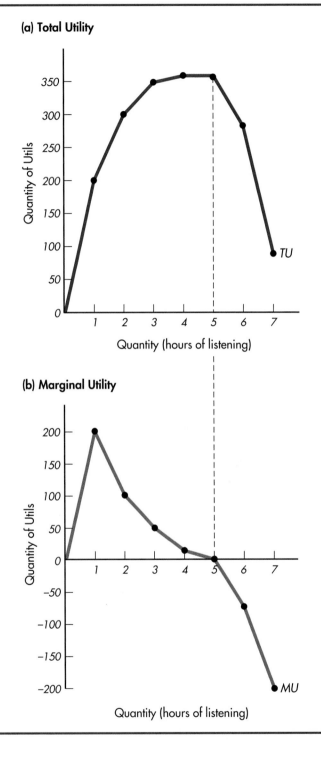

(a) Total Utility

(b) Marginal Utility

a period of several days, we might not observe diminishing marginal utility. But listening to the music in one 24-hour period causes Gabrielle to tire of it rather quickly. Usually, the shorter the time period, the more quickly marginal utility diminishes. Once the time period has been defined, diminishing marginal utility will apply; it applies to everyone and to every good and service, and perhaps even to income itself, as discussed in the Economic Insight "Does Money Buy Happiness?"

1.d. Consumers Are Not Identical

All consumers experience diminishing marginal utility, but the rate at which the marginal utility of any specific good or service declines is not identical for all consumers. The rate at which marginal utility diminishes depends on an individual's tastes and preferences. Gabrielle clearly enjoys country and western music. For a person who dislikes it, the first hour might yield disutility or negative utility. Also, we cannot compare the utility that two people get from something. We can't really say whether Bill likes the first piece of cake twice as much as Gary does. We can't compare their utils. All we can really do is observe whether Bill and Gary eat the cake.

1.e. An Illustration: "All You Can Eat"

When utility is positive, a person is happy; when utility is zero, a person receives no enjoyment. Let's look at an activity such as eating a piece of cake. If the first piece of cake creates 5 utils, then that first piece of cake is enjoyed; if the second piece creates 3 utils, then it is enjoyed less than the first piece. When a piece of cake has 0 utils or has a marginal utility of zero, then that piece is not enjoyed. People stop eating when marginal utility is zero.

Why would a restaurant ever have a policy of "all you can eat"? Won't people run the restaurant into the ground? No. The restaurant understands the concept of diminishing marginal utility. So it charges you a price for entering the restaurant and tells you that you can eat as much as you want—but you cannot have a "doggy bag." All consumers eventually stop eating—their marginal utility falls to zero. This is the point at which one more bite would be distasteful. The restaurant knows that everyone is limited in the amount he or she eats.

RECAP

1. Utility is a concept used to represent the degree to which goods and services satisfy wants.

2. Total utility is the total satisfaction that a consumer obtains from consuming a particular good or service.

3. Marginal utility is the utility that an additional unit of a good or service yields.

4. Total utility increases until dissatisfaction sets in. When another unit of a good would yield disutility, the consumer has been filled up with the good—more of it will not bring greater satisfaction.

5. According to the principle of diminishing marginal utility, marginal utility declines with each additional unit of a good or service that the consumer obtains. When marginal utility is zero, total utility is at its maximum.

?

1. How do consumers decide what to buy?

2. Utility and Choice _____

Can we simply conclude that people will consume goods until the marginal utility of each good is zero? No, we cannot, for if we did so, we would be ignoring scarcity and opportunity costs. No one has enough income to purchase everything until the

Economic Insight

Does Money Buy Happiness?

Diminishing marginal utility affects consumer purchases of every good. Does diminishing marginal utility affect income as well? This question has been a topic of economic debate for years. The case for progressive taxation—the more income you have, the greater the percentage of each additional dollar that you pay in taxes—is based on the idea that the marginal utility of income diminishes. In theory, if each additional dollar brings a person less utility, the pain associated with giving up a portion of each additional dollar will decline. And as a result of taxing the rich at a higher rate than the poor, the total pain imposed on society from a tax will be less than it would be if the same tax rate were applied to every dollar.

Economists have attempted to confirm or disprove the idea of the diminishing marginal utility of income, but doing so has proved difficult. Experiments have even been carried out on the topic. In one experiment, laboratory rats were trained to work for pay. They had to hit a bar several times to get a piece of food or a drink of water. After a while, after obtaining a certain amount of food and water, the rats reduced their work effort, choosing leisure instead of more food and water. Thus, the rats reacted as if their "income"—food and water—had a diminishing marginal utility.

Economists have also turned to the literature of psychology. Psychologists have carried out many surveys to measure whether people are more or less happy under various circumstances. One survey back in the 1960s asked people in different income brackets whether they were unhappy, pretty happy, or very happy. The results indicated that the higher income is, the happier people are. Several studies have found that, on average, people in wealthier nations are happier than people in poorer nations. However, although citizens of the wealthier nations tend to be happier than citizens of the less wealthy nations, other factors are very important in explaining national happiness. The longer a nation has been democratic, the happier are its citizens. Within any one country, there is only a modest link between well-being and being well-off. In other words, once people are comfortable, more money does not mean more happiness. The second $50,000 of income makes us less happy than the first.

The relationship between income and happiness for the United States over time looks like the accompanying figure. After a per capita income level of about $12,000 (adjusted to 1996 dollars), as income rises, the percentage who are happy does not change much. Results of many studies show that higher income undoubtedly raises happiness in developing countries, but the effect is only small or even negligible in rich countries.

Source: Adapted from David G. Myers, *The Pursuit of Happiness* (New York: William Morrow, 1992).

Box Sources: Bruno S. Frey and Alois Stutzer, *Happiness and Economics* (Princeton, NJ: Princeton University Press, 2002); John Stossel, "The Mystery of Happiness: Who Has It and How to Get It," ABC News, April 15, 1996, and replayed since; David G. Myers, *The Pursuit of Happiness* (New York: William Morrow, 1992); and N. M. Bradburn and D. Caplovitz, *Reports on Happiness* (Chicago: Aldine, 1965), p. 9.

marginal utility of each item is zero. Because incomes are limited, purchasing one thing means not purchasing other things. Gabrielle, our country and western music fancier, might be able to get more utility by purchasing some other good than by buying more music to listen to.

2.a. Consumer Choice

If you have $10 in your pocket to spend, you will spend it on the item or activity that gives you the most enjoyment—the greatest utility. Moreover, you may not spend all of it on just one thing. Suppose that with that $10, you are considering purchasing a CD, putting some gas in your car, and going to a movie. What will you decide? Well, you will purchase the amount of each that will give you the most enjoyment.

Although we don't go through an elaborate series of calculations when we decide to buy something, we act *as if* we did. We stand in line to purchase a $4 Starbucks latte at 10 A.M. because we need a little kick. We could have spent that $4 on a lot of other things, but at that moment, the latte seemed to give us the greatest satisfaction—the greatest utility. In the following long example, we go through the decision-making process as if the individual were a computer. The goal of this example is to show that people choose what to purchase with their limited budgets or incomes by comparing items to see which gives the most utility. If I am to spend another dollar, I will spend it to make myself as happy as that dollar can.

So let's turn again to Gabrielle. Gabrielle has $10 to spend on CDs, gasoline, and movies. She has found a place that sells used CDs, a gas station with low prices, and a movie theater that sells matinee tickets cheap. We want to know how many units of each she will purchase. The answer is in Table 2.

The price (P) of each secondhand CD is $2; the price of each gallon of gas is $1; the price of each movie is $3. The marginal utility (MU) provided by each unit and the ratio of the marginal utility to the price (MU/P) are presented at the top of the table. In the lower part of the table are the steps involved in allocating income among the three goods.

The first purchase involves a choice among the first unit of each of the three goods. The first CD yields a marginal utility (MU) of 200 and costs $2; thus, per dollar of expenditure, the first CD yields 100 utils ($MU/P = 100$). The first gallon of gas yields a marginal utility per dollar of expenditure of 200. The first movie yields a marginal utility per dollar of expenditure of 50; it yields 150 utils and costs $3. Which does Gabrielle choose?

To find the answer, compare the marginal utility per dollar of expenditure (MU/P) for each good, *not* the marginal utility (MU). The ratio of marginal utility to price puts the goods on the same basis (utility per dollar) and allows us to make sense of Gabrielle's decisions. Looking only at marginal utilities would not do this. For instance, another diamond might yield 10,000 utils and another apple might yield only 100 utils; but if the diamond costs $100,000 and the apple costs $1, the marginal utility per dollar of expenditure on the apple is greater than the marginal utility per dollar of expenditure on the diamond, and thus a consumer is better off purchasing the apple.

As indicated in Table 2, Gabrielle's first purchase is the gallon of gas. It yields the greatest marginal utility per dollar of expenditure (she needs gas in her car to be able to go anywhere). Because it costs $1, Gabrielle has $9 left to spend.

The second purchase involves a choice among the first CD, the second gallon of gas, and the first movie. The ratios of marginal utility per dollar of expenditure are 100 for the CD, 150 for the gas, and 50 for a movie. Thus, Gabrielle purchases a second gallon of gas and has $8 left.

For the third purchase, Gabrielle must decide between the first CD, the first movie, and the third gallon of gas. Because the CD yields a ratio of 100 and both the

TABLE 2   The Logic of Consumer Choice

CD (P = $2)			Gas (P = $1)			Movie (P = $3)		
Units	MU	MU/P	Units	MU	MU/P	Units	MU	MU/P
1	200	100	1	200	200	1	150	50
2	98	49	2	150	150	2	90	30
3	50	25	3	50	50	3	60	20
4	10	5	4	30	30	4	30	10
5	0	0	5	0	0	5	9	3
6	−70	−35	6	−300	−300	6	0	0
7	−200	−100	7	−700	−700	7	−6	−2

Steps	Choices			Decision	Remaining Budget
1st purchase	1st CD:	MU/P =	100	Gas	$10 − $1 = $9
	1st gas:	MU/P =	200		
	1st movie:	MU/P =	50		
2nd purchase	1st CD:	MU/P =	100	Gas	$9 − $1 = $8
	2nd gas:	MU/P =	150		
	1st movie:	MU/P =	50		
3rd purchase	1st CD:	MU/P =	100	CD	$8 − $2 = $6
	3rd gas:	MU/P =	50		
	1st movie:	MU/P =	50		
4th purchase	2nd CD:	MU/P =	49	Gas	$6 − $1 = $5
	3rd gas:	MU/P =	50		
	1st movie:	MU/P =	50		
5th purchase	2nd CD:	MU/P =	49	Movie	$5 − $3 = $2
	4th gas:	MU/P =	30		
	1st movie:	MU/P =	50		
6th purchase	2nd CD:	MU/P =	49	CD	$2 − $2 = 0
	4th gas:	MU/P =	30		
	2nd movie:	MU/P =	30		

Note: Purchases made with $10: 2 CDs, 3 gallons of gas, and 1 movie ticket.

gas and the movie yield ratios of 50, she purchases the CD. The CD costs $2, so she has $6 left to spend.

A utility-maximizing consumer like Gabrielle always chooses the purchase that yields the greatest marginal utility per dollar of expenditure. If two goods offer the same marginal utility per dollar of expenditure, the consumer will be indifferent between the two—that is, the consumer won't care which is chosen. For example, Table 2 indicates that for the fourth purchase, either another gallon of gas or a movie would yield 50 utils per dollar. Gabrielle is completely indifferent between the two and so arbitrarily selects gas. The movie is chosen for the fifth purchase. With the sixth purchase, a second CD, the total budget is spent. For $10, Gabrielle ends up with 2 CDs, 3 gallons of gas, and 1 movie.

In this example, Gabrielle is portrayed as a methodical, robotlike consumer who calculates how to allocate her scarce income among goods and services in a way that ensures that each additional dollar of expenditure yields the greatest marginal utility. This picture is more than a little far-fetched, but it does describe the result, if not the process, of consumer choice. People do have to decide which goods and services to purchase with their limited incomes, and people do select the options that give them the greatest utility.

2.b. Consumer Equilibrium

With $10, Gabrielle purchases 2 CDs, 3 gallons of gas, and 1 movie ticket. For the second CD, the marginal utility per dollar of expenditure is 49; for the third gallon of gas, it is 50; and for the first movie, it is 50. Is it merely a fluke that the marginal utility per dollar of expenditure ratios are nearly equal? No. *In order to maximize utility, consumers must allocate their limited incomes among goods and services in such a way that the marginal utility per dollar of expenditure on the last unit of each good purchased will be as nearly equal as possible.* This is called the **equimarginal principle** and also represents **consumer equilibrium.** It is consumer equilibrium because the consumer will not change from this point unless something changes income, marginal utility, or price.

In our example, the ratios at consumer equilibrium are as close to equal as possible—49, 50, and 50—but they are not identical because Gabrielle (like all consumers) had to purchase whole portions of the goods. Consumers cannot spend a dollar on any good or service and always get the fractional amount that a dollar buys—one-tenth of a tennis lesson or one-third of a bottle of water. Instead, consumers have to purchase goods and services in whole units—1 piece or 1 ounce or 1 package—and pay the per unit price.

The equimarginal principle is simply common sense. If consumers have money to spend, they will spend it on those things that give them the most satisfaction. If you have a choice of A or B and A makes you happier, you will take A. At the prices given in Table 2, with an income of $10, and with the marginal utilities given, Gabrielle maximizes her utility by purchasing 2 CDs, 3 gallons of gas, and 1 movie ticket. Everything else held constant, no other allocation of the $10 would yield Gabrielle more utility.

Consumers are in equilibrium when they have no incentive to change what they buy—to reallocate their limited budget or income. With *MU* standing for marginal utility and *P* for price, the general rule for consumer equilibrium is $MU_x/P_x = MU_y/P_y = MU_z/P_z$.

equimarginal principle or **consumer equilibrium:** to maximize utility, consumers must allocate their scarce incomes among goods in such a way as to equate the marginal utility per dollar of expenditure on the last unit of each good purchased

---

RECAP

1. To maximize utility, consumers must allocate their limited incomes in such a way that the marginal utility per dollar obtained from the last unit consumed is equal for all goods and services; this is the equimarginal principle.

2. As long as the marginal utility per dollar obtained from the last unit of all products consumed is the same, the consumer is in equilibrium and will not reallocate income.

3. Consumer equilibrium, or utility maximization, is summarized by a formula that equates the marginal utility per dollar of expenditure on the last item purchased of all goods:

$$MU_a/P_a = MU_b/P_b = MU_c/P_c = MU_x/P_x$$

3. The Demand Curve Again _____

We have shown how consumers make choices—by allocating their scarce incomes among goods in order to maximize their utility. These choices define a demand curve.

3.a. The Downward Slope of the Demand Curve

?

2. Why does the demand curve slope down?

The demand curve or schedule can be derived from consumer equilibrium by altering the price of one good or service.

Recall that as the price of a good falls, the quantity demanded of that good rises. This inverse relation between price and quantity demanded arises from diminishing marginal utility and consumer equilibrium.

Consumers allocate their income among goods and services in order to maximize their utility. A consumer is in equilibrium (has no reason to change) when the total budget has been spent and the marginal utility per dollar of expenditure on the last unit of each good is the same. A change in the price of one good will disturb the consumer's equilibrium; the marginal utilities per dollar of expenditure for the last unit of each good will no longer be equal. The consumer will then reallocate her income among the goods in order to increase total utility.

In the example presented in Table 2, the price of a CD is $2, the price per gallon of gas is $1, and the price of a movie ticket is $3. Now suppose the price of the CD falls to $1 while the prices of gas and movies and Gabrielle's budget of $10 remain the same. Common sense tells us that Gabrielle will probably alter the quantities purchased by buying more CDs. To find out if she does—and whether the equimarginal principle holds—her purchases can be traced step by step as we did previously.

In Table 3, only the *MU/P* ratio for CDs is different from the corresponding figure at the top of Table 2. At the old consumer equilibrium of 2 CDs, 3 gallons of gas, and 1 movie, the marginal utility per dollar of expenditure (*MU/P*) on each good is

CD: 98/$1 = 98/$1

Gas: 50/$1 = 50/$1

Movie: 150/$3 = 50/$1

Clearly, the ratios are no longer equal. In order to maximize utility, Gabrielle must reallocate her budget among the goods. When all $10 is spent, Gabrielle finds that she has purchased 3 CDs, 4 gallons of gas, and 1 movie ticket. The lower price of CDs has induced her to purchase an additional CD. Gabrielle's behavior illustrates what you already know: The quantity demanded of CDs increases as the price of the CD decreases.

If the price of the CD is increased to $3, we find that Gabrielle demands only 1 CD. The three prices and the corresponding quantities of CDs purchased give us Gabrielle's demand for CDs, which is shown in Figure 2. At $3 she is willing and able to buy 1 CD; at $2 she is willing and able to buy 2 CDs; and at $1 she is willing and able to buy 3 CDs.

TABLE 3   A Price Change

CD (P = $1)			Gas (P = $1)			Movie (P = $3)		
Units	MU	MU/P	Units	MU	MU/P	Units	MU	MU/P
1	200	200	1	200	200	1	150	50
2	98	98	2	150	150	2	90	30
3	50	50	3	50	50	3	60	20
4	10	10	4	30	30	4	30	10
5	0	0	5	0	0	5	9	3
6	−71	−70	6	−300	−300	6	0	0
7	−200	−200	7	−700	−700	7	−6	−2

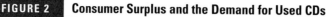

FIGURE 2   **Consumer Surplus and the Demand for Used CDs**

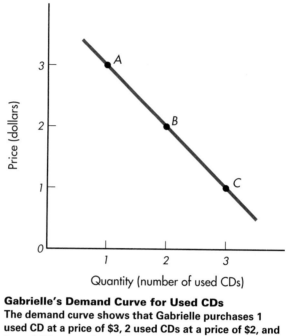

Gabrielle's Demand Curve for Used CDs
The demand curve shows that Gabrielle purchases 1
used CD at a price of $3, 2 used CDs at a price of $2, and
3 used CDs at a price of $1.

*The substitution effect
indicates that following a
decrease in the price of a
good or service, an indi-
vidual will purchase more
of the now less expensive
good and less of other
goods.*

*The income effect of a
price change indicates
that an individual's in-
come can buy more of all
goods when the price of
one good declines, every-
thing else held constant.*

3.b. Shifts of Demand and the Determination of Market Demand

Individual demand comes from utility maximization. Individuals allocate their scarce incomes among goods in order to get the greatest utility; this occurs when consumer equilibrium is reached, represented in symbols as $MU_x/P_x = MU_y/P_y = MU_z/P_z$. When the price of a good or service is changed, consumer equilibrium is disturbed. In response to the price change, individuals alter their purchases so as to achieve maximum utility.

When the price of one good falls while everything else is held constant, two things occur: (1) other goods become relatively *more* expensive, so consumers buy more of the less expensive good and less of the more expensive goods, and (2) the good purchased prior to the price change now costs less, so the consumer can buy more of all goods.

When a good becomes relatively less expensive, it yields more satisfaction per dollar than before, so consumers buy more of it than before as they decrease their expenditures on other goods. This is the *substitution effect* of a price change.

Figure 2 shows that at the price of $2 per used CD, Gabrielle spends $4 on CDs. When the price falls to $1, she spends only $2 for those two CDs. As a result, Gabrielle can purchase more of all goods, including the good whose price has fallen. This is the *income effect* of a price change.

The process of changing the price of one good or service while income, tastes and preferences, and the prices of related goods are held constant defines the individ-

Halloween has changed from a child's holiday to the second most popular holiday in the United States. Spending on Halloween supplies exceeds spending for every holiday except Christmas. The increased tastes for Halloween fun have led to an increased demand for costumes. In terms of economic theory, marginal utility for each dollar of spending on Halloween costumes has risen.

ual's demand for that good or service. Should income, tastes and preferences, or prices of related goods and services change, then the individual's demand will change. More or less income means that more or less goods and services can be purchased. A change in income affects the ratios of MU/P and disturbs consumer equilibrium. When the price of a related good changes, the ratio of marginal utility to price for that good changes, thus disturbing consumer equilibrium. And changes in tastes and preferences, represented as changes in the MUs, also alter consumer equilibrium. For each change in a determinant of demand, a new demand curve for a good or service is derived; the demand curve shifts.

The market demand curve is the sum of all the individual demand curves. This means that anything that affects the individual curves also affects the market curve. In addition, when we combine the individual demand curves into a market demand curve, the number of individuals to be combined determines the position of the market demand curve. Changes in the number of consumers alter the market demand curve. We thus say that the determinants of demand are tastes and preferences, income, prices of related goods, international effects, and number of consumers. Also, recall that diminishing marginal utility is defined for consumption during a specific period of time. Since consumer equilibrium and thus the demand curve depend on diminishing marginal utility, the demand curve is also defined for consumption over a specific period of time. Changes in the time period or changes in expectations will therefore also alter demand.

RECAP

1. The principle of diminishing marginal utility and the equimarginal principle account for the inverse relation between the price of a product and the quantity demanded.

2. A price change triggers both the substitution effect and the income effect.

3. The substitution effect occurs because once a good becomes less expensive, it yields more satisfaction per dollar than before and consumers buy more of it than before. They do this by decreasing their purchases of other goods. The income effect of the price change occurs because a lower price raises real income (total utility) and the consumer purchases more of all goods.

4. The market demand curve is the summation of all individual demand curves.

5. Economists derive the market demand curve for a good by assuming that individual incomes are fixed, that the prices of all goods except the one in question are constant, that each individual's tastes remain fixed, that expectations do not change, that the number of consumers is constant, and that the time period under consideration remains unchanged. A change in any one of these determinants causes the demand curve to shift.

4. Behavioral Economics and Neuroeconomics

Since the early 1900s, economists have assumed that people are rational—that they compare costs and benefits before undertaking any action. This assumption makes humans seem more like robots than like thinking, feeling beings. In recent years, two fields of study—behavioral economics and neuroeconomics—have attempted to change this assumption.

4.a. Behavioral Economics

Strict rationality assumes that the decision maker has complete or perfect information. **Bounded rationality** admits that complete and perfect information is not likely to be available, and that as a result, people make decisions that in hindsight look irrational, but in reality are the rational results of a brain that is economizing— finding shortcuts and easier ways to make decisions. **Behavioral economics** attempts to catalogue the biases that result from bounded rationality. Let's look at some well-documented behaviors and explore the interplay of emotions and logic in decision making.

4.a.1. Overconfidence

People tend to think that they *are* better and *do things* better than is really the case. For example, 100 percent of drivers say that they are in the top 30 percent of safe drivers; 68 percent of lawyers in civil cases believe that their side will prevail; 81 percent of new business owners think that their own business has at least a 70 percent chance of success, but only 39 percent think that any business like theirs would be likely to succeed. And consider this: Mutual fund managers, analysts, and business executives at a conference were asked to write down how much money they would have at retirement and how much the average person in the room would have. The average figures were $5 million and $2.6 million, respectively.

Making a decision—any decision—requires a certain amount of confidence in our understanding of the risks and benefits. But overconfidence and the illusion of control can add up to bad decisions and big losses. People prefer to drive rather than fly because they feel safer driving, even though the record confirms that flying is significantly safer. Similarly, people start new businesses even when the odds are against them. The U.S. Census Bureau reports that 50 percent of new ventures close within the first four years.

Overconfident chief executive officers (CEOs, or corporate bosses) provide prime examples. The top executives of Enron Corporation seemed to think that they could do and get away with just about anything. The result was the failure of the company. Tyco's former chief executive, Dennis Kozlowski, saw that the company was doing poorly, but denied it and, rather than readjust to the situation, did things that appeared to be and were fraudulent.

3. What are behavioral economics and neuroeconomics?

bounded rationality: the understanding that perfect information is not likely to be available, and that as a result people make decisions that in hindsight look irrational, but in reality are the rational results of a brain that is economizing

behavioral economics: the study of decision making assuming that people are rational in a broad sense

You might think that experience would lead people to become more realistic about their capabilities. But research indicates that overconfidence does not decline over time, perhaps because people generally remember failures very differently from successes. The typical view is that one's successes are due to one's own wisdom and ability, while one's failures are due to forces beyond one's control. Thus, people believe that with a little better luck or fine-tuning, the outcome will be much better next time.

4.a.2. Mental Accounting

A dollar is a dollar is a dollar—at least, that is the way economists tend to view assets. It should not matter whether that dollar comes from the right pocket or the left pocket. The term *mental accounting* refers to the idea that the value people place on money depends on where that money comes from. For instance, people tend to spend money received as gifts or through contests more readily than money they've earned, and people tend to continue gambling with winnings even though they would not continue gambling with money that they earned.

A story about a honeymooning couple in Las Vegas provides an illustration of mental accounting. Knowing that they were headed for Vegas, and knowing that they did not have a lot of money, the couple decided that they would spend only a certain amount. Once that was gone, they had to return home. After a few days, the amount had been spent, and the couple was spending their last night in their hotel prior to returning home. The wife was asleep, and the husband, wide awake, noticed a $5 chip that they had saved as a souvenir. Strangely, the number 12 was flashing in the groom's mind. Taking this as an omen, he rushed to the roulette tables, where he placed the $5 chip on the 12; sure enough, the winner was 12, paying 35 to 1. He let the winnings ride and kept on winning until he had won $262 million. He then let it ride once more and lost everything. Broke and dejected, he walked back to his room. "Where were you?" asked his bride. "Playing roulette," he responded. "How did you do?" she asked. "Not bad. I lost five dollars."

This story captures what is referred to as *playing with the house's money*. The idea is that people do not feel that something really belongs to them unless it comes out of their own pocket.

It is more painful to give up something that you possess than it is pleasurable to acquire the exact same thing when you don't already possess it. This means that the price elasticity of demand can be changed—made less elastic—if consumers feel that they own the product. The purchase decision can be influenced by having the buyers assume ownership, even temporarily, prior to purchase. If buyers can be persuaded to take the product home to try it out, they will be reluctant to return it when payment is due, since this will require that they incur a loss. A frequent tactic of home decoration and furniture stores is to encourage customers to take a piece of furniture or a carpet home to "see how it looks." This is also the approach of buy-now, pay-later plans. During holidays, for example, retailers frequently offer installment plans that delay payment for 90 days, so that buyers can integrate the new purchases into their reference points. Health clubs, fitness centers, and weight loss clinics offer an initial trial membership either free or at nominal rates.

Publisher's Clearing House addresses individuals who receive its direct mail promotion as "finalists" and warns them that they are about to lose millions of dollars if they do not return the winning number. Publisher's Clearing House is attempting to give consumers the impression that they possess an asset—the opportunity to win millions of dollars—that they will have to give up if they don't submit the entry form.

4.a.3. Status Quo

In general, people would rather leave things as they are. Once something is the status quo, people don't like to change it; they value the status quo or consider the costs of change too high. For example, if people receive an inheritance of low-risk, low-return bonds, they typically don't change anything. Similarly, if people receive higher-risk securities, they also leave most of the money alone. One explanation for this bias toward the status quo is aversion to loss—people are more concerned about the risk of loss than they are excited by the prospect of gain. If you switch your money from the stock market to housing, you would feel worse if the stock market increases than you would feel good if the housing market increases.

4.a.4. Loss Aversion and Framing
People don't react the same way to equal-sized gains and losses. For instance, if people have come to expect the price of a gallon of gasoline to be $2, a price of $3 is a loss of $1 rather than a loss of $3, and a price of $1 is a gain of $1. The gain and loss are calculated relative to a reference. People tend to create references for most things, not just prices. Moreover, although the gain and loss are the same, $1, people do not react to them in the same way. People dislike losses more than they like gains.

Framing—that is, the context in which a choice is presented—is important to the decision maker. For instance, when a customer calls a hotel for a reservation, the hotel reservationists generally quote their highest room rates, those that they charge during peak demand periods, and then discount those rates. This is an attempt to create a high reference price for the consumer. If the initially stated high price is the buyer's reference, then the buyer looks on the price actually paid as a gain. Similarly, airline reservationists initially quote the highest fare on a route before quoting discounts and associated travel restrictions. In written advertisements or in advertisements on radio, both hotels and airlines provide the lowest price along with a reference to which they want consumers to compare the advertised price. Statements like "this fare is 50 percent below previous fares" and "friends fly free," suggesting a 50 percent discount, are common in advertisements.

Some sense of fairness is important to most people. People will reject something that they perceive as not being fair and will react strongly when they feel that they are being taken advantage of. During a snowstorm, does the local hardware store raise the price of snow shovels? During a hurricane, do grocery stores raise the price of food and water? Not if they want to retain business. The old saying is: "If you gouge them at Christmas, they won't be back in March."

4.a.5. Familiarity
When people must make decisions without having perfect information, they often use things that they are familiar with more than economic theory would seem to suggest. Familiarity leads to decisions that might appear irrational because people are more comfortable with a familiar situation than an unfamiliar one. Consider the following quiz:

1. In four pages of a typical novel (about 2,000 words), how many words would you expect to find that have the form "_ _ _ _ ing" (a seven-letter word that ends in -ing)?

2. Now, how many words would you expect to find that have the form "_ _ _ _ _ n _" (a seven-letter word with an n in the sixth position)?

You may have noticed that the second option includes the first—in other words, the answer to the second has to be larger than the answer to the first. Yet, because people are familiar with words that end in -ing, they tend to think that these words are likely to appear more often.

This reliance on familiarity also arises in answers to questions such as: "Which is more common in New York City, murder or suicide?" Although suicide is much more prevalent than murder, many people think the answer is murder. The point is that the more familiar people are with something (here, news reports of murders in New York), the more likely they are to choose it.

People generally want more for less, but the framing of "more" and "less" makes a difference. Consider how people respond to the following situation.

> Who is happier: Person A, who wins the office football pool for $100 on the same day she ruins the carpet in her apartment and must pay her landlord $75, or Person B, who wins the office football pool for $25?

Most people believe that Person A is happier, even though both A and B end up with the same $25 gain. Consider the same problem with a slight revision.

> Who is happier: Person A, who ruins the carpet in her apartment and must pay the landlord $100, or Person B, who wins the office football pool for $25 but also ruins the carpet in his apartment and must pay the landlord $125?

In this case, most people believe that Person B is happier, even though A and B must pay the same amount, $100. If the net result involves a gain, people prefer to have the results of the actions presented separately—a $100 gain and a $25 loss rather than a $75 gain. But if the net result involves losses, people prefer to have the losses integrated or shown just once.

4.a.6. Anchoring

Ask a group of people to write down the last three digits of their phone number, and then ask them to estimate the date of Genghis Khan's death. Time and again, the results show a correlation between the two numbers; people assume that he lived in the first millennium, when in fact he lived from 1162 to 1227. Here is another quiz:

> You have five seconds to estimate the value of $1 \times 2 \times 3 \times 4 \times 5 \times 6 \times 7 \times 8$.
>
> Now, take five seconds to do the same for $8 \times 7 \times 6 \times 5 \times 4 \times 3 \times 2 \times 1$.

Typically, most people believe that the result of these two exercises is different—that the result of the first is smaller than the result of the second. The reason is that the guesstimates are "anchored" to the early numbers. In the first exercise, the early numbers are smaller; in the second, the higher numbers are listed first. (Still, few guessed that the product was anywhere near the correct number of 40,320.)

4.a.7. Sunk Costs

You and a friend are on the way to a concert for which you purchased tickets for $100, and the tickets are not refundable. Neither of you is feeling particularly well; both of you think that it would be more fun to simply loaf around in the apartment. Your friend says, "It's too bad we've already purchased the tickets, because if we don't go, we waste $100." You agree. Do you go to the concert, or do you go home?

This problem illustrates the sunk-cost effect, otherwise known as "throwing good money after bad." When we have put effort into something, we are often reluctant to pull out because of the loss that we will suffer, even if continued refusal to jump ship will lead to even more loss. Think about the $100 tickets again and consider the issue another way. The moment you paid $100 for the ticket, your net assets decreased by $100. That decrease occurred several days before the concert. Is the fact that your net assets have decreased by $100 sufficient reason for deciding to spend the night at a place you don't want to be? The $100 *you have already paid* is technically termed a *sunk cost*. Rationally, sunk costs *should not affect decisions about the future*. Sunk means that they are gone—they are not recoverable. The $100 is gone whether you go to the concert or not. So, why choose to do something that you would prefer not to do just because you have already bought tickets? The tendency to do so is the sunk-cost effect.

Executives making strategic investment decisions can also fall into the sunk-cost trap. When large projects overrun their schedules and budgets, the original economic case no longer holds. The project should be abandoned. However, because so much has already been spent, companies keep spending to complete such projects.

Now that we've taken a brief look at how emotions affect economic decisions, let's examine the ways in which biology affects decision making.

4.b. Neuroeconomics

Attempting to delve into the black box known as the consumer, some economists have joined forces with biologists and neurologists to attempt to see how the brain handles economic decisions. This is the study of **neuroeconomics.** It has long been known that different sectors of the human prefrontal cortex are involved in distinctive cognitive and behavioral operations. Figure 3 illustrates the anatomy of the brain. The frontal lobe carries out most decision making. Strategic thinking takes place in the prefrontal cortex, noted as areas 10 and 11. The orbital frontal cortex (CFC), or sections 11 and 12, accounts for the joy or pain of monetary rewards and punishments. Rewards and punishments are dealt with in different parts of the brain: The right CFC handles punishment, and the bilateral medial handles reward. In addition, pain registers more than an equal reward registers.

4.b.1. The Emotional Versus the Logical Brain   MRI scans have revealed the two parts of the brain in which most decisions take place. The emotional part is the limbic system (especially the amygdala). The logical part is the prefrontal cortex. Neuroeconomists have found that different kinds of decisions show up as increased electrical activity in either the emotional or the logical part. Often a decision is the result of conflicts between the two brain sections. For instance, decisions about the far-off future involve both the prefrontal cortex and the amygdala. The prefrontal cortex takes a long-term perspective, looking at logical cost-benefit comparisons. The amygdala confuses this logic by bringing in emotions, and in some cases it takes over and demands immediate gratification.

FIGURE 3   **Anatomy of the Brain**

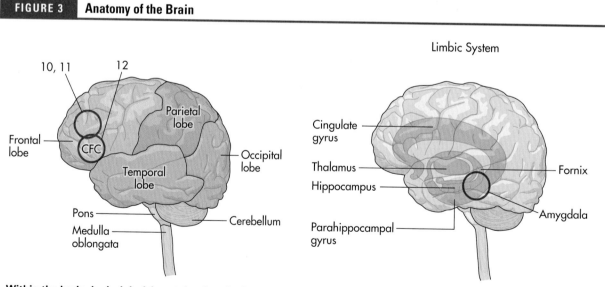

Within the brain, logical decisions take place in the prefrontal cortex. Emotional decisions take place in the limbic system or the amygdala.

Age-based differences in decision making stem from brain development. Adults have greater activity in their frontal lobes and lower activity in their amygdala than do teenagers. The amygdala is more primitive and deals with emotions; the frontal lobes deal more with reasoning. Another finding is that the limbic system has a hard time imagining the future, even though our prefrontal cortex clearly sees the future consequences of our current actions. Our emotional brain wants to max out the credit card, order dessert, and smoke a cigarette. Our logical brain knows that we should save for retirement, go for a run, and quit smoking. What we actually do depends on which is dominant at that point in time.

RECAP

1. Behavioral economics is the study of decision making assuming that people are rational in a broad sense. The human brain economizes, enabling people to make decisions without having complete and perfect information.

2. Neuroeconomics combines neurology and economics. It attempts to measure brain activity and map where such activity takes place in order to better understand how decisions are made.

Summary

1. How do consumers decide what to buy?

- Utility is a measure of the satisfaction received from possessing or consuming a good. *§1.a*

- *Diminishing marginal utility* refers to the decline in marginal utility received from each additional unit of a good that is consumed during a particular period of time. The more of some good a consumer has, the less desirable is another unit of that good. *§1.b*

- Even if a good is free, a consumer will eventually reach a point where one more unit of the good would be undesirable or distasteful, and he or she will not consume that additional unit. *§1.e*

- Consumer equilibrium refers to the utility-maximizing situation in which the consumer has allocated his or her budget among goods and services in such a way that the marginal utility per dollar of expenditure on the last unit of any good is the same for all goods. It is represented in symbols as $MU_x/P_x = MU_y/P_y = MU_z/P_z$. *§2.b*

2. Why does the demand curve slope down?

- The demand curve slopes down because of diminishing marginal utility and consumer equilibrium. *§3.a*

- The income and substitution effects of a price change occur because of diminishing marginal utility and the equimarginal principle. When the price of one good falls while all other prices remain the same, that good yields more satisfaction per dollar than before, so consumers buy more of it than before. *§3.b*

- Market demand is the summation of individual demands. *§3.b*

3. What are behavioral economics and neuroeconomics?

- The two fields of study are attempts to jump inside the human being, to discover why and how decisions are made. Behavioral economists have focused on observing decisions made by people in various situations; neuroeconomists have focused on measuring brain activity using technologies such as MRI scans. *§4.a, §4.b*

Key Terms

utility *§1.a*
diminishing marginal utility *§1.b*
marginal utility *§1.b*
disutility *§1.b*

total utility *§1.b*
equimarginal principle *§2.b*
consumer equilibrium *§2.b*
bounded rationality *§4.a*

behavioral economics *§4.a*
neuroeconomics *§4.b*

Exercises

1. Using the following information, calculate total utility and marginal utility.

   a. Plot the total utility curve.

   b. Plot marginal utility directly below total utility.

   c. At what marginal utility value does total utility reach a maximum?

Number of utils for the first unit:	300
Number of utils for the second unit:	250
Number of utils for the third unit:	220
Number of utils for the fourth unit:	160
Number of utils for the fifth unit:	100
Number of utils for the sixth unit:	50
Number of utils for the seventh unit:	20
Number of utils for the eighth unit:	0
Number of utils for the ninth unit:	−250

2. Is it possible for marginal utility to be negative and total utility positive? Explain.

3. Suppose Mary is in consumer equilibrium. The marginal utility of good A is 30, and the price of good A is $2.

   a. If the price of good B is $4, the price of good C is $3, the price of good D is $1, and the price of all other goods and services is $5, what is the marginal utility of each of the goods Mary is purchasing?

   b. If Mary has chosen to keep $10 in savings, what is the ratio of *MU* to *P* for savings?

4. Using the following utility schedule, derive a demand curve for pizza.

   a. Assume income is $10, the price of each slice of pizza is $1, and the price of each glass of beer is $2. Then change the price of pizza to $2 per slice.

   b. Now change income to $12 and derive a demand curve for pizza.

Slices of Pizza	Total Utility	Glasses of Beer	Total Utility
1	200	1	500
2	380	2	800
3	540	3	900
4	600	4	920
5	630	5	930

5. Using utility, explain the following commonly made statements:

   a. I couldn't eat another bite.

   b. I'll never get tired of your cooking.

   c. The last drop tastes as good as the first.

   d. I wouldn't eat broccoli if you paid me.

   e. My kid would eat nothing but junk food if I allowed her.

   f. Any job worth doing is worth doing well.

6. How would guests' behavior be likely to differ at a BYOB (bring your own bottle) party from one at which the host provides the drinks? Explain your answer.

7. A round of golf on a municipal golf course usually takes about five hours. At a private country club golf course, a round takes less than four hours. What accounts for the difference? Would the time spent playing golf be different if golfers paid only an admission fee (membership fee) and no monthly dues or if they paid only a charge per round and no monthly dues?

8. To increase marginal utility, you must decrease consumption (everything else held constant). This statement is correct, even though it sounds strange. Explain why.

9. Suppose that the marginal utility of good A is 4 times the marginal utility of good B, but the price of good A is only 2 times the price of good B. Is this point consumer equilibrium? If not, what will occur?

10. Last Saturday you went to a movie and ate a large box of popcorn and two candy bars and drank a medium soda. This Saturday you went to a movie and ate a medium box of popcorn and one candy bar and drank a large soda. Your tastes and preferences did not change. What could explain the different combinations of goods that you purchased?

11. Peer pressure is an important influence on the behavior of youngsters. For instance, many preteens begin smoking because their friends pressure them into being "cool" by smoking. Using utility theory, how would you explain peer pressure? How would this compare with the explanations provided by behavioral economics and neuroeconomics?

12. Many people who earn incomes below some level receive food stamps from the government. Economists argue that these people would be better off if the government gave them the cash equivalent of the food stamps rather than the food stamps. What is the basis of the economists' argument?

13. What is the purpose of the two fields of study neuroeconomics and behavioral economics? Why might people tend to be overconfident?

14. What does it mean to say that people like to "play with the house's money"?

15. Can you see a connection between the emotional and logical brain and the action known as loss aversion?

Take the ACE Practice Test for this chapter to review the important concepts and get immediate feedback with answers.

college.hmco.com/economics/students/

Why Sudden Wealth Will Not Make You Happy

South China Morning Post
(Hong Kong)
March 21, 2003

Lotteries are booming as a way to generate income without taxation, a prime example being Hong Kong's newly introduced soccer betting draw. Big-prize quiz shows guarantee massive viewer ratings. E-commerce, property, the stock exchange, music, sports, publishing and other sectors are making people wealthy overnight. . . .

The world over, most ticket buyers—and therefore winners—are working-class people who live and work in modest neighbourhoods. When they win, their world turns upside down. They are ill-equipped to handle the new situation. They do not know whom to trust. Nor are they prepared for what is likely to happen in their relationships.

Not much information is available on this subject, and the newly rich are becoming increasingly secretive because of the consequences they fear, such as harassment by strangers, exploitation by swindlers or vilification in the press. Many receive so many requests for money for seemingly worthy causes that they are hounded from their homes. One now anonymous lottery-winning couple in Ohio, reports *Money* magazine, was inundated with calls. They became frightened about robberies and stressed about managing their new wealth, and their children progressively lost all their old friends.

Choices expand and decisions are unavoidable. If lottery winners quit work and buy a new house in a fancy neighbourhood, they become alienated from their previous friends and family. They do not really fit in with their new neighbours, either. They can stay where they are and share their wealth. But then they are often relegated to the status of a free meal ticket and they begin to doubt the sincerity of those around them. Most studies of sudden wealth are limited to lottery winners who have volunteered to talk about their experiences, creating a sort of natural selection of the disgruntled and exploited.

But one study focused on customers of financial and legal consultants. These suddenly wealthy people were taking action to try to manage their new status and were not limited to lottery winners. Researcher Eileen Gallo's key finding was that "early money messages" made a big difference in how well people adapted to sudden wealth. If told while growing up to save and only spend responsibly, the winner was likely to be happy with the new wealth, with a positive view as to how it affected their relationships. The vast majority of those with a negative experience with their new affluence had not received that message.

Dr. Gallo found that married people did far better than single people at handling sudden wealth. Perhaps marriage gives you at least one trustworthy person with whom you can talk. There was also a positive connection with altruism. Viewing sudden affluence as a good opportunity to help others corresponded with a more satisfactory overall adaptation. . . .

A big win or a sudden business success creates euphoria. One study suggests it takes at least HK$ 1 million to guarantee the effect, but that is certainly relative, too. In any case, the effect does not last. A windfall brings challenges and, in the long run, overall happiness is virtually unaffected.

Jean Nicol

W̶e all want more—we assume that if we had all the money in the world, we would be happy and fulfilled, don't we? That assumption is wrong; more is not always better than less. More disease, more filth, more garbage, more pollution, more of many things is not better than less. With respect to goods, we do assume that more is better than less as long as there is no problem in storing or keeping the goods and services and as long as our tastes do not change. The cake example used in the text, where our consumer ate so much that he or she nearly got sick, illustrates nicely that more is preferred to less as long as there are no storage costs; it is simply impossible to "store" an infinite amount of cake, that is, to eat it. Eventually, more cake is not desired. This is the law of diminishing marginal utility in operation. It says that during a given period of time, as we get more of an additional good, the marginal amount of that good will provide us less additional happiness than a previous amount did.

In the Economic Insight "Does Money Buy Happiness?" it was shown that up to some income level, money and expressed happiness seem to rise together, but then, as money continues to rise, happiness does not. This article says the same thing. People want more money—more money enables people to purchase more of everything, and so more money equates to more happiness. This seems to occur, but only up to a point—once someone has a bunch of money, additional amounts do not mean very much.

What does more income do? It shifts the budget constraint out; it enables people to purchase more of everything. The consumer equilibrium formula states that a consumer will purchase additional amounts of items until the consumer's budget is spent and the marginal utility of each dollar of expenditures is nearly equal across all purchases:

$$MU_x/P_x = MU_y/P_y = MU_z/P_z$$

With more income, more of everything can be purchased. The consumer still purchases by spending the budget on each good and service up to the point where the last dollar spent on each item yields the same additional utility. So the question is, do people also experience diminishing marginal utility with money? The answer has to be no as long as there are no costs of storage and tastes do not change.

The theme of the article is that people's attitudes toward sudden wealth change over time, and that unless they are prepared for the sudden wealth, they may not be any happier with the wealth than they were before they had it. For instance, those people who saved and spent responsibly were more likely to be happier with their new wealth than those who were not able to manage their finances. In addition, viewing sudden affluence as a good opportunity to help others seemed to make people with sudden wealth happier than those who were less altruistic. What this means is that the utility of each individual for the same item (money or any other item) is different; comparing one person's utility (happiness) to another's is not possible. How can you measure whether one person is happier than another? Perhaps some day neuroeconomics will enable such comparisons to be made.

Indifference Analysis

1. Indifference Curves

In Figure 1, four combinations of CDs and gallons of gasoline are listed in the table and plotted in Figure 1(a). Preferring more to less, the consumer will clearly prefer C to the other combinations. Combination C is preferred to B because C offers one more gallon of gas than B and the same amount of CDs. Combination C is preferred to A because C offers both one more CD and one more gallon of gas than A. And

FIGURE 1 **Indifference Curve**

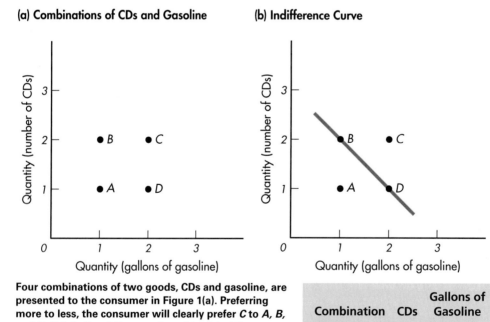

(a) Combinations of CDs and Gasoline

(b) Indifference Curve

Four combinations of two goods, CDs and gasoline, are presented to the consumer in Figure 1(a). Preferring more to less, the consumer will clearly prefer *C* to *A, B,* and *D*. Points *B* and *D* are preferred to *A*, but the consumer has no clear preference between *B* and *D*. The consumer is indifferent between *B* and *D*. Figure 1(b) shows that all combinations of goods among which the consumer is indifferent lie along an indifference curve.

Combination	CDs	Gallons of Gasoline
A	1	1
B	2	1
C	2	2
D	1	2

combination C is preferred to D because one more CD is obtained with no loss of gas. Combinations B and D are preferred to A; however, it is not obvious whether B is preferred to D or D is preferred to B.

Let's assume that the consumer has no preference between B and D. We thus say that the consumer is **indifferent** between combination B (2 CDs and 1 gallon of gas) and combination D (1 CD and 2 gallons of gas). Connecting points B and D, as in Figure 1(b), produces an indifference curve. An **indifference curve** shows all the combinations of two goods that the consumer is indifferent among, or, in other words, an indifference curve shows all the combinations of goods that will give the consumer the same level of total utility.

The quantity of goods increases as the distance from the origin increases. Thus, any combination lying on the indifference curve (like B or D) is preferred to any combination falling below the curve, or closer to the origin (like A). Any combination appearing above the curve, or farther from the origin (like C), is preferred to any combination lying on the curve.

indifferent: lacking any preference

indifference curve: a curve showing all combinations of two goods that the consumer is indifferent among

1.a. The Shape of Indifference Curves

The most reasonable shape for an indifference curve is a downward slope from left to right, indicating that as less of one good is consumed, more of another good is consumed. Indifference curves are not likely to be vertical, horizontal, or upward sloping. They do not touch the axes, and they do not touch each other.

An indifference curve that is a vertical line, like the one labeled I_v in Figure 2(a), would mean that the consumer is indifferent to combinations B and A. For most goods this will not be the case, because combination B provides more of one good with no less of the other good.

Similarly, horizontal indifference curves, such as line I_h in Figure 2(b), are ruled out for most goods. People are not likely to be indifferent between combinations A and B along the horizontal curve, since B provides more of one good with no less of the other good than A.

An upward-sloping curve, such as I_u in Figure 2(c), would mean that the consumer is indifferent between a combination of goods that provides less of everything

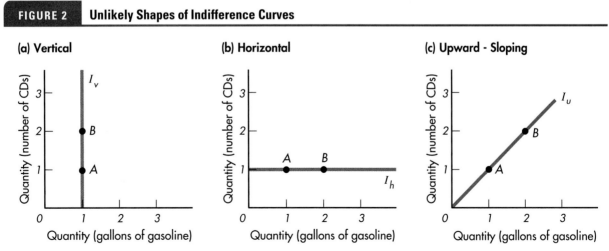

FIGURE 2   Unlikely Shapes of Indifference Curves

(a) Vertical

(b) Horizontal

(c) Upward - Sloping

A vertical indifference curve, as in Figure 2(a), would violate the condition that more is preferred to less, as would a horizontal indifference curve, as in Figure 2(b), or an upward-sloping curve, as in Figure 2(c). Thus, indifference curves are not likely to have any of these shapes.

FIGURE 3   Bowed-In Indifference Curve

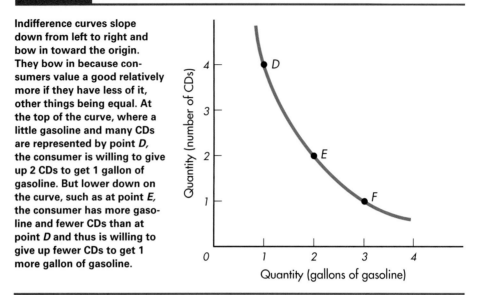

Indifference curves slope down from left to right and bow in toward the origin. They bow in because consumers value a good relatively more if they have less of it, other things being equal. At the top of the curve, where a little gasoline and many CDs are represented by point *D,* the consumer is willing to give up 2 CDs to get 1 gallon of gasoline. But lower down on the curve, such as at point *E,* the consumer has more gasoline and fewer CDs than at point *D* and thus is willing to give up fewer CDs to get 1 more gallon of gasoline.

and a combination that provides more of everything (compare points *A* and *B*). Rational consumers tend to prefer more to less.

1.b. The Slope of Indifference Curves

The slope, or steepness, of indifference curves is determined by consumer preferences. The amount of one good that a consumer must give up to get an additional unit of the other good and remain equally satisfied changes as the consumer trades off one good for the other. The less a consumer has of a good, the more the consumer values an additional unit of that good. This preference is shown by an indifference curve that bows in toward the origin, like the curve shown in Figure 3. A consumer

FIGURE 4   Indifference Curves Do Not Cross

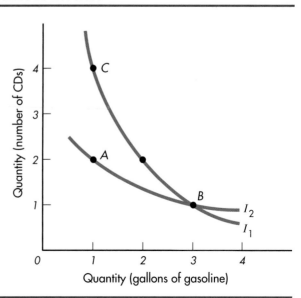

If two indifference curves intersected, such as at point *B,* then the consumer would be indifferent among all points on each curve. But point *C* clearly provides more CDs than point *A* and no less gasoline, so the consumer will prefer *C* to *A.* If the consumer prefers more to less, the indifference curves will not cross.

FIGURE 5 | **Indifference Map**

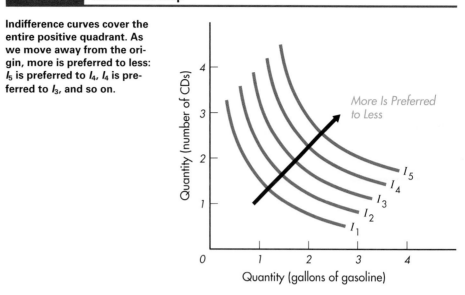

Indifference curves cover the entire positive quadrant. As we move away from the origin, more is preferred to less: I_5 is preferred to I_4, I_4 is preferred to I_3, and so on.

who has 4 CDs and 1 gallon of gasoline (point *D*) may be willing to give up 2 CDs for 1 more gallon of gasoline, moving from *D* to *E*. But a consumer who has only 2 CDs may be willing to give up only 1 CD to get that additional gallon of gasoline. This preference is shown as the move from *E* to *F*.

1.c. Indifference Curves Cannot Cross

Indifference curves do not intersect. If the curves crossed, two combinations of goods that clearly are not equally preferred by the consumer would seem to be equally preferred. According to Figure 4, the consumer is indifferent between *A* and *B* along indifference curve I_2 and indifferent between *B* and *C* along indifference curve I_1. Thus, the consumer appears to be indifferent among *A, B,* and *C*. Combination *C*, however, offers more CDs and no less gasoline than combination *A*. Clearly, the consumer, preferring more to less, will prefer *C* to *A*. Thus, indifference curves are not allowed to cross.

1.d. An Indifference Map

indifference map: a complete set of indifference curves

An **indifference map**, located in the positive quadrant of a graph, indicates the consumer's preferences among all combinations of goods and services. The farther from the origin an indifference curve is, the more the combinations of goods along that curve are preferred. The arrow in Figure 5 indicates the ordering of preferences: I_2 is preferred to I_1; I_3 is preferred to I_2 and I_1; I_4 is preferred to I_3, I_2, and I_1; and so on.

2. Budget Constraint _____

The indifference map reveals only the combinations of goods and services that a consumer prefers or is indifferent among—what the consumer is *willing* to buy. It does not tell us what the consumer is *able* to buy. Consumers' income levels or budgets limit the amount that they can purchase. Let's suppose a consumer has allocated \$6 to spend on gas and CDs. Figure 6 shows the **budget line**, a line giving all the combinations of goods that a consumer with a given budget can buy at given prices.

budget line: a line showing all the combinations of goods that can be purchased with a given level of income

FIGURE 6 | The Budget Line

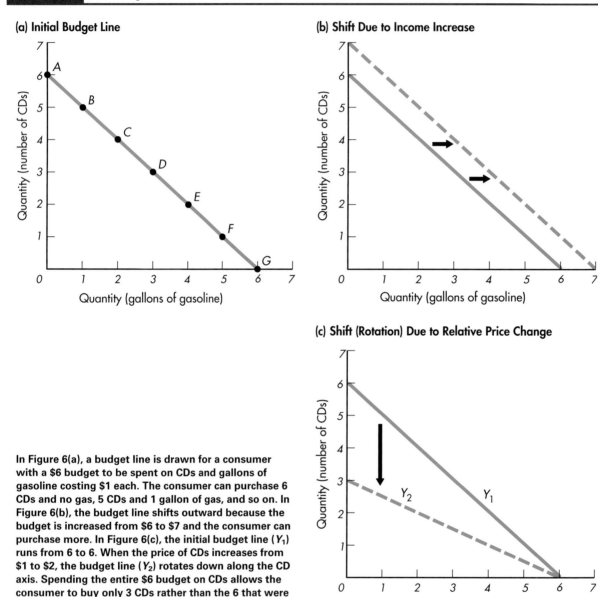

(a) Initial Budget Line

(b) Shift Due to Income Increase

(c) Shift (Rotation) Due to Relative Price Change

In Figure 6(a), a budget line is drawn for a consumer with a $6 budget to be spent on CDs and gallons of gasoline costing $1 each. The consumer can purchase 6 CDs and no gas, 5 CDs and 1 gallon of gas, and so on. In Figure 6(b), the budget line shifts outward because the budget is increased from $6 to $7 and the consumer can purchase more. In Figure 6(c), the initial budget line (Y_1) runs from 6 to 6. When the price of CDs increases from $1 to $2, the budget line ($Y_2$) rotates down along the CD axis. Spending the entire $6 budget on CDs allows the consumer to buy only 3 CDs rather than the 6 that were obtained at the per unit price of $1.

Anywhere along the budget line in Figure 6(a), the consumer is spending $6. When the price of CDs is $1 and the price of gas is $1 per gallon, the consumer can choose among several different combinations of CDs and gas that add up to $6. If only CDs are purchased, 6 CDs can be purchased (point *A*). If only gas is purchased, 6 gallons of gas can be purchased (point *G*). At point *B*, 5 CDs and 1 gallon of gas can be purchased. At point *C*, 4 CDs and 2 gallons of gas can be purchased. At point *F*, 1 CD and 5 gallons of gas can be purchased.

An increase in the consumer's income or budget is shown as an outward shift of the budget line. Figure 6(b) shows an increase in income from $6 to $7. The budget line shifts out to the line running from 7 to 7. A change in income or in the consumer's budget causes a parallel shift of the budget line.

A change in the price of one of the goods causes the budget line to rotate. For example, with a budget of $6 and the prices of both CDs and gas at $1, we have the budget line Y_1 in Figure 6(c). If the price of CDs rises to $2, only 3 CDs can be purchased if the entire budget is spent on CDs. As a result, the budget line Y_2 is flatter, running from 3 on the vertical axis to 6 on the horizontal axis. Conversely, a rise in the price of gas would cause the budget line to become steeper.

3. Consumer Equilibrium

Putting the budget line on the indifference map allows us to determine the one combination of goods and services that the consumer is both *willing* and *able* to purchase. Any combination of goods that lies on or below the budget line is within the consumer's budget. Which combination will the consumer choose in order to yield the greatest satisfaction (utility)?

The budget line in Figure 7 indicates that most of the combinations on indifference curve I_1 and point C on indifference curve I_2 are attainable. Combinations on indifference curve I_3 are preferred to combinations on I_2, but the consumer is *not able* to buy combinations on I_3 because they cost more than the consumer's budget. Therefore, point C represents the maximum level of satisfaction, or utility, available to the consumer. Point C is the point where the budget line is tangent to (just touches) the indifference curve.

FIGURE 7   **Consumer Equilibrium**

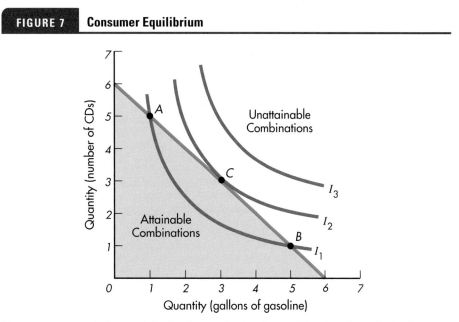

The consumer maximizes satisfaction by purchasing the combination of goods that is on the indifference curve farthest from the origin but attainable given the consumer's budget. The combinations along I_1 are attainable, but so are the combinations that lie above I_1. Combinations beyond the budget line, such as those along I_3, cost more than the consumer's budget. Point *C*, where the indifference curve I_2 just touches, or is tangent to, the budget line, is the chosen combination and the point of consumer equilibrium. *Source:* Adapted from David G. Myers, *The Pursuit of Happiness* (New York: William Morrow, 1992).

Summary

- Indifference curves show all combinations of two goods that give the consumer the same level of total utility. *§1*
- An indifference map is a complete set of indifference curves filling up the positive quadrant of a graph. *§1.d*
- The indifference curve indicates what the consumer is willing to buy. The budget line indicates what the consumer is able to buy. Together they determine the combinations of goods that the consumer is both willing and able to buy. *§1, 2*
- Consumer equilibrium occurs at the point where the budget line just touches, or is tangent to, an indifference curve. *§3*

Key Terms

indifferent *§1*

indifference curve *§1*

indifference map *§1.d*

budget line *§2*

Exercises

1. Use these combinations for parts a and b:

Combination	Clothes	Food
A	1 basket	1 pound
B	1 basket	2 pounds
C	1 basket	3 pounds
D	2 baskets	1 pound
E	2 baskets	2 pounds
F	2 baskets	3 pounds
G	3 baskets	1 pound
H	3 baskets	2 pounds
I	3 baskets	3 pounds

a. If more is preferred to less, which combinations are clearly preferred to other combinations? Rank the combinations in the order of preference.

b. Some clothes-food combinations cannot be clearly ranked. Why not?

2. Explain why two indifference curves cannot cross.

3. Using the data that follow, plot two demand curves for cake. Then explain what could have led to the shift of the demand curve.

I. Price of Cake	Quantity of Cake Demanded	II. Price of Cake	Quantity of Cake Demanded
$1	10	$1	14
$2	8	$2	10
$3	4	$3	8
$4	3	$4	6
$5	1	$5	5

chapter

8

Supply: The Costs of Doing Business

I n the previous chapter, we looked closely at demand. We learned that the demand for any one item comes from individuals choosing to allocate their limited income so as to maximize their happiness or satisfaction. We noted that demand changes when prices of related goods, income, expectations, and tastes and preferences change. In this chapter, we examine supply. We find that supply comes from the firms' desire to make money, and we learn what causes supply to change. ■

Fundamental Questions

1. **What is the law of diminishing marginal returns?**

2. **What is the relationship between costs and output in the short run?**

3. **What is the relationship between costs and output in the long run?**

1. Firms and Production

A firm hires labor, purchases materials, rents buildings and land, and spends money on advertising and other selling activities. The quantity of resources used and the amount spent on selling activities depends on how productive these activities are—how much they contribute to the value of the firm. In general, the more the firm wants to supply, the more resources it must have.

1.a. The Relationship Between Output and Resources

Supply is the quantities of output that sellers are willing and able to offer for sale at every price. To determine how much to supply at any given price, sellers must know how much it costs to supply each quantity. The relationship between output and costs depends on the relationship between output and the resources used to create that output. Such a relationship is illustrated in Table 1. A firm has a fixed space—say a 500-square-foot retail space in a mall. The quantity of items offered for sale—supplied—depends on the number of employees. One employee can display 30 items, two employees 65 items, three employees 100 items, and so on in that 500-square-foot space in one day's time. If we look at this in terms of how much each new employee adds, we see that the first employee adds 30, the second adds 35, the third adds another 35, the fourth 30, and so on. In other words, as the shop adds an additional employee, the number of items available for sale rises at an increasing rate, then at a decreasing rate, and finally, adding more employees actually causes output to decline.

1.b. Diminishing Marginal Returns

This relationship between employees and output is called the **law of diminishing marginal returns.** Too many employees on the floor at one time trying to display and sell items makes them inefficient—they get in one another's way.

Diminishing marginal returns are not unique to this small retail shop. In every instance where *increasing* amounts of one resource are combined with *fixed*

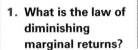

1. What is the law of diminishing marginal returns?

law of diminishing marginal returns: when successive equal amounts of a variable resource are combined with a fixed amount of another resource, marginal increases in output that can be attributed to each additional unit of the variable resource will eventually decline

Business owners combine quantities of land, labor, and capital to produce goods and services in the most profitable way. Technological improvements help them produce a larger quantity of goods and services at lower cost, thereby increasing profitability. Here, an Egyptian woman supervises several automatic sewing machines. One woman can produce the same quantity with the automatic machines 100 times faster than when the sewing was done by hand. Employing more people may speed up production; eventually, however, employing more people will not speed up production and could actually retard production as the workers interfere with each other's tasks.

TABLE 1	Diminishing Marginal Returns

As another employee is added to the 500 square feet of space, the number of items that can be displayed and offered for sale rises—initially at an accelerating rate, then at a decreasing rate—and eventually declines. The seventh employee adds no additional output, and the eighth causes output to decline.

Number of Employees	Total Output
0	0
1	30
2	65
3	100
4	130
5	150
6	160
7	160
8	140

amounts of other resources, the additional output that can be produced initially increases rapidly, then increases more slowly, and eventually decreases. A major manufacturing entity like General Motors will experience diminishing marginal returns as it hires more employees for one of its car divisions—eventually too many employees could reduce the number of cars produced.

Diminishing marginal returns applies anywhere that resources whose quantities can be changed are combined with resources whose quantities are fixed. For instance, it limits the effort to improve passenger safety during collisions by installing air bags in cars. The first air bag added to a car increases protection considerably. The second adds an element of safety, particularly for the front-seat passenger. But additional air bags provide little additional protection and eventually would lessen protection as they interfered with one another. As successive units of the variable resource, air bags, are placed on the fixed resource, the car, the additional amount of protection provided by each air bag declines.

RECAP

1. According to the law of diminishing marginal returns, as successive units of a variable resource are added to the fixed resources, the additional output produced will initially rise but will eventually decline.

2. Diminishing marginal returns occur because the efficiency of variable resources depends on the quantity of the fixed resources.

2. From Production to Costs _____

Every firm (and every individual and nation as well) is faced with the law of diminishing marginal returns. The law is, in fact, a physical property, not an economic one, but it is important to economics because it defines the relationship between costs and output in the short run.

TABLE 2 Costs

As employees are added, costs rise at a rate of $1,000 per employee. The cost of the building space is fixed at $6,000. Adding the cost of employees, variable cost, to the fixed cost gives the total cost, noted in column 5. Column 3 shows total variable costs, the costs of the resources that vary as output changes—employees in our example. Column 4 shows the fixed costs, the costs that do not change as output changes—selling space in the mall in our example. The last column shows total costs, the sum of variable and fixed costs.

Employees	Total Output	Variable Costs (Costs of Employees)	Fixed Cost (Cost of 500 Square Feet)	Total Cost (Fixed + Variable)
0	0	0	$6,000	$6,000
1	30	$1,000	$6,000	$7,000
2	65	$2,000	$6,000	$8,000
3	100	$3,000	$6,000	$9,000
4	130	$4,000	$6,000	$10,000
5	150	$5,000	$6,000	$11,000
6	160	$6,000	$6,000	$12,000
7	160	$7,000	$6,000	$13,000

2.a. The Calculation of Costs

Suppose, in our example of Table 1, that the cost per employee is $1,000 per month and the rent for the 500 square feet is $6,000 per month. Table 2 shows the costs for the different number of employees used.

We are most interested in the relationship between output and costs because we want to know the costs of supplying output. So we need to convert Table 2 into one that shows the relationship between output and costs. Table 3 shows what happens to costs as output increases in 30-unit increments.

TABLE 3 Output and Costs

Column 1 shows output in 30-unit increments. Column 2 shows the cost of employees—variable costs—that are required to increase output by 30 units. Column 3 is the fixed cost—the rent of the 500 square feet. Column 4 is total cost. Column 5 is average total cost (column 4 divided by column 1).

Total Output	Variable Costs	Fixed Costs	Total Cost	Average Total Cost
0	0	$6,000	$6,000	—
30	$1,000	$6,000	$7,000	$7,000/30 = $233
60	$1,920	$6,000	$7,920	$7,920/60 = $132
90	$2,820	$6,000	$8,820	$8,820/90 = $ 98
120	$3,745	$6,000	$9,745	$9,745/120 = $ 81
150	$5,000	$6,000	$11,000	$11,000/150 = $ 73.33
160*	$6,000	$6,000	$12,000	$12,000/160 = $ 75
160*	$7,000	$6,000	$13,000	$13,000/160 = $ 81

* Given 500 square feet, the most that can be produced is 160, according to Table 1.

FIGURE 1 Average Total Costs

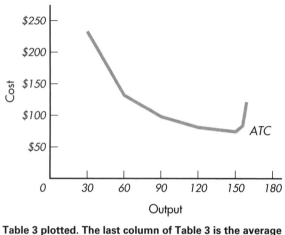

Table 3 plotted. The last column of Table 3 is the average total costs, *ATC*. Plotting the cost on the vertical axis and the quantity of output on the horizontal axis generates the *ATC* curve.

average total cost (ATC): the per unit cost, derived by dividing total cost by the quantity of output

marginal cost (MC): the change in cost caused by a change in output, derived by dividing the change in total cost by the change in the quantity of output

The last column in Table 3, **average total cost (ATC),** is plotted in Figure 1 with output measured on the horizontal axis and average total cost on the vertical axis. Figure 1 clearly shows that the average-total-cost curve is U-shaped. The "U" occurs because of the law of diminishing marginal returns. As the business increases its output, costs rise, but they rise slowly at first and then rapidly. This means that cost per unit declines initially and then rises, creating a U shape.

2.a.1. Marginal Cost   Average total cost is calculated by dividing total cost by output—*ATC* is cost per unit of output, shown in column 5 of Table 3. What does it cost to supply another unit? **Marginal cost (MC),** is the additional cost of supply-

TABLE 4 Marginal Cost

Column 4 is marginal cost, the change in total cost divided by the change in quantity. The change in total cost is the difference between row 1, column 2 and row 2, column 2; then between row 2, column 2 and row 3, column 2, and so on. The change in output is the difference between row 1, column 1 and row 2, column 1; and so on. The last column in the table shows the relationship between marginal cost and average total cost. If *MC* is above *ATC, ATC* is rising; if *MC* is below *ATC, ATC* is declining; *MC* = *ATC* at the minimum point of *ATC*.

Total Output, Q	Total Costs, TC	Average Total Cost, TC/Q	Marginal Cost, Change in TC/Change in Q	Relationship Between Average Total Cost and Marginal Cost
0	$6,000	—	—	
30	$7,000	$7,000/30 = $233	$1,000/30 = $ 33	*MC<ATC: ATC* falling
60	$7,920	$7,920/60 = $132	$920/30 = $ 31	*MC<ATC: ATC* falling
90	$8,820	$8,820/90 = $ 98	$900/30 = $ 30	*MC<ATC: ATC* falling
120	$9,745	$9,745/120 = $ 81	$925/30 = $ 31	*MC<ATC: ATC* falling
150	$11,000	$11,000/150 = $ 73.33	$1,255/30 = $ 41.83	*MC<ATC: ATC* falling
160*	$12,000	$12,000/160 = $ 75	$1000/10 = $100*	*MC>ATC: ATC* rising

* Notice that we increase output by only 10 units by adding the sixth worker.

ing another unit of output and is calculated by dividing the change in total cost by the change in output. A change in output, say moving from 0 to 30, causes costs to rise, from $6,000 to $7,000; the change in total cost of $1,000 divided by the change in output of 30 gives the marginal cost of $33. Table 4 presents marginal cost.

In column 5 of Table 4, the relationship between average total cost and marginal cost is noted. When marginal cost is greater than average total cost, average total cost rises—the *ATC* curve slopes up. When marginal cost is below average total cost, then average total cost falls—the *ATC* curve slopes down. Marginal cost equals average total cost when average total cost is at its minimum.

This relationship between marginal and average exists for any average and marginal measurement. Consider your grades, for example. Think of the grade point average (GPA) that you get each semester as your *marginal* GPA, and your cumulative, or overall, GPA as your *average* GPA. You can see the relationship between marginal and average by considering what will happen to your cumulative GPA if this semester's GPA is less than your cumulative GPA. Suppose your GPA this semester is 3.0 for 16 hours of classes and your cumulative GPA, not including this semester, is 3.5 for 48 hours of classes. Your marginal (this semester's) GPA will be less than your average GPA. Thus, when your marginal GPA is added to your average GPA, your average GPA falls, from 3.5 to 3.375. *As long as the marginal is less than the average, the average falls.* If your GPA this semester is 4.0 instead of 3.0, your average GPA will rise from 3.5 to 3.625. *As long as the marginal is greater than the average, the average rises.*

Whenever marginal is less than average, the average is falling, and whenever marginal is greater than average, the average is rising.

If the average is falling when marginal is below average and rising when marginal is above average, then marginal and average can be the same only when the average is neither rising nor falling. If your GPA this semester is 3.5 and your cumulative GPA up to this semester was 3.5, then your new GPA will be 3.5. Average and marginal are the same when the average is constant. This occurs only when the average curve is at its maximum or minimum point.

We know that if marginal is less than average, average is falling, and if marginal is above average, average is rising. This is illustrated in Figure 2. Note that the

FIGURE 2   Average Total and Marginal Cost

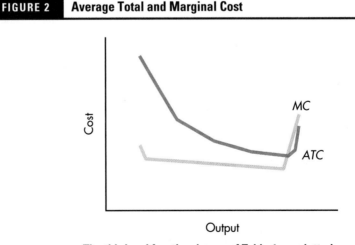

The third and fourth columns of Table 4 are plotted. The relationship between the *ATC* and the *MC* is shown in column 5. If *MC* is less than *ATC*, *ATC* is falling; if *MC* is above *ATC*, then *ATC* is rising. *MC* = *ATC* at the minimum point of *ATC*.

total costs (TC): the expenses that a business has in supplying goods and/or services

total fixed costs (TFC): payments to resources whose quantities cannot be changed during a fixed period of time—the short run

total variable costs (TVC): payments for additional resources used as output increases

average fixed cost (AFC): the total fixed cost divided by total output

marginal-cost curve lies below the average-total-cost curve while *ATC* is declining, and that the marginal-cost curve lies above the average-total-cost curve while *ATC* is rising. Finally, notice how the marginal-cost curve intersects the average-total-cost curve at the minimum point of the average-total-cost curve. This always occurs: The marginal-cost curve intersects the average-total-cost curve at its minimum point. So when *MC* equals *ATC,* it is the firm's most efficient point—the firm could not supply at a lower cost per unit of output.

2.b. Definition of Costs

We have mentioned several terms associated with costs—total costs, variable costs, fixed costs, marginal costs, and average total costs. Let us discuss these terms to be sure we understand what they measure. **Total costs (TC)** are the expenses that a business has in supplying goods and/or services. They are the payments to land, labor, and capital. These costs can be divided into variable and fixed costs. **Total fixed costs (TFC)** are payments to resources whose quantities cannot be changed during a fixed period of time—the short run. Typically, fixed costs include rent and some of the payments to workers, suppliers, and others; often there are fixed contracts, such as labor contracts and rental agreements, that cannot be changed for a period of time such as a year. Other costs are variable. **Total variable costs (TVC)** are payments for additional resources used as output increases. For instance, we need more electricity and water when we sell more goods and services. We may need to

Economic Insight

Overhead

Economists classify costs as either fixed or variable. Fixed costs do not change as the volume of production changes. Variable costs, on the other hand, depend on the volume of production. In business, costs are often classified into overhead and direct operating costs. Overhead costs are those that are not directly attributable to the production process. They include items such as taxes, insurance premiums, managerial or administrative salaries, paperwork, the cost of electricity not used in the production process (such as electricity used in the administration building), and so on. Overhead costs can be either fixed or variable. Insurance premiums, taxes, and managerial salaries are fixed costs. They must be paid regardless of how much is produced. Electricity used to operate the production process is a variable cost, increasing as the quantity of output produced is increased. The electricity used in a classroom would be a direct cost whereas the electricity used in the administration building would be an indirect cost.

Statements like "we need to spread the overhead" sound somewhat like the concept of declining average fixed costs—fixed cost per unit of output declines as output rises. But overhead may also include variable costs. Thus, the need to "spread the overhead" refers to reducing the total costs that are not directly attributable to the production process. The more a firm can keep its overhead costs the same and increase its volume of production, the more overhead costs look and act like fixed costs. The higher the percentage of overhead costs that are fixed, the more closely related the economist's and the businessperson's classifications will be. But the two are not—and are not meant to be—the same.

The different classifications provide different information. The economist is interested in the decision to produce—whether to produce at all, and how much to produce. This is the information provided by fixed and variable costs. The businessperson is interested in attributing costs to different activities, that is, in determining whether the business is running as cost-efficiently as it can. The classification of costs into overhead and direct provides this information.

employ workers for more hours or hire temporary workers. These are variable costs. Average costs are simply the costs per unit of output. **Average fixed cost (*AFC*)** is the total fixed cost divided by total output. **Average variable cost (*AVC*)** is total variable cost divided by total output. **Short-run average total cost (*SRATC*)** is the total cost divided by the total output when the firm is operating in the short run—that is, when at least one resource is fixed. Marginal costs are the changes in costs that occur as output is changed.

RECAP

1. Costs are the full opportunity costs of resources used to create and sell goods and services.

2. Economists like to discuss costs in terms of fixed and variable costs. Fixed costs are those costs that a firm has in creating and or offering for sale goods and services that do not change as quantities of a good or service offered for sale change. Variable costs are costs that do increase as quantities offered for sale increase.

3. Average costs are total costs divided by the quantity of a good or service being offered for sale—the per unit costs.

4. Marginal costs are the incremental costs, the change in costs that results from a change in the quantity of a good or service offered for sale.

3. The Long Run

The short run refers to any period of time (a day, a month, a year, or whatever) during which at least one resource cannot be changed—its quality or quantity is fixed. In the long run, everything is variable—nothing is fixed. A firm can choose to relocate, build a new plant, rent more floor space, acquire heavy equipment, go out of business, enter a new business, or undertake any other action in the long run.

Perhaps the most important difference between the short run and the long run is that the law of diminishing marginal returns does *not* apply when all resources are variable. Diminishing returns applies only when quantities of variable resources are combined with a fixed resource. In the long run, everything is variable.

If you look at Table 1 and ask, "What could happen if we had more employees and a bigger space in the mall or if we went to a different mall?" you then are thinking about the long run. Table 5 shows the long-run version of Table 1. Recall that in Table 1, the floor space was fixed—our fixed resource. Now, in the long run, nothing is fixed; the owner of the firm is able to choose how many employees to hire, how big a building to rent, and how many other resources to acquire; all combinations are possible in the long run. Table 5 illustrates the difference between the short run and the long run. The short run would be the output combinations available in any one column of the table, such as the first two columns—number of employees and 500 square feet of retail space. In the long run, any size of space can be used by any number of employees to supply output.

The way you read Table 5 is to look at the number of employees and the amount of floor space to find how much output can be supplied. For instance, with 1 employee and 500 square feet of space, 30 units of output can be supplied. Doubling the size of the firm—2 employees and 1,000 square feet—means that 250 units of output can be supplied; doubling both resources again, to 4 employees and 2,000 square feet, means that 640 units of output can be supplied. So, doubling the size of the firm initially allows the firm to supply more than double the output.

TABLE 5	Long Run or Planning Period			
	Floor Space (sq. ft.)			
Employees	500	1,000	1,500	2,000
0	0	0	0	0
1	**30**	100	250	340
2	65	**250**	360	450
3	100	360	480	570
4	130	440	580	**640**
5	150	500	650	710
6	160	540	700	760
7	160	550	720	790
8	140	540	680	800

If the firm can double its resources (and thus double its costs) but more than double its output, it is experiencing what is called *economies of scale*—getting more efficient as it gets bigger. Conversely, if the firm doubles its resources but does not double its output, then it is experiencing *diseconomies of scale*—it is getting less efficient as it gets bigger.

3.a. Economies of Scale and Long-Run Cost Curves

3. What is the relationship between costs and output in the long run?

scale: size; all resources change when scale changes

If the size of the firm doubles when the quantities of all resources are doubled, this is called doubling the scale of the firm. **Scale** means size. In the long run, a firm has many sizes to choose from—those given in Table 5, for instance. The short run requires that scale be fixed—only one or a few resources can be changed. If we are looking at Table 5 and we decide that column 4 is what we think will be the best, then we sign a lease for 1,500 square feet. At this point, we are in the short run. We can vary the number of employees, but we are stuck with the 1,500 square feet of space until the rental agreement can be revised.

The relationship between the long run and the short run is illustrated in Figure 3. For each size or scale, the firm can vary the quantities of the variable resources and supply different quantities of output. Notice in Figure 3(a) that there are several short-run cost curves. Each curve has a minimum point at a different quantity of output. This quantity of output is the scale or size of the firm in the short run. Whether the firm supplies less or more, its costs are defined by the short-run cost curve. The firm cannot change floor space except in the long run—that is, the firm cannot move from $SRATC_1$ to $SRATC_2$ except in the long run. In the long run, the firm can select any of the short-run curves to operate on. But once it has selected the size, it is in the short run and operates along just one of the short-run average-total-cost curves.

Each short-run cost curve is drawn for a particular quantity of building space—that is, a specific column in Table 5. Once the space is selected, the firm brings together combinations of the other resources to supply output. If a small quantity of the building space is selected, the firm might operate along $SRATC_1$. If the firm selects a slightly larger quantity of the fixed resource, then it will be able to operate along $SRATC_2$. With a still larger quantity, the firm can operate along $SRATC_3$, $SRATC_4$, $SRATC_5$, or some other short-run average-total-cost curve.

In the long run, the firm can choose any of the $SRATC$ curves. All it needs to do is choose the level of output it wants to supply and then select the least-cost combination

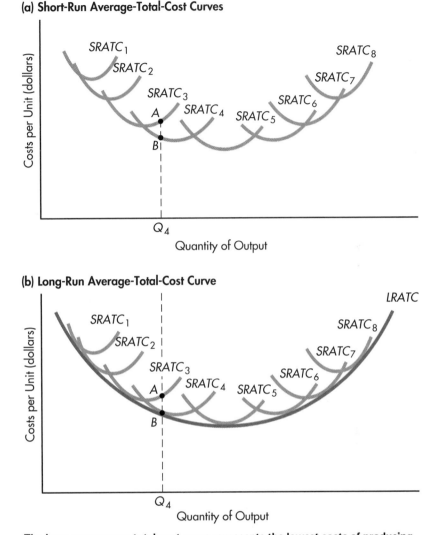

(a) Short-Run Average-Total-Cost Curves

Costs per Unit (dollars)

$SRATC_1$ $SRATC_8$
$SRATC_2$ $SRATC_7$
$SRATC_3$ $SRATC_6$
A $SRATC_4$ $SRATC_5$
B

Q_4

Quantity of Output

(b) Long-Run Average-Total-Cost Curve

Costs per Unit (dollars)

LRATC

$SRATC_1$ $SRATC_8$
$SRATC_2$ $SRATC_7$
$SRATC_3$ $SRATC_6$
A $SRATC_4$ $SRATC_5$
B

Q_4
Quantity of Output

The long-run average-total-cost curve represents the lowest costs of producing any level of output when all resources are variable. Short-run average-total-cost curves represent the lowest costs of producing any level of output in the short run, when at least one of the resources is fixed. Figure 3(a) shows the possible *SRATC* curves facing a firm. Figure 3(b) shows the *LRATC* curve, which connects the minimum cost of producing each level of output. Notice that the *SRATC* curves need not indicate the lowest costs of producing in the long run. If the short run is characterized by *SRATC*$_3$, then quantity Q_4 can be produced at point A. But if some of the fixed resources are allowed to change, managers can shift to *SRATC*$_4$ and produce at point B.

long-run average-total-cost curve (*LRATC*): the lowest-cost combination of resources with which each level of output is produced when all resources are variable

of resources with which to reach that level. All possible least-cost combinations are represented in Figure 3(b) by a curve that just touches each *SRATC* curve. This curve is the **long-run average-total-cost curve (*LRATC*)**—the lowest cost per unit of output for every level of output when all resources are variable.

The distinction between the short run and the long run is that everything is variable in the long run. In the short run, something is fixed. The long-run average-total-cost

economies of scale: the decrease in per unit costs as the quantity of production increases and all resources are variable

diseconomies of scale: the increase in per unit costs as the quantity of production increases and all resources are variable

constant returns to scale: unit costs remain constant as the quantity of production is increased and all resources are variable

curve gets its shape from **economies of scale** and **diseconomies of scale.** Economies of scale account for the downward-sloping portion of the long-run average-total-cost curve. The firm is able to become more efficient as it gets larger—the cost of supplying each unit of output decreases as the firm gets bigger. Diseconomies of scale account for the upward-sloping portion; the firm becomes less efficient as it gets larger. If the cost per unit of output is constant as output rises, there are **constant returns to scale.**

Figures 4(a), 4(b), and 4(c) show three possible shapes of a long-run average-total-cost curve. Figure 4(a) is the usual U shape, indicating that economies of scale are followed by constant returns to scale and then diseconomies of scale. Figure 4(b) is a curve indicating only economies of scale. Figure 4(c) is a curve indicating only constant returns to scale. Each of these long-run average-total-cost curves would connect several short-run average-total-cost curves, as shown in Figures 4(d), 4(e), and 4(f).

3.b. The Reasons for Economies and Diseconomies of Scale

As a firm gets larger, its employees may be able to specialize based on comparative advantage, making the firm more efficient. Firms that can specialize more as they grow larger may be able to realize economies of scale. Specialization of marketing, sales, pricing, and research, for example, allows some employees to focus on research while others focus on marketing and still others focus on sales and on pricing. For instance, when Mrs. Fields Cookies was just starting out, it was a one-person operation in northern California. When it moved to Park City, Utah, it was a multi-person operation with cookie outlets throughout most of the western United States. As it grew, the company was able to achieve economies of scale. Its employees could specialize more in just one activity, its advertising did not have to increase as its size increased, and larger machinery enabled it to produce a larger quantity of dough in a shorter period of time.

In 2001 and 2002, oil companies merged—Exxon and Mobil, Chevron and Texaco. The firms resulting from these combinations became two of the largest companies in the world. The reason for merging given by the chief executive officers of these companies was to achieve economies of scale. They believed that having larger oil fields and more refining capability would enable their employees to specialize more and their drilling and refining equipment to be more fully utilized. In 2005 and 2006, Verizon and MCI finalized a merger. The executives of these firms also claimed that there would be economies of scale. Economies of scale is the most common reason given for mergers.

Economies of scale may also result from the use of larger machines that are more efficient than smaller ones. Large blast furnaces can produce more than twice as much steel per hour as smaller furnaces, but they do not cost twice as much to build or operate. Large electric-power generators are more efficient (more output per quantity of resource) than small ones.

Size, however, does not automatically improve efficiency. The specialization that comes with large size often requires the addition of specialized managers. A 10 percent increase in the number of employees may require an increase of greater than 10 percent in the number of managers. A manager to supervise the other managers is needed. Paperwork increases. Meetings are held more often. The amount of time and labor that are not devoted to producing output grows. In other words, the overhead increases. In addition, it becomes increasingly difficult for the CEO to coordinate the activities of all the division heads and for the division heads to communicate with one another. In this way, size can cause diseconomies of scale.

FIGURE 4 | Long-Run and Short-Run Cost Curves

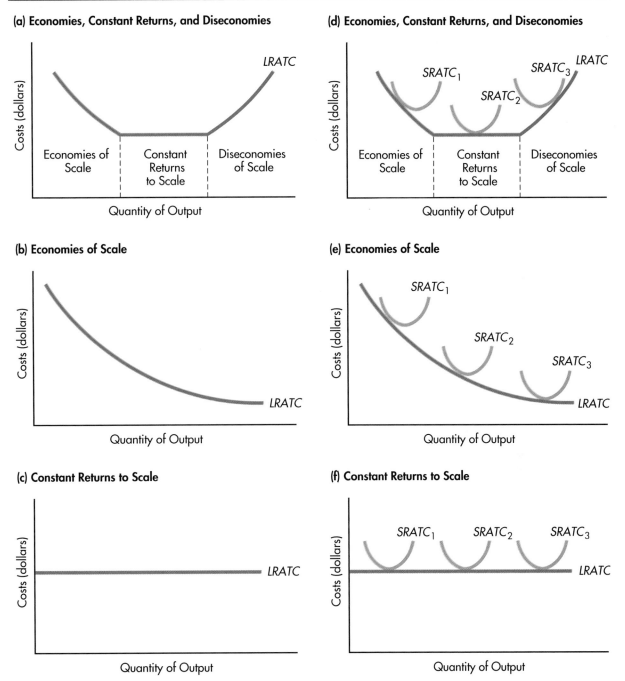

(a) Economies, Constant Returns, and Diseconomies

(b) Economies of Scale

(c) Constant Returns to Scale

(d) Economies, Constant Returns, and Diseconomies

(e) Economies of Scale

(f) Constant Returns to Scale

In Figure 4(a), a U-shaped *LRATC* curve is shown. The downward-sloping portion is due to economies of scale, the horizontal portion to constant returns to scale, and the upward-sloping portion to diseconomies of scale. In Figure 4(b), only economies of scale are experienced. In Figure 4(c), only constant returns to scale are experienced. The *LRATC* curve connects the lowest cost for each level of output given by the *SRATC* curves. Three such short-run cost curves for each *LRATC* curve are illustrated in Figures 4(d), 4(e), and 4(f).

Again consider what happened to Mrs. Fields Cookies. As the company continued to add more and more outlets, its CEO could not keep track of everything. Assistant managers, vice presidents, and other executives were hired. The company had achieved economies of scale by utilizing larger equipment in its central location in Park City. But as more and more outlets were added at greater distances from Park City, the distribution of the cookie dough became more and more costly. At some size, most companies reach a point where diseconomies of scale set in. Mrs. Fields Cookies went beyond that point and eventually was sold, dismantled, and reorganized.

3.c. The Minimum Efficient Scale

The law of diminishing marginal returns applies to every resource, every firm, and every industry. Whether there are economies of scale, diseconomies of scale, constant returns to scale, or some combination of these depends on the industry under consideration. No law dictates that an industry will have economies of scale, eventually followed by diseconomies of scale, although that seems to be the typical pattern. Theoretically, it is possible for an industry to experience only diseconomies of scale, only economies of scale, or only constant returns to scale.

Most industries experience both economies and diseconomies of scale. As we noted earlier, Mrs. Fields Cookies was able to achieve economies of scale as it grew from one location to 700. But the company then faced diseconomies of scale because the cookie dough was produced at one location and distributed to the outlets in premixed packages. The dough factory was large, but the distribution of dough produced diseconomies of scale that worsened as outlets farther and farther away from the factory were opened.

minimum efficient scale (MES): the minimum point of the long-run average-total-cost curve; the output level at which the cost per unit of output is the lowest

If the long-run average-total-cost curve reaches a minimum, the level of output at which the minimum occurs is called the **minimum efficient scale (MES).** The *MES* varies from industry to industry; it is significantly smaller, for instance, in the production of shoes than it is in the production of cigarettes. A shoe is made by stretching leather around a mold, sewing the leather, and fitting and attaching the soles and insoles. The process requires one worker to operate just two or three machines at a time. Thus, increasing the quantity of shoes made per hour requires more building space, more workers, more leather, and more machines. The cost per shoe declines for the first few shoes made per hour, but rises thereafter. Cigarettes, on the other hand, can be rolled in a machine that can produce several thousand per hour. Producing 100 cigarettes an hour is more costly per cigarette than producing 100,000 per hour.

3.d. The Planning Horizon

The long run is referred to as a planning horizon because the firm has not committed to a specific size. It has all options available to it. In determining the size or scale to select, the manager must look at expected demand and expected costs of production and then select the size that appears to be the most profitable. Once a scale is selected, the firm is operating in the short run, since at least one of the resources is fixed. If you look back at Figure 3(b), you see that the long-run average-total-cost curve does *not* connect the minimum points of each of the short-run average-total-cost curves ($SRATC_1$, $SRATC_2$, and so on). The reason is that the minimum point of a short-run average-total-cost curve is not necessarily the lowest-cost method of producing a given level of output. For instance, point A on $SRATC_3$ is much higher than point B on $SRATC_4$, but output level Q_4 could be produced at either A or B. When the quantities of all resources can be varied, the choices open to the manager are much greater than when only one or a few of the resources are variable. The manager can select the lowest cost for a given output level in the long run.

RECAP

1. Many industries are characterized by U-shaped long-run average-total-cost curves, but they need not be. There is no law dictating a U-shaped *LRATC* curve. The law of diminishing marginal returns dictates the U shape of the short-run cost curves.

2. The long-run average-total-cost curve gets its U shape from economies and diseconomies of scale.

3. The minimum efficient scale (*MES*) is the output of a firm that is at the minimum point of a long-run average-total-cost curve.

4. The *MES* varies from industry to industry. Some industries, like the electric-power distribution industry, have large economies of scale and a large *MES*. Other industries, like the fast-food industry, have a relatively small *MES*.

5. Economies of scale may result from specialization and technology. Diseconomies of scale may occur because coordination and communication become more difficult as size increases.

6. The long run is the planning period—the firm can select any size. Once a size is selected, contracts are signed, and resources are acquired, the firm is in the short run.

Summary

1. What is the law of diminishing marginal returns?

- According to the law of diminishing marginal returns, when successive equal amounts of a variable resource are combined with a fixed amount of another resource, there will be a point beyond which the extra or marginal product that can be attributed to each additional unit of the variable resource will decline. *§1.b*

2. What is the relationship between costs and output in the short run?

- Average total cost is the cost per unit of output—total costs divided by the quantity of output produced. *§2.a*

- The U shape of the short-run average-total-cost curve is due to the law of diminishing marginal returns. *§2.a*

- Marginal cost is the change in total cost divided by the change in output. *§2.a.1*

- Average total cost falls when marginal cost is less than average total cost and rise when marginal cost is greater than average total cost. Thus, the marginal-cost curve intersects the average-total-cost curve at the minimum point of the average total cost curve. *§2.a.1*

- Costs rise as a firm supplies more output. The law of diminishing marginal returns dictates that costs rise at a decreasing and then an increasing rate as output rises. *§2.a, 2.b*

- Fixed costs are costs that do not vary as the quantity of goods produced varies. *§2.b*

- Variable costs rise as the quantity of goods produced rises. *§2.b*

- Total costs are the sum of fixed and variable costs. *§2.b*

3. What is the relationship between costs and output in the long run?

- The short run is a period of time just short enough that the quantity of at least one of the resources cannot be altered. *§3*

- Everything is variable in the long run. *§3*

- Economies of scale occur when the size of the firm is doubled and the output that the firm can supply more than doubles. *§3.a*

- Diseconomies of scale occur when the size of the firm is doubled and the output that the firm can supply increases by less than double. *§3.a*

- The U shape of the long-run average-total-cost curve is due to economies and diseconomies of scale. *§3.a*

- Constant returns to scale occur when increases in output lead to no changes in unit costs and the quantities of all resources are variable. *§3.a*

- Specialization can lead to economies of scale—larger size enables people to specialize in the jobs where they use their comparative advantage. *§3.b*

- The minimum efficient scale (*MES*) occurs at the minimum point of the long-run average-total-cost curve. *§3.c*

- The long run is the planning horizon, where all resources are variable. Once a size or scale is selected, the firm is operating in the short run. *§3.d*

Key Terms

law of diminishing marginal returns *§1.b*

average total cost (*ATC*) *§2.a*

marginal cost (*MC*) *§2.a.1*

total costs (*TC*) *§2.b*

total fixed costs (*TFC*) *§2.b*

total variable costs (*TVC*) *§2.b*

average fixed cost (*AFC*) *§2.b*

average variable cost (*AVC*) *§2.b*

short-run average total cost (*SRATC*) *§2.b*

scale *§3.a*

long-run average total cost (*LRATC*) *§3.a*

economies of scale *§3.a*

diseconomies of scale *§3.a*

constant returns to scale *§3.a*

minimum efficient scale (*MES*) *§3.c*

Exercises

1. Use the following information to determine the total fixed costs, total variable costs, average fixed costs, average variable costs, average total costs, and marginal costs.

Total Output	Costs	TFC	TVC	AFC	AVC	ATC	MC
0	$100						
1	$150						
2	$225						
3	$230						
4	$300						
5	$400						

2. Use the following table to answer the questions listed below.

Total Output	Cost	TFC	TVC	AFC	AVC	ATC	MC
0	$ 20						
10	$ 40						
20	$ 60						
30	$ 90						
40	$120						
50	$180						
60	$280						

a. Calculate the total fixed costs, total variable costs, average fixed costs, average variable costs, average total costs, and marginal costs.

b. Plot each of the cost curves.

c. At what quantity of output does marginal cost equal average total cost and average variable cost?

3. Using the table in exercise 1, explain what happens to *ATC* when *MC > ATC, MC < ATC,* and *MC = ATC.*

4. Using the table in exercise 2, find the quantity where *MC = ATC.* Find the quantity where *ATC* is at its minimum. Find the quantity that is the most efficient operating point for the firm.

5. Describe some conditions that might cause large firms to experience inefficiencies that small firms would not experience.

6. What is the minimum efficient scale? Why would different industries have different minimum efficient scales?

7. Describe the relation between marginal and average costs. Describe the relation between marginal and average fixed costs and between marginal and average variable costs.

8. Explain why the *ATC* and *MC* curves are U-shaped.

9. Explain why the short-run marginal-cost curve must intersect the short-run average-total-cost curve at the minimum point of the *ATC.* Does the marginal-cost curve intersect the average-variable-cost curve at its minimum point? What about the average-fixed-cost curve? Why doesn't the marginal-cost curve also intersect the average-fixed-cost curve at its minimum point?

10. Why does the minimum point of the average-total-cost curve show the quantity at which the firm is most efficiently supplying output in the short run?

11. Consider a firm with a fixed-size production facility as described by its existing cost curves.

    a. Explain what would happen to those cost curves if a mandatory health insurance program is imposed on all firms.

    b. What would happen to the cost curves if the plan required the firm to provide a health insurance program for each employee worth 10 percent of the employee's salary?

    c. How would that plan compare to one that requires each firm to provide a $100,000 group program that would cover all employees in the firm, no matter what the number of employees was?

12. Does the following statement make sense? "You made a real blunder. The $600 you paid for repairs is worth more than the car."

13. Explain the statement "We had to increase our volume to spread the overhead."

14. Three college students are considering operating a tutoring business in economics. This business would require that they give up their current jobs at the student recreation center, which pay $6,000 per year. A fully equipped facility can be leased at a cost of $8,000 per year. Additional costs are $1,000 a year for insurance and $.50 per person per hour for materials and supplies. Their services would be priced at $10 per hour per person.

    a. What are fixed costs?
    b. What are variable costs?
    c. What is the marginal cost?
    d. How many students would it take to break even?

15. Express Mail offers overnight delivery to customers. It is attempting to come to some conclusion on whether to expand its facilities or not. Currently its fixed costs are $2 million per month and its variable costs are $2 per package. It charges $12 per package and has a monthly volume of 2 million packages. If it expands, its fixed costs will rise by $1 million and its variable costs will fall to $1.50 per package. Should it expand?

Merge or Die

Lloyd's List
February 12, 2003

Tanker operators were yesterday urged to merge or pool resources in order to survive in a market where oil companies are looking for economies of scale in leasing.

Charterers of tankers and product carriers seeking to lower their risks need high quality tonnage, owned by large companies with low-risk profiles. For smaller family-operated tanker owners there is the choice of evolving or being eaten. To evolve they can merge with other smaller players or join one of many vessel-pool organisations. Alex Papachristidis-Bove, president and chartering manager of Seatramp Tankers, told London's Tanker Operator conference yesterday: "Big fleets rule! Oil companies need high quality tonnage so large stable companies will continue to lead the market.

"Large companies have lower risk so show accountability and quality. They can grow because they are attractive to investment."

He believed this highly fragmented market was moving towards consolidation because the oil industry had already gone through the process. He said Scandinavian companies—Bergesen, Fredriksen, Stolt-Nielsen and Moller—were leading the market, with strong evidence that Greek players and US companies were building fleets through acquisition.

Joining forces meant "optimising vessel utilisation to satisfy a broader market base" and it provided a "stronger asset base for accessing capital and renewing fleets," he said.

Mr. Papachristidis-Bove also thought consolidation led to economies of scale and "profitability from service rather than opportunistic sale and purchase activity." But if tanker owners wanted to stay independent they could benefit from economies of scale through vessel pools.

"Small companies need to pool resources," added Alex Staring, director of operations of Tanker International, a pool of 44 very large crude carriers owned by Moller, Euronav, Oldendorff and OSG.

Some of the advantages included improved cash flow, as earnings were distributed across pool members, and lower voyage waiting times, which could reduce waiting costs to $400 per journey.

Martyn Wingrove

Merge or die? What does this mean? According to the article, oil shippers need to experience economies of scale, and to do this, the smaller companies must get larger. A quick way to get larger is to merge with another firm. When Chevron merged with Texaco, the Chevron Company immediately became nearly twice as large. It had twice as many resources: twice as much oil available in reserves, twice as many refining stations, and twice as many retail gas stations.

Why is it necessary to be large? If, as the article states, there are economies of scale, then the larger firms will have a cost advantage over the smaller firms. Being twice as large means that the firm's costs have less than doubled—it can produce twice as much at less than twice the cost. Consider the figure shown here, which shows a long-run average-total-cost curve with economies of scale and two short-run average-total-cost curves, one for a smaller firm, $SRATC_S$, and one for a larger firm, $SRATC_L$. The larger firm has experienced economies of scale and therefore has costs that are significantly lower than the smaller firm's. In addition, because it has lower costs, the larger entity can offer a price significantly below the price that the smaller firm can offer. The larger firm's lowest price would be P_L, whereas the smaller firm's best price would be P_S.

The article points out how small companies might be able to experience economies of scale and remain small: The companies can form vessel pools. Vessel pools enable the small companies in the pool to ship oil at the same cost as one larger company. However, there can be problems in such arrangements with who gets what and with attempts to have one's partners do more work and pay more costs but receive less profit. When these problems become too large, firms will merge rather than forming sharing arrangements. But, at least theoretically, it is possible to remain small and independent and form sharing arrangements to obtain economies of scale. This type of sharing arrangement is common; high-tech firms located in Silicon Valley because other high-tech firms were there, and so the firms had a large supply of highly skilled labor available. The firms achieved economies of scale without being large themselves. If the transport firms can pool vessels in such a way that each firm can become more specialized, then the vessel pools may result in economies of scale.

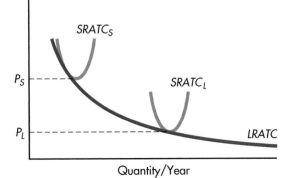

Quantity/Year

The Mechanics of Going from Production to Costs

1. Output and Resources

The costs of producing and selling output depend on the productivity of resources. The more home runs a baseball player hits in a season, the more valuable he is as a resource. The more welding equipment an employee for Lincoln Electric can make each month, the more valuable he or she is as an employee. They are more valuable because they generate more money for their employers; the baseball team sells more tickets, and Lincoln Electric sells more equipment. The material in this chapter is based on the relationship between resources, output, and costs; in this appendix, we look more closely at this relationship.

total physical product (*TPP*): the maximum output that can be produced when successive units of a variable resource are added to fixed amounts of other resources

The **total physical product (*TPP*)** (also called *total product*) schedule and curve show how the quantity of the variable resource (employees) and the output produced are related for a certain quantity of the fixed resource. In Figure 1(a), with total output measured on the vertical axis and the number of employees measured on the horizontal axis, the combinations of output and employees trace out the *TPP* curve. Both the table and the *TPP* curve in Figure 1(a) show that as additional units of the variable resource are used with a fixed amount of another resource, total output at first rises, initially quite rapidly and then more slowly, and then declines. As the first units of the variable resource (employees) are used, each additional employee can provide more output. But at some point, there are "too many chefs stirring the broth," and each additional employee adds only a little to total output. Eventually, an additional employee actually detracts from the productivity of the other employees.

average physical product (*APP*): output per unit of resource

marginal physical product (*MPP*): the additional quantity that is produced when one additional unit of a resource is used in combination with the same quantities of all other resources

The law of diminishing marginal returns shows up more clearly with the average-product and marginal-product curves, also called the **average-physical-product (*APP*)** and **marginal-physical-product (*MPP*)** curves. The average-product schedule is calculated by dividing total output by the number of employees:

$$APP = \frac{\text{total output}}{\text{number of employees}}$$

Plotting *APP* gives us Figure 1(b), a curve that rises quite rapidly and then slowly declines. The marginal-product schedule is the change in total output divided by the change in the quantity of variable resources (the number of employees):

$$MPP = \frac{\text{change in output}}{\text{change in number of employees}}$$

FIGURE 1 | Total, Average, and Marginal Product

The table provides plotting data for the graphs. Total, average, and marginal product schedules and curves are shown. The total physical product schedule, shown in Figure 1(a), is derived by fixing one resource.

The average and marginal physical product schedules are calculated from the total physical product schedule. Average is total output divided by number of employees; marginal is the change in the total output divided by the change in the number of employees.

Number of Employees	Total Output	Average Physical Product	Marginal Physical Product
0	0	—	—
1	100	100	100
2	250	125	150
3	360	120	110
4	440	110	80
5	500	100	60
6	540	90	40
7	550	78.6	10
8	540	67.5	−10

(a) The Total Physical Product Curve

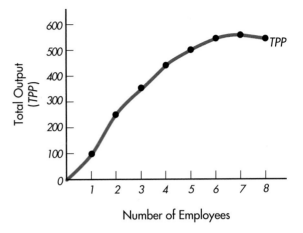

(b) The Average Physical Product Curve

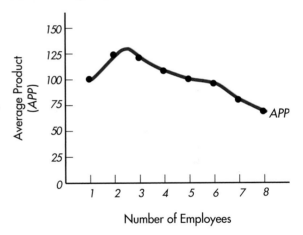

(c) The Marginal Physical Product Curve

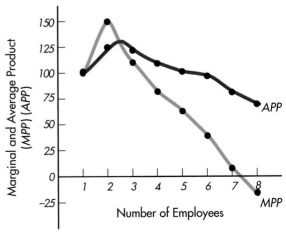

The *MPP* is shown in Figure 1(c); it is drawn with the *APP* curve so that we can compare *MPP* and *APP*. The *MPP* curve initially rises more rapidly than the *APP* curve, then falls more rapidly than *APP,* and eventually reaches zero. When *MPP* is zero or negative, the additional variable resources are actually detracting from the production of other resources, causing output to decline.

You can see the relationship between average physical product and marginal physical product in Figure 1(c). As long as the *MPP* is greater than the *APP,* the *APP* is rising; whenever the *MPP* is less than the *APP,* the *APP* is falling. Thus, the *MPP* and the *APP* are equal at the peak or top of the *APP* curve. This occurs at between two and three employees.

2. Productivity and Costs _____

The total-, average-, and marginal-physical-product schedules and curves show the relationship between quantities of resources (inputs) and quantities of output. To examine the costs of doing business rather than the physical production relationships, we must measure the costs of the resources and define how many resources are needed to supply output. This is done in the following table. The cost per

---

FIGURE 2   **Average and Marginal Costs**

Quantity of Output	Total Cost	Average Cost	Marginal Cost
100	$1,000	$10	$ 10
250	$2,000	$ 8	$ 6.7
360	$3,000	$ 8.33	$ 9.1
440	$4,000	$ 9	$ 12.5
500	$5,000	$10	$ 16.7
540	$6,000	$11.1	$ 25
550	$7,000	$12.7	$100

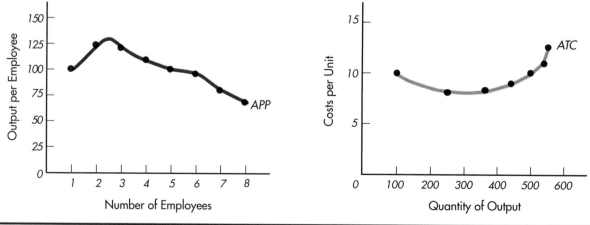

(a) Compare *APP* with *ATC*

(continues)

FIGURE 2 Average and Marginal Costs

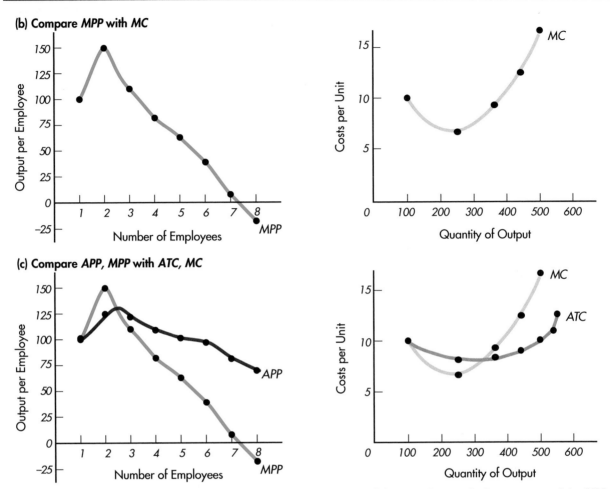

Figure 2(a) shows the average-total-cost curve and the *APP* curve. Figure 2(b) shows the marginal-cost curve and the *MPP* curve. The cost curves are described as U-shaped, the product curves as hump-shaped. The shapes of the curves are due to the law of diminishing marginal returns. Figure 2(c) shows the relationship between average and marginal curves.

employee is $1,000. We can calculate total costs by multiplying $1,000 times the number of employees.

Notice that as output rises, costs also rise, but output rises by a larger amount at first and then by smaller and smaller amounts, whereas costs rise by a constant $1,000. This means that the cost per unit, or average cost, falls and then rises. In addition, the incremental cost, or cost per additional unit of output, initially declines and then rises. This is shown in Figure 2(b).

In Figure 2(a), the *APP* and *ATC* curves are drawn. In Figure 2(b), the *MPP* and *MC* curves are drawn. Whereas the *MPP* and *APP* curves might be described as hump-shaped, the *MC* and *ATC* curves are described as U-shaped. The shapes are due to the law of diminishing marginal returns and what is measured on the axes. In the case of the *APP* and *MPP* curves, output is on the vertical axis and number of employees is on the horizontal axis. In the case of the *ATC* and *MC* curves, costs are on the vertical axis and output on the horizontal axis. You can see that the relationship between marginal and average applies to both the product and the cost curves: Whenever the marginal is above the average, the average is rising, and whenever the marginal is below the average, the average is falling. Note also that $MPP = APP$ at the maximum point of the APP curve, while $MC = ATC$ at the minimum point on the ATC curve.

Number of Employees	Total Output	Total Cost
0	0	$0
1	100	$1,000
2	250	$2,000
3	360	$3,000
4	440	$4,000
5	500	$5,000
6	540	$6,000
7	550	$7,000

Summary

1. The productivity curves—*TPP, APP,* and *MPP*—reflect the law of diminishing marginal returns. They show that as a variable resource is increased, output initially rises at an accelerating pace, then at a slower pace, and then may eventually decline. *§1*

2. The shape of the productivity curves and the U shape of the cost curves are the result of the law of diminishing marginal returns. *§2*

Key Terms

total physical product (*TPP*) *§1*   average physical product (*APP*) *§1*   marginal physical product (*MPP*) *§1*

Exercise

1. Explain the relationship between the shapes of the productivity curves and the shape of the cost curves. Specifically, compare the *APP* curve with the *ATC* curve and the *MPP* curve with the *MC* curve.

chapter

9

Profit Maximization

You start a business. To get it off the ground, you use your own money and perhaps the money of friends and relatives. Then you put in many hours to get the business on a successful footing. If the business provides enough to match what you could have earned working for someone else (taking into account the joy of owning your own business), you consider it a success. Similarly, when you purchase the stock of a publicly traded company, you are expecting that the firm will pay you more than you could have gotten using that money in another way. If it does, then the investment is a success. We measure the success of a business in terms of profit. ■

? Fundamental Questions

1. How do firms decide how much to supply?

2. What is a market structure?

3. What is the difference between economic profit and accounting profit?

4. What is the role of economic profit in allocating resources?

1. Profit Maximization _____

?

1. How do firms decide how much to supply?

Economists assume that the primary goal of a business is to make a profit. Profit is total revenue less total costs. We know from the previous chapter that total costs are the sum of the costs of resources—land, labor, and capital. Total revenue is the quantity of goods and services sold multiplied by the price at which they are sold, PQ. So, profit $= PQ -$ cost of land, labor, and capital.

1.a. Calculation of Total Profit

Consider Table 1, in which column 1 is total output (Q), column 2 is price (P), column 3 is total revenue (TR), and total cost (TC) is listed in column 4. Profit, the difference between total revenue and total cost, is listed in column 5. For each row, column 4 is subtracted from column 3 to get profit. According to Table 1, profit is maximized if the firm supplies either 7 or 8 units of output.

1.a.1. Marginal Revenue and Marginal Cost
Another way to discover the profit-maximizing quantity of output is to compare marginal revenue and marginal cost. Look at columns 6 and 7—the two are equal at quantity 8, the profit-maximizing quantity.

Why would marginal revenue equal marginal cost when profit is maximized? *Marginal cost* is the additional cost of producing one more unit of output. *Marginal revenue* is the additional revenue obtained from selling one more unit of output. If producing and selling one more unit of output increases costs less than it increases revenue—that is, if marginal cost is less than marginal revenue—then producing and selling that unit will increase profit. Conversely, if the production of one more unit costs more than the revenue obtained from the sale of the unit, then producing and selling that unit will decrease profit. When marginal revenue is greater than marginal cost, producing more will increase profit. Conversely, when marginal

| TABLE 1 | Profit Maximization |

1	2	3	4	5	6	7
Total Output (Q)	Price (P)	Total Revenue (TR)	Total Cost (TC)	Profit (TR − TC)	Marginal Revenue (MR)	Marginal Cost (MC)
0	$1,900	$ 0	$1,000	−$1,000		
1	1,700	1,700	2,000	−300	$1,700	$1,000
2	1,650	3,300	2,800	500	1,600	800
3	1,600	4,800	3,500	1,300	1,500	700
4	1,550	6,200	4,000	2,200	1,400	500
5	1,500	7,500	4,500	3,000	1,300	500
6	1,450	8,700	5,200	3,500	1,200	700
7	1,400	9,800	6,000	3,800	1,100	800
8	1,350	10,800	7,000	3,800	1,000	1,000
9	1,300	11,700	9,000	2,700	900	2,000

Brisk Business in Measuring Economic Profit

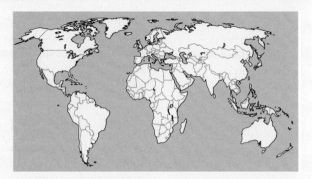

The recognition that economic profit provides valuable information has led to a brisk business in management consulting. Spurred by lucrative fees, consultants are scrambling to help companies install new performance measures to replace the old standbys such as earnings per share (EPS) and return on equity (ROE). The dominant firm in this business is Stern-Stewart, promoting its Economic Value Added (EVA). Another major firm in the business is the Boston Consulting Group, whose experts combine cash flow return on investment (CFROI) with a concept that they call Total Business Return. McKinsey uses the term *economic profit,* while the LEK/Alcar Group pushes for Shareholder Value Added (SVA). These are far from the only consulting firms in the business, but they are the dominant ones.

The value of measuring economic profit as well as accounting profit has become increasingly clear to executives in recent years. A change in focus from accounting profit to economic profit has altered the behavior of many firms.* Before Quaker Oats adopted economic profit as its measure of performance, the manager of Quaker's granola bar plant in Danville, Illinois, used long production runs to turn out the various sizes of bars in order to minimize downtime and setup costs. This bolstered operating profits, but also resulted in huge inventories of bars that sat in a warehouse until they were shipped to customers. Inventory is not free, however, since money is tied up in it. Thus, when the company charged the manager for the inventory—that is, for the money tied up in inventory—he switched to short production runs, which reduced net operating profits but increased economic profit. Prior to focusing on economic profit, the Coca-Cola Company shipped its soft drink syrup to bottlers in stainless steel cans that could be used over and over. The problem was that the steel cans were expensive; they required significant amounts of capital. When the company began focusing on economic profit, it sold the stainless steel cans and used cardboard instead. The cardboard increased operating costs, but by less than the cost of capital declined. As a result, economic profit rose.

*These examples are from Al Ehrbar, *EVA: The Real Key to Creating Wealth* (New York: John Wiley & Sons, 1999), p. 141; *www.eva.com.* Reprinted with permission of John Wiley & Sons, Inc.

---

revenue is less than marginal cost, producing more will lower profit. Thus, *profit is at a maximum when marginal revenue equals marginal cost.*[1]

Consider column 6 of Table 1, where marginal revenue is listed.

Marginal revenue = change in total revenue/change in total output

$$MR = \Delta TR/\Delta Q$$

Marginal revenue (*MR*) is calculated by subtracting total revenue in column 3, row 1 from total revenue in column 3, row 2 and dividing that by the change in units of output from row 1 to row 2. Do this calculation for each pair of rows and you derive marginal revenue.

It is important to understand the relationship between demand, price, and marginal revenue. The law of demand says that for a firm to increase the quantity it sells,

---

[1] You might notice that profit is at the maximum level for quantities of 7 and 8 units. This occurs because we are dealing with integers, 1, 2, 3, and so on, when discussing output. There would be a unique quantity for which profit is at its maximum level if we could divide the quantities into very small units instead of having to deal with integers. That unique quantity would be where $MR = MC$. Thus, we always choose the quantity at which marginal revenue and marginal cost are the same as the profit-maximizing quantity.

the price has to be reduced. Consider Table 1 again. Notice that at a price of $1,700, 1 unit of output is sold. Then, when the price is reduced to $1,650, 2 units of output are sold: unit 1 at $1,650 plus unit 2 at $1,650 means total revenue of $3,300. The firm did not sell the first unit at $1,700 and then the second at $1,650; it sold both at the lower price, $1,650 each. Since total revenue changed from $1,700 to $3,300, marginal revenue is $1,600. (Change in total revenue is $3,300 − $1,700 = $1,600, and change in output is 1 unit). MR = $1,600, but the price is $1,650. Because the firm had to set the price of units 1 and 2 at $1,650 apiece in order to sell 2 units, it lost $50 by reducing the price of the first unit from $1,700 to $1,650 and gained $1,650 by selling the second unit. The marginal revenue is less than the price.

Column 7 of the table lists marginal cost. We know from the previous chapter that

Marginal cost = change in total cost/change in total output
$$MC = \Delta TC/\Delta Q$$

Marginal cost is calculated by subtracting the total cost in row 1 from that in row 2, and dividing that by the change in units of output.

To summarize: comparing marginal revenue and marginal cost determines whether the firm needs to supply more or less in order to maximize profit. The amount the firm should supply to maximize profit is indicated by the quantity at which marginal revenue equals marginal cost.

1.b. The Graphics of Profit Maximization

We now know that profit is maximized by finding the quantity where *MR* = *MC*. Let's show how this works graphically. We will use the cost curves derived in the previous chapter and put them together with the demand and marginal-revenue curves derived from Table 1 to illustrate how a firm maximizes profit. In Figure 1 we have drawn the

FIGURE 1	**Profit Maximization**

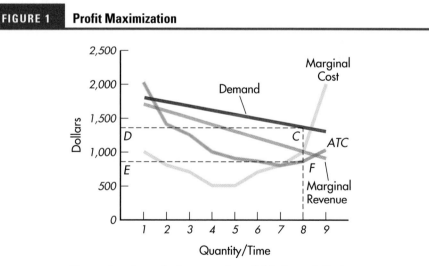

Demand and marginal revenue from Table 1 are plotted along with the *ATC* and *MC* curves from the previous chapter. The profit-maximizing quantity is given by where *MR* = *MC*. Profit is found by drawing a vertical line up from quantity 8 to *ATC* and then up to demand. A horizontal line from *ATC* over to the axis shows total cost, 08*FE*. Continuing the horizontal line to demand and then over to the axis shows total revenue, 08*CD*. Subtracting total cost from total revenue yields total profit, *EFCD*.

demand and marginal-revenue curves and then added the average-total-cost and marginal-cost curves.

The profit-maximizing quantity of output is given by the quantity at which *MR = MC*. This occurs at quantity 8. If we then draw a vertical line up from the quantity 8 to the *ATC* curve, we have identified the cost per unit of output. If we then draw a horizontal line from the *ATC* curve over to the axis, we will have identified total cost, 08*EF*. This rectangle is cost per unit of output, or *ATC*, multiplied by the number of units of output, 8. Because *ATC* is total cost divided by *Q*, multiplying it by *Q* just leaves total cost [$ATC \times Q$ = (total cost/Q) $\times Q$ = total cost].

Back to the quantity of 8 and the vertical line. We drew it up to the *ATC* curve. Now continue up to the demand curve. That identifies the price—it is the price that consumers will pay for that quantity. If we draw a horizontal line from the demand curve over to the axis, we will have identified total revenue, $P \times 8$ = 08*CD*. Subtracting total cost 08*EF* from 08*CD* leaves the rectangle *EFCD*. This is total profit.

<table>
<tr><td>**RECAP**</td><td>1. The profit-maximizing rule is to produce where marginal revenue equals marginal cost.

2. Firms will supply a quantity given by the equality between marginal revenue and marginal cost.</td></tr>
</table>

?

2. What is a market structure?

2. Selling Environments or Market Structure

Profit maximization occurs when marginal revenue equals marginal cost. This means that to identify the output level that a firm will supply, all we need to do is to identify its marginal revenue and marginal cost. This is actually not very difficult, since in the short run every firm, no matter what its size, no matter what its location, and no matter what it does, has a relationship between costs and output dictated by the law of diminishing marginal returns. Thus, the cost curves can have only one shape—the U shape. The marginal-cost curve is a U-shaped curve with output on the horizontal axis and costs on the vertical axis.

The shape of the marginal-revenue curve depends on the shape of the demand curve. The shape of the demand curve depends on the type of selling environment in which a firm operates. So let's look at selling environments and define the demand and marginal-revenue curves for firms in each type of environment.

2.a. Characteristics of the Market Structures

The selling environment in which a firm produces and sells its product, called a *market structure,* is defined by three characteristics:

- The number of firms that make up the market. In some industries, such as agriculture, there are hundreds of individual firms. In others, such as the photofinishing supplies industry, there are very few firms.

- The ease with which new firms may enter the market and begin producing the good or service. It is relatively easy and inexpensive to enter the desktop publishing business, but it is much more costly and difficult to start a new airline.

- The degree to which the products produced by the firms are different. Firms may sell identical products—wheat is wheat no matter which farm it comes

| TABLE 2 | Characteristics of Market Structures |

Market Structure	Number of Firms	Entry Condition	Product Type
Perfect competition	Very large number	Easy	Standardized
Monopoly	One	No entry possible	Only one product
Monopolistic competition	Large number	Easy	Differentiated
Oligopoly	Few	Impeded	Standardized or differentiated

from—or differentiated products—McDonald's Big Mac is not identical to Jack-in-the-Box's Ciabatta burger.

Table 2 summarizes the characteristics of the four market structures.

2.a.1. Perfect Competition   Perfect competition is a market structure characterized by the following:

- A very large number of firms, so large that whatever any *one* firm does has no effect on the market
- Firms that produce an identical product
- Easy entry

In perfect competition, very large number of firms in the market means that consumers have many options when they are deciding where to purchase the good or service, and there is no cost to the consumer of going to a different seller. In this market structure, the product is identical, so consumers do not prefer one seller to another or one brand to another. In fact, there are no brands—only identical, generic products. The large number of sellers also means that any one seller is a very small part of the market, and so its actions will not affect the others. A single firm can sell everything it wants to at the market price, but it cannot try to increase price, and it won't lower price. If a single small firm tried to raise the price even a very small amount, consumers would simply switch to another seller—why pay even a penny more if you can simply turn around and get the identical item for a penny less? This situation is illustrated with a demand curve that is a horizontal line, as shown in Figure 2(a). Notice that when price goes above the existing market price, demand disappears—there is no demand except at that one price.

2.a.2. Monopoly   Monopoly is a market structure in which:

- There is just one firm.
- Entry by other firms is not possible.

In a monopoly, because there is only one firm, consumers have only one place to buy the good, and there are no close substitutes. The monopolist can do anything it wants, since consumers cannot go to another seller—anything, that is, as long as it earns a profit.

The demand curve facing the single firm in a monopoly is the market demand because the firm is the only supplier in the market. This is shown in Figure 2(b). Being the only producer, the monopolist must carefully consider what price to charge. Unlike a price increase in a perfectly competitive market, a price increase in a monopoly will not drive every customer to another producer. But if the price

FIGURE 2   The Demand Curve Facing an Individual Firm

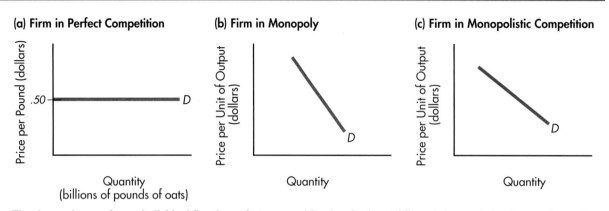

(a) Firm in Perfect Competition

(b) Firm in Monopoly

(c) Firm in Monopolistic Competition

The demand curve for an individual firm in perfect competition is a horizontal line at the market price, as shown in Figure 2(a). Figure 2(b) shows the market demand, which is the demand curve faced by a monopoly firm. The firm is the only supplier and thus faces the entire market demand. Figure 2(c) shows the downward-sloping demand curve faced by a firm in monopolistic competition. The curve slopes downward because of the differentiated nature of the products in the industry.

is too high, consumers will not buy the product. Even if a monopolist had something that was needed—say insulin or gasoline or electricity—consumers would quit buying it if the price got too high.

2.a.3. Monopolistic Competition   A monopolistically competitive market structure is characterized by the following:

- A large number of firms
- Easy entry
- Differentiated products

Product differentiation distinguishes a perfectly competitive market from a monopolistically competitive market. (In both, entry is easy and there are a large number of firms.) Even though there are many firms in a monopolistically competitive market structure, the demand curve faced by *any one firm* slopes downward, as in Figure 2(c). Because each product is slightly different from all other products, each firm is like a minimonopoly—the only producer of that specific product. The greater the differentiation among products, the less price-elastic the demand.

2.a.4. Oligopoly   In an oligopoly,

- There are few firms—more than one, but few enough so that each firm alone can affect the market.
- Product can be either differentiated or identical. Automobile producers constitute one oligopoly, steelmakers another.
- Entry is more difficult than entry into a perfectly competitive or monopolistically competitive market, but in contrast to monopoly, entry can occur.
- Firms are *interdependent,* and this interdependence distinguishes oligopoly from the other selling environments.

A cab driver in Tokyo dusts the rear seat of his cab prior to picking up passengers. Taxicabs are tightly regulated in Japan, having to serve specific districts and maintain specified quality standards. A particular company may have a government-created monopoly in a certain part of the city. Nevertheless, each cab company attempts to compete with other cab and limousine companies by providing extra service. Cleanliness and order are emphasized. Many cab drivers wear white gloves; others use feather dusters on the seats before each customer enters the cab; still others provide special music and other services.

The oligopolist faces a downward-sloping demand curve, but the shape of the curve depends on the behavior of competitors. Oligopoly is the most complicated of the market structure models to examine because there are so many behaviors that firms might display. Because of its diversity, many economists describe oligopoly as the most realistic of the market structure models.

2.b. Demand and Profit Maximization

Profit is maximized at the output level where marginal revenue and marginal cost are equal (MR = MC).

Does a perfectly competitive firm maximize profit in a different manner from a monopolist or a monopolistically competitive firm? The answer is not really. Each firm maximizes profit by finding the quantity where marginal revenue equals marginal cost ($MR = MC$) and then setting the price according to demand. The difference is that for a perfectly competitive firm, demand is a horizontal line—it is perfectly elastic. For the perfectly competitive firm, the only decision is what quantity to produce. The output choice of the perfectly competitive firm is shown in Figure 3(a). The perfectly elastic demand, a horizontal line at the market price, means that marginal revenue, demand, and price are the same. For firms that have a downward-sloping demand curve, marginal revenue lies below demand, as shown in Figure 3(b). Thus, the process of determining the profit-maximizing quantity of output to offer for sale is to find the quantity where $MR = MC$ and then determine what price consumers are willing and able to pay to purchase the quantity of output offered by the firm [tracing a vertical line up to demand, shown in Figure 3(b)]. That price is the profit-maximizing price, P^*.

FIGURE 3 — Choosing Price and Quantity to Maximize Profit

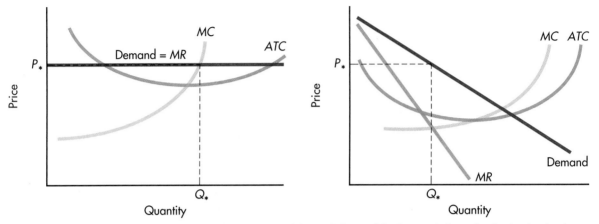

(a) Perfect Competition — Horizontal Demand

(b) Downward Sloping Demand

As shown in Figure 3(a), when the firm is perfectly competitive and demand for its goods is perfectly elastic, the demand and marginal revenue are the same. The firm maximizes profit by finding the quantity where $MR = MC$ and the price is the same as MR. As shown in Figure 3(b), when the firm is not perfectly competitive, the demand for its goods slopes down. As a result, marginal revenue is less than demand. The firm maximizes profit by finding the quantity where $MR = MC$ and then setting the price according to demand.

RECAP

1. Economists have identified four market structures: perfect competition, monopoly, monopolistic competition, and oligopoly.

2. Perfect competition is a market structure in which many firms are producing a nondifferentiated product and entry is easy. The demand curve for a perfectly competitive firm is a horizontal line at the market price. $P = MR$.

3. Monopoly is a market structure in which only one firm supplies the product and entry cannot occur. Demand is downward sloping, and the marginal-revenue curve lies below the demand curve. $P > MR$.

4. Monopolistic competition is a market structure in which many firms are producing differentiated products and entry is easy. The demand curve is downward sloping, and marginal revenue is less than demand and less than price. $P > MR$.

5. Oligopoly is a market structure in which a few firms are producing either standardized or differentiated products and entry is possible but not easy. The distinguishing characteristic of oligopoly is that the firms are interdependent. The shape of the demand curve depends on how the firms interact—what form their interdependence takes.

?

3. What is the difference between economic profit and accounting profit?

3. Measuring Economic Profit _____

We now know the mechanics of maximizing profit: Find the quantity where marginal revenue equals marginal cost, determine the price, and then subtract total cost from total revenue. Now let's be sure we understand what profit is. There are two measures of profit, accounting profit and economic profit.

3.a. Calculating Profit

accounting profit: net operating income

Accounting profit is net operating income, or

$$\text{Accounting profit} = PQ - \text{cost of land} - \text{cost of labor} - \text{cost of capital}$$

The difference between accounting profit and economic profit is the last term, cost of capital. Accounting profit measures the cost of capital as interest expense only. It does not include the cost of ownership, called **equity capital. Economic profit** includes all opportunity costs:

equity capital: ownership; funds investors or owners put into a firm

$$\text{Economic profit} = \text{accounting profit} - \text{cost of equity capital}$$

economic profit: accounting profit minus the cost of equity capital

To illustrate the difference between accounting profit and economic profit, let's look at a sole proprietorship, a pet grooming business. The owner of the business, Roberto Brawning, left his job at Intel, where he earned $80,000 a year, to start the pet grooming business. He used $50,000 of his own money and a loan of $100,000, which he agreed to pay back with 7 percent interest. His business is bringing in $100,000 a year. Brawning has rent and labor expenses of $30,000. So with the interest expense of $7,000 = (7%)($100,000), Brawning's accounting profit is

$$\$100,000 - \$30,000 - \$7,000 = \$63,000$$

This does not include all of Brawning's opportunity costs, since he gave up the job with Intel and he used $50,000 of his own money. He could have used this $50,000 for anything else—such as buying stock in Microsoft. Brawning's highest-valued alternative would have returned 8 percent to him last year. It is necessary to account for this $4,000 (8% × $50,000) as well as the $80,000 job he gave up to give a true picture of the success of the grooming business. This is what economic profit does. Brawning's economic profit is

$$\text{Accounting profit} - \text{cost of ownership: } \$63,000 - \$4,000$$
$$- \$80,000 = -\$21,000$$

If we changed the example slightly and said that Brawning really enjoys running his own business and puts a value of $28,000 on that enjoyment, then we must add that to the $100,000 the grooming business makes in revenue. In this case, the economic profit is positive, $7,000.

Accounting profit is always equal to or greater than economic profit. It is possible for economic profit to be negative and accounting profit positive. Only if there are no equity costs are economic and accounting profit the same; otherwise accounting profit is larger than economic profit.

$$\text{Economic profit} = \text{accounting profit} - (\text{cost of equity})(\text{amount of equity})$$

The calculation of accounting and economic costs is essentially the same for a large, publicly traded company as it is for the pet grooming business. Consider the following data taken from General Motors's annual income statement.

General Motors	Millions of Dollars
Sales	$193,518
Expenses	178,813
Interest expense	11,900
Net income	2,805
Cost of equity	44,235

According to the income statement, GM's accounting profit (called net income) is a positive $2,805 million. But to get a true picture of GM's performance, subtract the cost of equity capital:

$$\$2,805 - \$44,835 = -\$42,030$$

Economic profit is negative.

3.b. The Role of Economic Profit

?

4. **What is the role of economic profit in allocating resources?**

negative economic profit: total revenue is less than total costs, including opportunity costs

Economic profit allocates resources—it is a signal indicating whether resources would have a higher value in another use. When economic profit is negative, resources flow elsewhere; when it is positive, resources flow to the activity creating the profit.

3.b.1. Negative Economic Profit   **Negative economic profit** means that the resources used would have a higher value in another use. If total revenue does not pay for all costs, then owners don't get paid for their time, effort, and investments. When this occurs, the owners take their money and time and go elsewhere. If the economic profit of the pet grooming business is negative, the owner is not earning enough to pay for all of the opportunity costs. He would be better off selling the business or selling pieces of it and going to work for someone else. This is exactly the same as with GM. And in fact, GM discontinued the Oldsmobile brand in 2004, and sold assets including stakes in Fiat and Fuji Heavy Industries (Subaru), as well as its locomotive manufacturing business, in 2005.

zero economic profit: total revenue equals total costs, including opportunity costs

3.b.2 Zero Economic Profit   When total revenue exactly equals total cost, the firm is just breaking even—economic profit is zero. **Zero economic profit** might sound bad, but it is not. A zero economic profit simply means that the owners could not have expected to have done better elsewhere. The investors have no incentive to sell their business and purchase something else, since they would expect to earn no more than they are currently earning. Remember, accounting profit is greater than economic profit, so even if economic profit is zero, accounting profit is positive. The accounting profit that occurs when economic profit is zero is called **normal profit.**

normal profit: the accounting profit that corresponds to a zero economic profit

positive economic profit: total revenue exceeds total costs, including opportunity costs

3.b.3. Positive Economic Profit   When total revenue is greater than total cost, the firm is said to be earning **positive economic profit.** Positive economic profit is a powerful signal in the marketplace. Whenever other investors see the positive economic profit, they want to get in on it as well. As a result, they take their funds from whatever use they are currently in and invest them in existing and new firms that will compete with the profitable firm.

Recall from Chapter 3 the scenario of the bottled water that was carried to the top of a hiking trail and sold to thirsty hikers. As more hikers showed up than there were water bottles available, stand owners were induced to increase supplies to earn greater profits, and new owners were prompted to open their own water stands. With additional firms producing the good or service, the supply increases; this will lower the price of that good or service and reduce the positive economic profit. The entry of new firms will stop once economic profit is zero.

RECAP

1. Economic profit refers to the difference between total revenue and the full cost of inputs.

2. Accounting profit is total revenue less total costs but does not include the opportunity cost of the owner's capital.

3. Economic profit is accounting profit less the opportunity cost of the owner's capital.

4. Economic profit can be positive, negative, or zero. A positive economic profit means that the revenue exceeds the full cost of inputs, that is, that inputs are earning more than their opportunity costs. A negative economic profit means that the inputs are not earning their opportunity costs. A zero economic profit means that the inputs are just earning their opportunity costs.

5. Accounting profit is greater than economic profit. Normal profit is the accounting profit when economic profit is zero.

Summary

1. How do firms decide how much to supply?

- The supply rule for all firms is to supply the quantity at which the firm's marginal revenue and marginal cost are equal. *§1.a.1*

2. What is a market structure?

- A market structure is a model of the producing and selling environments in which firms operate. The three characteristics that define market structure are the number of firms, the ease of entry, and whether the products are differentiated. *§2.a*

- A perfectly competitive market is a market in which a very large number of firms are producing an identical product and entry is easy. *§2.a.1*

- The demand curve facing a perfectly competitive firm is a horizontal line at the market price. Price = *MR*. *§2.a.1*

- A monopoly is a market in which there is only one firm and entry by others cannot occur. *§2.a.2*

- The demand curve facing a monopolist is the market demand, since there is only one firm. The demand curve slopes down. Price > *MR*. *§2.a.2*

- A monopolistically competitive market is a market in which a large number of firms are producing differentiated products and entry is easy. *§2.a.3*

- The demand curve facing a monopolistically competitive firm is downward sloping because of the differentiated nature of the products offered by the firm. *§2.a.3*

- An oligopoly is a market in which a few firms are producing either differentiated or nondifferentiated products and entry is possible but not easy. *§2.a.4*

- The shape of the demand curve facing a firm in an oligopoly depends on how the firms interact. *§2.a.4*

- The marginal-revenue curve for all firms except those in perfect competition is downward sloping and lies below the demand curve. The marginal-revenue curve for the perfectly competitive firm is the same as the demand curve, a horizontal or perfectly elastic curve. *§2.b*

3. What is the difference between economic profit and accounting profit?

- Accountants measure only the direct costs. Economists measure all opportunity costs. *§3.a*

- Accounting profit is total revenue − cost of land, labor, and capital. Cost of capital is interest expense only. *§3.a*

- Economic profit is accounting profit − cost of ownership. *§3.a*

4. What is the role of economic profit in allocating resources?

- Economic profit indicates whether resources will remain in their current activity or be distributed to a different activity. When economic profit is positive, all resources, including the firm's investors and owners, are getting paid more than they could have expected to get in another activity. Others seeing this will redirect their time and investments to that activity. Conversely, when economic profit is negative, all resources are not getting paid their opportunity costs. Resource owners will take their resources and place them into an activity that promises to pay more. *§3.b*

Key Terms

Exercises

1. Use the following to calculate profit at each quantity of output.

Total Output (Q)	Price (P)	Total Revenue (TR)	Total Cost (TC)
0	$1,900	$ 0	$1,000
1	$1,700	$ 1,700	$2,000
2	$1,650	$ 3,300	$2,800
3	$1,600	$ 4,800	$3,500
4	$1,550	$ 6,200	$4,000
5	$1,500	$ 7,500	$4,500
6	$1,450	$ 8,700	$5,200
7	$1,400	$ 9,800	$6,000
8	$1,350	$10,800	$7,000
9	$1,300	$11,700	$9,000

2. Use the table in exercise 1 to calculate marginal revenue and marginal cost.

3. Use the information in exercises 1 and 2 to graphically show maximum profit. Label the profit-maximizing quantity and price, total cost, total revenue, and profit.

4. Can accounting profit be positive and economic profit negative? Can accounting profit be negative and economic profit positive? Explain.

5. Use the following information to calculate accounting profit and economic profit.

   Sales $100

   Employee expenses $40

   Inventory expenses $20

   Value of owner's labor in any other enterprise $40

6. Calculate accounting profit and economic profit for each of the following firms (amounts are in millions of dollars).

	General Motors	Barclay's Bank	Microsoft
Sales	$50,091	$5,730	$2,750
Wages and salaries	$29,052	$3,932	$ 400
Cost of capital—equity	$12,100	$ 750	$ 35
Interest on debt	$ 7,585	$ 275	$ 5
Cost of materials	$ 6,500	$ 556	$1,650

7. Which type of market characterizes most businesses operating in the United States today?

8. Given that a firm in a monopoly has no competitors producing close substitutes, does the monopolist set exorbitantly high prices?

9. Give 10 examples of differentiated products. Then list as many nondifferentiated products as you can.

10. Describe profit maximization in terms of marginal revenue and marginal cost.

11. Use the information in the table to calculate total revenue, marginal revenue, and marginal cost. Indicate the profit-maximizing level of output. If the price was $3 and fixed costs were $5, what would variable costs be? At what level of output would the firm produce?

Output	Price	Total Costs	Total Revenue (P × Q)
1	$5	$10	
2	$5	$12	
3	$5	$15	
4	$5	$19	
5	$5	$24	
6	$5	$30	
7	$5	$45	

12. Try to classify the following firms into one of the four market structure models. Explain your choice.

   a. Rowena's Gourmet Foods (produces and sells a line of specialty foods)

   b. Shasta Pool Company (swimming pool and spa building)

   c. Merck (pharmaceuticals)

   d. America West Airlines

   e. UDC Homebuilders

   f. Legal Seafoods (restaurant chain)

13. Draw a demand curve and the corresponding marginal revenue curve for a firm selling in the following market structures:

   a. Monopoly

   b. Perfect competition

ACE

Take the ACE Practice Test for this chapter to review the important concepts and get immediate feedback with answers.

college.hmco.com/economics/students/

Business Ethics Guarantee Value to All Interested Parties

The Korea Herald
January 24, 2003

The Enron and WorldCom scandals inflicted serious damage on the pride of corporate America. Before these events, nobody really dared to doubt the superiority of the United States economy, completely trusting its transparency, accountability, and integrity. Corporate America's rules were regarded as the global standard, which is why Korea accepted them unconditionally, especially in the wake of the Asian financial crisis. The recent accounting mishaps in the U.S., however, proved that the system alone will not warrant everything, and that in order for it to function efficiently, the right ethics need to be in place.

The same goes for Korea. Before and even after the financial crisis in 1997, the Korean government implemented a series of reforms to regulate the domestic business sector and guide it under the principles of transparency, global standards and accountability. Noted for its relatively tight regulatory framework, Korea is sometimes dubbed as the "kingdom of regulation," but despite the high-handed regulations, corruption does not seem to show any signs of dwindling. Political corruptions stemming from ruling politicians and the president's own family continue to plague the nation, along with those in the economy involving venture companies. There are too many to even recollect, showing how futile the regulatory framework is when not coupled with the right business ethics. . . .

Most people automatically assume that business ethics simply symbolize righteousness or virtue, but actually, they are the natural result of the process in seeking to maximize the profit of a company. The management and owners and other shareholders adhere to ethical management practices not because they are people with such high moral standards and believe in contributing to society, but because pursuing them leads to increased profits.

For instance, by removing corrupted connections within a company, such as between the firm's suppliers and the firm itself, the company can benefit by cutting away the additional costs it had been bearing due to the corruption. Ethical business management can also work to improve a company's reputation, which in turn would enhance its price competitiveness to ultimately boost its sales. Thus, in order to survive in the market today, companies have to ensure customers that they are clean and ethical. Consumers, stock holders and creditors don't hesitate to punish unethical companies and boycott their products, meaning that in the end, only the ethical companies will remain in the market. . . .

The market is already globalized so that no product nor company that fails to meet the global standards in any way survives even in the local or regional markets. As a result, corporate ethics have become not an option, but an indispensable way to do business in order for a company to avoid government regulations and pursue a competitive edge in the international markets. . . .

Kim Suk-Joong

It is often claimed that striving for profits means not caring about ethics. During the corporate scandals of 2000–2003, excesses on the part of many executives were discovered and reported. The chief executive of Tyco used the company as his personal bank account. The top executives of Enron lived lavish lifestyles using company resources. Martha Stewart was indicted for insider trading and misleading investigators. The list of wrongdoers seems to go on and on. But, notice two things: first, that it is these examples of unethical behaviors that make the headlines, and second, that for the most part these executives and their companies were harshly punished. Martha Stewart's company has lost over $80 million in value; Enron has been decimated; Tyco is valued significantly lower than it was prior to 2001.

As noted in this article, ethics and profit are not contradictory; they are instead complementary. If the public wants ethical behavior on the part of firms, the public will get such behavior. A company that fails to follow an ethical path will find itself without many customers and with a lower stock market value than a comparable company that follows the ethical path.

In this chapter we discussed profit maximization. Profit is the difference between revenue and costs. If a firm loses customers, it loses revenue. Everything else the same, profits will decline. Similarly, if a firm's costs rise, everything else the same, its profits will decline. Unethical behavior could reduce revenue because the public will not purchase the firm's goods and services. Unethical behavior could also raise costs—the firm would have to do more advertising and more lobbying of government and make more payments to ensure that its behavior is not discovered. These increase costs and reduce profit.

The author of the article notes: "The market is already globalized so that no product nor company that fails to meet the global standards in any way survives even in the local or regional markets. As a result, corporate ethics have become not an option, but an indispensable way to do business in order for a company to avoid government regulations and pursue a competitive edge in the international markets." This statement emphasizes that a firm must meet not only the standards of the nation in which it is located, but the standards in all nations with which it does business and from which its stockholders come—in general, those of almost everywhere. A company that operates to maximize profit while minimizing ethics or a social conscience will fail to maximize profit.

10

Perfect Competition

The market structure of perfect competition is a model that is intended to capture the behavior of firms when there are a great many competitors offering a virtually identical product. It also captures what is known as a commodity. As we will see, there are many items that have become commoditized or are sold in a market that looks quite a bit like the model of perfect competition. ■

1. The Perfectly Competitive Firm in the Short Run

We begin our analysis of perfect competition by taking the viewpoint of an individual firm that is currently in business, having already procured the necessary land, tools, equipment, and employees to operate the firm. After we discuss how

much the firm produces and at what price it sells its products, we discuss the entry and exit processes. We examine how someone begins a business and how someone leaves or exits a business. We then alter our perspective and look at the market as a whole. Let's start our discussion by reviewing the characteristics of a perfectly competitive market.

1.a. The Definition of Perfect Competition

A market that is perfectly competitive exhibits the following characteristics:

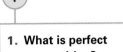

1. What is perfect competition?

Perfect competition is a firm behavior that occurs when many firms produce identical products and entry is easy.

1. There are many sellers. No one firm can have an influence on market price. Each firm is such a minute part of the total market that however much the firm produces—nothing at all, as much as it can, or some amount in between—it will have no effect on the market price.

2. The products sold by all the firms in the industry are identical. The product sold by one firm can be substituted perfectly for the product sold by any other firm in the industry. Products are not differentiated by packaging, advertising, or quality.

3. Entry is easy, and there are many potential entrants. There are no huge economies of scale relative to the size of the market. Laws do not require producers to obtain licenses or pay for the privilege of producing. Other firms cannot take action to keep someone from entering the business. Firms can stop producing and can sell or liquidate the business without difficulty.

4. Buyers and sellers have perfect information. Buyers know the price and quantity at each firm. Each firm knows what the other firms are charging and how they are behaving.

1.b. The Demand Curve of the Individual Firm

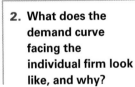

2. What does the demand curve facing the individual firm look like, and why?

price taker: a firm in a perfectly competitive market structure

The individual firm in a perfectly competitive industry is a price taker because it cannot charge more than the market price, and it will not charge less.

A firm in a perfectly competitive market structure is said to be a **price taker** because the price of the product is determined by market demand and supply, and the individual firm simply has to sell at that price or simply not sell. In 2005 the world market price of corn was about $1 per bushel, and nearly 20 billion bushels were produced worldwide. Approximately 46 percent of all the corn harvested in the world comes from the United States. Nevertheless, the average farm in the United States produces an extremely small percentage of the total quantity harvested each year.

What would occur if one U.S. farmer decided to set the price of corn at $1.20 per bushel when the market price was $1 per bushel? According to the model of a perfectly competitive market, no one would purchase the higher-priced corn because the identical product could be obtained without difficulty elsewhere for $1 per bushel. In this instance, what the model predicts is what actually occurs in the real-world corn market. The grain silo owner who buys the farmers' grain would simply pass on that farm's grain and move to the next truckful of grain at $1 per bushel. By setting a price above the market price, the individual farmer may sell nothing.

Is an individual farmer likely to set a price of $.80 per bushel when the market price is $1 per bushel? Not in a perfectly competitive market. All of the produce from a single farm can be sold at the market price. Why would a farmer sell at $.80 per bushel when he or she can get $1 per bushel? The individual farm is a price taker because it cannot charge more than the market price, and it will not charge less.

You could think of price takers as being the sellers in a big auction. The potential buyers bid against each other for the product until a price is determined. The product is then sold at that price. The seller has no control over the price.

FIGURE 1 Market Demand and Supply and Single-Firm Demand for Corn

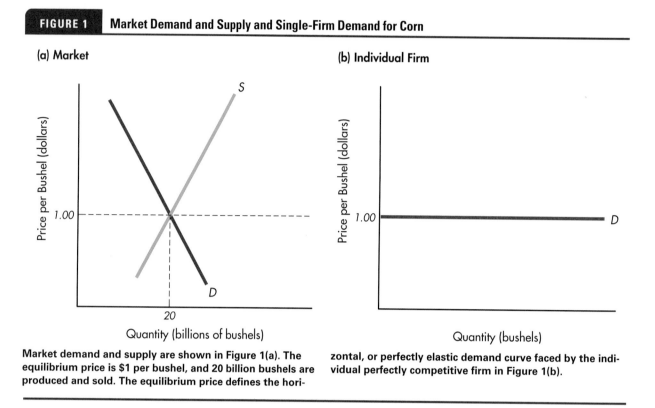

(a) Market

(b) Individual Firm

Market demand and supply are shown in Figure 1(a). The equilibrium price is $1 per bushel, and 20 billion bushels are produced and sold. The equilibrium price defines the hori-

zontal, or perfectly elastic demand curve faced by the individual perfectly competitive firm in Figure 1(b).

Market demand and supply in a perfectly competitive market are shown in Figure 1(a). The demand curve of a single firm is shown in Figure 1(b). The horizontal line at the market price is the demand curve faced by an individual firm in a perfectly competitive market structure. It shows that the individual firm is a price taker—that the demand curve is perfectly elastic. The question facing the individual firm in a perfectly competitive industry is how much to produce, not what price to charge.

1.c. Profit Maximization

? 3. How does the firm maximize profit in the short run?

Profit maximization occurs at the output level where MR = MC.

We know that profit is maximized at the quantity where $MR = MC$. Profit rises when the revenue brought in by the sale of one more unit (one more bushel) is greater than the cost of producing that unit. Conversely, if the cost of producing one more unit is greater than the amount of revenue brought in by selling that unit, profit declines with the production of that unit. Only when marginal revenue and marginal cost are the same is profit at a maximum, as illustrated in Figure 2.[1]

[1]Marginal revenue and marginal cost could be equal at small levels of production and sales, such as with the first bushel, but profit would definitely not be at its greatest level. The reason is that marginal cost is falling with the first unit of production—the marginal cost of the second unit is less than the marginal cost of the first unit. Since marginal revenue is the same for both the first and the second units, profit actually rises as quantity increases. Profit maximization requires both that marginal revenue equal marginal cost and that marginal cost be rising. Since marginal revenue and marginal cost are the same for the ninth bushel and marginal cost is rising, the ninth bushel is the profit-maximizing level of output.

FIGURE 2 | Profit Maximization

Total Output (Q)	Price (P)	Total Revenue (TR)	Total Cost (TC)	Total Profit (TR−TC)	Marginal Revenue (MR)	Marginal Cost (MC)	Average Total Cost (ATC)
0	$1	$ 0	$ 1.00	−$1.00	$1		
1	$1	$ 1	$ 2.00	−$1.00	$1	$1.00	$2.00
2	$1	$ 2	$ 2.80	−$ .80	$1	$ .80	$1.40
3	$1	$ 3	$ 3.50	−$ .50	$1	$ .70	$1.1667
4	$1	$ 4	$ 4.00	$ .00	$1	$ .50	$1.00
5	$1	$ 5	$ 4.50	$ .50	$1	$ .50	$ .90
6	$1	$ 6	$ 5.20	$ .80	$1	$ .70	$ .8667
7	$1	$ 7	$ 6.00	$1.00	$1	$ .80	$ .8571
8	$1	$ 8	$ 6.86	$1.14	$1	$ .86	$ .8575
9	$1	$ 9	$ 7.86	$1.14	$1	$1.00	$ .8733
10	$1	$10	$ 9.36	$ .64	$1	$1.50	$ .936
11	$1	$11	$12.00	−$1.00	$1	$2.64	$1.09

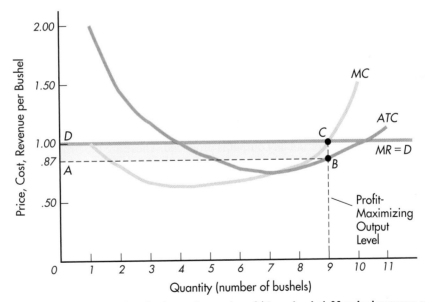

The profit-maximization point for a single firm is shown for a price of $1 per bushel. Marginal revenue and marginal cost are equal at the profit-maximization point, 9 bushels. At quantities less than 9 bushels, marginal revenue exceeds marginal cost, so increased production would raise profits. At quantities greater than 9, marginal revenue is less than marginal cost, so reduced production would increase profits. The point at which profit is maximized is shown by the highlighted row in the table. The profit per unit is the difference between the price line and the average-total-cost curve at the profit-maximizing quantity. Total profit ($1.14) is the rectangle ABCD, an area that is equal to the profit per unit times the number of units.

MR = MC *is the profit-maximizing or loss-minimizing output level.*

With a price of $1 per bushel, the individual farm maximizes profit by producing 9 bushels. We can illustrate how much profit the individual firm in perfect competition earns, or whether it makes a loss, by calculating total costs at the quantity where $MR = MC$ and comparing that with total revenue.

In Figure 2, the price per bushel of $1 exceeds the cost per bushel (average total cost, $.8733) by the distance BC ($.1267) when 9 bushels are produced. This amount ($.1267) is the profit per bushel. The total profit is the rectangle $ABCD$ (highlighted in the table).

Figure 3 illustrates what happens to the individual firm in a perfectly competitive market as the market price changes. The only curve in Figure 3 that changes as a result of the price change is the perfectly elastic demand curve (which is also the price line and the marginal-revenue curve). Let's assume that the market price changes to $.70 per bushel, so that the individual farm's demand curve shifts down. Whether the firm is making a profit is determined by finding the new quantity at which the new marginal-revenue curve, MR_2, equals the marginal-cost curve, at point F, and then tracing a vertical line from point F to the ATC curve at point G. The distance FG is the profit or loss per unit of output. If the demand curve is above the ATC curve at that point, the firm is making a profit. If the ATC curve exceeds the price line, as is the case in Figure 3, the firm is suffering a loss.

A firm cannot make a profit as long as the price is less than the average-cost curve, because the cost per bushel (ATC) exceeds the revenue per bushel (price). At a price of $.70 per bushel, marginal revenue and marginal cost are equal as the sixth bushel is produced (see Figure 3 and the highlighted bar in the table), but the average total cost is greater than the price. The cost per bushel (ATC) is $.8667, which is higher than the price or revenue per bushel of $.70. Thus, the firm makes a loss, shown as the rectangle $EFGH$ in Figure 3.

Recall that an economic loss means that opportunity costs are not being covered by revenues; that is, the owners could do better in another line of business. An economic loss means that a firm is confronted with the choice of whether to continue producing, shut down temporarily, or shut down permanently. The decision depends on which alternative has the lowest opportunity cost.

1.d. Short-Run Break-Even and Shutdown Prices

In the short run, certain costs, such as rent on land and equipment, must be paid whether or not any output is produced. These are the firm's fixed costs. If a firm has purchased equipment and buildings but does not produce, the firm still has to pay for the equipment and buildings. Thus, the decision about whether to produce or to temporarily suspend operations depends on which option promises the lesser costs. In order to continue producing in the short run, the firm must earn sufficient revenue to pay all of the *variable* costs (the costs that change as output changes), because then the excess of revenue over variable costs will enable the firm to pay some of its fixed costs. If the firm cannot pay all the variable costs out of revenue, then it should suspend operations temporarily because if it continues to produce, it must pay not only its fixed costs but also those variable costs in excess of revenue.

Does suspending operations mean quitting the business altogether—shutting down permanently? It may, but it need not. The decision depends on the long-term outlook. If the long-term outlook indicates that revenue will exceed costs, then production is warranted. However, if the outlook is for continued low prices and inability to cover costs, a firm would be better off quitting the business altogether.

To see how producing at a loss can at times be better than not producing at all, let's return to the individual farm in Figure 4. At a price of $.70 per bushel, the output at which $MR = MC$ is 6 bushels, as shown by the highlighted bar in the table.

FIGURE 3 **Loss Minimization**

In Figure 3 the price changed from $1 per bushel to $.70 per bushel. The profit-maximization, or loss-minimization, point is the level of output where *MR* = *MC*. If, at this output level, the price is less than the corresponding average-cost curve, the film makes a loss. At a price of $.70 per bushel, a loss is incurred—the loss-minimizing level of output is 6 bushels, as shown by the highlighted bar in the table. The total loss is the rectangle *EFGH*.

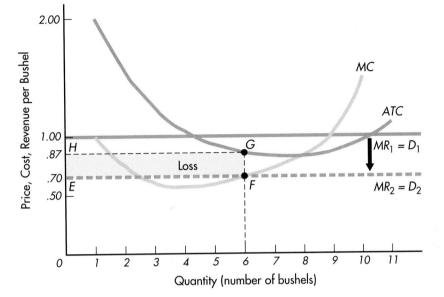

Total Output (Q)	Price (P)	Total Revenue (TR)	Total Cost (TC)	Total Profit (TR−TC)	Marginal Revenue (MR)	Marginal Cost (MC)	Average Total Cost (ATC)
0	$.70	$ 0	$ 1.00	−$1.00			
1	$.70	$ .70	$ 2.00	−$1.30	$.70	$1.00	$2.00
2	$.70	$1.40	$ 2.80	−$1.40	$.70	$ .80	$1.40
3	$.70	$2.10	$ 3.50	−$1.40	$.70	$ .70	$1.1667
4	$.70	$2.80	$ 4.00	−$1.20	$.70	$ .50	$1.00
5	$.70	$3.50	$ 4.50	−$1.00	$.70	$ .50	$ .90
6	$.70	$4.20	$ 5.20	−$1.00	$.70	$ .70	$ .8667
7	$.70	$4.90	$ 6.00	−$1.10	$.70	$ .80	$ .8571
8	$.70	$5.60	$ 6.86	−$1.26	$.70	$ .86	$ .8575
9	$.70	$6.30	$ 7.86	−$1.56	$.70	$1.00	$ .8733
10	$.70	$7.00	$ 9.36	−$2.36	$.70	$1.50	$ .936
11	$.70	$7.70	$12.00	−$4.30	$.70	$2.64	$1.09

At 6 bushels, total revenue is $4.20 and total cost is $5.20. The farm loses $1 by producing 6 bushels. The question is whether to produce at all. If production is stopped, the fixed cost of $1 must still be paid. Thus, the farmer is indifferent between producing 6 bushels and losing $1 or shutting down and losing $1. Should the price be less than the minimum point of the average-variable-cost curve (*AVC*), as would occur at any price less than $P = \$.70$ per bushel, the farm is not earning enough to cover its variable costs (see Figure 4 and the accompanying table). By continuing to produce, the farm will lose more than it would lose if it suspended operations or shut down until the outlook improved. The minimum point of the average-variable-cost curve is the **shutdown price**. If the market price is less than the minimum point of the *AVC* curve, then the firm will incur fewer losses if it does not produce than if it continues to produce in the short run.

At prices above the minimum point of the average-variable-cost curve, the excess of revenue over variable cost means that some fixed costs can be paid. A firm is better off producing than shutting down because by producing, it is able to earn enough revenue to pay all the variable costs and some of the fixed costs. If the firm does not produce, it will still have to pay all of the fixed costs. When the price equals the minimum point of the average-total-cost curve, the firm is earning just enough revenue to pay for all of its costs, fixed and variable. This point is called the **break-even price.** At the break-even price, economic profit is zero—all costs are being covered, including opportunity costs. Because costs include the opportunity costs of the resources already owned by the entrepreneur—his or her own labor and capital—zero economic profit means that the entrepreneur could not do better in another activity. Zero economic profit is normal profit, profit that is just sufficient to keep the entrepreneur in this line of business.

The shutdown price is the price that is equal to the minimum point of the *AVC* curve. The break-even price is the price that is equal to the minimum point of the *ATC* curve. In the examples just discussed, the firm continues to operate at a loss because variable costs are being covered and the long-term outlook is favorable. Many firms decide to operate for a while at a loss, then suspend operations temporarily, and finally shut down permanently. A firm will shut down permanently if it cannot pay all its costs in the long run. In the long run, the minimum point of the *ATC* curve is the permanent shutdown point. Price must exceed the minimum point of the *ATC* curve in the long run if the firm is to remain in business. Of the 80,000 businesses that shut down permanently in 1997, most went through a period in which they continued to operate even though revenue was not large enough to pay variable costs.

1.e. The Firm's Supply Curve in the Short Run

As long as revenue equals or exceeds variable costs, an individual firm will produce the quantity at which marginal revenue and marginal cost are equal. This means that the individual firm's supply curve is the portion of the *MC* curve that lies above the *AVC* curve. An individual firm's supply curve shows the quantity that a firm will produce and offer for sale at each price. When the price is less than the minimum point of the *AVC* curve, a firm incurs fewer losses from not producing than from producing. The firm thus produces and supplies nothing, and there is no supply curve. When the price is greater than the minimum point of the *AVC* curve, the firm will produce and offer for sale the quantity yielded at the point where the *MC* curve and the *MR* line intersect for each price. The supply curve is thus the *MC* curve. The portion of the *MC* curve lying above the minimum point of the *AVC* curve is the individual firm's supply curve in the short run.

In our example of an individual farm illustrated in Figure 4, nothing is produced at a price of $.50 per bushel. At $.70 per bushel, the farm produces 6 bushels in the

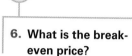

shutdown price: the minimum point of the average-variable-cost curve

6. What is the break-even price?

break-even price: a price that is equal to the minimum point of the average-total-cost curve

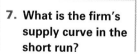

7. What is the firm's supply curve in the short run?

FIGURE 4   **Shutdown Price**

When the firm is making a loss, it must decide whether to continue producing or to suspend operations and not produce. The decision depends on which alternative has higher costs. When the price is equal to or greater than the minimum point of the average-variable-cost curve, $.70, the firm is earning sufficient revenue to pay for all of the variable costs. When the price is less than the minimum point of the average-variable-cost curve, the firm is not covering all of its variable costs. In that case the firm is better off shutting down its operations. For this reason, the minimum point of the *AVC* curve is called the *shutdown price*. The *break-even price* is the minimum point of the *ATC* curve because at that point all costs are being paid.

Total Output (Q)	Price (P)	Total Revenue (TR)	Total Cost (TC)	Total Profit (TR−TC)	Marginal Revenue (MR)	Marginal Cost (MC)	Average Total Cost (ATC)	Average Variable Cost (AVC)
0	$.70	$ 0	$ 1.00	−$1.00				
1	$.70	$ .70	$ 2.00	−$1.30	$.70	$1.00	$2.00	$1.00
2	$.70	$1.40	$ 2.80	−$1.40	$.70	$ .80	$1.40	$ .90
3	$.70	$2.10	$ 3.50	−$1.40	$.70	$ .70	$1.1667	$ .833
4	$.70	$2.80	$ 4.00	−$1.20	$.70	$ .50	$1.00	$ .75
5	$.70	$3.50	$ 4.50	−$1.00	$.70	$ .50	$ .90	$ .70
6	$.70	$4.20	$ 5.20	−$1.00	$.70	$ .70	$ .8667	$ .70
7	$.70	$4.90	$ 6.00	−$1.10	$.70	$ .80	$ .8571	$ .714
8	$.70	$5.60	$ 6.86	−$1.26	$.70	$ .86	$ .8575	$ .7325
9	$.70	$6.30	$ 7.86	−$1.56	$.70	$1.00	$ .8733	$ .7622
10	$.70	$7.00	$ 9.36	−$2.36	$.70	$1.50	$ .936	$ .836
11	$.70	$7.70	$12.00	−$4.30	$.70	$2.64	$1.09	$1.00

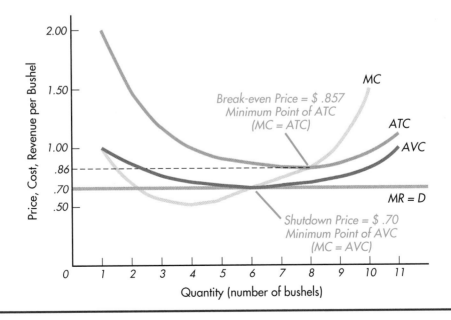

short run; at $1 per bushel, the farm produces 9 bushels. The higher the price, the greater the quantity produced and offered for sale.

A firm may continue to produce and offer its products for sale even if it is earning a negative economic profit, as long as it earns enough revenue to pay its variable costs and expects revenue to grow enough to pay all costs eventually. If the business does not improve and losses continue to pile up, the firm will shut down permanently. In the long run, the firm must be able to earn enough revenue to pay all of its costs. If it does not, the business will not continue to operate. If the firm does earn enough to pay its costs, the firm will produce and offer for sale the quantity of output yielded at the point where $MR = MC$. This means that the firm's supply curve is the portion of its MC curve that lies above the minimum point of the ATC curve.

?

8. What is the firm's supply curve in the long run?

RECAP

1. The firm maximizes profit or minimizes losses by producing at the output level at which MR and MC are equal.

2. In order to remain in business, the firm must earn sufficient revenue to pay for all of its variable costs. The shutdown price is the price that is just equal to the minimum point of the AVC curve.

3. The firm's break-even price is the price that is just equal to the minimum point of the ATC curve.

4. The portion of the marginal-cost curve lying above the minimum point of the AVC curve is the firm's short-run supply curve.

5. The portion of the marginal-cost curve lying above the minimum point of the ATC curve is the firm's long-run supply curve.

2. The Long Run

In the short run, at least one of the resources **cannot** be altered. This means that new firms cannot be organized and begin producing. Thus the supply of firms in an industry is fixed in the short run. In the long run, of course, all quantities of resources can be changed. Buildings can be built or purchased and machinery accumulated and placed into production. New firms may arise as entrepreneurs who are not currently in the industry see that they could earn more than they are currently earning and decide to expand into new businesses.

Exit and entry are long-run phenomena.

Entry and exit can both occur in the long run. On average, 4.5 percent of the total number of farms in the United States go out of business each year, and more than half of them file for bankruptcy.

How does exit occur? Entrepreneurs may sell their businesses and move to another industry, or they may use the bankruptcy laws to exit the industry. In the United States, a sole proprietor or partnership may file Chapter 13 personal bankruptcy; a corporation may file Chapter 7 bankruptcy or a Chapter 11 reorganization; a farmer may file Chapter 12. From the mid-1970s to the present, the average birthrate for all industries (the percent of total businesses that begin during a year) has been just over 11.2 percent, and the average death rate (the percent of total businesses that disappear during a year) has been 9.6 percent.

Bankruptcy laws in the developed nations are similar to those in the United States. Although most nations have some type of laws regarding going out of business, the laws are not enforced or used in many emerging-market nations. In most

The price taker can do nothing but accept and sell at the market price. When times are bad, the market price may be so low that some firms must exit the market. In this photo, a firm is going out of business, liquidating all its assets, and eventually shutting its doors.

less-developed countries, a farmer goes out of business by simply walking away. The farmer did not hold title to the land in the first place, and so when the land no longer provides support for the family, it is left untilled and uncared for.

2.a. The Market Supply Curve and Exit and Entry

When additional firms enter the industry and begin producing the product, the market supply curve shifts out.

Recall from Chapter 3 that the market supply curve shifts when the number of suppliers changes. The market supply curve is the sum of all the individual firms' supply curves. In the corn-producing business, when new farms enter the market, the total quantity of corn supplied at each price increases. In other words, entry causes the market supply curve to shift out to the right.

When firms leave the industry, the market supply curve shifts in.

Conversely, exit means that there are fewer producers and lower quantities supplied at each price, and there is a leftward or inward shift of the market supply curve. Suppose some existing farms are not covering their costs and believe that the future is not bright enough to warrant continued production. As a result, they shut down their operations and sell their equipment and land. As the number of farms in the industry declines, everything else held constant, the market supply curve shifts to the left—as long as those remaining in the business produce the same quantity as they did before the farms exited, or less.

2.b. Normal Profit in the Long Run

One of the principal characteristics of the perfectly competitive market structure is that entry and exit can occur easily. Entry and exit occur whenever firms are earning more or less than a *normal profit* (zero economic profit). When a normal profit is being earned, there is no entry or exit. This condition is the long-run equilibrium.

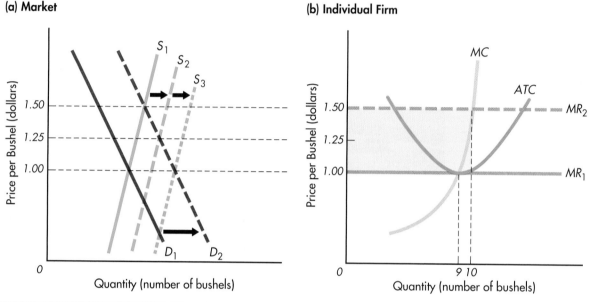

FIGURE 5   Economic Profit in the Long Run

Market demand and supply determine the price and the demand curve faced by the single perfectly competitive firm. At a price of $1 per bushel, the individual farm is earning normal profit. After an agricultural disaster in Russia increases the demand for U.S. corn, the price rises to $1.50.

At $1.50 per bushel, the single farm makes a profit equal to the yellow rectangle. Above-normal profits induce new farms to begin raising corn and existing farms to increase their production.

(a) Market

(b) Individual Firm

The process of establishing the long-run position is shown in Figure 5. The market demand and supply curves for corn are shown in Figure 5(a), and the cost and revenue curves for a representative firm in the industry are shown in Figure 5(b). Let's assume that the market price is $1. Let's also assume that at $1 per bushel, the demand curve facing the individual farm (the price line) is equal to the minimum point of the ATC curve. The quantity produced is 9 bushels. The individual farm and the industry are in equilibrium. There is no reason for entry or exit to occur, and there is no reason for individual farms to change their scale of operation.

To illustrate how the process of reaching the long-run equilibrium occurs in the perfectly competitive market structure, let's begin with the corn market in equilibrium at $S_1 = D_1$. Then let's suppose that a major agricultural disaster strikes Russia, and Russia turns to the United States to buy agricultural products. As a result of the increased Russian demand, the total demand for U.S. corn increases, as shown by the rightward shift of the demand curve to D_2 in Figure 5(a). In the short run, the market price rises to $1.50 per bushel, where the new market demand curve intersects the initial market supply curve, S_1. This raises the demand curve for the individual farm to the horizontal line at $1.50 per bushel. In the short run, the individual farms in the industry increase production (by adding variable inputs) from 9 bushels to 10 bushels, the point in Figure 5(b) where $MC = MR_2 = 1.50, and earn economic profit of the amount shown by the yellow rectangle.

The above-normal profit attracts others to the farming business. The result of the new entry and expansion is a rightward shift of the market supply curve. How far

In the long run, perfectly competitive firms earn normal profits.

does the market supply curve shift? It shifts until the market price is low enough that firms in the industry earn normal profit.

Let us suppose that the costs of doing business do not rise as the market expands. Then, if the market supply curve shifts to S_2, the new market price, $1.25, is less than the former price of $1.50 but still high enough for firms to earn above-normal profits. These profits are sufficient inducement for more firms to enter, causing the supply curve to shift farther right. The supply curve continues to shift until there is no incentive for additional firms to enter—that is, until firms are earning the normal profit, where price is equal to the minimum ATC, shown as S_3 in Figure 5(a). When the adjustment stops, firms are just earning the normal profit.

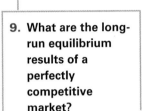

9. What are the long-run equilibrium results of a perfectly competitive market?

2.c. The Predictions of the Model of Perfect Competition

According to the model of perfect competition, whenever *above-normal* profits (positive economic profits) are earned by existing firms, entry occurs until a *normal* profit (zero economic profit) is earned by all firms. Conversely, whenever economic losses occur, exit takes place until a normal profit is made by all remaining firms.

It is so important to keep in mind the distinctions between economic and accounting terms that we repeatedly remind you of them. A *zero economic profit* is a *normal accounting profit*, or just *normal profit*. It is the profit that is just sufficient to keep a business owner or investors in a particular line of business, the point where revenue exactly equals total opportunity costs. Business owners and investors earning a normal profit are earning enough to cover their opportunity costs—they could not do better by changing—but they are not earning more than their opportunity costs. A *loss* refers to a situation in which revenue is not sufficient to pay all of the opportunity costs. A firm can earn a positive accounting profit and yet be experiencing a loss, not earning a normal profit.

Perfect competition results in economic efficiency.

The long-run equilibrium position of the perfectly competitive market structure shows firms producing at the minimum point of their long-run average-total-cost curves. If the price is above the minimum point of the ATC curve, then firms are earning above-normal profits, and entry will occur. If the price is less than the minimum of the ATC curve, exit will occur. Only when price equals the minimum point of the ATC curve will neither entry nor exit take place.

Producing at the minimum of the ATC curve means that firms are producing with the lowest possible costs. Changing the way they produce won't allow them to produce less expensively. Altering the resources they use won't allow them to produce less expensively.

Firms produce at a level where marginal cost and marginal revenue are the same. Since marginal revenue and price are the same in a perfectly competitive market, firms produce where marginal cost equals price. This means that firms are employing resources until the marginal cost to them of producing the last unit of a good just equals the price of the last unit. Moreover, since price is equal to marginal cost, consumers are paying a price that is as low as it can get; the price just covers the marginal cost of producing that good or service. There is no waste—no one could be made better off without making someone else worse off. Economists refer to this result as **economic efficiency.**

economic efficiency: the situation in which the price of a good or service just covers the marginal cost of producing that good or service and people are getting the goods and services that they want

2.c.1. Consumer and Producer Surplus
Efficiency is the term economists give to the situation in which firms are producing with as little cost as they can (at the minimum point of the ATC curve) and consumers are getting the products they desire at a price that is equal to the marginal cost of producing those goods. To say that

| FIGURE 6 | Producer and Consumer Surpluses |

Since the firm is willing to sell the product at the marginal cost and since the firm receives the market price, the difference between the two is a bonus to the firm, a bonus of market exchange. This bonus is producer surplus. Figure 6 illustrates total producer surplus in a competitive market, the sum of the producer surplus received by each firm in the market. Producer surplus is the area below the price line and above the supply curve. Also pictured is total consumer surplus. Recall that consumer surplus is the difference between what the consumer would be willing to pay for a good, the demand curve, and the price actually paid. The sum of producer and consumer surplus represents the total benefits that come from exchange in the market: benefits that accrue to the consumer plus those that accrue to the firm.

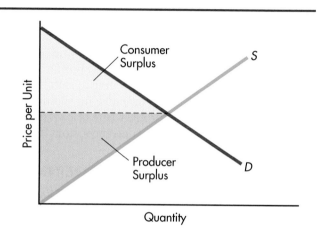

a competitive market is efficient is to say that all market participants get the greatest benefits possible from market exchange.[2]

We measure the benefits from market exchange as the sum of the consumer surplus and the producer surplus. Consumer surplus is the difference between what consumers would be willing and able to pay for a product and the price they actually have to pay to buy the product. **Producer surplus** is the difference between the price that firms would have been willing and able to accept for their products and the price they actually receive.

Since the firm is willing to sell the product at the marginal cost, as long as marginal cost is greater than average variable cost, and since the firm receives the market price, the difference between the two is a bonus to the firm, a bonus resulting from market exchange. This bonus is producer surplus.

producer surplus: the difference between the price firms would have been willing to accept for their products and the price they actually receive

Consumer surplus = area above equilibrium price and below the demand curve
Producer surplus = area below equilibrium price and above the supply curve

Figure 6 illustrates consumer and producer surplus in a competitive market. The sum of producer and consumer surplus represents the total benefits that come from exchange in a market: the benefits that accrue to the consumer plus those that accrue to the firm.

The primary result of perfect competition is that things just do not get any better: Total consumer and producer surplus is at a maximum. Any interference with the market exchange reduces the total surplus. Consider rent control on apartments, for instance. The market for rental apartments is pictured in Figure 7. As shown in Figure 7, the market solution would yield a monthly rent of $400. The consumer surplus would be the area ABC; the producer surplus would be the area ABD. Now, suppose the city imposes a rent control at $300 per month. The producer surplus

---

[2]Economists have classified efficiency into several categories. *Productive efficiency* refers to the firm's using the least-cost combination of resources to produce any output level. This output level may not be the goods that consumers want, however. *Allocative efficiency* is the term given to the situation in which firms are producing the goods that consumers most want and consumers are paying a price that is just equal to the marginal cost of producing those goods. Allocative efficiency may occur when firms are not producing at their most efficient level. Economic efficiency exists when both productive and allocative efficiency occur.

FIGURE 7 **Rent Control and Market Efficiency**

The market for rental apartments is pictured in this graph; the market solution would yield a monthly rent of $400. The consumer surplus would be the area *ABC*; the producer surplus would be the area *ABD*. Now, suppose the city imposes rent control at $300 per month. The producer surplus changes to area *EFD* while the consumer surplus changes to *EFHC*. The total surplus has been reduced by the rent control.

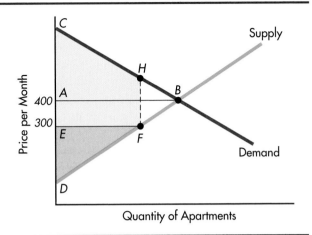

changes to area *EFD*, while the consumer surplus changes to *EFHC*. Clearly the total surplus has been reduced. The question that policymakers must decide is whether the additional benefits to consumers offset the additional losses to producers. We will discuss this further in the chapter "Government and Market Failure."

RECAP

1. Entry occurs when firms are earning above-normal profit or positive economic profit.

2. A temporary shutdown occurs when firms are not covering their variable costs in the short run. In the long run, exit occurs when firms are not covering all costs.

3. The short-run market supply curve is the horizontal sum of the supply curves of all individual firms in the industry.

4. In a perfectly competitive market, firms produce goods at the least cost, and consumers purchase the goods that they most desire at a price that is equal to the marginal cost of producing those goods. There is no waste—no one could be made better off without making someone else worse off. Economists refer to this result as economic efficiency.

5. Producer surplus is the benefit that the firm receives for engaging in market exchange; it is the difference between the price the firm would be willing to sell its goods for and the price the firm actually receives.

6. Consumer surplus is the area below the demand curve and above the equilibrium price; producer surplus is the area above the supply curve and below the equilibrium price.

Summary

1. What is perfect competition?

- Perfect competition is a market structure in which there are many firms that are producing an identical product and where entry and exit are easy. *§1.a*

2. What does the demand curve facing the individual firm look like, and why?

- The demand curve of the individual firm is a horizontal line at the market price. Each firm is a price taker. *§1.b*

3. How does the firm maximize profit in the short run?

- The individual firm maximizes profit by producing at the point where $MR = MC$. *§1.c*

4. At what point does a firm decide to suspend operations?

- A firm will shut down operations temporarily if price does not exceed the minimum point of the average-variable-cost curve. *§1.c*

5. When will a firm shut down permanently?

- A firm will shut down operations permanently if price does not exceed the minimum point of the average-total-cost curve in the long run. *§1.d*

6. What is the break-even price?

- The firm breaks even when revenue and cost are equal—when the demand curve (price) just equals the minimum point of the average-total-cost curve. *§1.d*

7. What is the firm's supply curve in the short run?

- The firm's short-run supply curve is the portion of its marginal-cost curve that lies above the minimum point of the average-variable-cost curve. *§1.e*

8. What is the firm's supply curve in the long run?

- The firm produces at the point where marginal cost equals marginal revenue, as long as marginal revenue exceeds the minimum point of the average-total-cost curve. Thus, the firm's long-run supply curve is the portion of its marginal-cost curve that lies above the minimum point of the average-total-cost curve. *§1.e*

9. What are the long-run equilibrium results of a perfectly competitive market?

- In the long run, all firms operating in perfect competition will earn a normal profit by producing at the lowest possible cost, and all consumers will buy the goods and services that they most want at a price equal to the marginal cost of producing those goods and services. *§2.c*

- Producer surplus is the difference between what a firm would be willing to produce and sell a good for and the price that the firm actually receives for the good. Consumer surplus is the difference between what an individual would be willing to pay for a good and what the individual actually has to pay. Total consumer and producer surpluses are at a maximum in a perfectly competitive market. *§2.c.1*

Key Terms

price taker *§1.b*

shutdown price *§1.d*

break-even price *§1.d*

economic efficiency *§2.c*

producer surplus *§2.c.1*

Exercises

1. Cost figures for a hypothetical firm are given in the following table. Use them for the exercises below. The firm is selling in a perfectly competitive market.

Output	Fixed Cost	AFC	Variable Cost	AVC	Total Cost	ATC	MC
1	$50		$ 30				
2	$50		$ 50				
3	$50		$ 80				
4	$50		$120				
5	$50		$170				

a. Fill in the blank columns.
b. What is the minimum price needed by the firm to break even?
c. What is the shutdown price?
d. At a price of $40, what output level would the firm produce? What would its profits be?

2. Label the curves in the following graph.

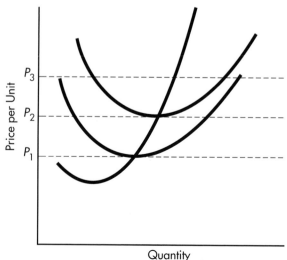

a. At each market price, P_1, P_2, and P_3, at what output level would the firm produce?

b. What profit would be earned if the market price was P_1?

c. What are the shutdown and break-even prices?

3. Why might a firm continue to produce in the short run even though the market price is less than its average total cost?

4. Explain why the demand curve facing the individual firm in a perfectly competitive industry is a horizontal line.

5. Explain what occurs in the long run in a constant-cost industry, an increasing-cost industry, and a decreasing-cost industry when the market demand declines (shifts in).

6. What can you expect from an industry in perfect competition in the long run? What will price be? What quantity will be produced? What will be the relation between marginal cost, average cost, and price?

7. Assume that the market for illegal drugs is an example of a perfectly competitive market structure. Describe what the perfectly competitive market model predicts for illegal drugs in the long run. What is likely to be the impact of the U.S. government's war on drugs in the short run? In the long run?

8. If no real-life industry meets the conditions of the perfectly competitive model exactly, why do we study perfect competition? What is the relevance of the model to a decision to switch careers? Why might it shed some light on pollution, acid rain, and other social problems?

9. Using the model of perfect competition, explain what it means to say, "Too much electricity is generated," or "Too little education is produced." Would the firm be producing at the bottom of the ATC curve if too much or too little was being produced?

10. Private swimming pools can be dangerous. There are serious accidents each year in those areas of the United States where backyard pools are common. Should pools be banned? In other words, should the market for swimming pools be eliminated? Answer this in terms of producer and consumer surplus.

11. Discuss whether the following are examples of perfectly competitive industries.

a. The U.S. stock market

b. The automobile industry

c. The consumer electronics market

d. The market for college students

12. Macy's was making millions of dollars in profits when it declared bankruptcy. Explain Macy's decision.

13. Entry and exit of firms occur in the long run, but not in the short run. Why? What is meant by the long run and the short run? Would you say that entry is more or less difficult than exit?

14. Use the following data for the exercises below.

Price	Quantity Supplied	Quantity Demanded
$20	30	0
$18	25	5
$16	20	10
$14	15	15
$12	10	20
$10	5	25
$ 8	0	30

a. What is the equilibrium price and quantity?

b. Draw the demand and supply curves. If this represents perfect competition, are the curves individual-firm or market curves? How is the quantity supplied derived?

c. Show the consumer surplus. Show the producer surplus.

d. Suppose that a price ceiling of $12 was imposed. How would this change the consumer and producer surplus? Suppose a price floor of $16 was imposed. How would this change the consumer and producer surplus?

15. Explain the following statement: "The market can better determine the value of polluting than the politicians. Rather than assign an emission fee to a polluting firm, simply allow firms to purchase the rights to pollute."

ACE

Take the ACE Practice Test for this chapter to review the important concepts and get immediate feedback with answers.

college.hmco.com/economics/students/

Avoid "Commoditization"

Crain Communications Inc.
October 14, 2002

From advanced telecommunications gear to raw chemicals, the "commoditization" of products continues unabated.

How can companies differentiate themselves? Unfortunately, many companies have cut back on one tool at their disposal: marketing. Companies that sell commodities often view marketing as an unnecessary expense. This strategic miscalculation perpetuates, and even accelerates, shrinking margins and smaller profits. Strategic marketing programs that promote your "universe of value" will create a competitive edge.

Your universe of value is more than quality products; it encompasses the total value that you provide to customers. It includes benefits that improve customers' buying experiences, eliminate administrative burdens and improve operational efficiency. These benefits are delivered at every point of contact with customers.

The first step is to strategically identify your real-world differentiating factors. Don't rely exclusively on sales personnel for feedback from the field. Survey customers to determine the benefits that you are delivering.

Perhaps your company has an online ordering system. The value to your customer is that the system significantly reduces inefficient administrative tasks to lower order processing costs. Make customers aware of this intrinsic value.

Technical services may provide another marketing opportunity. Failure to effectively market these services can diminish their inherent value.

Innovative packaging can also be a differentiating factor. Take rock salt, for example. Little difference exists between rock salt products. But companies that incorporate "easy-to-carry handles" into bulk packaging can drive brand preference.

Once differentiating factors have been identified, brand them. Simply branding for the sake of brand awareness is worthless (think about Pets.com).

The goal is not simply to develop new names and creative logos. Brands represent your company. They convey value. Most important, they help to promote the benefits that your products and services deliver to customers.

Promote your differentiating factors through strategic publicity, advertising and other marketing tactics. Develop return on investment tools that quantify value. Use testimonials to demonstrate how customers achieved specific results.

By marketing your universe of value, you begin to differentiate your company from the competition. Remember to heed one key principle: market brand value.

Customers will begin to see that the services you provide are more valuable than the penny discount they typically ask for.

Kelly Howard

A new product is introduced, such as the cell phone. The firm introducing the product earns a nice profit. The profit is shown in the figure below. Everyone wants to get in on a good thing, and so other firms introduce their own cell phones. As more and more phones are introduced, consumers have many choices of virtually identical products. This is shown by the demand curve becoming more and more price-elastic, as shown in the figures that follow.

The price elasticity finally approaches infinity—where the demand curve is a horizontal line. This is what the article means by "commoditization." The product has many substitutes that are essentially identical. When this occurs, the market is perfectly competitive, and the demand seen by any one firm is a horizontal line at the market price.

Notice what happens to the firm's ability to raise price and to its profits. The firm cannot raise its price without losing most or all of its customers. The firm's profits decline to the point where it earns a zero economic profit. This is why business advisers consider commoditization bad.

The article goes on to advise firms to differentiate their products, to somehow make the demand curve less price-elastic. Distinctive packaging, brand names, and advertising can all help create a difference in the consumer's mind between one firm's product and other similar products. The effect of differentiation is discussed in the following two chapters.

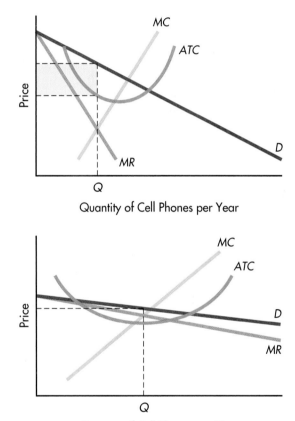

11

Monopoly

P erfect competition captures the behavior of individual firms when there are a great many firms selling an identical product. To find out how a firm's behavior would be different in the opposite situation—that is, when there are no competitors, just one firm selling an item—economists use the model of monopoly. The market structure of monopoly is a model that is intended to be used as a contrast to perfect competition. The comparison enables us to understand the effects of competition. ■

Fundamental Questions

1. What is monopoly?

2. How is a monopoly created?

3. What does the demand curve for a monopoly firm look like, and why?

4. Why would someone want to have a monopoly in some business or activity?

5. Under what conditions will a monopolist charge different customers different prices for the same product?

6. How do the predictions of the models of perfect competition and monopoly differ?

1. The Market Structure of Monopoly

Does a monopolist earn unseemly profits by charging outrageously high prices? Does a monopolist go its own way no matter what customers want? What is the relation between the Parker Brothers game Monopoly and the economic model of monopoly? We'll discuss these questions in this chapter, and we'll begin by defining what a monopolist is.

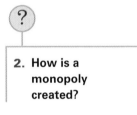

1. What is monopoly?

1.a. Market Definition

monopoly: a market structure in which there is a single supplier of a product

monopoly firm (monopolist): a single supplier of a product for which there are no close substitutes

Monopoly is a market structure in which there is a single supplier of a product. A **monopoly firm (monopolist)** may be large or small, but whatever its size, it must be the *only supplier* of the product. In addition, a monopoly firm must sell a product for which there are *no close substitutes*. The more likely that there is a substitute for a firm's product, the less likely it is that the firm has a monopoly.

You purchase products from monopoly firms every day, perhaps without realizing it. Congress created the U.S. Postal Service to provide first-class mail service. No other firm is allowed to provide that service. In the United States, the currency you use is issued and its quantity is controlled by a government entity known as the Federal Reserve; in other countries, there is a central bank like the Federal Reserve that controls the money supply. It is illegal for any organization or individual other than the central bank to issue currency.

2. How is a monopoly created?

1.b. The Creation of Monopolies

barrier to entry: anything that impedes the ability of firms to begin a new business in an industry in which existing firms are earning positive economic profits

The pharmaceutical firm Glaxo-Wellcome's profits doubled in the three years following the introduction of AZT. Glaxo-Wellcome was a monopoly supplier of AZT, a drug to slow down AIDS, and it was earning above-normal profits. But if a product is valuable and the owners are getting rich from selling it, won't others develop substitutes and also enjoy the fruits of the market? Yes, unless something gets in the way. The name given to that something is a **barrier to entry.** There are three general classes of barriers to entry:

- Natural barriers, such as economies of scale
- Actions on the part of firms that create barriers to entry
- Governmentally created barriers

1.b.1. Economies of Scale Economies of scale can be a barrier to entry. There are economies of scale in the generation of electricity. The larger the generating plant, the lower the cost per kilowatt-hour of electricity produced. A large generating plant can produce each unit of electricity much less expensively than several small generating plants. Size thus constitutes a barrier to entry, since to be able to enter the market and compete with existing large-scale public utilities, a firm needs to be large so that it can produce each kilowatt-hour as inexpensively as the large-scale plants.

1.b.2. Actions by Firms Entry is barred when one firm owns an essential resource. The owners of the desiccant clay mine in New Mexico had a monopoly position because they owned the essential resource, clay. No one could produce a close substitute for many years; eventually a synthetic clay was developed. Inventions and discoveries are essential resources, at least until others develop close substitutes. Microsoft owned the important resource known as Windows.

1.b.3. Government   Barriers to entry are often created by governments. The U.S. government issues patents, which provide a firm with a monopoly on certain products, inventions, or discoveries for a period of 17 years. Such was the case with the Glaxo-Wellcome monopoly. The company was granted a patent on AZT and thus was, by law, the only supplier of the drug. Domestic government policy also restricts entry into many industries. The federal government issues broadcast licenses for radio and television and grants airlines landing rights at certain airports. City governments limit the number of taxi companies that can operate, the number of cable television companies that can provide service, and the number of garbage collection firms that can provide service. State and local governments issue liquor licenses, cosmetology licenses (for hair cutters), contractor licenses, and many other licenses to carry on business, and restrict the number of electric utility, cable, satellite, garbage collection, and other companies. These are just a few examples of government-created monopolies in the United States.

1.c. Types of Monopolies

The word *monopoly* is often part of another term, such as *natural monopoly, local monopoly, regulated monopoly, monopoly power,* and *monopolization.* A **natural monopoly** is a firm that has become a monopoly because of economies of scale and demand conditions. The adjective *natural* indicates that the monopoly arises from cost and demand conditions, not from government action. If costs decline as the quantity produced rises, only very large producers will be able to stay in business. Their lower costs will enable them to force smaller producers, who have higher costs, out of business. Large producers can underprice smaller producers, as illustrated in Figure 1. The larger firm, operating along ATC_2, can set a price anywhere between P_1 and P_2 which is lower than the smaller firm, operating along ATC_1, can sell its products at and still survive. If the market can support only one producer or if the long-run average-total-cost curve continually slopes downward, the monopoly that results is said to be natural.

natural monopoly: a monopoly that arises from economies of scale

---

FIGURE 1   **Economies of Scale**

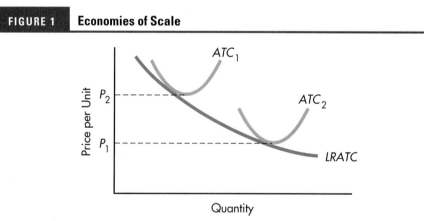

A large firm producing along ATC_2 can produce output much less expensively per unit than a small firm operating along ATC_1. The large firm, therefore, can set a price that is below the minimum point of the small firm's average-total-cost curve yet still earn profit. Any price between P_1 and P_2 will provide a profit for the large firm and a loss for the small firm.

Electric utilities are often considered to be natural monopolies because there are large economies of scale in the generation of electricity. One large power plant can generate electricity at a lower cost per kilowatt-hour than can several small power plants. The transmission of electricity is different, however. There are diseconomies of scale in the transmission of electricity. The farther electricity has to be transmitted, the higher the cost per kilowatt-hour. Together, generation and transmission imply an MES (minimum efficient scale) that is sufficiently large for a local monopoly but not for a national or international monopoly.

local monopoly: a monopoly that exists in a limited geographic area

A **local monopoly** is a firm that has a monopoly within a specific geographic area. An electric utility may be the sole supplier of electricity in a municipality or local area. A taxicab company may have a monopoly for service to the airport or within a city. Cable TV companies may have monopolies within municipalities. An airline may have a monopoly over some routes.

regulated monopoly: a monopoly firm whose behavior is monitored and prescribed by a government entity

A **regulated monopoly** is a monopoly whose prices and production rates are controlled by a government entity. Electric utility companies, telephone companies, cable TV companies, and water companies are or have been regulated monopolies. A state corporation or utility commission sets their rates, determines the costs to be allowed in the production of their services, and restricts entry by other firms.

monopoly power: market power, the ability to set prices

price maker: a firm that sets the price of the product it sells

Monopoly power is market power, the ability to set prices rather than just be a price taker. Market power exists whenever the demand curve facing the producer is downward sloping. All firms except those operating in perfectly competitive markets have some monopoly power. A firm that has monopoly power is a **price maker** rather than a price taker. A firm that has to lower prices to sell more is a price maker—it will maximize profit by finding the quantity where $MR = MC$ and then setting price according to demand.

monopolization: an attempt by a firm to dominate a market or become a monopoly

Monopolization refers to the attempt by a firm to take over a market—that is, the attempt to become the only supplier of a good or service. As we'll discuss in the chapter "Antitrust and Regulation," the law forbids monopolization even though it does not always forbid monopolies.

Many businesses are given monopolies by the governments of the nations in which they operate. The government tells the business that it can have an exclusive operation, without worrying about entry or competition. In this photo, oil distributors are given a monopoly by a Middle Eastern government; the employees are watching where and to whom the supplies of oil are allocated.

1. A monopoly firm is the sole supplier of a product for which there are no close substitutes.

2. A monopoly firm remains the sole supplier because of barriers to entry.

3. Barriers to entry may be economic, such as economies of scale; they may be due to the exclusive ownership of an essential resource; or they may be created by government policy.

4. A natural monopoly is a monopoly that results from economies of scale. A regulated monopoly is a monopoly whose pricing and production are controlled by the government. A local monopoly is a firm that has a monopoly in a specific geographic region.

5. Monopoly power, or market power, is when a firm can set prices rather than just be a price taker.

?

3. What does the demand curve for a monopoly firm look like, and why?

2. The Demand Curve Facing a Monopoly Firm

In any market, the industry demand curve is a downward-sloping line because of the law of demand. Although the industry demand curve is downward sloping, the demand curve facing an individual firm in a perfectly competitive market is a horizontal line at the market price. This is not the case for a monopoly. Because a monopolist is the only producer, it *is* the industry, so its demand curve is the industry demand curve; it slopes down.

The demand curve facing the monopoly firm is the industry demand curve.

2.a. Marginal Revenue

In 2004, Apple introduced the iPod. Throughout the year, Apple had a monopoly on the iPod. Let's consider the firm's pricing and output decisions, using hypothetical cost and revenue data.

Suppose an iPod sells for $150, and at that price the firm is selling 5 iPods per day, as shown in Figure 2. If Apple wants to sell more, it must move down the demand curve. Why? Because of the law of demand. People will do without the iPod rather than pay more than they think it's worth. As the price declines, more people are willing and able to purchase an iPod—sales increase. The table in Figure 2 shows that if the monopoly firm lowers the price to $135 per unit from $140, it will sell 8 iPods per day instead of 7.

What is the firm's marginal revenue? To find marginal revenue, the total revenue earned at $140 per iPod must be compared to the total revenue earned at $135 per iPod—the change in total revenue must be calculated. At $140 apiece, 7 iPods are sold each day, and total revenue each day is

$$\$140 \text{ per iPod} \times 7 \text{ iPods} = \$980$$

At $135 apiece, 8 iPods are sold, and total revenue is

$$\$135 \text{ per iPod} \times 8 \text{ iPods} = \$1,080$$

The difference, change in total revenue, is $100. Thus, marginal revenue is

$$\frac{\Delta TR}{\Delta Q} = \frac{\$100}{1 \text{ iPod}} = \$100$$

FIGURE 2 **Demand Curve for a Monopolist**

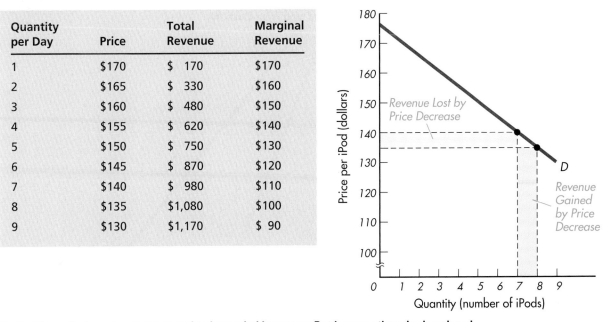

Quantity per Day	Price	Total Revenue	Marginal Revenue
1	$170	$ 170	$170
2	$165	$ 330	$160
3	$160	$ 480	$150
4	$155	$ 620	$140
5	$150	$ 750	$130
6	$145	$ 870	$120
7	$140	$ 980	$110
8	$135	$1,080	$100
9	$130	$1,170	$ 90

As the iPod price is reduced, the quantity demanded increases. But because the price is reduced on all quantities sold, not just on the last unit sold, marginal revenue declines faster than price.

The change in revenue is the difference between the increased revenue due to the increased quantity sold, the yellow area in Figure 2, and the decreased revenue due to a lower price, the blue area in Figure 2.

Marginal revenue is less than price for a monopoly firm.

The price is $135 per iPod, but marginal revenue is $100 per iPod. Price and marginal revenue are not the same for a monopoly firm. This is a fundamental difference between a monopolist and a perfect competitor. For a perfect competitor, price and marginal revenue are the same.

Marginal revenue is less than price and declines as output rises because the monopolist must lower the price in order to sell more units. When the price of an iPod is $140, the firm sells 7 iPods. When the price is dropped to $135, the firm sells 8 units. The firm does not sell the first 7 iPods for $140 and the eighth one for $135. It might lose business if it tried to do that. The customer who purchased the iPod at $135 could sell it for $137.50 to a customer who was about to pay $140, and the firm would lose the $140 sale. Customers who would have paid $140 could decide to wait until they too can get the $135 price. As long as customers know about the prices paid by other customers and as long as the firm cannot easily distinguish among customers, the monopoly firm is not able to charge a different price for each additional unit. All units are sold at the same price, and in order to sell additional units, the monopolist must lower the price on all units. As a result, marginal revenue and price are not the same.

2.a.1. Marginal and Average Revenue Recall from the chapters "Elasticity: Demand and Supply" and "Profit Maximization" that whenever the marginal is greater than the average, the average rises, and whenever the marginal is less than the average, the average falls. Average revenue is calculated by dividing total revenue by the number of units of output sold.

FIGURE 3 — Downward-Sloping Demand Curve and Revenue

(a) Demand and Price Elasticity

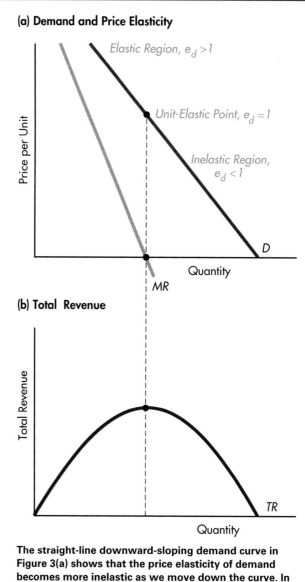

(b) Total Revenue

The straight-line downward-sloping demand curve in Figure 3(a) shows that the price elasticity of demand becomes more inelastic as we move down the curve. In the elastic region, revenue increases as price is lowered, as shown in Figure 3(b); in the inelastic region, revenue decreases as price is lowered. The revenue-maximizing point, the top of the curve in Figure 3(b), occurs where the demand curve is unit-elastic, shown in Figure 3(a).

At a price of $150 per iPod, average revenue is $AR = \$750/5 = \$150$. At a price of $145, average revenue is $AR = \$870/6 = \$145$. Average revenue is the same as price; in fact, *the average-revenue curve is the demand curve.* Because of the law of demand, where quantity demanded rises as price falls, average revenue (price) always falls as output rises (the demand curve slopes downward). Because average revenue falls as output rises, marginal revenue must always be less than average revenue. For the monopolist (or any firm facing a downward-sloping demand curve), marginal revenue always declines as output increases, and the marginal-revenue curve always lies below the demand curve.

Also recall from previous chapters that the marginal-revenue curve is positive in the elastic region of the demand curve, is zero at the output level where the demand curve is unit-elastic, and is negative in the inelastic portion of the demand curve.[1] This is illustrated in Figure 3.

RECAP

1. The demand curve facing a monopoly firm is the market demand curve.

2. For the monopoly firm, price is greater than marginal revenue. For the perfectly competitive firm, price and marginal revenue are equal.

3. As price declines, total revenue increases in the elastic portion of the demand curve, reaches a maximum at the unit-elastic point, and declines in the inelastic portion.

4. The marginal-revenue curve of the monopoly firm lies below the demand curve.

5. For both the perfectly competitive firm and the monopoly firm, price = average revenue = demand.

3. Profit Maximization

The objective of the monopoly firm is to maximize profit. Where does the monopolist choose to produce, and what price does it set? Recall from the chapter "Profit Maximization" that all profit-maximizing firms produce at the point where marginal revenue equals marginal cost.

3.a. What Price to Charge?

A schedule of revenues and costs for the iPod producer accompanies Figure 4. Total revenue (TR) is listed in column 3; total cost (TC), in column 4. Total profit ($TR - TC$), shown in column 5, is the difference between the entries in column 3 and those in column 4. Marginal revenue (MR) is listed in column 6, marginal cost (MC) in column 7, and average total cost (ATC) in column 8.

The quantity of output to be produced is the quantity that corresponds to the point where $MR = MC$. How high a price will the market bear at that quantity? The market is willing and able to purchase the quantity given by $MR = MC$ at the corresponding price on the demand curve. As shown in Figure 4(a), the price is found by drawing a vertical line from the point where $MR = MC$ up to the demand curve and then extending a horizontal line over to the vertical axis. That price is $135 when output is 8.

3.b. Monopoly Profit and Loss

The profit that the monopoly firm generates by selling 8 iPods at a price of $135 is shown in Figure 4(a) as the colored rectangle. The vertical distance between the ATC curve and the demand curve, multiplied by the quantity sold, yields total profit.

?

4. Why would someone want to have a monopoly in some business or activity?

---

[1] The slope of the demand curve is one-half the slope of the marginal-revenue curve. Consider the demand formula $P = a - bQ$; total revenue is $PQ = aQ - bQ^2$, so marginal revenue is $MR = a - 2bQ$.

FIGURE 4 — Profit Maximization for the iPod Seller

(1) Total Output (Q)	(2) Price (P)	(3) Total Revenue (TR)	(4) Total Cost (TC)	(5) Total Profit (TR − TC)	(6) Marginal Revenue (MR)	(7) Marginal Cost (MC)	(8) Average Total Cost (ATC)
0	$175	$ 0	$100	$100			
1	$170	$ 170	$200	$ 30	$170	$100	$200
2	$165	$ 330	$280	$ 50	$160	$ 80	$140
3	$160	$ 480	$350	$130	$150	$ 70	$117
4	$155	$ 620	$400	$220	$140	$ 50	$100
5	$150	$ 750	$450	$300	$130	$ 50	$ 90
6	$145	$ 870	$520	$350	$120	$ 70	$ 87
7	$140	$ 980	$600	$380	$110	$ 80	$ 86
8	$135	$1,080	$700	$380	$100	$100	$ 88
9	$130	$1,170	$900	$270	$ 90	$200	$100

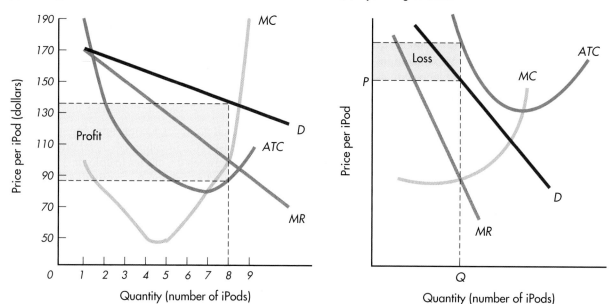

(a) Making a Profit   **(b) Operating at a Loss**

The data listed in the table are plotted in Figure 4(a). The firm produces where *MR* = *MC*, 8 units; charges a price given by the demand curve directly above the production of 8 units, a price of $135 per iPod; and earns a profit (yellow rectangle). In Figure 4(b), the firm is shown to be operating at a loss (blue rectangle). It produces output *Q* at price *P*, but the average total cost exceeds the price.

A monopolist can earn above-normal profits in the long run.

Just like any other firm, a monopoly firm could experience a loss. A monopoly supplier of sharpeners for disposable razor blades probably would not be very successful, and the U.S. Postal Service has failed to make a profit in five of the last ten years. Unless price exceeds average total costs, the firm loses money. A monopolist producing at a loss is shown in Figure 4(b)—the price is less than the average total cost.

Like a perfectly competitive firm, a monopolist will suspend operations in the short run if its price does not exceed the average variable cost at the quantity the firm produces. And, like a perfectly competitive firm, a monopolist will shut down permanently if revenue is not likely to equal or exceed all costs in the long run (unless the government subsidizes the firm, as it does in the case of the U.S. Postal Service). In contrast, however, if a monopolist makes a profit, barriers to entry will keep other firms out of the industry. As a result, the monopolist can earn above-normal profits in the long run.

3.c. Supply and the Monopoly Firm

For the firm in perfect competition, the supply curve is that portion of the marginal-cost curve that lies above the average-cost curve, and the market supply curve is the sum of all the individual firms' supply curves. The supply curve for the firm selling in any of the other market structures is not as straightforward to derive, and, therefore, neither is the market supply curve. The reason is that firms selling in market structures other than perfect competition are price makers rather than price takers. This means that the hypothetical experiment of varying the price of a product and seeing how the firm selling that product reacts makes no sense.

In the case of the monopolist, the firm supplies a quantity determined by setting marginal revenue equal to marginal cost, but it also sets the price to go along with this quantity. Varying the price will not change the decision rule, since the firm will choose to produce at its profit-maximizing output level and set the price accordingly. There is, therefore, only one quantity and price at which the monopolist will operate. There is a supply point, not a supply curve. Moreover, because the monopolist is the only firm in the market, its supply curve (or supply point) is also the market supply curve (or point).

The complications of the price makers do not alter the supply rule: A firm will produce and offer for sale a quantity that equates marginal revenue with marginal cost. This supply rule applies to all firms, regardless of the market structure in which the firm operates.

3.d. Monopoly Myths

There are a few myths about monopoly that we have debunked here. The first myth is that a monopolist can charge any price it wants and will reap unseemly profits by continually increasing the price. We know that a monopolist maximizes profit by producing the quantity that equates marginal revenue and marginal cost. We also know that a monopolist can price and sell only the quantities given by the demand curve. If the demand curve is very inelastic, as would be the case for a lifesaving pharmaceutical, then the price the monopolist will charge will be high. Conversely, if demand is very price-elastic, the monopolist will experience losses if it charges exorbitant prices. A second myth is that a monopolist is not sensitive to customers. The monopolist can stay in business only if it earns at least a normal profit (unless a government entity subsidizes the the money losing monopolist). Ignoring customers, producing a good that no one will purchase, setting prices that all customers think are exorbitant, and providing terrible service or products that customers do not want will not allow a firm to remain in business for long. The monopolist faces a demand curve for its product and must search for a price and quantity that are dictated by that demand curve. The third myth is that the monopolist cannot make a loss. A monopolist is no different from any other firm in that it has costs of doing business and it must earn sufficient revenues to pay those costs. If the monopolist sets too high a price or provides a product that few people want, revenues may be less than costs and losses may result.

1. Profit is maximized at the output level where $MR = MC$.

2. The price charged by the monopoly firm is the point on the demand curve that corresponds to the quantity where $MR = MC$.

3. A monopoly firm can make profits or experience losses. A monopoly firm can earn above-normal profit in the long run.

4. The monopoly firm will shut down in the short run if all variable costs aren't covered. It will shut down in the long run if all costs aren't covered.

5. The amount that a firm is willing and able to supply depends on marginal revenue and marginal cost. A firm will produce and offer for sale a quantity that equates marginal revenue and marginal cost.

4. Market Power and Price Discrimination

price discrimination: charging different customers at different prices for the same product

With market power, a firm can choose to charge more and sell less or to charge less and sell more. Under certain conditions, a firm with market power is able to charge different customers different prices. This is called **price discrimination.** Figure 5 shows the demand curve facing a firm with market power. Notice that the demand curve tells us that at price P_1, consumers are willing and able to purchase quantity Q_1. If the price is P_2, they are willing and able to purchase Q_2. If the firm sells to everyone at the same price, say P_2, it does not make as much money as it would if it could charge some customers, those who were willing and able to pay a higher price, P_1, and other customers P_2. It could sell quantity Q_1 at price P_1 and quantity $Q_2 - Q_1$ at price P_2. What would be even better for the firm would be to charge each

---

FIGURE 5   **Price Discrimination**

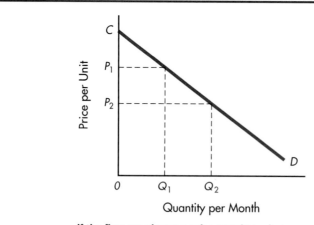

If the firm can charge a price equal to what each person is willing and able to pay, the firm esssentially collects the consumer surplus instead of the consumer. In this figure, the firm is charging one set of customers price P_1 and another set of customers price P_2.

---

customer what that customer was willing and able to pay. This is price discrimination; price discrimination enables the firm to capture consumer surplus for itself.

4.a. Necessary Conditions for Price Discrimination

?

5. Under what conditions will a monopolist charge different customers different prices for the same product?

You read in section 2.a that the monopoly firm has to sell all of its products at a uniform price; otherwise, one customer could sell to another, thereby reducing the monopoly firm's profit. However, if customers do not come into contact with each other or are somehow separated by the firm, the firm may be able to charge each customer the exact price that he or she is willing to pay.

When different customers are charged different prices for the same product or when customers are charged different prices for different quantities of the same product, price discrimination is occurring. Price discrimination occurs when price changes result not from cost changes, but from the firm's attempt to extract more of the consumer surplus. Certain conditions are necessary for price discrimination to occur:

- The firm cannot be a price taker (perfect competitor).
- The firm must be able to separate customers according to price elasticities of demand.
- The firm must be able to prevent resale of the product.

4.b. Examples of Price Discrimination

Examples of price discrimination are not hard to find. Senior citizens often pay a lower price than the general population at movie theaters, drugstores, and golf courses. It is relatively easy to identify senior citizens and to ensure that they do not resell their tickets to the general population.

Tuition at state schools is different for in-state and out-of-state residents. It is not difficult to find out where a student resides, and it is very easy to ensure that in-state students do not sell their places to out-of-state students.

Airlines discriminate between business passengers and others. Passengers who do not fly at the busiest times, who purchase tickets in advance, and who can stay at their destination longer than a day pay lower fares than business passengers, who cannot make advance reservations and who must travel during rush hours. It is relatively easy for the airlines to separate business from nonbusiness passengers and to ensure that the latter do not sell their tickets to the former.

Electric utilities practice a form of price discrimination by charging different rates for different quantities of electricity used. The rate declines as the quantity purchased increases. A customer might pay $.07 per kilowatt-hour for the first 100 kilowatt-hours, $.06 for the next 100, and so on. Many utility companies have different rate structures for different classes of customers as well. Businesses pay less per kilowatt-hour than households.

Grocery coupons, mail-in rebates, trading stamps, and other discount strategies are also price-discrimination techniques. Shoppers who are willing to spend time cutting out coupons and presenting them receive a lower price than those who are not willing to spend that time. Shoppers are separated by the amount of time they are willing to devote to coupon clipping. Is it possible that the popcorn at the movies is also a price-discrimination tactic? If the excess price of the popcorn and other foodstuffs at the movies was simply added to the price of an admission ticket, the movie theater would lose some of those customers who do not purchase popcorn. By charging a high price for the popcorn, the movie theater is distinguishing those customers who have a lower price elasticity of demand for the entire package of the movie and the popcorn from those with a higher elasticity of demand.

4.c. The Theory of Price Discrimination

How does price discrimination work? Suppose there are two classes of buyers for movie tickets, senior citizens and everybody else, and each class has a different price elasticity of demand. The two classes are shown in Figure 6. Profit is maximized when $MR = MC$. Because the same firm is providing the goods in two submarkets, MC is the same for senior citizens and the general public, but the demand curves differ. Because the demand curves of the two groups differ, there are two MR curves: MR_{sc} for senior citizens, in Figure 6(a), and MR_{gp} for the general population, in Figure 6(b). Profit is maximized when $MR_{sc} = MC$ and when $MR_{gp} = MC$. The price is found by drawing a vertical line from the quantities where $MR = MC$ up to the respective demand curves, D_{sc} and D_{gp}.

Notice that the price to the general population, P_{gp}, is higher than the price to the senior citizens, P_{sc}. The reason is that the senior citizens' demand curve is more elastic than the demand curve of the general population. Senior citizens are more sensitive to price than is the general population, so to attract more of their business, the merchant has to offer them a lower price.

By discriminating, a monopoly firm makes greater profits than it would make by charging both groups the same price. If both groups were charged the same price, P_{gp}, the monopoly firm would lose sales to senior citizens who found the price too high, Q_{sc} to Q_2. And if both groups were charged P_{sc}, so few additional sales to the general population would be made that revenues would fall. A firm with market power could collect the entire consumer surplus if it could charge each customer exactly the price that that customer was willing and able to pay. This is called *perfect price discrimination*.

| FIGURE 6 | Price Discrimination in Action |

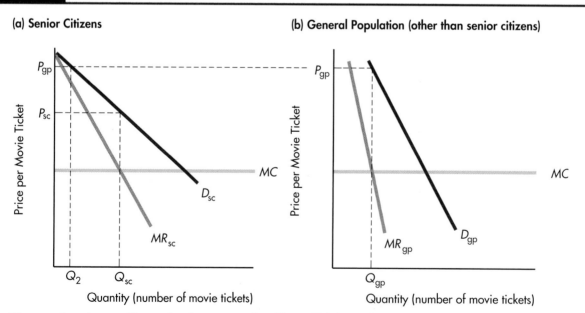

There are two classes of buyers for the same product. Figure 6(a) shows the elasticity of demand for senior citizens. Figure 6(b) shows the elasticity of demand for the general population. The demand of the senior citizens is more elastic than that of the general population. As a result, faced with the same marginal cost, the firm charges senior citizens a lower price than it charges the rest of the population. The quantity sold to senior citizens is Q_{sc}, the intersection between MC and MR_{sc}, and the price charged is P_{sc}. The quantity sold to the general population is Q_{gp}, and the price charged is P_{gp}.

1. Price discrimination occurs when a firm charges different customers different prices for the same product or charges different prices for different quantities of the same product.

2. Three conditions are necessary for price discrimination to occur: (a) the firm must have some market power, (b) the firm must be able to separate customers according to price elasticities of demand, and (c) the firm must be able to prevent resale of the product.

?

6. How do the predictions of the models of perfect competition and monopoly differ?

5. Comparison of Perfect Competition and Monopoly

Because perfect competition and monopoly are bookends—opposites that are intended to surround all business behavior—it is useful to compare the outcome of the two.

5.a. Costs of Monopoly: Inefficiency

In the long run, the perfectly competitive firm operates at the minimum point of the long-run average-total-cost curve, and the firm's price is equal to its marginal cost. Profit is at the normal level. A monopolist does not operate at the minimum point of the average-total-cost curve and does not set price equal to marginal cost. Because entry does not occur, a monopoly firm may earn above-normal profit in the long run.

Figure 7(a) shows a perfectly competitive market. The market demand curve is D; the market supply curve is S. The market price determined by the intersection of D and S is P_{pc}. At P_{pc}, the perfectly competitive market produces Q_{pc}. Consumers are able to enjoy the consumer surplus indicated by the triangle $P_{pc}BA$ by purchasing the quantity Q_{pc} at the price P_{pc}. Firms receive the producer surplus indicated by triangle OBP_{pc} by producing the quantity Q_{pc} and selling that quantity at price P_{pc}.

To compare these results to monopoly, we must assume that all of the firms in a perfectly competitive industry are merged into a single monopoly firm and that the monopolist does not close or alter plants and does not achieve any economies of scale. In other words, what would occur if a perfectly competitive industry were transformed into a monopoly—just one firm that determines price and quantity produced? The industry demand curve becomes the monopoly firm's demand curve, and the industry supply curve becomes the monopoly firm's marginal-cost curve. Recall that a firm will supply the quantity given by the point where marginal revenue equals marginal-cost curve (above the average-variable-cost curve). This is illustrated in Figure 7(b).

The monopoly firm restricts quantity produced to Q_m, where $MR = MC$, and charges a price P_m, as indicated on the demand curve shown in Figure 7(b). *The monopoly firm thus produces a lower quantity than does the perfectly competitive market, Q_m compared to Q_{pc}, and sells that smaller quantity at a higher price, P_m compared to P_{pc}.* In addition, the consumer surplus in monopoly is the triangle P_mCA, which is smaller than the consumer surplus under perfect competition, $P_{pc}BA$. The rectangle $P_{pc}ECP_m$ is part of consumer surplus in perfect competition. In monopoly, that part of consumer surplus is transferred to the firm. The total producer surplus is area $OFCP_m$.

FIGURE 7 Monopoly and Perfect Competition Compared

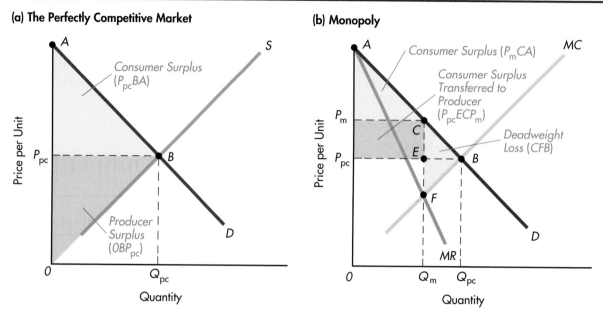

(a) The Perfectly Competitive Market

(b) Monopoly

Figure 7(a) shows a perfectly competitive industry; it produces at the point where industry demand, *D*, and industry supply, *S*, intersect. The quantity produced by the industry is Q_{pc}; the price charged is P_{pc}. Consumer surplus is the triangle $P_{pc}BA$. Figure 7(b) shows what happens if the industry is monopolized. The single firm faces the industry demand curve, *D*, and has the marginal-revenue curve *MR*. The intersection of the marginal-cost curve and the marginal-revenue curve indicates the quantity that will be produced, Q_m. The price charged for Q_m is P_m. Thus, the monopoly firm produces less and charges more than the perfectly competitive industry. Consumer surplus, shown as the triangle P_mCA, is smaller in the monopoly industry. The area $P_{pc}ECP_m$ is the consumer surplus in perfect competition that is transferred from consumer to producer. The producer surplus is area $OFCP_m$. The deadweight loss is the area *CFB*.

---

deadweight loss: the reduction of consumer surplus without a corresponding increase in profit when a perfectly competitive firm is monopolized

Thus, firms are better off (more producer surplus) while consumers are worse off (less consumer surplus) under monopoly compared to perfect competition. Consumers are worse off by area $P_{pc}BCP_m$, and firms are better off by area $P_{pc}ECP_m$ less area *EFB*. The consumer and producer surplus represented by triangle *CFB* is lost by both consumers and firms and goes to no one. This loss is the reduction in consumer surplus and producer surplus that is not transferred to the monopoly firm or to anyone else; it is called a **deadweight loss.**

RECAP

1. A monopoly firm produces a smaller quantity and charges a higher price than a perfectly competitive industry if the two industries have identical costs.

2. The consumer surplus is smaller if an industry is operated by a monopoly firm than it is if an industry is operated by perfectly competitive firms. Profits are larger in the monopoly case.

3. The costs to society that result when a perfectly competitive industry becomes a monopoly are a reduction of consumer surplus and producer surplus that is not transferred to anyone. This loss is called a *deadweight loss.*

Summary

1. What is monopoly?

- Monopoly is a market structure in which there is a single supplier of a product. A monopoly firm, or monopolist, is the only supplier of a product for which there are no close substitutes. *§1.a*

2. How is a monopoly created?

- Natural barriers to entry (such as economies of scale), barriers erected by firms in the industry, and barriers erected by government may create monopolies. *§1.b, 1.b.1, 1.b.2, 1.b.3*

- A natural monopoly refers to a monopoly that exists due to economies of scale. A local monopoly is a monopoly that applies only to a niche of the market or to a small geographical area. A regulated monopoly is a firm whose price and output are controlled by a government entity. Monopoly power refers to market power or the ability a firm has to set prices rather than act as a price taker. *§1.c*

3. What does the demand curve for a monopoly firm look like, and why?

- Because a monopolist is the only producer of a good or service, the demand curve facing a monopoly firm is the industry demand curve. *§2*

- Price and marginal revenue are not the same for a monopoly firm. Marginal revenue is less than price. *§2.a*

- The average-revenue curve is the demand curve. *§2.a.1*

- A monopoly firm maximizes profit by producing the quantity of output yielded at the point where marginal revenue and marginal cost are equal. *§3.a*

- A monopoly firm sets a price that is on the demand curve and that corresponds to the point where marginal revenue and marginal cost are equal. *§3.a*

4. Why would someone want to have a monopoly in some business or activity?

- A monopoly firm can make above-normal or normal profit or even a loss. If it makes above-normal profit, entry by other firms does not occur and the monopoly firm can earn above-normal profit in the long run. Exit occurs if the monopoly firm cannot cover its costs in the long run. *§3.b*

5. Under what conditions will a monopolist charge different customers different prices for the same product?

- Price discrimination occurs when the firm is not a price taker, can separate customers according to their price elasticities of demand for the firm's product, and can prevent resale of the product. *§4.a*

6. How do the predictions of the models of perfect competition and monopoly differ?

- A comparison of monopoly and perfectly competitive firms implies that monopoly imposes costs on society. These costs include less output being produced and that output being sold at a higher price. *§5.a*

Key Terms

monopoly *§1.a*

monopoly firm (monopolist) *§1.a*

barrier to entry *§1.b*

natural monopoly *§1.c*

local monopoly *§1.c*

regulated monopoly *§1.c*

monopoly power *§1.c*

price maker *§1.c*

monopolization *§1.c*

price discrimination *§4*

deadweight loss *§5.a*

Exercises

1. About 85 percent of the soup sold in the United States is Campbell's brand. Is Campbell Soup Company a monopoly firm?

2. Price discrimination is practiced by movie theaters, motels, golf courses, drugstores, and universities. Are they monopolies? If not, how can they carry out price discrimination?

3. Why is it necessary for the seller to be able to keep customers from reselling the product in order for price discrimination to occur? There are many products for

which you get a discount for purchasing large quantities. For instance, most liquor stores will provide a discount on wine if you purchase a case. Is this price discrimination? If so, what is to keep one customer from purchasing cases of wine and then reselling single bottles at a price above the case price but below the liquor store's single-bottle price?

4. Many people have claimed that there is no good for which substitutes are not available. If so, does this mean there is no such thing as monopoly?

5. Suppose that at a price of $6 per unit, quantity demanded is 12 units. Calculate the quantity demanded when the marginal revenue is $6 per unit. (*Hint:* The price elasticity of demand is unity at the midpoint of the demand curve.)

6. In the following figure, if the monopoly firm faces ATC_1, which rectangle measures total profit? If the monopoly firm faces ATC_2, what is total profit? What information would you need in order to know whether the monopoly firm will shut down or continue producing in the short run? In the long run?

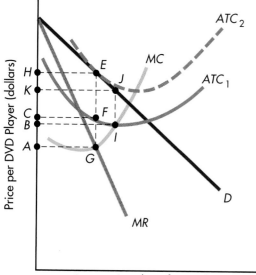

7. In recent years, U.S. car manufacturers have charged lower prices for cars in western states in an effort to offset the competition from Japanese cars. This two-tier pricing scheme has upset many car dealers in the eastern states. Many have called it discriminatory and illegal. What conditions are necessary for this pricing scheme to be profitable to the U.S. companies?

8. Consider the following demand schedule. Does it apply to a perfectly competitive firm? Compute marginal and average revenue.

Price	Quantity	Price	Quantity
$100	1	$70	5
$ 95	2	$55	6
$ 88	3	$40	7
$ 80	4	$22	8

9. Suppose the marginal cost of producing the good in question 8 is a constant $10 per unit of output. What quantity of output will the firm produce?

10. Do you agree or disagree with this statement: "A monopoly firm will charge an exorbitant price for its product"? Explain your answer.

11. Do you agree or disagree with this statement: "A monopoly firm will run a much less safe business than a perfect competitor"? Explain your answer.

12. State colleges and universities have two levels of tuition or fees. The less expensive is for residents of the state; the more expensive is for nonresidents. Assume that the universities are profit-maximizing monopolists and explain their pricing policy. Now, explain why the colleges and universities give student aid and scholarships.

13. Several electric utilities are providing customers with a choice of billing procedures. Customers can select a time-of-day meter that registers electric usage throughout the day, or they can select a regular meter that registers total usage at the end of the day. With the time-of-day meter, the utility is able to charge customers a much higher rate for peak usage than for nonpeak usage. The regular meter users pay the same rate for electric usage no matter when it is used. Why would the electric utility want customers to choose the time-of-day meter?

14. Suppose that a firm has a monopoly on a good with the following demand schedule:

Price	Quantity	Price	Quantity
$10	0	$4	6
$ 9	1	$3	7
$ 8	2	$2	8
$ 7	3	$1	9
$ 6	4	$0	10
$ 5	5		

a. What price and quantity will the monopolist produce at if the marginal cost is a constant $4?

b. Calculate the deadweight loss from having the monopolist produce, rather than a perfect competitor.

Psst! Wanna Buy a Diamond?

Toronto Star
December 1, 2005

For almost 100 years, London-based DeBeers and its South African mines had a stranglehold on the diamond industry.

But three major events put an end to the DeBeers cartel: The fall of communism and the Soviet Union in 1989 enabling diamonds to pour out of Russia; the discovery of diamonds in the Northwest Territories in 1991 and the drying up of some of DeBeers' diamond mines in South Africa.

In a nutshell, there is now competition. DeBeers had to re-think its Diamonds are Forever slogan and has given notice to competitors that they are going to have to ante up bucks to push their own gems.

DeBeers' marketing strategy has shifted to branding and the organic nature of diamonds, a change illustrated when the Diamond Trading Company, the marketing arm of DeBeers, brought the world's largest uncut diamond to Toronto last month. The 300-carat treasure, found in South Africa in the 1970s, is the oldest object on the planet, carbon-dated back 3.4 billion years. DeBeers also sponsored Diamonds: Nature's Miracle, an international competition that challenged designers to create an organic piece of jewellery illustrating the "intrinsic value of diamonds and their 3-billion-year struggle to be born."

Canadian Annik Lucier won with a 3-metre long, shimmering diamond strand. She based her design on the ancient belief that diamonds are fallen stars. Her 80-carat strand of 402 diamonds features oval, marquise, princess cut, round brilliant, borealis and rough diamonds and is sold at Birks for $600,000.

DeBeers and its competitors have also realized the marketing potential of branded diamonds and proprietary cuts.

A proprietary cut is exclusive to one supplier and patented so it cannot be copied by other diamond cutters, explains Kim Sutch, director of Toronto's Diamond Information Centre. DeBeers supplies the diamonds for several proprietary cuts, including the Adura and Tycoon. The Adura (Latin for light on fire), a square princess cut with 27 more facets than the traditional 58-facet princess. The extra facets give the diamond much more sparkle.

The Tycoon is rectangular and similar to an emerald cut. It's referred to as "a diamond with a diamond on top" because of its innovative faceting and prominent top.

Exclusive to Birks is the Amorique. Unveiled in October by Birks creative director Holly Brubach, it is a modern version of the classic round cushion cut, says Paul Lombardi, vice-president of gemstone procurement for Birks.

The Amorique's 70 facets surpass the 58 facets that are the norm for round stones. The extra facets give a lot more dazzling light and the cut eliminates shadowing on the diamond. It represents three years of development and a $10 million investment. The Amorique collection includes a solitaire, a three-stone ring, drop earrings and pendants, set in 18k gold or platinum and in sizes ranging from 0.25 to 3 carats. Prices start at $6,500. There is an international waiting list for stones of 2 to 3 carats.

Donna Jean Mackinnon

Ask people to name a monopoly and the name that comes up most often is DeBeers. DeBeers never was a true monopolist—the only seller—but it has been the dominant firm in the diamond market for nearly 70 years. The South African company controls over 60 percent of the $7 billion a year global market for uncut diamonds. Over the years, it has used its dominance of the industry to drive up the price of diamonds by buying up surplus diamonds. The policy dates back to 1934, when the Great Depression caused a slump in diamond prices and the chairman of DeBeers at that time, Sir Ernest Oppenheimer, offered to buy all the rough stones on the market. Had prices continued to fall, the move would have probably led to DeBeers's bankruptcy. But the price recovered, and Sir Ernest's gamble laid the foundation for the company's dominance of the diamond industry for the remainder of the century. DeBeers spent billions of dollars to accumulate a large stockpile of diamonds that were never sold. At the end of 1999, DeBeers's diamond mountain, hoarded in its London vaults, was worth around $4 billion. The diamonds were used to maintain or manipulate the price. But that practice is changing. DeBeers has announced that it is giving up its traditional role of buyer of last resort of every stone on the market. The reason given for the change is what are called conflict diamonds, diamonds sold by various forces in Africa to fuel civil wars. DeBeers has announced that it will not purchase or trade in conflict diamonds.

While the policy might have some emotional or ethical appeal, the real reason that DeBeers is ending its buyer of last resort strategy is to reduce its declining economic profits. DeBeers knows that if conflict, or blood, diamonds become an emotional consumer issue, they could trigger a public opinion backlash similar to the one that crippled the fur trade. Moreover, rivals such as BHP, an Australian group, and Rio Tinto of the United Kingdom are gaining more and more market share. DeBeers's strategy is two-pronged: to attempt to reduce the supply of diamonds, and to increase the demand.

DeBeers is attempting to become a monopolist again, but through differentiation—it wants to be the only buyer of rough diamonds that are licensed. It is also differentiating its diamonds by the cut. A proprietary cut is exclusive to one supplier and patented so that it cannot be copied by other diamond cutters; in essence creating a monopoly. The monopoly strategy is illustrated in the figure below. The elastic demand, $Demand_e$ and associated marginal revenue, MR_e, represent the demand for diamonds before successful differentiation. The less elastic demand, $Demand_{ie}$ is the result of successful differentiation. The proprietary cut means that people are willing to pay to have a special cut just as they are willing to pay to own a BMW. Differentiation allows the price to be set higher, P_{ie} as opposed to P_e.

The various cuts also act as a price discrimination strategy. By selling different cuts at different prices, DeBeer's is allowing customers to self select – those choosing one cut pay more than those choosing another. In this way, a buyer choosing the Adura cut pays a different amount than the buyer choosing the Tycoon cut. Even if the costs of the cuts are virtually identical, the buyer is paying significantly different amounts. Thus, demand, $Demand_e$, represents the demand for the Adura while the demand, $Demand_{ie}$, represents the demand for the Tycoon. Due to consumer desires (the price elasticities), the price of the Tycoon is higher than the price of the Adura.

On the demand side, DeBeers spends enormous sums to advertise the gems under its famous slogan, "A diamond is forever."

It is difficult for a monopolist to give up its monopoly power and positive economic profits. DeBeers doesn't plan to do so without a fight.

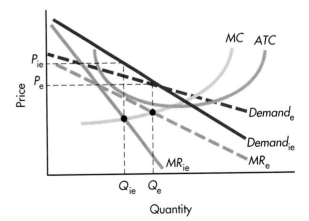

12

Monopolistic Competition and Oligopoly

? Fundamental Questions

1. What is monopolistic competition?

2. What behavior is most common in monopolistic competition?

3. What is oligopoly?

4. In what form does rivalry occur in an oligopoly?

5. Why does cooperation among rivals occur most often in oligopolies?

First there was the hype. Then came the lines and, within hours of the product's launch, the inevitable shortages—followed by the auctions on eBay. This was the process that occurred when the Xbox 360, Microsoft's competitor to Sony's Playstation, hit the stores in early December 2005. Many people thought that this was just another contrived shortage. They wondered whether Microsoft was deliberately holding back on shipments, trying to create an artificial appearance of extraordinary demand.

To understand whether a firm could or would deliberately create a shortage, we have to know the selling environment in which the firm functions. Clearly, Microsoft is not a perfectly competitive firm; there are not many other firms selling identical products. But neither is it a monopoly, because Microsoft is competing here with Sony. So to understand the behavior of Microsoft, Sony, and others, we need to consider other selling environments. Besides perfect competition and mo-

nopoly, the two other selling environments are monopolistic competition and oligopoly. We discuss these two selling environments in this chapter.

Monopolistic competition is like perfect competition in that there are many firms and new firms may enter easily, but it differs from perfect competition in that each firm produces a slightly different product. It is like monopoly in that each firm in monopolistic competition has some market power—each firm has a unique (slightly differentiated) product. It is unlike monopoly in that there are many close substitutes for the goods and services that each firm produces.

With oligopoly, there are few firms—not one, but not many either. A firm in an oligopoly may sell a product that is identical to that sold by other firms in the oligopoly, or it may sell slightly different products from its competitors. We'll discuss monopolistic competition in the first part of this chapter and oligopoly in the second part. ■

1. Monopolistic Competition

?

1. What is
monopolistic
competition?

Monopolistic competition is a market structure in which (1) there are a large number of firms, (2) the products produced by the firms are differentiated, and (3) entry and exit occur easily. The definitions of *monopolistic competition* and *perfect competition* overlap. In both structures, there are a large number of firms. The difference is that each firm in monopolistic competition produces a product that is slightly different from all other products, whereas in perfect competition, the products are standardized. The definition of *monopolistic competition* also overlaps with that of *monopoly*. Because each firm in monopolistic competition produces a unique product, each has a "mini" monopoly over its product. Thus, like a monopolist, a firm in a monopolistically competitive market structure has a downward-sloping demand curve, marginal revenue is below the demand curve, and price is greater than marginal cost. What distinguishes monopolistic competition from monopoly is ease of entry. Any time firms in monopolistic competition are earning above-normal profit, new firms enter, and this entry continues until firms are earning normal profit. In monopoly, a firm can earn above-normal profit in the long run. Table 1 summarizes the differences among perfect competition, monopoly, and monopolistic competition.

*Monopolistically
competitive firms
produce differentiated
products.*

1.a. Profits and Entry

Firms in monopolistic competition tend to use product differentiation more than price to compete. They attempt to provide a product for each market niche. Even though

TABLE 1   Summary of Perfect Competition, Monopoly, and Monopolistic Competition

	Perfect Competition	Monopoly	Monopolistic Competition
Number of firms	Many	One	Many
Type of product	Identical	One	Differentiated
Entry conditions	Easy	Difficult or impossible	Easy
Demand curve for firm	Horizontal (perfectly elastic)	Downward sloping	Downward sloping
Price and marginal cost	$MC = P$	$MC < P$	$MC < P$
Long-run profit	Zero	Yes	Zero

Firms operating in monopolistically competitive environments typically try to differentiate their products from those of their rivals. The more consumers think of a product as being distinctive or unique, the less elastic the demand for the product and the more ability the firm has to raise its price without losing customers. In this photo, we see that Apple is using public transport to advertise its iPod.

the total market may not be expanding, they divide the market into smaller and smaller segments by introducing variations of products. You can think of a market demand curve for clothes, but within that market there are many niches and many demand curves. In fact, there is a separate demand curve for each firm and for each product the firm sells. Each individual demand curve is quite price-elastic because of the existence of many close substitutes.

1.a.1. In the Short Run

Figure 1(a) shows the cost and revenue curves of a monopolistically competitive firm providing a single product in the short run. As with all profit-maximizing firms, production occurs at the quantity where $MR = MC$. The price the firm charges, P_1, is given by the demand curve at the quantity where $MR = MC$. Price P_1 is above average total cost, as indicated by the distance AB. Thus, the firm is earning above-normal profit, shown as the rectangle $CBAP_1$.

In Figure 1(b), the firms in a monopolistically competitive market are earning normal profit. The price is the same as the average total cost at Q_1, so a normal profit is obtained. If the firm is earning a loss, then the average-total-cost curve lies above the demand curve at the quantity produced, as shown in Figure 1(c). At Q_1, the firm is earning a loss, the rectangle P_1BAC. The firm must decide whether to temporarily suspend production of that product or to continue producing it because the outlook is favorable. The decision depends on whether revenue exceeds variable costs.

1.a.2. In the Long Run

Whenever existing firms in a market structure without barriers to entry are earning above-normal profit, new firms enter the business and, in some cases, existing firms expand until all firms are earning the normal profit. In a perfectly competitive industry, the new firms supply a product that is identical to the product being supplied by existing firms. *In a monopolistically competitive industry, entering firms produce a close substitute, not an identical or standardized product.*

As the introduction of new products by new or existing firms occurs, the demand curves for existing products shift in until a normal profit is earned. For each firm and each product, the demand curve shifts in, as shown in Figure 2, until it just touches

FIGURE 1 A Monopolistically Competitive Firm

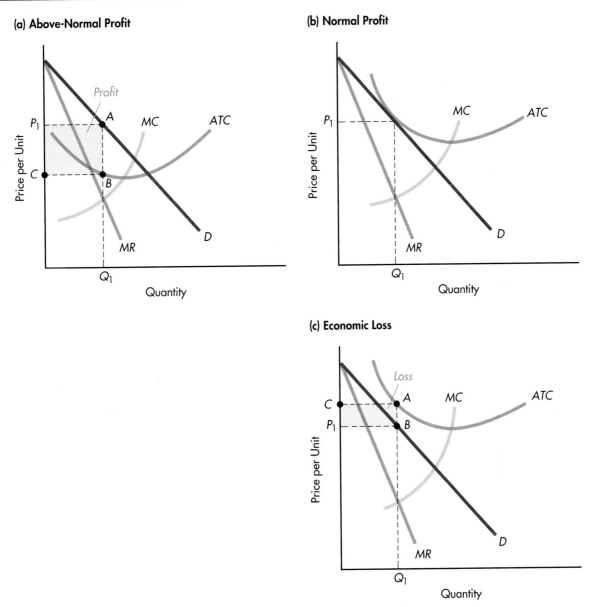

(a) Above-Normal Profit

(b) Normal Profit

(c) Economic Loss

A monopolistically competitive firm faces a downward-sloping demand curve. The firm in Figure 1(a) maximizes profit by producing Q_1, where $MR = MC$, and charging a price, P_1, given by the demand curve above Q_1. Profit is the rectangle $CBAP_1$. In Figure 1(b), the firm is earning a normal profit because where $MR = MC$, price is P_1 on the demand curve above Q_1 and is equal to average total cost. In Figure 1(c), the firm is earning the loss of rectangle P_1BAC. At the profit-maximizing (loss-minimizing) output level, Q_1, average total cost exceeds price.

the average-total-cost curve at the price charged and the output produced, P_2 and Q_2. When profit is at the normal level, expansion and entry cease.

When a firm is earning a loss on a product and the long-run outlook is for continued losses, the firm will stop producing that product. Exit means that fewer differentiated products are produced, and the demand curves for the remaining products shift out. This continues until the remaining firms are earning normal profits.

FIGURE 2   **Entry and Normal Profit**

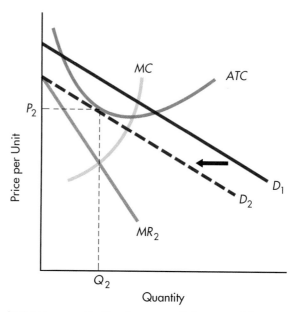

In the long run, the firm in monopolistic competition earns a normal profit. Entry shifts the firm's demand curve in from D_1 to D_2. Entry, which takes the form of a differentiated product, continues to occur as long as above-normal profits exist. When the demand curve just touches the average-total-cost curve, as at P_2 and Q_2, profit is at the normal level.

1.b. Monopolistic Competition Versus Perfect Competition

Monopolistically competitive firms produce less and charge a higher price than perfectly competitive firms.

Monopolistic competition does not yield economic efficiency because consumers are willing and able to pay for variety.

Figure 3 shows both a perfectly competitive firm in long-run equilibrium and a monopolistically competitive firm in long-run equilibrium. The perfectly competitive firm, shown as the horizontal demand and marginal-revenue curve, $MR_{pc} = D_{pc}$, produces at the minimum point of the long-run average-total-cost curve at Q_{pc}; the price, marginal cost, marginal revenue, and average total cost are P_{pc}. The long-run equilibrium for a monopolistically competitive firm is shown by the demand curve D_{mc} and the marginal-revenue curve MR_{mc}. The monopolistically competitive firm produces at Q_{mc}, where $MR_{mc} = MC$, and charges a price determined by drawing a vertical line up from the point where $MR_{mc} = MC$ to the demand curve. That price is just equal to the point where the long-run average-total-cost curve touches the demand curve, P_{mc}. In other words, at Q_{mc}, the monopolistically competitive firm is just earning the normal profit.

The difference between a perfectly competitive firm and a monopolistically competitive firm is clear in Figure 3. Because of the downward-sloping demand curve facing the monopolistically competitive firm, the firm does not produce at the minimum point of the long-run average-total-cost curve, Q_{pc}. Instead, it produces a smaller quantity of output, Q_{mc}, at a higher price, P_{mc}. The difference between P_{mc} and P_{pc} is the additional amount that consumers pay for the privilege of having differentiated products. If consumers placed no value on product choice—if they desired generic products—they would not pay anything extra for product differentiation, and the monopolistically competitive firm would not exist.

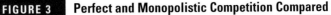

FIGURE 3 — Perfect and Monopolistic Competition Compared

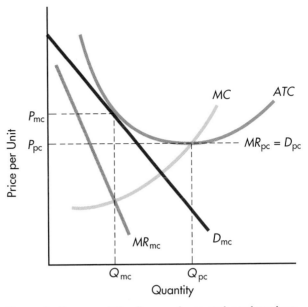

The perfectly competitive firm produces at the point where the price line, the horizontal *MR* curve, intersects the *MC* curve. This is the bottom of the *ATC* curve in the long run, quantity Q_{pc} at price P_{pc}. The monopolistically competitive firm also produces where $MR = MC$. The downward-sloping demand curve faced by the monopolistically competitive firm means that the quantity produced, Q_{mc} is less than the quantity produced by the perfectly competitive firm, Q_{pc}. The price charged by the monopolistically competitive firm is also higher than that charged by the perfectly competitive firm, P_{mc} versus P_{pc}. In both cases, however, the firms earn only a normal profit.

Even though price does not equal marginal cost and the monopolistically competitive firm does not operate at the minimum point of the average-total-cost curve, the firm does earn normal profit in the long run. And although the monopolistically competitive firm does not strictly meet the conditions of economic efficiency (since price is not equal to marginal cost), the inefficiency is not due to the firm's ability to restrict quantity and increase price, but instead is a direct result of consumers' desire for variety. It is hard to argue that society is worse off with monopolistic competition than it is with perfect competition, since the difference is due solely to consumer desires. Yet variety is costly, and critics of market economies argue that the cost is not worthwhile. Would the world be a better place if we had a simpler array of products to choose from, if there was a simple generic product—one type of automobile, say—for everyone?

1.c. Nonprice Competition—Product Differentiation

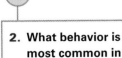

2. What behavior is most common in monopolistic competition?

A firm in a monopolistically competitive market structure attempts to differentiate its product or itself from its competitors. Successful product differentiation reduces the price elasticity of demand. The demand curve, shown as the rotation from D_1 to D_2 in Figure 4, becomes steeper.

FIGURE 4 Advertising, Prices, and Profits

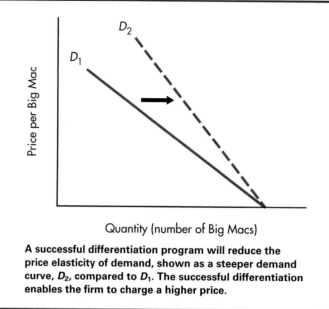

A successful differentiation program will reduce the
price elasticity of demand, shown as a steeper demand
curve, D_2, compared to D_1. The successful differentiation
enables the firm to charge a higher price.

Numerous characteristics may serve to differentiate products: quality, color,
style, safety features, taste, packaging, purchase terms, warranties, and guarantees.
All it takes is for the consumer to *think* there is a difference for there to *be* a difference. A firm might change its hours of operation—for example, a supermarket
might offer service 24 hours a day—to call attention to itself. Firms can also use location to differentiate their products. A firm may locate where traffic is heavy and
the cost to the consumer of making a trip to the firm is minimal. If location is used
for differentiation, however, why do fast-food restaurants tend to be clustered together? Where you find a McDonald's, you usually find a Taco Bell or a Wendy's
nearby. The model of monopolistic competition explains this behavior. Suppose
that five identical consumers—A, B, C, D, and E—are spread out along a line as
shown in Figure 5. Consumer C is the median consumer, residing equidistantly from
consumers B and D and equidistantly from consumers A and E. Assume that the five
consumers care about the costs incurred in getting to a fast-food restaurant and are
indifferent about the food offered. McDonald's is the first fast-food provider to open
near these five consumers. Where does it locate? It locates as close to consumer C
as possible because that location minimizes the total distance of all five consumers
from McDonald's.

Taco Bell wants to open in the same area. If it locates near consumer D, it will
pull customers D and E from McDonald's but will have no chance to attract A, B,
or C. Similarly, if it locates near consumer A, only A will go to Taco Bell. Only if
Taco Bell locates next door to McDonald's will it have a chance to gather a larger
market share than McDonald's. As other fast-food firms enter, they too will locate
close to McDonald's.

Being able to earn positive economic profits is what drives firms to differentiate
their goods and services. Every firm—producer, fabricator, seller, broker, agent, or
merchant—tries to distinguish its offering from all others. The reason that firms try
to differentiate themselves or their products is to make it more difficult for competitors to take away business.

FIGURE 5   **Location Under Monopolistic Competition**

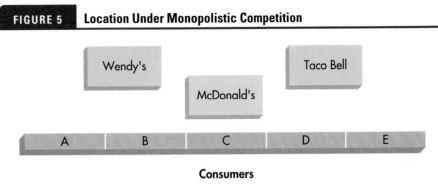

Five customers—A, B, C, D, and E—reside along a straight line. Customer C is in the middle, equidistant from B and D and from A and E. McDonald's decides to locate a restaurant at the spot that is closest to all five customers. This is the median position, where consumer C resides. Other fast-food firms locate nearby because any other location will increase the total distance of some consumers from the fast-food restaurant, thereby causing some customers to go elsewhere.

Successful differentiation reduces the price elasticity of demand and gives the firm more market power. What does this mean for a firm? It means that the firm can raise the price of the good or service that it sells without incurring the loss of revenue that would result if the elasticity were higher. For years Intel was able to charge more for its microchips than competitors could charge for essentially the same microchip. Intel was able to do that because of its successful campaign to differentiate itself—"Intel Inside." Intel was able to shift the demand curve for its products out and make it more inelastic.

1.c.1. Brand Name   Starbucks has created a powerful brand name. People know that a Starbucks store will provide an identical product, whether that Starbucks is in Seattle or Beijing. The Starbucks brand name provides value to consumers, so they are willing to pay a higher price for Starbucks products than for similar products without the Starbucks name. A brand name is valuable to a firm; it makes the demand less elastic and can enable the firm to earn higher profits. How is a brand name created, and why does it have value?

Most goods and services have many different attributes—look, feel, taste, sensation, reliability, performance, and so on. You learn about many products by trying them, but this learning may be costly. For example, you may go into a coffee shop and pay for a crummy cup of coffee that you throw away. Or perhaps you buy a new TV that you later find does not have the picture quality you hoped for. A brand name can provide reliability and save you from these costly mistakes.

If you see someone selling neckties from a table set up on the street corner, you have less confidence in that "firm" than you would have in the Nordstrom store across the street, so you might be willing to pay more for the same tie at Nordstrom than at the street vendor. The reason is at least partly that Nordstrom has devoted huge resources to that large building. You see many types of firms trying to assure customers of their reliability by locating in large buildings or beautiful offices or by spending lavishly on advertisements. For some products, a guarantee or warranty is an important signal that the product is of high quality.

Reliability is the important differentiator for some goods and services, such as Starbucks, McDonald's, and so on. But for customers to know that the product is reliable, they must first try the product. A firm may advertise that its product "tastes great" or "refreshes you." Goods may be advertised by showing groups of people having fun on a beach or in the mountains—such as with Coors beer, for example. The goods may be placed in a setting of upper class or wealth—Grey Poupon being requested by a passenger in a limousine, for instance. These advertisements are intended to get people to try the good or service.

Reliability may be represented by the consistent flavor of a McDonald's hamburger, the infrequency with which a machine breaks down, or the soundness of the opinions of a professional adviser. The consumer has to experience these products and services over a relatively long period of time before reliability is established. Once a consumer has had a positive experience with a good, the price elasticity of demand for that good typically decreases—the consumer becomes loyal to the product. For instance, Coke and Pepsi drinkers are usually loyal to one of the two brands, even though the products are similar. Prudential Insurance shows "the rock" and Allstate shows the "good hands" to illustrate their reliability. Although these symbols have nothing to do with the actual service, they promote an aspect of the service that consumers find valuable—the idea that the service will continue to be offered in the future, so that an experience now can be used to evaluate the service in the future. Lawyers and financial advisers need to present an image of success. Who wants to use an unsuccessful attorney or financial adviser? Thus, attorneys and financial advisers typically have richly appointed offices located in large central-city buildings. They dress in expensive clothes and carry expensive briefcases.

Many people claim that marketing and advertising create phony or artificial distinctions among products and that the benefits conferred by brand names are illusory. These critics note that there may be no difference between Tide laundry detergent and the generic detergent sold under the grocery store's label, that Ralph Lauren's Polo brand shirts may be constructed of exactly the same fabric and knit design as several less-expensive brands, and that aspirin is aspirin whether or not it is Bayer. Nonetheless, consumers are often willing to pay a higher price for a brand-name product than for a similar product without a brand name. Why? Because the brand name signals something valuable—reliability, confidence, assurance.

The objective of creating a brand name is to reduce the price elasticity of demand. The greater the consumer's reluctance to shift brands, the lower the price elasticity of demand. Consumers who are loyal to a brand or to a firm will purchase that brand or purchase from that firm even if the prices are above those of competing brands.

Because it takes a long time to establish a reputation and a brand name, some firms attempt to rent a reputation that has been established in one market and use it in a new market. Endorsement of products by famous personalities is a clear example. Everyone knows that when celebrities endorse a product, it is not because the celebrities have scoured the market for the best product, but rather because they have canvassed potential sponsors to see who will offer the highest fee. So why are consumers influenced by the endorsement? Because the endorser is, to some degree, putting his or her reputation at risk. If the product is of low quality, the celebrity's reputation and value to other sponsors can be damaged. For the manufacturer, payment of the endorsement fee is a demonstration of its commitment to the market. Willingness to pay the endorsement fee is therefore actually a measure of product quality.

Firms will sometimes use their established reputation in one market to enter a new market. BMW's reputation for producing cars reinforces its reputation for producing motor bikes, and vice versa. BMW also endorses a range of "Active Line" sportswear. Caterpillar has a line of clothing, "CAT," that portrays the image of its tough, no-nonsense equipment. There is little reason to believe that the capabilities that distinguish BMW cars or CAT equipment are applicable to the manufacture of clothes. But it would clearly be foolish for the companies to attach their name to poor-quality clothes.

Guarantees and warranties can also be ways to get people to experience a good or service. When Japanese automobile companies first entered the U.S. market in the 1960s, they faced the problem of convincing consumers of the quality of the cars. Although the manufacturers knew that their products were of high quality, their potential customers did not. In fact, many potential customers believed that Japanese goods were shoddy imitations of western products. "Made in Japan" had become synonymous with cheap and crummy. Accordingly, Japanese manufacturers offered more extensive warranties than had been usual in the market. And, of course, Japanese autos like Toyota and Honda are now considered to have the highest quality.

Guarantees are difficult to fake. A low-quality product will break down frequently, making the guarantee quite costly for the firm. Thus, the higher the quality of the product, the better the guarantee that the firm can offer.

If a firm establishes a warranty policy, then other firms have to either follow or admit to having a lower-quality product. If another firm is unable to imitate its rivals' existing warranties, it may decide not to enter the market in the first place. This is what the Japanese auto producers did to the U.S. auto producers in the 1970s. U.S. auto producers did not offer as extensive warranties as the Japanese auto producers. As a result, customers soon came to see that "Made in Japan" meant quality. A similar strategy was employed in the late 1990s and early 2000s with respect to the Korean-manufactured Hyundai. Hyundai offered a 100,000-mile full warranty at a time when other manufacturers were offering 36,000-mile warranties.

The key aspect of firms in monopolistic competition is that they devote considerable resources to differentiating their goods and services. But, since entry is easy, does that differentiation do the firm any good?

An innovation or successful differentiation in any area—style, quality, location, service—leads initially to above-normal profit, but it eventually brings in copycats that drive profit back down to the normal level. In a monopolistically competitive market structure, innovation and above-normal profit for one firm are followed by entry of other firms and normal profit. Differentiation and above-normal profit then occur again. They induce entry, which again drives profit back to the normal level. The cycle continues until product differentiation no longer brings above-normal profit.

Although an above-normal profit attracts competitors, even a short-lived period of above-normal profit is better than no positive economic profit. That is why firms in monopolistic competition devote so many resources to differentiating their products.

RECAP

1. The market structure called *monopolistic competition* describes an industry in which many sellers produce a differentiated product and entry is easy.

2. In the short run, a firm in monopolistic competition can earn above-normal profit.

3. In the long run, a firm in a monopolistically competitive market structure will produce a lower output at a higher cost than a firm in a perfectly competitive market structure will. In both market structures, firms earn only a normal profit.

4. Monopolistic competitors may engage more in nonprice competition than in price differentiation.

5. The key aspect of monopolistic competition is differentiation.

6. As a firm successfully differentiates its product and earns a positive economic profit, other firms will mimic the successful firm and reduce the differentiation. As a result, the positive economic profit will be competed down toward a normal economic profit.

2. Oligopoly and Interdependence

In Mexico, only two or three companies provide goods and services in areas such as finance, telecommunications, broadcasting, and retailing. Some argue that this is the reason that the Mexican economy has not progressed in the same way as the economy of the United States. And in Poland, a candidate for finance minister argued that the country's current economic problems are due to the dominance of just one or a few firms in the fuel sectors and the financial markets. When a few firms dominate a market, an oligopoly is said to exist. *Oligopoly* is a market structure characterized by (1) few firms, (2) either standardized or differentiated products, and (3) difficult entry. Oligopoly may take many forms. It may consist of one dominant firm coexisting with many smaller firms or a group of giant firms that dominate the industry. Whatever the number of firms, the characteristic that describes oligopoly is *interdependence;* an individual firm in an oligopoly does not decide what to do without considering what the other firms in the industry will do. When a large firm in an oligopoly changes its behavior, the demand curves of the other firms are affected significantly.

In monopolistically competitive and perfectly competitive markets, what one firm does affects each of the other firms so slightly that each firm essentially ignores the others. Each firm in an oligopoly, however, must watch the actions of the other firms closely because the actions of one can dramatically affect the others. This interdependence among firms leads to actions not found in the other market structures.

2.a. The Creation of Oligopolies

In the chapter titled "Monopoly," it was noted that a monopoly could, theoretically, arise as a result of natural barriers to entry such as economies of scale, actions on the part of firms that create barriers to entry, or governmentally created barriers. Oligopolies can arise for similar reasons. Many exist because of government regulations. The roots of Mexico's oligopolies, for example, reach back to the 1950s and 1960s, when the government funded private businesses and closed the domestic market to international competition. During that era, the government created a culture in which the state supported companies—government officials forced mergers to create larger companies, and later helped their friends who headed those companies. Large companies owned by powerful dynasties such as the mining company Grupo Mexico, the transportation company TMM, and Bancomer, the country's biggest bank, date from this period. Nowadays, this policy is known as "crony capitalism." In Russia, crony capitalism dominated after the fall of the Soviet Empire. Former government officials grabbed assets and took control of former state-owned enterprises such as mining, oil, and utilities.

It is not just developing nations whose governments create oligopolies. In Japan, businesses require government approval for many actions, including entering a new business. For instance, from the early 1990s through 2005, the government allowed only three phone companies—NTT DoCoMo Inc., KDDI Corp., and Vodafone KK—to offer services, although it is now widening the market to allow six new firms to enter the business. In the European Union, the large monopolies and oligopolies created by national governments must now restructure as Union-wide companies. (The large French and German electric companies are fighting to retain their government privileges.) In the United States, Fannie Mae (Federal National Mortgage Association), set up in 1936 by Congress, and Freddie Mac, a company established by Congress in 1970 to support homeownership and rental housing, have totally dominated the mortgage industry for years, controlling as many as 70 percent of all mortgages created. They continue to do this because of subsidies or special credit arrangements they have with the federal government and the Federal Reserve.

Whereas in a monopoly or a government-created oligopoly, competition may be very limited or nonexistent, in an oligopoly that is not supported by the government, the firms must constantly innovate and seek other barriers to entry. Cutthroat competition—competition through innovation, patents, and other means is often the companion of oligopoly.

Oligopoly can arise as the result of economies of scale. Since the cost per unit of output declines as a firm gets larger, only the larger firms can remain in business. A small business cannot offer goods and services at as low a price as a larger business can. Thus, the number of companies is determined by the size of the market—where the market demand curve intersects the long-run average-total-cost curve.

Wal-Mart is the dominant retail firm and Microsoft is the dominant software company, but neither is the only firm in its industry. Both firms dominate because of the efficiencies they have experienced as they have grown and because of the strategies they undertake to maintain their dominance.

2.b. Oligopoly and Competition

Strategic behavior occurs when what is best for A depends on what B does, and what is best for B depends on what A does. It is much like a card game—bridge, say—where strategies are designed depending on the cards the players are dealt. Underbidding, overbidding, bluffing, deceit, and other strategies are used. In fact, the analogy between games and firm behavior in oligopoly is so strong that economists have applied **game theory** to their analyses of oligopoly. Game theory, developed in the 1940s by John von Neumann and Oskar Morgenstern, describes oligopolistic behavior, the behavior of firms in an oligopoly, as a series of strategic moves and countermoves. In this section, we briefly discuss some of the theories of oligopolistic behavior.

Oligopolistic behavior includes both ruthless competition and cooperation. Competition does not just mean that firms lower their prices. In oligopoly, firms typically compete more on other dimensions than they do on price. In the real world, we observe as much competition through innovation as we do through price. In computer hardware and software, for example, firms race to see which will be the first to come out with a new product or which can obtain the patent on an innovation. Consumers are constantly being presented with upgrades and improvements to existing products as well as with brand-new products. Pharmaceutical companies race to create new drugs. They don't compete on price, but rather on innovation. Such competition can take many forms. To analyze all of the behaviors we find in oligopoly would be too much of an undertaking here. What we want to do is to get a flavor of how firms in an oligopoly might behave. To do that, we'll consider two rather simple models—the kinked demand curve and the prisoner's dilemma.

2.b.1. The Kinked Demand Curve
All firms know the law of demand. Thus, they know that sales will increase if price is lowered because people will purchase more of all goods (the income effect) and will substitute away from the more expensive goods to purchase more of the less expensive goods (the substitution effect). But the firms in an oligopoly may not know the shape of the demand curve for their product because the shape depends on how their rivals react to one another. They have to predict how their competitors will respond to a price change in order to know what their demand curve looks like.

Let's consider the auto industry. Suppose General Motors's costs have fallen (its marginal-cost curve has shifted down), and the company is deciding whether to

? 4. In what form does rivalry occur in an oligopoly?

strategic behavior: the behavior that occurs when what is best for A depends on what B does, and what is best for B depends on what A does

game theory: a description of oligopolistic behavior as a series of strategic moves and countermoves

lower the prices of its cars. If GM did not have to consider how the other car companies would respond, it would simply lower the price in order to be sure that the new *MC* curve intersected the *MR* curve, as illustrated in Figure 6(a). But GM suspects that the demand and marginal-revenue curves in Figure 6(a) do not represent its true market situation. Instead, GM believes that if it lowers the prices on its cars from their current level of P_1, the other auto companies will follow suit. If the other companies also lower the price of their cars, the substitution effect for the GM cars does not occur; sales of GM cars might increase a little, but only because of the income effect. In other words, GM does not capture the market share indicated in Figure 6(b) by D_1, but finds the quantity demanded increasing along D_2 (below price P_1). Also, GM suspects that should it increase the price of its cars, none of the other auto companies would raise theirs. In this case, the price increase would mean substantially reduced sales for GM because of both the income effect and the substitution effect. The quantity demanded decreases, as indicated along D_1. Consequently, the demand curve for GM is a combination of D_1 and D_2. It is D_1 above P_1 and D_2 below P_1, a demand curve with a *kink*.

FIGURE 6   **The Kinked Demand Curve**

(a) Competitors Do Not Follow Price Changes

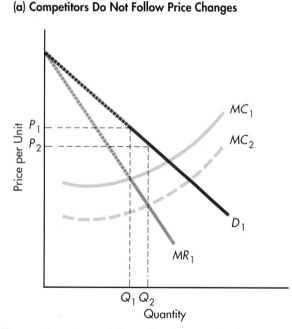

(b) Competitors Follow Price Changes

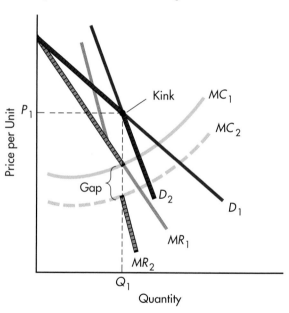

If competitors do not follow price changes, the demand curve faced by an oligopolistic firm is the curve D_1 in Figures 6(a) and 6(b). If competitors do follow price changes, the demand curve faced by the firm is D_2 in 6(b). If competitors match price decreases but not price increases, then the firm faces a combination of the two demand curves. If competitors do not follow a price increase, then above the current price, P_1, the relevant demand curve is D_1. If competitors do follow a price decrease, then below price P_1 the relevant demand curve is D_2. The demand curve is the shaded combination of the two demand curves; it has a

kink at the current price. The resulting marginal-revenue curve is also a combination of the two marginal-revenue curves. The marginal-revenue curve is MR_1 to the left of the kink in the demand curve and MR_2 to the right of the kink. Between the two marginal-revenue curves is a gap. The firm produces where $MR = MC$. If the MC curve intersects the MR curve in the gap, the resulting price is P_1 and the resulting quantity produced is Q_1. If costs fall, as represented by a downward shift of MC_1 to MC_2, the price and quantity produced do not change.

What should GM do? It should price where $MR = MC$. But the resulting marginal-revenue curve is given by a combination of MR_1 and MR_2. The MR_1 curve slopes down gently until it reaches the quantity associated with the kink. As we move below the kink, the MR_2 curve becomes the appropriate marginal-revenue curve. Thus, the shaded portions of the two marginal-revenue curves combine to give the firm's marginal-revenue curve. Notice that GM's marginal-cost curves, MC_1 and MC_2, intersect the combined MR curves at the same price and quantity, P_1 and Q_1. Thus, GM's strategy is to do nothing: *not* to change price, even though costs have changed.

The kinked demand curve is a very simplified model of real life. Nevertheless, it suggests how oligopolistic firms might behave. Because there are just a few firms, and because what one firm does significantly affects its rivals, firms tend not to change their price very often. This is what the kink sort of tells us—that firms are reluctant to change price. The implication is that firms in an oligopoly compete on characteristics other than price. We see how this type of behavior might occur in the next model we consider, the prisoner's dilemma. The firms in an oligopoly might avoid price competition altogether and devote their resources to nonprice competition. Even with nonprice competition, however, strategic behavior comes into play, as noted in the next section.

2.b.2. Prisoner's Dilemma Consider the situation in which firms must decide whether to devote more resources to advertising. When a firm in any given industry advertises its product, its demand increases for two reasons. First, people who had not used that type of product before learn about it, and some will buy it. Second, other people who already consume a different brand of the same product may switch brands. The first effect boosts sales for the industry as a whole, while the second redistributes existing sales within the industry.

Consider the cigarette industry as an example, and assume that Figure 7 illustrates the possible actions that two firms might take and the results of those actions. The top left rectangle represents the payoffs, or results, if both A and B advertise; the bottom left is the payoffs when A advertises but B does not; the top right is the payoffs when B advertises but A does not; and the bottom right is the payoffs if neither advertises. If firm A can earn higher profits by advertising than by not advertising, whether or not firm B advertises, then firm A will surely advertise. This is referred to as a **dominant strategy**—a strategy that produces the best results no matter what strategy the opposing player follows. Firm A compares the left side of the matrix to the right side and sees that it earns more by advertising, no matter what firm B does. If B advertises and A advertises, then A earns 70, but if B advertises and A does not advertise, it earns 40. If B does not advertise, then A earns 100 by advertising and only 80 by not advertising. The dominant strategy for firm A is to advertise. And according to Figure 7, the dominant strategy for firm B is also to advertise. Firm B will earn 80 by advertising and 50 by not advertising if A advertises, and will earn 100 by advertising but only 90 by not advertising if A does not advertise. But notice that both firms would be better off if neither advertised; firm A would earn 80 instead of 70, and firm B would earn 90 instead of 80. Yet, the firms cannot afford to *not* advertise because they would lose more if the other firm advertised and they didn't. This situation is known as the prisoner's dilemma; see the Economic Insight "The Prisoner's Dilemma" for a more complete description of why it has this name.

None of the cigarette manufacturers wants to do much advertising, for example. Yet strategic behavior suggests that they must. Firm A advertises, so firm B must also do so. Each firm ups the advertising ante. How can this expensive advertising competition be controlled? Each firm alone has no incentive to do it, since unilateral

Game theory can illustrate ways in which oligopolistic firms interact. Game theory considers each firm a participant in a game in which the winners are the firms with the greatest profit.

dominant strategy: a strategy that produces better results no matter what strategy the opposing firm follows

The Prisoner's Dilemma

Strategic behavior characterizes oligopoly. Perhaps the best-known example of strategic behavior occurs in what is called the prisoner's dilemma.

Two people have been arrested for a crime, but the evidence against them is weak. The sheriff keeps the prisoners separated and offers each of them a special deal: If the prisoner confesses, that prisoner can go free as long as only he confesses, and the other prisoner will get ten or more years in prison. However, if both prisoners confess, each will receive a reduced sentence of two years in jail. The prisoners know that if neither confesses, they will be cleared of all but a minor charge and will serve only two days in jail. The problem is that they do not know what deal the other is being offered, or whether the other will take the deal.

The options available to the two prisoners are shown in the four cells of the figure. Prisoner B's options are shown in the horizontal direction, and prisoner A's are shown in the vertical direction. In the upper left cell is the result if both prisoners confess. In the lower left cell is the result if prisoner A does not confess but prisoner B does; in the upper right cell is the result of prisoner A's confessing but prisoner B's not confessing; and in the lower right cell is the result when neither prisoner confesses. The dominant strategy for both prisoners is to confess and receive two years of jail time.

If the prisoners had been loyal to each other, each would have received a much smaller penalty. Because both chose to confess, each is worse off than he or she would have been if he or she had known what the other was doing. Yet, in the context of the interdependence of the decisions, each made the best choice.

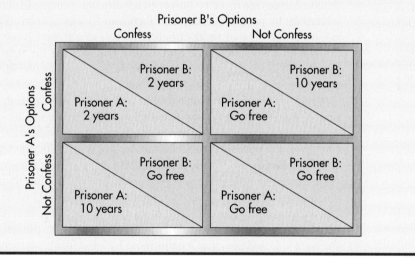

action will mean a significant loss of market share. But if they can ban advertising together or if the government passes a law banning cigarette advertising, all of the cigarette companies will be better off. In fact, a ban on cigarette advertising on television has been in effect since January 1, 1971. The ban was intended by the government as a means of reducing cigarette smoking—of helping the consumer. Yet who does this ban really benefit?

5. Why does cooperation among rivals occur most often in oligopolies?

2.c. Cooperation

If the firms in an oligopoly cooperate, they may all be better off. Because there are only a few firms in an oligopoly, the firms can communicate more easily than can the many firms in a perfectly competitive or monopolistically competitive industry. This allows the oligopolistic firms to cooperate instead of competing.

FIGURE 7 Prisoner's Dilemma

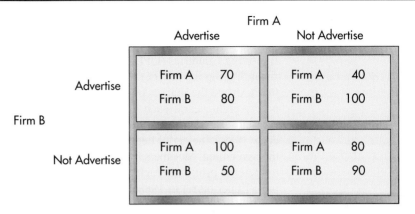

Figure 7 illustrates the dominant strategy game. The dominant strategy for firm A is to advertise. No matter what firm B does, firm A is better off advertising. If firm B does not advertise, firm A earns 80 not advertising and 100 advertising. If firm B does advertise, firm A earns 40 not advertising and 70 advertising. Similarly, firm B is better off advertising no matter what firm A does. Both A and B have dominant strategies—advertise.

Acting jointly allows firms to earn more profits than they would if they acted independently or against each other. To avoid the destructiveness of strategic behavior, the few firms in an oligopoly can collude, or come to some agreement about price and output levels. Typically these agreements provide the members of the oligopoly with higher profits and thus raise prices to consumers. Collusion, which leads to secret cooperative agreements, is illegal in the United States, although it is acceptable in many other nations.

2.c.1. Price-Leadership Oligopoly One way for firms to communicate without illegally colluding is to allow one firm to be the leader in changes in price or advertising activities. When the leader makes a change, the others duplicate what the leader has done. This enables all firms to know exactly what their rivals will do. It eliminates the kink in the demand curve because both price increases and price decreases will be followed, and it avoids the prisoner's dilemma situation where excessive expenditures are made on advertising or other activities. This type of oligopoly is called a *price-leadership oligopoly.*

The steel industry in the 1960s is an example of a dominant-firm price-leadership oligopoly. For many years, steel producers allowed U.S. Steel to set prices for the entire industry. The cooperation of the steel companies probably led to higher profits than would have occurred with rivalry. However, the absence of rivalry is said to be one reason for the decline of the steel industry in the United States. Price leadership removed the need for the steel companies to compete by maintaining and upgrading their equipment and materials and by developing new technologies. As a result, foreign firms that chose not to behave as price followers emerged as more-sophisticated producers of steel than U.S. firms.

For many years, airlines also relied on a price leader. In many cases, the price leader was not the dominant airline, but instead was one of the weaker or new airlines. In recent years, however, airlines have communicated less through a price leader and more through their computerized reservation systems, according to the Justice Department.

cartel: an organization of independent firms whose purpose is to control and limit production and maintain or increase prices and profits

2.c.2. Cartels and Other Cooperative Mechanisms

A **cartel** is an organization of independent firms whose purpose is to control and limit production and maintain or increase prices and profits. A cartel can result from either formal or informal agreement among members. Like collusion, cartels are illegal in the United States. The cartel most people are familiar with is the Organization of Petroleum Exporting Countries (OPEC), a group of nations rather than a group of independent firms. During the 1970s, OPEC was able to coordinate oil production in such a way that it drove the market price of crude oil from $1.10 a barrel to $32 a barrel. For nearly eight years, each member of OPEC agreed to produce a certain, limited amount of crude oil as designated by the OPEC production committee. Then in the early 1980s, the cartel began to fall apart as individual members began to cheat on the agreement. Members began to produce more than their allocation in an attempt to increase profit. As each member of the cartel did this, the price of oil fell, reaching $12 per barrel in 1988.

OPEC has attempted to set oil prices at a level that will earn its member countries significant profits, but not so high that oil exploration and production will be dramatically increased; however, it has often found its policies subverted by world events. When Iraq invaded Kuwait in 1990, oil prices shot up, but they then were reduced as the other OPEC countries increased production and the Kuwaiti oil fields were repaired and brought back into production. Then in 2002, in anticipation of and during the U.S. and U.K. invasion of Iraq, oil prices rose again. In late 2003, oil production resumed, and oil prices returned to earlier levels. Most of the fluctuations in oil prices in recent years have been the result of the vagaries of world events, but some continue to be the result of the policies of the OPEC nations.

Production quotas for different firms or different nations are not easy to maintain. Most cartels do not last very long because their members chisel on the agreements. If each producer thinks that it can increase its own production, and thus its profits, without affecting what the other producers do, all producers end up producing more than their assigned amounts; the price of the product declines, and the cartel falls apart.

Economists have identified certain conditions that make it likely that a cartel will be stable. A cartel is likely to remain in force when:

- There are few firms in the industry.
- There are significant barriers to entry.
- An identical product is produced.
- There are few opportunities to keep actions secret.
- There are no legal barriers to sharing agreements.

2.c.3. The Theory of Cartels

In 1998, the U.S. Justice Department showed that ten firms had held meetings in places as disparate as Vienna and Tokyo to set the price of the food additive sorbate in the global market and to allocate market shares. Federal officials said that the conspiracy affected $1 billion in sales made between 1979 and 1997. Although ten firms produce and sell sorbate, let's assume that there are just two in order to show how and why the firms might fix prices. In Figure 8, we've drawn the market demand curve, *D,* and we've drawn the marginal and average costs as being constant. If the two firms were a monopolist rather than being two firms, the monopolist's marginal-revenue curve would be as shown in Figure 8(a), intersecting the marginal-cost curve at a quantity of 130 and a price of $40. If the two companies act as one, they will select the monopoly price of $40 and quantity of 130 and then split the market, with each having 65. The average cost is $20, so each firm earns a profit of $1,300 ($20 × 65).

FIGURE 8 **Behavior of a Cartel**

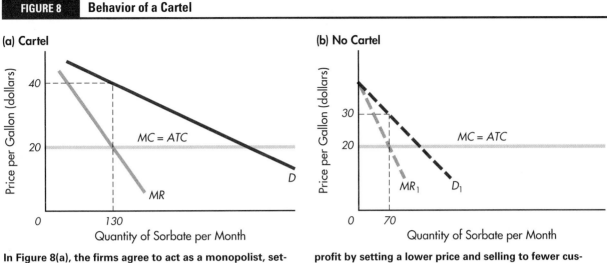

(a) Cartel

(b) No Cartel

In Figure 8(a), the firms agree to act as a monopolist, setting the price where the monopolist would maximize profit and then sharing the resulting profits. When the cartel members act alone, as shown in Figure 8(b), they maximize profit by setting a lower price and selling to fewer customers than was the case when they acted as monopolists. The result is a lower profit.

If instead the two firms compete with each other, then their demand curves will lie inside the market or monopoly demand curve. Figure 8(b) shows the demand and marginal revenue for firm 1. Firm 2 is identical to firm 1. As a result of competition, each firm sets a lower price and serves more customers. The profit each firm makes is $700 ($10 × 70). When the two firms compete, their combined profits are $1,400; when they collude by fixing the price and setting the quantities each will produce, their profits are $1,300 each, or $2,600 combined.

The extra profits from collusion create an incentive for firms to cheat on their agreements. Suppose that one of the firms decides to sell more than its allotted quantity of 65. It will be able to sell the higher quantity only if the price is lower or if the other firm serves fewer customers. Either case hurts at least one of the colluding firms, and the cartel breaks apart.

Because there is a strong incentive for firms that are members of a cartel or that are colluding to cheat on their agreements, a way to stop cheaters, to penalize them, must be found if the cartel is to remain in place. In most cartels, the strongest member takes over and polices it. In OPEC, it is Saudi Arabia that serves as police. When a member does not adhere to the prescribed quantity, Saudi Arabia opens its valves and floods the market with petroleum. Saudi Arabia can do this because it is the nation with the largest supply of petroleum. The flooded market means a lower price and thus lower profits for all countries. With the drug cartels of Colombia and Mexico, one family polices the agreement; cheaters typically end up dead. Without a policing authority, the cartel will fall apart.

Even though cartels are generally illegal in the United States, a few have been sanctioned by the government. The National Collegiate Athletic Association (NCAA) is a cartel of colleges and universities. It sets rules of behavior and enforces those rules through a governing board. Member schools are placed on probation or their programs are dismantled if they violate the agreement. The citrus cartel, composed of citrus growers in California and Arizona, enforces its actions through its governing board. Sunkist Growers Inc., a cooperative of many growers, represents more than half of the California and Arizona production and also plays an important role in enforcing the rules of the cartel.

2.c.4. Facilitating Practices   Actions by firms can contribute to cooperation and collusion even though the firms do not formally agree to cooperate. Such actions are called **facilitating practices.** Pricing policies can give the impression that firms are explicitly fixing prices, or cooperating, when in fact they are merely following the same strategies. For instance, the use of **cost-plus/markup pricing** tends to lead to similar or identical pricing behavior among rival firms. If firms set prices by determining the average cost of an item and adding a fixed markup to the cost, they are engaging in cost-plus pricing. If all firms face the same cost curves, then all firms will set the same prices. If costs decrease, then all firms will lower prices the same amount and at virtually the same time. Such pricing behavior is common in the grocery business.

Another practice that leads to implicit cooperation is the most-favored-customer policy. Often the time between purchase and delivery of a product is quite long. To avoid the possibility that customer A purchases a product at one price and then learns that customer B purchased the product at a lower price or benefited from product features that were unavailable to customer A, a producer will guarantee that customer A will receive the lowest price and all features for a certain period of time. Customer A is thus a **most-favored customer (MFC).**

The most-favored-customer policy actually gives firms an incentive not to lower prices, even in the face of reduced demand. A firm that lowers the price of its product must then give rebates to all most-favored customers, which forces all other firms with most-favored-customer policies to do the same. In addition, the MFC policy allows a firm to collect information on what its rivals are doing. Customers will return products for a rebate when another firm offers the same product for a lower price.

Consider the behavior of firms that produced antiknock additives for gasoline from 1974 to 1979. Lead-based antiknock compounds had been used in the refining of gasoline since the 1920s. From the 1920s until 1948, Ethyl Corporation was the sole domestic producer of the compounds. In 1948, DuPont entered the industry. Then PPG Industries followed in 1961, and Nalco in 1964. Beginning in 1973, the demand for lead-based antiknock compounds decreased dramatically. However, because each company had most-favored-customer clauses, high prices were maintained even as demand for the product declined.

A most-favored-customer policy discourages price decreases because it requires producers to lower prices retroactively with rebates. If all rivals provide all buyers with most-favored-customer clauses, a high price is likely to be stabilized in the industry.

---

facilitating practices: actions by oligopolistic firms that can contribute to cooperation and collusion even though the firms do not formally agree to cooperate

cost-plus/markup pricing: a pricing policy whereby a firm computes its average cost of producing a product and then sets the price at some percentage above this cost

most-favored customer (MFC): a customer who receives a guarantee of the lowest price and all product features for a certain period of time

---

RECAP

1. Oligopoly is a market structure in which there are so few firms that each must take into account what the others do, entry is difficult, and either undifferentiated or differentiated products are produced.

2. An oligopoly may come into being because government allows only a few firms to control or dominate an industry, or it may arise as a result of economies of scale.

3. Interdependence and strategic behavior characterize oligopoly.

4. The shape of the demand curve and the marginal-revenue curve facing an oligopolist depend on how rival firms react to changes in price and product.

5. The kinked demand curve is one example of how oligopolistic firms might react to price changes. The kink occurs because rivals follow price cuts but not price increases.

6. The prisoner's dilemma is an example of how competition among firms that are interdependent can result in an outcome that is not the best for the competing firms.

7. Oligopolistic firms have incentives to cooperate. In a price-leadership oligopoly, one firm determines the price and quantity, knowing that all other firms will follow suit. The price leader is usually the dominant firm in the industry.

8. Collusion, or making a secret cooperative agreement, is illegal in the United States. Cartels, also illegal in the United States, rest on explicit cooperation achieved through formal agreement.

9. The incentive for cartel members to cheat typically leads to the collapse of the cartel. To minimize cheating, one member must police the others.

10. Facilitating practices implicitly encourage cooperation in an industry.

3. Summary of Market Structures

We have now discussed each of the four market structures in some detail. Table 2 summarizes the characteristics of each model and the main predictions yielded by that model. The model of perfect competition predicts that firms will produce at a point where price and marginal cost are the same (at the bottom of the average-total-cost curve) and profit will be zero in the long run. The model characterizes competition as an ideal—consumers get what they want at the lowest possible prices, and the efficiency for society is maximized. The model of monopoly predicts that price will exceed marginal cost and that the firm can earn positive economic profit in the long run. This model is the opposite of the ideal of perfect competition—the seller obtains the largest producer surplus and creates a deadweight loss. With monopolistic competition and oligopoly, we turn from the theoretical bookends of perfect competition and monopoly to more real-life behaviors. With monopolistic competition, price will exceed marginal cost and the firm will not produce at the bottom point of the average-total-cost curve, but this is due to consumers' desire for product differentiation. In the long run, the firm in monopolistic competition will earn a normal profit. In

TABLE 2 Summary of Perfect Competition, Monopoly, Monopolistic Competition, and Oligopoly

	Perfect Competition	Monopoly	Monopolistic Competition	Oligopoly
Number of firms	Many	One	Many	Few
Type of product	Identical	One	Differentiated	Identical or differentiated
Entry conditions	Easy	Difficult or impossible	Easy	Difficult
Demand curve for firm	Horizontal (perfectly elastic)	Downward sloping	Downward sloping	Downward sloping
Price and marginal cost	$MC = P$	$MC < P$	$MC < P$	$MC < P$
Long-run profit	Zero	Yes	Zero	Depends on whether entry occurs

oligopoly, a firm may be able to earn above-normal profit for a long time—as long as entry can be restricted. In oligopoly, price exceeds marginal cost, and the firm does not operate at the bottom of the average-total-cost curve.

Under perfect competition, consumers purchase products at the lowest possible price; there is no advertising, no excessive overhead, and no warranties or guarantees. Under monopoly, people purchase a single product and advertising is virtually nonexistent. With monopolistic competition and oligopoly, advertising commonly plays an important role.

Summary

1. What is monopolistic competition?

- Monopolistic competition is a market structure in which many firms are producing a slightly different product and entry is easy. §1

- Monopolistically competitive firms will earn a normal profit in the long run. §1.a.2

2. What behavior is most common in monopolistic competition?

- Entry occurs in monopolistically competitive industries through the introduction of a slightly different product. §1.a

- A monopolistically competitive firm will produce less output and charge a higher price than an identical perfectly competitive firm if demand and costs are assumed to be the same. §1.b

3. What is oligopoly?

- Oligopoly is a market structure in which a few large firms produce identical or slightly different products and entry is difficult but not impossible. The firms are interdependent. §2

4. In what form does rivalry occur in an oligopoly?

- Oligopolies may arise from government restrictions or from natural economic factors such as economies of scale. §2.a

- The prisoner's dilemma illustrates an outcome in which competition among interdependent firms results in an outcome that is less than the best for each firm. §2.b.2

- Strategic behavior characterizes oligopoly. The firms are interdependent. The actions of each oligopolist will affect its competitors, and each will be affected by the actions of its rivals. §2.c

- The kinked demand curve results when firms follow a price decrease but do not follow a price increase. §2.b.1

5. Why does cooperation among rivals occur most often in oligopolies?

- The small number of firms in an oligopoly and the interdependence of these firms creates the situation in which the firms are better off if they cooperate (as in the prisoner's dilemma). §2.b.2, 2.c

- Price leadership is another type of strategic behavior. One firm determines price for the entire industry. All other firms follow the leader in increasing and decreasing prices. The dominant firm in the industry is most likely to be the price leader. §2.c.1

- Practices like collusion and cartels minimize profit-reducing rivalry and ensure cooperation. Both are illegal in the United States but acceptable in many other nations. §2.c.2

- Cost-plus pricing ensures that firms with the same costs will charge the same prices. The most-favored-customer policy guarantees a customer that the price he or she paid for a product will not be lowered for another customer. Cost-plus pricing and the most-favored-customer policy are facilitating practices. §2.c.4

Key Terms

strategic behavior §2.b

game theory §2.b

dominant strategy §2.b.2

cartel §2.c.2

facilitating practices §2.c.4

cost-plus/markup pricing §2.c.4

most-favored customer (MFC) §2.c.4

Exercises

1. Disney, Universal, and MGM, among others, have movie studios in Hollywood. Each of these major studios also has one or several subsidiary studios. Disney, for example, has Touchstone. What market structure best describes these movie production companies? Why would each studio have subsidiary studios? Consider the movies that have come out under the Disney name and those that have come out under Touchstone. Are they different?

2. Suppose that Disney was experiencing above-normal profits. If Disney is a member of a monopolistically competitive industry, what would you predict would happen to its demand curve (the demand curve for Disney movies) over time? Suppose that Disney is a member of an oligopoly. How would this change your answer?

3. Why is monopolistic competition said to be inefficient? Suppose that you counted the higher price the consumer pays for the monopolistically competitive firm's product as part of consumer surplus. Would that change the conclusion regarding the efficiency of monopolistic competition?

4. Why might some people claim that the breakfast cereal industry is monopolistically competitive but that the automobile industry is an oligopoly? In both cases, about eight to ten firms dominate the industry.

5. The graph that follows shows an individual firm in long-run equilibrium. In which market structure is this firm operating? Explain. Compare the long-run quantity and price to those of a perfectly competitive firm. What accounts for the difference? Is the equilibrium price greater than, equal to, or less than marginal cost? Why or why not?

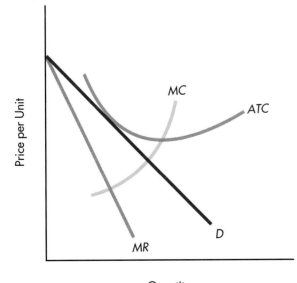

6. Explain what is meant by strategic behavior. How does the kinked demand curve describe strategic behavior?

7. The NCAA is described as a cartel. In what way is it a cartel? What is the product being produced? How does the cartel stay together?

8. Almost every town has at least one funeral home, even if the number of deaths could not possibly keep the funeral home busy. What market structure does the funeral home industry best exemplify? Use the firm's demand and cost curves and long-run equilibrium position to explain the fact that the funeral home can handle more business than it has. (*Hint:* Is the firm operating at the bottom of the average-total-cost curve?)

9. What is the cost to a firm in an oligopoly that fails to take rivals' actions into account? Suppose the firm operates along demand curve D_1, shown below, as if no firms will follow its lead in price cuts or price rises. In fact, however, other firms do follow the price cuts, and the true demand curve below price P_1 lies below D_1. If the firm sets a price lower than P_1, what will happen?

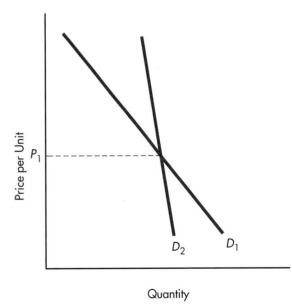

10. Suppose a firm in monopolistic competition has the following demand schedule. Suppose the marginal cost is a constant $70. How much will the firm produce? Is this a long- or short-run situation? If the firm is earning above-normal profit, what will happen to this demand schedule?

Price	Quantity	Price	Quantity
$100	1	$70	5
$ 95	2	$55	6
$ 88	3	$40	7
$ 80	4	$22	8

11. The cement industry is an example of an undifferentiated oligopoly. The automobile industry is a differentiated oligopoly. Which of these two is more likely to advertise? Why?

12. The South American cocaine industry consists of several "families" that obtain the raw material, refine it, and distribute it in the United States. There are only about three large families, but there are several small families. What market structure does the industry most closely resemble? What predictions based on the market-structure models can be made about the cocaine business? How do you explain the lack of wars among the families?

13. Use the payoff matrix below for the following exercises. The payoff matrix indicates the profit outcome that corresponds to each firm's pricing strategy.

		Firm A's Price	
		$20	*$15*
Firm B's Price	**$20**	Firm A earns $40 profit	Firm A earns $35 profit
		Firm B earns $37 profit	Firm B earns $39 profit
	$15	Firm A earns $49 profit	Firm A earns $38 profit
		Firm B earns $30 profit	Firm B earns $35 profit

a. Firms A and B are members of an oligopoly. Explain the interdependence that exists in oligopolies using the payoff matrix facing the two firms.

b. Assuming that the firms cooperate, what is the solution to the problem facing the firms?

c. Given your answer to part b, explain why cooperation would be mutually beneficial and then explain why one of the firms might cheat.

14. What is the purpose of a brand name? What would occur if any maker of aspirin could put a Bayer Aspirin label on its product?

ACE
Practice Test

Take the ACE Practice Test for this chapter to review the important concepts and get immediate feedback with answers.

college.hmco.com/economics/students/

Mexican Authorities Work to Break Up Drug Cartel

Houston Chronicle
September 3, 2005

MEXICO CITY—Federal authorities have charged 15 police officers from the violent border city of Nuevo Laredo with organized crime and kidnapping, alleging they worked for the Gulf Cartel, officials said Friday.

The federal Attorney General's Office said in a statement that witnesses linked to a rival drug organization, the Sinaloa Cartel, allege the officers abducted them and handed them over to the Zetas, the Gulf Cartel's army of enforcers.

The witnesses were part of a group of 44 people found bound and gagged in a Nuevo Laredo house raided by federal agents and soldiers in June, the Attorney General's Office said.

The Gulf Cartel, led by the imprisoned Osiel Cardenas, and the Sinaloa Cartel, led by escaped convict Joaquin "Shorty" Guzman, are fighting a bloody turf war to control Nuevo Laredo and its billion-dollar drug-smuggling routes into Texas, investigators say. The Gulf Cartel, authorities allege, had a number of local policemen on its payroll.

"The police used their position as municipal officers to detain people they thought were linked to the Shorty Guzman organization," the Attorney General's Office said. "They gave (the detainees) to the Zetas, who tortured them and used them to get information, get a ransom or kill them."

Since Jan. 1, drug-related violence has left more than 100 people dead, including 15 police officers, in Nuevo Laredo, a city of 500,000 across the Rio Grande from Laredo. One of the victims, Police Chief Alejandro Dominguez, was gunned down just hours after taking office.

The 15 accused policemen were part of a group of 41 Nuevo Laredo officers arrested in June after a shootout with federal agents. The fate of the other 26 detained officers will be decided soon, authorities said.

President Vicente Fox has declared the "mother of all battles" against drug traffickers and has promised to crack down on any corrupt police officer working for the cartels.

Since Jan. 1, there have been more than 830 drug-related killings in Mexico, mostly in states near the U.S. border.

Ioan Grillo

Source: Copyright 2005, The Houston Chronicle Publishing Company.

N uevo Laredo is a battleground. Warring drug organizations there are fighting for control of the billion-dollar drug-smuggling routes into the United States. In recent years, the drug trade, once the province of Colombian drug families, has been taken over by Mexican cartels. In particular, the Gulf Cartel and the Sinaloa Cartel have taken over drug smuggling. But now the two cartels are battling with each other. Let's use the material of this chapter to consider some of the cartels' actions.

Let's begin with the fact that the two factions are battling. Wouldn't cooperation seem to be preferred by each of them? We can present the alternatives in the matrix below.

		Sinaloa	
		Share Market	**Take Market**
Gulf	**Share Market**	Sinaloa = 75 Gulf = 75	Sinaloa = 150 Gulf = 0
	Take Market	Sinaloa = 0 Gulf =150	Sinaloa = 50 Gulf = 50

If the Sinaloa Cartel shares the market with the Gulf Cartel, each earns 75 (hundreds of millions of dollars). If Sinaloa tries to take the market while Gulf tries to share, Sinaloa gets 150 and Gulf gets nothing. Conversely, if Gulf tries to take the market while Sinaloa tries to share, Gulf gets 150 and Sinaloa gets nothing. If both cartels try to take the market, then they both end up with 50, since the costs of battle take away from their profits. Notice from the matrix that the two will choose to fight—to take the market. Although each would be better off sharing the market than fighting for it, each has an incentive to try to take the market. This prisoner's dilemma points to the situation that the two cartels find themselves in.

The prisoner's dilemma points out that if the cartels could cooperate and share, they would be better off. We can show this on a standard demand/supply diagram as well. Consider the following diagram with the market demand curve, D. If the cartels cooperated and acted as a single monopolist, they would have the marginal-revenue curve, MR, associated with demand, D, which would intersect the supply or MC at a quantity of 150 and a price of $30. So by cooperating or colluding, the result would be greater profits for each—each must agree to sell 75 at a price of $30.

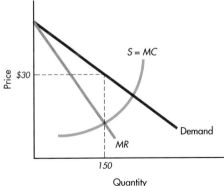

However, if they are colluding and have increased the price to $30, the drug suppliers will each think to themselves, "Why don't I sell 100 at a price of $30?" The problem is that when the cartels begin selling more than their quota, the market price declines. The only way that the price can be kept high and one of the drug groups increases quantity is that the other group reduces quantity. This means that one group gains while the other loses— something that neither group will accept. As a result, both groups begin selling more, and the price declines.

This is a common problem with cartels—the members have a huge incentive to cheat. Because there is a strong incentive for firms that are members of the drug cartel to cheat on agreements, a way to stop cheaters must be found, or else the cartel falls apart. In the illegal drug trade, the way the cheaters are dealt with is violence and drug wars. When one drug cartel moves into the territory of another, drug wars break out. When one cartel expands its business without dealing with another cartel, violence erupts. According to the article, between January 1, 2005, and September 3, 2005, over 830 drug-related killings occurred in Mexico and more than 100 people were killed in Nuevo Laredo.

c h a p t e r

13

Antitrust and Regulation

There are two reasons that the government intervenes in the operation of a business. One is that the free market creates inefficiencies that require government intervention. Another is that groups of people or special interests don't like the results of the free market and use the government to create the type of outcome that they favor. We will discuss these two rationales in this and the following chapters. ■

? Fundamental Questions

1. What is antitrust policy?

2. What is the difference between economic regulation and social regulation?

3. What is intellectual property?

4. Is it legal to download music, movies, and other copyrighted materials without permission?

1. Antitrust

Comparing the price and output of a monopolist with those of a perfectly competitive market illustrates the idea that competition is beneficial for society and monopoly is not. The monopolist restricts output and raises price, thereby transferring

antitrust policy:
government policies and programs designed to control the growth of monopoly and enhance competition

1. What is antitrust policy?

some consumer surplus to itself and creating deadweight loss. The more like a monopolist a company or a group of companies acts, the greater the inefficiency relative to perfect competition. A cartel is a group of companies that attempt to behave like a monopolist; collusion is an attempt by companies to restrict output and raise price much as a monopolist would. It is the inefficiencies of monopoly and cartels that form the basis of **antitrust policy.**

1.a. Antitrust Policy

Three laws define the U.S. government's approach to antitrust—the Sherman, Clayton, and Federal Trade Commission Acts. These laws are intended to limit the creation and behavior of *trusts,* or combinations of independent firms. You can see in Table 1 that the laws were enacted in the period between 1890 and 1914, a period in which the railroads, steel, oil, mining, and finance were becoming large and dominant businesses. The story at the time involved large, successful companies and their smaller competitors—not too much unlike Microsoft and Wal-Mart and their competitors today. Questions arose as to whether the large firms were acting unfairly and needed to be controlled or restricted in their behavior or whether the smaller competitors found that they could compete only if the government restricted the behavior of the larger firms.

1.b. Procedures

Any one of four different entities may sue a firm for alleged antitrust behavior: the U.S. Department of Justice, the Federal Trade Commission (FTC), state attorneys general, and private individuals or firms. Since 1941, the FTC and the Justice Department together have filed nearly 2,800 cases, but private suits have far outnumbered those filed by the Justice Department and the FTC combined. One reason is that if the private plaintiffs are able to win in court, they can receive compensation of up to three times the amount of the damages caused by the action. The Justice Department and the FTC do not obtain treble damages but can impose substantial penalties. They can force firms to break up through dissolution or divestiture, and the Justice Department can file criminal actions for violations of the Sherman Act. A guilty finding can result in fines and prison sentences.

TABLE 1	Antitrust Acts

Sherman Antitrust Act (1890)

Section 1 outlaws contracts and conspiracies in restraint of trade.
Section 2 forbids monopolization and attempts to monopolize.

Clayton Antitrust Act (1914)

Section 2, as amended by the Robinson-Patman Act (1936), bans price discrimination that substantially lessens competition or injures particular competitors.
Section 3 prohibits certain practices that might keep other firms from entering an industry or competing with an existing firm.
Section 7, as amended by the Celler-Kefauver Act (1950), outlaws mergers that substantially lessen competition.

Federal Trade Commission Act (1914)

Section 5, as amended by the Wheeler-Lea Act (1938), prohibits unfair methods of competition and unfair or deceptive acts.

1.c. Violations—Proof

Price fixing is by definition illegal—there is no justification for it. Other aspects of the antitrust statutes are not as clear-cut and are, therefore, difficult to prove. For instance, Section 1 of the Sherman Act outlaws "every contract, combination . . . or conspiracy" that is "in restraint of trade," but it defines none of these terms. Similarly, Section 2 of the Sherman Act outlaws "monopolization" but does not forbid monopolies and does not define "to monopolize." As a result of these ambiguities, the application of antitrust law has often depended on politics—the views of the judges appointed to the various courts, particularly the Supreme Court, and what party was in power—as much as or more than economics.

There have been several distinct phases of antitrust policy in the United States, as illustrated in Figure 1. The first began with passage of the Sherman Antitrust Act in 1890 and lasted until about 1914. In this period, litigation was infrequent. The courts used a *rule of reason* to judge firms' actions: Being a monopoly or attempting to monopolize was not in itself illegal; to be illegal, an action had to be shown to have negative economic effects. The second phase of antitrust policy began in 1914 with the passage of the Clayton Antitrust Act and the Federal Trade Commission Act. Operating under these two acts, the courts used the *per se rule* to judge firms' actions: Activities that were potentially monopolizing tactics were illegal; the mere existence of these activities was sufficient evidence to lead to a guilty verdict. The per se approach was strengthened during the 36 years that Justice William O. Douglas served on the Supreme Court. Appointed by President Franklin Roosevelt in 1939, Douglas maintained a strong antitrust stance until his departure from the Supreme Court in 1975. Following Douglas's departure, the court made a gradual move back to rule of reason. Justice Sandra Day O'Connor argued in 1984 that it was time to abandon the per se label and refocus the inquiry on the adverse economic effects and potential economic benefits. In general this is how U.S. antitrust cases have been tried and decided since 1990. Nevertheless, the Clinton Administration devoted more resources to antitrust than did the Bush Administration.

Antitrust cases are complex and often confusing. The typical approach is to demonstrate that a firm is a dominant firm and thus can raise or lower prices and quantities and carry out other practices at will. A dominant firm is one that has

---

FIGURE 1   Phases of Antitrust Interpretation

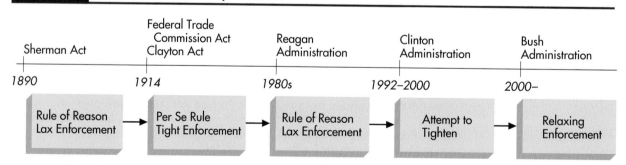

The degree to which antitrust law has been enforced has varied over the years. With the Sherman Act of 1890, the government formally began antitrust policy. But enforcement was lax, based on a rule of reason, until about 1914. Between 1914 and the early 1980s, strict enforcement based on a per se rule was used. With the Reagan and Bush administrations, enforcement was relaxed again to the rule-of-reason standard. The Clinton administration tightened enforcement.

---

sufficient market share to be able to control prices and quantities. When a firm or a few firms are able to dictate the competitive conditions in a market, the market is called *concentrated*. Several ways to measure how concentrated a market is have been developed. The measure that is most relied on is called the *Herfindahl index* and is defined as the sum of the squared market shares of each firm in the industry[1]

$$\text{Herfindahl index} = (S_1)^2 + (S_2)^2 + \cdots + (S_n)^2$$

where S refers to the market share of the firm, the subscripts refer to the firms, and there are n firms. The higher the Herfindahl index number, the more concentrated the industry.

A monopoly would have one firm with 100 percent of the market share, so the Herfindahl index would be $(100)^2 = 10,000$. An industry in which each of five firms has 20 percent of the market would have a Herfindahl index value of 2,000:

$$(20)^2 + (20)^2 + (20)^2 + (20)^2 + (20)^2 = 2,000$$

An industry in which there are five firms, but the largest firm has 88 percent of the market and each of the others has 3 percent would have a Herfindahl index of 7,780:

$$(88)^2 + (3)^2 + (3)^2 + (3)^2 + (3)^2 = 7,780$$

The higher number indicates a much more concentrated market—an indication that one or a few firms dominate a market. The Justice Department defines its policies on the basis of the concentration measures. In 1982, 1984, and 1992, the Justice Department stated that industries with Herfindahl indexes below 1,000 are considered *highly competitive;* those with indexes between 1,000 and 1,800 are *moderately competitive;* and those with indexes above 1,800 are *highly concentrated.* The department was informing businesses that they needed to consider their impact on market share when they undertook actions; reducing competition could bring government lawsuits.

Using the Herfindahl index to gauge the extent to which a few firms dominate a market sounds simple, but it is not. Before the concentration of an industry can be calculated, there must be some definition of the market. In a $100 billion market, an $80 billion firm would have an 80 percent market share. But in a $1,000 billion market, an $80 billion firm would have only an 8 percent market share. The Herfindahl index in the former case would exceed 2,000, but in the latter case it would be less than 1,000. Obviously, those accusing a firm of attempting to monopolize a market would want the market defined narrowly, making it small. Conversely, those that are accused of monopolization would argue for broadly defined markets in order to give the appearance that they possess a very small market share.

For example, Coca-Cola, Dr Pepper, PepsiCo, and Seven-Up are usually identified as producers of carbonated soft drinks (CSD). These firms provide bottlers with the syrup that is used to make the drinks. Is this the appropriate market in which to assess the competitive consequences of the CSD's behavior, or should the market be more widely defined—perhaps to encompass all potable liquids (fruit juices, milk, coffee, tea, etc.)?

In the Microsoft antitrust case, the Justice Department defined the market very narrowly. All of Microsoft's rivals were defined as not being in the same market— the market of single-user desktop PCs that run on an Intel chip. Thus, Apple's market share did not count because Apple ran on a Motorola chip. Nor did Sun

---

[1] The four-firm concentration ratio is another commonly used measure of concentration, but it has come under criticism because it does not account for the size distribution of firms. It merely divides the total output of the four largest firms by the total market output.

Microsystems' share count because Sun was not Intel-based. Linux did not count because it came into being after the government's complaints against Microsoft. And, the 15 percent of the PC market that consisted of machines offered without any operating system were not counted. Thus, instead of having a Herfindahl index of 10,000 in the very narrow market as defined by the Justice Department, Microsoft's market share was 65 percent or less if the market was defined more broadly. This market share still showed a concentrated market, a Herfindahl index of about 5,000, but not the monopoly that the Justice Department defined.

Defining the market and the degree of concentration is just the beginning. Perhaps the most difficult part of any antitrust lawsuit is establishing intent—did the firm intend the actions that it took to reduce competition? Did a firm set prices below costs in an attempt to run competitors out of business, or was it simply matching competitors' prices? Did a firm unfairly restrict access to customers by bundling products together or requiring exclusive deals with suppliers, or were these policies beneficial for the consumer? Did the combined efforts of companies benefit consumers, or were they attempts to create cartels? Questions like these are at the center of antitrust lawsuits.

1.d. Business Policy from a Global Perspective

A firm doing business in the United States must be wary of its actions once it gets large. The impact of its behavior on the Herfindahl index is carefully scrutinized when it wants to purchase other companies or merge with other firms. Moreover, the executives of the company must always be aware of how its actions might be viewed by the antitrust authorities. But if you think that a business might be confused about what to do in the United States, consider a company that carries on business in many different nations. Each nation has a different set of laws. Approximately 70 jurisdictions have enacted merger review laws and merger notification regimes.

In an attempt to make the national antitrust laws more consistent with one another, the International Competition Network (ICN) was formed in October 2001. This is an informal network of antitrust agencies from developed and developing countries around the world. It began with antirust officials from 14 jurisdictions— Australia, Canada, the European Union, France, Germany, Israel, Italy, Japan, Korea, Mexico, South America, the United Kingdom, the United States, and Zambia—but today, 90 member competition agencies from 80 jurisdictions participate. In addition to the ICN, the United States and the European Union have been attempting to encourage close cooperation between the agencies and to see the laws converge to become essentially the same. But that desire may be just a dream; national politics enters the arena, and while consistency might be generally desired, nations do not want to forgo what they believe is the best way to pursue antitrust actions. Right now, the laws are not the same and are applied in very different ways. Typically the United States relies more on economic theory and the rule of reason approach (what the impact is), while the European Union relies more on the per se approach (guilty if it exists, without consideration of impact); it specifies particular actions as simply being prohibited irrespective of economic arguments. Other nations often attempt to simply be different from or more restrictive than the United States, not wanting to appear to be merely a puppet of U.S. antitrust authorities.

Microsoft illustrates the problems of globalization and national antitrust laws. The first antitrust case against Microsoft was filed in the United States in 1998 by the Justice Department and 20 state attorneys general as well as several private firms competing with Microsoft. The case was completed in 2002 with the finding that Microsoft had illegally maintained its Windows monopoly. Microsoft was required to allow PC makers and consumers to install competing products on their computers instead of the Internet Explorer browser and Media Player. Microsoft also had to reveal parts of its software code to other companies so that these companies could create products that would work with the Windows-based PCs.

The cases against Microsoft were far from over, however. In the European Union, EU regulators ruled that Microsoft had abused its near-monopoly in desktop computer systems to illegally dominate the media software market and threaten the position of competitors selling office networking software. It fined Microsoft and ordered it to both share code with rivals and offer an unbundled version of Windows without the Media Player software. In South Korea, antitrust regulators ruled that Microsoft had abused its market dominance, fined the company, and ordered it to offer alternative versions of Windows. And other countries are beginning to look at Microsoft from the perspective of their antitrust laws.

Global Business Insight

The Debate over Antitrust

What is the purpose of an antitrust lawsuit, to protect the public or to protect firms that are unable to offer competitive prices and products? This debate began with the 1890 antitrust laws and continues today. Economic theory points out that a perfectly competitive market that is monopolized will have higher prices, lower output, and deadweight losses. This simple theory has been used in textbooks and other literature to support antitrust laws. But, the theory may not accurately depict what happens when firms get large. Economic theory also points out that size itself is no demon. Size may come about as a result of efficiencies such as economies of scale. Let's look briefly at the history of antitrust to see how politics and economics have intersected.

In the nineteenth century, the beef industry underwent a series of changes related to butchering, farming, and meatpacking. Four large companies, Swift, Armour, Morris, and Hammond, decided to integrate their businesses in order to centralize the butchering and meatpacking process. The centralization allowed them to use assembly-line methods and achieve economies of scale. This "beef trust" was able to ship its final product to anywhere in the United States from its facilities in Chicago, and to do so at significantly lower prices. Many butchers and cattlemen were negatively affected. In states like Missouri, butchers and cattlemen protested against a "conspiracy" designed to reduce the price of beef. In May 1889, Missouri passed an antitrust law, prohibiting cooperative actions. Other states followed, and in July 1890 the first federal antitrust law was introduced, by Ohio Senator John Sherman.

Sherman's concern was the oil industry more than the beef industry, since Standard Oil of Ohio was buying up independent oil companies and driving smaller firms out of business. But support for the bill came from every state in which trusts were active. A study of letters to Senator Sherman showed that it was competitors to the trusts and not consumers who were complaining.[1] The small oil and petroleum refining companies complained that their competitor's success was based on the use of tank cars instead of the traditional oil barrels. Congressman William Mason declared that even though trusts had made products cheaper, it would not matter if prices continued to decline because this would not correct the damage that the trusts had done by driving honest men from legitimate business enterprises.

So, is antitrust legislation something that benefits consumers, or does it benefit firms that are unable to compete with a large company? According to many critics, it is the smaller competitors that benefit. They note that in recent major cases, we see the small rivals suing their larger competitors: IBM was sued under antitrust laws by companies such as Greyhound, Tele3x, Cal Comp., and Memorex; Microsoft has been sued by Oracle, Nokia, Red Hat, RealNetworks, IBM, Netscape, and Sun Systems.

[1] Thomas J. DiLorenzo, "The Origins of Antitrust: An Interest-Group Perspective," *International Review of Law and Economics* 5 (June 1985), pp. 73–90; "Inside the History of Antitrust: Special Interests Unleashed," Economic Note, June 2005, Institut Economique Molinari, *www.institutmolinari.org*.

1. Antitrust policy in the United States is based on the Sherman, Clayton, and Federal Trade Commission Acts.

2. Antitrust lawsuits may be brought by private firms or individuals, the Justice Department, and the Federal Trade Commission. When a firm's actions are proven to be damaging to competition, the penalties imposed depend on who brought suit. If private concerns are involved, then penalties of three times the damages created by the actions may be imposed.

3. The Herfindahl index is a measure of concentration, attempting to provide an indication of how one or a few firms might control a market. It is the sum of the squares of the market shares of the firms in an industry. The higher the number, the more concentrated the market.

4. Currently the U.S. tends to take a rule of reason approach, as do some other nations, but still others rely more on a per se rule.

economic regulation: the prescription of price and output for a specific industry

social regulation: the prescribing of health, safety, performance, and environmental standards that apply across several industries

2. **What is the difference between economic regulation and social regulation?**

2. Regulation

There are two categories of regulation, economic regulation and social regulation. **Economic regulation** refers to the prescribing of prices and output levels for entire industries. **Social regulation** refers to the prescribing of performance standards, workplace health and safety standards, emission levels, and a variety of output and job standards that apply across most if not all industries.

2.a. Economic Regulation

A natural monopoly exists when economies of scale make it efficient for a single firm to supply the entire market. Regulation of monopolies is based on the idea that certain industries—utilities, railroads, communication, and others—are natural monopolies. Most economic regulation of natural monopolies began during the Great Depression of the 1930s. The idea was to make the natural monopolist's price and supply much like what a perfectly competitive industry would provide.

Figure 2 shows the demand, marginal-revenue, long-run average-total-cost, and long-run marginal-cost curves for a natural monopoly. The huge economies of scale mean that it would be inefficient to have many small firms supply the product. Yet allowing the natural monopoly to produce at $MR = MC$ and set a price of P_m from the demand curve yields too little output and too much profit for the firm, in comparison to the perfectly competitive result. In addition, since price is greater than marginal cost, resources are not being allocated efficiently. In fact, too few resources are devoted to this product—too few because if more was produced, MC would equal price. Can regulation solve this problem?

If the natural monopolist is to look like a perfectly competitive industry, then its price should be set equal to its marginal cost. At P_r in Figure 2, $P = MC$, and the monopolist would then produce at quantity Q_r. The problem with the regulated price P_r is that the regulated firm could actually make a loss. You can see in Figure 2 that demand lies below ATC, which means that revenues are less than total costs. Figure 2 illustrates a fairly common situation with public utility companies. Most public utilities acquire enough capacity to be able to provide the electricity needed during the *peak periods.* For instance, air conditioning is used most heavily during the 5 to 9 P.M. time period during the summer months. The demand during this period may be twice as great as the highest demand in any other time period. To be able to sup-

FIGURE 2   **Natural Monopoly and Regulation**

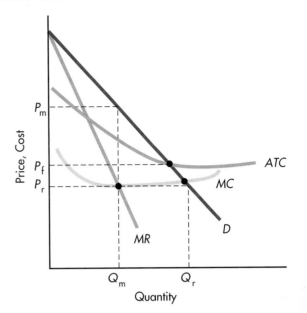

The demand, marginal-revenue, and long-run average-total-cost and marginal-cost curves for a natural monopoly are shown. The huge economies of scale mean that it would be inefficient to have many small firms supply the product. Yet, producing at $MR = MC$ and setting a price of P_m from the demand curve yields too small an output and too much profit for the firm, in comparison to the perfectly competitive result. Too few resources are devoted to this product—too few because if more was produced, MC would equal price. To achieve allocative ef-ficiency (giving consumers the goods they most want), the regulatory agency must attempt to have the monopolist set a price equal to marginal cost. This price would be P_r. The monopolist would then produce at quantity Q_r. The problem with the regulated price P_r is that the revenues do not cover average costs. The fair-rate-of-return price is set to allow the monopolist a normal profit. The price corresponding to the normal profit is the one where demand and average total costs are equal, P_f.

fair rate of return: a price that allows a monopoly firm to earn a normal profit

ply enough electricity for the peak period, the electric company has to have nearly double the generating capacity it would need in order to satisfy demand in other time periods. And this generating capacity simply sits idle most of the time. To avoid the problem of forcing utilities into bankruptcy, regulatory commissions allow for a **fair rate of return.** The fair-rate-of-return price is set to allow the monopolist a normal profit, that is, a zero economic profit. The price corresponding to the normal profit is one at which demand and average total cost curves intersect, P_f. Remember, a perfectly competitive firm in the long run would have price equal to marginal cost and equal to the minimum of the average total cost.

The fair rate of return avoids driving a regulated firm into bankruptcy, but it creates a different problem. When the firm is allowed to set the price as a percentage of average costs, it has an incentive to increase costs. The regulated firm thus ends up with "too much" capital—it builds too much capacity or more office space than is needed because these capital costs can be included in the rate base.

The California Debacle

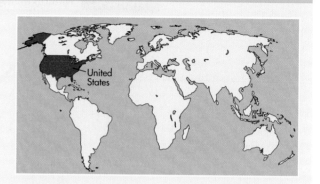

In many countries, electric power has been deregulated without difficulty. That has not been the case in the United States. Events in California slowed the movement toward deregulation. Beginning in 1998, California utilities operated within a system that was unlike any other in the world. They could buy power only in the shortest-term market imaginable, paying prices for their next day's energy that varied hour by hour. They were prohibited from using longer-term contracts. In the summer of 2000, almost everything that could raise wholesale prices happened at once. Hot weather in the Southwest and low water levels in the Northwest cut importable power. Natural gas prices spiked, and the price of pollution permits rose from $4 to $40. In addition, because of public objections to the construction of major power plants, none had been built in 15 years, while the growth of the silicon economy had raised demand to very high levels. Unethical behavior on the part of suppliers to the electrical utilities drove prices even higher. Enron, for instance, bought and sold gasoline supplies to itself through hidden companies (a practice called *round-trip trading*) in order to drive the price upward. The California utilities had no choice but to pay the higher prices.

Although the utilities faced high wholesale prices, the rates that they could charge customers were still frozen. Thus, by February 2000, their estimated net cash shortfalls were over $6 billion and rising, and analysts had downgraded their bonds to junk status. PG&E declared bankruptcy. The so-called deregulation experiment in California was finished.

Attempting to make the natural monopoly look like a perfectly competitive firm in its pricing and output decisions is not straightforward. It creates incentives for the natural monopoly to be inefficient, to acquire too much capacity and other capital costs. This became clear in the years following the implementation of regulation. The inefficiencies that resulted from economic regulation accumulated to the point that many of these industries were deregulated.

2.b. Deregulation and Privatization in the United States

Regulation alters incentives and forces firms to change the way they do business. For instance, if firms are not allowed to compete using price, then they compete using other things. When airlines were unable to compete with prices, they competed instead with schedules, movies, food, and size of aircraft. The result was a much larger number of flights and expansion of aircraft capacity than was demanded by passengers. The load factor (the average percentage of seats filled) fell to less than 50 percent in the early 1970s.

Price competition among truckers was also stifled by regulation. The Interstate Commerce Commission (ICC) had a complex rate schedule and restrictions affecting whether trucks could be full or less than full and the routes that trucks could take. As a result, by the mid-1970s, 36 percent of all truck-miles were logged by empty trucks.

These problems and the higher costs that resulted finally led to a change. Trucking was deregulated in 1980 and air flight in 1982. Trucks were allowed to haul what they wanted, where they wanted, at rates set by the trucking companies. In air transportation, deregulation of route authority and fares was completed by 1982. But the government did not free up the airports and the air traffic control system. These remain government controlled and typically government owned. Much of the telecommunications industry was deregulated in 1984. Long distance communication became free of restraint immediately, but local markets still retain some restrictions.

The deregulation of electricity generation and other utilities has not been uniform. Some states have lessened regulation more than others, but most continue to impose some type of regulation. Deregulation is a politically difficult thing to accomplish. The regulated companies argue that competition will cost too much because of their **stranded assets.** Electric and cable companies argue that if regulation is eliminated, they need to be compensated for the cable they have laid, the lines they have built, and the power plants they have created. Fair-rate-of-return regulation induced these companies to purchase a great deal of capital that they would not otherwise have purchased. The companies argue that they invested for the public good on the assumption that their monopolies would be preserved, and that to now tell them that they aren't guaranteed a return on these assets is not right; exposing them to competition without compensating them for their previous investments amounts to an unconstitutional "taking" of their property.

Privatization is the term for changing from a government-run business to a privately owned and run business. Advocates of privatization claim that private firms can, in many instances, provide better services at reduced costs. Cities and local governments in the United States have **contracted out** (privatized) many services in recent years. Local governments are now allowing private firms to provide garbage services, water services, and even road building and maintenance. Rural/Metro Company in Scottsdale, Arizona, has been running a private fire department for several decades. It is now purchasing contracts to run fire departments and emergency medical services throughout Arizona and in other states. Corrections Corporation of America in Nashville, Tennessee, is building prisons. Many members of Congress are looking at the U.S. Postal Service and arguing that private firms could deliver mail better and less expensively. Even highways are subjects for privatization. Arguing that the first good highways in the United States were privately built and operated in the late 1700s, some economists argue that congestion and air pollution today could be reduced if highways were privatized. And in a few locations, such as between Los Angeles and San Diego, highways have been privately built and maintained. As will be discussed in the chapter "Aging, Social Security, and Health Care," proposals for improving the Social Security system include privatization.

stranded assets: assets acquired by a firm when it was regulated that have little value when the firm is deregulated

privatization: transferring a publicly owned enterprise to private ownership

contracting out: the process of enlisting a private firm to provide a product or service for a government entity

2.c. Social Regulation

Social regulation is concerned with the conditions under which goods and services are produced and the impact of these conditions on the public. Social regulation is often applied across all industries. For instance, the Environmental Protection Agency (EPA) enforces emission standards that apply to all businesses, and the Occupational Safety and Health Administration (OSHA) imposes workplace requirements on all businesses.

Who decides whether a regulation is necessary? How is the regulation to be implemented? According to economists, a cost-benefit calculation is necessary to determine whether a regulation should be implemented.

2.c.1. Cost–Benefit Calculations
There have been several studies that focused on estimating the costs of regulations on the economy. These range from about $400 billion to over $800 billion, depending on what is included as a cost.[2] Who pays

---

[2] Clyde Wayne Crews, Jr., "Ten Thousand Commandments: An Annual Snapshot of the Federal Regulatory State," Cato Institute, 2003.

When a business is required to pay for environmental protection or cleanup, its costs of supplying goods and services rise. This can lead to higher prices for the consumer. Who pays the higher proportion of the costs, the consumers or the owners of the firm, depends on the price elasticities of demand for and supply of the firm's goods and services. In this photo, a geologist is disturbing a seal so that he can obtain samples of coastal water quality.

these costs? It may be the business, it may be the consumer, or both may end up paying. The impact of social regulation on a business is illustrated in Figure 3. The firm is producing quantity Q_1 at a cost of C_1 and selling at a price of P_1. The firm, an automobile company, is told that it must increase the fuel efficiency of its fleet of cars. This requirement means that the company must modify its manufacturing plants

FIGURE 3 Regulatory Costs

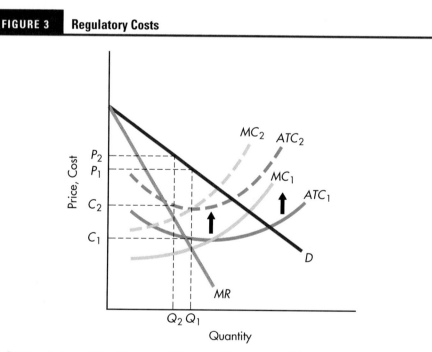

The firm producing at Q_1 with costs of C_1 and selling at price P_1 is required to implement changes in production in order to meet pollution requirements. The increased costs of the regulation are illustrated as upward shifts of the *ATC* and *MC* curves, leading to less output being produced, Q_2 rather than Q_1, at higher costs, C_2 rather than C_1, and thus being sold at higher prices, P_2 rather than P_1.

Part Three Product Markets

and alter the parts it uses in its autos. The result is an increase in the company's fixed and variable costs, shown as an upward shift of the ATC and MC curves. The regulation causes the firm to bear increased costs, illustrated as an upward shift of the ATC and MC curves, leading to less output being produced, Q_2 rather than Q_1, at higher costs, C_2 rather than C_1, and the output being sold at higher prices, P_2 rather than P_1. In virtually every case of regulation, consumers pay higher prices for the goods and services sold by the regulated firm. How much more does the consumer pay? The answer depends on the price elasticities of demand and supply.

If the price elasticity of demand is low—demand is inelastic—then the consumer will not be very likely to switch to a substitute good or service as the price rises. In such a case, the firm will be able to pass along a larger portion of the increased costs to the consumer in the form of higher prices than it will if the price elasticity of demand is high, everything else the same. On the other hand, the firm is likely to have to bear a greater portion of the increased costs if it has a low price elasticity of supply. The low price elasticity of supply means that the firm is not able to easily switch its production and sales from the now more regulated and more costly good or service to a less regulated and less costly good or service.

Since prices are higher and costs are higher as a result of regulation, both producers and consumers lose benefits—consumer and producer surplus is reduced. Consider Figure 4(a), in which the demand and supply curves for the market for automobiles are illustrated. Consumer surplus is shown as triangle ABP_1, and producer surplus is shown as triangle ACP_1. Total societal surplus is thus the area outlined as ABC.

Autos pollute, and the cost of the pollution to society is shown as the area FGQ_1H. So suppose that a regulation is imposed on auto producers that requires

FIGURE 4   Costs and Benefits of Regulation

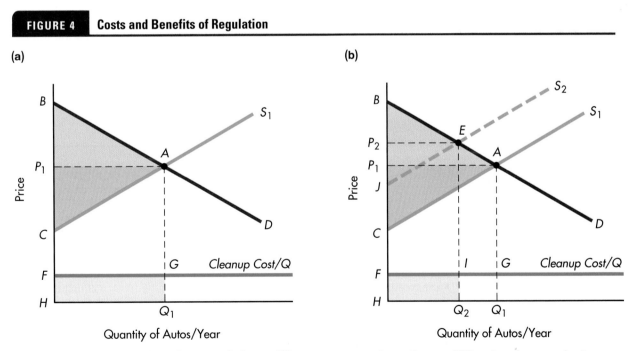

(a)

(b)

Quantity of Autos/Year

Figure 4(a) shows the market prior to regulation, and Figure 4(b) shows the effects of regulation. The regulation causes the supply curve (the sum of the MC curves of each of the automobile firms) to shift up. This reduces con-

sumer surplus to the area EBP_2 and producer surplus to EJP_2. The area $CAEJ$ is the cost of the regulation. The benefits of the regulation are the costs of the pollution that is no longer created by the automobiles, area GIQ_2Q_1.

them to produce cleaner-burning engines. The regulation causes the supply curve (the sum of the MC curves of each of the automobile firms) to shift in, as shown in Figure 4(b). This reduces consumer surplus to the area EBP_2 and producer surplus to EJP_2. The area $CAEJ$ is the cost of the regulation. What are the benefits? The benefits are the cost of the pollution that is no longer created by the automobiles. This is shown as the rectangle GIQ_2Q_1.

The cost-benefit calculation indicates whether a regulation benefits society or not. If the costs exceed the benefits, then, according to economic theory, the regulation should not be imposed. If a regulation is to be imposed, the amount or restrictiveness of the regulation should be at a level where marginal benefits equal marginal costs. Carrying out cost-benefit analyses on regulations is an approach that has been agreed to in principle by the U.S. federal government's Office of Management and Budget and by the main financial agencies of most industrial countries. In many instances, the cost-benefit calculation is done in terms of lives saved and lives lost.

For example, a program to detect and treat breast cancer among women over the age of 50 has been estimated to cost less than $15,000 per life-year saved, while the cost per life-year saved of a regulation to reduce airborne exposure to benzene is approximately $17.5 million According to the federal government, the cost of some environmental regulations is high, as shown in Table 2.

Regulations may not just be costly in terms of dollars; they can also cost lives. The argument, according to economists, is that regulations are costly to implement and conform to, and so reduce income. When people are poorer, they spend less on health care and safety measures and engage in riskier behavior. For example, they buy smaller cars and visit the doctor less often. Hence, regulations that reduce people's incomes can increase fatalities from other causes. A cost-benefit calculation for a regulation that is intended to save lives should compare the number of lives saved with the number of lives lost as a result of the regulation.

Studies have shown that any regulation costing more than about $8.4 million for each life saved is likely to cause overall fatalities to rise. Looking at the cost of regulations suggests that many do the opposite of their intended objective. Most of the Federal Aviation Administration's regulations cost less than $8.4 million per life

| TABLE 2 | The Cost of Regulation |

Regulation of	Saves	At a Cost per Life of
Grain dust	4.00 lives/year	$5.3 million
Uranium mines	1.10 lives/year	6.9 million
Benzene	3.80 lives/year	17.1 million
Glass plants	0.11 life/year	19.2 million
Ethylene oxide	2.80 lives/year	25.6 million
Copper smelters	0.06 life/year	26.5 million
Uranium mill tailings, active	2.10 lives/year	53 million
Low-arsenic copper	0.08 life/year	764 million
Land disposal	2.52 lives/year	3,500 million
Formaldehyde	0.01 life/year	72,000 million

Source: U.S. Office of Management and Budget, Office of Information and Regulatory Affairs, *Report to Congress on the Costs and Benefits of Federal Regulations,* 1998. Each year the OMB provides cost-benefit calculations for rules implemented during the year; see *www.whitehouse.gov/omb.*

saved, and thus arguably yield a net saving of lives. The same is true for most of the National Highway Traffic Safety Administration's rules. The record of the Occupational Safety and Health Administration (OSHA) is not so good. OSHA regulations are about evenly divided between those that are cheap enough to save lives on balance and those (such as OSHA's ethylene dibromide and formaldehyde rules) that are so costly that they have no doubt killed far more people than would have died in the absence of the regulations. The Environmental Protection Agency's (EPA) regulations are almost all more costly in terms of lives lost than they are beneficial in terms of lives saved. The arsenic standard, for example, costs almost $27 million per life saved, according to the official numbers. This income loss leads to about three added fatalities from other causes for each life saved. Similarly, the EPA asbestos standard was supposed to save 10 lives each year. However, its cost per life saved (about $144 million) suggests that 18 people will die each year to save those 10.[3]

A cost-benefit test would limit regulations to those that create benefits greater than their cost. But as shown by the examples presented in Table 2, many regulations do not pass a cost-benefit test but are implemented anyway. Why? Many economists argue that a number of these regulations are implemented to benefit special interest groups rather than to solve problems resulting from market failure. We will discuss such issues further in the chapter "Government and Market Failure."

2.d. Regulation and Deregulation in Other Countries

In most European nations, nationalization rather than regulation was the traditional solution to natural monopoly. With nationalization, the government takes over and operates an industry. Privatization is the opposite of nationalization. Privatization, as discussed earlier, is the transfer of public-sector activities to the private sector. Privatization may take one of three forms: *wholesale privatization,* in which an entire publicly owned firm is transferred to private ownership; *contracting out,* in which a specific aspect of a government operation is carried out by a private firm; and *auctioning,* in which the rights to operate a government enterprise go to the highest private-sector bidder.

While the United States was deregulating, the rest of the world was privatizing. Chile, Argentina, Colombia, the United Kingdom, and 15 other nations allow workers to invest their social security payroll deductions in privately managed funds. The Netherlands offered 25 percent of the Dutch postal and telephone system for private ownership in 1994. Britain has privatized its airlines, telephones, steel, and electric and gas utilities.

Between 1980 and 2000, more than eighty countries launched ambitious efforts to privatize their state-owned enterprises (SOEs). More than 2,000 SOEs have been privatized in developing countries, and more than 7,000 worldwide. State-owned enterprises are chronically unprofitable, partly because they are told to increase employment and locate where they will help the local population rather than to maximize efficiency. Governments provide SOEs with a variety of subsidies, such as reduced prices for resources and guarantees to cover operating losses. Privatization is intended to substitute the single objective of profit maximization for all these other objectives. Subjecting the newly privatized firms to the tests of the market and competition forces the companies to cut costs and increase efficiency or get out of

---

[3] Ulf-G. Gerdtham and Magnus Johannesson, "Do Life-Saving Regulations Save Lives?" *Journal of Risk and Uncertainty* Vol. 24, 231–249, 2002; John F. Morrall, III, "A Review of the Record," *Regulation,* November/December 1986, 25–34. Daniel K. Benjamin, "Killing Us with Kindness," *PERC Reports,* Vol. 20, No. 3, September 2002, perc@perc.org.

business altogether. At first glance, this would seem to indicate that the firms will have to cut employment. Interestingly, the experience has been that the privatized firms do perform much more efficiently, but that they also increase both output and employment relative to the SOEs. Employment in privatized firms has risen by about 10 percent relative to the SOEs.

The privatization movement in Latin America in the 1990s has been reversed in Venezuela and Bolivia as socialist governments have been elected. In Venezuela, President Hugo Chavez is taking land from richer individuals and from firms and redistributing it to poorer.individuals and is nationalizing oil and other major industries. Similarly, Eva Morales in Bolivia has nationalized several industries and redistributed land. In coming years, a comparison between Venezuela and Bolivia, who have nationalized, and Chile, who has privatized, may yield some insights into the relative successes of privatization versus nationalization programs.

2.e. Multinationals, International Regulation, GATT, and the WTO

International regulation occurs at two levels, one in which a specific government regulates the activities of individual firms operating within the country, and another in which several nations are involved. The General Agreement on Tariffs and Trade (GATT) is a form of the latter. In April 1947, delegates from the United States, Asia, Europe, and Latin America traveled to Geneva, Switzerland. Aware of the effects of trade restrictions on economic health that had been experienced during the Great Depression, they all sought to liberalize trade, reduce barriers, and create an environment in which economies would prosper. The first global trade agreement resulted, called GATT. Today the successor to GATT is called the World Trade Organization (WTO). Its 149 member nations have agreed to settle trade disputes in the WTO courts rather than raise barriers, impose tariffs, or otherwise restrict trade. The WTO was created on January 1, 1995, by the Uruguay Round of the GATT. It is located in Geneva.

RECAP

1. Economic regulation means that the government dictates the price that a firm may charge and/or the quantity that a firm must supply.

2. Economic regulation typically applies to an entire industry.

3. Since the mid-1970s, deregulation has occurred in airlines, trucking, railroads, and communications.

4. Social regulation deals with workplace safety, product safety, the environment, and other aspects of doing business; it applies to all industries.

5. A cost-benefit calculation measures whether the benefits of a rule or regulation exceed the costs. Economists assert that only those regulations that create more benefits than costs should be implemented.

6. The costs of a rule or regulation include the reduction in output produced, higher costs of production, and higher prices. They also include the lost consumer and producer surplus. The benefits of the rule or regulation are the reductions in the costs of cleaning up wastes and reductions in the risk to human life.

7. In other countries, nationalization occurred instead of regulation. In those countries, deregulation means privatization.

8. Attempts to increase trade among nations have led to the creation of GATT and then the WTO.

3. The Securities and Exchange Commission

After the stock market crash of 1929, President Roosevelt, the business community, and other government leaders believed that they needed to do something to restore faith in the financial markets and in the U.S. economy. What they came up with in 1934 was a government agency called the Securities and Exchange Commission (SEC). The Securities and Exchange Commission regulates the financial activities of public companies (those whose shares of stock are traded on a stock exchange). The aim of the SEC is to protect investors from fraudulent and questionable public companies and from dishonest and unscrupulous individuals dealing within financial markets. The SEC requires that companies provide it with prudent and truthful financial and material information, and all material information, whether it will positively or negatively affect the company, is provided to investors by the SEC. Today, this information is provided electronically through the SEC's EDGAR database. The problem is that the SEC does not have the resources to examine every document that is required to be submitted to it. It has to rely on the work of auditors, investment bankers, and others who have incentives to ensure that firms are reporting appropriate and accurate information. In the late 1990s, this reliance proved to be a disaster.

3.a. Auditors

Auditors are accountants who act like detectives, examining a company's books, inventories, and other areas of operation to determine whether what the firm is reporting is accurate. The auditors are employed by an auditing or accounting company, such as PricewaterhouseCoopers or KPMG. These accounting firms are separate entities from—and are supposed to be independent of—the firm being audited. In the 1990s, however, many accounting firms began providing business consulting services to the same firms that they were auditing. This created a conflict of interest, as the auditors found it difficult to give a negative report about a firm while at the same time soliciting consulting business from it. The conflict became evident in the late 1990s, when Arthur Andersen was found to be providing misleading auditing reports regarding Enron Corporation. The demise of Arthur Andersen was due to the lawsuits and other penalties resulting from its actions regarding Enron.

3.b. Investment Banks

Investment banks are companies that help a firm raise funds by issuing stocks or bonds, assist in mergers and acquisitions, or perform other financial services. Investment banks also provide advice to investors about individual companies and stocks through *analyst recommendations*. This creates a conflict of interest; analysts can find it difficult to provide a negative opinion on a firm for which the analyst's company was providing investment banking services. The conflict came to home to roost in the late 1990s, as investment banking companies began to seek an increasing amount of business. For instance, Credit Suisse First Boston, Citigroup, and JP Morgan Chase helped design Enron's hidden partnerships and owned shares of stock in Enron at the same time that their analysts were recommending that the general public buy Enron stock. The banks made money not only from their investments in Enron stock, but also from the services they provided to Enron.

3.c. The Sarbanes-Oxley Act

The public outcry that resulted from the collapse of Enron and the activities of other firms was so loud that Congress immediately enacted a law restricting many activities engaged in by auditors, investment banks, and the CEOs of companies. The Sarbanes-Oxley Act, passed by Congress in 2002, requires that auditing and consulting services be provided by different firms. No longer can one company, like Arthur Andersen, provide both auditing and consulting services to the same client. To limit the possibility of fraud on the part of investment banks, analysts, and companies, the act requires the CEOs of corporations to sign and verify the accuracy of the financial statements; in essence, the CEO must take personal responsibility for the statements.[4] In the scandals of the early 2000s, CEOs typically said that they had no knowledge of any fraud, that it was the people who worked under them who had broken the law.

3.d. Financial Regulations in Other Countries

Financial instruments—stocks, bonds, mutual funds, etc.—trade within the regulatory structure that exists in each country. Regulations from country to country have many common features, although there are many rules and regulations that are unique to a particular country. But since the six largest exchanges (New York, Nasdaq, Tokyo, London, Frankfurt, and Paris) account for 90 percent of all securities transactions in the world, their rules and regulations essentially determine who may offer stocks to the public, what information companies must provide to the public, and how all parties must behave.

RECAP

1. The Securities and Exchange Commission (SEC) regulates the equity market in the United States. It requires firms to submit documents regarding the firm's financial activities each quarter.

2. The SEC must rely on the work of auditors and others to ensure that firms comply with its rules and regulations.

3. Auditors are accountants employed by accounting firms who peruse the financial statements of companies to ensure that what is being reported is the truth.

4. Investment banks provide firms with the tools and advice that they need in order to issue stock and carry out other financial activities.

5. In some of the scandals of the late 1990s, auditors failed to do their jobs, investment banks acted improperly, and stock analysts gave misleading recommendations.

4. Intellectual Property Rights: The Market for Ideas

?

3. What is intellectual property?

Intellectual property (IP) is the most valuable asset in business today; as much as three-quarters of the value of publicly traded companies in the United States comes from intangible assets—ideas and conceptual assets. But IP creates difficulties because valuable goods and services can be offered for free. The Microsoft antitrust

---

[4] For more information on the various laws that govern the securities industry, visit *www.sec.gov/about/laws.shtml.*

cases center around the decision by Microsoft to include the Internet Explorer browser and Media Player in Windows at no additional charge. Napster became the flashpoint in a war over music distribution by offering a music-swapping service for free, while Grokster was the center of movie distribution using software for **peer-to-peer (P2P)** file sharing.

4.a. High Fixed, Low Marginal Cost

When research, creation, and development costs are high but the marginal cost of the final service or the cost of duplication of the final output is very low, even near zero, problems arise in defining how a firm can make a profit supplying the good or service. This issue exists for anything that can be digitally produced, but it occurs in other industries as well, such as pharmaceuticals, where the costs of getting a drug to market are huge, but the marginal cost of manufacturing drugs is very low, or amusement parks, where the cost of constructing a park and rides is very large, but the cost of providing a ride to another customer is near zero.

A traditional economic good is one for which the marginal cost decreases as output rises until it reaches a minimum and then rises. The marginal-cost curve intersects the minimum of the average-total-cost curve and continues rising as output rises. For traditional economic goods, price is set according to demand at the quantity where $MR = MC$. But when marginal cost continually falls, it is always below average cost; it does not reach a minimum and then rise to intersect the minimum of the average-total-cost curve, so that setting $MR = MC$ does not lead to profit maximization.

In Figure 5, the cost curves of a movie studio are shown. The fixed costs are very high because of the costs of the facilities and the costs involved in hiring actors, directors, film crews, and so on. Notice that the ATC is very high at a quantity of 1 unit. But the second unit costs almost nothing, shown by the MC dropping rapidly toward zero. The $MC = MR$ point is near zero, and price is not high enough to pay for ATC. What happens is that once the movie is created, the costs of offering additional copies of the movie are very low. The movie studio is unable to charge a high enough price to pay for the huge development and creation costs.

4.b. Intellectual Property Law

Since the firm is unable to recoup its high development costs, there is no incentive for the firm to produce the product. Why should a pharmaceutical company like Eli Lilly spend millions of dollars on research and tests of a particular drug if it can't make a profit selling that drug? It is partly for this reason that Congress established the patent system, including copyrights, trademarks, patents, and trade secrets. The system confers a monopoly on inventions, brand names, creative works, and trade secrets for a limited period of time. Copyrights are used to protect artistic, musical, or literary works. Trademarks are used to protect things like brands. Patents apply to inventions, and trade secrets are practices that are kept confidential. The use of intellectual property law to create monopolies has grown along with intellectual property. The number of patent applications has nearly doubled over the past decade and continues to climb. Microsoft filed about 3,000 patents in 2005; Nokia has over 12,000 patents globally and 10,000 more applications. IBM has about 40,000 patents and obtains about 3,000 more every year. Hewlett-Packard has about 25,000 patents worldwide.

If it is effective, patent or copyright protection enables the owner to act like a monopolist by reducing quantity and raising price. The firm can set a price that is higher than ATC so that it can earn a profit. Intellectual property law is designed to

FIGURE 5 | **Intellectual Property and Profits**

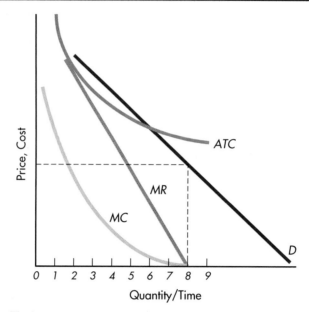

The huge development and research costs cause the average-total-cost curve to begin high and remain high as quantity increases. This occurs even though marginal costs are extremely low, perhaps near zero. As a result, the firm is unable to set a price where it can make a profit.

Q	Costs	ATC	MC
0	10,000		
1	10,020	10,020	20
2	10,030	5,015	10
3	10,035	3,012	5
4	10,036	2,504	1

limit competition by creating limited monopolies. The problem is that intellectual property is often easy to steal; in fact, duplication costs may be near zero. And, as a result, copyright law is becoming increasingly ineffective. People act as if there is no problem with duplicating copyrighted materials or sharing files without paying a fee. It was estimated in 2005 that approximately 400,000 films were illegally downloaded every day. CacheLogic, an Internet monitoring group, has estimated that over 60 percent of all Internet traffic in the United States in 2005 was attributable to peer-to-peer usage, while in Asia, over 80 percent of all traffic on the Web was from P2P and 90 percent of P2P file content was copyrighted materials that were being illegally transferred.

4.c. Giving the Product Away Free

What can be done about copyright infringement and P2P sharing? The entertainment industry has used lawsuits—thousands of them—to attack the problem. Nevertheless, although some 30,000 lawsuits were filed in 2005, P2P sharing increased significantly. Because the law has been unable to control the growing use of P2P sharing, new business models must be developed. Firms that recognize the cost structure of their business and then attempt to use it to sell their goods and services have had some success. For instance, tying the digital product in with something else that cannot be readily duplicated or bundling the free digital product with other items, such as advertising, will have to be used. Google has become one of the most successful businesses by providing its services for free. At Barnes & Noble, SparkNotes study guides took over from Cliff Notes because SparkNotes were given away digitally. This was not an easy thing for executives at Barnes & Noble to do; people feared that giving away the digital product would subtract from sales in store. Why would people spend money to buy something that they could get online, legally, for free? But, the digital product stimulated sales of the physical product. The physical book is a slightly different product from the online book. People want the convenience, the physical product, the better-quality paper, and other such features. Recognizing the digital nature of a product and then designing business strategy to deal with that digital nature may lead to more success than trying to fight it through lawsuits and antitrust type laws.

RECAP

1. Intellectual property refers to the thoughts, artistic creations, and ideas that individuals develop.

2. As with many high-fixed-cost businesses, intellectual property often has large start-up or development and creation costs and small marginal costs.

3. The cost structure means that it may be difficult to make a profit on intellectual property.

4. Intellectual property law consists of laws covering patents, copyrights, and trade secrets. These confer a monopoly of limited duration to the owner of the property.

5. P2P or peer-to-peer sharing has rendered intellectual property law almost useless. The amount of file sharing is huge and growing daily.

6. New business approaches to digital and intellectual property are emerging whereby content is given away free and profit is made from products or services that are bundled with or tied to the digital product.

Summary

1. What is antitrust policy?

- Antitrust policy is an attempt to enhance competition by restricting certain activities that could be anticompetitive. *§1.a*

- The antitrust statutes include Sections 1 and 2 of the Sherman Antitrust Act, which forbid conspiracies and monopolization; Sections 2, 3, and 7 of the Clayton Antitrust Act, which prohibit anticompetitive pricing and nonprice restraints; and Section 5 of the Federal Trade Commission Act, which prohibits deceptive and unfair acts. *§1.a, Table 1*

- Interpretation of the antitrust statutes has gone through several phases. In the early years, a rule of reason prevailed; acts had to be unreasonable to be a violation of the statutes. Between 1914 and 1980, a per se rule was applied more often. Under this policy, the mere existence of actions that could be used anticompetitively was a violation. In the early 1980s, the interpretations returned to the rule-of-reason standard. *§1.c*

- The Herfindahl index is used to measure size and influence; industries with a Herfindahl index above 1,800 are considered highly concentrated. *§1.c*

- Although each country has its own antitrust laws, the International Competition Network, an organization of about 90 nations, has attempted to create more similar laws. *§1.d.*

2. What is the difference between economic regulation and social regulation?

- Economic regulation refers to the prescription of price and output for a particular industry. Social regulation refers to the setting of health and safety standards for products and the workplace, and environmental and operating procedures for all industries. *§2*

- Because monopoly is inefficient and perfect competition efficient, governments have attempted to regulate natural monopolies to make them more like perfect competitors. The huge economies of scale involved rule out breaking up the natural monopolies into small firms. Instead, price has been set at a fair rate of return, $P = ATC$. *§2.a*

- Social regulation has increased even as economic regulation has decreased. *§2.c*

- Regulations create costs and provide benefits. The economist's view is that a regulation should be implemented only if its benefits exceed its costs. *§2.c.1*

- Deregulation in other developed countries took the form of privatization: the selling, auctioning, or contracting out of a government enterprise to private interests. *§2.d*

- The WTO is intended to lower tariffs and increase trade. *§2.e*

- The SEC regulates the financial dealings of public companies; its purpose is to protect the public from fraudulent activities in the financial markets. *§3*

3. What is intellectual property?

- Intellectual property refers to the ideas and artistic creations developed by individuals. *§4*

- The cost structure of many intellectual property activities is such that a firm may not be able to make a profit. Huge development costs and very small marginal costs mean that the item has to be given away free. As a result, many intellectual property assets will not be created. *§4.a*

4. Is it legal to download music, movies, and other copyrighted materials without permission?

- Intellectual property law deals with patents, copyrights, and trade secrets. The intention of these laws is to confer monopolies on owners of intellectual property for a limited time. *§4.b*

- Digital copying and P2P sharing have driven the cost of duplicating to near zero. As a result, intellectual property law has not been effective in limiting illegal uses of the property. *§4.b*

Key Terms

antitrust policy *§1*	fair rate of return *§2.a*	contracting out *§2.b*
economic regulation *§2*	stranded assets *§2.b*	intellectual property (IP) *§4*
social regulation *§2*	privatization *§2.b*	peer-to-peer (P2P) *§4*

Exercises

1. Using the average-total-cost and marginal-cost curves, demonstrate what huge fixed costs and near zero marginal costs mean for the average-total-cost curve.

2. Using the demand and cost curves of an individual firm in oligopoly, demonstrate what the effects of each of the following are:

   a. The Clean Air Act
   b. The Nutrition and Labeling Act
   c. A ban on smoking inside the workplace
   d. A sales tax

3. Kodak has developed an important brand name through its advertising, innovation, and product quality and service. Suppose Kodak sets up a network of exclusive dealerships, and one of the dealers decides to carry Fuji and Mitsubishi as well as Kodak products. If Kodak terminates the dealership, is it acting in a pro- or anticompetitive manner?

4. Explain why a market in which broadcast licenses can be purchased might be more efficient than having the FCC assign licenses on some basis designed by the FCC.

5. Which of the three types of government policies—antitrust, social regulation, and economic regulation—is the basis for each of the following?

   a. Beautician education standards
   b. Certified Public Accounting requirements
   c. Liquor licensing
   d. Justice Department guidelines
   e. The Clean Air Act
   f. The Nutrition and Labeling Act

6. Some airline executives have called for reregulation. Why might an executive of an airline prefer to operate in a regulated environment?

7. Suppose the Herfindahl index for domestic production of televisions is 5,000. Does this imply a very competitive or a noncompetitive environment?

8. Discuss the claim that social regulation is unnecessary. Does the claim depend on whether the industry is perfectly competitive or is an oligopoly?

9. Suppose a monopolist is practicing price discrimination and a lawsuit against the monopolist forces an end to the practice. Is it possible that the result is a loss in efficiency? Explain.

10. The Justice Department sued several universities for collectively setting the size of scholarships offered. Explain why the alleged price fixing on the part of universities might be harmful to students.

11. The FDA is considering the adoption of a higher standard of success in clinical trials for any pharmaceutical that the agency will permit to be sold in the United States. Explain how a cost-benefit calculation would be carried out.

12. Suppose that in exercise 11, the benefits of the regulation were 1,000 lives saved per year. Would you support adoption of the regulation? Explain.

13. Explain what the costs of the regulation are in the scenario in exercises 11 and 12.

14. What does a loss of consumer surplus mean? In the case of exercises 11–13, exactly how do the losses of consumer surplus occur?

15. Using cost curves and demand and marginal-revenue curves, illustrate why P2P sharing is a problem for firms that create and distribute intellectual property.

16. Explain why a university might purchase a site license for downloading movies or music if students at the university are known to be downloading these things for free.

ACE

Take the ACE Practice Test for this chapter to review the important concepts and get immediate feedback with answers.

college.hmco.com/economics/students/

Don't Let It Happen Again; Why Didn't the Post-'65 Fixes Stop This Blackout?

Newsday (New York)
August 17, 2003

It will be days, at best, before blame for the sweeping power blackout that left 50 million people in the United States and Canada without electricity can be definitively assigned. But there's no question about the extent of the disruption to business, to public transportation systems, to cell phone and conventional telephone networks—to any of the myriad activities that rely on electricity to work.

In a modern, high-tech society, electric power touches nearly every aspect of life. It is vast amounts of power that help make this country the success that it is—and the largest consumer of energy per capita of any nation in the world. But, says former Energy Secretary Bill Richardson, "We are a major superpower with a third-world electrical grid . . . It needs serious modernization."

His description may be overwrought, but his broad prescription is correct. The nation must respond with constructive action.

It's far from clear whether the cascading power failures were caused by weaknesses in the transmission system that links the electrical grid of New York with those of other sections of the eastern United States.

But that is one of several issues that will have to be examined in the wake of the largest blackout in North American history. And although it's increasingly certain that terrorism was not a cause of the power outage, its rapid spread and the dislocation and inconvenience in its wake show how vulnerable the nation is to a terrorist attack on its power delivery system.

After the massive 1965 blackout that swept much of the Northeast, the utility industry took steps that, it said, would prevent such a thing from happening again. One was formation of the North American Electric Reliability Council, which describes itself as "a voluntary organization, relying on reciprocity, peer pressure and the mutual self-interest of all those involved . . . to make the North American bulk electric system the most reliable in the world."

The obvious question now is whether such voluntary measures are adequate to bring the nation's power grid up to major superpower standards, or whether government should be taking a more active role in controlling and modernizing the electric system. . . .

Since New York deregulated its electric system, in hopes of gaining new efficiencies from competition, it has depended on private energy companies to build new generating plants. But in the wake of the failure of Enron Corp., those companies have had difficulty financing new projects. A Not-in-My-Backyard climate makes building any major energy project dicey. And a streamlined state system for approving sites for new power plants has been allowed to lapse by the State Legislature. As a result of such factors, few new power plants have been built or even started in New York in recent years.

And deregulation makes it harder to plan when and where to bolster the state's transmission system, since it's unclear where new plants will be built.

That's a full plate for the power industry and federal and state officials to confront. But America was promised, after the 1965 blackout that darkened the Northeast, that this kind of thing would never happen again. Now it has, and there's no reason to think it couldn't be repeated. The industry and its regulators must redeem that promise.

Source: Copyright 2003 Newsday, Inc.

When electricity was unavailable to a large section of the United States and parts of Canada, people were stuck in elevators and subways, drinking water was unavailable in Cleveland and Detroit, cell phones wouldn't work, and transportation came to a stop. According to the article, the problem stems from the electrical grid. Throughout the United States, electricity generation stations—fueled by coal, oil, gas, water, wind, or nuclear fission—are interconnected in a system called power grids. Power from over 6,000 power-generating units is moved around the country on almost a half-million miles of bulk transmission lines that carry high-voltage charges of electricity. At more than 100 control centers, officials direct the transmission and monitor the distribution of power, rerouting electricity from areas of low demand to areas of high demand.

The idea of the electrical grid is to ensure that areas in which demand is higher than normal are able to meet that demand. Conceptually, if New York City has a heat wave and requires large amounts of power to run air conditioners at the same time that Cleveland is using less power, then sending the power from Cleveland to New York City benefits everyone.

According to the article, the blackout was due to a bad combination of deregulation and regulation. The reason this combination exists is related to the structure of the electric-power industry. Electricity is generated in one location and then must be transmitted to users—homes and businesses. Although many different companies can build generating plants and compete to send power, transmission does not seem to lend itself to competition, at least according to government regulators, who argue that transmission is a natural monopoly. With a natural monopoly, the first firm to build power lines would experience economies of scale (the more power delivered over the lines it provided, up to the maximum capacity, the lower the cost per foot of line provided), so only one firm would end up owning the lines. As a result, the government regulators decided to deregulate generation and allow virtually anyone to generate power, while continuing to control transmission. Many firms believed that they could earn a profit by building generating plants and selling the electricity. No one thought that a profit could be made by building transmission lines because federal and state governments controlled the lines and the prices that could be charged to the users of those lines. The result has been an increasing and improving number of generation plants connected through a deteriorating set of transmission lines.

The article states that neither generating plants nor transmission lines have been built in the past several years. This isn't true nationwide. Although it has become difficult to build plants, many new plants have been built in the United States in the past five or six years; in fact, the amount of potential new electric power that can be generated in the United States is nearly enough to supply half of Europe. The problem is that because transmission has remained under government control, there has been no incentive for companies to build additional transmission lines or to upgrade existing lines. Thus, even with greater generating capacity, the U.S. electric-power system is severely limited and susceptible to power failures.

chapter

14

Government and Market Failure

Fundamental Questions

1. What is economic freedom?

2. What is a market failure?

3. What are externalities?

4. Why are chickens not an endangered species?

5. Why do governments create, own, and run national parks?

6. Why does the government require the listing of ingredients on food packaging?

7. What is rent seeking?

conomic freedom refers to the degree to which private individuals are able to carry out voluntary exchange without government involvement. The *Wall Street Journal* and the Heritage Foundation coauthor an annual measure of economic freedom, called the Index of Economic Freedom. According to the Index of Economic Freedom, the United States is only about the tenth freest economy in the world. Nations such as Luxembourg, Ireland, New Zealand, Ukraine, and even Hong Kong are rated as being freer than the United States. What this means is that government is more involved in the economy in the United States than it is in these other nations. Higher taxes mean less economic freedom, more rules and regulations mean less economic freedom, restrictions on travel mean less economic freedom, restrictions on international trade mean less economic freedom, the paperwork necessary to comply with government rules and regulations means less economic freedom, and so on.

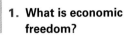

1. What is economic freedom?

Economic freedom is linked to standards of living. Many studies have shown that, in general, the greater a nation's economic freedom, the higher its standard of living. The freest nations average more than $30,000 per capita income, the mainly free economies average about $14,000, and the mainly unfree and repressed economies average just over $4,000, little more than one-eighth that of the freest nations. While this relationship between free economies and standards of living should make sense, since economic theory shows that free markets are more efficient and ensure that resources flow to where they are most highly valued, there are many situations, economists point out, in which markets do not work so well.

market failure: a situation in which resources are not allocated to their highest-valued use

A **market failure** occurs when the market outcome is not the socially efficient outcome—that is, when resources are not allocated to their highest-valued use. Market failures are an important reason that government becomes involved in the economy. A second reason that government intervenes in free markets is because it provides benefits to special interests.

2. What is a market failure?

What is a market failure, what causes it, and how can it be resolved? We answer this question in this chapter. We'll find that action by the government is sometimes necessary to ensure that the market does work well. However, when the market provides an outcome that a special interest group doesn't like, even if the market is working well, that special interest group may try to change the outcome; that is, it may get the government to carry out some action that benefits the special interest group. For instance, why would it require more schooling to be a haircutter than to be a nurse? Why has it been illegal for wine to be shipped from a winery to a customer in another state? Why does it take a special permit to run a taxi service? These and many more cases of government involvement result from political action by special interest groups. ■

3. What are externalities?

private costs: costs that are borne solely by the individuals involved in the transaction that created the costs

1. Externalities

The price you pay for a Big Mac is the **private cost** of that Big Mac. When you throw the wrapper into a garbage can two blocks away, you are creating a cost that you are not paying. People who had nothing to do with that Big Mac must pay the cost of picking up the garbage. This situation represents a market failure because the price of the good and the equilibrium quantity produced and consumed do not reflect the full cost of producing or consuming the good. If you had to pay for each wrapper you threw away, you would have an incentive to consume or produce less of the product and thus pollute less.

Consider an oil tanker that runs aground and dumps crude oil into a pristine ocean area teeming with wildlife, people who litter a public beach, the constant barking of your neighbor's dog, secondhand smoke, and people who leave their cups, used papers, and food wrappers on the floor of your classrooms. A cost is involved in these actions: the crude oil may kill wildlife and ruin fishing industries, the trash may discourage families from using the beach and lower property values near the beach, the barking dog may disrupt your study or leisure time, the secondhand smoke may reduce your enjoyment of some activity or even cause health problems, and the trash in the classroom may distract from the discussions and lectures. But in none of these cases is the cost of the action borne solely by the individuals or firms who took the action. Instead, some or all of the cost is borne by people who were not participants in the activity. The fishermen did not spill the oil, yet they have to bear the cost. The beachgoers who encounter trash and broken bottles and the local property owners were not the litterers, yet they must bear the cost. It was not your dog that was barking, but you have to put up with the racket. You do not smoke, and yet you have to put up with secondhand smoke. Many students and professors do not litter, and yet they must wade through the trash. The cost is outside of or external to the activity and is thus called an **externality.**

externality: the cost or benefit of a transaction that is borne by someone not directly involved in the transaction

Externalities may be negative or positive. The examples just given are *negative externalities.* A *positive externality* may result when the benefits of an activity are received by consumers or firms that are not directly involved in the activity. For instance, inoculations for mumps, measles, flu, and other communicable diseases provide benefits to all of society. If some people get a flu shot, you may have less chance of getting the flu even though you did not get a flu shot. You receive a positive externality from those who were vaccinated. The total cost of a transaction, the private cost plus the external cost, is called the **social cost.**

social cost: the total cost of a transaction, the private cost plus the external cost

$$\text{Social cost} = \text{private cost} + \text{value of externality}$$

If all the costs of a transaction are borne by the participants in that transaction, the private costs and the social costs are the same. When private costs differ from social costs, the full opportunity cost of using a scarce resource is borne not by the producer or the consumer, but by society in general. When you don't have to pay the full cost of a good or service, you will consume more than you would if you had to pay the full cost. In this sense, "too much" of the good or service is consumed.

1.a. Externalities and Market Failure

When there is a divergence between social costs and private costs, the result is either *too much* or *too little* production and consumption. In either case, resources are not being used in their highest-valued activity. For instance, those who pollute do not bear the entire costs of the pollution, and therefore they pollute more than they otherwise would. Those who smoke do not pay a cost for secondhand smoke, and therefore they tend to smoke more than they otherwise would. Those who get flu shots provide some protection for those who do not get the shots. The problem is that those who benefit from others getting the inoculations don't pay for the benefit. If they did, it would lower the price for those who purchase the shots, and more people would get the inoculations.

These are cases of market failure, where either demand or supply or both fail to reflect all the costs and benefits. We can illustrate a market failure using a typical market diagram. Consider a gas station selling gasoline with pumps that have no emission-control equipment. Each time a consumer pumps gas, a certain quantity of pollutants is released into the air. Consumers are willing and able to purchase gasoline at various prices, as shown by the demand curve, D, in Figure 1. Gas is supplied according to the supply curve S_p. The equilibrium price and quantity are P_p and Q_p. The pollution imposes costs on society, but neither those selling the gas nor those buying the gas pay these costs. If the gas station did have to account for the pollution costs, its costs of supplying the gas would rise. The supply of gas would be given by the supply curve S_s, because with higher costs, firms are willing and able to supply less at each price. The (social) equilibrium, the equilibrium taking into account all costs and benefits, is the intersection of demand and supply at price P_s and quantity Q_s.

In contrast to negative externalities, private costs exceed social costs when external benefits are created. Figure 2 represents the market for inoculations against some communicable disease. People would be willing and able to purchase the inoculations according to D_s if there were no externalities. However, because some

FIGURE 1 Negative Externalities

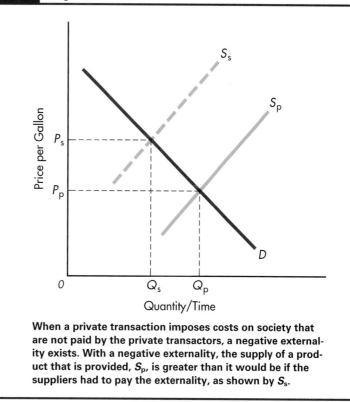

When a private transaction imposes costs on society that are not paid by the private transactors, a negative externality exists. With a negative externality, the supply of a product that is provided, S_p, is greater than it would be if the suppliers had to pay the externality, as shown by S_s.

people in society can benefit from the inoculations without purchasing them, the demand for the inoculations is less, D_p instead of D_s. This means that fewer people receive the inoculations than would be the case if the price took all the benefits into account. The social equilibrium would have Q_s getting the inoculations, but the smaller number Q_p actually do—"too little" of the good is purchased.

1.b. Solutions to the Externality Problem

The solution to the externality problem requires that all the costs of a transaction, private and social, be borne by those involved in the transaction. The question is, how can this be done—how can the externality be "internalized"? Many people argue that it is the government's responsibility to reduce the externality problem. One approach that the government uses is to impose a tax on or provide a subsidy to those creating the externality.

1.b.1. Pollution Tax   Suppose a firm is creating an externality by polluting as it produces its product. If the government imposed a tax on that company based on the amount of pollution the firm created, the firm would have to consider the extra cost when deciding whether to increase its output (and thereby pollution). This is shown in Figure 3 as the supply curve $S + t$, the supply curve plus the tax. The tax reduces the amount produced from Q to Q_s, and thereby reduces the amount of pollution created by the firm. The tax is a way in which the government can force the polluter to *internalize* the externality, that is, to pay for it rather than have society pay for it.

The firm can avoid the tax by either reducing the amount it produces or purchasing pollution abatement equipment—equipment that will reduce the amount of

FIGURE 2   **Positive Externalities**

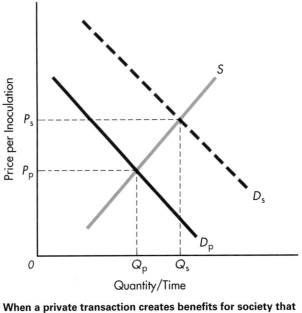

When a private transaction creates benefits for society that
exceed those involved in the private transaction, positive
externalities exist. D_p represents the demand for inoculations against a communicable disease when there is no
externality. D_s represents the demand with an externality.
Fewer people get the inoculations than would be desired
by society.

pollution created. With less pollution, the firm will pay fewer taxes. Either choice,
paying the tax or buying the equipment, means that the externality is internalized by
the firm.

In the case of a positive externality, the government might provide a subsidy
rather than impose a tax. Suppose each person getting an inoculation is given some
money. More people would be willing to be inoculated, as shown in Figure 4. The
subsidy, s, induces buyers to increase the quantities that they are willing and able to
buy at each price. The total amount produced and consumed rises from Q to Q_s.

The problem with taxes and subsidies is that those setting the taxes and subsidies
(the government in most cases) must guess at what the socially optimal level would
be. A tax that is too high will create an inefficiency of too little production; a tax that
is not high enough will do the opposite.

1.b.2. Command   Rather than imposing a tax, the government could simply require or command that the company not create waste. For instance, the government
could tell a copper mining operation to produce no more than 3 gallons of waste per
ton of copper. The firm will then have no choice; it will have to either reduce the
amount of waste it produces or go out of business. However, the command approach
provides no incentive for the firm to utilize any new technology that might reduce
waste beyond the mandated amount. With the pollution tax, the firm is taxed only
on the waste it produces—if it can reduce waste, it can reduce its taxes.

With a positive externality, the government might dictate who must use or consume the beneficial activity. For instance, by mandating that all children under the

FIGURE 3   Pollution Tax

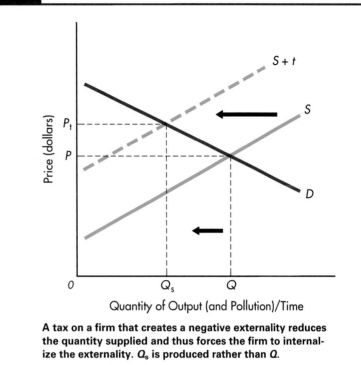

A tax on a firm that creates a negative externality reduces
the quantity supplied and thus forces the firm to internalize the externality. Q_s is produced rather than Q.

FIGURE 4   Subsidy

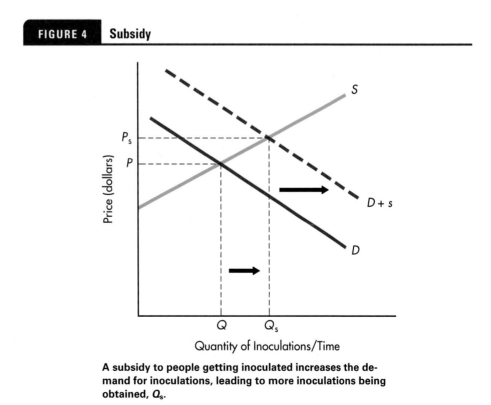

A subsidy to people getting inoculated increases the demand for inoculations, leading to more inoculations being
obtained, Q_s.

age of six be inoculated, the government is using a command approach: it is forcing the children to be inoculated. But by forcing everyone to be inoculated, the government is not selecting the socially optimal amount of inoculations. As a result, more than the socially optimal number of people get inoculations, and the costs of the inoculations are higher than would be necessary.

1.b.3. Marketable Pollution Permits   Realizing that a command system is inefficient—it doesn't create incentives to reduce the problem—and that taxes and subsidies may not be set at the efficient levels, the government has attempted to establish a market for the right to create some externalities, such as air pollution. The government specifies that a certain quantity of pollutants will be permitted in a particular area. It then issues permits that enable the owners of the permits to pollute. For example, if the target pollution level in the Los Angeles basin is 400 billion particulates per day, the government could issue a total of 400 permits, each permitting the emission of 1 billion particulates per day. Then the government could sell the permits. Demanders, typically firms, would purchase the permits, allowing them to pollute up to the amount specified by the permits they own. If a firm purchased 20 permits, it could emit up to 20 billion particulates per day. If that firm implemented a cleaner technology or for some other reason did not use all of its permits, it could sell them to other firms.

The marketable permit idea is illustrated in Figure 5. The pollution target set by the Environmental Protection Agency is indicated by the vertical supply curve for

---

FIGURE 5   **The Market for Pollution Permits**

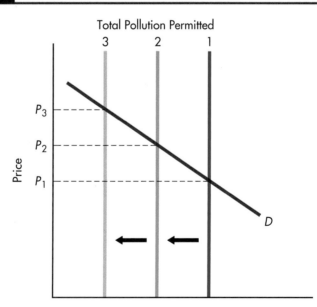

The government establishes the amount of pollution to be permitted. It then issues permits, each allowing a certain amount of pollution. To be able to pollute, a firm, individual, or group must have a permit. The price of permits is determined by demand and supply. As the government reduces the amount of pollution allowed, the price of the permits increases.

pollution rights in Figure 5 labeled "1." The demand for permits to pollute is shown by the downward-sloping demand curve, D. With a price, P_1, for pollution rights determined, firms choose whether to pollute the amount they have purchased, to not produce as much and sell the excess permits, or to adopt cleaner technology and thus be able to sell the permits they don't use.

If the government decides to reduce pollutants more than it has in the past, it will reduce its pollution target. This is shown in Figure 5 as an inward shift of the total pollution permitted line. Demanders will bid for the now fewer pollution permits, driving the price of the permits up. As the price rises, some firms will decide not to purchase the permits, but instead to purchase new pollution abatement equipment or to reduce the amount they produce.

The higher price gives firms an incentive to adopt more efficient pollution abatement equipment. The permit market also enables others to influence the total amount of pollution created. Anyone can purchase permits. Some might speculate that in the future, the price of the permits will rise. If the price rises, the owners of the permits will be able to sell them for a gain. Some environmental groups, such as the Nature Conservancy and the Sierra Club, have purchased permits simply to reduce the total amount of pollution that can occur in a specific area or industry. By purchasing the permits and taking them out of circulation, they essentially reduce the total number of permits and the total amount of pollution permitted.

1.c. The Coase Theorem

With the permit approach, the government establishes the amount of pollution to be permitted. It then issues permits, each allowing a certain amount of pollution. To be able to pollute, a firm, individual, or group must have a permit. The price of permits is determined by demand and supply. As the government reduces the amount of pollution allowed, the price of the permits increases.

Is government intervention the only way to solve an externality problem? Ronald Coase, a professor at the University of Chicago, said no. He was the first to see that if people can negotiate with one another at no cost over the right to perform activities that cause externalities, they will arrive at an efficient solution. Professor Coase was awarded the 1991 Nobel Prize in economics for this insight, which is called the **Coase theorem.**

Coase theorem: the idea that if people can negotiate with one another at no cost over the right to perform activities that cause externalities, they will always arrive at an efficient solution

To illustrate the Coase theorem, consider the following situation. Suppose that a city has a noise ordinance forbidding the operation of lawnmowers and leaf blowers prior to 8 A.M. on Sunday mornings. Neighbor Ralph ignores the ordinance and mows and blows his lawn every Sunday morning, which neighbor Louis finds increasingly irritating. Louis has the advantage in this case because he has the property right. The noise ordinance gives Louis the right to demand that Ralph be quiet. So Louis could call the cops and require Ralph to obey the ordinance. Another solution would be for Ralph to pay Louis for the right to make noise.

It was the noise ordinance or property right that gave Louis the power in the negotiation. Suppose there were no city noise ordinance. Then Louis could not demand that Ralph be quiet. Instead, Louis might pay Ralph not to start mowing until after 10 A.M. This is the point that Coase made: if ownership is established—that is, if private property rights are well defined and enforced—private parties can negotiate a solution to the externality problem. The solution will make both parties happy—one receives money, and the other receives the right to make noise or to obtain quiet. The Coase theorem indicates that if negotiation is possible, then resources will be allocated to their highest-valued use even if an externality should occur.

1.c.1. Outcomes When Negotiation Is Not Efficient

Efficient solutions to externalities will occur whenever the affected parties can negotiate with one another at no cost. But negotiation is not always practical or free. A motorist with a polluting automobile imposes costs on everyone who breathes the air, but as a practical matter, all these people can't stop the motorist and offer him money to fix his car. The Coase theorem doesn't work in this case, and as a result, most governments command an outcome, such as requiring cars to meet certain emission standards.

Why do speed limits exist? Why are there other traffic laws, such as no-passing zones, right-of-way rules, and stop and go signals? What accounts for zoning laws? One answer is that these laws solve the externality problem when negotiation is not practicable.

RECAP

1. An externality occurs when the costs and/or benefits of a private transaction are borne by those who are not involved in that private transaction.

2. A positive externality is a situation in which a private transaction creates benefits for members of society who are not involved in the transaction. In the case of positive externalities, not enough of the good or service is produced and consumed.

3. A negative externality is a situation in which a private transaction creates costs for members of society who are not involved in the transaction. In the case of a negative externality, too much of the good or service is produced and consumed.

4. The government may attempt to minimize the problems of negative externalities by imposing taxes, dictating behavior, or creating a market in permits to internalize the externality.

5. The government may attempt to minimize the ill effects of positive externalities by subsidizing the beneficial activity or supplying the activity itself.

6. The Coase theorem says that if private parties are able to negotiate, the parties will resolve externality problems.

---

2. Private Property Rights

4. Why are chickens not an endangered species?

A market failure may result because of the absence of well-defined private property rights. A private property right is the right to claim ownership of an item—to do what you wish with that item. The private property right is well defined if there is a clear owner and if the right is recognized and enforced by society.

2.a. Market Failure and the Problem of Common Ownership

Suppose you have purchased a pizza to be delivered to your house. If you have a well-defined private property right in that pizza, only you can decide who can enjoy the pizza. However, if you do not have a well-defined private property right in the pizza, anyone can simply run over and begin eating the pizza. You can see that if there were no private property right, no one would spend the money to buy a pizza. That's no problem with pizzas because there are private property rights. But with some goods and services, the ownership is not so clear-cut. Consider the pollution caused by auto emissions in your area of residence. Each driver of a car is imposing an externality on you. The problem is that neither you nor the driver owns the airspace in which the emissions occur. If you owned the airspace, you could restrict the driving activity or you could charge the driver a price that would pay for the externality. If the driver owned the airspace, you would have to pay the driver not to drive and pollute. In either case, the externality would no longer be external; it would be part of the private costs.

Global Business Insight

Why Aren't Cows and Chickens on the Endangered Species List?

There are plenty of cows and chickens—and although they are consumed in huge numbers, their populations are not declining. Other species are experiencing declining numbers.

The *Red List of Threatened Species,* compiled by the World Conservation Union, gives details of 11,167 species of animals and plants that are known to be at risk of extinction. The 10 animals that are of most concern because of their commercial value include the Hawksbill sea turtles, which are threatened because of the demand for their beautiful shells: the species is the sole source of "tortoiseshell" used to make curios and jewelry. Among the three species of Asian rhinos, the Sumatran rhino is the most threatened, as a result of both habitat loss and poaching for rhino horn, which is used in traditional Chinese medicine. A keystone species for Amazon rain-forests, big-leaf mahogany, is highly prized for furniture in the United States, which is the world's leading importer of the wood. Marketed under the more appealing name of "Chilean sea bass," the toothfish has suffered from its popularity among seafood lovers in the United States and Japan. Yellow-headed Amazon parrots are in demand as pets. There are 32 known species of seahorses, and at least 20 are threatened by the unregulated trade in both live seahorses for aquariums and dried seahorses, which are sold as curios and as treatments in traditional Chinese medicine. Whale sharks are the world's largest fish—growing as long as 50 feet—and are found in tropical and warm temperate seas. They have been overfished for their meat, fins, liver, cartilage, and skin. The Malayan giant turtle, along with dozens of other Asian tortoises and freshwater turtles, is threatened largely by unsustainable collection for food, primarily in China.

What is the difference between cows and chickens and these endangered species? Private ownership. When a species is privately owned, it will flourish because its owner will ensure that its numbers remain at the level that will earn the owner the most income. When a species is commonly owned—or not owned—no one has an incentive to ensure that the species endures. The command approach defines the endangered species list. Once a species is placed on the list, there are bans on hunting it, fishing for it, or otherwise endangering it. But, unless the bans carry huge penalties and are easily enforced, the hunting and fishing will continue.

To illustrate why common ownership is a problem, let's consider a situation in which a small village has communal property—everyone owns everything. There are five villagers, and each has $100. Each villager could use the $100 to buy a lamb or could deposit it in a bank account and earn $10 over one year. Lambs are allowed to graze for free on a small grass field called the commons. The price the lamb will sell for after one year depends on the amount of weight it gains during the year, which, in turn, depends on the number of lambs sent onto the commons, as shown in Table 1.

TABLE 1 Lambs on the Commons

Number of Lambs	Price After One Year	Income/Year
1	$130	$30
2	$120	$20
3	$112	$12
4	$110	$10
5	$109	$9

If just one lamb grazes on the field, it will sell for $130, a gain of $30, or 30 percent for the year. This is three times the interest rate earned on the savings. Clearly, one lamb will be purchased and sent out to graze. With two lambs, the sale price is $120 each, so the total income for each owner is $20, for a return of 20 percent. With three lambs, the sale price is $112 each, so each owner receives a 12 percent return. With four lambs, the return to each owner is the same as the return from putting the money in the bank, 10 percent. And with five lambs, the owners of the lambs are worse off than they would have been if they had simply put the money in the bank. So, four lambs use the commons. Each lamb returns $10 profit at the end of the year. Thus, with $40 from the lambs and $10 from interest, the total income of the village is $50, exactly what it would be if no lambs had been raised and the money had just been put in the bank.

Would things turn out differently if the village decided to charge rent for using the commons? What is the most that one person would pay to allow her lamb to graze on the commons? The opportunity cost of the $100 used to purchase the lamb was $10 (what could have been earned from the bank), so the economic profit from the single lamb is $20—$30 from the sale of the lamb minus the $10 opportunity cost. But with rent, the situation changes. A single commune member would pay no more than $10 to rent the land, since with that rent the total return is just $10—$30 from the sale of the lamb minus $10 opportunity cost minus $10 rent. At a rent of $10, just one lamb would use the commons. Total village income would be the rent plus the $10 return per resident, or $60. When someone owns the commons—when there are private property rights—utilization is reduced, and the benefits to society rise. The problem with communal property is that, because no one owns the commons, too many people use it; no one takes into account the costs that each additional user imposes on others.

The lack of private property ownership is a common problem in the natural resources area. No one has a private property right to the ocean, no one owns the fish in the sea, no one owns the elephants that roam the African plains, and no one owned the American buffalo or bald eagle. Since no one owns them, a "too rapid" rate of use or harvest occurs; the "commons" is overutilized.

The *tragedy of the commons* is the name given to the problem created when something is owned commonly rather than privately. Fish, for instance, are overfished because no one owns them. Because there are no private property rights, everyone can catch the fish and no one has an incentive to ensure that enough fish are left to propagate. In Zanzibar, a string of people with nets slowly walks through the stream so that no fish are missed.

We encounter the commons or common ownership with many items. Consider the African elephant. Without ownership of the elephant, no one has an incentive to protect the animal and ensure that it multiplies. Consider a forest. If the forest is privately owned, the owner will harvest the trees at a rate that ensures that more trees are available for harvesting in the future.

Common ownership fails to create an incentive for people to produce and consume the amount that is best for society. This is why communism failed. Under communism, no one has a private property right to anything, including his or her own labor. As a result, no one has an incentive to improve his or her human capital—to increase the value of personal skills and training—and no one has an incentive to ensure that companies are run efficiently. In China prior to 1990, people could not own the apartments in which they lived. All urban living took place in government-owned buildings. Since no one had a private property right to a home, no one had an incentive to take care of it. The buildings were dilapidated, the hallways were filthy, and the landscaping was nonexistent. When the Chinese leaders allowed some private ownership of apartments, those that were privately owned immediately became much improved. The hallways became clean, the landscaping reappeared, and the apparent quality of the buildings changed virtually overnight. In China's rural areas, farmers were required to work on government farms, but they were allowed a very small portion of the farm where they could grow whatever they wanted. They could sell or trade what they grew on these small sections. Incredibly, the very small plots of land, less than 10 percent of the farms, accounted for nearly 90 percent of the total produce.

2.b. Solutions to Lack of Private Property Rights

The solution to the lack of private property rights seems pretty straightforward: create and enforce private property rights. This has occurred in some instances where what had been considered to be a common good became privately owned; the result was less utilization of the commons. For instance, in many nations in which elephants reside, no one owns the elephants. The result is that they are *overutilized*—they are becoming extinct. In most nations with elephants, large national parks have been created in which hunting is forbidden. But even in the face of these bans on hunting, the reduction in the number of elephants has continued. A decade ago, Africa's elephant population was more than a million; it has now fallen to less than half of that.

In contrast to the common ownership strategy, the governments of Botswana, Zimbabwe, and South Africa created private property rights by allowing individuals to own elephants. These elephant farmers ensure that the elephants breed and reproduce so that they can be sold for their tusks, for hunting in special hunting parks, or to zoos in developed nations. This has led to a revival of the elephant population in these nations.

Thousands of acres of Amazon forest are burned or cut each year to provide land for Brazil's ranchers and subsistence farmers and to extract woods for use elsewhere. No one owns the rainforest, leading it to be overutilized. If the Brazilian government created private property rights to the forest, it would be taken care of. Consider what has happened in Sweden and neighboring Finland. Sweden and Finland have more standing forest today than at any time in the past. Unlike the situation in Canada, where the forest is dwindling, most of the forest land in Sweden is privately owned. Private owners do not cut at a loss and do not cut to maintain employment levels or for other political reasons. They cut at the rate that yields them the greatest return. If they simply razed their forests, they would have no income in coming years. So they cut or harvest at rates that ensure viable populations.

It is not always easy to establish private property rights. What happens in cases where private property rights cannot be created, such as with ocean fish? Without private ownership, the oceans will be overutilized, and species of fish will become extinct. The response of governments has been to restrict fishing around their shores, but this does not solve the problem. Instead, as the cost of fishing rises—as it becomes increasingly more difficult to find the fish—alternatives such as fish farms begin to appear. Private property rights arise to solve the commons problem.

RECAP

1. Private property rights enable someone to own an item, that is, to dispose of, destroy, share, give away, or do anything that the person wants with the item.
2. When there are no private property rights to an item, that item cannot be bought or sold. No one has an incentive to produce the item or to purchase it.
3. When something is commonly owned, that something is overutilized.
4. The solution to a lack of private property rights is to create such rights. However, sometimes the creation of private property rights is not straightforward.

3. Public Goods

principle of mutual exclusivity: the rule that an owner of private property is entitled to enjoy the consumption of that property privately

According to the **principle of mutual exclusivity,** the owner of private property is entitled to enjoy the consumption of that property *privately*. The principle of mutual exclusivity refers to a well-defined private property right. It says that if you own a good, I cannot use it or consume it without your permission; and if I own a good, you cannot use it or consume it unless I grant permission. When I purchase a pizza,

Global Business Insight

Land Titling in Argentina

In 1981, about 1,800 families occupied a piece of wasteland in San Francisco Solano, County of Quilmes, in the Province of Buenos Aires, Argentina. The occupants were landless citizens organized through a Catholic chapel. As they wanted to avoid creating a shantytown, they divided the land into small parcels. The squatters resisted several attempts at eviction during the military government. After Argentina's return to democracy, the Congress of the Province of Buenos Aires passed a law giving the squatters title to the property. But, as a result of bureaucracy, mismanagement, and other events, not all squatters received title. Approximately half the squatters (those living north of the main street) received title, and half (those living south of the main street) did not. By 2005, startling differences between the group with land title and that without had arisen. Ownership was crucial in this regard. Those with title had repaired their houses,

improved their property, and sent their children to school. Those without title had allowed their houses to fall into disrepair, failed to improve their property, and allowed their children to skip school. Those with title had fewer children, and their children received more education. Those with title had higher standards of living, and their children had even higher standards of living, whereas those without title saw their standards of living stagnate or even decline, and their children experienced no improvement.

Source: Sebastian Galiani and Ernesto Schargrodsky, "Property Rights for the Poor: Effects of Land Titling," Ronald Coase Institute, Working Paper Number 7, August 2005.

it is mine to do with as I wish. You have no right to the pizza unless I provide that right. If the principle of mutual exclusivity does not apply to a particular good or service, then anyone can use or consume that good or service.

public good: a good whose consumption by one person does not diminish the quantity or quality available for others

If the principle of mutual exclusivity does not apply, and if the use of the good by one person does not reduce the quantity or quality available for other consumers, then the good is called a **public good.** The TV airwaves illustrate the characteristics of a public good quite well. A television station broadcasts on a certain frequency, and anyone can pick up that station. It doesn't matter whether one person or one million people tune in to the station—the signal is the same, and additional users do not deprive others of any of the good. If your neighbor tunes in to the channel you are watching, you don't receive a weaker signal.

3.a. The Problem

If something is available for you to use and you don't have to pay for it, why would you pay? That's the problem with public goods: people can get these goods without paying for them. When goods are public, an individual has an incentive to be a **free rider**—a consumer or producer who enjoys the benefits of a good or service without paying for that good or service. As an example, suppose that national defense was not provided by the government and paid for with tax money; instead, you would not be protected by the armed forces unless you paid a fee. A problem would arise because national defense is a public good; you would be protected whether or not you paid for it as long as others paid. Of course, because each person has an incentive not to pay for it, few will voluntarily do so, and so the good may not be provided, or, if it is provided, the quantity produced will be "too small" from society's viewpoint.

free rider: a consumer or producer who enjoys the benefits of a good or service without paying for that good or service

Suppose that there are two people in society, Jesse and Rafael, whose willingness to pay for different quantities of a public good—public radio—is shown in Table 2. Jesse would be willing to pay as much as $5 for one day of radio programming, while Rafael would be willing to pay $3. Jesse would be willing to pay just $4 each for two days of programming, and Rafael would be willing to pay only $2 per day. Thus, in Table 2 we can see society's willingness to pay for different quantities of the public good. However, willingness to pay and actually paying are different things; since neither Jesse nor Rafael has to pay for any quantity, each may choose to listen without paying anything. There would then be no demand for the radio programming.

Examples of public goods that are often given are national defense, lighthouses, fire protection, and police protection. If one rich person established a missile defense system on her property, all her neighbors would enjoy the protection without paying anything. Lighthouses signal landmasses to passing ships. Because any ship

TABLE 2	The Demand for a Public Good

Quantity	Willingness to Pay per Unit	
	Jesse	Rafael
1	$5	$3
2	$4	$2
3	$3	$1
4	$2	$0

can see the light and heed the warning, none of them has an incentive to pay for the service. If my neighbors subscribe to fire or police protection services, then I can enjoy the benefit without having to subscribe myself. There is a market failure: too few resources are devoted to the production of the public good.

3.b. Solutions to Public Good Problems

5. Why do governments create, own, and run national parks?

The organization Defenders of Wildlife collects money from its members and uses the money to pay landowners who allow wolves to live on their properties. The host landowner receives a payment of $5,000 for each litter of pups reared by wolves. As a result of this program, the population of wolves in the Yellowstone Basin has risen. This is an example of converting public goods into private goods. Building large stadiums around baseball or football fields restricts the viewing of the games from outside of the stadiums—you have to purchase a ticket to see the contest. Without the stadiums, the games would be available for anyone to watch—for free. The Rural Metro Company of Scottsdale, Arizona, provides private subscription fire protection to residents of Scottsdale, Fountain Hills, and surrounding communities. The company will put out fires for subscribers at no cost, but to put out fires for non-subscribers, it charges a price that equals its cost. In general, however, the solution for the free-rider problems of public goods is to have the government produce the good. National defense, wildlife reserves in Kenya, wilderness areas in the United States, and the park system in every country are examples of government provision of public goods.

3.b.1. Government Financing or Provision of Public Goods?

A public good requires only a means of financing the production. It need not be the government that supplies the good.

Private for-profit firms offer emergency vehicle service (ambulances) in some cities, wastewater management and drinking water in some cities, fire protection in some cities, and even roads in some locations. These are examples of situations in which a public good is provided by a private company. But, if the good is a public good, how can the private company collect for its services? The government has to tax either the public or the users of the good and compensate the private company. So the question is, does the government provide the public good, or does the government simply finance the public good and allow private companies to provide it?

RECAP

1. A public good is one for which the principle of mutual exclusivity does not hold; when one person uses the item, that use does not reduce the quantity available for others.

2. Since a public good can be used without paying for it, people have no incentive to purchase it. A free-rider problem arises.

3. A free-rider problem occurs when someone can contribute less to an activity than that person can get back in return because that person relies on others to make up the difference. The problem is that if many people free-ride, the item or activity is not produced.

4. A possible solution to the public good problem is to turn the public good into one that is privately provided.

5. The government solution to the public good problem is to supply the good or to finance a private company so that it will supply the good.

4. Asymmetric Information _____

What happens when one party to an exchange knows a lot more about the good or service than the other party? The knowledgeable party may take advantage of the less informed party. If so, a market failure can occur. This is the problem of *asymmetric information*.

4.a. Adverse Selection

When you purchase a used car, you are probably unsure of the car's quality. You could hire a mechanic to look at the car before you buy it, but because that procedure is quite expensive, you probably choose to forgo it. Most people assume that cars offered for sale by private individuals are defective in some way, and they are not willing to pay top dollar for such a car. In Figure 6, the market for high-quality used cars and that for low-quality used cars is shown. People offer their cars for sale as shown along the supply curve. But, although demand for high-quality used cars would be D_{HQ} if demanders could differentiate high- from low-quality used cars, the actual demand is D_A. Thus, people who do have high-quality used cars for sale cannot obtain the high price that they deserve. The result is that low-quality cars continue to be sold in the secondhand market, but high-quality cars do not. This result of the good being driven out of a market by the bad is called **adverse selection.**

adverse selection: the situation in which higher-quality goods, consumers, or producers are driven out of the market by lower-quality examples because of limited information about the quality

Adverse selection can occur in many different markets. For instance, banks do not always know which people who are applying for loans will default and which will pay on time. What happens if a bank increases the interest rate it charges on loans in an attempt to drive high-risk applicants out of the market? High-risk applicants

---

FIGURE 6   **Adverse Selection**

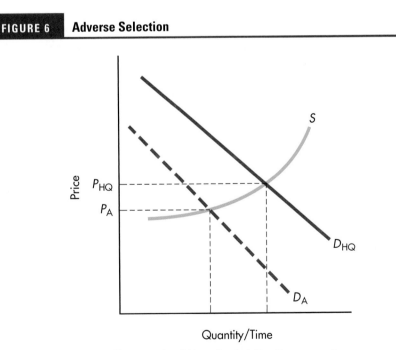

High-quality cars should be priced at P_{HQ}. Because potential buyers cannot distinguish between high- and low-quality cars, the actual price of high-quality cars is P_A. The result is that only low-quality cars remain in the used-car market.

---

continue to apply for loans because they don't have other alternatives that are less expensive. But low-risk applicants have other sources for loans, and so they stop applying to this bank. As a result, only high-risk applicants remain in the market.

People purchase automobile or health insurance even if they are excellent drivers and enjoy good health. However, as the cost of insurance rises, the good drivers and healthy people may reduce their coverage, while the poor drivers and unhealthy people maintain their coverage. As a result, high-risk applicants take the place of more desirable low-risk applicants in the market for insurance.

4.b. Moral Hazard

moral hazard: the problem that arises when people change their behavior from what was expected of them when they engaged in a trade or contract

A person who drives much less carefully after obtaining car insurance is creating a **moral hazard.** A person who takes less care to be healthy after obtaining health insurance is creating a moral hazard. Moral hazard occurs because the person buying the insurance knows more about his behavior than the insurance company does. When people can change their behavior from what was anticipated when a trade or contract was made without the knowledge of the other party to the agreement, a moral hazard exists.

4.c. Solutions to the Asymmetric Information Issue

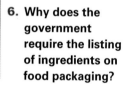

6. Why does the government require the listing of ingredients on food packaging?

Asymmetric information can cause the market to fail—to not allocate goods and services to their highest-valued use. Why can't someone with a high-quality used car simply tell the buyer about the car's condition? The reason is that the seller has an incentive to exaggerate the condition of the car, and the buyer has an incentive to believe that it is of lower quality than it is. The problem can be resolved privately if the seller can credibly demonstrate the high quality of the car. A seller must provide credible information about the quality of the good.

What about the used-car market or the market for insurance or loans—how can individuals or firms spend enough to provide quality assurance or to provide guarantees that buyers will believe? Many argue that they cannot, and that this is why government rules and regulations are necessary. The Federal Trade Commission restricts advertising, requiring that claims be demonstrable. Many state governments and the federal government require a time period after an exchange has occurred during which the buyer can change her mind; if before two days are up I decide that I don't want the product, I can return it and get my money back. In the case of insurance and loans, government rules and regulations indicate who is eligible for loans and whether different customers can be charged different rates.

On the other hand, private companies have emerged that provide information about a used car for a fee. The potential buyer merely types in the serial number on a webpage, and the company provides instantaneous information about whether the car has been in an accident or damaged elsewhere.

4.c.1. Copayments and Deductibles
Sometimes a moral hazard problem can be reduced by having the person or firm creating the hazard and the person or firm being taken advantage of share in the costs. This is a reason that insurance companies require a deductible and banks and other lending institutions require a down payment: so that the company and the customer share in the expenses and risks. You are more likely to drive carefully and safeguard your health if you have to pay some of the costs of an accident or illness. Similarly, if you must pay a copayment, you are less likely to behave in a way that causes you to bear a large number of such copayments. And finally, insurance companies will often cancel a contract after a few claims have been made in a certain period of time. After two or three claims, the company believes that the moral hazard problem has occurred and that resolution of

this problem requires canceling the contract. In many instances, when someone cannot get insurance, the government steps in to subsidize the insurance or to provide the insurance through a government agency.

When moral hazard or adverse selection exists, there may be an opportunity for someone to profit from providing information. Carfax provides the history of a car for a fee. Equifax provides individual credit histories for a fee. These firms illustrate that the market can often solve what is called a market failure problem. When the missing information can be privately provided, the market failure problem disappears. It is when the asymmetric information cannot be made symmetric—with everyone having the same information—that the market will have a problem.

5. Government Failure

We have discussed several possible types of market failure. For each, there are usually two types of solution. In one, the government is only minimally involved. In the other, the government does everything. For instance, if the government can assign private property rights to an externality problem, the problem can be solved privately. But if private property rights cannot be assigned, then the government may have to command that businesses and individuals behave in specific ways. Similarly, a public good might be provided privately and financed by government, or the government might have to provide it and pay for it.

Because the government is so involved in these market failure issues, we have to evaluate how efficiently the government can do the job. Whereas it is one thing to argue that a market failure cannot be resolved privately, it is quite another to argue that the inefficiency created by the failure is worse than the inefficiency of having the government try to solve the problem. At least, this is what James Buchanan, who received the 1986 Nobel Prize in economics, argues. Inefficiencies often arise not because legislators are incompetent or ignorant, but because of problems with individual incentives. Consider, for instance, the senator from Arizona who wants to reduce government spending, so he votes *no* on all spending bills. The result is that Arizona residents do not get federal government money to build highways and bridges, while the residents of those states with senators who aren't as conscientious as the Arizona senator receive federal government dollars for their bridges and roads.

The behavior of the senators is similar to the situation facing a group of diners who are going to split the bill for the dinner equally. Herb and nine friends are having dinner at Chimichangas in Phoenix. To simplify the task of paying for their meal, they have agreed in advance to split the cost of their meal equally, with each paying one-tenth of the total check. Herb recognizes that if he orders more expensive items than the others, he will be gaining at the expense of his nine friends. So he orders appetizers, the most expensive entree, and the most exorbitant dessert and drinks. The problem is that each of his nine friends recognizes the same thing. Each orders far more than he would if he were dining alone. As a result, the total bill rises.

Legislators will support one another's special or so-called pork-barrel programs, causing total government spending to rise significantly. Consider a voter in a congressional district that contains one one-hundredth of the country's taxpayers. Suppose that district's representative is able to deliver a public project that generates benefits of $100 million for the district, but costs the government $150 million. Because the district's share of the tax bill for the project will be only $150 million/100 = $1.5 million, residents of the district are $98.5 million better off with the project than without it. And that explains why so many voters favor legislators who have a successful record of "bringing home the bacon."

Why would legislator A support such a project in legislator B's home district? After all, B's project will cause A's constituents' taxes to rise by a small amount, while they get absolutely no benefit. The answer is that if A does not support B's project, then B will not support A's. The practice of legislators supporting one another's projects is called **logrolling.**

logrolling: an inefficiency in the political process in which legislators support one another's projects in order to ensure support for their own

A primary cause of inefficiency in government is that the gains from government projects are often concentrated in the hands of a few beneficiaries, while the costs are spread among many. This means that the beneficiaries have an incentive to organize and lobby in favor of their projects. For example, in the 1990s, the Cosmetology Association in many states lobbied the state legislators to require more stringent licensing requirements for manicurists. The reason for the lobbying was the number of new spas and salons that were being established by immigrants. These spas were driving prices down; some of them were offering manicures for $10 rather than the $25 charged at the established spas. If manicurists were required to go to school for six months, the number of new spas that would open for business would decline, and prices at established spas could be upheld. The laws benefited the existing cosmetologists at the expense of new upstart manicurists. While the Cosmetology Association was willing to devote resources to its lobbying effort, no group opposed the legislation.

?

7. What is rent seeking?

rent seeking: the use of resources simply to transfer wealth from one group to another without increasing production or total wealth

When a new government project is financed, a very few people get large benefits, while the taxpayers pay an only slightly larger amount in taxes. This means that individual taxpayers have little at stake and therefore have little incentive to incur the cost of mobilizing themselves in opposition. **Rent seeking** is the process of devoting resources to taking wealth away from one group in order to benefit another group. Resources devoted to getting the government to provide benefits to special interest groups are called *rent,* and the special interest group is said to be *rent seeking.*

Rent seeking is a very rewarding activity in many cases. Rent seeking does not create new products or income; it merely transfers wealth from one group to another. Typically the transfer takes resources from large, diverse groups, like taxpayers, and gives them to small, organized groups, such as cosmetologists.

Beyond the fact that the legislative process often results in pork-barrel programs, we must worry that government employees may not have incentives to get the most for what the government spends. Since the government is not a profit-maximizing entity, it has no incentive to minimize costs. Instead, what often occurs is bureaucracy building. An agency director will have more say in policy if her agency is large than if it is small. So, she may have an incentive to increase the spending, and therefore the size, of her agency. And, whereas an appointed government official might engage in bureaucracy building, an elected official wants to get reelected.

That might mean supporting special interest projects in order to secure votes, even if those projects are inefficient.

Which is worse, market failure or government failure? Economists have been debating this question for decades and aren't likely to come to a mutual agreement any time soon. The debate continues.

RECAP

1. The government is inefficient, and having the government resolve market failure problems may impose greater costs on society than if the government did not try to resolve the problems.

2. Government inefficiencies result from the legislative process, from the incentives of government employees, and from rent seeking.

3. The question asked by many economists is, which is worse, market failure or government failure? Some support government solutions and others market solutions.

Summary

1. What is economic freedom?

- Economic freedom is the degree to which individuals are able to engage in voluntary transactions without government involvement. *Preview*

- The index of economic freedom is a measure of the involvement of government in an economy. *Preview*

2. What is a market failure?

- A market failure occurs when the market is not able to reach the equilibrium that is most efficient, when resources are not allocated to their highest-valued use. *Preview*

- The government is often called upon to resolve market failures. *Preview*

- A freely functioning market results in resources being allocated to their highest-valued use. When something occurs that leads resources not to be so allocated, we say that a market failure has resulted. *Preview*

3. What are externalities?

- Private benefits of a transaction are the gains from trade that the individuals involved in the transaction achieve. Private costs are the opportunity costs that the individuals involved in the transaction must bear. *§1*

- Social costs and benefits are the total costs and benefits created by a transaction. When some costs are borne by those who are not involved in the private transaction, so that social costs exceed private costs, a negative externality occurs. When some benefits are received by those who are not involved in the private transaction, so that

social benefits exceed private benefits, a positive externality occurs. *§1*

- When social costs and benefits are not equal to private costs and benefits, the market outcome is either overutilization or underutilization: resources are not allocated to their highest-valued use. *§1.a*

- There are several approaches to reducing the inefficiencies created by externalities. One approach is to impose a tax on the individual or institutions creating the externality. In another approach, the government requires or commands that those creating negative externalities reduce the amount created or that more production of positive externalities occur. In yet another, the government creates a market for the negative externalities by establishing ownership of the right to create the negative externality and allowing that ownership to be exchanged. *§1.b.1–§1.b.3*

- The Coase theorem states that as long as private property rights can be established, private individuals will be able to solve an externality problem without government intervention. *§1.c*

4. Why are chickens not an endangered species?

- Chickens are privately owned. A market failure problem occurs when no one owns something or when everyone owns something. Endangered species are species that are not privately owned. *§2.a*

- Common ownership results in a market failure. Too much of the commonly owned good is consumed, and not enough is produced. *§2.a*

- The solution to a common ownership problem is to create private property rights in any case where such rights can be created. *§2.b.1*

5. Why do governments create, own, and run national parks?

- One approach taken to resolve common ownership problems is for the government to claim ownership of the common good and to provide it as the government defines. *§2.a*

- Private property rights provide ownership. In order to buy or sell something, one must be able to decide how that something is to be used. *§2.a*

- Without private property rights, anyone can claim partial ownership of an item and thereby consume that item. Without private ownership, no one would be willing to purchase an item, since others could consume that item. *2.a*

- Free riding means that one person will contribute less than that person expects to get in return because the person expects others to make up the difference. *§3.a*

- People free-ride because they can—their self-interest tells them to get the most for the least. *§3.a*

- The problem with free riding is that if many people or everyone free-rides, nothing gets done. *§3.a*

- Solutions to public good problems include private provision of the public good and government provision of the good. *§3.b*

6. Why does the government require the listing of ingredients on food packaging?

- When buyers have less information than sellers, a situation can arise in which high-quality products are driven out of the market, leaving just low-quality products. This is called *adverse selection*. *§4.a*

- When buyers have more information than sellers about a particular item, buyers may alter their behavior with regard to that item once they have purchased it. For instance, once someone is insured, that person may act differently, taking on more risk. This is called *moral hazard*. *§4.b*

- Problems of adverse selection and moral hazard are often resolved privately through copayments, deductibles, and other such arrangements that reduce the incentives to change behavior or not reveal information. *§4.c*

7. What is rent seeking?

- Since the government has no competition, it is generally less efficient than the private market. *§5*

- Government failures may result from logrolling, bureaucracy building, and rent seeking. *§5*

Key Terms

market failure *Preview, §1*

rent seeking *Preview*

private costs *§1*

externality *§1*

social cost *§1*

Coase theorem *§1.c*

principle of mutual exclusivity *§3*

public good *§3*

free rider *§3.a*

adverse selection *§4.a*

moral hazard *§4.b*

logrolling *§5*

Exercises

1. How would you derive the demand for milk at the local grocery store? How would you derive the demand for tuna? How would you derive the demand for national defense?

2. Explain why an externality might be a market failure. What does market failure mean?

3. Use the following information to answer the following questions:

Quantity	Private Cost	Social Cost	Benefit
1	$2	$4	$12
2	$6	$10	$22
3	$12	$18	$30
4	$20	$28	$36
5	$30	$40	$40

a. What is the external cost per unit of output?

b. What level of output will be produced?

c. What level of output should be produced to achieve economic efficiency?

d. What is the value to society of correcting the externality?

4. What level of tax would be appropriate to internalize the externality in exercise 3?

5. If, in exercise 3, the Private Cost and Social Cost columns were reversed, you would have an example of what? Would too much or too little of the good be produced? How would the market failure be resolved, by a tax or by a subsidy?

6. What is meant by the term *overfishing?* What is the fundamental problem associated with overfishing of the oceans? What might lead to *underfishing?*

7. How much pollution would exist if all externalities were internalized? Why would it not be zero? Use the same explanation to discuss the amount of health and safety that the government should require in the workplace.

8. Suppose the following table describes the marginal costs and marginal benefits of waste (garbage) reduction. What is the optimal amount of garbage? What is the situation if no garbage is allowed to be produced?

Percentage of Waste Eliminated	Marginal Costs (millions of dollars)	Marginal Benefits (millions of dollars)
10%	10	1,000
20%	15	500
30%	25	100
40%	40	50
50%	70	20
60%	110	5
70%	200	3
80%	500	2
90%	900	1
100%	2,000	0

9. Elephants eat 300 pounds of food per day. They flourished in Africa when they could roam over huge areas of land, eating the vegetation in one area and then moving on so that the vegetation could renew itself. Now, the area over which elephants can roam is declining. Without some action, the elephants will become extinct. What actions might save the elephants? What are the costs and benefits of such actions?

10. What can explain why the value of pollution permits in one area of the country is rising 20 percent per year, while in another it is unchanged from year to year? What would you expect to occur as a result of this differential?

11. Smokers impose negative externalities on nonsmokers. Suppose the airspace in a restaurant is a resource owned by the restaurant owner.

a. How would the owner respond to the negative externalities of smokers?

b. Suppose the smokers owned the airspace. How would that change matters?

c. How about if the nonsmokers owned the airspace?

d. Finally, consider what would occur if the government passed a law banning all smoking. How would the outcome compare with the outcomes described above?

12. Discuss the argument that education should be subsidized because it creates a positive externality.

13. If the best solution to solving the positive externality problem of education is to provide a subsidy, explain why educational systems in all countries are nationalized, that is, are government entities.

ACE

Take the ACE Practice Test for this chapter to review the important concepts and get immediate feedback with answers.

college.hmco.com/economics/students/

Bates College Students Retire Air Pollution Permit Worth a Ton of Sulfur Dioxide

AScribe Newswire
April 24, 2003

For the third year, students in the 200-level Environmental Economics course at Bates College have successfully bid on and purchased a government permit for the atmospheric release of a ton of sulfur dioxide [SO_2], a pollutant that causes acid rain.

The 50 students in the two sections of the course each put $5 toward a bid for the U.S. Environmental Protection Agency's 11th annual SO_2-permit auction, hosted by the Chicago Board of Trade. As it has each year, the class will retire its permit.

"We're not going to resell it, so that a ton of sulfur dioxide will never be emitted into the atmosphere," says Lynne Lewis, associate professor of economics at Bates and the originator of the college's annual bidding effort.

The auction, held every March, is a mechanism in the EPA's Acid Rain Program, which uses a market-based "cap and trade" approach to curtail air pollution. "It's always sort of cool to see the theory applied in real life," says senior biology major Mark Thomson, of Minneapolis, who took the course with Lewis.

"There's something very tangible about seeing Bates' name on the actual auction," says Thomson. "And the fact that we obtained a permit is excellent, because you study different market-based incentive programs to reduce pollution, but to actually do it—and to say that we're willing to pay because we don't want acid rain in Maine—is a great opportunity."

Lewis came to Bates in 2000 and initiated the bid process in 2001. "One of the exciting parts of this program is that anyone can buy a permit," she says. "It's fairly straightforward."

[The EPA website offers ample information about the process, with a good starting point being the "Acid Rain Program SO_2 Allowances Fact Sheet" page at http://www.epa.gov/airmarkt/arp/allfact.html.]

This year's "clearing price" per permit—that is, the lowest successful bid—was $171.80. The Ohio-based American Electric Power, the nation's largest electrical supplier, won 99.9 percent of the 125,000 permits on offer. Bates' bid was $185.50, fourth-lowest of the 20 successful bids.

Determining how much to bid, Lewis says, is "the challenging part of the exercise, but also makes it fun to do with my class."

She divided her students into teams and assigned each to research the bid history for the auction, suggest a bid, and offer a defense of the amount. The final bid was the average of all bids. Student contributions left over were donated to the Acid Rain Retirement Fund, a program at the University of Southern Maine that was the only other Maine bidder this year.

Tradable permits "are something that economists have been touting for a long time as a good thing," Lewis says. "With economic incentives for pollution control, you can achieve an environmental standard at a lower cost, which is good for everybody." . . .

Source: Copyright 2003 AScribe Inc.

The United States was the first nation to create a market for the buying and selling of rights to pollute water and air, but it is not alone. Several governments have proposed the creation of a market system to control air and water pollution. Why would a government create such a market? Why doesn't the government simply forbid firms to pollute the air and water?

A command system will reduce the amount of pollution created, but at what costs? As discussed in the chapter, by requiring firms to limit their emissions to some prescribed amount of pollution, the government is not allowing resources to be allocated to their most valuable use. In some cases, a firm might have to shut down because it can't meet the government's restrictions. In other cases, a firm could increase the amount of pollution it creates because it was emitting a smaller quantity than that permitted by the government. In no case does a firm have a choice or an incentive to meet the government's requirements in an efficient manner.

We discussed how such a market system is created. Essentially, the government specifies an allowable amount of pollution for a particular area or in a particular water system, and then sells permits that allow firms to pollute. A firm compares the price of an additional permit to the cost of reducing pollution by the amount specified on the permit. If the price of the permit is greater than the cost of reducing pollution, the firm will choose to reduce the pollutants it emits. In other words, firms compare marginal benefits (MB) and marginal costs (MC) and purchase additional permits until $MB = MC$. Thus, the market system provides an incentive for firms to use a cleaner technology when the price of the permits becomes more expensive than the purchase of new, cleaner technology.

As described in the chapter, the price of a permit is determined by demand and supply. As the government reduces the number of permits supplied, the price of the permits rises, *everything else held constant*. As the price rises, the quantity demanded declines, and more firms choose to reduce their emissions rather than purchase additional permits.

An important aspect of the market approach to minimizing the externality problem is that it is up to the firm to decide when it is best to switch to the new technology. This ensures that resources are used in their most efficient manner—that is, where they have the highest value. The command approach does not do this. There is an additional aspect of the market system approach: it allows anyone who is interested in reducing pollution to bid for the permits. This drives the price up and induces more firms to adopt the more efficient or less polluting technologies more quickly. For instance, groups like the Sierra Club, the Nature Conservancy, Greenpeace, the Czech Republic's Children of the Earth, and even a group of college students at Bates College can raise funds to purchase permits and then simply not use them. With fewer permits available, the price of the permits rises, and the quantity of pollution created is reduced.

15

Resource Markets

Do you recycle? Are you concerned with global warming, saving the rainforest, and reducing pollution? Perhaps you've noticed the number of homeless people on the streets and wondered why they are homeless and what can be done about homelessness. Have you ever been discriminated against because of your age, race, or sex? Have you been touched by illegal drugs—gang wars, drive-by shootings, crime? Do you or do your parents have health insurance and medical coverage, or is it simply too expensive? In the following chapters we discuss some aspects of these issues as we examine the resource markets. Remember that resource markets provide the resources, or ingredients, for producing goods and services. They include the markets for labor, capital, and land in general terms, but more specifically they involve people and their jobs, physical and financial capital, and natural resources. In this chapter, we'll look at how firms choose their resources and how firms draw on economic

theory to help them decide what resources and how much of a given resource to use. In the chapters that follow, we'll look at each market more closely, examining some of the societal questions and issues that arise in the process. ▪

(?)

1. Who are the buyers and sellers of resources?

resource market: a market that provides one of the resources for producing goods and services: labor, capital, and land

1. Buyers and Sellers of Resources ___

There are three general types of resource markets: those for land, labor, and capital. The price and quantity of each resource are determined in its **resource market.** Rent and the quantity of land used are determined in the land market. The wage rate and the number of people employed are determined in the labor market. The cost of capital (the interest rate) and the quantity of capital used are determined in the capital market. Although each of these markets is somewhat unique, they are all markets, and thus they simply involve the demand for and supply of that particular resource.

1.a. The Resource Markets

To understand the resource markets, you need to realize that the roles of firms and households are reversed from what they are in the product markets. Figure 1 is the simplest circular flow diagram that you saw in Chapter 4. It illustrates the roles of firms and households in the product and resource markets. The market for goods and services is represented by the top lines in the figure. Households buy goods and services from firms, as shown by the line going from firms to households; and firms sell goods and services and receive revenue, as shown by the line going from households to firms. The resource market is represented by the bottom half of the diagram in Figure 1. Households are the sellers of resources, and firms are the buyers of resources. Households sell resources, as shown by the line going from households to firms; and firms pay households income, as shown by the line going from firms to households.

FIGURE 1   **The Market for Resources**

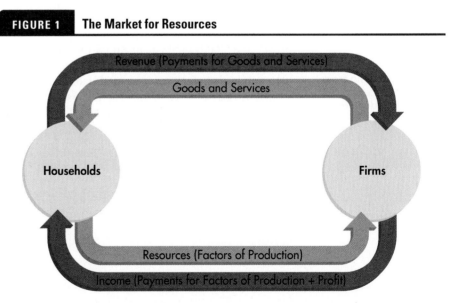

The buyers of resources are firms that purchase resources in order to produce goods and services. The sellers of resources are households that supply resources in order to obtain income with which to purchase goods and services.

In resource markets the sellers are the owners of land, labor, or capital while the buyers are firms. In this particular situation, a restaurant owner is deciding which fresh produce to purchase for her restaurant. The seller is the farmer who has grown the produce.

Households supply resources in order to earn income. By offering to work, individuals supply their labor; by saving, households supply firms with the funds used to purchase machines, equipment, and buildings; by offering their land and the minerals, trees, and other natural resources associated with it, households supply land. The supply of a resource consists of the sum of the quantities supplied by every resource owner. The supply of unskilled workers consists of the sum of the quantities that each and every unskilled worker is willing to work at each wage rate. The supply of office space in Phoenix, Arizona, offered for rent consists of the supplies offered by every owner of office space in Phoenix.

Resources are wanted not for themselves, but for what they produce. A firm uses resources in order to produce goods and services. Thus, the demand for a resource by a firm depends on the demand for the goods and services that the firm produces. For this reason, the demand for resources is often called a **derived demand:** An automobile manufacturer uses land, labor, and capital to produce cars; a retail T-shirt store uses land, labor, and capital to sell T-shirts; a farmer uses land, labor, and capital to produce agricultural products. The market demand for a resource consists of the demands of each firm that is willing and able to pay for that resource. An electric utility firm in Iowa demands engineers, as does a construction firm in Minnesota. The market demand for engineers consists of the demands of the Iowa utility and the Minnesota construction firm. Each firm's demand depends on separate and distinct factors, however. The electric utility firm hires more engineers to modernize its plant; the construction firm hires more engineers to fulfill its contracts with the state government to build bridges. Yet all firms have the same decision-making process for hiring or acquiring resources.

derived demand: demand stemming from what a resource can produce, not demand for the resource itself

RECAP

1. Resource markets are classified into three types: those for land, labor, and capital.

2. The buyers of resources are firms; the suppliers are households.

2. How Firms Decide What Resources to Acquire

How do you decide how much you are willing to pay for something? Don't you decide how much it is worth to you? This is what businesses do when they decide how much to pay a worker or how much to pay for a machine. A firm uses the quantity of each resource that will enable the firm to maximize profit.

2.a. The Firm's Demand

We know from previous chapters that firms maximize profit when they operate at the level where marginal revenue (*MR*) equals marginal cost (*MC*). The same thing occurs in the resource markets. *MR* is called the marginal revenue product (*MRP*), and *MC* is called the marginal factor cost (*MFC*).

marginal revenue product (*MRP*): the additional revenue that an additional resource can create for a firm

The additional value that an additional resource creates for a firm is called the **marginal revenue product (*MRP*).** If Jennifer Aniston can bring in $30 million in additional revenue to the movie studio for performing in one movie, then we can say that Jennifer Aniston's marginal revenue product for that movie is $30 million. If an additional server at Applebee's can bring in $30 an hour to the restaurant, we say that the server's *MRP* is $30 an hour.

The MRP *of a resource is a measure of how much the additional output generated by the last unit of that resource is worth to the firm.* The marginal-revenue-product curve for a resource that is not unique is drawn in Figure 2. It slopes down because the additional revenue that an additional resource can generate for a firm declines as more resources are acquired. This is the law of diminishing marginal product we encountered in the chapter "Supply: The Costs of Doing Business." As Applebee's adds more and more servers, the additional revenue that each additional server can create for the restaurant declines. The *MRP* for a unique resource also declines as that resource is used more and more during a specific time period. If Jennifer Aniston performed in several movies during a year's time, it is likely that the additional revenue she could bring into the movie studio for each additional movie would decline.

2.b. Marginal Factor Costs

marginal factor cost (*MFC*): the additional cost of an additional unit of a resource

The cost of an additional unit of a resource, called the **marginal factor cost,** depends on whether the firm is purchasing resources in a market with many suppliers or in a market with one or only a few suppliers. The marginal factor cost is the actual cost to the firm of acquiring an additional resource.

2.b.1. Hiring Resources in a Perfectly Competitive Market If the firm is purchasing resources in a market in which there is a very large number of suppliers of an identical resource—a perfectly competitive resource market—the price to the firm of each additional unit of the resource is constant. Why? Because no seller is large enough to individually change the price. Servers at Applebee's would be an example. There are many people who are willing and able to work for Applebee's, and the firm can hire as much of the resource as it wants without affecting either the quantity available or the price of that resource.

Let's use the information in the table and graph of Figure 3 to determine how many servers an Applebee's restaurant would hire. The firm can employ as many servers as it wants at $15 per day—the *MFC* is a straight horizontal line at $15. The first server hired has a marginal revenue product of $130 per day and costs $15 per day. It is profitable to hire her. A second brings in an additional $60 per day and

FIGURE 2   **Resource Market Demand and Market Supply**

Quantity of Resource

The demand curve for a resource slopes down, reflecting the inverse relation between the price of the resource and the quantity demanded. The supply curve for a resource slopes up, reflecting the direct relation between the price of the resource and the quantity supplied. Equilibrium occurs where the two curves intersect; the quantities demanded and supplied are the same at the equilibrium price. If the resource price is greater than the equilibrium price, a surplus of the resource arises and drives the price back down to equilibrium. If the resource price is less than the equilibrium price, a shortage occurs and forces the price back up to equilibrium.

costs $15 per day, and so is also profitable. The third server brings in $40 per day, the fourth $20 per day, the fifth $10 per day, and the sixth nothing. Thus, the third, fourth, and fifth servers are profitable, but the sixth, seventh and so on aren't. The firm hires four servers. You can see in the graph that the marginal revenue product lies above the wage rate until after the fourth server is hired.

The firm hires additional servers until the *MRP* of one more server is equal to the marginal factor cost of that server, *MRP* = *MFC*. This is a general rule; it holds whether the firms sells its output in a perfectly competitive, monopoly, monopolistically competitive, or oligopoly market; and it holds for all resources, land and capital as well as labor.

Resources will be employed up to the point at which MRP = MFC.

2.b.2. Hiring Resources as a Monopoly Buyer   When just one firm is acquiring a resource, that firm is called a **monopsonist.** A monopsonist is a monopoly buyer. In the early days of mining in the United States, it was not uncommon for firms to create entire towns in order to attract a readily available supply of labor. The sole provider of jobs in the town was the mining company. Thus, when the company hired labor, it affected the prices of all workers, not just the worker it recently hired. In the 1970s along the Alaskan pipeline, and in the

monopsonist: a firm that is the only buyer of a resource

FIGURE 3   The Employment of Resources

The marginal revenue product and the marginal factor cost together indicate the number of servers the restaurant would hire. The *MRP* and the *MFC* for a restaurant are listed in the table. The *MRP* curve and the *MFC* curve are shown in the graph. The marginal revenue product exceeds the marginal factor cost (wage rate) until after the fourth server is hired. The firm will not hire more than four, for then the costs would exceed the additional revenue produced by the last server hired.

(1)	(2)	(3)
Number of Servers	*MRP*	*MFC*
1	$130	$15
2	$60	$15
3	$40	$15
4	$20	$15
5	$10	$15
6	$0	$15

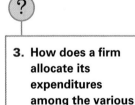

1980s in foreign countries where U.S. firms were hired to carry out specialized engineering projects or massive construction jobs, small towns dependent on a single U.S. firm were created. There are cases in which a monopsony exists even though a company town was not created. For instance, many universities in small communities are monopsonistic employers—they are the primary employer in the town. When these universities hire a mechanic, they affect the wage rates of all mechanics in the town. Wal-Mart is often called a monopsony because it locates a store in a small town and quickly becomes the major, if not almost the only, employer in the town.

> *A firm buying in a perfectly competitive resource market will pay the marginal revenue product; a monopsonistic firm will pay less than the marginal revenue product.*

A monopsony firm is able pay resources less than their marginal revenue products because the resource owners have no choice. They can't rent their land to someone else or go work for someone else.

2.c. Hiring When There Is More Than One Resource

?

> **3. How does a firm allocate its expenditures among the various resources?**

To this point we've examined the firm's hiring decision for one resource, everything else, including the quantities of all other resources, held constant. However, a firm uses several resources and makes hiring decisions regarding most of them all the time. How does the firm decide what combinations of resources to use? Like the consumer deciding what combinations of goods and services to purchase, the firm will ensure that the benefits of spending one more dollar are the same no matter which resource the firm chooses to spend that dollar on.

You may recall that the consumer maximizes utility when the marginal utility per dollar of expenditure is the same for all goods and services purchased:

$$MU_{coffee}/P_{coffee} = MU_{gas}/P_{gas} = \cdots = MU_n/P_n$$

A similar rule holds for the firm that is attempting to purchase resource services in order to maximize profit and minimize costs. The firm will be maximizing profit

Wal-Mart

Wal-Mart's strategy for success has been to locate in small towns, rural areas, and parts of major metropolitan areas that are not well served by other firms and to provide goods and services at the lowest prices possible. This strategy has been a huge success; Wal-Mart has been the most successful retail store during the past two decades. Wal-Mart has grown to the point that it is the largest employer in the world and virtually the only employer in many small towns. This success has made it a focal point of political concern. The wages and benefits that Wal-Mart provides have been criticized as being inadequate by politicians in many states. Thirty-three states have proposed or enacted laws directed at forcing Wal-Mart to provide more benefits, hire different groups, pay different wages, or carry out some other activity that will cost Wal-Mart money.

At the beginning of 2006, Maryland enacted a law requiring that Wal-Mart provide benefits equal to 8 percent of wages. While many companies provide benefits that are at least 8 percent of wages, Wal-Mart does not because of its strategy of low costs. Employees continue to apply for positions at the giant company, and unions have been unable to convince employees to unionize. The effect of the law is most likely not going to be to help the Wal-Mart employees in Maryland, but instead, to drive Wal-Mart out of the state. Wal-Mart has canceled the location of a major new center in Somerset that was scheduled to employ about 800 people. Indiana defeated a law similar to Maryland's, but about thirty states are considering enacting similar laws.

when its marginal revenue product per dollar of expenditure on all resources is the same:

$$MRP_{land}/MFC_{land} = MRP_{labor}/MFC_{labor} = \cdots = MRP_n/MFC_n$$

As long as the marginal factor cost of a resource is less than its marginal revenue product, the firm will increase profit by hiring more of the resource. If a dollar spent on labor yields less marginal revenue product than a dollar spent on capital, the firm will increase profit more by purchasing the capital than by purchasing the labor.

In equilibrium, the last dollar spent on resources must yield the same marginal revenue product no matter which resource the dollar is spent on.

If a resource is very expensive relative to other resources, then the expensive resource must generate a significantly larger marginal revenue product than the other resources. For instance, for a firm to remain in Manhattan (New York City), it must generate a significantly larger marginal revenue product than it could obtain in Dallas or elsewhere, because rents are so much higher in Manhattan. A professional athlete who gets paid $30 million a year has to bring in more revenue for the team than another who earns $2 million a year.

A firm that is in equilibrium in terms of allocating its expenditures among resources will alter the allocation only if the cost of one of the resources rises relative to the others. For instance, if government-mandated medical or other benefits mean that labor costs rise while everything else remains constant, then firms will tend to hire less labor and use more capital and land if they can. Everything else the same, if the costs of doing business in the United States rise, firms will locate offices or plants in other countries.

2.d. Product Market Structures and Resource Demand

Firms purchase the types and quantities of resource services that allow them to maximize profit; each firm equates the *MRP* per dollar of expenditure on all resource services used. The *MRP* depends on the market structure in which the firm sells its output. A perfectly competitive firm produces more output and sells that output at a lower price than a firm operating in any other type of market, everything else the same. Since the perfectly competitive firm produces more output, it must use more resources.

For the perfectly competitive firm, price and marginal revenue are the same, $P = MR$. Thus, the marginal revenue product is often called the value of the marginal product, VMP, to distinguish it from the marginal revenue product.

The demand for a resource by a single firm is the MRP of that resource, no matter whether it sells its goods and services as a monopolist or as a perfect competitor (for the perfectly competitive firm, $VMP = MRP$, so that MRP is its resource demand as well). However, since for the firms that are not selling in a perfectly competitive market, price is greater than marginal revenue, VMP would be greater than MRP, which indicates that the perfectly competitive firm's demand curve for a resource lies above (or is greater than) the demand curve for a resource by a monopoly firm, an oligopoly firm, or a monopolistically competitive firm.

RECAP

1. The MRP of a resource is a measure of how much the additional output generated by the last unit of the resource is worth to the firm.

2. Resources are hired up to the point at which $MRP = MFC$.

3. In a perfectly competitive resource market, resources are paid an amount equal to their marginal revenue product. In a monopsonistic resource market, resources are paid less than their marginal revenue product.

4. A firm will allocate its budget on resources up to the point where the last dollar spent yields an equal marginal revenue product no matter on which resource the dollar is spent.

5. A perfectly competitive firm will hire and acquire more resources than firms selling in monopoly, oligopoly, or monopolistically competitive product markets, everything else the same.

3. Resource Supplies

The owners of land, labor, and capital are households or individuals. Individuals act so as to maximize their utility. They receive utility when they consume goods and services, but they need income to purchase these goods and services. To acquire income, households must sell the services of their resources. They must give up some of their leisure time and go to work or offer the services of the other resources they own in order to acquire income. The quantity of resources that are supplied depends on the wages, rents, interest, and profits offered for those resources. If, while everything else is held constant, people can get higher wages, they will offer to work more hours; if they can obtain more rent for their land, they will offer more of their land for use, and so on. The quantity supplied of a resource rises as the price of the resource rises.

3.a. Economic Rent

economic rent: the portion of earnings above transfer earnings

transfer earnings: the amount that must be paid to a resource owner to get him or her to allocate the resource to another use

When a resource has a perfectly inelastic supply (vertical supply curve), its pay or earnings is called **economic rent.** If a resource has a perfectly elastic supply curve, its pay or earnings is called **transfer earnings.** For upward-sloping supply curves, resource earnings consist of both transfer earnings and economic rent. Transfer earnings is what a resource could earn in its best alternative use (its opportunity cost). It is the amount that must be paid to get the resource to "transfer" to another use. Economic rent is earnings in excess of transfer earnings. It is the portion of a resource's earnings that is not necessary to keep the resource in its current use. A movie star can earn more than $20 million per movie but probably could not earn that kind of income in another occupation. Thus, the greatest part of the movie star's earnings is economic rent.

There are two different meanings for the term *rent* in economics. The most common meaning refers to the payment for the use of something, as distinguished from payment for ownership. In this sense, you purchase a house but rent an apartment; you buy a car from Chrysler but rent cars from Avis. The second use of the term *rent* is to mean payment for the use of something that is in fixed—that is, perfectly inelastic—supply. The total quantity of land is fixed; therefore, payment for land is economic rent. When something is in fixed supply, even a higher rent cannot increase its quantity. Because the term *economic rent* is associated with payments for something that don't increase the quantity supplied, it is often applied to politics. For instance, a payment for favors from a government official is called economic rent; it is a payment that does not create anything or increase the quantity supplied of anything. The government official uses tax money to provide you benefits; thus, the payment merely transfers wealth from one person to another. It does not increase the quantity of something.

RECAP

1. Firms purchase resources in such a way that they maximize profits. Households sell resources in order to maximize income.

2. Transfer earnings is the portion of total earnings required to keep a resource in its current use.

3. Economic rent is earnings in excess of transfer earnings.

4. A Look Ahead

In the next few chapters, we will examine some interesting features of resource markets. We'll look at labor markets and discuss why different people receive different wages, why firms treat employees the way they do, the impact of labor laws, and the causes and results of discrimination. We'll discuss financial markets and physical and financial capital and explore why firms carry out research and development. We'll look at the markets for land and natural resources. Selling resource services creates income, so we'll examine who has income and why. And we'll look at how the government gets involved in providing needed human services such as health care and social security.

Often we will discuss resource markets at the level of the individual firm or individual household, but typically we will refer to the market as a whole. For instance, if we talk about the "labor market," we are talking about the demand for every worker by every firm and the supply of every possible employee by every individual. The market demand curve slopes downward, indicating that as the price of a resource falls, the quantity demanded rises, everything else held constant. The market supply curve slopes upward, indicating that as the price of a resource falls, the quantity supplied falls, everything else held constant.

Summary

1. Who are the buyers and sellers of resources?

- The term *resource markets* refers to the buyers and sellers of three classes of resources: land, labor, and capital. *§1*

- The buyers of resources are firms that purchase resources in order to produce goods and services. *§1.a*

- The sellers of resources are households that supply resources in order to obtain income with which to purchase goods and services. *§1.a*

2. How are resource prices determined?

- A single firm's demand for a resource is the marginal-revenue-product curve for that resource. *§2.a*

- A firm purchasing resources in a perfectly competitive resource market will hire resources up to the point where *MRP = MFC*. A firm that is one of only a few buyers or the only buyer of a particular resource (a monopsonist) will face a marginal-factor-cost curve that is above the supply curve for that resource. As a result, the resource is paid less than its marginal revenue product. *§2.b.1, 2.b.2*

3. How does a firm allocate its expenditures among the various resources?

- A firm will allocate its budget on resources in such a way that the last dollar spent will yield the same marginal revenue product no matter on which resource the dollar is spent. *§2.c*

- Households own resources and decide how much of the resource services to offer for use. The supply of a resource depends on the income received by the owners of that resource. *§3*

- Payments for the use of resources consist of two parts: transfer earnings and economic rent. Transfer earnings are the rate of pay necessary to keep a resource in its current use. Economic rent is the excess of pay above transfer earnings. *§3.a*

Key Terms

resource market *§1*

derived demand *§1.a*

marginal revenue product (*MRP*) *§2.a*

marginal factor cost (*MFC*) *§2.b*

monopsonist *§2.b.2*

economic rent *§3.a*

transfer earnings *§3.a*

Exercises

1. What does it mean to say that the demand for resources is a derived demand? Is the demand for all goods and services a derived demand?

2. Using the information in the following table, calculate the marginal revenue product (*MRP = MPP × MR*).

Units of Resources	Total Output	Price	Resource Price
1	10	$5	$10
2	25	$5	$10
3	35	$5	$10
4	40	$5	$10
5	40	$5	$10

3. Using the data in exercise 2, determine how many units of resources the firm will want to acquire.

4. Suppose the output price falls from $5 to $4 to $3 to $1 in exercise 2. How would that change your answers to exercises 2 and 3?

5. Using the data in exercise 2, calculate the marginal factor cost.

6. Suppose the resource price rises from $10 to $12 to $14 to $18 to $20 as resource units go from 1 to 5. How would that change your answer to exercise 5? How would it change your answer to exercise 3?

7. Using exercise 6, calculate the transfer earnings and economic rent of the third unit of the resource when four units of the resource are employed. Do the same calculations when only three units of the resource are employed. How do you account for the different answers?

8. Can you explain why Jennifer Aniston earns $30 million a year and a schoolteacher $40,000 a year?

9. What is a monopsonist? How does a monopsonist differ from a monopolist?

10. Supposedly Larry Bird once said that he would play basketball for $10,000 per year. Yet he was paid over $1 million per year. If the quote is correct, how much were Bird's transfer earnings? How much was his economic rent?

11. Wal-Mart is vilified by many people as being evil, destroying jobs and cities. Others note that it has the lowest prices and is the largest employer in the country. What is the difference? Is Wal-Mart a monopsonist?

12. Early in her journalistic career, Gloria Steinem posed as a Playboy Bunny to examine the inside of a Playboy Club. Steinem discovered that the Bunnies had to purchase their costumes from the club, pay for the cleaning, purchase their food from the club, and so on. This "company store" exploited the employees (the Bunnies), according to Steinem. Explain what Steinem meant by exploitation.

13. Explain the idea behind the lyrics "You load 16 tons, and what do you get? You get another day older and deeper in debt. Saint Peter, don't you call me, 'cause I can't go. I owe my soul to the company store."

14. In some small cities, Wal-Mart is the only firm offering many types of goods. Suppose the demand for those goods is very price inelastic. How does that affect how Wal-Mart treats its employees—what is the marginal factor cost and the wage rate?

Take the ACE Practice Test for this chapter to review the important concepts and get immediate feedback with answers.

college.hmco.com/economics/students/

"We Love Wie" Fans Fill U.S. Open Golf Qualifier

Bloomberg
June 5, 2006

Bill Lord finished his night shift as a police supervisor in Clark, New Jersey, and headed right to Canoe Brook Country Club to watch Michelle Wie attempt to become the first woman to qualify for golf's U.S. Open.

"I haven't slept in almost 24 hours," Lord said in an interview while walking the course in Summit, New Jersey. "But this is history in the making, possibly. I told my wife I had to come and watch."

The 16-year-old Wie ultimately fell short in her quest to join Tiger Woods and Phil Mickelson at Winged Foot Golf Club in two weeks, tying for 59th in the field of 153 players. Yet she was in contention for one of the 18 U.S. Open berths until making three straight bogeys late in her second round.

"Even though she didn't make it, she competes with these guys," said Terry Sumner of Brooklyn, New York. "She carried herself remarkably well. I can't imagine doing that at 16."

Brett Quigley, a veteran on the U.S. PGA Tour, topped the 36-hole sectional qualifier at 11-under-par. PGA players Kevin Stadler, Kent Jones, Mark Brooks, J.J. Henry and Tom Pernice Jr. were among the other players earning U.S. Open spots.

While almost 50 U.S. PGA Tour players were in the field at Canoe Brook, Wie was the biggest draw. As other groups played alone, Wie's group was followed by a gallery of about 2,000 people. The course, which didn't charge admission, was closed to fans at 11 a.m. after it reached capacity.

Top Draw

"The crowd out there was four to five times what we've seen," said Jeannie McCooey, communications director for the Metropolitan Golf Association, which organized the event. "And we usually get maybe a dozen reporters. Today we've got nearly 200 and probably 199 of them are following Michelle."

Wally Kim, a golf professional at Stanton Ridge Golf and Country Club in Whitehouse Station, New Jersey, took a day off from work and brought his two girls, 7-year-old Kirsten and 3-year-old Claudia, to watch Wie. Kirsten even got a ball from Wie at the ninth hole.

"This is just a great experience," Kim said as he marched up the 12th fairway with Claudia on his back. "My girls are half Korean and they love Michelle. This is a great thing to share with them."

Since it is not a professional event, there were no ropes along the fairways to keep the fans—some wearing pink "We love Wie" buttons—away from the golfers.

"It's amazing, you can almost walk with them," Lord said.

Missed Birdies

Wie, who reached the sectional by winning her local qualifier in Hawaii, shot a 2-under 68 during her opening round even though she missed six birdie putts of less than 15 feet.

The 6-foot-tall Wie followed with a 75 in the second round at the longer and more difficult North Course, making three bogeys over her final six holes. She remained upbeat however, even stopping to give a ball to a young female fan after missing a three-foot par putt at her 32nd hole.

"A couple of shots here and there didn't go where I wanted, but I played through," Wie said at her post-round news conference. "It was a long day out there."

Wie's opening round matched her best score from the eight events she's played against men, having also shot a 68 at the PGA Tour's 2004 Sony Open. She was four strokes better than her two playing partners, former PGA Tour veteran David Gossett and Rick Hartmann, a club pro from Long Island.

Gossett and Hartmann both finished 4-over-par, three shots behind Wie, who also finished ahead of veteran PGA players Alex Cejka, Scott Gutschewski, Len Mattiace and John Senden.

"She's right there," said Sumner, a public school teacher. "Tee to green her game is as good as any PGA man. At 16, that's amazing. She's only going to get better."

Erik Matuszewski

Teenage golfer Michelle Wie has amazed even seasoned golf observers with her stunning talent and ability to draw huge crowds of fans eager to cheer her on. Since turning professional at age 15, Wie is thought to have signed endorsement deals worth $13 million a year, a huge sum for any golfer, let alone a young woman at the start of her career. How can anyone be worth $13 million or more per year? How can we justify earnings for a teenager that are so much more per year than what, for instance, a schoolteacher might earn? Something must be wrong.

Well, is it? According to economic theory, resources are paid their *MRP,* or their value to the firm. The more revenue that a resource generates for a firm, the more valuable that resource is. Demand and supply determine the value of resources. The greater the demand relative to the supply, the higher the price of the resource, and, conversely, the lower the demand relative to the supply, the lower the price of the resource. Schoolteachers are plentiful; nearly anyone with a college degree can be a schoolteacher. One merely needs to obtain a certificate. But to be a professional golfer, one must have very special skills. There are very few people who can play golf the way Michele Wie can.

Nevertheless, why would the scarcity of golfers relative to teachers create the huge distortion in incomes? The answer is that Michele brings in more revenue to the firms she endorses than the teacher does to the school district or school. Society is willing to pay high prices to watch golfing matches, and the better a player is, the higher the prices that the firms who gain endorsements from that player can charge. So, Michele Wie is expected to attract many consumers who will purchase what Michele endorses.

The accompanying figure shows Michele's marginal revenue product, MRP_{MW}, and a schoolteacher's, MRP_T. The huge difference in compensation is due to society's demands. People want to watch Michele Wie hit that little white ball, and Michele is one of just a few people who can play at the level she plays. The supply of teachers is huge compared to the supply of Michele Wie–type golfers.

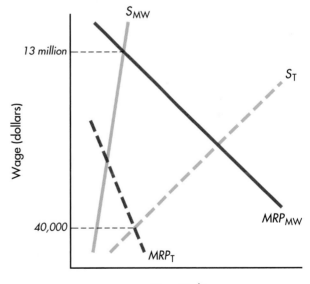

chapter

16

The Labor Market

Fundamental Questions

1. Are people willing to work more hours for higher wages?

2. What are compensating wage differentials?

3. What is the impact of technological change and the New Economy on workers?

4. What is offshoring?

5. What is the impact of a minimum wage law on unskilled labor?

6. What is the effect of illegal immigration on the economy?

7. Are discrimination and freely functioning markets compatible?

Is something out of balance when teachers, firefighters, and police officers earn salaries that are just 1 percent of the salary of the average professional basketball player? Why are some jobs that could be done by Americans being sent to other countries? Why are unskilled people from less-developed countries flooding into the developed countries to do menial or unskilled jobs? Are these events things to worry about? In this chapter we examine these issues. ■

1. The Supply of Labor _____

The supply of labor comes from individual households. Each member of a household must determine whether to give up a certain number of hours each day to work. That decision is the individual's labor supply decision and is called the *labor-leisure tradeoff.*

1.a. Individual Labor Supply: Labor-Leisure Tradeoff

?

1. Are people willing to work more hours for higher wages?

There are only twenty-four hours in a day, and there are only two things that people can do during this time: (1) work for pay or (2) not work for pay. *Any* time spent not working is called *leisure time*. Leisure time includes being a "couch potato," going to clubs, volunteering to serve food at a homeless shelter, or participating in any other activity except working at a paying job. People want leisure time, but they also want food, housing, cars, fun, and many other things. To be able to buy goods and services, people usually have to work.

> *People have 24 hours a day during which they can either work or do something other than work (leisure).*

It is important to recognize that the cost of leisure time is the money that could be earned working. A person's wage or salary is his or her opportunity cost of leisure. This creates an interesting dilemma—you want to earn more money so that you can purchase goods and services, yet you want to have time to enjoy the things you buy. So you have to trade off work and leisure time: if you take more leisure, you work less, and vice versa. So how many hours do people spend working and how many hours do they devote to other activities?

In addition to going to school, do you work? Let's say that you earn $10 per hour and work 10 hours a week. What would you do if the wage rate for your job increased to $15 per hour? You might ask to work *more* hours each week. What would you do if the wage rate increased to $50 per hour? You might drop your classes and work 40 or more hours a week. The higher wage means that an hour of leisure costs more—$50 rather than $10. As the price of a normal good goes up, people purchase less of it. As the price of leisure goes up, people work more.

Leisure is a little different from other normal goods—such as books, gasoline, and Starbucks coffee—because of the limited number of hours in a day. You can't work 24 hours a day—at least, not for very long. What happens with most people is that as they earn more money, they want more time to enjoy what the money can buy. This becomes a problem: if I work more, I have more money, but I have less time to enjoy what the money can buy; if I work less so that I can have more time to enjoy what I purchase, I have less income.

When the wage rate increases, people choose to work more (or work harder or better), but since they now have more money, they can purchase more and may decide that they would rather take a little more leisure time. Thus, a wage increase creates two opposing effects; one leads to increased hours of work, and one leads to decreased hours of work. This means that the quantity of labor supplied may rise or fall as the wage rate rises.

The labor supply curve shown in Figure 1 is what the labor supply curve for an individual usually looks like. It rises as the wage rate rises until the wage is sufficiently high that people begin to choose more leisure; then the curve begins to turn backward. This is called the **backward-bending labor supply curve.**

> **backward-bending labor supply curve:** a labor supply curve indicating that a person is willing and able to work more hours as the wage rate increases until, at some sufficiently high wage rate, the person chooses to work fewer hours

1.a.1. Do People Really Trade Off Labor and Leisure?

About one-half of the workers in the United States report being paid an hourly wage. While it might seem that people who work a set number of hours a week at a particular hourly wage do not have the luxury of deciding at each minute whether to work or to take leisure time, it is not inappropriate to examine the labor market as if they do. This is because there is flexibility in that some people might be able to choose between part-time and full-time work, and because over a month, a year, or several years, people do choose to put in more or less time on the job. Some people choose occupations that enable them to have more flexibility; many prefer to be self-employed in order to be able to choose whether to put in more or less time on the job. People can also *moonlight,* that is, work an additional job or put in extra hours after their full-time job is completed.

FIGURE 1 The Backward-Bending Labor Supply Curve

As the wage rate rises, people are willing and able to supply more labor, at least up to some high wage rate. A higher wage rate means that the opportunity cost of leisure time increases, so that people will purchase less leisure (will work more). Conversely, as the wage rate rises and people's incomes rise, more of all goods are purchased, including leisure time. As a result, fewer hours of work are supplied. Which of these opposing effects is larger determines whether the labor supply curve slopes upward or downward. The most commonly shaped labor supply curve is one that slopes upward until the wage rate reaches some high level and then, as people choose more leisure time, begins to bend backward.

1.b. From Individual to Market Supply

If the labor supply curve for each individual slopes upward, then the market supply curve (the sum of all individual supply curves) also slopes upward. Even if each individual labor supply curve bends backward at some high wage, it is unlikely that all of the curves will bend backward at the same wage. Not everyone has the same tradeoffs between labor and leisure; not all offer to work at the same wage rate; not all want the same kind of job. As the wage rate rises, some people who choose not to participate in the labor market at lower wages are induced to offer their services for employment at a higher wage. The labor market supply curve slopes up because the number of people who are both willing and able to work rises as the wage rate rises and because the number of hours that each person is willing and able to work rises as the wage rate rises, at least up to some high wage rate.

1.c. Equilibrium

The labor market consists of the labor demand and labor supply curves. We've just discussed labor supply. Labor demand is based on the firm's marginal revenue

Global Business Insight

Hours Spent Working

The average employed person in the United States is now on the job 1,824 hours a year, but the average employed person in seven other nations puts in more time. The nation in which the average annual number of hours worked is largest is Korea, followed by the former Communist bloc countries of Poland, Hungary, and the Czech Republic, and then Greece, Mexico, and New Zealand. The Netherlands, Norway, Germany, Denmark, and France remain the nations with the lowest average annual hours of work, just slightly more than 26 hours a week. In the United States, the average workweek is 35 hours. If you consider that the average vacation time is less than two weeks in the United States and around four weeks in the European countries, the number of hours spent working when not on vacation is 37 in the United States and 29 in Europe.

Average Annual Hours Worked

Source: OECD Productivity Database, July 2005: *http://www.oecd .org/dataoecd/30/13/29860000.xls.*

product curves, as discussed in the previous chapter. The marginal revenue product is the value that the individual employee contributes to the firm. The term *productivity* typically refers to all workers together and means the output per worker or average product. If we talk about the productivity of an individual person, then we are referring to the marginal product, the additional product provided by that individual worker. The intersection of the labor demand and labor supply curves determines the equilibrium wage, W_e, and the quantity of hours people work at this equilibrium wage, Q_e, as shown in Figure 2.

The labor market pictured in Figure 2 suggests that as long as all workers are the same and all jobs are the same, there will be one equilibrium wage. But workers are not all the same, jobs are not all the same, and wages are definitely not all the same. College-educated people earn more than people with only a high school education, and people with a high school education earn more than those with only a grammar school education. Older workers earn more than younger workers. Men earn more than women. Whites earn more than nonwhites.

Chapter 16 The Labor Market

FIGURE 2   **Labor Market Equilibrium**

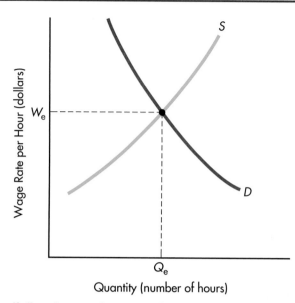

If all workers are the same to firms—that is, if a firm doesn't care whether it hires Roberto, Renee, or Ryan—and if all firms and jobs are the same to workers—that is, if a worker doesn't care whether a job is with IBM or Ted's Hot Dog Stand—then one demand curve and one supply curve define the labor market. The intersection of the two curves is the labor market equilibrium at which the wage rate is determined.

In general, workers will be paid their marginal revenue products—that is, they are paid according to how much they contribute to the profits of their employers. The more productive a worker is, the higher his or her compensation will be, and vice versa. However, in reality, there are large salary differences for people with similar levels of productivity, and people who are vastly different in terms of productivity are paid the same. This occurs because, even though two people generate about the same output, the value that one provides exceeds the value provided by the other. We'll discuss a few cases in the remainder of this chapter.

RECAP

1. An increase in the wage rate causes workers to increase the hours they are willing and able to work and reduce their hours of leisure; at the same time, the wage increase also means that income is higher and more leisure can be purchased. This causes the individual labor supply curve to be backward bending.

2. The labor market supply curve slopes upward because as the wage rate rises, more people are willing and able to work and people are willing and able to work more hours.

3. Equilibrium in the labor market defines the wage rate and the quantity of hours that people work at that wage.

2. Wage Differentials

If people were identical, if jobs were identical, and if information were perfect, there would be no wage differentials.

2. What are compensating wage differentials?

compensating wage differentials: wage differences that make up for the higher risk or poorer working conditions of one job over another

If all workers are the same to a firm—that is, if a firm doesn't care whether it hires Roberto, Renee, or Ryan—and if all firms and jobs are the same to workers—that is, if IBM is no different from Ted's Hot Dog Stand to individual workers—then the one demand for labor and the one supply of labor define the one equilibrium wage. However, firms do differentiate among workers and workers do differentiate among firms and jobs, and so there is more than one labor market and more than one equilibrium wage level. Wages differ from job to job and from person to person. The reasons for wage differences include compensating wage differentials and differences in individual levels of productivity.

2.a. Compensating Wage Differentials

Some jobs are dangerous or unhealthy. For instance, loggers and pilots of small planes used as small crop dusters have the greatest chance of dying on the job, according to Table 1. Other jobs, such as coal mining or garbage collecting, might be considered quite unpleasant. In most market economies, enough people voluntarily choose to work in unpleasant jobs that the jobs get filled. People choose to work in unpleasant occupations because of **compensating wage differentials**—wage differences that make up for the high risk or poor working conditions of a job. Workers mine coal, clean sewers, and weld steel beams fifty stories off the ground because, compared to alternative jobs for which they qualify, these jobs pay well.

Figure 3 illustrates the concept of compensating wage differentials. There are two labor markets, one for a risky occupation and one for a less risky occupation. At each wage rate, fewer people are willing and able to work in the risky occupation than in the less risky occupation. Thus, if the demand curves are identical, the supply curve of the risky occupation will be to the left of the supply curve of the less risky occupation. As a result, the equilibrium wage rate is higher in the risky occupation ($10) than

---

TABLE 1	Most Dangerous Jobs	
Job	**Fatality Rate (per 100,000 employees)**	**Number of Deaths**
Logging workers	92.4	85
Aircraft pilots	92.4	109
Fishers	86.4	38
Iron and steel workers	47.0	31
Garbage collectors	43.2	35
Farmers and ranchers	37.5	307
Roofers	34.9	94
Power line workers	30.0	36
Truckers and driver/sales workers (pizza and newspaper delivery, for example)	27.6	905
Taxi drivers, chauffeurs	24.2	67

Source: U.S. Department of Labor, Bureau of Labor Statistics, *Census of Fatal Occupational Injuries, 2004.*

in the less risky occupation ($5). The difference between the wage in the risky occupation ($10 per hour) and the wage in the less risky occupation ($5 per hour) is an *equilibrium differential*—the compensation that a worker receives for undertaking the greater risk.

Commercial deep-sea divers are exposed to the dangers of drowning and several physiological disorders that result from compression and decompression. They choose this job because they earn about 90 percent more than the average high school graduate. Coal miners in West Virginia and in the United Kingdom are exposed to coal dust, black lung disease, and cave-ins. They choose to work in the mines because the pay is twice what they could earn elsewhere. Wage differentials ensure that deep-sea diving jobs, coal-mining jobs, and jobs in other risky occupations are filled.

Any characteristic that distinguishes one job from another may result in a compensating wage

FIGURE 3   **Compensating Wage Differentials**

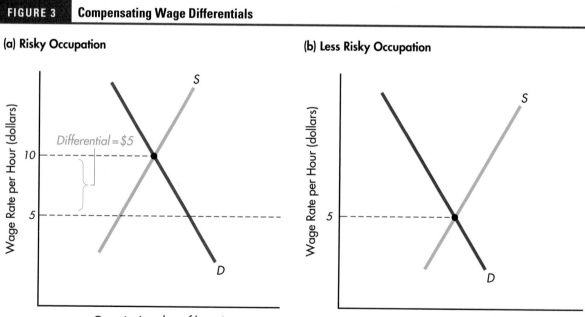

Figure 3(a) shows the market for a risky occupation. Figure 3(b) shows the market for a less risky occupation. At each wage rate, fewer people are willing and able to work in the risky occupation than in the less risky occupation. Thus, the supply curve of the risky occupation is higher (supply is less) than the supply curve of the less risky occupation. As a result, the wage in the risky occupation ($10 per hour) is higher than the wage in the less risky occupation ($5 per hour). The differential ($10 − $5 = $5) is an equilibrium differential—the amount necessary to induce enough people to fill the jobs. If the differential were any higher, more people would flow to the risky occupation, driving wages there down and wages in the less risky occupation up. If the differential were any lower, shortages would prevail in the risky occupation, driving wages there up.

differential. A job that requires a great deal of travel and time away from home usually pays more than a comparable job without the travel requirements because most people find extensive travel and time away from home to be costly. If people were indifferent to extensive travel, there would be no compensating wage differential.

2.b. Human Capital

People differ with respect to their training and abilities. These differences influence the level of wages for two reasons: (1) skilled workers have higher marginal revenue products than unskilled workers, and (2) the supply of skilled workers is smaller than the supply of unskilled workers. As a result, skilled labor generates higher wages than less-skilled labor; in 2005, skilled workers earned on average five times what the average unskilled worker earned ($45 per hour versus $8.50 per hour). In Figure 4, we illustrate the differences between the skilled- and unskilled-labor markets; the skilled-labor market is shown to generate a wage of $15 per hour, and the unskilled-labor market a wage of $8 per hour. The difference exists because the demand for skilled labor relative to the supply of skilled labor is greater than the demand for unskilled labor relative to the supply of unskilled labor.

human capital: skills and training acquired through education and on-the-job training

The expectation of higher income induces people to acquire **human capital**— skills and training acquired through education and job experience. People go to college or vocational school or enter training programs because they expect the training to increase their future income. These activities are *investments in human capital.* Like investments in real capital (machines and equipment), education and training are purchased in order to generate output and income in the future.

2.b.1. Investment in Human Capital   Individuals who go to college or obtain special training expect the costs of going to college or obtaining the training to be

---

FIGURE 4   **Human Capital**

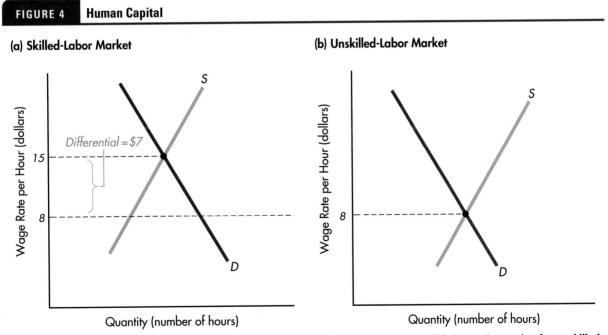

(a) Skilled-Labor Market

(b) Unskilled-Labor Market

Two labor markets are pictured. Figure 4(a) shows the market for skilled labor. Figure 4(b) shows the market for unskilled labor. The smaller supply in the skilled-labor market results in a higher wage there. The equilibrium differential between the wages in the two markets is the return to human capital.

more than offset by the income and other benefits they will obtain in the future. Individuals who acquire human capital reap the rewards of that human capital over time. Figure 5(a) is an illustration of what the income profiles of a worker with a college degree and a worker without a college degree might look like. We might expect the income of the worker without the degree to increase rapidly from the early working years until the worker gets to be about fifty; then income might rise more slowly until the worker reaches retirement age. Until around age thirty, the worker without the college degree clearly enjoys more income than the college-educated worker. The shaded areas represent estimated income lost to the college-educated worker while he or she is attending classes and then gaining work experience. It may take several years after entering the labor market for a college-degree recipient to achieve and then surpass the income level of a worker without a degree, but on average a college-educated person does earn more than someone without a college education. Figure 5(b) shows the ratios of the median income of college- to high school–educated workers. This is called the college income premium. As mentioned in Chapter 1, college-educated people earn more over their lifetimes than people without a college degree.

The economic model of labor suggests that the reason that so many young adults go to college is that college-educated people have better-paying jobs and jobs with greater benefits and security than non-college-educated people.

2.b.2. Choice of a Major

If you decide to attend college, you must then decide what field to major in. Your decision depends in part on the opportunity costs that you face. If your opportunity costs of devoting a great deal of time to a job are high, you may choose to major in a field that is not overly time-consuming. For instance, for several years after college, men and women who have studied to become medical doctors, lawyers, and accountants face long training periods and very long workdays, and they have to devote significant amounts of time each year to staying abreast of new developments in their profession. If you think that you are not likely to be willing to undertake and complete a four- or five-year apprenticeship after college in order to reap the rewards from your expenditure of time and money, then it would be very costly for you to be a premed student or to major in accounting or law. The greater the opportunity costs of any particular occupation, the smaller the number of people who will select that occupation, everything else the same. For instance, it takes more time, money, and effort to become a medical doctor than to become a teacher in the K–12 schools. For this reason, many more people choose to become teachers than choose to become doctors. As a result, there is a wage differential between the two fields that is sufficient to compensate those who become doctors for the extra opportunity costs of a medical career.

2.b.3. Changing Careers

Today it is estimated that one in three people in the U.S. labor force will change careers at least once during their work lives. People choose a major and thus a career on the basis of the information they have at their disposal, family influences, and other related factors. People acquire additional information once they are involved in their occupation, and sometimes their tastes change. They decide to embark on another career path. Who will make such a change? What types of occupations might see more changes?

Relying on the labor market model, we can suggest some answers to these questions. There might be a temptation to say that those who devoted the most effort, time, and money to their first occupation would be the least likely to change. But it is the marginal cost that matters; the effort, time, and money that have been devoted to that first career are gone, whether one remains in the first occupation or moves to another. In the words of the chapter on monopolistic competition and oligopoly,

FIGURE 5   Income Profiles and Educational Level

(a) Profiles

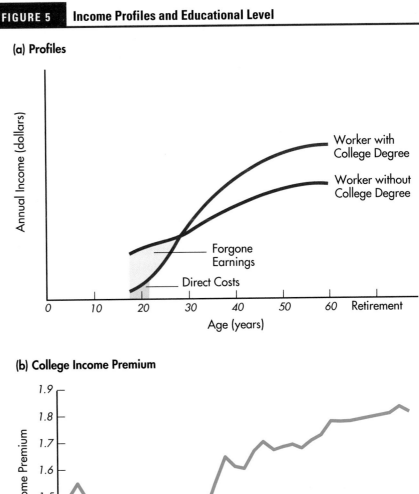

(b) College Income Premium

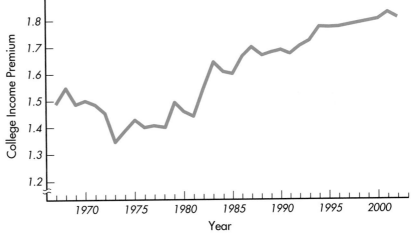

Income rises rapidly until age fifty, then rises more slowly until retirement. Figure 5 compares the income earned by a worker without a degree with the income earned by a college graduate. Figure 5(a) suggests what the actual pattern looks like. Initially, the college graduate gives up substantial income in the form of direct costs and forgone earnings to go to college. Eventually, however, the income of the college graduate exceeds that of the high school-educated worker. Figure 5(b) illustrates the college income premium, the ratio of median income of college-educated to median income of non-college-educated individuals.

Sources: *Statistical Abstract of the United States, 2006; Economic Report of the President, 2003.*

these are sunk, or unrecoverable, costs. Thus, we would expect people who have the greatest expected net gains from a change to make that change. Those who see that they are in dead-end positions or in occupations whose outlook for future income increases is not as good as the outlook in other occupations are more likely to move to a new career. We might expect people not to remain in or enter those professions where the marginal costs of remaining in the profession are high. For instance, those occupations that require continuous time and/or financial commitments if their members are to remain productive, such as the high-tech occupations, the hard sciences, engineering, accounting, or law, might lose relatively more people to areas that do not require similar time and money expenditures, such as management and administration.

2.b.4. The New Economy: Outsourcing

The term the **New Economy** refers to the technological developments that took place in the 1990s. High-technology companies flourished, and the number of jobs demanding technical skills grew. As a result, the distribution of income became wider as the incomes of the skilled rose faster than the incomes of the unskilled. The New Economy is also called the **knowledge economy** because of the large number of new industries whose major product is knowledge itself, such as the software, biotechnology, and information technology hardware industries, and because of the increase in the number of engineers, scientists, programmers, and designers needed to manage or convey information.

The labor market adjusts to these technological changes. New markets are created for highly skilled workers, and old markets are eliminated. The knowledge economy makes it possible for many jobs—ranging from routine clerical jobs like processing insurance claims and handling customer calls to positions in highly skilled occupations like software development and radiology—to be performed anywhere in the world, with the results being transmitted electronically to wherever they are demanded. So if the work can be done as well by another firm at a lower cost, companies will purchase the work from that firm. If firms in India or China can perform the work at a much lower price, companies in the United States and other developed nations will purchase the work from these countries. This is why an increasing number of IT jobs are being done offshore. This process is called **outsourcing** if the firm is located in the same country and **offshoring** if the firm is located in another country. For instance, rather than have a telephone receptionist sitting outside the main office of a firm's headquarters, a firm could pay to have the service provided by an Indian company that could do it at a fourth of the cost. Offshoring eliminates domestic jobs, but it also enables companies to reduce the prices of goods and services.

Outsourcing is not just something that U.S. firms do. Every developed country sends jobs to low-wage nations—India, Mexico, Latin America, and much of Asia. Studies have found that for each dollar a U.S. company spends offshore, it saves 58 cents; this translates into lower prices for the goods it produces. The lower prices enable customers to demand other goods and services and thus create jobs in other areas.

Figure 6 illustrates the dynamic process of offshoring jobs and its impact on prices of goods and services. Initially, the firm is hiring U.S. labor to produce its goods and/or services. The wage rate is indicated as W_{US} in the labor market. In the output market, the firm maximizes profit with its costs ATC_{US} and MC_{US} at the point where $MR = MC_{US}$. The resulting price that the firm charges is P_{US}. If the firm can obtain the same labor services from India at a much lower cost, its cost curves shift down to ATC_{India} and MC_{India}, and it prices its product at the point where $MR = MC_{India}$, or P_{India}, which is much lower than P_{US}. The demand for U.S. workers declines or disappears and is replaced by the demand for Indian

Outsourcing is the process of purchasing services from another firm rather than employing someone to perform those services inside the firm. Outsourcing is called offshoring when the jobs are purchased from a firm in another country.

3. **What is the impact of technological change and the New Economy on workers?**
4. **What is offshoring?**

New Economy: the technological changes shifting emphasis away from manufacturing and toward high technology

knowledge economy: the developments in information processing and transmission

outsourcing: the process in which one firm purchases services from another firm (rather than having the services performed in-house)

offshoring: the process in which one firm purchases services from another firm in another country (rather than having the services performed in-house).

FIGURE 6   **The Dynamics of Offshoring**

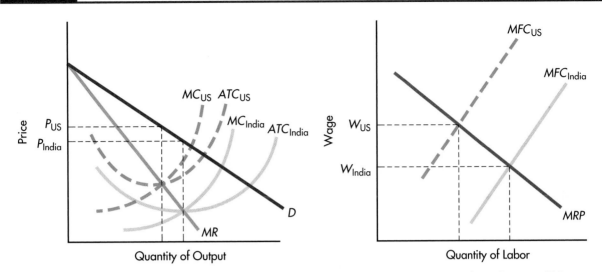

The U.S. firm has costs given by MC_{US} and ATC_{US} when using U.S. workers. These costs come from the cost of labor, W_{US}. The firm maximizes profit at $MR = MC_{US}$ and sells the good at P_{US}. If the firm can obtain the same labor services from India, the firm's cost curves shift down to MC_{India} and ATC_{India}, and the firm maximizes profit at the point where $MR = MC_{India}$, or a price of P_{India}.

workers. The lower prices for the goods and services in the United States enable customers to purchase other goods and services and increase the demand for workers in these other areas.

Today manufacturing jobs are being sent to China and service-sector jobs to India through the dynamic process illustrated in Figure 6. Manufacturing's share of gross domestic product in the United States declined from 27 percent in 1960 to 13 percent in 2005, and the percentage of U.S. workers employed in manufacturing dropped from 28.4 percent to 11 percent over the same period. Workers whose jobs are eliminated must go where they are more highly valued; they may require education or training, but just like any other resource, labor goes where it has the highest value. This is not new or unique to the New Economy. The same thing happened over 100 years ago with agriculture. In 1870, 47.6 percent of total U.S. employment was in agriculture; by 2002, agriculture employed just 1.7 percent.

2.c. The Minimum Wage

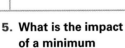

5. What is the impact of a minimum wage law on unskilled labor?

Because the demand for highly skilled workers has increased and the demand for unskilled workers has not kept pace, the inequality of income has become greater. In the 1970s, a high school dropout was 3.5 times more likely to be unemployed than a college graduate; this is now more than 4.5 times. Those with a college degree now make about 74 percent more than those who have only a high school education, a figure that has nearly doubled since 1979. The unemployment rate for those who hold at least a bachelor's degree is 2.7 percent, compared with 8.3 percent for those without a high school diploma. Several politicians and others have argued that the minimum wage (the government-set price floor on wages), should be raised in order to ensure that unskilled workers can make a decent living. A minimum wage has existed in the United States since 1938, when it was set at $.25 per hour. In 2006, the minimum wage was $5.15 per hour. A worker who earns this minimum wage and works 40 hours per week, 50 weeks per year, earns $10,300 per year. Currently, the government defines the poverty level of income for a family of four to be about $19,874.

Today, while about 80 percent of all jobs that are not in agriculture are required to pay at least the minimum wage, some are granted exemptions. States may have their own minimum wage if that wage exceeds the federal level. In 2006, Washington state's minimum wage was the highest at $7.63 per hour. If cities are not happy with the level of either the federal or the state minimum wage, they may set their own. More than 100 cities have their own minimum wage ordinances. The highest effective rate, $8.50, is paid in Santa Fe, New Mexico.

The intention of a minimum wage is to raise the wage rate above the equilibrium level. Let's suppose that government wants a family to earn at least $20,000 per year. This requires an hourly wage of $10 per hour if it is assumed that a worker will spend 40 hours a week for 50 weeks a year at the job. So in Figure 7(a) the minimum wage (W_m) is set at $10, above the equilibrium wage (W) of $4. In markets such as the unskilled-labor markets for agricultural workers, construction workers, and restaurant busboys, the minimum wage would create a labor surplus, as the quantity of jobs offered would be reduced and the quantity of people wanting jobs would increase.

While the minimum wage drives wages up for those who have a job, it hurts the chances of employment for others. Studies show that the minimum wage adversely affects teenagers the most and then affects those with the least skills or value to a firm. An increase in the minimum wage of 1 to 3 percent results in a 10 percent increase in teenage unemployment.

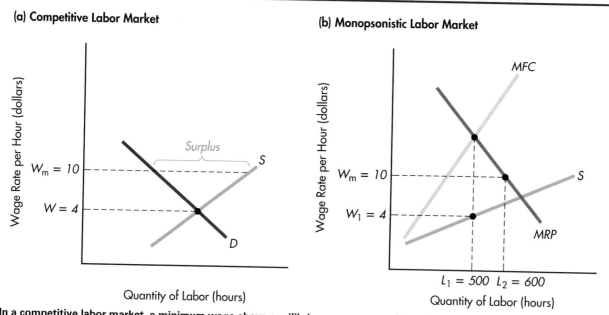

FIGURE 7   The Effect of Minimum Wage

(a) Competitive Labor Market

(b) Monopsonistic Labor Market

In a competitive labor market, a minimum wage above equilibrium causes a surplus—increases unemployment. This is shown in Figure 7(a). In a monopsonistic market, a minimum wage can increase both the wage and the employment rate, as shown in Figure 7(b). The wage rises from W_1 = $4 (the wage rate that the monopsonistic firm wants to pay) to W_m = $10 the legal minimum wage; and the quantity of labor employed rises from L_1 to L_2.

Notice that the market we discuss in Figure 7(a) is a perfectly competitive one. The *MRP* of all firms constitutes the demand for labor, and the *MFC* for all workers is the supply of labor. The minimum wage could have a different effect if just one employer, a monopsony, was hiring unskilled labor. If an employer is a monopsonist, a worker's wage (*W*) is less than *MRP*. The imposition of a minimum wage set at a level that is less than *MRP* but greater than the wage rate that the monopsonistic firm wants to pay may actually increase the level of employment. Recall from the previous chapter that a monopsonist drives up the costs of all other workers when it hire one more—it does not hire a worker at one wage and another identical worker at a different wage. The minimum wage limits the increase in marginal costs, and, as shown in Figure 7(b), at a W_m of $10, employment actually rises. How important is this in the unskilled-labor market? If labor is not mobile and a single firm, such as a large agricultural firm, controls a particular region, say the Yuma valley in Arizona, then could we think of the unskilled-labor market in that region as being monopsonistic?

RECAP

1. Compensating wage differentials are wage differences that make up for the higher risk or poorer working conditions of one job over another. Risky jobs pay more than risk-free jobs, and unpleasant jobs pay more than pleasant jobs.

2. Human capital is the education, training, and experience embodied in an individual.

3. An individual's choice of an occupation reflects a tradeoff between expected opportunity costs and expected benefits. An individual is likely to choose an occupation in which expected benefits outweigh expected opportunity costs.

4. A firm that used to have an accountant but then eliminated the accounting position and purchased its accounting services from another firm, would be said to be *outsourcing*. Outsourcing refers to firm A purchasing from firm B something firm A used to do itself. If firm B is a foreign firm, outsourcing is called *offshoring*.

5. If the market is competitive, increasing the minimum wage benefits those who have and can retain jobs and harms those who are least skilled and have the least value to the firm.

6. If the employer is a monopsonist, a minimum wage set between supply and marginal factor cost can increase employment while increasing wages.

3. Immigration

Approximately 700,000 people cross legally into the United States from Mexico every day to shop and work, returning afterwards to their homes in Mexico. About 3,500 people cross the border *illegally* every day, and many of them don't return to Mexico. In the United States, the illegal population from Mexico is estimated to be between 6 and 7 million. Another 3 to 4 million undocumented aliens living in the United States are from other Latin American countries and Asia.

Why do so many people leave their home countries and migrate to the United States? What societal effects do immigrants, and especially illegal immigrants, have? Answers to these questions are varying and controversial. But since the effect of immigration on labor markets depends on the demand for and supply of labor, it is not so controversial.

3.a. The United States Is a Nation of Immigrants

In Figure 8 you can see the pattern of legal immigration to the United States from about 1850. It has not happened at a steady pace, but instead has been cyclical, with peaks in the number of people coming to the United States from other countries occurring in 1870, 1920, and 2004–2005.

The amount of immigration relative to the existing population is also shown in Figure 8. The total foreign-born population as a percentage of the total U.S. population declined from a peak in 1880 and 1910 of about 15 percent to a low of 5 percent around 1970 and has risen since.

3.b. Why Immigrate?

People leave their home country and go to another country to live primarily because they seek a higher quality of life. Their own country may be politically repressive or economically stagnant, or there may be no upward mobility among income classes in their home country. For instance, most immigrants to the United States in the 1800s and 1900s were from northern and western Europe. Economic events like the potato famine in Ireland, recessions in the United Kingdom and western Europe, and religious persecution led to migrant flows to the United States. Beginning about 1950, immigration to the United States switched from being primarily from Europe to being mostly from Latin America and Asia. The change was caused by changes in U.S. immigration policy and the relatively more severe political and economic problems in the Asian and Latin American countries.

| FIGURE 8 | Foreign-Born Population of the United States |

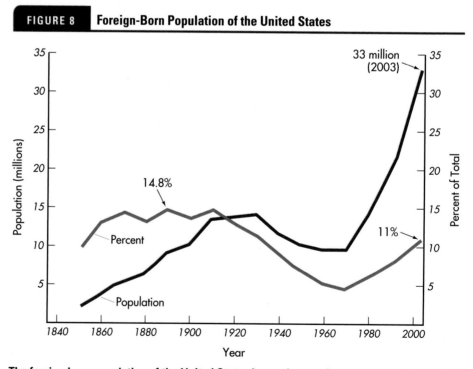

The foreign-born population of the United States in numbers and percentages is shown for the period from 1860 to 2000. The amounts (total numbers and percentages) rose until the early 1900s, then declined until the late 1960s and have risen since. *Source:* "Foreign-Born Population of the United States," *Current Population Survey, March 2004 and previous years;* http://www.census.gov/population/www/socdemo/foreign/ppl-176.html.

For example, the greatest number of recent immigrants to the United States comes from Mexico. Compare incomes—the per capita income in the United States is $36,000, and in Mexico it is $9,000. These are average figures, but just for perspective, a single person in the United States earning $9,000 would be legally considered to be in poverty; at the minimum wage of $5.15 per hour, a person would earn $10,300 working 40 hours a week, 50 weeks a year.

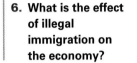

6. What is the effect of illegal immigration on the economy?

3.b.1. Why Immigrate Illegally?

As Figure 9 shows, illegal immigration is a significant percentage of immigration and has been growing rapidly in the past few years. However, fewer than half of illegal immigrants cross the nation's borders clandestinely; most illegal immigrants enter legally and overstay their visas.

For much of U.S. history, there were few restrictions on immigration, so illegal immigration was not an issue. The first restriction was the Chinese Exclusion Act of 1882. Chinese immigrants had been brought in to work during the labor shortages of the 1840s, but they became increasingly disliked by the native unskilled laborers. The Chinese Exclusion Act suspended immigration of Chinese laborers for 10 years, removed the right of Chinese entrants to be naturalized, and provided for the deportation of Chinese who were in the United States illegally. It was not until 1943 that the Chinese exclusion laws were repealed. In 1924, the United States established a quota system specifying how many people from each country could immigrate to the United States each year. The law placed a ceiling of 150,000 per year on immigrants from Europe, completely barred immigrants from Japan, and based the admission of immigrants from other countries on the proportion of people of that national origin that were present in the United States as measured by the 1890 census. In 1965, the national origins quota system was

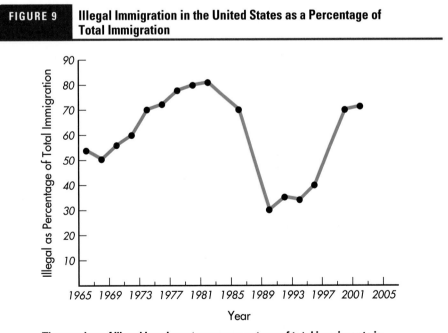

FIGURE 9 | Illegal Immigration in the United States as a Percentage of Total Immigration

The number of illegal immigrants as a percentage of total immigrants is shown for the period 1965–2004. The percentage rose until the early 1980s, then declined until the mid-1990s and rose until the current period.

Source: Jeffrey S. Passel and Roberto Suro, Pew Hispanic Center, Rise, Peak and Decline: Trends in U.S. Immigration 1992–2004.

replaced with a uniform limit of 20,000 immigrants per country for all countries outside the Western Hemisphere and a limit on immigration from the Western Hemisphere (most notably from Mexico). The Immigration Reform and Control Act of 1986 (IRCA) was the first to address the issue of illegal immigration. It introduced penalties for employers who knowingly hire illegal immigrants.

The United States currently admits about 700,000 immigrants annually as legal ("green card") residents who will be eligible to apply for citizenship after living in the United States for five years. Only about 110,000 of those receiving green cards do not have family members who are U.S. citizens. Of these, about 65,000 are highly skilled workers on H1-B visas, and about 44,000 are low-skilled workers.

To understand what these developments mean, we need to look at the unskilled labor market as depicted in Figure 10. The equilibrium wage is $15 per hour if only legal immigrants and natives are considered. Now, what happens when illegal immigration takes place? The supply of low-skilled labor rises—the supply curve shifts out—and the equilibrium wage drops to $9 per hour. At $9, fewer natives choose to work—the quantity supplied of native workers declines from A to B. The shortage of native workers, B to C, is made up by illegal immigrants.

Have you heard the claim that illegal immigrants take jobs that Americans won't take? Those making this claim are focusing on the distance from B to C in Figure 10. What they are not including in their discussion is the distance from A to B caused by the lower wage. What the claim actually should say is that illegal immigrants take jobs that Americans won't take at the wage rate for these jobs. If the wage rate was $15, then enough native workers would be willing to work to match the quantity demanded. Yet, that higher cost has economic effects on the goods and services produced by this unskilled labor.

| FIGURE 10 | Unskilled Labor Market and Illegal Immigration |

Without illegal immigrants, the equilibrium wage is $15, and the equilibrium quantity is quantity 0–Q_1. With illegal immigration, the supply increases and the wage rate declines to $9. At $9, there would be a shortage of B − C if no illegal immigrants supplied labor.

Labor is a resource—it is used to produce goods and services, and the wages and salaries provided to workers are part of the costs of doing business. So, when the cost of labor declines, the costs of doing business also decline. A typical firm will produce more and earn greater profits when its costs decline. As firms increase their output and new firms enter the business, the market supply of the products being produced by the unskilled labor will rise, and the market price of the good or service will decline. This is what happens with illegal immigration. Illegal immigration has reduced costs in certain businesses—construction, restaurants, agriculture, meatpacking, textiles, and poultry production in particular. The lower costs lead to lower prices for houses and buildings, child care, housekeeping, gardening, produce, poultry, meats, and restaurants.

3.c. Immigration Policy

Illegal immigration in the United States is one of the topics of greatest concern to the American public. In 2005, the costs and benefits of illegal immigration were examined in a number of studies. The costs included the effects of illegal immigration on unskilled workers, and the benefits included the lower prices for some goods and services. Other costs were the property damage caused by immigrants sneaking into the United States and the expenditures on health care for immigrants at emergency clinics and hospitals, which are legally unable to deny care to anyone or to inquire whether someone is a legal resident. Another cost was the expenditures on public education for the children of immigrants who attended public schools. Still another cost involved burglaries and other crimes committed by illegal immigrants.

Benefits created by the illegal immigrants include the taxes they pay. It is estimated that about three-fourths of illegal immigrants pay social security and other withholding taxes, but since an illegal immigrant must have fake identification and social security numbers, any payments made to social security will not be assigned to a potential recipient. Instead, when the social security number does not match the SSA's records, the payments go into a slush fund called the "suspense file." Since 2002, the suspense file has been growing by at more than $60 billion a year. The net effect of these costs and benefits varies according to the study, but most studies conclude that the first generation of illegal immigrants imposes costs that exceed the benefits they create, but every generation thereafter creates more benefits than it costs.

Those most affected by the benefits want immigrants to have a way to take a job, while those most affected by the costs want immigrants kept out of the country. Views on illegal immigration range from using the military to guard the borders to support for the McCain-Kennedy-Flake bill, which would provide a form of amnesty for illegal aliens already in the United States and set up a guest worker program.

3.c.1. Enforcement of Borders
As illegal immigration has increased, so have government expenditures on border enforcement. Between 1986 and 2005, the U.S. Border Patrol more than tripled in size, and the hours spent patrolling increased more than eight times. In addition to the Border Patrol, the U.S. Customs Service and the Immigration and Naturalization Service have intensified their inspections, and the Drug Enforcement Agency (DEA) and the Bureau of Alcohol, Tobacco, and Firearms (BATF) have increased their presence. Border apprehensions increased from 200,000 in 1970 to more than 2 million in 2004, and yet the apprehension rate—apprehensions per total illegal crossings—declined because the number of crossings had increased more quickly.

What would be the effects of more intense border enforcement? In Figure 10, the supply curve would shift in to the "Supply Without Illegal Immigrants" curve as a result of the border enforcement. With fewer illegal immigrants, in order to hire people to work in restaurants and agricultural fields and other unskilled areas, firms would have to pay more. Suppose the wage is driven up to $15. The firms that before the increased enforcement had employed the illegal unskilled workers would now have to pay more; their costs of doing business would rise. Profits would decline, with the result that those that remained in business would not produce as much, and fewer firms would be in business. The market supply of the products created by unskilled labor would decline, and the prices of these products would rise.

4. Discrimination

7. Are discrimination and freely functioning markets compatible?

What would you think if you found out that women earn only about 75 percent of what men earn, that African Americans earn only about 60 percent of what whites earn, or that there are pay differentials among Hispanics, Asians, African Americans, and whites? Would you think that this result was evidence of discrimination? Could the differentials be explained in any other way? We'll provide some answers in this section.

4.a. Definition of Discrimination

discrimination:
prejudice that occurs when factors unrelated to marginal revenue product affect the wages or jobs that are obtained

Is **discrimination** present when there is prejudice, or just when prejudice has harmful results? Consider a firm with two branch offices. One office employs only African Americans; the other, only whites. Workers in both branches are paid the same wages and have the same opportunities for advancement. Is discrimination occurring?

Is a firm that provides extensive training to employees discriminating when it prefers to hire young workers who are likely to stay with the firm long enough for it to recoup the training costs? Is a university economics department that has no African American faculty members guilty of discrimination if African American economists constitute only 1 percent of the profession? Would your answer change if the department could show that it advertised job openings widely and made the same offers to African Americans and whites? Clearly, discrimination is a difficult subject to define and measure.

From an economist's viewpoint, a worker's value in the labor market depends on the factors affecting the marginal revenue product. When a factor that is unrelated to marginal revenue product acquires a positive or negative value in the labor market, discrimination is occurring. In Figure 11, if D_M is the demand for males and D_F is the demand for females, and if males and females have identical marginal revenue products, then the resulting wage differences can be attributed to discrimination. Race, gender, age, physical handicaps, religion, sexual preference, and ethnic heritage are factors that can take on positive or negative values in the labor market and yet are unrelated to marginal revenue products.

4.b. Theories of Discrimination

Wage differentials based on race or gender pose a theoretical problem for economists because the labor market model attributes differences in wages to demand and supply differences that depend on productivity and the labor-leisure tradeoff. How can economists account for different pay scales for men and women, or for one race versus another, in the absence of differences in marginal productivity

---

FIGURE 11   Discrimination

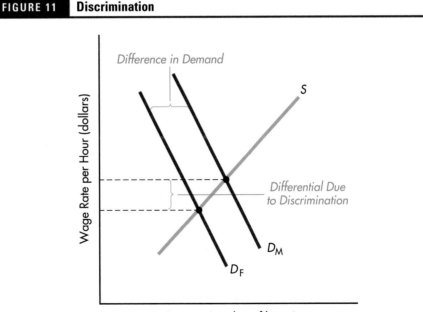

Quantity (number of hours)

The curve D_M is the demand for males, and D_F is the demand for females. The two groups of workers are identical except in gender. The greater demand and the higher wage rate for males, even though males and females are equally productive, are due to discrimination.

---

between sexes or races? They identify discrimination as the cause of the differences, even though they find discrimination difficult to rationalize because it is costly to those who discriminate.

In the freely functioning labor market, there is a profit to be made from *not* discriminating; therefore, discrimination should not exist. But, because discrimination *does* exist, economists have attempted to find plausible explanations for it. They have identified two sources of labor market discrimination. The first is *personal prejudice:* employers, fellow employees, or customers dislike associating with workers of a given race or sex. The second is *statistical discrimination:* employers project certain perceived group characteristics onto individuals. Economists tend to argue that personal prejudice is not consistent with a market economy but have acknowledged that statistical discrimination can coexist with a market economy.

Discrimination might occur if employers attempt to hire only certain kinds of workers, employees attempt to work only with certain kinds of coworkers, or customers attempt to purchase goods and services only from certain kinds of workers. Discrimination is costly in that either less productive employees are used or more expensive but not more productive employees are used.

4.b.1. Personal Prejudice   Certain groups in a society could be precluded from higher-paying jobs or from jobs that provide valuable human capital by personal prejudice on the part of employers, fellow workers, or customers.

Employer Prejudice   If two workers have identical marginal revenue products and one worker is less expensive than the other, firms will want to hire the lower-cost worker. If they do otherwise, profits will be lower than they need to be. Suppose white males and others are identically productive, but managers prefer white males. Then white males will be more expensive than women and minorities, and hiring white males will lower profits.

Under what conditions will lower profits as a result of personal prejudice be acceptable? Perhaps a monopoly firm can forgo some of its monopoly profit in order to satisfy the manager's personal prejudices, or perhaps firms that do not maximize profits can indulge in personal preferences. However, for profit-maximizing firms selling their goods in the market structures of perfect competition, monopolistic competition, or oligopoly, personal prejudice will mean a loss of profit unless all rivals also discriminate. Could firms form a cartel to discriminate? Recall from the discussion of oligopoly that cartels do not last long—there is an incentive to cheat—unless an entity like the government sanctions and enforces the cartel.

In the United States, well-meaning legislation intended to protect women actually created a situation in which women were denied access to training and education and thus were not able to gain the human capital necessary to compete for high-skill, high-paying jobs. Until the 1960s, women were barred from jobs by legislation that attempted to protect them from heavy labor or injury. In reality, this legislation precluded women from obtaining certain kinds of human capital. Without this human capital, a generation or more of women were unable to obtain many high-paying jobs.

Worker Prejudice   Workers may not want to associate with other workers of different races or sexes. White males may resist taking orders from females or sharing responsibility with a member of a minority group. White male workers who have these discriminatory preferences will tend to quit employers who employ women or minorities on a nondiscriminatory basis.

The worker prejudice explanation of discrimination assumes that white males are willing to accept lower-paying positions in order to avoid working with anyone other than a white male. Such discrimination is costly to those who discriminate.

Consumer Prejudice   Customers may prefer to be served by white males in some situations and by minorities or women in others. If their preferences for white males extend to high-paying jobs such as physician and lawyer and their preferences for women and minorities are confined to lower-paying jobs like maid, nurse, and flight attendant, then women and minorities will be forced into occupations that work to their disadvantage.

This explanation of discrimination assumes that consumers are willing to pay higher prices in order to be served by a person of a specific race or gender. In certain circumstances and during certain periods of time, this may be true; but over wide geographic areas or across different nations and over long periods of time, consumer prejudice does not appear to be a very likely explanation of discrimination.

Be sure you recognize that economists are not saying that discrimination based on personal prejudice never occurs. They are saying that when it does occur, it costs the person doing the discriminating.

4.b.2. Statistical Discrimination   Discrimination that is not related to personal prejudices can occur because of a lack of information. Employers must try to predict the potential productivity of job applicants, but rarely do they know what a worker's actual productivity will be. Often, the only information that is available when they hire someone is information that may be imperfectly related to productivity in general and may not apply to a particular person at all. Reliance on indicators of productivity such as education, experience, age, and test scores may keep some very good people from getting a job and may result in the hiring of some unproductive people. This is called **statistical discrimination.**

statistical discrimination: discrimination that results when an indicator of group performance is incorrectly applied to an individual member of the group

Suppose two types of workers apply for a word-processing job: those who can process 80 words per minute and those who can process only 40 words per minute. The problem is that these actual productivities are unknown to the employer. The employer can observe only the results of a five-minute word-processing test that is given to all applicants. How can the employer decide who is lucky or unlucky on the test and who can actually process 80 words per minute? Suppose the employer discovers that applicants from a particular vocational college, the DeVat School, are taught to perform well on preemployment tests, but that their overall performance as employees is the same as that of the rest of the applicants—some do well and some do not. The employer might decide to reject all applicants from DeVat because the good and bad ones can't be differentiated. Is the employer discriminating against DeVat? The answer is yes. The employer is using statistical discrimination.

Let's extend this example to race and gender. Suppose that, on average, minorities with a high school education are discovered to be less productive than white males with a high school education because of differences in the quality of the schools they attend. An employer using this information when making a hiring decision might prefer to hire a white male. Statistical discrimination can cause a systematic preference for one group over another even if some individuals in each group have the same measured characteristics.

4.c. Occupational Segregation

crowding: forcing members of a group into certain kinds of occupations

occupational segregation: the separation of jobs by sex

Statistical discrimination and imperfect information can lead to **crowding**—forcing women and members of minority groups into occupations where they are unable to obtain the human capital necessary to compete for high-paying jobs. Today, even in the United States and other industrialized nations, some occupations are considered women's jobs and other occupations are considered men's jobs. This separation of jobs by sex is called **occupational segregation.**

One reason for occupational segregation is differences in the human capital acquired by males and females. Much of the human capital portion of the discrepancy between men and women is due to childbearing. Data suggest that marriage and children handicap women's efforts to earn as much as men. Many women leave the labor market during pregnancy, at childbirth, or when their children are young. These child-related interruptions are damaging to subsequent earnings because three out of four births occur to women before the age of thirty, the period in which men are gaining the training and experience that lead to higher earnings later in life. Second, even when mothers stay in the labor force, responsibility for children frequently constrains their choice of job: they accept lower wages in exchange for shorter or more flexible hours, a location near home, limited out-of-town travel, and the like. Third, women have a disproportionate responsibility for child care and often have to make sacrifices that men do not have to make. For instance, when a couple has a young child, the woman is more likely than the man to be absent from work, even when the man and woman have equal levels of education and wages.

Perhaps most important of all, because most female children are expected to become mothers, they have been less likely than male children to acquire marketable human capital while in school. In the past, this difference was reflected in the choice of a curriculum in primary and secondary schools, in a college major, and in the reluctance of females to pursue graduate school training or to undergo the long hours and other rigors characteristic of apprenticeships in medicine, law, business, and other financially rewarding occupations. Females were channeled

Economic Insight

Pay and Performance

In 2004, Tiger Woods earned over $80 million. Although he was the highest-paid athlete that year, most professional athletes earn pretty good incomes; the ten highest-paid athletes earned more than $15 million each. This seems small compared to the income of some celebrities: Oprah Winfrey pulled in $215 million; Mel Gibson made $185 million, and many others exceeded $90 million. Why do these people make so much money? One explanation is called the superstar effect.

If you own a firm and an employee generates a huge income for you, you'd be willing to pay that employee a high salary. Similarly, if an athlete is bringing in fans or a performer is increasing the numbers of viewers, the owners of the firm that employs that person will willingly pay him or her a high salary. So athletes, celebrities, and TV performers are paid a lot because they make their employers lots of money. Yet, some athletes make a lot more money than other athletes and a few celebrities make a lot more money than others, even though their appeal to the public is not much different. The reason is that the public has limited time to devote to watching sports or television shows. As a result, they watch the best, even if the best is only slightly better than others.

Sometimes small differences in ability translate into huge differences in compensation. The playing ability of the top tennis players or golfers is not much better than the playing ability of the players ranked between forty and fifty. Nonetheless, the differences in compensation and in the demand for the top performers are incredibly large. If you watch golf tournaments, you will notice that huge throngs surround Tiger Woods, while lesser-known players play the game without the attention of adoring fans. In a similar manner, people choosing among television shows must select one over others, so if Oprah Winfrey is just slightly preferred to other personalities, she will draw thousands more viewers than a competing personality. The demand for the superstars is huge relative to the demand for the lesser-ranked players or personalities.

This effect may also explain big pay differences among attorneys, physicians, and even economists. Two lawyers of relatively equal ability may earn significantly different fees, or two economic consultants with apparently similar abilities may earn vastly different consulting fees. Consider the economist who offers advice to lawyers in cases involving firm behavior. The outcome of a lawsuit filed against a firm might involve billions of dollars. Even if the differences between economists are very small, if hiring the better economist means a win, then the better economist will receive huge compensation relative to the lesser economist. A $40 billion victory means that the value of the better economist is significantly greater than the value of the lesser economist.

into languages, typing, and home economics, while males were channeled into mechanical drawing, shop, chemistry, and physics. This situation is changing, but the remnants of the past continue to influence the market. Since the late 1970s, about half of all law school classes and about one-third of medical school classes have been female. Nonetheless, mostly females major in languages, literature, education, and home economics, while mostly males major in physics, mathematics, chemistry, and engineering.

If new female entrants into the labor force have human capital equal to the human capital of new male entrants and thus greater than the human capital of females who are already in the labor force, then the average human capital and wages of females will rise. But even though the wage gap between males and females is decreasing, a gap will continue to exist because the average male in the labor force has more marketable human capital than the average female. The average rate of pay of males will continue to exceed that of females.

4.d. Wage Differentials and Government Policies

Not until the 1960s did wage disparities and employment practices become a major public policy issue in the United States. In 1963, the Equal Pay Act outlawed separate pay scales for men and women performing similar jobs, and Title VII of the 1964 Civil Rights Act prohibited all forms of discrimination in employment.

Prior to the 1960s, sex discrimination was officially sanctioned by so-called protective labor laws, which limited the total hours that women were allowed to work and prohibited them from working at night, lifting heavy objects, and working during pregnancy. The argument was that women were not strong enough to do certain jobs. Interestingly, if you look at the supporters of these laws, they were the people who worked in the jobs that women were being kept out of. With the Civil Rights Act of 1964, it became unlawful for any employer to discriminate on the basis of race, color, religion, sex, or national origin. Unions also were forbidden from excluding anyone on the basis of those five categories. Historically, it had been very difficult for members of racial minorities to obtain admission into unions representing workers in the skilled trades. This exclusion prevented members of racial minorities from obtaining the human capital necessary to compete for higher-paying jobs.

The Civil Rights Act applied only to actions after its effective date, July 1, 1965. It also permitted exceptions in cases where religion, sex, or national origin is a bona fide occupational qualification reasonably necessary to the normal operation of a business. This qualification might apply to certain jobs in religious organizations, for example. In addition, the act permits an employer to differentiate wages and other employment conditions on the basis of a bona fide seniority system, provided that such differences are not the result of an intention to discriminate. As a result of these exceptions, the Civil Rights Act has had neither as large nor as quick an impact on wage and job differentials as many had anticipated. It has, however, led to a clearer definition of discrimination.

disparate treatment: different treatment of individuals because of their race, sex, color, religion, or national origin

Two standards, or tests, of discrimination have evolved from court cases: disparate treatment and disparate impact. **Disparate treatment** means treating individuals differently because of their race, sex, color, religion, or national origin. The difficulty created by this standard is that personnel policies that appear to be neutral because they ignore race, gender, and so on may nevertheless continue the effects of past discrimination. For instance, a seniority system that fires first the last person hired will protect those who were historically favored in hiring and training practices. Similarly, a practice of hiring by word of mouth will perpetuate past discrimination if current employees are primarily of one race or sex.

This concern with perpetuating past discrimination led to the second standard, **disparate impact.** Under this standard, it is the result of different treatment, not the motivation, that matters. Thus, statistical discrimination is illegal under the impact standard even though it is not illegal under the treatment standard.

4.d.1. Comparable Worth

The persistent wage gap between men and women in particular, but also between white males and minorities, has prompted well-meaning reformers to seek a new remedy for eliminating the gap—laws requiring companies to offer equal pay for jobs of comparable worth. **Comparable worth** is a catchword for the idea that pay ought to be determined by job characteristics rather than by supply and demand and that people in jobs with comparable requirements should receive comparable wages.

To identify jobs of comparable worth, employers would be required to evaluate all of the different jobs in their firms, answering questions such as these: What level of formal education is needed? How much training is necessary? Is previous experience needed? What skills are required? How much supervision is required? Is the work dangerous? Are working conditions unpleasant? By assigning point values to the answers, employers could create job classifications based on job characteristics and could pay comparable wages for jobs with comparable "scores." A firm employing both secretaries and steelworkers, for example, would determine the wages for these jobs by assessing job characteristics. If the assessment showed that secretaries' work was comparable to that of steelworkers, then the firm would pay secretaries and steelworkers comparable wages.

Proponents of comparable worth claim that market-determined wages are inappropriate because, as a result of statistical discrimination, team production, and personal prejudice, the market is unable to assess marginal products. They argue that mandating a comparable worth system would minimize wage differentials resulting from statistical discrimination and occupational segregation, and they charge that a freely functioning market will continue to misallocate pay.

Opponents of comparable worth argue that interfering with the functioning of the labor market will lead to shortages in some occupations and excess supplies in others. For instance, Figure 12 shows two markets for university professors, a market for computer science professors and a market for English professors. The supply and demand conditions in the two markets determine a wage for English professors that is less than the wage for computer science professors. The wage differential exists even though professors in both disciplines are required to have a Ph.D. and have essentially the same responsibilities.

Advocates of comparable worth would say that the two groups of professors should earn the same wage, the wage of the computer science professors, W_{CS}. But at this wage there would be a surplus of English professors, $QE_2 - QE_1$. The higher wage would cause the university to reduce the number of English professors it employs, from QE to QE_1. The net effect of comparable worth would be to reduce the number of English professors employed, but to increase the wages of those who were employed. The policy would also have a detrimental effect in the future. The wage would send an incorrect signal to current college students. It would tell them to remain in English instead of forgoing English for computer science.

Comparable worth has not fared well in U.S. courtrooms. On the whole, U.S. federal courts have not accepted the notion that unequal pay for comparable jobs violates existing employment discrimination law. Perhaps not surprisingly, therefore, the concept has made little headway in the private sector. It has had greater success in the public sector at the local and state levels. In Colorado Springs, San Jose, and Los Angeles and in Iowa, Michigan, New York, and Minnesota, pay adjustments

FIGURE 12   **Comparable Worth**

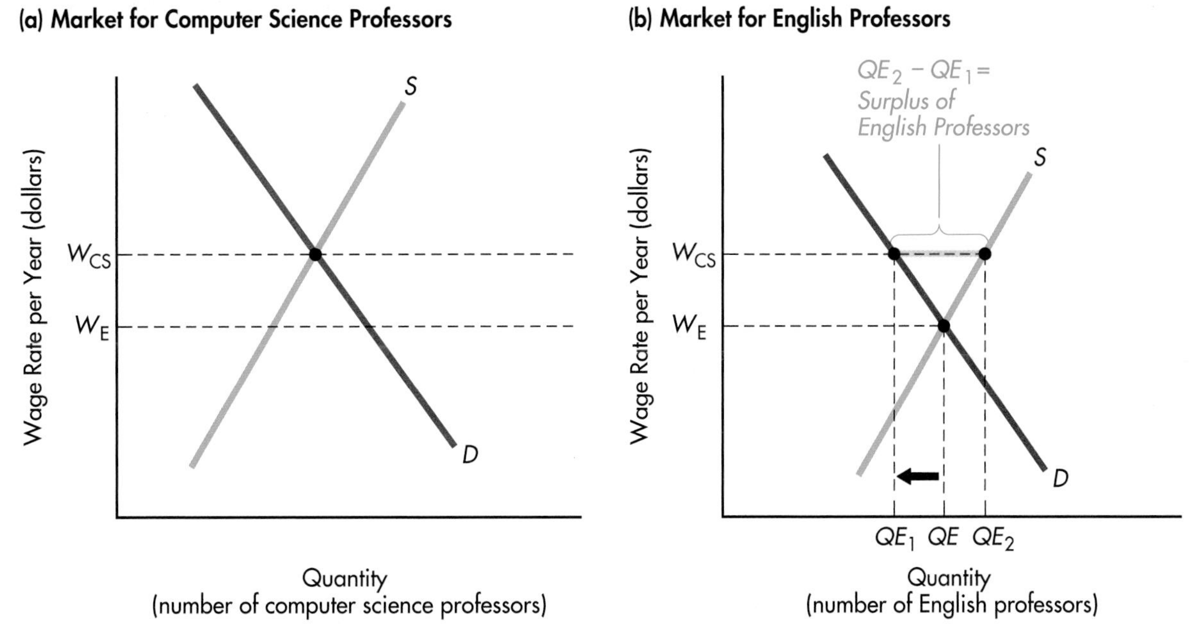

(a) Market for Computer Science Professors

(b) Market for English Professors

Two markets are shown, a market for computer science professors and a market for English professors. Demand and supply conditions determine that the wages for computer science professors are higher than the wages for English professors. Proponents of comparable worth might argue that the wages of both groups of professors should be equal to the higher wages of computer science professors, since the requirements and responsibilities of the two jobs are virtually identical. However, the effect of imposing a higher wage in the market for English professors, W_{CS}, is to create a surplus of English professors, $QE_2 - QE_1$. In addition, the higher wage sends the signal to current college students that majoring in English will generate the same expected income as majoring in computer science. Students who might have studied computer science turn to English. In the future, an excess of English professors remains and even grows, while the number of computer science professors shrinks.

have been made on the basis of comparable worth. More than two-thirds of the state governments have begun studies to determine whether the compensation of state workers reflects the worth of their jobs. Why has comparable worth had more success in the government sector? State governments suffer from the problem of team production, and if personal prejudice is to occur, it is more likely to occur in nonprofit organizations such as government, where firms do not employ to the profit-maximizing point where $MFC = MRP$. Thus, it is in the state, local, and federal governments that comparable worth can be an effective policy. Comparable worth was adopted nationwide in Australia in the early 1970s, and aspects of it have arisen in parts of the United Kingdom.

RECAP

1. Discrimination occurs when factors unrelated to marginal physical product acquire a positive or negative value in the labor market.

2. Earnings disparities may exist for a number of reasons, including personal prejudice, statistical discrimination, and human capital differentials. Human capital differentials may exist because of occupational choice, statistical discrimination, or unequal opportunities to acquire human capital.

3. There are two general classes of discrimination theories: prejudice theory and statistical theory. Prejudice theory claims that employers, workers, and consumers express their personal prejudices by, respectively, earning lower profits, accepting lower wages, and paying higher prices. Statistical discrimination theory asserts that firms have imperfect information and must rely on general indicators of marginal physical product when they pay wages and hire people, and that reliance on these general indicators may create a pattern of discrimination.

4. Occupational segregation is the separation of jobs by sex. Some jobs are filled primarily by women, and other jobs are filled primarily by men.

5. The first national antidiscrimination law was the Civil Rights Act of 1964. It forbade firms from discriminating on the basis of sex, race, color, religion, or national origin.

6. Two tests of discrimination have evolved from court cases. According to the disparate treatment standard, it is illegal to intentionally treat individuals differently because of their race, sex, color, religion, or national origin. According to the disparate impact standard, it is the result, not the intention, of actions that is illegal.

7. Comparable worth is the idea that jobs should be evaluated on the basis of a number of characteristics, and that all jobs receiving the same evaluation should receive the same pay, regardless of demand and supply conditions. Proponents argue that comparable worth is a solution to a market failure problem. Opponents argue that it will create surpluses and shortages in labor markets.

Summary

1. Are people willing to work more hours for higher wages?

- The individual labor supply curve is backward bending because at some high wage, people choose to enjoy more leisure rather than to earn additional income. *§1.a*

2. What are compensating wage differentials?

- Equilibrium in the labor market defines the wage and quantity of hours worked. If all workers and all jobs were identical, then one wage would prevail. However, because jobs and workers differ, there are different wages. *§1.c*

- A compensating wage differential exists in situations where a higher wage is determined in one labor market than in another because of differences in job characteristics. *§2.a*

- Human capital is the training, education, and skills that people acquire. Human capital increases productivity. Because acquiring human capital takes time and money, the necessity of obtaining human capital for some jobs reduces the supply of labor to those jobs. *§2.b*

3. What is the impact of technological change and the New Economy on workers?

- The New Economy is the technological changes occurring in information and knowledge transmission and development. It increases the demand for skilled workers and reduces that for unskilled workers. *§2.a*

4. What is offshoring?

- The ability to transmit information quickly almost anywhere in the world enables firms to seek out the least costly resources wherever they are located, and thus to have many jobs performed at a lower price in a less developed country, with the output being transmitted back to the firm in a developed country. This is called offshoring. *§2.b*

- The ability to use offshoring to produce goods and services at lower prices enables firms to reduce prices on these goods and services. *§2.b*

5. What is the impact of a minimum wage law on unskilled labor?

- The minimum wage in the United States is currently $5.15 per hour. States and individual cities can set a higher wage. *§2.c*

- The objective of a minimum wage law is to ensure that the poor are able to earn a decent living. *§2.c*

- The effect of a minimum wage is to create a labor surplus because it reduces the quantity of jobs offered and increases the number of people who want a job. A minimum wage has an effect only if it is higher than the equilibrium wage, thereby acting as a wage floor. *§2.c*

- Should a labor market be monopsonistic, a minimum wage could increase employment because it reduces the marginal cost of hiring another worker. *§2.c*

6. What is the effect of illegal immigration on the economy?

- It is primarily those without skills who immigrate illegally. U.S. immigration policy allows only about 65,000 skilled workers to obtain visas each year. Only about 45,000 unskilled workers can obtain legal entry. All other workers must enter the United States illegally. *§3.b*

- An increase in unskilled labor causes the wage rate of unskilled labor to decline. This reduces the willingness to work for many native workers who would have earned more had there been no illegal immigration. *§3.b*

- The lower costs that result from illegal immigration carry over into the prices of the goods and services produced by illegal immigrants. Without illegal immigra-

tion, prices of agricultural products, poultry, meat, textiles, and home services would be as much as 25 percent higher. *§3.b*

7. Are discrimination and freely functioning markets compatible?

- Earnings disparities may result from discrimination, occupational choice, human capital differences, educational opportunity differences, age, and immigration. *§4.a, 4.c*

- Discrimination occurs when some factor that is not related to marginal revenue product affects the wage rate someone receives. *§4.a*

- There are two general types of discrimination—personal prejudice and statistical discrimination. *§ 4.b*

- Personal prejudice is costly to those who demonstrate the prejudice and should not last in a market economy. For it to last, some restrictions on the functioning of markets must exist. *§4.b.1*

- Statistical discrimination is the result of imperfect information and can occur as long as information is imperfect. *§4.b.2*

- Occupational segregation exists when some jobs are held mainly by one group in society and other jobs are held by other groups. A great deal of occupational segregation exists between males and females in the United States. *§4.c*

Key Terms

backward-bending labor supply curve *§1.a*

compensating wage differentials *§2.a*

human capital *§2.b*

New Economy *§2.b.4*

knowledge economy *§2.b.4*

outsourcing *§2.b.4*

offshoring *§2.b.4*

discrimination *§4.a*

statistical discrimination *§4.b.2*

crowding *§4.c*

occupational segregation *§4.c*

disparate treatment *§4.d*

disparate impact *§4.d*

comparable worth *§4.d.1*

Exercises

1. What could account for a backward-bending labor supply curve?

2. What is human capital? Is a college degree considered to be human capital?

3. Define equilibrium in the labor market. Illustrate equilibrium on a graph. Illustrate the situation in which there are two types of labor, skilled and unskilled.

4. Describe how people choose a major in college. If someone majors in English literature knowing that the starting salary for English literature graduates is much

lower than the starting salary for accountants, is the English literature major irrational?

5. What is the difference between legal and illegal immigration?

6. What is the effect of immigration laws restricting the number of immigrants?

7. Explain what is meant by discrimination, and explain the difference between personal prejudice and statistical discrimination.

8. How does technological change benefit firms? Does it benefit workers?

9. Explain what outsourcing is. Explain what offshoring is. Do you believe that unemployment is being created by CEOs who send jobs to less-developed nations such as India and China?

10. Explain why occupational segregation by sex might occur. Can you imagine a society in which you would not expect to find occupational segregation by sex? Explain. Would you expect to find occupational segregation by race in most societies?

11. Why are women's wages only 60 to 80 percent of men's wages, and why has this situation existed for several decades? Now that women are entering college and professional schools in increasing numbers, why doesn't the wage differential disappear?

12. Why do economists say that discrimination is inherently inefficient and therefore will not occur in general?

13. Demonstrate, using two labor markets, what is meant by comparable worth. What problems are created by comparable worth? Under what conditions might comparable worth make economic sense? Explain.

14. Consider the decision of a working woman or man who has young children or elderly relatives to take care of. Explain in terms of the labor supply curve how this person's decision to work is affected by the presence of dependents. What happens to the opportunity cost of working? How is the labor supply curve affected?

15. Demonstrate how a minimum wage affects the unskilled-labor market. Is the labor market perfectly competitive? Can you find any examples of monopsonistic hiring? What would a minimum wage do in a monopsonistic market?

Take the ACE Practice Test for this chapter to review the important concepts and get immediate feedback with answers.

college.hmco.com/economics/students/

Obese Workers Getting Smaller Pay; Stanford Study Ties Lower Wages to Higher Health Care Costs

San Francisco Chronicle
May 12, 2005

Employers may be compensating for the expected higher health costs of obese workers by giving them slimmer paychecks, according to a just-released study.

Previous studies have shown that severely overweight workers get paid less than other employees. But in the latest look at the issue, researchers at Stanford University have found that the pay gap exists only in workplaces with employer-paid health insurance.

"We view this as evidence that the higher expected expense of obese people is being passed along in the form of lower wages," said study co-author Kate Bundorf, assistant professor of health research and policy at Stanford.

The study was published online as a working paper on the Web site of the National Bureau of Economic Research, a nonprofit Massachusetts research organization.

Nearly 59 million Americans are classified as obese. Medical spending attributed to excess weight was estimated at about $92.6 billion in 2002 dollars, according to research published in 2003. That study found yearly medical expenses are $732 higher on average for obese people than for people of normal weight.

Many assume that normal-weight workers are sharing the medical costs of such obesity-related conditions as diabetes and hypertension, Bundorf said. Her research suggests that obese workers are paying these costs themselves by collecting smaller paychecks.

According to the Stanford survey, obese people with health coverage were paid an adjusted average of $1.20 less per hour than non-obese workers during the study period of 1989 through 1998, with the amount rising incrementally to $2.58 in 1998. That suggests the gap widened as workers aged, the authors said.

The study used older data from a Bureau of Labor Statistics youth survey because it contained detailed information about employees' height, weight and health, as well as their jobs, wages and education.

Researchers compared hourly wages of obese and non-obese workers, factoring in experience and job type. They found no significant difference when comparing the wages, retirement and life insurance benefits of obese and non-obese workers whose employers did not provide health insurance. But there was a discrepancy among workers whose employers offered health insurance.

The study did not address whether employers intentionally adjusted wages for obese workers to account for health costs.

San Francisco resident Marilyn Wann, a board member of the National Association to Advance Fat Acceptance, said the study shows that obese people face bias on the job.

"For anyone to act like there isn't that discrimination, which is pervasive and unchallenged . . . is completely ridiculous," Wann said.

But Paul Fronstin of the Employee Benefit Research Institute in Washington said he doubts that employers would risk litigation by deliberately paying obese workers less.

"They are very hesitant about any type of discrimination, be it weight, age or racial discrimination," he said.

An increasing number of employers are battling fat in the workplace by offering programs to promote weight loss, noted Lisa Horn with the Society for Human Resource Management in Alexandria, Va.

ompensating wage differentials refers to the differences in pay that result from differences in the characteristics of jobs or job conditions. For instance, an identical person working at a risky job would earn more than one working at a less risky job. The reason is that the worker has to be compensated for taking the risk. As shown in the first figure, it is the marginal factor cost (*MFC*) that is higher.

The other factor that enters into wage differentials is productivity. People are paid according to their contribution to the firm's profits, the marginal revenue product (*MRP*). If a person has skills that enable him or her to be more productive, then he or she will be paid more, as shown in the second figure.

So how could one's weight be a factor in pay? What does the finding that *the pay gap exists only in workplaces with employer-paid health insurance* have to do with pay differentials? It has to do with the marginal factor cost. In addition to salaries, many firms also pay for workers' health insurance, retirement benefits, disability insurance, and other benefits. Firms are choosing to allocate their per employee expenditure for wages and benefits so that total pay per individual is the same. Suppose that the salary for a normal-weight person is $10 per hour and benefits are $9 per hour, including $4 for health insurance, for a total expenditure of $19 per hour. To maintain the same $19 total expenditure per employee and yet pay $5 for health insurance, the firm would have to pay $9 salary and $10 benefits.

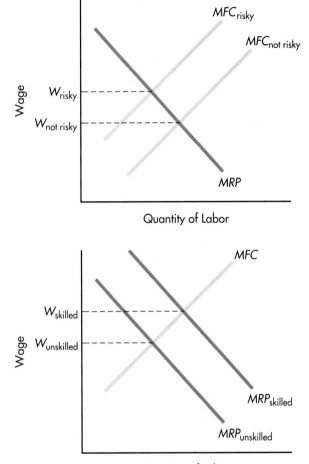

Yet Marilyn Wann, a board member of the National Association to Advance Fat Acceptance, said that the study shows that obese people face bias on the job. She stated, "For anyone to act like there isn't that discrimination, which is pervasive and unchallenged . . . is completely ridiculous." Is this discrimination?

Discrimination occurs when marginal revenue product is the same and pay is not for any given marginal factor cost. Pay is not different here if total pay includes salary and benefits and the firm has merely shifted categories and not changed the total. However, the study also said that the pay differential exceeds the marginal cost of insuring the obese individual. If that is the case and the *MRP* is the same, we could say that there does appear to be discrimination against obese people. On the other hand, if it is found that the *MRP* differs or if there are other costs that should be included in the *MFC,* then the differential may be merely a compensating wage differential. For instance, perhaps obese people have to spend more time away from the job, so that the *MRP* is different. Or perhaps the firm must provide special equipment or services for the obese, so that the *MFC* is higher. To know the answer, more information is required.

17

Capital Markets

The three broad categories of resources are land, labor and capital. Capital refers to the equipment, machinery, structures, and buildings necessary to produce goods and services. How do businesses acquire capital, and how much do they acquire? In this chapter, we examine the decision to acquire capital and the role that financial capital plays in this decision. ▪

1. The Capital Market

A firm will hire another worker when the marginal revenue product of that additional worker exceeds the marginal factor cost of the worker. In exactly the same way, a firm will decide to rent more building space or more equipment if the marginal revenue product of the additional capital exceeds its marginal factor cost.

1. What is the capital market?

2. What is the impact of technological change on the capital market?

If a firm is going to own the building or the equipment, it is planning on using that capital for a few years and thus can think of it as renting it to itself. It is just like the case when people purchase a house; they are using the house for a few years instead of renting, so it is as if they were renting to themselves.

1.a. The Demand for Capital

The demand for capital is shown in Figure 1(a) as a downward-sloping curve with the quantity of capital measured on the horizontal axis and the price of capital measured on the vertical axis. Just as the price of labor is a rental price, the price of capital is also a rental price. An increase in the price of capital, say from $80,000 to $100,000 per machine in Figure 1(a), decreases the quantity of capital demanded, from 350,000 to 300,000 machines. For instance, a farmer will postpone getting a new tractor if the price increases, or an airline will postpone purchasing a new airplane when the price of airplanes increases.

The demand curve for capital shifts when one of the nonprice determinants of demand changes. Perhaps the most important nonprice determinant of demand for capital is the interest rate. A firm has a choice of where to put its money. If it rents capital, then it cannot deposit the money into an interest-earning account. So, if the interest rate rises, the opportunity cost of renting capital rises, and less capital will be rented. Because this occurs at every rental price, the demand curve shifts when the interest rate changes. Each time the interest rate increases, from 5 to 6 to

FIGURE 1   The Market Demand for Capital

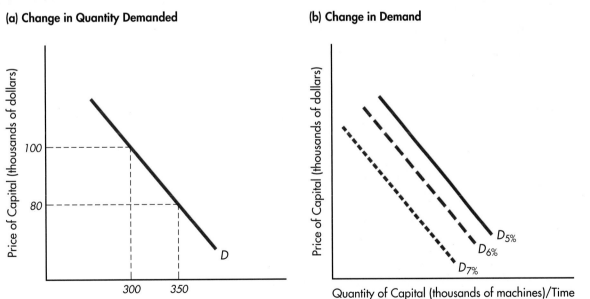

(a) Change in Quantity Demanded

(b) Change in Demand

In Figure 1(a), the demand for capital is shown as a downward-sloping line, wih the quantity of capital measured on the horizontal axis and the price of capital measured on the vertical axis. As the price of capital changes, say from $80,000 to $100,000 per unit of capital (per machine), the quantity of capital demanded changes, from 350,000 to 300,000 machines. In Figure 1(b), the relationship between the demand for capital and the interest rate is illustrated. As the rate of interest rises, the demand for capital declines—the demand curve shifts in. The interest rate associated with each demand curve is given as a subscript.

7 percent, the demand curve for capital shifts in, as shown in Figure 1(b) by the move from $D_{5\%}$ to $D_{6\%}$ to $D_{7\%}$.

The demand curve also shifts when any other determinant of demand changes. For instance, technological change will affect the demand for capital. Technological change is an increase in the amount that resources are able to produce, everything else the same. For instance, each generation of computers is faster and more powerful than previous generations. Many firms need the latest and most advanced technology to be able to compete, so that when technological change is occurring rapidly, firms demand more capital.

Expectations will also alter the demand for capital. In 2005, Google was estimating that the coming years would see exponential growth in sales. As a result, it relocated to a larger building and acquired additional equipment. A business that expects strong demand for its goods will want more capital, causing the demand curve for capital to shift out.

In sum, a change in the interest rate, a change in technology, a change in expectations, or a change in any other nonprice determinant of demand will change the demand for capital.

1.b. The Supply of Capital

The suppliers of capital are firms like John Deere, which supplies farm equipment; Boeing, which supplies airplanes; Dell, IBM, and Gateway, which supply computers; Intel and AMD, which supply computer chips; Lincoln Electric, which supplies arc welding equipment, and so on. The quantity of capital supplied by these firms depends on the price of the capital. As the price of capital rises, the quantity that producers are willing and able to offer rises, as shown in Figure 2 by the upward-sloping curve, *S*.

| FIGURE 2 | The Interest Rate, the Price of Capital, and the Rate of Return on Capital |

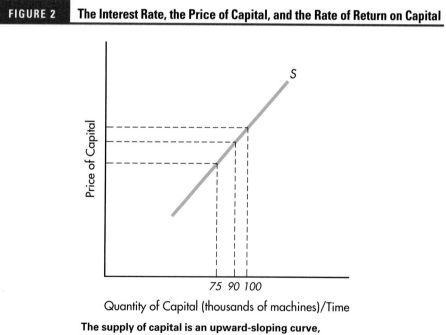

Quantity of Capital (thousands of machines)/Time

The supply of capital is an upward-sloping curve, indicating that the quantity of capital supplied rises as the price of capital rises, everything else the same. As the price of airplanes rises, the quantity of airplanes supplied by Boeing, Airbus, or the smaller firms rises.

(a) Interest Rate and Rate of Return

(b) Cost and Supply

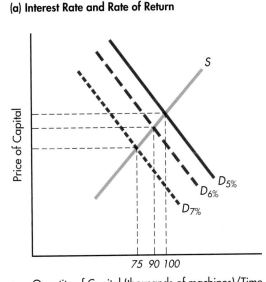
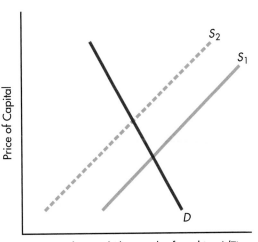

The demand for and the supply of capital determine both the price of capital and the quantity of capital produced and purchased. The rate of return on capital is the additional annual revenue generated by additional capital, divided by the purchase price of the capital. As shown in Figure 3(a), as the interest rate rises, the demand for capital declines (the demand curve shifts in) and the price of capital declines. As a result of the lower price, the rate of return rises. As shown in Figure 3(b), if the costs of supplying capital rise, everything else the same, the supply curve shifts in. This increases the price of capital and lowers the equilibrium quantity.

1.c. Equilibrium

The demand for and supply of capital determine the price of capital and the quantity supplied. Changes in demand or supply change the equilibrium price and quantity. For example, if the interest rate rises, the demand for capital decreases and the price of capital falls, as shown by the move from $D_{5\%}$ to $D_{6\%}$ to $D_{7\%}$ in Figure 3(a). Similarly, if the costs of supplying capital rise, the equilibrium price and quantity are affected. As an example, suppose that a law requiring that all farm equipment have costly safety equipment is enacted. The costs to John Deere rise and the quantity of farm equipment supplied decreases, everything else held constant. The supply curve shifts in, as illustrated in Figure 3(b) by the move from S_1 to S_2.

RECAP

1. The capital market is the market in which physical capital is acquired.
2. The demand for capital is represented by a downward-sloping curve, illustrating that the quantity of capital demanded rises as the price of capital falls.
3. The demand for capital shifts when the interest rate rises, when technological change occurs, when expectations change, or in general when any nonprice determinant of demand changes.
4. The supply of capital is represented by an upward-sloping curve, illustrating that the quantity of capital supplied rises as the rental price of capital rises.
5. The demand for and supply of capital determine the rental price of capital.

2. Equity

Stocks and bonds are called *financial capital* because they provide the funds with which capital can be purchased. When the financial markets determine higher or lower prices, the decision to acquire capital is affected.

2.a. Stocks

Whether you say shares, equity, or stock doesn't matter; these terms all mean the same thing—ownership of a piece of a company. Technically, owning a share of stock means that you own a share of everything the firm owns—every item of furniture, every piece of equipment, every building. In actuality, you are entitled only to a share of the company's earnings; you can't walk into the company's headquarters and walk out with a chair. There are two main types of stock: common and preferred stock. When people talk about stocks in general, they are referring to common stock. Preferred shares usually guarantee a fixed annual payment, or **dividend.** Common stock may or may not provide such a payment; that choice is at the discretion of the company.

dividend: the amount paid to shareholders on each share of stock owned

Global Business Insight

ADRs, or American Depositary Receipts

Suppose you want to purchase the stock of a foreign company, one that is listed on the London Stock Exchange. You need to convert your dollars to pounds and then get a broker to purchase that stock for you. When you have the broker sell the stock, you have to pay whatever taxes are required in the U.K. and then convert the pounds back to dollars. Or suppose you run a Scottish firm that needs a large sum of money in order to enter Asian markets. You know that the United States provides more funds to businesses than any other country, so you want to sell stock in the United States. To do so, you would have to go through the process of meeting all U.S. requirements and then finding an exchange on which you could list your company, translating your currency to dollars, and converting all your accounting statements to dollars. In addition to these difficulties, certain countries have regulations limiting foreign ownership (e.g., China, South Korea, Taiwan, and India) or controls on the movement of financial capital (e.g., Malaysia from 1998 to 2001) that make owning stock in a company in these nations difficult for U.S. investors. In the past, these transactions were very difficult, and so few U.S. investors owned stock in foreign companies and few foreign businesses raised money in the United States. American Depositary Receipts (ADRs) allow easy access to non-U.S. stocks for U.S. investors.

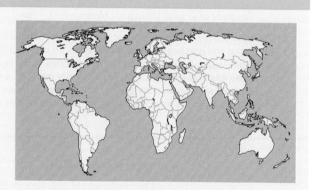

An ADR is a stock that trades in the United States but represents a specified number of shares in a foreign corporation. ADRs are bought and sold on American markets just like regular stocks, and are issued or sponsored in the United States by a bank or brokerage. A U.S. bank purchases shares of a company, say Sainsbury in England. The bank then issues ADRs representing ownership of the shares of Sainsbury stock and sells them in the United States as a Sainsbury ADR. Each ADR is backed by a specific number of the issuer's local shares; for instance, 1 Sainsbury ADR = 1.5 Sainsbury shares in the United Kingdom.

ADRs offer U.S. investors a convenient, easy-to-use avenue for owning international stocks. And for foreign companies, ADRs are an easy way to raise money from U.S. investors. Today, ADRs are used by approximately 2,200 non-U.S. issuers from more than 80 countries. Of the 2,200 ADRs, approximately 600 are listed on U.S. stock exchanges. The remainder are sold "over the counter." (A stock that is not traded on an exchange is said to trade over the counter.)

2.a.1. Stock Exchanges   Stocks are bought and sold on stock exchanges.

The New York Stock Exchange (NYSE), founded in 1792, is located on Wall Street in Manhattan and is the largest stock exchange in the world. Until 2006, trading on the NYSE could occur only on the trading floor. Beginning in 2006, customers have been able to choose between the floor-based auction market and sub-second electronic trading.

The Nasdaq is a virtual market—for example, there is no central location and no floor brokers. Trading takes place only through computers. Buyers and sellers submit orders electronically, and there are no specialists like there are on the NYSE.

The third largest exchange in the United States is the American Stock Exchange (AMEX). Almost all the firms listed on the AMEX are small firms.

In addition to the various U.S. stock exchanges, many other countries have stock exchanges. In fact, trading is taking place somewhere in the world 24 hours a day. Figure 4 shows how trading begins each day in Hong Kong, moves west to London, and then moves on to New York. Not only can you trade in different exchanges around the world, but trading for a stock listed on one exchange may occur "off

---

FIGURE 4   **Stock Exchanges Around the World**

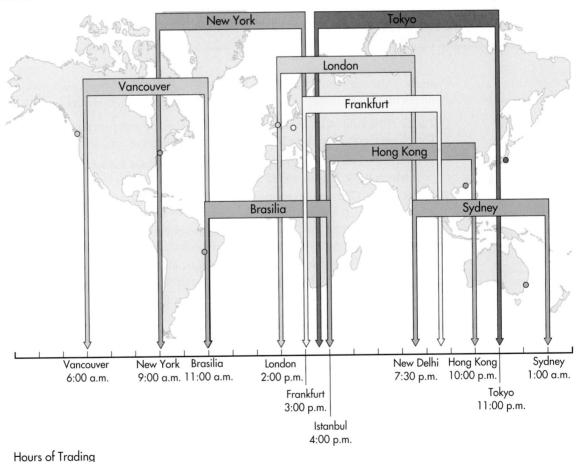

Hours of Trading
(9:00 a.m. Eastern Time)

Stocks can be traded literally 24 hours a day. The day opens with Hong Kong; then, as Hong Kong is ready to shut down, London opens up, followed later by New York.

The P/E Ratio

How does a potential buyer decide which stocks to purchase? How does the buyer know when is a good time to buy? One method used is to see whether the stock price is appropriately related to the firm's earnings. The P/E ratio is an indicator of this relationship. The P/E ratio is the ratio of a company's share price (P) to its earnings per share (E). To calculate the P/E, you divide a company's current stock price by its earnings per share (EPS). Most of the time the P/E is calculated using the EPS from the last four quarters (known as the trailing P/E). Occasionally, however, you will see earnings expected over the next four quarters (known as the leading P/E) used as EPS.

Theoretically, a stock's P/E tells us how much investors are willing to pay for each dollar of earnings. For this reason, the P/E is also called the *multiple* of a stock. In other words, a P/E ratio of 20 suggests that investors in the stock are willing to pay $20 for every $1 of earnings that the company generates during the period (leading or lagging). If a company has a P/E higher than the market or industry average, this is interpreted as meaning that the market is expecting that the company will have better performance than the average firm in the market or industry over the next few months or years. But you can't just compare the P/Es of two different companies to determine which is a better value, because the companies may have very different growth rates. If two companies both have a P/E of 20, but one is growing twice as fast as the other, then the faster-growing firm is undervalued relative to the slower-growing one. Finally, a low P/E ratio could mean that the market believes that the company is headed for trouble in the near future. If earnings are expected to come in lower than forecast in the future, this won't be reflected in a trailing P/E ratio, as the future performance may differ greatly from the past.

hours." Although the NYSE might close at 4:00 p.m. eastern time, trading on some stocks may occur through computer-based exchanges throughout the night.

2.a.2. How to Read a Stock Table/Quote Most newspapers report stock prices. The reports look something like Figure 5 and include the columns listed here.

Columns 1 and 2: 52-week high and low. These are the highest and lowest prices at which the stock has traded over the previous 52 weeks (one year).

Column 3: Company name and type of stock. This column gives the name of the company. If there are no special symbols or letters following the name, the stock is common stock. Different symbols identify different classes of shares. For example, "pf" means that the shares are preferred stock.

Column 4: Ticker symbol. This is the unique alphabetic name that identifies the stock. If you are looking for stock quotes online, you use the ticker symbol.

Column 5: Dividend per share. This indicates the annual dividend payment per share. If this space is blank, the company does not currently pay dividends.

Column 6: Dividend yield. This gives the percentage return provided by the dividend. It is calculated as annual dividends per share divided by price per share.

Column 7: Price/earnings ratio. This is calculated by dividing the current stock price by the earnings per share for the last four quarters.

Column 8: Trading volume. This figure gives the total number of shares traded for the day, in hundreds. To get the actual number traded, add "00" to the end of the number given.

Columns 9 and 10: High and low for the day. This indicates the price range within which the stock has traded that day.

Column 11: Close. The close is the last trading price recorded when the market closed for the day. If the closing price is up or down more than 5 percent from the previous day's close, the entire listing for that stock is given in bold type.

FIGURE 5 Stock Market Listing

52W high	52W low	Stock	Ticker	Yield Div	%	P/E	Vol 00s	High	Low	Close	Net chg
45.39	19.75	ResMed	RMD			52.5	3831	42.00	39.51	41.50	−1.90
11.63	3.55	RevlonA	REV				162	6.09	5.90	6.09	+0.12
77.25	55.13	RioTinto	RTP	2.30	3.2		168	72.75	71.84	72.74	+0.03
31.31	16.63	RitchieBr	RBA			20.9	15	24.49	24.29	24.49	−0.01
8.44	1.75	RiteAid	RAD				31028	4.50	4.20	4.31	+0.21
38.63	18.81	RobtHalf	RHI			26.5	6517	27.15	26.50	26.50	+0.14
51.25	27.69	Rockwell	ROK	1.02	2.1	14.5	6412	47.99	47.08	47.54	+0.24

Column 1 Column 2 Column 3 Column 4 Column 5 Column 6 Column 7 Column 8 Column 9 Column 10 Column 11 Column 12

Stocks are listed in newspapers in a standard form, showing annual highs and lows, dividends, P/E ratios, and daily volume and activity.

Column 12: Net change. This is the dollar value change in the stock price from the previous day's closing price.

Stock quotes are also available on the Internet and are reported in the same way that the newspapers report them.

2.a.3. Stock Indexes   A stock index is a measure of the price movements of a group of stocks. The number of stocks in the group may vary; for example, there are 30 stocks in the Dow Jones Industrial Average and 6,500 in the Wilshire Index. Since the prices of individual stocks do not necessarily go up or down at the same time, the importance or weight of a single stock in an index will vary. Most indexes weight companies based on their **market capitalization (market cap),** which is the stock price multiplied by the number of shares of that stock that are outstanding. If a company's market cap is $1,000,000 and the value of all stocks in the index is $100,000,000, then that company has a weight of 1 percent of the index. An exception to weighting stocks by market cap is the Dow Jones Industrial Average, which uses the stock price relative to the sum of the prices of all the stocks in the index.

The most popular indexes are the Dow Jones Industrial Average (DJIA), the Standard & Poor's 500 (S&P 500), the Wilshire 5000, and the Nasdaq Composite Index. The DJIA contains 30 companies, the S&P 500 includes 500 companies, the Nasdaq Composite includes all companies listed on the Nasdaq stock exchange, and the Wilshire 5000 contains more than 6,500 stocks (the 5000 in the name is misleading). The S&P 500 tries to represent all major areas of the U.S. economy. It does not use the 500 largest companies, but rather includes 500 companies that are widely owned and that represent all sectors of the economy. The stocks in the index are chosen by the S&P Index Committee, which typically makes between 25 and 50 changes every year. Non-U.S. companies were included in the past, but today, and in the future, only U.S. companies are included. The Nasdaq Composite Index includes all the stocks that are traded on the Nasdaq stock market. Most are technology- and Internet-related, although there are financial, consumer, biotech, and industrial companies as well. The Wilshire 5000 Index contains more than 6,500 stocks that trade in the United States. It includes all of the stocks on the New York Stock Exchange and most of the Nasdaq and AMEX issues. Another index, the

4. What does a stock index represent?

market capitalization (market cap): the stock price multiplied by the number of shares of stock that are outstanding

Russell 2000, measures the performance of smaller stocks (small-cap stocks), which are often excluded from the big indexes. The average market capitalization in the Russell 2000 is approximately $530 million. To put that into perspective, Wal-Mart alone had a market capitalization of over $225 billion in 2006.

These well-known indexes are only a few among many indexes; every major country has an index that represents its stock exchange.

2.b. Mutual Funds

mutual fund: an investment tool that aggregates many different individual stocks into one entity

global fund: a mutual fund that includes international investments

specific fund: a mutual fund that focuses on a particular industry or a particular part of the world

socially responsible fund: a group of stocks or bonds of companies that meet specified requirements for ethical behavior or environmental behavior

index fund: a mutual fund that tries to match the performance of a broad market index

load: the fees paid to the manager of a mutual fund

front-end load: a fee that you pay when you purchase a mutual fund

back-end load: a fee that you pay if you sell a mutual fund within a certain time frame

no-load fund: a mutual fund that sells its shares without a commission or sales charge

More than 80 million people, or half of the households in the United States, invest in mutual funds. A **mutual fund** is a group of stocks of individual firms that are placed into one investment pool by an investment company. For instance, one of the larger mutual fund investment companies is the Vanguard Group, which has many different mutual funds. One of its mutual funds is focused on high-tech firms, another on manufacturing firms, another on international firms, and so on. Individual investors are thus able to purchase a large set of stocks by simply purchasing shares in a mutual fund. There are more than 10,000 mutual funds offered to investors in the United States.

There are three general types of mutual funds: equity funds (made up of stocks), fixed-income funds (composed of corporate and government bonds), and money market funds (made up mostly of short-term U.S. government securities, but also including some corporate bonds).

If a fund includes international investments, it is called a **global fund** or an international fund. Some mutual funds focus on a specific sector of the economy, such as financial, technology, or health-care stocks, while others focus on a specific area of the world, say Latin America, or an individual country, such as Mexico. These are called **specific funds. Socially responsible funds** invest only in companies that meet certain criteria. Most socially responsible funds don't invest in companies producing such things as tobacco, alcoholic beverages, weapons, or nuclear power. An **index fund** attempts to mimic the performance of a broad market index, such as the S&P 500 or the Dow Jones Industrial Average. These mutual funds purchase shares of stock in those companies that are included in the index and weight them so as to create as close a copy of the index as possible.

Funds may be load or no-load. **Load** refers to fees paid to a fund manager. With a **front-end load**, you pay a fee when you purchase the fund. If you invest $1,000 in a mutual fund with a 5 percent front-end load, $50 will be used to pay for the sales charge, and $950 will be invested in the fund. With a **back-end load**, you pay a fee if you sell the fund within a certain time frame. For example, a fund may have a 5 percent back-end load that decreases to 0 percent in the sixth year. The load is 5 percent if you sell in the first year, 4 percent if you sell in the second year, and so on. If you don't sell the mutual fund until the sixth year, you don't have to pay the back-end load at all. A **no-load fund** sells its shares without a commission or sales charge (fees are typically paid by clients on a prearranged basis).

2.b.1. How to Read a Mutual Fund Table A typical newspaper report on mutual funds looks like Figure 6. The columns in the mutual fund table provide the following information:

Columns 1 and 2: 52-week high and low. These columns show the highest and lowest asset values that the mutual fund has experienced over the previous 52 weeks (one year). They typically do not include the previous day's price.

Column 3: Fund name. This column gives the name of the mutual fund. The name of the company that manages the fund is written above the funds that the company manages in bold type.

FIGURE 6   The Reporting of Mutual Funds

52W high	52W low	Fund	Spec.	Fri. NAVPS $chg	Fri. NAVPS %chg	Wkly NAVPS high	Wkly NAVPS low	Wkly NAVPS cls	$chg	%chg
Montrusco Bolton Funds										
11.71	10.12	Bal Plus	*N	−0.08	−0.76	10.58	10.50	10.50	0.02	0.15
12.50	10.25	Growth Plus	*N	−0.10	−0.96	10.89	10.78	10.78	0.02	0.22
31.39	24.78	Quebec Growth	*FR	0.05	0.17	26.97	26.75	26.97	0.43	1.61
13.78	7.24	RSP Intl Growth	*N	−0.08	−1.01	7.45	7.36	7.36	−0.03	−0.41
11.16	9.09	Value Plus	*N	−0.07	−0.75	9.39	9.32	9.32	0.01	0.14
9.65	8.90	World Inc	*N	−0.04	−0.40	9.52	9.39	9.48	0.04	0.43
Montrusco Select Funds CS(a)										
12.87	10.49	Balanced	*N	−0.04	−0.37	10.85	10.80	10.81	0.05	0.45
16.32	12.11	Balanced+	*N	−0.05	−0.43	12.57	12.52	12.52	0.06	0.45
10.36	9.86	Bond Index+	X*N	−0.03	−0.32	10.35	10.30	10.30	0.04	0.37

Column 1   Column 2   Column 3   Column 4   Column 5   Column 6   Column 7   Column 8   Column 9   Column 10   Column 11

Financial newspapers report on mutual fund performance in a standard manner, showing annual and weekly activity.

Column 4: Fund specifics. Different letters and symbols have various meanings. For example, "N" means no load, "F" means front-end load, and "B" means that the fund has both front- and back-end fees.

Column 5: Dollar change. This states the dollar change in the asset value of the mutual fund from the close of the previous day's trading. NAVPS stands for net asset value per share, the value of the mutual fund divided by the number of shares of the fund.

Column 6: Percentage change. This states the percentage change in the asset value of the mutual fund from the close of the previous day's trading.

Column 7: Week high. This is the highest asset value at which the fund was sold during the past week.

Column 8: Week low. This is the lowest asset value at which the fund was sold during the past week.

Column 9: Close. The asset value of the fund at the end of the trading day is shown in this column.

Column 10: Week's dollar change. This represents the dollar change in the asset value of the mutual fund from the previous week.

Column 11: Week's percentage change. This shows the percentage change in the asset value of the mutual fund from the previous week.

RECAP

1. Shares, equity, and stock mean the same thing—ownership of a piece of a company.

2. There are two main types of stock: common and preferred stock.

3. A stock index is a measure of the price movements of a group of stocks.

4. A mutual fund is an entity that invests money in stocks, bonds, and other securities for groups of people.

3. The Stock Market _____

The prices of stocks vary from day to day, and even from minute to minute. What causes stock prices to rise or fall? The answer is the same things that affect prices in any other market—demand and supply. The demand for stocks comes from investors—individuals, mutual funds, and other institutions like insurance companies—who are looking for the highest return on their funds. The return to a shareholder is the dividend the stock pays and the appreciation in the price of the stock. Suppose, for instance, that you purchased Microsoft at $5 per share in 1996 and then sold it for $100 per share in 2006. Your appreciation would have been $95 per share over the 10-year period. Since Microsoft paid no dividends during this period, your total return would have been that appreciation.

The demand curve for the shares of a company's stock slopes downward, since the higher the price of the stock, everything else the same, the lower the quantity of stock demanded. Nonprice determinants of demand are the prices of other companies' stocks and other possible investments, expectations regarding stock price movements, income, and tastes and preferences. When one of the nonprice determinants of demand for a firm's stock changes, the demand curve shifts. For instance, if people expect the price of the stock to increase, demand will increase, as shown in Figure 7.

| FIGURE 7 | The Equity Market |

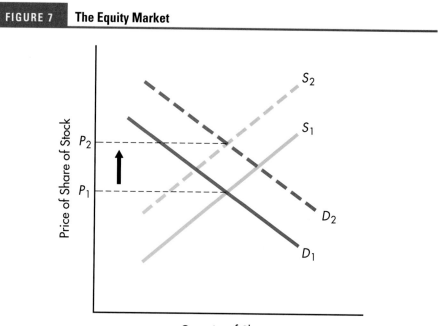

Demand for stocks comes from investors looking to acquire wealth; the quantity demanded of a stock rises when the price of the stock declines. Supply of stocks comes from investors wanting to obtain money. The quantity supplied rises as the price of the stock rises. Demand shifts when the determinants of demand change; supply shifts when the determinants of supply shift.

The supply of a stock comes from current shareholders who want to sell their shares of stock and from firms issuing new shares.[1] The supply curve for a company's stock slopes upward, indicating that the higher the price, the greater the quantity offered for sale, everything else the same. The nonprice determinants of supply are the prices of related stocks and other investments and the expectations of shareholders. When one of the nonprice determinants of supply changes, the supply curve shifts. For instance, if current shareholders begin to believe that the future price of the stock will be higher than they had previously believed, then they will tend to hold on to their shares, that is, to offer less for sale, and the supply curve will shift to the left, as illustrated in Figure 7.

You can see in Figure 7 that the effect of expectations that the price of a stock will rise in the future is an increase in the price of the stock today from P_1 to P_2. Buyers want to purchase more shares now, so demand increases from D_1 to D_2, and sellers are offering less for sale, so supply decreases from S_1 to S_2. The result is a higher price today, P_2.

For one investor to sell a share of a particular company's stock to another investor, the buyer has to expect that the purchase of this stock will return more than any other comparable purchase, and the seller has to expect that the purchase of other financial assets, goods, or services with the money obtained from the sale of this stock will generate more satisfaction than holding onto the shares of this stock. An important point here is that buyers and sellers are comparing all possible investments and seeking the one that they think will give them the best return. Buyers and sellers evaluate the firm's stock on the basis of a comparison with all other comparable investments. A **comparable investment** is an investment that has the same features, such as risk and ease of selling (called liquidity), as the one being considered.

comparable investment: a stock that has the same features, such as risk and liquidity, as the one that buyers and sellers are evaluating

5. What causes stock prices to rise and fall?

3.a. Risk

Risk and return are related—if you take more risk, you expect more return. What is risk? It is the possibility that some unexpected event will occur. Most people are risk averse, meaning that they will pay to have less risk. Suppose you are given the opportunity to win some money, and there are two ways of doing it. With choice A, you get $1,000, and with choice B, you have a 50 percent chance of getting 0 and a 50 percent chance of getting $2,000. Which do you prefer?

Choice A = $1,000

Choice B = $0 × 50% = $0 or $2,000 × 50% = $1,000

The average outcome of the choices is the same. Therefore, risk-averse people will choose A. To get risk-averse people to select B, we would have to offer them more, say $100 × 50% or $2,100 × 50% = $1,100. This extra $100 is called the risk premium—the amount that a risk-averse person requires in order to take on risk. A purchase of a firm's stock will include a risk premium, and the more risky the firm, the higher the premium. So if you have a choice of investing in Microsoft or a brand-new biotech company, you would need to have the possibility of earning a great deal more on the new company to get you to invest in it.

---

[1] The primary market refers to the market in which a firm issues stock for the very first time (an IPO, or the initial public offering of stocks by a firm) or issues additional stock. The secondary market is what we are typically referring to when we speak of the stock market. This is the market in which outstanding shares are bought and sold.

FIGURE 8   **Revisions of Expectations**

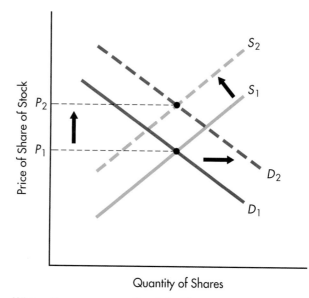

Quantity of Shares

When a firm earns more than it had been expected to earn, investors in that firm's stock are likely to change their expectations of what the future may bring. This will induce investors to purchase more shares of the stock and sell fewer—an increase in demand and a decrease in supply.

Rather than investing in the risky biotech firm or the less risky Microsoft, investors could decide not to take any risk at all. By not taking any risk, investors would expect to receive a return that is even lower than the return that an established firm like Microsoft would provide and much lower than the return that the high-risk firm would provide. Risk-averse people must be paid to take on more risk, and the more risk they take on, the more they must be paid.

3.b. Stock Price Changes

Stock prices change every day because of supply and demand. If more people want to buy a stock (demand) than want to sell it (supply), the price moves up. Conversely, if more people want to sell a stock than want to buy it, the price will fall. What causes demand and supply to change? When investors change their expectations so that they now expect the price of the stock to rise more than they previously did, more investors will want to buy. At the same time, fewer will want to sell. As illustrated in Figure 8, when expectations are revised upward, demand will increase, supply will decrease, and price will rise from P_1 to P_2. When expectations are revised downward, fewer investors will want to buy and more will want to sell. In this case, supply will increase (shift right), demand will decrease (shift down), and price will fall from P_2 to P_1.

Firms are required to report their earnings (accounting profit) at the end of each quarter (for most companies, the end of March, June, September, and December). These quarterly reports are used by stock market analysts and investors to evaluate how well their previous forecasts of the firm's performance match what has actually been happening. When the quarterly results are not consistent with the investors' forecasts or expectations, the investors will revise their expectations of the firm's

Stock Market Booms and Busts

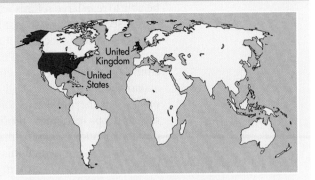

The stock market decline from 2000 to 2003 produced a dramatic decrease in investor wealth, especially after the boom of the 1990s. But this stock market decline was not an isolated event in history. Stock market booms and busts are a recurrent feature of developed economies. In the United States, there have been 14 market crashes since 1800, and in the United Kingdom there have been 11. The patterns of booms and busts for the United States and the United Kingdom are noted in the accompanying table. The greatest declines in percentage terms occurred during the 1929–1932 period in the United States and the 1909–1920 period in the United Kingdom. The 2000–2002 decline ranked as the sixth greatest decline in the United States and the ninth in the United Kingdom.

Crashes—United States			Crashes—United Kingdom		
Peak	Trough	% Change	Peak	Trough	% Change
1809	1814	−37.8	1808	1812	−54.5
1835	1842	−46.6	1824	1826	−33.6
1853	1859	−53.4	1829	1831	−27
1863	1865	−22.5	1835	1839	−39.1
1875	1877	−26.8	1844	1847	−30.5
1881	1885	−22.2	1865	1867	−24.5
1892	1894	−16.4	1874	1878	−19.7
1902	1904	−19.4	1909	1920	−80.5
1906	1907	−22.3	1928	1931	−55.4
1916	1918	−42.5	1936	1940	−59.9
1919	1921	−24.5	2000	2002	−26.7
1929	1932	−66.5			
1936	1938	−27			
2000	2002	−30.8			

Source: *World Economic Outlook,* International Monetary Fund, April 2003, pp. 64–66.

future performance up or down. If the earnings reports indicate lower earnings than had been expected, the forecasts will be revised downward, and the stock price will decline. When a firm does better than it had been expected to do, the forecasts will be revised upward, and the stock price will rise. As an illustration, consider the following report: "Google stock soared Friday, continuing Wall Street's love affair with the company, after its earnings easily topped estimates." The report states that investors realized that the revenues they had expected Google to earn were less than what Google actually earned, and so they began to think that the value of the company was higher than they had previously thought, and as a result they wanted to own more of it. The greater demand drove the price up.

3.c. Market Efficiency

There are hundreds of millions of people who own shares of stock. Some of these people analyze all available information about companies, and some don't even know which stocks they own. It would seem that those people who study the stock markets would be so much better informed than the average investor that they would be able to reap large returns relative to the average investor. But this is not necessarily so. To see why, suppose that a particular investor gains a reputation as a stock market guru—a very successful investor—and that the investor's activities are easily observed by others. What will happen? As with any market that does not have significant barriers to entry, when some firm (some person) begins making positive economic profits, others will mimic that firm (that person) and compete with it. As others copy the initial investor's strategy and mimic every move, the initial investor's returns drop—economic profit is driven down to zero. This view of the behavior of the stock markets suggests that no investor can continually outperform the market.

Another way in which this idea is expressed is by saying that one can do as well at picking stocks by throwing darts at the stock tables as by picking them in any other way.[2] If there was one best way to pick stocks, then everyone would focus on that method, and the price would reflect all such information. There would be no way to do better than everyone else. This is what people mean when they say that the market is *efficient*.

Prices are the result of demand and supply, and demand and supply take into account all relevant or important information. Stock prices reflect or incorporate all relevant information about a company, expectations concerning the company's performance and the economy's performance, and any other event that could affect the firm. The point is that stock prices will incorporate and reflect all relevant information once that information appears. Thus, even though investors possess widely differing amounts of information, there is no way in which one investor can continually make above-normal profits or "beat the market." Of course there are some investors who seem to do better than others, but in few cases does a single investor continually do better than others. The basic idea of efficient markets is that there are no sure profits. As the Global Business Insight "Stock Market Booms and Busts" shows, investing is a risky business, as prices continually adjust to new information and circumstances.

If the market is efficient, how can stock market bubbles and panics be explained? A bubble or panic is a sudden increase or decrease in prices that occurs simply because people are jumping on the bandwagon without an underlying economic basis. In the bubble of the 1990s, the price of Amazon.com stock was very high even though the company had never made a profit. Perhaps some of that stock price was based on expectations of future profits, but a great deal of it was the result of investors gambling or speculating on the basis of wishful thinking. In that period, people would hear about the secretary in a start-up company who became a millionaire, and so they would start purchasing stocks in start-up companies so that they too would become rich. The problem is that wishful thinking by itself cannot drive stock prices up for very long. Eventually a firm must earn positive economic profits. The stock market collapsed in 2000 because it became evident that firms were not earning economic profits that were high enough to support the inflated stock prices. In the short run, psychological aspects may drive stock prices, but over the long run, stock prices will reflect profit.

3.d. Ethics and the Stock Market

If people like what a company does, they purchase its shares of stock, driving the price up. If people don't like what a company does, they sell the shares, driving prices lower. In this way, prices of stocks reflect individual desires and attitudes.

?

6. What do ethics have to do with financial capital?

------

[2] This statement was made in a 1973 book by Burton Malkiel, *A Random Walk Down Wall Street* (W. W. Norton and Company).

FIGURE 9 **Stock Market Performance**

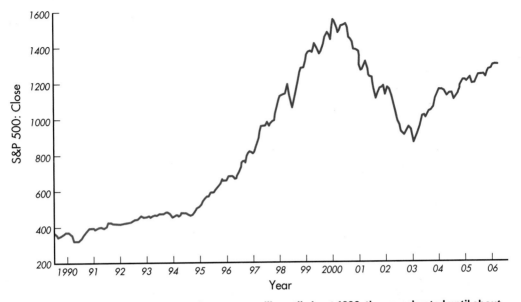

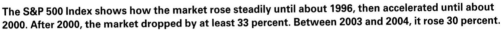

The S&P 500 Index shows how the market rose steadily until about 1996, then accelerated until about 2000. After 2000, the market dropped by at least 33 percent. Between 2003 and 2004, it rose 30 percent.

The capital markets work to penalize companies that act in ways that are not desired by society. However, when the executives of a company engage in fraudulent activities and those activities are not known, the share prices will not reflect the behavior until it is recognized.

Figure 9 shows the pattern of the S&P 500 index from 1992 to 2006. The Internet revolution had created many new opportunities for businesses and allowed firms to reduce their costs and increase their revenues. Stock prices began rising in 1992, and as the market continued to go up, people began to feel that it would rise forever and that if they didn't purchase stocks, they would be left behind. This drove the market up more and more rapidly. Shareholders were demanding that companies grow faster and generate increasingly higher accounting profits. Companies that reported higher earnings saw their stocks rise in price, and executives in these companies saw their own wealth increase. It was in this setting that several high-profile corporate scandals occurred.

3.d.1 Enron Corporation The best-known corporate scandal involved Enron Corporation. Enron originally was a gas pipeline and electricity-generating and electricity-transmission company—what most people considered to be a staid old electric utility. It was turned into a company that traded power—bought and sold it rather than producing it—and generated staggering profits in doing so. None of this got Enron into trouble. It was what Enron executives did with respect to the company's financial accounts and its relationships with auditors and investment banks that led to disaster. Enron executives made it appear that the company was earning more profits than it actually was. They did this by not accounting for many costs and overstating revenues. Enron's accountants hid costs by reporting them as costs not of Enron but of different entities—partnerships that were not directly part of Enron Corporation. These accounting shenanigans were not all that the executives did in order to drive Enron's stock price higher. Enron also used some unscrupulous techniques to convince stock analysts that Enron was in excellent shape, and these analysts then recommended the purchase of Enron stock to their clients. This process continued until Enron's true situation could no longer be hidden. Once the seventh largest company in the world, Enron had virtually disappeared by 2002.

3.d.2 WorldCom, Tyco, and Others   Tyco and WorldCom also used aggressive accounting to increase current earnings above what they would have been if a more conservative accounting treatment had been used. WorldCom had grown into a telecommunications giant by acquiring or merging with more than 65 other companies, including MCI. Because of accounting maneuvers, each new acquisition allowed WorldCom to report higher per share profits, even when its business was doing poorly. To keep the momentum going, however, WorldCom needed larger and larger deals. The biggest and last was a $145 billion bid for Sprint. When the Justice Department decided not to allow this merger to proceed, WorldCom's ability to delude investors came to an end. When the company was unable to continue hiding its costs through accounting maneuvers associated with acquisitions, the reality that WorldCom was losing money became widely known. The company declared bankruptcy in 2000.

Tyco's CEO used company funds for his own uses; these expenditures were hidden in the accounts. Other companies used tactics such as reporting earnings in one quarter when they actually occurred in another quarter in order to give the appearance of continual improvement.

These scandals contributed to the 2000 collapse of the stock market. Investors sold stock, fearing that more scandals involving other firms might occur. The resulting stock sales drove prices down. By 2003, the stock market had declined 33 percent from its 2000 high. As you can see in Figure 9, it has recovered from the collapse.

As mentioned earlier, unethical behavior on the part of the executives of firms will be reflected in stock prices when that behavior is recognized. Similarly, other behaviors that society dislikes will be reflected in lower stock prices. Exxon was hurt by the Exxon-Valdez oil transporter leak in Alaska; Ford and B.F. Goodrich were damaged by the accidents involving the Explorer model caused by faulty tires; The Body Shop was hurt when it was found that it had carried materials that had been tested on animals. When firms are owned by shareholders, the firms must perform the way society wants them to perform or else people will not choose to own shares of stock.

RECAP

1. The equity market is the market in which stocks are bought and sold.
2. The demand for equities comes from investors who are seeking the greatest return on their savings.
3. The supply of equities comes from stock owners who want to sell their stock and purchase something else.
4. Demand depends on expectations, income, and the prices of and returns on other investments. Supply depends on expectations and the prices of and returns on other investments. A change in one of these determinants of demand and/or supply will cause the curve to shift. If buyers want to buy more stock (demand) than sellers want to sell (supply), then the price will move up. Conversely, if sellers want to sell more of a stock than buyers want to buy, the price will fall.
5. The equity market is said to be an efficient market in the sense that it is difficult for an investor to continually earn above-normal profits. If there were a secret formula for becoming rich in the stock market, everyone would soon learn that formula, and it would no longer be an effective strategy.

6. By manipulating their financial statements, several companies were able to mislead the investing public about their performance. This helped to fuel the booming stock market in the late 1990s.

7. Enron was the best-known instance of misleading and deceptive practices on the part of its executives, but other companies engaged in similar practices. The result was a collapse in the value of these companies once their practices were discovered, and a decline in the stock market in general.

4. Bonds

bond: an IOU issued by a borrower to a lender

Firms can raise cash by selling ownership rights (shares of stock—equity—in the case of a public company), by retaining earnings in the firm (not distributing them to owners in the form of dividends), and by selling bonds or taking out loans (debt). A **bond** (sometimes called a fixed-income security or debt security) is an IOU issued by a borrower to a lender. When you buy a newly issued bond, you are lending money to the borrower. When you purchase a bond that is not a new issue, you are buying that bond not from the issuing firm but from an investor or lender that initially provided the loan. You are choosing to own a portion of the debt obligation of a company because you think that the return on that bond exceeds the return on whatever else you might have done with the money used to purchase the bond. The seller of the bond has decided that he is better off selling that debt and thus receiving money now than waiting for the debtor (the issuing firm) to pay off the loan.

Global Business Insight

Country Bond Ratings

Governments issue bonds in order to raise money. Government bonds are rated in terms of risk much like corporate bonds are. The following are government bond ratings provided by Moody's and other rating services.

Country	Long-Term Bond Rating	Country	Long-Term Bond Rating
Argentina	Ca	Mexico	Baa
Australia	Aa	Pakistan	Caa
Brazil	B	Philippines	Ba
Canada	Aa	Russia	Ba
Chile	Baa	Singapore	Aa
China	A	South Africa	Baa
Hong Kong	A	Taiwan	Aa
Hungary	A	Thailand	Baa
India	Ba	Turkey	B
Indonesia	B	UK	Aaa
Japan	Aa	USA	Aaa
Korea	Baa	Vietnam	B
Malaysia	Baa		

FIGURE 10   **Bond Ratings**

Bond Rating		Grade	Risk
Moody's	*Standard & Poor's*		
Aaa	AAA	Investment	Lowest risk
Aa	AA	Investment	Low risk
A	A	Investment	Low risk
Baa	BBB	Investment	Medium risk
Ba, B	BB, B	Junk	High risk
Caa/Ca/C	CCC/CC/C	Junk	Highest risk
C	D	Junk	In default

Rating agencies provide measures of the amount of risk associated with particular bonds.

maturity date: the specified time at which the issuer of a bond will repay the loan

face or par value: the amount that the lender will be repaid when a bond matures

coupon: the fixed amount that the issuer of a bond agrees to pay the bondholder each year

There is a specified time at which the borrower will repay your loan; this is the **maturity date.** In most cases, the bond's **face or par value** is $1,000; this is the amount that the lender will be repaid once the bond matures. The borrower pays the lender a fixed amount, called a **coupon,** each year. These interest payments are usually made every six months until the bond matures. The rate of interest that must be paid—that is, the *coupon rate*—depends on how risky the borrower is. The chart in Figure 10 illustrates the different bond rating scales from the two major rating agencies, Moody's and Standard & Poor's, their associated grades, and the risk levels that the ratings indicate.

4.a. Bond Ratings

U.S. government bonds are considered no-risk investments because it is so unlikely that the United States will default on its obligations. Corporations must offer a higher yield than the government in order to entice lenders to purchase corporate bonds because corporate bonds are more risky. AAA corporate bonds—often referred to as blue chip bonds—are the lowest-risk corporate bonds. The highest-risk corporate bonds are called junk bonds. Junk bonds are typically rated at BB/Ba or lower. On average, a bond carries less risk than a share of stock because in the event of the firm's collapse, the shareholders cannot get anything until all debtholders have been paid.

4.b. Reading a Bond Table

In every financial newspaper there are bond tables similar to the one shown in Figure 11. The columns in the bond table provide the following information:

Column 1: Issuer. This is the company, state (or province), or country that issued the bond.

Column 2: Coupon. The coupon refers to the fixed interest rate that the issuer pays to the lender. The coupon rate varies by bond.

Column 3: Maturity date. This is the date when the borrower will pay the lenders (investors) their principal back. Typically only the last two digits of the year are quoted: 25 means 2025, 04 is 2004, and so on.

Column 4: Bid price. This is the price that someone is willing to pay for the bond. It is quoted in relation to 100, no matter what the par value is. Think of the bond price as a percentage: a bid of $93 means that the bond is trading at 93 percent of its par value.

FIGURE 11 — Reading a Bond Table

	Coupon	Mat. Date	Bid $	Yld%
Corporate				
GTE Florida Inc	6.860	Feb 01/28	102.562	6.635
General Motors Corp	8.375	Jul 15/33	76.000	11.205
General Mtrs Acep Corp	8.000	Nov 01/31	98.358	8.152
General Elec Co	5.000	Feb 01/13	100.112	4.979
Ford Mtr Co Del	7.450	Jul 16/31	74.437	10.306

Column 1   Column 2   Column 3   Column 4   Column 5

Bonds are reported in financial newspapers and on the Internet in a standard manner.

Column 5: Yield. The yield indicates the annual return until the bond matures. Yield is calculated as the amount of interest paid on a bond divided by the price; it is a measure of the income generated by a bond. If the bond is callable, the yield will be given as "c—," where the "—" is the year in which the bond can be called. For example c10 means that the bond can be called as early as 2010.

You will hear some bonds referred to as bills or notes. The name indicates the length of time until the bond matures. *Bills* are debt securities maturing in less than one year. *Notes* are debt securities maturing in one to ten years. *Bonds* are debt securities maturing in more than ten years. A bond that provides no interest payments but instead is issued at a value that is lower than its face value is called a **zero-coupon bond.**

zero-coupon bond: a bond that provides no interest payments but is issued at a value lower than its face value

7. What causes bond prices to rise and fall?

4.c. The Bond Market

The market for bonds is not very different from the stock market, and the two are closely linked. Demanders of bonds are investors who are looking for the best return on their savings. They will purchase a bond when the return on the bond is expected to be greater than the return on other comparable investments—for instance, better than the return on stocks adjusted for risk. Consider a $100 bond maturing in one year that pays a 5 percent rate of interest, or coupon rate. The bondholder receives $5 per year in interest until the bond matures. If the price of the bond is $100, the same as the face value, then the yield is 5 percent ($5/$100). But if the price of the bond is lower than the face value, say $95, the yield is $10/$95 = 10.52 percent. Thus, for a bond paying a 5 percent coupon, as the price rises, everything else the same, the quantity demanded will decline, so the demand curve slopes down. The demand for bonds depends on the coupon, the prices of and interest rates on other bonds and other investments, expectations of investors, income, and other factors. When one of the determinants of demand other than the bond's own price changes, the demand curve shifts. For instance, in Figure 12, an increase in interest rates on other investments will cause the demand for a bond offering a 5 percent coupon to decline—the demand curve shifts down from D_1 to D_2.

The suppliers of bonds are companies, governments, and other institutions offering new issues of IOUs and investors who own previously issued bonds and want to sell them. The supply curve slopes upward, illustrating the idea that as the price of an

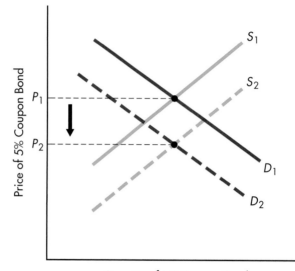

Quantity of 5% Coupon Bonds

The demand for bonds comes from lenders—investors who want to earn interest on their savings. The supply of bonds comes from the holders of bonds—firms and governments that are attempting to borrow and bond owners that are offering to sell. The quantity demanded of a bond paying a fixed coupon declines as the price of the bond rises; the quantity supplied of a bond paying a fixed coupon rises as the price of the bond rises. Demand and supply together determine the price of the bond. If expectations, interest rates on other investments, or something else other than the price of the bond changes, the demand for the bond and/or the supply of the bond will change—the curves will shift.

IOU rises, everything else the same, the quantity offered for sale rises. The supply depends on the prices of other bonds and investments, interest rates on other bonds and investments, and expectations of bond sellers. If interest rates on other investments rise, the quantity of bonds offering a 5 percent coupon that suppliers are willing and able to sell will rise—the supply curve shifts out, and the bond price falls.

As illustrated in Figure 12, the result of an increase in interest rates, everything else the same, is to cause the price on a 5 percent coupon bond to fall. This illustrates the fact that bond prices and interest rates are inversely related. Everything else the same, when interest rates rise, bond prices fall.

Bonds and stocks are often substitute goods, meaning that as the price of stocks rise, the demand for bonds rises. The reason for this is that investors sell their shares of stock and purchase bonds when interest rates are higher than the expected return on stocks. Suppose that investors are expecting stock prices to decline in the future. Then current shareholders will offer to sell more stock. The supply of shares of stock increases and demand drops, forcing stock prices down. Expecting stock prices to drop, investors purchase bonds and other assets, driving the price of bonds up. As the price of bonds rises, the interest rate declines (remember the inverse relationship between interest rate and bond price).

In some cases, bonds and stocks are complementary goods. An investor will purchase both stocks and bonds when both are expected to yield better returns than other investments and when the investor wants to diversify his or her portfolio—to not put all his or her eggs in one basket. Thus, we can't always say that when stock prices rise, bond prices will fall, and vice versa. In some circumstances, bond and stock prices will rise and fall together.

RECAP

1. Bonds are IOUs provided by the lender or issuer of the bond to the purchaser of the bond.
2. The demanders of bonds are individuals and mutual funds seeking the highest return given a certain amount of risk.
3. The suppliers of bonds are the original issuers or borrowers—corporations and governments—and bond owners who choose to sell bonds that they own.
4. The market for a bond consists of the demand for and supply of that bond. The price of the bond is determined by demand and supply.

Summary

1. What is the capital market?

- Capital is the machines, equipment, structures, and buildings that firms use to produce goods and services. *Preview*

- The demand for capital comes from firms that want to use capital in order to supply goods and services. The supply of capital comes from firms that provide the machines or buildings to other firms. *§1.a, 1.b*

- The demand for and supply of capital determine the rental price of capital and the quantities supplied and demanded. Nonprice determinants of demand include interest rates—the higher the interest rate, everything else the same, the lower is the quantity demanded. *§1.a, 1.c*

- The supply of funds with which firms acquire capital comes from selling stocks and bonds and taking out loans from financial institutions. *§1.b, 1.c*

2. What is the impact of technological change on the capital market?

- Technological change refers to improvements that allow more output to be produced for each unit of input. *§1.a*

- Firms demand more capital when technological change is occurring. Thus, technological change is a nonprice determinant of demand. *§1.a*

3. What are stocks? How are stocks bought and sold?

- Shares, equity, and stock mean the same thing—ownership of a piece of a company. *§2.a*

- There are two main types of stocks: common stock and preferred stock. *§2.a*

- Stocks are bought and sold on stock exchanges. A company will complete specified requirements and pay fees to have its stock listed on a particular exchange. Typically, the NYSE lists larger, well-known companies; Nasdaq lists high-tech and biotech companies; and the AMEX lists small-cap stocks. Non-U.S. companies are listed on stock exchanges in their own countries. *§2.a.1*

4. What does a stock index represent?

- A stock index is a measure of the price movements of a group of stocks. The best-known indexes are the Dow Jones Industrial Average, the S&P 500, the Nasdaq Composite, and the Wilshire 5000, but there are other indexes for U.S. companies and indexes for every stock exchange in the world. *§2.a.1*

- A mutual fund is a group of stocks or bonds of individual companies or governments placed into one investment pool. *§2.b*

5. What causes stock prices to rise and fall?

- The equity market is the market in which stocks are bought and sold. *§3*

- The demand for equities comes from investors who are seeking the greatest return on their savings—individuals, mutual funds, and institutions like insurance companies. *§3*

- The supply of equities comes from stock owners who want to sell their stock and purchase something else. This is known as the secondary market. The primary market is the market for new issues—stocks that had not previously been sold by the firms. It is the secondary market that people are referring to when they speak of the stock market. *§3*

- Demand depends on expectations, income, and prices of and returns on other investments. Supply depends on expectations and on prices of and returns on other investments. A change in one of these determinants of demand and/or supply will cause demand and/or supply to change. *§3.b*

- If buyers want to buy more of a stock (demand) than sellers want to sell (supply), then the price will move up. Conversely, if sellers want to sell more of a stock than buyers want to buy, the price will fall. *§3.b*

- The equity market is said to be an efficient market in the sense that it is difficult for an investor to continually earn above-normal profits. If there were a secret formula for becoming rich in the stock market, everyone would soon learn that formula, and it would no longer be an effective strategy. *§3.c*

- Bubbles and panics occur because people are simply jumping on the bandwagon without an underlying economic basis. Although these tendencies can affect the prices of stocks in the short run, it is the performance of the firm that determines the stock price in the long run. *§3.c*

6. What do ethics have to do with financial capital?

- Unethical behavior by executives of firms can undermine the capital markets. *§3.d*

- When people begin to expect that firms will perform poorly because of mismanagement or corruption or when people begin not to trust reports, they will not purchase stocks and bonds. *§3.d.2*

7. What causes bond prices to rise and fall?

- Bonds are IOUs provided by a lender or issuer of the bond to the purchaser of the bond. *§4*

- The demanders of bonds are individuals and mutual funds that are seeking the highest return given a certain amount of risk. *§4.c*

- The suppliers of bonds are corporations and governments attempting to borrow money and the owners of previously issued bonds who choose to sell their bonds. *§4.c*

- The market for a bond consists of the demand for and supply of that bond. As with the stock market, demand depends on the prices of and expected returns on other investments, income, and investor expectations; supply depends on the prices of and expected returns on other investments and supplier (bond issuer) expectations. *§4.c*

- The price of a bond is determined by demand and supply. *§4.c*

- There is an inverse relationship between bond prices and interest rates. As the interest rate rises, bond prices fall, and vice versa. *§4.c*

Key Terms

dividend *§2.a*	socially responsible fund *§2.b*	comparable investment *§3*
market capitalization (market cap) *§2.a.3*	index fund *§2.b*	bond *§4*
	load *§2.b*	maturity date *§4*
mutual fund *§2.b*	front-end load *§2.b*	face or par value *§4*
global fund *§2.b*	back-end load *§2.b*	coupon *§4*
specific fund *§2.b*	no-load fund *§2.b*	zero-coupon bond *§4.b*

Exercises

1. What is saving? What role does it play in financial markets?

2. Investors know for sure that the CEO of firm A will undertake an investment that will yield $100 million profit next year and then $2 million each year after that for 10 years. They also know for sure that the CEO of

firm B will undertake an investment that will yield nothing for two years and then a profit of $20 million per year for 10 years. Which company will have the higher stock price today, next year, the second year, the third year?

3. The investors in exercise 2 are surprised by firm B's performance in year 5. Instead of being $20 million, the

firm's profits are $40 million. What happens to firm B's stock price in years 6 and 7?

4. Nova Corporation has just announced that it has had a record good year. Its earnings have increased nearly 10 percent. Explain how this announcement can lead to a decline in the price of Nova Corporation's stock.

5. The Benly Company needs to raise funds for a major expansion. The company is debating whether to issue stock or to issue bonds. If the company issues bonds, then its debt will increase and it will be under additional stress to ensure that its revenues can cover the costs of its debt. If it issues stock, the current owners will lose power and influence. What should the company do? Explain your answer.

6. The Federal Reserve has just lowered interest rates. Explain the effect of that on bond prices.

7. In exercise 6, not only bond prices but also stock prices are affected. Explain why.

8. Suppose the price elasticity of demand for stocks is 1.5. This means that for every 10 percent increase in stock prices, the quantity demanded will decline by 15 percent. Does this price elasticity make sense? Explain.

9. Suppose the cross-price elasticity of demand between stocks and bonds is negative 1.2. If stock prices are

expected to rise by 10 percent, what is expected to happen to bond prices? Does this make sense? Explain.

10. Which would you expect bonds and stocks to be, substitutes or complements? Explain.

11. From 2000 to 2003, stock prices declined by about 33 percent. Explain why this occurred. If stock prices have been falling for a period of time, what would have to happen to get them to turn around and begin rising again?

12. The price of a stock is determined by the demand for and supply of that stock. Both demand and supply depend on investors' expectations of the future performance—future economic profits—of the firm. Explain what happens to a firm's stock when the company earns less than investors had expected.

13. IBM recently announced that its earnings declined during the past quarter, yet its stock price rose. How could this occur?

14. During the second quarter of 2003, both bond prices and stock prices fell. Explain why this occurred.

15. Explain why stock prices fall when a company is found to be carrying out unethical and illegal activities.

ACE

Practice Test

Take the ACE Practice Test for this chapter to review the important concepts and get immediate feedback with answers.

college.hmco.com/economics/students/

Accountants Figure Law to Benefit Them

Chicago Sun-Times
November 18, 2002

"The Sarbanes-Oxley Act might as well be called the Enron-Andersen Act," says attorney Peggy Zagel.

The law, which Congress adopted in July in the wake of corporate scandals at Enron, WorldCom, Tyco, and other prominent companies, is intended to make corporate fraud more difficult to commit and conceal.

The law probably will have some potent side effects, too. Many Chicago area businesses—including law, accounting, and consulting firms—see the new accounting and financial reporting rules mandated by Sarbanes-Oxley as an opportunity to boost revenue.

"It can almost be seen as the Lawyer and Accountant Full Employment Act," wisecracked Zagel, who recently was hired by Chicago law firm Altheimer & Gray to generate business by helping companies comply with Sarbanes-Oxley.

Another Chicago-based company, Parson Consulting, is licking its chops over the opportunities presented by the law. "This is a radical transformation of corporate governance," said Dan Weinfurter, president of Parson Consulting. Among the main provisions of Sarbanes-Oxley:

- Top management must certify corporate financial results.
- Deadlines were tightened for filing results.
- Regulations were tightened regarding potential conflicts of interest for accounting firms. For instance, an auditor of record is now barred from handling work other than tax and auditing responsibilities for a single client.
- Financial resources must be provided to key board committees so they can hire outside counsel to advise on issues such as compensation and audit functions.

Weinfurter sees an opportunity for Parson Consulting, a firm that specializes in financial and accounting consulting, in helping corporations adhere to the law. Companies will need help not only in setting up programs to comply with the law, but in executing those programs on a daily basis.

"Our focus has been on Fortune 1000 companies," he said. "We feel that we're very well positioned. We don't do tax and audit work for anyone. We're completely conflict-free."

Additionally, Weinfurter pointed out that the accelerated filing deadlines with the SEC probably will force many companies to rely on consultants, rather than adding employees, to process the welter of complex financial data more quickly. Processes will also have to be updated, Weinfurter said. "When you're used to closing your books in 45 days, and you now have to get that down to 20, you can't just work harder. You have to fundamentally change the process," he said.

It is too early to gauge the exact impact the new law will have on the company's revenues, Weinfurter said, but what he has seen so far is encouraging.

"We've noticed a big change in our corporate clients," he said. Chief financial officers who were difficult to reach in the past now return calls, he said.

Sean Callahan

The Sarbanes-Oxley Act of 2002 was intended to reform the practices of accounting firms, corporate boards, and Wall Street stock analysts and thereby protect the small investor and consumer from unethical practices and fraud. The major provisions of the act are:

1. Companies must disclose whether a board's audit committee has at least one "financial expert" and, if not, the reason for the absence.

2. It is generally unlawful for an accounting firm to provide any major nonaudit service (bookkeeping, for example) to a client while completing that company's audit.

3. The CEO and CFO must swear to the accuracy of the company's quarterly and annual financial reports. An officer who certifies a report that does not conform to the requirements of Sarbanes-Oxley faces a fine of not more than $1 million and a sentence of not more than 10 years in jail, or both.

4. The act established the Public Company Accounting Oversight Board, or PCAOB—nicknamed Peekaboo.

5. New rules separate Wall Street's stock analysis from its deal-making side and punish companies that retaliate against analysts who criticize them.

6. The act makes tampering with corporate records a crime. The maximum penalty for mail and wire fraud has increased from five to ten years.

Economics is the study of unintended consequences; economists judge whether a public policy (rules, regulations, laws) is beneficial—that is, whether it creates more benefits than costs. The Sarbanes-Oxley Act was intended to protect investors by forcing public companies to stand behind their financial reports. But although the six major provisions of the act listed here may seem to benefit small investors and consumers, there are some unintended consequences of the act that suggest a different interpretation. One unintended effect is that firms have to bear higher costs of doing business. The initial estimate was that the compliance cost would be about $1.2 billion, but in 2005 it was $35 billion. Firms are hiring more lawyers, accountants, and consultants specializing in corporate governance and are allocating more resources to internal staffs that focus on the act. Where do the resources come from that are used to comply with the Sarbanes-Oxley Act? They are taken from any or all other uses of resources by each firm. As a result of taking resources away from other uses, the firm may be less efficient or may have lower profits than was the case prior to the act.

Some of the additional costs will be passed along to consumers; the amount depends on the price elasticities of demand and supply (as discussed in the chapter "Elasticity: Demand and Supply"). In addition, lower profits mean lower stock prices; because the additional costs imposed on firms are not the same for every firm, some firms will be affected more than others. Some investors may be harmed by the act in that their stocks will not rise in value as much as otherwise would have been the case. A recent study at the University of Rochester concluded that the total effect of the law has reduced the stock value of American companies by $1.4 trillion (see Mallory Factor, "Rule of Law," *Wall Street Journal*, March 18–19, 2006, p. A9).

So, how should we evaluate whether the Sarbanes-Oxley Act benefits society? The answer depends on whether the unintended consequences have greater costs than the benefits of the act. This comparison of costs and benefits will determine whether the act is good public policy. As of April 2006, it looked as if Congress was deciding that the costs outweighed the benefits. Proposals from both Democrats and Republicans at that time were to change the law.

chapter

18

The Land Market and Natural Resources

G lobal warming, the destruction of the rain forests, the depletion of the ozone layer, the extinction of animal species, and other environmental issues are of great concern to many people. So are the costs that people have to pay in the name of the environment: higher prices for cars as a result of emission controls, annual fees to test for emissions from cars, higher gas prices because of refining requirements, higher taxes to pay for cleaning up the environment, and so on. All of these issues occur in the "land market." In this chapter we examine the market for land and natural resources. ■

? **Fundamental Questions**

1. **What is the difference between the land market and the markets for uses of land?**

2. **What is a housing bubble?**

3. **What is the difference between renewable and nonrenewable natural resources?**

4. **What is the optimal rate of use of natural resources?**

1. Land

The category of resources that we call "land" refers not just to the land surface, but to everything associated with the land—the natural resources. Natural resources are the nonproduced resources with which a society is endowed. A market exists for each type of natural resource and for each use of land.

?

1. What is the difference between the land market and the markets for uses of land?

1.a. Fixed Supply of Land

The market for land is, in the most general terms, a market with a fixed supply. There is only so much land available. Obviously land is used in many different ways—for cities and housing, parks, wilderness areas, agricultural areas, and on and on. For each use of land, there is a market in which the typical demand and supply curves apply. For instance, the market for land on which to put housing has a demand curve that slopes down and a supply curve that slopes up. As the price of land available for housing rises, the quantity of land demanded for housing declines and the quantity of land available increases. However, in the general market for land, where there is a fixed supply of land, we have a downward-sloping demand curve but a perfectly inelastic supply curve.

Recall from the discussion of resource markets that when a resource has a perfectly inelastic supply curve, its earnings are called **economic rent.** If a resource has a perfectly elastic supply curve, its earnings are called **transfer earnings.** For resources with upward-sloping supply curves, earnings consist of both transfer earnings and economic rent. Transfer earnings are what a resource could earn in its best

economic rent: the portion of earnings above transfer earnings

transfer earnings: the amount that must be paid to a resource owner to get him or her to allocate the resource to another use

This sea of red tile roofs is the result of new homes built in Las Vegas, Nevada, the fastest growing city in the United States. The demand for new housing means a demand for land on which to put new housing. Because the use of land for housing is more valuable than the use of the land as open desert, the land is reallocated. Water is a different matter. Las Vegas has no natural supply of water; instead, water is brought in from the Colorado River. Yet, there is a huge demand for the water to be used in swimming pools. As the population of Las Vegas continues to grow, the demand for water will continue to rise. Eventually, water prices will begin rising, to match demand and supply.

alternative use. This is the amount that must be paid to get the resource owner to "transfer" the resource to another use. Economic rent is earnings in excess of transfer earnings. It is the portion of a resource's earnings that is not necessary to keep the resource in its current use.

You've seen that there are two different meanings for the term *rent* in economics. The more common meaning refers to the payment for the use of something—the rent on an apartment, for instance. The second use of the term *rent* is to mean payment for something whose quantity is fixed—that is, that has a perfectly inelastic supply. The total quantity of land is fixed, so payment for land is economic rent.

The reason that the earnings of a good, service, or resource whose supply is fixed are called economic rent is to distinguish the result of changes in rent from that of changes in the price of a good, service, or resource that is not fixed in quantity. When the price of a good increases, everything else the same, the quantity supplied will increase. But when economic rent increases, quantity supplied cannot increase. Therefore, an increase in economic rent is simply a transfer from the buyer to the seller without any change in quantity.

As we saw in the chapter "Government and Market Failure," the term *rent seeking* is used to distinguish the result of actions designed to gain additional income or wealth by seeking profits from the result of actions designed to do so by seeking rents. An increase in profits will bring on additional production and increased quantities supplied; an increase in rents simply transfers income from buyers to sellers. Rent seeking is not a productive activity; profit seeking is. Thus, economists refer to lobbying by individuals or groups to gain favors from the government as rent seeking. The resources devoted to the lobbying will not increase productive activities and quantities supplied; they merely transfer income and wealth from one individual or group to another. Rent seeking does not increase an economy's growth and improve its standards of living; profit seeking does.

1.b. Uses of Land

When we break the market for land into markets for uses of land, then the supplies are not fixed, and prices and profits function as they do in any other market: They allocate land to alternative uses. For instance, an increase in the demand for housing will drive the price of land used for housing up, inducing landowners to offer more of their land in the housing market. The land has to come from somewhere, so an increase in land devoted to housing means less land devoted to parks or agriculture or wilderness. The use of land is shifted to where the land has the highest value.

1.c. A Housing Bubble?

bubble: a situation in which the price of an asset is being bid up through speculation or gambling rather than because of the value of the services the asset returns

The term **bubble** means that the price of an asset is being bid up through speculation or gambling rather than because of the value of the services the asset returns. When the price of a stock rises significantly higher than can be justified by the dividends the firm can be expected to pay in the future, a stock bubble is said to have occurred. (This in fact did happen in the latter part of the 1990s.) The same applies to any asset—when the price of the asset rises significantly above the value of the services the asset provides, a bubble is occurring. Between 1998 and 2006, house prices in the United States rose more than 45 percent after adjusting for inflation. Is this a housing bubble?

As we have just discussed, land prices are determined by the demand for and supply of land. The prices of the structures on that land are also set by demand and supply. If housing prices are rising, then demand has been rising relative to supply. What has been driving the price of houses up? People want housing for the services

2. What is a housing bubble?

it provides—a roof over their head, among others—and people can obtain these services either by renting or by purchasing. The choice facing people is whether to purchase and give up the use of the money they have to put into buying the house, or to rent and use the money that is not used to purchase to buy stocks or some other asset. People will purchase when it is relatively less costly than renting.

When people purchase an asset, any asset, they expect that asset to provide benefits or payments in the future. For a stock, the payoff is the future earnings of the firm. People buy a stock thinking that they will get paid each year through dividends or appreciation, so the price they are willing to pay depends on how long they think it will take for the firm to pay them back. The P/E ratio gives an indication of this.[1] If you pay $40 for a share of stock, and the earnings per share is $2, then the P/E ratio is 20/1, which tells us that if the performance of the firm stays the same, it will take 20 years for the firm's earnings to add up to the purchase price.

If you think about a house in the same way, then you want to find how long it will take for the value of the housing services you receive each year to add up to the price of the house; this should be about the same as adding up all rents to be paid in the future. A ratio of the prices of houses to the rents on houses (P/R) can be calculated as shown in Figure 1. The figure suggests that current prices are high relative to rents. Is this a housing bubble? There definitely appears to be a large and growing deviation between prices and rents, but exactly how large and how long lasting a deviation must be to constitute a bubble is far from obvious.

Imagine a real estate market near the Boeing factory outside Seattle. The company announces that within five years, it is moving its operations to Chicago. This

FIGURE 1 The Price-Rent (P/R) Ratio

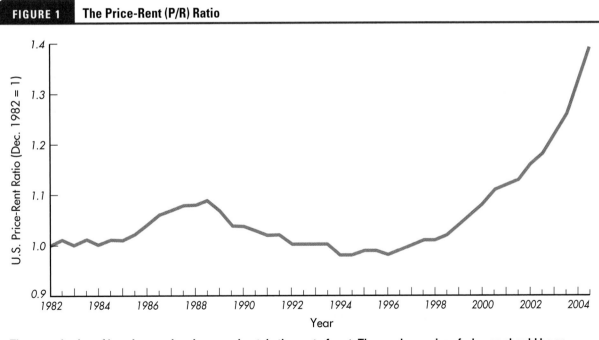

The annual value of housing services is approximately the cost of rent. The purchase price of a house should be approximately equal to the total rents that would have to be paid over the life of the house. When the deviation gets large, people begin looking at the housing market as a speculative market or a bubble. *Source: http://calculatedrisk .blogspot.com.*

---

[1] The P/E ratio is price per share divided by earnings per share of a given stock. See Chapter 33 capital markets for further discussion of the P/E ratio.

would be an adverse shock to the demand for housing and would drive house prices down immediately. However, current rental prices would remain the same, since these prices are set by contracts and there is time before people leave the area. Such an event should send the price-rent ratio down. Alternatively, consider the Chicago suburbs where Boeing announced that it would be locating. This area would certainly experience a higher demand for housing, and the price-rent ratio would increase. If the movement of the price-rent ratio is accounted for by future growth in rents and future returns, then this is not a bubble (and conversely for a decline). But if demand increases solely for speculative reasons, then a bubble exists.

RECAP

1. The total supply of land is fixed.

2. The payment to landowners is economic rent because there are no transfer payments that serve to allocate resources.

3. The amount of land devoted to any given use is not fixed. The use of land depends on the demand for and supply of that use.

4. A housing bubble means that the value of the housing services that houses generate over time is far less than the purchase price of those houses.

?

3. What is the difference between renewable and nonrenewable natural resources?

nonrenewable (exhaustible) natural resources: natural resources whose supply is fixed

2. Nonrenewable Resources

Nonrenewable (exhaustible) natural resources can be used only once and cannot be replaced. Examples include coal, natural gas, and oil. The market for nonrenewable natural resources consists of the demand for and supply of these resources. Supply depends on the amount of the resource in existence, and the supply curve is perfectly inelastic. Only a fixed amount of oil or coal exists, so the more that is used in any given year, the less that remains for future use. This means that an upward-sloping supply curve exists for a particular period of time, such as a year. The quantity that resource owners are willing to extract and offer for sale during any particular year depends on the price of the resource. The supply curve in Figure 2(a) is upward sloping to reflect the relationship between the price of the resource today and the amount extracted and offered to users today. Resource owners are willing to extract more of a resource from its natural state and offer it for sale as the price of the resource increases.

When some of the resource is used today, less is available next year. The supply curve of the resource in the future shifts in, as shown in Figure 2(b) by the move from S_1 to S_2. The shift occurs because the cost of extracting any quantity of the resource rises as the amount of the resource in existence falls. The first amounts extracted come from the most accessible sources, and each additional quantity then comes from a less accessible source. For instance, in the late 1800s, oil became an important resource. At first, it was extracted with small pumps that gathered up oil seeping out of the ground. Once that extremely accessible source was gone, wells had to be dug. Over time, wells had to be deeper and had to be placed in progressively more difficult terrain. From land, to the ocean off California, to the rugged waters off Alaska, to the wicked North Sea, the search for oil has progressed. As more and more is extracted, the marginal cost of extracting any given amount increases, and the supply curve shifts up.

FIGURE 2   **The Market for Nonrenewable Resources**

(a) Demand and Supply

(b) Costs of Extraction Rise Over Time

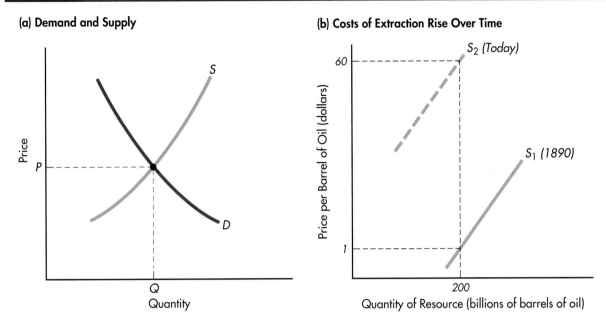

The demand curve slopes down, and the supply curve slopes up. The intersection of demand and supply determines the quantity used today and the price at which the quantity was sold, as shown in Figure 2(a). As quantities are used today, less remains for the future. Because the available quantities come from increasingly more expensive sources, the supply curve shifts in over time, as shown in Figure 2(b). The curve S_1 represents the supply in 1890 and S_2 represents the supply today. For the quantity supplied at 200 billion barrels, the price was $1 per barrel in 1890, and today the price is $60.

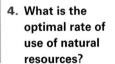

4. What is the optimal rate of use of natural resources?

If 200 billion barrels of crude oil are extracted this year, then the extraction of another 200 billion barrels in the future will be more difficult—more expensive—than the extraction of the 200 billion barrels was this year. This increase is illustrated by an inward shift of the supply curve in Figure 2(b).

The demand for a nonrenewable natural resource is determined in the same way as the demand for any other resource. It is the marginal revenue product of the resource. Thus, anything that affects the *MRP* of the nonrenewable resource will affect the demand for that resource.

Equilibrium occurs in the market for a nonrenewable natural resource when the demand and supply curves intersect, as shown in Figure 3. The equilibrium price, $15, and quantity, 200 billion barrels, represent the price and quantity today. Extracting and selling the equilibrium quantity of 200 billion barrels today reduces the quantity available tomorrow by 200 billion barrels. This means that extracting the resource tomorrow is probably going to be more costly than extracting it today. Thus, the supply curve for the resource in the future lies above the supply curve for today—S_2 rather than S_1, if any of the resource is being consumed today. With a higher supply curve and the same demand, the price is higher, $20 rather than $15. Thus, the price in the future is likely to be higher than the price today if some of the resource is extracted and sold today.

The resource owner must decide whether to extract and sell the resource today or leave it in the ground for future use. Suppose that by extracting and selling the oil

FIGURE 3 Price Today and in the Future

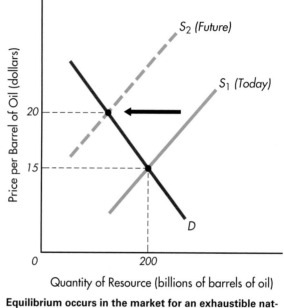

Equilibrium occurs in the market for an exhaustible natural resource when the demand and supply curves intersect. The equilibrium price, $15, and quantity, 200 billion
barrels, represent the price and quantity of the resource
used today. Selling the equilibrium quantity of 200 billion barrels today reduces the quantity available tomorrow by 200 billion barrels. With a smaller and probably
less accessible quantity available, extracting the
resource tomorrow is probably going to be more costly
than extracting it today. Thus, the supply curve for the
resource in the future lies above the supply curve for
today, S_2 rather than S_1 if any of the resource is being
consumed today. With a higher supply curve, the price
is higher, $20 rather than $15. Thus, the price in the
future is likely to be higher than the price today.

that lies below the land today, a landowner can make a profit of $10 per barrel after
all costs of extraction have been paid. The owner could buy stocks or bonds with
that $10, put the money into a savings account, or use it to acquire education or mar-
ketable skills. If the interest rate is 10 percent, the owner could realize $11 one year
from now from the $10 profit obtained today. Should the oil be extracted today? The
answer depends on how much profit the resource owner expects to earn on the oil
one year from now, and this depends on what the price of oil and the cost of extraction are one year from now.

If the owner expects to obtain a profit of $13 a barrel one year from now, the
oil should be left in the ground. If the profit on the oil one year from now is
expected to be only $10.50, the oil should be extracted and the proceeds used to
buy stocks or bonds or put in a savings account. The more that a simple bank
account or interest-bearing investment yields, the more oil is extracted and sold.
As the interest rate rises, more is extracted and sold today, and less is left for the
future.

Because suppliers and potential suppliers continually calculate whether to extract now or in the future and how much to extract, an equilibrium arises in which the year-to-year rate of return for the resource equals the rate of interest on alternative uses of the funds. If the rate of interest is 10 percent a year, everything else held constant, the resource price will rise at a rate of about 10 percent a year (the rate of return must be 10 percent).

Suppose the interest rate rises above the current rate of return on the nonrenewable resource, oil. The higher interest rate means that producers will pump more oil out of the ground today and purchase stocks, bonds, or savings accounts with the money they get from selling the oil. More extraction means that the supply curve today shifts out and today's price falls. At the same time, the supply curve in the future shifts in (since less will be available in the future) and the future price rises. This will occur until the rate of return on leaving the oil in the ground equals the interest rate—that is, until the value of pumping the oil and selling it is the same as the value of the oil left in the ground. A higher interest rate implies the use of more resources today. Conversely, a lower interest rate implies the use of fewer resources today.

RECAP

1. Nonrenewable natural resources are natural resources whose supply is fixed.

2. The market's role is to ensure that resources are allocated across time to where they are most highly valued. If more is used today, the return on saving the resource for future use rises.

3. The higher the interest-earning potential on financial investments, the more of the nonrenewable resource is extracted today.

4. The more a nonrenewable resource is consumed today, the less it is available in the future and the higher its price is in the future.

---

3. Renewable Resources _____

renewable (nonexhaustible) natural resources: natural resources whose supply can be replenished

Renewable (nonexhaustible) natural resources can be used repeatedly without depleting the amount available for future use. Plants and animals are classified as nonexhaustible natural resources because it is possible for them to renew themselves and thus replace those used in production and consumption activities. The prices of renewable resources and the quantities used are determined in the markets for renewable resources. The role of the market is to determine a price at which the quantity of the resource used is just sufficient to enable the resource to renew itself at a rate that best satisfies society's wants.

Owners of forest lands could harvest all their trees in one year and reap a huge profit. But if they did so, several years would pass before the trees would have grown enough to be cut again. The rate at which the trees are harvested depends on the interest rate. A large harvest one year means fewer trees available in the future and a longer time for renewal to occur. This would suggest a lower price today and a higher price in the future. If the interest rate rises, everything else held constant, owners will want to increase harvesting in order to get more money with which to purchase stocks and bonds. This means harvesting more trees now and having fewer available in the future, thereby driving up the price of the trees that are not cut today. If the interest rate falls, owners will want to harvest fewer trees today. This means that today's price will rise and the future price will fall. As was the case with the nonrenewable resources, the market adjusts so that the resources are allocated to their highest-valued use now and in the future. The timing of the use of resources depends on the rate of interest.

Suppose you raise beef cattle and you want to remain in that business for most of your lifetime and eventually to pass it along to your children. You will sell only part of your herd each year to ensure that you will have a herd to raise next year, the year after, and so on. If you sell more in any one year, the size of your herd the next year will be smaller. If you sell the entire herd, you will have nothing in the future. What you want to do is to maximize your economic profit over the time periods during which you and your family remain in the business of cattle raising. Thus, you allocate the sale of your cattle over the various time periods. If the price of beef cattle increases rapidly one year because of mad cow disease in Britain, then you would sell more of your herd that year. Conversely, if the price of beef cattle falls substantially one year because of reports that eating beef causes heart disease, then you would sell fewer cattle that year. But, even though the size of your herd varies with the price of cattle and the interest-earning potential of other financial investments, you don't sell off your entire herd unless you plan to get out of the cattle business. You retain enough cattle so that they can propagate and replenish the herd.

The same principle applies to any renewable resource that is privately owned. The owner has the incentive to ensure that sufficient supplies exist in the future to maximize profits over all time periods. Some people argue that forests should not be privately owned because logging firms would raze or clear-cut the forests, leaving nothing for the future. But this makes no sense. No logging company that owns and logs its own forests would sell off all its trees unless it planned to get out of the logging business. When renewable resources are privately owned, the market ensures that resources are allocated between the current period and the future so that those resources are used in the most valuable manner. The private owners want to maximize their profit over the current and future periods.

A problem arises with the current use of a resource, whether renewable or nonrenewable, when the resource is not privately owned. Recall from the chapter "Government and Market Failure," that private property rights are necessary if markets are to work. When common ownership exists, the common property is overused. Many natural resources are overused because they are not privately owned. For instance, many fish are overfished; some are nearly extinct. Many animals are overhunted; some are nearly extinct. Many forests are razed; these are owned commonly (by a government). Air, lakes, streams, and oceans are often overused or polluted because they are not privately owned.

In summary, the markets for nonrenewable and renewable resources operate to ensure that current and future wants are satisfied in the least costly manner and that resources are used in their highest-valued alternative now and in the future. When a nonrenewable resource is being rapidly depleted, its future price rises and the value of using the resource in the future rises, so that less of the resource is used today. When a renewable resource is being used at a rate that does not allow it to replenish itself, the future price rises and the value of the future use rises, so that less of the resource is used today.

1. Renewable natural resources are natural resources that can be replenished.

2. The rate of use of renewable resources in a functioning market system is one that equalizes the rate of return on the resource and the return on comparable investments.

3. A problem arises with the current use of resources, whether they are renewable or nonrenewable, when the resource is not privately owned. When common ownership exists, the common property is overused. Many natural resources are overused because they are not privately owned.

Summary

1. What is the difference between the land market and the markets for uses of land?

- The total amount of land is fixed. *§1.a*

- Changes in the price of land do not change the quantity supplied. *§1.a*

- There are many uses of land, and how much land is allocated to each use depends on the demand for and supply of land for each use. *§1.b*

2. What is a housing bubble?

- When the value of the services an asset provides (its payoff) over time is far less than the purchase price of the asset, a bubble may exist. *§1.c*

- People purchase houses for two reasons: to obtain the services houses provide—a roof over your head—and to gain from the appreciation of the house. People can rent if they want the housing services but think that the expected appreciation will be less than the opportunity cost of the difference between the purchase price and the rental value of housing services. *§1.c*

- Although housing prices have been rising rapidly during the past few years, it is difficult to tell whether there is a housing bubble. *§1.c*

3. What is the difference between renewable and nonrenewable natural resources?

- Nonrenewable natural resources are inert resources—coal, oil, and so on—that are fixed in supply. *§2*

- Renewable natural resources are resources that can regenerate, such as wildlife, flora, and fauna. *§3*

4. What is the optimal rate of use of natural resources?

- The optimal rate of use of nonrenewable resources is not zero. It is the rate at which the nonrenewable resource can satisfy society's wants now and in the future. *§2*

- The optimal rate of use of renewable resources is the rate that equates the expected return from using the resources and the expected return from not using them. *§3*

Key Terms

economic rent *§1.a*

transfer earnings *§1.a*

bubble *§1.c*

nonrenewable (exhaustible) natural resources *§2*

renewable (nonexhaustible) natural resources *§3*

Exercises

1. The market for some good or service is shown by the demand and supply curves below.
   a. Illustrate what transfer earnings and economic rent are.
   b. Explain what would occur if the demand for the good or service were to increase.

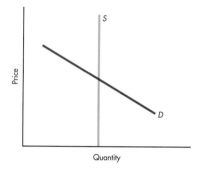

2. The market for some good or service is shown by the demand and supply curves below.
   a. Illustrate what transfer earnings and economic rent are.
   b. Explain what would occur if the demand for the good or service were to increase.

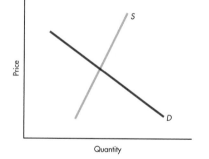

3. Since the early 2000s, people have been talking about a housing bubble. In its June 9, 2003, issue, the *Economist* magazine discussed the possibility that the real estate market might be in a speculative bubble. Explain what a bubble is. Explain how a bubble in housing could occur.

4. It is often stated that an artist is not famous until after he or she dies. Why do artists' works rise in price much more rapidly after the artist is dead than during the artist's life? How does this relate to the land market?

5. How would you describe economic rent in the case of a movie star earning millions of dollars each year?

6. If the world's population is rising and the quantity of land is not changing, won't the world eventually run out of room? Explain, using the market for land.

7. Will the world ever run out of a nonrenewable resource? Explain.

8. Suppose the supply of oil that had not yet been used was suddenly lost as a result of a rupture in the earth. What would occur?

9. The difference between a renewable and a nonrenewable resource is that the renewable resource can be replenished. Is there a difference between the markets for the two types of resources? What is the "optimal" rate of use of either renewable or nonrenewable resources?

10. In 2003, Alan Greenspan, chairman of the Federal Reserve, convinced the Open Market Committee to reduce the interest rate to near zero percent in an attempt to stimulate spending in the economy and increase the growth of income and employment. What might this policy do to the use of natural resources? Explain.

11. Urban sprawl is described as the establishment of housing and commercial development increasingly far from the city center. What might be the effect on sprawl if it was the policy of a city to build the infrastructure—sewers, power, and other essential services—to these developments at the average cost to the city? If it built the infrastructure at the marginal cost to the city?

12. If a city's political leaders decided to limit sprawl by restricting residential and commercial development to an area within a prescribed distance from the city center, what would be the effect on land prices in the areas inside the development boundary and outside the development boundary?

ACE

Take the ACE Practice Test for this chapter to review the important concepts and get immediate feedback with answers.

college.hmco.com/economics/students/

Debate: Is Anti-Sprawl Really "Smart" Growth?

The Herald-Sun (**Durham, NC**)
March 29, 2003

Imagine Durham as bread and housing growth as peanut butter.

If you spread the peanut butter across the bread in one smooth stroke that would be suburban sprawl, said Frank Duke, director for the City/County Planning Department, trying to put the complicated issues of population growth, the environment and anti-sprawl efforts into layman's terms.

But with anti-sprawl ordinances or what is often called "smart growth" the peanut butter is spread out in chunks, where sensitive areas and different community resources are protected, Duke said.

Currently, Durham has a traditional land-use plan. It treats all areas the same and ends up encouraging suburban sprawl, Duke said.

Durham is in the process of defining a unified development ordinance to guide growth and deter sprawl, Duke said. The plan would prohibit housing developments in environmentally sensitive areas and promote cluster developments, where housing units are grouped together so that other areas can remain undeveloped.

But smart growth has its downside, said David Almasey of the National Center for Public Policy and Research.

A recent report commissioned by the center claims that anti-growth policies hurt the poor and minorities by increasing housing costs and decreasing housing options. The center is a Washington-based conservative foundation that researches public policy.

The study, "Smart Growth and Its Effects on Housing Markets: The New Segregation," examined restricted growth policies in Portland, Ore., said Almasey, who spoke at a Triangle Community Coalition luncheon this week. The Triangle Community Coalition's stated mission is to promote public policy that supports a balance between economic growth, development, the environment, and community needs while it protects the rights and interests of property owners.

The study examined what would happen to housing costs if Portland's policies were applied nationwide. It found more than 1 million disadvantaged families—260,000 of them minority families—would have been unable to buy homes because the cost of the average home would have risen $7,000. The study found the cost of renting would have risen 6 percent.

Instead of restricting growth, the anti-sprawl policies caused housing prices in restricted areas to rise and people who could not afford the costs to move, Almasey said.

But anti-sprawl efforts are more than site restrictions, said Cara Crisler, executive director of the N.C. Smart Growth Alliance, which is based in Carrboro. The center's report was a misrepresentation about what "smart growth" is, she said.

Duke, who wasn't familiar with the report or the organization, said, "any zoning and land development regulation that is not approached with sensitivity will adversely affect affordable housing."

Durham's current ordinances promote segregation, said Duke, who added that he's working to create anti-sprawl policies that will not inhibit growth but instead will recognize that different regulations are needed to protect distinct areas.

Durham County Commissioner Joe Bowser, who was recently elected the president of the Durham chapter of the NAACP, said the civil rights organization hasn't taken a position on "smart growth" but plans to talk about it in the future.

Bowser questioned whether "smart growth" really "ends up pitting community against homebuilders" by raising housing costs. He said it would be more appropriate to link lack of home ownership with lack of job-training opportunities rather than anti-sprawl efforts.

Virginia Bridges

"Sprawl" refers to a situation in which the distance from city center to outermost suburbs in a metropolitan area is increasing. Many people find sprawl unsightly and unpleasant. They want to restrict growth and sprawl and increase the density in which people live. In many cities, boundaries have been placed around urban areas, beyond which no housing and commercial development may occur.

In this article, one city that is considering reducing sprawl is Durham, North Carolina, which currently treats all areas the same and ends up encouraging sprawl. What is the economic rationale for sprawl? Why do people move farther and farther from the city center? Primarily because land prices are lower the farther from the city you live. Open space and agricultural areas have a lower price per acre than land that is used for housing or commercial development. As open space or agricultural land becomes more valuable as housing property, landowners will sell the land to housing developers. The developers, because they are able to acquire land more inexpensively than if they were purchasing land in the city center, then build housing that is relatively inexpensive compared to similar housing closer to the city center. People choose to purchase the less expensive housing even though it often means longer commutes. This increases the price of housing and drives development further away from the city center. This process has occurred in many metropolitan areas.

A few metropolitan areas have attempted to alter the economic process of sprawl. For example, Portland, Oregon, placed a boundary around the city and forbade development outside that boundary. What is the effect of such restrictions?

In the figure, the situation in Portland prior to the growth restrictions is shown by the supply curve without growth restrictions. The price is P_1. Now suppose that the city planners decide to impose a growth boundary equal to the amount of land currently used for housing and commercial buildings. Nothing would change as long as demand did not change. But if demand increases, such as to Demand$_2$, additional land cannot be shifted from open space or agricultural uses to housing and commercial uses. As a result, the price rises considerably more than it would without growth restrictions.

This is what the study noted in the article concludes. It found that if such antigrowth policies had been imposed nationwide, the cost of the average home would have risen $7,000, and the cost of renting would have risen 6 percent. Another aspect of the study is to point out just which group in society would be harmed by this policy. More than 1 million disadvantaged families—260,000 of them minority families—would have been unable to buy homes because of the restriction on land use, according to the study.

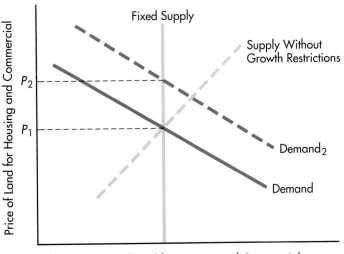

Quantity of Land for Housing and Commercial

19

Aging, Social Security, and Health Care

The population of the United States is aging rapidly. Currently, more than 12 percent of the population is retired—living off pensions, savings, and social security. By the year 2030, 21 percent of the population will be older than 65. The aging of the population is likely to have a dramatic effect on living standards. For instance, the elderly will increasingly influence the types of goods and services produced. In particular, expenditures on health care will continue to rise. Already, people in the United States allocate more than 14 percent of their income to medical care. Is there a limit to how much they are willing to commit? The aging of the population also means that an increasing percentage of people will be retired and a smaller percentage will be producing goods and services and paying taxes. What are the implications for social security and for productivity? In this chapter, we look at the impact of an aging population on medical care and social security. ■

1. Aging and Social Security ⎯⎯⎯⎯⎯

In the United States, persons 65 years or older represent more than 13 percent of the total population, about one in every eight Americans, and the oldest group of Americans is getting older. In 2005, the 65 to 74 age group was more than 8 times larger than in 1900, but the 75 to 84 age group was more than 12 times larger and the 85-plus age group was more than 22 times larger. The median age in 1850 was 18.9. It is now 40.

The pattern of aging is clearly visible in Figure 1, which shows the age of the U.S. population at three points of time: 1970, 1990, and what is anticipated for 2010. The pattern has been described as a python swallowing a pig: the pig represents the baby boom generation working its way up the age scale, the python.

The growth of the older population in the United States has brought several issues to the forefront of political debate. Among them are social security and health care.

1.a. Social Security

1. Why worry about social security?

Old-Age, Survivors, and Disability Insurance (OASDI), also known as social security, had been established in 108 countries by the beginning of 1975. Some of the oldest plans are those of Germany (1889), the United Kingdom (1908), France (1910), Sweden (1913), and Italy (1919). The United States did not enact a national retirement program until 1935.

The social security system in the United States, which covers both social security and hospital insurance (Medicare), is financed by a payroll tax, Federal Insurance

---

FIGURE 1   **Aging Patterns in the United States**

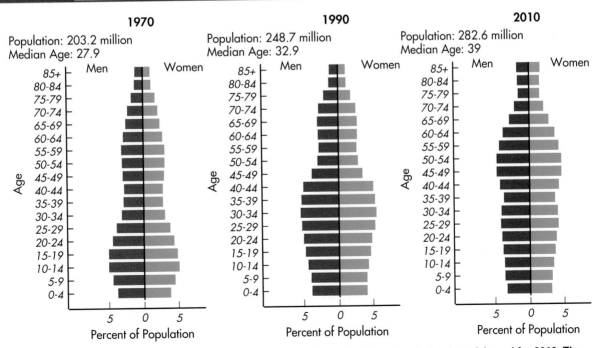

The age distribution of the U.S. population at three points of time: 1970, 1990, and what is anticipated for 2010. The pattern has been described as a python swallowing a pig. The pig represents the baby boom generation working its way up the age scale, the python. *Source:* U.S. Bureau of the Census.

Contributions Act (FICA), which is levied on the employer and the employee in equal portions. The initial FICA tax rate was 1 percent of the first $3,000 of wage income paid by both parties. In 2006, the tax rate was 7.65 percent (6.2 percent on the first $94,200 of earnings for the social security contribution and 1.45 percent on all earnings for the Medicare contribution) for each employee and employer. For a self-employed person, the tax rate is 12.4 percent for social security and 2.9 percent for Medicare.

1.b. The Viability of Social Security

Social security was intended to supplement the retirement funds of individuals.

The social security taxes that the working population pays today are used to provide benefits for current retirees. As a result, the financial viability of the system depends on the ratio of those working to those retired. The age distribution of the United States population has affected this viability. As illustrated in Figure 2, the ratio has declined from 16.5 in 1950 to about 3 today and is expected to decline to 2 by 2030. The situation in the United States is no different from that in many other parts of the world, as noted in the Global Business Insight "The World Is Aging."

In the past two decades, the social security tax has risen more rapidly than any other tax. Social security tax revenues were less than 5 percent of personal income in 1960 and currently exceed 11 percent of personal income. The revenues from the personal income tax were 3.4 percent of personal income in 1940 and rose to the current amount of more than 15 percent in the early 1980s. Social security expenditures also have risen more rapidly than expenditures for any other government program. Social security outlays currently constitute 7 percent of GDP, whereas

| FIGURE 2 | Social Security Viability |

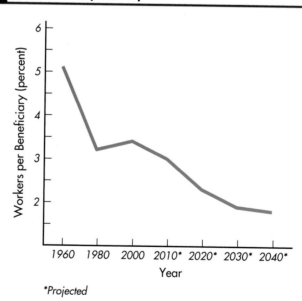

*Projected

The ratio of workers to social security beneficiaries is shown. The ratio has declined from 16.5 in 1950 to about 3 today and is expected to decline to 2 or less by 2030. This trend means that the source of social security benefits is getting relatively smaller. The viability of the system depends on whether the trends of recent years continue. *Source:* Social Security Administration.

The World Is Aging

The United States is not the only country whose population is growing older. Most of the developed nations in the world are experiencing the same aging of their populations. As seen in the accompanying figure, in 1985 the elderly population constituted about 12 percent in the United States but nearly 17 percent in Sweden. Although three-quarters of the world's population resides in developing areas, these areas contain only about 50 percent of the world's elderly. The developed countries are aging because the birthrates in these countries have decreased and life expectancy has increased. Japan's life expectancy of 77 years is the highest among the major countries, but life expectancies in most developed nations approach 75 years. In contrast, Bangladesh and some African nations south of the Sahara have life expectancies of 49 years.

As longevity has increased and families have had fewer children, the ratio of persons 65 and older to persons age 20 to 64 has risen in most of the developed countries. These elderly support ratios will rise modestly over the next 15 years because the large number of people born between 1946 and 1961 will still be in the labor force. But as the large working-age population begins to retire after 2005, the elderly support ratio will rise sharply.

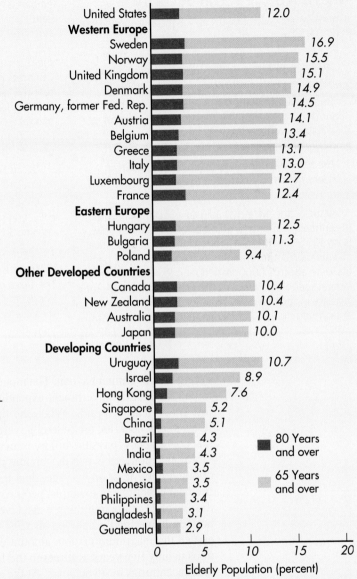

Source: U.S. Department of Commerce, U.S. Bureau of the Census, *International Population Reports*.

national defense is less than 5.5 percent, and education and training expenditures are less than 1 percent. From 1980 to 2000, social security expenditures rose 13 percent, Medicare rose 109 percent, national defense declined 29 percent, and education declined 34 percent.

One of the concerns about social security is that social security taxes are not put into a place that is touched only when benefits are paid. Instead, the money raised from the social security tax is used to purchase government bonds—essentially

Myths About Social Security

There are several myths about social security. Here we examine just a few.

We've contributed to that fund all our lives! It's our money! It's not the government's money!

This is one of the most strongly and widely held myths about the social security system. In fact, the typical retiree collects more than twice the amount represented by employer and employee contributions plus interest.

The benefits of the system are determined by a scientific formula designed to ensure that the fund remains viable.

Actually, the system of adjusting social security benefits annually as the cost of living increases dates only from 1975, and it came about as the result of political machinations, not foresight. In 1975, the annual benefits were about $7,000. Attempting to hold the line on federal spending, President Nixon proposed a 5 percent increase in social security benefits and threatened a veto of anything higher. Democrats saw an opportunity to

embarrass the president. They decided to pass a 10 percent increase and force Nixon to make an unpopular veto. The 10 percent increase was introduced in the Senate, but then rumors that Nixon would double-cross them and sign the bill anyway began circulating. So Congress increased the benefits by 20 percent, knowing that this huge increase would be vetoed. Nixon, however, signed the bill and proudly boasted of how well he had taken care of the elderly. Congress, irritated at being outflanked, passed the cost-of-living adjustment program to show that it, too, cared about the elderly.

Social Security ensures that only the elderly poor are cared for.

In fact, there are at least a million individuals currently collecting social security benefits who have incomes exceeding $100,000 per year.

There is a surplus in the Social Security Trust Fund.

There is no trust fund in which money is invested. The taxes collected are used to purchase Treasury bonds. It is these government bonds that make up the social security fund.

giving the government a loan. The money the government gets from the loan is used to pay for general government expenditures. The social security funds are actually just U.S. Treasury bonds. When the time comes for social security to cash in its IOUs to pay benefits, the federal government, which holds no assets earmarked for that contingency, pays the bill by issuing additional debt or raising taxes.

Another concern is that the amount paid into the social security system by an individual is far less, on average, than the amount received by that individual in retirement benefits. For example, people who retired in the 1980s, after working since the age of 21 at the minimum wage level, recovered all social security taxes paid—both employer and employee shares—in less than four years; an individual who earned the maximum taxable amount each year would recover the total contributions in only five years. Retirees in the 1990s recovered their total contributions and interest earnings in seven years. At the age of 82, the average worker who retired at age 65 will have received more than twice his and his employer's contributions to social security. Other social security issues are noted in the Economic Insight "Myths About Social Security."

So what's the alternative? There have been many proposals—increasing taxes, increasing the eligibility age, means testing, and holding down cost-of-living increases. The eligibility age—the age at which individuals can start collecting social security—was increased from 59 to 67 for those born in 1960 or later. Means testing—not paying social security benefits to anyone earning above a certain level of income—has been resisted but is under serious consideration. One of the more controversial proposals has been to privatize the system. This is what Chile, Australia, Turkey, Sweden, Italy, Argentina, Mexico, the Philippines, Great Britain, and several other nations have done. Privatization allows individuals to choose among an approved list of possible investments rather than giving the money to the government. What the individual earns on those investments will be the individual's retirement funds. Unlike the government program, which is a pay-as-you-go system and which provides defined benefits to contributors, the private system will pay what individual investments earn. Some systems, like Chile's, are fully privatized: workers are required to save a portion of their own salary for retirement, but they give no money directly to the government. Others, like Great Britain's, are partially privatized: workers still pay taxes, but only part of this money is used to support a government-run system; the rest may be used for a private plan chosen by the worker. In Australia, workers are required to contribute 9 percent of their income to a fund of their choice.

The difference between what $1 put into the Social Security System earns and what that $1 would earn if it were invested in the stock market, for example, is very large. If individuals born in 1970 were allowed to invest in stocks the amount that they currently pay in Social Security taxes, those individuals could receive nearly six times the benefits that they are scheduled to receive under social security. Even low-wage earners would receive nearly three times what they would receive from social security.

But as good as this looks, people are critical of private investment because of the fear that many people will invest badly and end up with nothing. They look at what happened to the stock market in 2000 and wonder what would have happened to people who were planning to retire in 2001. Social security, in contrast, seems to be a sure thing. Most of the privatization plans have met this criticism by ensuring that no one contributing to the new plan will receive less than he or she would have received under the former government-run plan.

The form of privatization differs from country to country, but the results have been uniformly positive. In every case, the returns that individuals have received have exceeded those of the government system. In addition, national savings rates have increased and government borrowing and debt creation have decreased.

RECAP

1. The U.S. population is aging as a result of lower birthrates, higher life expectancy, and the impact of the baby boom generation.

2. Social security, otherwise known as Old-Age, Survivors, and Disability Insurance, is financed by a tax imposed on employers and employees.

3. Social security uses the current working population's contributions to provide benefits to the current retirees. As the population ages, the ratio of contributors to beneficiaries declines.

4. Solutions to the social security problem include means testing, increasing the eligibility age, and privatization.

2. Health Economics

?

2. Why is health care heading the list of U.S. citizens' concerns?

Spending for health care in the United States amounts to $1.9 trillion. Figure 3 shows that health-care expenditures were only 5.9 percent of GDP in 1965 but exceed 16 percent of GDP today. (How this compares with other countries is shown in the Global Business Insight box "Health-Care Spending in OECD Countries.") What are the reasons that health-care expenditures have risen so dramatically over that time?

FIGURE 3   The Growth of U.S. Health-Care Spending

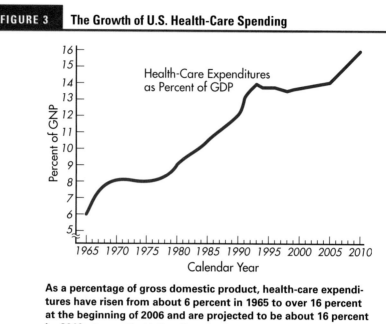

As a percentage of gross domestic product, health-care expenditures have risen from about 6 percent in 1965 to over 16 percent at the beginning of 2006 and are projected to be about 16 percent by 2010. *Source: Health Care Financing Review,* May 2001; Office of National Health Statistics, Office of the Actuary, *www.hcfa.gov/.*

2.a. Overview

Figure 4 shows where the nation's health-care dollar is spent and where the money comes from. Expenditures for hospital services constitute 31 percent of the nation's health-care bill; nursing-home expenditures, 8 percent; spending for physicians' services, 21 percent; spending for other personal health-care services, 11 percent; spending on prescription drugs 10 percent; and spending on medical equipment at retail stores 13 percent.

Figure 4(b) shows who provides the funds for these expenditures. Of the $1.9 trillion spent on health care, private health insurance, the single largest payer for health care, accounts for 40 percent. Private direct payments account for 15 percent. Direct payments consist of out-of-pocket payments made by individuals, including copayments and deductibles required by many third-party payers (third-party payers are insurance companies and government).

Government spending on health care constitutes 45 percent of the total; the federal government pays about 70 percent of this. **Medicare,** the largest publicly sponsored health-care program, funds health-care services for about 40 million aged and disabled enrollees. The Medicare program pays for 20 percent of all national health expenditures. **Medicaid,** a jointly funded federal and state program, finances 16 percent of all health care, covering the costs of medical care for poor families, the neediest elderly, and disabled persons who are eligible for social security disability benefits. Other government programs pay for 9 percent.

Health-care spending varies tremendously among various groups in the U.S. population. Figure 5 illustrates how health-care expenditures vary across the economy. If each person spent the same amount on health care, the line of perfect equality shown in Figure 5 would describe the distribution of spending. In fact, the distribution of health expenditures is heavily skewed. The top 1 percent of persons ranked by health-care expenditures account for almost 30 percent of total health-care

Medicare: a federal health-care program for the elderly and the disabled

Medicaid: a joint federal-state program that pays for health care for poor families, the neediest elderly, and disabled persons

Spending on Pharmaceuticals in Selected OECD Countries, 2003

How do other countries compare with the United States in regard to health-care spending and spending on pharmaceuticals? The following table indicates that the United States spends a higher percentage of GDP on health care and on pharmaceuticals than any other country.

	% GDP	Per Capita	Pharmaceuticals as % of Health-Care Exp.
Australia	9.3%	$2,699	14.0%
Austria	7.6	2,280	16.1
Belgium	9.6	2,827	16.6
Canada	9.9	3,003	16.9
Czech Republic	7.5	1,298	21.9
Denmark	9.0	2,763	9.8
Finland	7.4	2,118	16.0
France	10.1	2,903	20.9
Germany	11.1	2,996	14.6
Greece	9.9	2,011	16
Hungary	7.8	1,115	27.6
Iceland	10.5	3,115	14.5
Ireland	7.3	2,386	11.0
Italy	8.4	2,258	22.1
Japan	7.9	2,139	18.4
Korea	5.6	1,074	28.8
Luxembourg	6.1	3,190	11.6
Mexico	6.2	583	21.4
Netherlands	9.8	2,976	11.4
New Zealand	8.1	1,886	14.4
Norway	10.3	3,807	9.4
Poland	6.0	667	—
Portugal	9.6	1,797	23.4
Slovak Republic	5.9	777	38.5
Spain	7.7	1,835	21.8
Sweden	9.2	2,594	13.1
Switzerland	11.5	3,781	10.5
Turkey	6.6	425	24.8
United Kingdom	7.7	2,231	15.8
United States	15.0	5,635	12.9

Source: Gerard F. Anderson, Uwe E. Reinhardt, Peter S. Hussey, and Varduhi Petrosyan, "It's the Prices, Stupid: Why the United States Is So Different from Other Countries," *Health Affairs (Project HOPE)* 22, no. 3 (2003), pp. 89–105. *OECD Health Data*, 2005. Health Affairs by Anderson, Reinhardt, Hussey, Petrosyan. Copyright 2003 by Project Hope. Reproduced with permission of Project Hope in the format Textbook via Copyright Clearance Center.

FIGURE 4 The U.S. Health Dollar

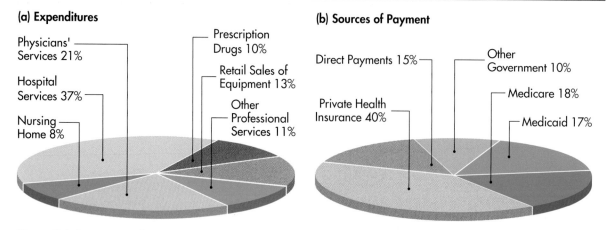

(a) Expenditures

Physicians' Services 21%

Hospital Services 37%

Nursing Home 8%

Prescription Drugs 10%

Retail Sales of Equipment 13%

Other Professional Services 11%

(b) Sources of Payment

Direct Payments 15%

Private Health Insurance 40%

Other Government 10%

Medicare 18%

Medicaid 17%

Figure 4(a) shows expenditures on health care by source; Figure 4(b) shows sources of payment for health expenditures. *Source:* *Health Care Financing Review,* various issues; *http://www.cms.hss.gov/NationalHealthExpendData/downloads/ tables.pdf,* accessed March 13, 2006.

FIGURE 5 The Inequality of U.S. Health-Care Spending

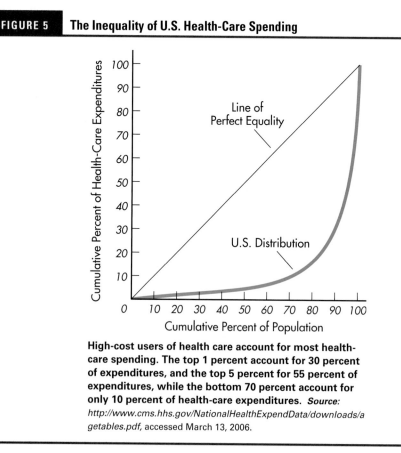

High-cost users of health care account for most health-care spending. The top 1 percent account for 30 percent of expenditures, and the top 5 percent for 55 percent of expenditures, while the bottom 70 percent account for only 10 percent of health-care expenditures. *Source:* *http://www.cms.hhs.gov/NationalHealthExpendData/downloads/a getables.pdf,* accessed March 13, 2006.

FIGURE 6   **Age and Health-Care Spending**

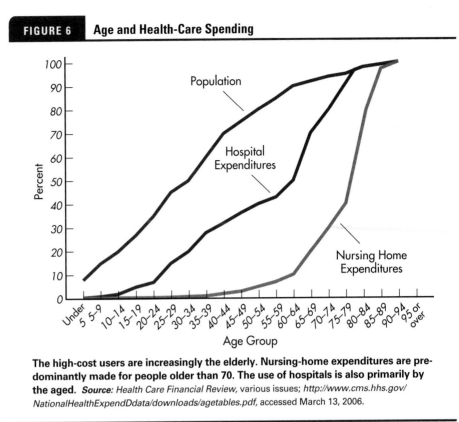

The high-cost users are increasingly the elderly. Nursing-home expenditures are predominantly made for people older than 70. The use of hospitals is also primarily by
the aged. *Source: Health Care Financial Review*, various issues; *http://www.cms.hhs.gov/
NationalHealthExpendDdata/downloads/agetables.pdf*, accessed March 13, 2006.

expenditures, and the top 5 percent incur 55 percent of all health-care expenditures.
The bottom 50 percent of the population account for only 4 percent of these expenditures, and the bottom 70 percent account for only 10 percent of costs.

Figure 6 shows that the distribution of spending for hospital care and nursing
homes is heavily dominated by the elderly. The top curve in Figure 6 represents the
cumulative percentage of the population in each age group. As the age rises from
under 5 to 10 to 20, and so on, there are increasing numbers of people. Eventually
100 percent of the population has been accounted for. The bottom curve represents
the cumulative percentage of nursing home expenditures accounted for by people in
each age group. Similarly, the middle line represents the cumulative percentage of
expenditures on hospitals accounted for by each age group.

2.b. The Market for Medical Care

Rising costs or expenditures mean that the demand for medical care has risen relative to the supply (Figure 7). The initial demand for medical care is D_1, and the supply of medical care is S_1. The intersection determines the price of medical care, P_1,
and the total expenditures, P_1 times Q_1. An increase in demand relative to supply is
shown as an outward shift of the demand curve, from D_1 to D_2. As a result, the price
of medical care rises, from P_1 to P_2, as do the total expenditures on medical care,
from P_1 times Q_1 to P_2 times Q_2. What accounts for the rising demand relative to
supply?

> Health-care costs have
> risen because the de-
> mand for health care has
> risen relative to supply.

2.b.1. Demand Increase: The Aging Population
The aging of the population
stimulates the demand for health care. The elderly consume four times as much health
care per capita as the rest of the population. About 90 percent of the expenditures

FIGURE 7   The Market for Medical Care: A Demand Shift

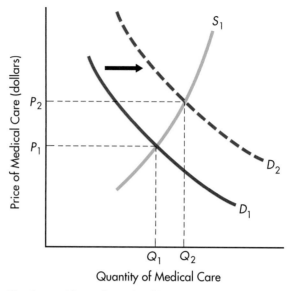

The demand for and supply of health care determine the price of medical care, P_1, and the total expenditures, P_1 times Q_1. Rising health-care expenditures may be due to increased demand. A larger demand, D_2 means a higher price and a greater total quantity of expenditures, P_2 times Q_2.

for nursing-home care are for persons 65 or over, a group that constitutes only 12 percent of the population. The aged (those 65 or older) currently account for 35 percent of hospital expenditures. In contrast, the young, although they constitute 29 percent of the population, consume only 11 percent of hospital care. Per capita spending on personal health care for those 85 years of age or over is 2.5 times that for people age 65 to 69 years. For hospital care, per capita consumption is twice as great for those age 85 or over as for those age 65 to 69; for nursing-home care, it is 23 times as great.

2.b.2. Demand Increase: The Financing Mechanism

For demand to increase, the aged must be both *willing* to buy medical care and *able* to pay for it. The emergence of Medicare and Medicaid in 1966 gave many elderly the ability. Medicare covers the cost of the first 100 days of hospital or nursing-home care for the elderly and disabled, providing benefits to 32 million people. Like social security, Medicare is funded by payroll taxes and is available on the basis of age (or disability), *not* need. By contrast, Medicaid helps only the neediest people, including many elderly people whose Medicare benefits have run out. As a result, Medicaid is the program that is most associated with long-term health care (such as for people living in nursing homes).

The effect of the Medicare and Medicaid programs has been to increase the demand for services and to decrease the price elasticity of demand because individuals do not pay for much of their health care. Private sources pay for about 55 percent of personal health care for the population as a whole, and Medicare and Medicaid pick up most of the remainder. Private sources, however, pay for 74 percent of care for people under age 65. For the elderly, the private share of spending

FIGURE 8 The Market for Medical Care: A Supply Shift

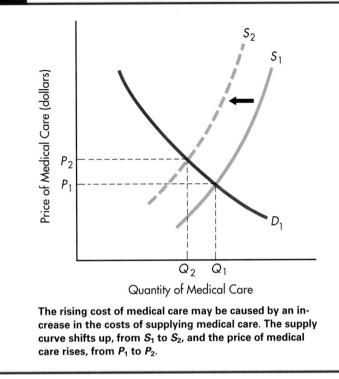

The rising cost of medical care may be caused by an increase in the costs of supplying medical care. The supply curve shifts up, from S_1 to S_2, and the price of medical care rises, from P_1 to P_2.

is only 15 percent for hospital care, 36 percent for physicians' services, and 58 percent for nursing-home care.[1] Medicaid spending for those 85 or over is seven times the spending for people age 65 to 69 and three times greater than the spending for people age 75 to 79. This difference is attributable to the heavy concentration of Medicaid money in nursing-home care, which those 85 or over use much more than others. Medicare spending for the oldest group is double that for the 65 to 69 age group.

2.b.3. Demand Increase: New Technologies   New medical technologies provide the very sick with increased opportunities for survival. Everyone wants the latest technology to be used when their life or the lives of their loved ones are at stake. But because these technologies are cost-increasing innovations and because costs are not paid by the users, the increased technology increases demand.

2.b.4. Supply   Even if the demand curve for medical care were not shifting out, the cost of medical care could be forced up by a leftward shift of the supply curve, as shown in Figure 8. The supply curve, composed of the marginal-cost curves of individual suppliers of medical care, shifts up, from S_1 to S_2, if the cost of producing medical care is rising—that is, if resource prices are rising or if diseconomies of scale are being experienced.

Hospitals   The original function of hospitals was to provide the poor with a place to die. Not until the twentieth century could wealthy individuals who were sick find

---

[1] *Health Care Financing Review,* various issues.

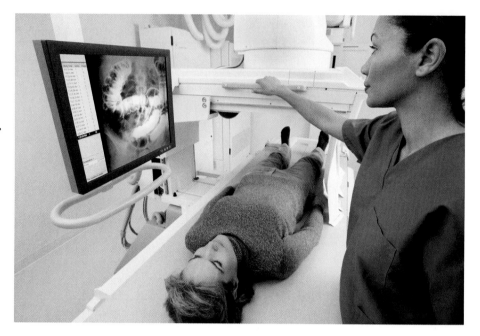

Medical care in the United States is expensive, but it is technologically superior to that in other nations. If patients do not have to pay the higher costs of the higher quality care and instead insurance or government pays it, then patients will want the highest quality care. As long as they get paid, doctors and care facilities will provide the high quality care.

more comfort, cleanliness, and service in a hospital than in their own homes. As technological changes in medicine occurred, the function of the hospital changed: the hospital became the doctor's workshop.

The cost of hospital care is attributable in large part to the way in which current operations and capital purchases are financed. Only a small fraction of the cost of hospital care is paid directly by patients; the bulk comes from *third parties,* of which the government is the most important. The term *third-party payers* refers to insurance companies and government programs: neither the user (the patient) nor the supplier (the physician or hospital) pays.

Hospital size is typically measured in numbers of beds; efficiency, in expenditures per case or expenditures per patient-day. To make precise determinations of the effect of size on efficiency is difficult because hospitals that differ in size are also likely to differ with respect to location, kind of patient admitted, services provided, and other characteristics. Hospitals that do not provide a large number of complex services need not be very large to be efficient. But if hospitals do provide a large number of services, it is very inefficient for them to be small. A hospital with 200 beds can efficiently provide most of the basic services needed for routine short-term care. If that hospital grows to 600 beds, yet still provides only the same basic services, inefficiencies are likely to develop because of increasing difficulties of administrative control. What is more likely to happen, however, is that specialized services will be introduced—services that could not have been provided at a reasonable cost when the hospital had only 200 beds.

In the past 20 years, the average number of beds per hospital increased by 50 percent, inpatient days declined by about 10 percent, lengths of stay declined by about 10 percent, and occupancy rates declined by nearly 20 percent. The problem that more beds per hospital and shorter stays creates for the hospital is that the occupancy rate is only about 66 percent, whereas the efficient occupancy rate is between 80 and 88 percent.

Physicians Physicians affect the cost of medical care not only through their impact on the operation of the hospital, but also through their fees. Expenditures on physicians' services rose more rapidly than any other medical-care expenditure category in the 1980s and 1990s. Is the increased cost of physicians due to a shortage of doctors? The answer is not necessarily yes. From 1966 to 1997, the supply of physicians increased 100 percent, whereas the U.S. population increased about 25 percent. As a result, the number of active physicians per 100,000 people increased substantially, from 169 in 1975 to 240 in 1997, and it has remained near that level since 1997.

The factors that have led to rising physicians' fees include an increase in demand relative to the supply of certain types of physicians, the ability of physicians to restrict price competition, and the payment system. The number of physicians per population has risen in many areas of the country. Yet, because the American Medical Association restricts advertising by physicians, consumers are unable to obtain complete information about prices or professional quality, and physicians are less likely to compete through advertising or lower prices. Moreover, the restrictions on advertising enable established physicians to keep new, entering physicians from competing for their customers by charging lower prices.

The payment system influences both physicians' fees and the supply of physicians. Over 31 percent of all physicians' fees are set by the government. More than 75 percent are set by third-party providers. Physicians are reimbursed on the basis of procedures and according to specialty. A gynecologist would have to examine 275 women a week to achieve the income earned by a cardiac surgeon doing two operations per week. More than 60 percent of all physicians in the United States are specialists. The payment system has induced more physicians to specialize in certain areas than would have occurred otherwise. Income varies widely among specialties as well. Cardiac surgeons tend to earn more than other specialists, for instance.

The costs of doing business have risen for physicians. For instance, the cost of malpractice insurance has increased about 25 percent a year during the past two decades. Although only about 1 percent of health-care expenditures can be directly attributed to malpractice suits, there are some implicit costs associated with the fear of such suits. This fear has caused an increase in both the number of tests ordered by physicians and the quantity of medical equipment purchased by them.

Prescription Drugs The fastest-growing health expenditure category between 1995 and 2003 was prescription medicines. Prescription drug expenditures grew by an annual average of 15 percent during this period, but the rate of growth slowed in 2004 and 2005, actually falling below the growth rate of health-care spending. Beginning in 2006, however, the Medicare Prescription Drug, Improvement and Modernization Act, which provides Medicare beneficiaries with comprehensive drug coverage, went into effect. The cost is estimated to be very high, about 1.9 percent of GDP.

Some of the United States' expenditures on health care involve spending on research. The United States is the world's leader in biomedical research: in public-sector spending through the National Institutes of Health and other government agencies; in private-sector research and development; in the scientific discoveries that this research has produced; and in manufacturing the drugs, diagnostics, and medical devices that apply these innovations to improving human health. Many of these discoveries do not first come to market in the United States, however, but instead are introduced in other countries. The only way a company can begin to sell a new drug or device in the United States is to get permission from the Food and Drug Administration (FDA), and the FDA is increasingly reluctant to give this permission. It has a very strong incentive to keep unsafe products off the market, even if in doing so it may block beneficial new products. As a result, the FDA has made it increasingly difficult to bring a new drug to market. The time required to bring a new drug to market, including preclinical testing, clinical development, and regulatory review, has increased from a low of 6.3 years in 1963–1965 to 16.1 years. This delay means that the percentage of drugs that are available first in the United States is low. While more than 60 percent of biopharmaceutical products approved in the United States, Europe, or Japan originated in the United States, less than 18 percent were first marketed in the United States. The latest estimate of the cost to develop a new drug and bring it to market exceeds $800 million; in 1987 the cost was $231 million.[2]

2.c. Do the Laws of Economics Apply to Health Care?

Many people claim that the laws of economics do not apply to health care. People tend to look at health care as a right, something that everyone is entitled to regardless of costs. You may recall our survey and discussion about allocation mechanisms in Chapter 3; most people look at health care as something different from other goods and services. They do not want the market system to determine who gets health care and who doesn't.

Is health care a scarce good? The answer is a clear yes; at a zero price, more people want health care than there is health care available, the definition of a scarce good. Scarcity means that choices must be made, that there is an opportunity cost for choosing to purchase the scarce good. The choice is made on the basis of rational self-interest. These principles of economics suggest that health care is an economic good and is subject to the laws of economics.

The demand curve for medical care looks like any other demand curve; it slopes down because the higher the price, the lower the quantity demanded. The demand curve is probably quite inelastic, but it does slope downward. There also is a standard-looking supply curve. Physicians, hospitals, and medical firms offer an increasing quantity of medical care for sale as the price rises. As shown in Figures 7 and 8 and repeated in Figure 9, the demand and supply curves look no different from the curves representing a market in any other economic good.

In Figure 9, the price for medical care is the level at which the demand and supply curves intersect, the point of equilibrium. At price P_1, the quantity of medical care demanded is equal to the quantity supplied. Those people who are willing and able to pay price P_1 (all those lying along the demand curve from A to B) get the medical care. Those who are not willing and able to pay the price (all those lying along the demand curve from B to C) do not get the care.

The problems that arise in the health-care market are due not to a repeal of the laws of economics, but instead to the nature of the product. People believe that they and others have an inalienable right to medical care, that it is not right to ignore those people making up the demand curve from B to C on D_1. As a result, government programs such as Medicare and Medicaid have been created. These programs, along with private insurance programs, mean that most of the payments for medical care are made by third parties, as described earlier in this chapter. The third-party payment system allows many of those who would not otherwise be willing and able to purchase health care, those lying along the demand curve from B to C, to be able to purchase the care. This shifts the demand curve out, which drives health-care costs up, as shown by the shift from D_1 to D_2 in Figure 9.

---

[2] Denise Myshko, "Pricing—The Cost of Doing Business," *PharmaVOICE,* March 1, 2002 (www.websterconsultinggroup.com/pharmapricing_030102.html#head1).

FIGURE 9 **Do Laws of Economics Apply to Health Care?**

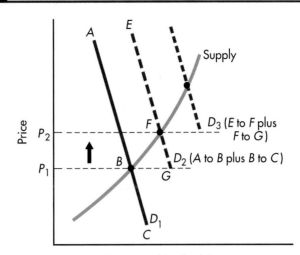

The price of medical care is the level at which the demand and supply curves intersect, the point of equilibrium. At price P_1, the quantity of medical care demanded is equal to the quantity supplied. Those people who are willing and able to pay price P_1 (all those lying along demand curve D_1 from *A* to *B*) get the medical care. Those who are not willing and able to pay the price (all those lying along the demand curve from *B* to *C*) do not get the medical care.

The third-party payment system allows many who would not otherwise be willing and able to purchase health care (those lying along the demand curve from *B* to *C*) to be able to purchase the care. This shifts the demand curve out and drives health-care costs up, as shown by the shift in the demand curve from D_1 to D_2.

The government and private insurance programs thus face ever-rising health-care costs. Each new equilibrium means that some are unable to afford the care; if their demand is covered, the demand curve shifts out again, to D_3. This continues as long as someone is willing and able to pay the price. That someone has been the government, principally through Medicare, and private employers through employee benefit plans. The result has been double-digit price increases for health care for over a decade.

2.c.1. The Market for Human Organs   Many respected doctors, lawyers, economists, and ethicists argue that a legal and open market in organs, such as kidneys, hearts, and livers, could help cure the chronic organ shortage that is gripping transplant medicine. If the price is right and the seller is willing, why should someone not be allowed to sell a kidney? The debate over the issue is intense. Many who are against an open and free market in organs argue that it will result in exploitation of the poor. They point to cases in which black market activity has occurred, such as in India's poorest sectors, where, for about $1,500, poor Indians have sold a kidney and in just a few years, are back in poverty, with huge debts and with one less kidney. But how people choose to spend the money gained from selling an organ has nothing to do with the market for the organs. People may fritter away money, but that has nothing to do with where they earned the money. The debate over the market for organs must focus on the supply of organs and the lives saved or lost because of the existence of a market in organs or due to the fact that a market is not allowed.

Supporters of a free and open market argue that it would increase supplies of transplant organs and save many lives. In the United States alone, there are 50,000 people on dialysis waiting for a donor kidney. About three thousand people die each year while waiting for a kidney transplant. Thousands also die while waiting for livers, hearts, and other vital organs, and the number of people dying is increasing each year.

How would the legal market work? One part of the market would be the purchase of organs from living individuals. A person would offer a kidney or a part of a liver (since only pieces of livers, not whole livers, are needed for transplant) for a price. The price would be set by demand and supply. A second part of the market would be organs harvested from people who die suddenly, such as those killed in accidents. These people would have sold their organs, such as lungs, hearts, and kidneys, in what can be called a "futures" market. The rights to harvest these organs after death could be purchased from donors while they were still living, at prices set by supply and demand. Donors would be paid for future rights to their organs. So you could sell the rights to your kidneys once you die and receive the payment today.

What would the outcome of such a market be? Let's use Figure 10 to illustrate the market for organs. The demand for organs would be price-inelastic, since those who need the organs would be willing to pay just about anything they were able to pay to get them. The supply of organs is expected to be price-elastic, at least once the price reaches some threshold level. For instance, a 10 percent increase in the price, say from $100,000 to $110,000, would induce more than a 10 percent increase in the number of organs offered for sale. And if a futures market developed, the sup-

FIGURE 10   **The Market for Human Organs**

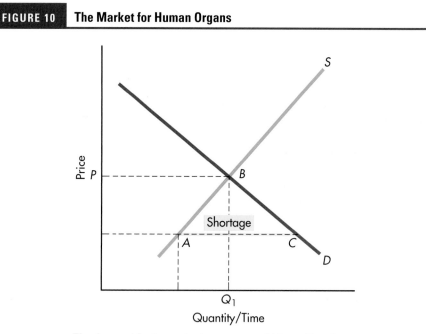

The demand for transplant organs would be quite price-inelastic, since people who are awaiting a donor organ would be willing and able to pay nearly any price to save their lives. The demand and supply would determine the equilibrium price and quantity.

ply would be price-elastic, since everyone who now volunteers to donate organs would continue to do so, and many others would also do so because they would receive some income for almost no cost. The market for human organs would look something like Figure 10, where the equilibrium price would be P_1 and the equilibrium quantity Q_1. What would the price be? In the United States in 2000, a kidney was auctioned on eBay. The government terminated the auction after only a few hours, but when it was stopped, the price had reached $5 million. At the other end of the price range, the black market (illegal market) price of a kidney in India was about three times the average annual income, or $1,500. Some studies predict that the supply of organs and the alternatives to organs created by technological changes spurred by the profits possible would drive prices to a very low level, perhaps $200, in just a matter of years.[3]

A black market arises when an item that some people are willing and able to buy and others are willing and able to supply cannot be legally traded. Black markets are less efficient or more costly than legal markets simply because traders have to be discreet, cannot meet buyers and sellers openly, and have no means to enforce agreements. As a result, the number of traders in the market is less than it would be in a legal market. Most of the evidence available regarding human organs shows that the market would be immensely larger if it were legal than the black market in human organs currently is.

The problem that most people have with the idea of a market in human organs is the potential for what they call exploitation. They point out that the organs would be going one way—from poor people to rich people, from the Third World to the First World or to rich people in the Third World. This is the way markets work—from those who are willing and able to sell to those who are willing and able to buy. Arguing that this result is bad is a normative argument, not a positive one. Similarly, the counterargument that a father who is desperate to provide a plate of rice for his starving family should be entitled to sell one of his kidneys on the open market is a normative argument. No matter what the normative viewpoints, there is a market for human organs; transplant surgery is a business driven by the simple market principle of supply and demand. The positive aspect of the issue is not who would gain and who would lose in a free, open market, because both buyers and sellers gain as measured by consumer and producer surplus, but instead, how does the current black market situation compare with a free, open, legal market?

RECAP

1. Health care is the fastest-growing portion of total national expenditures. It is rising primarily because of the rising cost of physician services, nursing homes, and hospital services.

2. The demand for medical care has risen at a very rapid rate. One reason for the increase is the introduction of Medicare and Medicaid and private insurance plans that make demand relatively inelastic. The aging of the population has also increased the demand for medical care.

3. The cost of providing medical care has risen because of increases in hospital costs and physicians' fees. Rising hospital costs are partly a result of the reimbursement plans of third-party providers and partly a result of the control of the operation of hospitals by physicians.

---

[3] David L. Kaserman and A. H. Barnett, *The U.S. Organ Procurement System: A Prescription for Reform* (Washington D.C., The AEI Press, 2002.)

4. Physicians' fees have risen even though the supply of physicians has risen. The demand for medical services does not match the supply; reimbursement methods have led to higher rates of return in certain specialties and thus have drawn an increasing number of physicians to those specialties.

5. The laws of economics do apply to the medical arena. They apply even in the case of markets for human organs.

Summary

1. Why worry about social security?

- Social security is a government-mandated pension fund. In the United States it is funded by a tax on employer and employee. The current tax collections are used to provide benefits to current retirees. *§1.a*

2. Why is health care heading the list of U.S. citizens' concerns?

- The rapidly rising costs of medical care result from increases in demand relative to supply. *§2.a*

- The increasing demand results from the aging of the population and from payment systems that decrease the price elasticity of demand. *§2.b.1, 2.b.2*

- The reduced supply (higher costs of producing medical care) results from inefficiencies in the allocation of physicians among specialties and inefficiencies in the operation and organization of hospitals. *§2.b.4*

Key Terms

Medicare *§2.a*

Medicaid *§2.a*

Exercises

1. What is social security? What is Medicare? What is the economic role of these government programs?

2. Why have expenditures on medical care risen more rapidly than expenditures on any other goods and services?

3. Explain how both the supply of physicians and physicians' fees can increase at the same time.

4. Why are there more medical specialists and fewer general practitioners in the United States now than was the case 50 years ago?

5. What is the economic logic of increasing social security benefits?

6. What does it mean to say that people have a right to a specific good or service? Why do people believe that they have a right to medical care but do not believe that they have a right to a 3,000-square-foot house?

7. Suppose the objective of government policy is to increase an economy's growth and raise citizens'

standards of living. Explain in this context the roles of retirement, social security, and Medicare.

8. Explain why the U.S. system of payment for medical procedures leads to higher health-care costs than a system of payment for physicians' services.

9. Analyze the following solutions to the problem of social security.
   a. The retirement age is increased to 70.
   b. The FICA tax is increased.
   c. Income plus social security payments cannot exceed the poverty level.
   d. The total amount of social security benefits received cannot exceed the amount paid in by employer and employee plus the interest earnings on those amounts.

10. Oregon proposed a solution to the health-care costs problem that was widely criticized. Under this solution the state would pay only for common medical problems. Special and expensive problems would not be

covered. Using the market for medical care, analyze the Oregon plan.

11. What would be the impact of a policy that did away with Medicare and Medicaid and instead provided each individual with the amount that he or she had contributed to the Medicare program during his or her working life?

12. Why is a third-party payer a problem? Private insurance companies are third-party payers, and yet they want to maximize profit. So wouldn't they ensure that the allocation of dollars was efficient?

13. "We must recognize that health care is not a commodity. Those with more resources should not be able to purchase services while those with less do without. Health care is a social good that should be available to every person without regard to his or her resources." Evaluate this statement.

14. Explain and illustrate how a market for human organs could increase the amount of organs available and save lives. Explain and illustrate what would have to occur in order for the lives saved to decline as a result of a legal market for human organs.

15. Suppose firms provide health-care coverage and drug benefits as part of their competition for employees. Suppose the government enacts a law that provides drug benefits to everyone, whether employed or not. What is the effect on employment and wages?

ACE

Take the ACE Practice Test for this chapter to review the important concepts and get immediate feedback with answers.

college.hmco.com/economics/students/

Thriving Market for Body Parts

The Australian
September 26, 2005

The illegal sale of human organs is flourishing across the globe, with the poor providing the body parts and hospitals in Third World nations colluding to bolster the trade.

Sydney University economist Stephen Jan will tell a seminar in Sydney today that the sale of organs, primarily kidneys, is difficult to prevent because none of the parties involved—the donors, the recipients or the hospitals—have any interest in withdrawing from the market.

"In parts of India, the sale of organs has become a de facto form of welfare," Dr Jan said after recently completing a study of the bleak practice across India.

"Families rely on one person—often a woman—to donate her kidney, so that the whole family can benefit.

"The recipients obviously don't want the trade to stop, and the middlemen, who find the donors and take a cut of the money, obviously have no interest in it, either."

Dr Jan said there was no direct evidence that Australians were buying Indian organs "but you can assume it's possible, just as it's possible that deals are done here."

Some villages in India have become "overtaken by the trade." "They get this idea that it's an acceptable way to make money and suddenly you find almost every house has somebody who has sold a kidney."

Donors get about $US1070 ($1410) for a kidney, in a nation where average yearly income is $US420.

"Even if you disagree on ethical grounds, it's still going to happen in India because of the poverty, so the issue becomes one of minimising harm," Dr Jan said.

Caroline Overington

Source: Copyright 2005 Nationwide News Pty Limited.

No one denies that an organ-shortage problem exists. Nearly 90,000 people are on waiting lists to get transplants. Every year, about 7,000 patients who need organ transplants die without getting them. The only legal way to get a transplant now is through voluntary donation. No country subscribes to an open, free market in human organs. But given the huge demand and the large shortage, people seek other ways to obtain what they need. The Internet allows a look at both sides of the issue: Advertisements placed by those seeking organs and those willing to sell organs abound. One ad from Korea provided information about health, blood type, and other crucial information regarding a man's kidney and liver. Another offered to sell at a price significantly lower than what was being mentioned in other ads.

Ignore for a moment what item we are talking about here. Look at a simple demand and supply diagram where the price is below the equilibrium. The shortage created is quickly erased as the price increases and the quantity supplied rises while the quantity demanded declines. If the price is not allowed to rise—if, in fact, the market is not allowed to legally exist—then the shortage will continue. Allocation of the scarce human organs will take place first come, first served or as government dictates. There will be no incentive for more human organs to be supplied or for anyone to come up with a technological innovation that might substitute for the human organs.

But if a market in the organs were made legal, the equilibrium would be reached as the quantity of organs supplied rose. So why does the public see it as such a terrible thing for a market in human organs to be made legal?

One fear often voiced on this subject is that you will be attacked and your organs stolen from you. There are two counterarguments against this. First, for a market to exist, private property rights must exist, and these rights must be enforced. You own a car. Do you constantly fear that someone will throw you out of the car and steal it? Do you constantly fear that someone will break down the door to your house and take all your property? You do not fear these things because you know that the police and the courts will enforce the laws that give you the right of ownership. Do these terrible things happen? Yes, but they are not very common relative to the number of cars and houses owned. In the case of human organs, you own your body—it is your private property right. No one will be able to steal your organs—there are serious penalties for doing so, just as there are for murder. The market would provide the incentive for people to offer their organs—perhaps not right away, but instead through a futures market, in which they agree to sell their organs when they die.

In the article, economist Stephen Jan notes that none of the parties involved—the donors, the recipients, or the hospitals—have any interest in withdrawing from the market. He notes that the practice helps the poor; it is one means by which parents can support their families. If a legal market existed, the poor could sell organs—get money now and give up organs in the future as well as sell a kidney or liver now—and use the money to send their kids to school or simply to feed the family. A market for human organs will work in the developed as well as the developing world. In the United States today, there is a thriving market to induce women to furnish ova for infertile couples.

20

Income Distribution, Poverty, and Government Policy

Fundamental Questions

1. Are incomes distributed equally in the United States?

2. How is poverty measured, and does poverty exist in the United States?

3. Who are the poor?

4. What are the determinants of poverty?

5. Do government programs intended to reduce poverty benefit the poor?

6. Why are incomes unequally distributed among nations?

ncome is what resource owners receive as payment for the use of their resources. Resource owners have incentives to increase the value of their resources—that is, to increase their income. They will innovate and adopt the latest technology in order to enhance the value of capital. They will acquire additional skills and education in order to increase their wages and salaries. They will redirect their land from agricultural uses to commercial uses when they gain from so doing, and they will make improvements to their land to enhance its value. Resource owners want to ensure that they get the highest value for the use of their resources, now and in the future.

In every society, different people own different resources and differently valued resources. This means that incomes vary from person to person. The United States is a wealthy society. Yet, half a million Americans today are living on city streets, in parks, under bridges, or in temporary shelters. Income is unequally distributed

in the United States. However, even the poor in the United States are better off than the entire populations of other nations. In Bolivia, the average life expectancy is only 53 years, a full 20 years less than in the United States. In Burma, only about one-fourth of the population has access to safe water. In Burundi, less than one-fourth of the urban houses have electricity. In Chad, less than one-third of the children reach the sixth grade. In Ethiopia, average income is just $120 a year.

Why is Ethiopia so poor and the United States so rich? Would the poor in the United States be rich in Ethiopia? Who are the poor and the rich? Is the inequality of incomes something that can or should be corrected? These questions are the topic of this chapter. Previous chapters have discussed how the market system works to ensure that resources flow to their highest-valued uses, that output is produced in the least-cost manner, and that people get what they want at the lowest possible price. But the market does not produce equal incomes. Markets ensure that goods and services are allocated to those with the ability to pay, not necessarily to those with needs, and definitely not in equal amounts to everyone.

One of the major controversies in economics over the last 100 years has been which system makes people better off, capitalism and free markets or socialism and government-controlled markets? In general, the answer is that capitalism and free markets lead to higher standards of living than government-run economies. The poorest nations in the world are the most repressive, and the wealthiest are the freest. Yet, some wealthy nations attempt to ensure that incomes do not differ much from one individual to another. Sweden, for instance, is a wealthy society in which government has a large role and family incomes do not differ much from one family to another. Hong Kong, on the other hand, has risen from a destitute little outcropping of China 50 years ago to one of the wealthiest societies in the world, and it has very little government involvement and wide differences in income from one family to another. In this chapter we discuss income distribution and how economic well-being is measured. ■

1. Income Distribution and Poverty ___

1. Are incomes distributed equally in the United States?

There are wealthy countries and there are poor countries; there are wealthy people and there are poor people. Incomes are not distributed equally in the world. How unequal is the distribution? Two measures of income equality are used to answer this question: the Lorenz curve and the Gini coefficient.

1.a. A Measure of Income Inequality

Equal incomes among members of a population can be plotted as a 45-degree line that is equidistant from the axes (see Figure 1). The horizontal axis measures the total population in cumulative percentages. Cumulative means that as we move along the horizontal axis, the percentages are increasing. The numbers end at 100, which designates 100 percent of the population. The vertical axis measures total income in cumulative percentages. As we move up the vertical axis, the percentage of total income being counted rises to 100 percent. The 45-degree line splitting the distance between the axes is called the *line of income equality*. At each point on the line, the percentage of total population and the percentage of total income are equal. The line of income equality indicates that 10 percent of the population earns 10 percent of

FIGURE 1 The U.S. Lorenz Curve

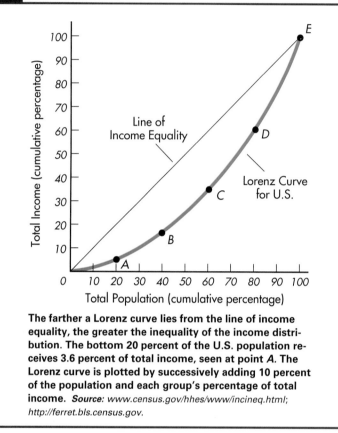

The farther a Lorenz curve lies from the line of income equality, the greater the inequality of the income distribution. The bottom 20 percent of the U.S. population receives 3.6 percent of total income, seen at point *A*. The Lorenz curve is plotted by successively adding 10 percent of the population and each group's percentage of total income. *Source: www.census.gov/hhes/www/incineq.html; http://ferret.bls.census.gov.*

the income, 20 percent of the population earns 20 percent of the income, and so on, until we see that 90 percent of the population earns 90 percent of the income and 100 percent of the population earns 100 percent of the income.

Points off the line of income equality indicate an income distribution that is unequal. Figure 1 shows the line of income equality and a curve that bows down below the income-equality line. The bowed curve is a **Lorenz curve.** The Lorenz curve in Figure 1 is for the United States. It shows that the bottom 20 percent of the population receives 3.6 percent of income, seen at point *A*. The second 20 percent accounts for another 9.6 percent of income, shown as point *B*. The third 20 percent accounts for another 15.7 percent of income, so point *C* is plotted at a population of 60 percent and an income of 28.9 (3.6 + 9.6 + 15.7) percent. The fourth 20 percent accounts for another 23.4 percent of income, shown as point *D*. The richest 20 percent accounts for the remaining 47.7 percent of income, shown as point *E*. With the last 20 percent of the population and the last 47.7 percent of income, 100 percent of the population and 100 percent of income are accounted for. Point *E*, therefore, is plotted where both income and population are 100 percent.[1] The more bowed out the Lorenz curve, the greater the income inequality.

Lorenz curve: a curve measuring the degree of inequality of income distribution within a society

---

[1] A Lorenz curve for wealth could also be shown. It would bow down below the Lorenz curve for income, indicating that wealth is more unequally distributed than income. Wealth and income are different and should be kept distinct. Wealth is the stock of assets. Income is the flow of earnings that results from the stock of assets.

Another way you will see income distributions reported is with the **Gini coefficient.** The Gini coefficient is the area between the Lorenz curve and the line of perfect equality divided by the total area under the line of income equality. A Gini of 0 would occur if every family had the exact same amount of income, since there would be no difference between the line of income equality and the Lorenz curve. A Gini of 1 would occur if one family had all the income, since the Lorenz curve would be the rectangle going from 0 to 100 on the horizontal axis and from 100 on the horizontal axis up to the line of income equality—the entire area. According to Figure 2, the coefficient was between .35 and .37 until the 1990s; it then increased and has reached .466. This means that the distribution of income in the United States became slightly more equally distributed from 1947 to 1968, then became less equal from then until the mid-1990s, and then became more unequal after that.

Income is much more equally distributed in industrial nations than it is in developing countries. In developing countries, the richest 20 percent of the population have more than 50 percent of total household income while the poorest 20 percent have less than 4 percent. Figure 3 shows two Lorenz curves, one for the United States and one for Mexico. The curve for Mexico bows down far below the curve for the United States; the Gini coefficient for the United States is .408 and that for Mexico is .519, showing that incomes are much more unequal in Mexico than in the United States.

1.b. Measuring Poverty

So, incomes are distributed unequally in most countries. What does that tell us about the quality of life of the people in different nations? Are those near the bottom of the income distribution living in poverty? Are the rich in a poor country living in poverty?

FIGURE 2   **The Gini Coefficient**

The Gini coefficient is a measure of the dispersion of income that ranges between 0 and 1. A lower value indicates less dispersion in the income distribution: A Gini of 0 would occur if every family had the exact same amount of income, while a Gini of 1 would occur if all income accrued to only one family. Figure 2 shows that from 1947 to 1968, the dispersion of income fell gradually. Since then the dispersion has risen slowly. *Source: Economic Report of the President, 2000 and 2006.*

FIGURE 3   Lorenz Curves for Mexico and the United States

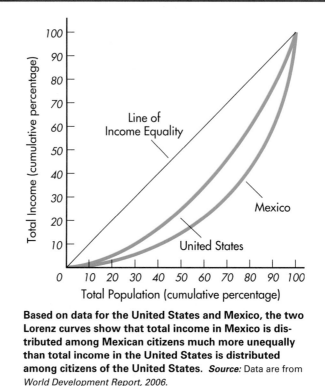

Based on data for the United States and Mexico, the two Lorenz curves show that total income in Mexico is distributed among Mexican citizens much more unequally than total income in the United States is distributed among citizens of the United States. *Source:* Data are from *World Development Report, 2006.*

Defining poverty is difficult. We can, without too much trouble, say which groups have higher or lower income levels and how incomes are distributed in a society, but this does not provide much information about a person's quality of life. All the Lorenz curve can tell us is what one's income is relative to others'; it is a relative measure. Per capita income—income per person—is an absolute measure. It doesn't compare incomes, but simply states the level. Per capita income does not indicate how people feel about their income status or whether they enjoy good health and a decent standard of living. Those who are comfortable in one country could be impoverished in another. The poverty level in the United States would represent a substantial increase in living standards in many other nations. Yet members of a poor family in the United States would probably not feel less poor if they knew that their income level exceeded the median income in other countries.

1.b.1. What Is Income?   In the United States, data related to poverty are collected and published annually by the Department of Health and Human Services. Table 1 lists the average poverty levels of income for a nonfarm family of four since 1959. Families with incomes above the cutoffs would be above the poverty level, in the eyes of the federal government. These cutoffs are called *poverty thresholds.* They are arbitrary numbers selected by the government to provide an indication of how many people are in poverty.

Where does the poverty income threshold come from? A 1955 study found that the average family in the United States spent about one-third of its income on food, so when the government decided to begin measuring poverty in the 1960s, it calculated the cost to purchase meals that met a predetermined nutritional standard for a

?

2. How is poverty measured, and does poverty exist in the United States?

Incomes are unequally distributed in every nation. In developing countries, the distinction between rich and poor is greater than in the industrial nations, although the per capita income is significantly less in the developing countries. For instance, although the per capita income in Nigeria is only 7 percent of the per capita income in the United States, the wealthy in Lagos, Nigeria, live very well with large houses, servants, expensive clothes, and other accouterments of wealth. During the 1970s, many Nigerians became very wealthy as the price of oil surged and Nigerian oil production rose. Economic crisis and the collapse of oil prices since the late 1970s have led to a decline in Nigeria that has wiped out the gains of the previous twenty years.

TABLE 1 **Average Income Poverty Cutoffs for a Nonfarm Family of Four in the United States, 1959–2005**

Year	Poverty Level	Year	Poverty Level
1959	$ 2,973	1988	$12,090
1960	$ 3,022	1989	$12,675
1966	$ 3,317	1990	$13,359
1969	$ 3,743	1991	$13,924
1970	$ 3,968	1992	$13,950
1975	$ 5,500	1993	$14,764
1976	$ 5,815	1994	$15,200
1977	$ 6,191	1995	$15,600
1978	$ 6,662	1996	$16,036
1979	$ 7,412	1997	$16,400
1980	$ 8,414	1998	$16,660
1981	$ 9,287	1999	$16,895
1982	$ 9,862	2000	$17,463
1983	$10,178	2000	$17,463
1984	$10,609	2002	$18,244
1985	$10,989	2003	$18,900
1986	$11,203	2004	$19,424
1987	$11,611	2005	$19,874

Source: www.census.gov/hhes/www/poverty.html.

year and multiplied that cost by 3. That is where it drew the poverty line. Since then, the official poverty-line income has been adjusted for inflation each year.

The poverty thresholds count earnings from cash transfers but not in-kind transfers. **Cash transfers** are unearned funds given to certain sectors of the population. They include some social security benefits and disability pensions, as well as unemployment compensation to those who are temporarily out of work. **In-kind transfers,** or noncash transfers, are services or products provided to certain sectors of society. They include food purchased with food stamps and medical services provided under Medicaid. Although economists agree that in-kind transfers increase the economic well-being of those who receive them, there is much debate over how they should be accounted for and the extent to which they should be added to money income for the purpose of defining *poverty*. The official measure of the poverty rate does not include in-kind transfers. So when you hear that the poverty level of income is $19,874, that number does not include any measures of in-kind transfers. People earning $19,874 could be receiving food, clothing, or housing benefits and still be considered to be in poverty.

How many Americans fall below the poverty line? Figure 4 compares the number of people living in poverty and the percentage of the total population living in poverty (the incidence of poverty) for each year.

cash transfers: money allocated away from one group in society to another

in-kind transfers: the allocations of goods and services from one group in society to another

---

FIGURE 4 **The Trends of Poverty Incidence**

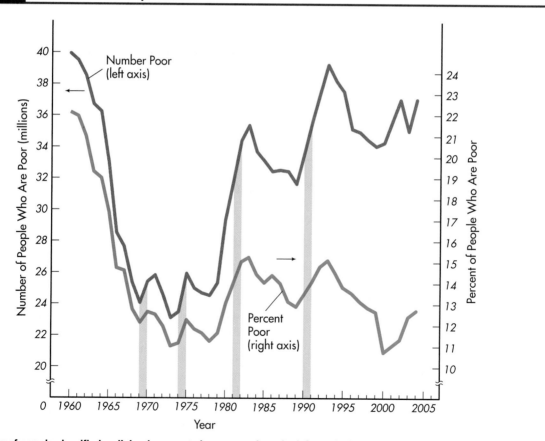

The number of people classified as living in poverty is measured on the left vertical axis. The percentage of the population classified as living in poverty is measured on the right vertical axis. *Source: www.census.gov/hhes/www/poverty.html.*

The health of the economy is a primary determinant of the incidence of poverty.

There are many controversies over how poverty should be measured. Some argue that the poverty rate is really not nearly as high as Figure 4 indicates—that government transfers and other programs are not properly taken into account. Also, the poverty measure makes no distinction between the needs of a 3-month-old and those of a 14-year-old or between a rural family in a cold climate and an urban family in the subtropics. It draws no distinction between income and purchasing power. A welfare mom living on $400 a month is treated identically to a graduate student who earns $400 a month at a part-time job and borrows an additional $1,500 from her parents. Nor does it consider the problem of income from the underground economy—the income that is not reported or measured in income statistics.

RECAP

1. The Lorenz curve shows the degree to which incomes are distributed equally in a society. The more the Lorenz curve bows out, the greater that income is unequally distributed.

2. The Gini coefficient is a measure of the degree to which the Lorenz curve bows down away from the line of income equality. The higher the Gini coefficient, the greater the income inequality.

3. The income level selected as the poverty threshold is arbitrary—an attempt to measure the income people would need to purchase three meals of a certain nutritious value.

4. The incidence of poverty is the percentage of the population whose income falls below the poverty threshold.

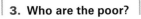

2. The Poor

3. Who are the poor?

A higher percentage of women fall into poverty than do men; a higher percentage of African Americans and Hispanics fall into poverty than do others; a higher percentage of those without high school education fall into poverty than do those with high school educations.

2.a. Temporary and Permanent Poverty

If those who are poor at any one time are poor only temporarily, then their plight is only temporary. If people in poverty are able to improve their situation even while others slip into poverty temporarily, the problem of poverty for society is not as serious as it is if poverty is a permanent condition once a person has fallen into it. Approximately 25 percent of all Americans fall below the poverty line at some time in their lives. Many of these spells of poverty are relatively short; nearly 45 percent last less than a year. However, a large number of people remain in poverty for at least 10 years.

4. What are the determinants of poverty?

The primary characteristic of those who fall below the poverty line is the lack of a job.

2.a.1. The Economy and Poverty The major factor accounting for the incidence of poverty is the health of the economy. People are generally made better off by economic growth. Economic stagnation and recession throw the relatively poor out of their jobs and into poverty. Economic growth increases the number of jobs and draws people out of poverty and into the mainstream of economic progress. Recessions increase poverty and economic booms reduce poverty.

The recession of 1969–1970 was relatively mild. Between 1969 and 1971, the unemployment rate rose from 3.4 to 5.8 percent, and the total number of people unemployed rose from 2,832,000 to 5,016,000. This recession halted the decline in poverty rates for two years. When the economy once again began to expand, the poverty rates dropped. The 1974 recession brought on another bout of unemployment that threw people into poverty. This recession was relatively serious, causing

The less education a person has, the greater his or her chance of experiencing poverty.

the unemployment rate to rise to 8.3 percent by 1975 and the number of unemployed to rise to 7,929,000. Once again, however, the poverty rate declined as the economy picked up after 1975. The recession of 1980–1982 threw the economy off track again. In 1979, the total number of people unemployed was 6,137,000; by 1982, 10,717,000 were without jobs. As the economy came out of this recession, the poverty rate began to decline, and it continued to decline as the economy grew throughout the 1980s. The poverty rate then rose as the economy fell into recession in 1990 and struggled into 1992. The poverty rate of 14.2 percent in 1991 was the highest level in nearly three decades; the number of people living in poverty grew to 35.7 million. Somewhat surprisingly, the number of people in poverty and the incidence of poverty both grew in 1993 and 1994, years of economic growth. Throughout the rest of the 1990s, however, both the poverty rate and the number of people in poverty declined. As the economy again entered a recession in 2000, the number of people in poverty began to rise. But as the economy grew following 2001, the number in poverty fell to about 35 million in 2003 and 37 million in 2004.

Common sense says that the primary reason people might have no or little income is that they don't have a job or don't have a job that pays well. Why don't people have jobs or good jobs? The primary reason is that their skills and education don't offer value to employers. People who do not have a high school education are many more times likely to have an income at the poverty level than people with a high school diploma. And a technical school or college degree offers even more likelihood that one won't fall into poverty. Because it is primarily the very young who don't have skills or education, they are the primary population group with poverty-level incomes. In 2004, 17.8 percent of the U.S. population under the age of 18 had incomes below the poverty threshold while less than 9 percent of the rest of the population had poverty-level incomes.

African Americans and Hispanics carry a much heavier burden of poverty relative to the size of their populations than do whites. Families headed by a female are much more likely to be in poverty (35 percent) than families headed by a male (8 percent). Why? At least part of the answer is skills and education: white males have higher levels of education than do African American or Hispanic males or females of all ethnic groups.

A significant percentage of those in poverty have less than eight years of education. Fully 25 percent of the people with less than eight years of education fall below the poverty level of income. Only 4 percent of those with one or more years of college fall below the poverty cutoff. Lack of education prevents people from securing well-paying jobs. Without the human capital obtained from education or training programs, finding a job that is stable and will not disappear during a recession is very difficult. Even someone who has the desire to work but has no exceptional abilities and has not acquired the skills necessary for a well-paying job is unlikely to escape poverty completely. Minorities, women, the young, and the disabled have disproportionately less education than the rest of the population, and as a result have a higher likelihood of falling into poverty.

RECAP

1. Many people experience poverty only temporarily. Nearly 45 percent of the spells of poverty last less than a year. However, nearly 50 percent of those in poverty remain there for at least 10 years.

2. The health of the economy is a primary determinant of the incidence of poverty.

3. The incidence of poverty is much higher among African Americans and Hispanics than it is among whites, and higher among females than males.

3. Government Antipoverty Policies ___

The poor, the homeless, those in poverty, and even wide differences in income among the population are of concern to economists, policymakers, and the general public. Why are economists and others concerned with income inequality and poverty? One reason might be normative. People might have compassion for those who have less than they do, or people might not like to see the squalid living conditions endured by some in poverty. In other words, the existence of poverty may mean lower levels of utility for members of society who are not poor. If increases in poverty mean decreases in utility, then people will want less poverty. They will be willing and able to purchase less poverty by allocating portions of their income or their time to alleviating the problem.

Another reason for concern about income inequality and poverty might be positive—not dependent on value judgments. Perhaps the inequality is a result of inefficiency, and correction of the situation that creates the inefficiency will improve the functioning of the economy. For instance, if education provides benefits for society that are not taken into account in individual decisions to acquire education, then too few people will acquire education (this is the externality problem discussed in the chapter "Government and Market Failure"). People who would have acquired education if the positive benefits for society had been subsidized, but did not do so, are wasted resources. These people would have earned more income, fewer would have fallen into poverty, and the distribution of income might have been more equal. In this sense, the number of people in poverty and the existence of income inequality provide indications that allocative efficiency has failed to occur. This inefficiency could become so large that society breaks down. Several commentators argue that if incomes become too widely distributed, an upheaval could occur, such as looting and rioting, or even revolution.

If poverty is distasteful to society, then citizens, by paying taxes and through their votes, may ask the government to reduce poverty. And if poverty is inefficient, the government may become involved to try to reduce the inefficiency. Whatever the rationale, positive or normative, the fact is that the government is involved in antipoverty programs and in the attempt to reduce income inequality.

3.a. Tax Policy

If people are provided with enough income to bring them above the poverty level, the number of people in poverty will be reduced. Funds used to supplement the incomes of the poor must come from somewhere. Many societies adopt a Robin Hood approach, taxing the rich to give to the poor.

progressive tax: a tax whose rate increases as income increases

A **progressive tax** is a tax that rises as income rises—the marginal tax rate increases as income increases. If someone with an annual income of $20,000 pays $5,000 in taxes while someone else with an annual income of $40,000 pays $12,000 in taxes, the tax is progressive. The first person is paying a 25 percent rate, and the second is paying a 30 percent rate.

proportional tax: a tax whose rate does not change as the tax base changes

A **proportional tax** is a tax whose rate does not change as the tax base changes. The rate of a proportional income tax remains the same at every level of income. If the tax rate is 20 percent, then all individuals pay 20 percent, whether they earn $10,000 or $100,000.

regressive tax: a tax whose rate decreases as the tax base increases

A **regressive tax** is one whose rate decreases as the tax base increases. The social security tax is regressive; a specified rate is paid on income up to a specified level, but no social security taxes are paid on income beyond that level. In 2005, the cutoff level of income was $94,000 and the tax rate was 6.2 percent. A person

Government welfare or transfer programs are a combination of in-kind and cash. Economists often argue that transfers ought to be just cash and then people could decide how to spend their cash. In this photo, a food stamp recipient holds up her bridge card. The bridge card works like food stamps, but its value is in the form of a debit card so people who are on welfare can access cash allowances and food stamps.

earning $300,000 paid no more in social security taxes than someone earning $94,000, and therefore had a lower social security tax rate.

3.b. Transfers

Once funds are collected, how are they transferred to the poor?

The main transfer programs are social insurance, cash welfare or public assistance, in-kind transfers, and employment programs. Social security—officially known as Old-Age, Survivors, and Disability Insurance (OASDI) and listed as FICA on your paycheck stubs—is the largest social insurance program. It helps a family replace income that is lost when a worker retires, becomes severely disabled, or dies. Coverage is nearly universal, so the total amount of money involved is immense—more than $200 billion annually. Two-thirds of the aged rely on social security for more than half of their income.

Unemployment insurance provides temporary benefits to regularly employed people who become temporarily unemployed. Funded by a national tax on payrolls levied on firms with eight or more workers, the system is run by state governments. Benefits normally amount to about 50 percent of a worker's usual wage.

Supplemental Security Income (SSI) ranks first among cash welfare programs. Most of the SSI population is blind or otherwise disabled (65 percent), and the rest are over age 65. Unlike social security recipients, who are *entitled* to receive benefits because they are a certain age or otherwise qualify, recipients of SSI must meet certain disability requirements or be of a certain age and must have incomes below about $4,500 per year.

About 60 percent of all poor households receive in-kind transfers. The largest of these programs is Medicaid (for a discussion of Medicaid and the medical-care industry, see the chapter "Aging, Social Security, and Health Care"). Medicaid provides federal funds to states to help them cover the costs of long-term medical and nursing-home care. Second in magnitude is the food stamp program, which gives households coupons that are redeemable at grocery stores. The amounts vary with

income and household size. Other programs include jobs and training directed toward disadvantaged workers and the Head Start program, an education program available to poor children. Total government outlays for social service (welfare) programs run more than $700 billion annually.

3.c. The Effectiveness of Welfare Programs

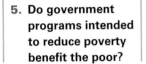

5. Do government programs intended to reduce poverty benefit the poor?

In 1964, President Lyndon Johnson declared "unconditional war on poverty." In 1967, total transfers were about $10 billion. Now they are more than $250 billion. Is the war being won? Unfortunately, there is no easy or straightforward answer to that question. In fact, there is disagreement about whether antipoverty programs have reduced or increased poverty. Some people maintain that without these programs, income inequality and poverty would have been much more severe. Others argue that welfare has been a drag on the economy and may have made poverty and inequality worse than they otherwise would have been. It is impossible to compare what did happen with what would have happened in the absence of the government's programs. All economists can do is look at the incentives created by the programs and observe what actually occurred.

3.c.1. Incentives and Government Income Transfer Programs

Taxes are one method of collecting revenues with which antipoverty or welfare programs can be paid for. Taxes affect those who pay the taxes; they may lead to less labor being supplied. As we discussed in the chapter "The Labor Market," the supply of labor comes from the decisions that individuals make regarding the number of hours of work they are willing and able to perform at each wage. The individual trades off labor and leisure, essentially buying leisure time—giving up the income gained by working. Thus, when the cost of leisure to an individual is decreased, individuals will buy more leisure; that is, they will work less. A tax increases the cost of working or, conversely, decreases the cost of leisure. It should be expected that people will choose the now less expensive leisure time over the now more costly work time when taxes increase. This will affect the cost of labor to firms. In Figure 5, suppose the equilibrium in the labor market prior to a tax on labor is Q_2. Now, suppose a tax of rate t is imposed on each hour of time worked (each dollar of income). As a result of the tax, the worker decides to supply less labor at every wage rate, shown as an inward shift of supply, to $S + t$. The number of hours worked declines to Q_1. The tax has led to fewer hours worked and thus less income earned.

When funds are distributed to the unemployed or to those who are employed at low-paying jobs, it affects the incentives of these individuals to work. When a low-income individual receives a transfer payment, that individual has less of an incentive to forgo leisure time for work time. This raises the question about whether welfare leads to a permanent dependency on welfare and an unwillingness to work.

3.c.2. Disincentives Created by the Welfare System

Those who argue that welfare programs are a drag on the economy and may make poverty and income inequality worse typically focus on the disincentives created by the transfers. Incentives to work hard and increase productivity may be reduced for both the rich and the poor by programs that take from the rich and give to the poor. Those who are paying taxes may ask themselves, "Why should I work an extra hour every day if all the extra income does is pay additional taxes?" Someone who gets to keep only 60 cents of the next dollar earned has less incentive to earn that dollar than someone who gets to keep it all.

In addition, those who receive benefits may lose the incentive to change their status. Why should someone take a job paying $6,000 per year when he or she can remain unemployed and receive $8,000? Someone who is out of work might wonder,

FIGURE 5 Taxes and Jobs

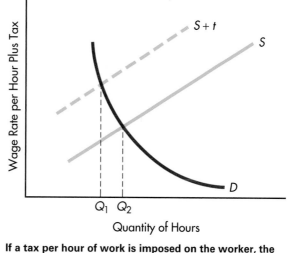

If a tax per hour of work is imposed on the worker, the individual will choose to supply less labor at each wage rate. The supply curve shifts in, and the number of hours worked decreases.

"Why should I spend eight hours a day in miserable working conditions when I can relax every day and bring home nearly the same amount of income?" If incentives to work are weak, then the total income created in the economy is less than it otherwise would be. Less income and lower economic growth mean more people in poverty.

Antipoverty programs must pay special attention to the incentives they create. Everything else the same, a program causing fewer distortions is better than a program creating more distortions.

3.d. The Negative Income Tax and Family Allowance Plans

The solution to the welfare system problems most often proposed by economists is the **negative income tax (NIT)**—a tax system that transfers increasing amounts of income to households earning incomes below some specified level. The lower the income, the more that is transferred. As income rises above the specified level, a tax is applied. Economists like the NIT because, at least in theory, it attacks the distribution of income and reduces poverty without causing too many distortions in the economy.

The NIT would work like this. Suppose policymakers determine that a family of four is to be guaranteed an income of $10,000. If the family earns nothing, then it will get a transfer of $10,000. If the family earns some income, it will receive $10,000 less a tax on the earned income. If the tax rate is 50 percent, then for each dollar earned, $.50 will be taken out of the $10,000 transfer.

With a 50 percent tax rate, there would always be some incentive to work under the NIT system because each additional dollar of earnings would bring the recipient of the transfer $.50 in additional income. At some income level, the tax taken would be equal to the transfer of $10,000. This level of income is referred to as the *break-even income level.* In the case of a $10,000 guaranteed income and a 50 percent tax rate, the break-even income level is $20,000. Once a family of four earns more than $20,000, its taxes exceed the transfer of $10,000.

negative income tax (NIT): a tax system that transfers increasing amounts of income to households earning incomes below some specified level as their income declines

The break-even level of income is determined by the income floor and the tax rate:

$$\text{Break-even income level} = \frac{\textit{income floor}}{\textit{negative income tax rate}}$$

If the guaranteed income floor is $13,000 and the tax rate is 50 percent, then the break-even income level would be $26,000. If the guaranteed income floor is $13,000 but the tax rate is 33 percent, then the break-even income level would be $39,000.

For the negative income tax to eradicate poverty, the guaranteed level of income has to be equal to the poverty level, $19,874 in 2005. But if the tax rate is less than 100 percent, the break-even income level will be above the poverty level, and families who are not officially considered "poor" will also receive benefits. At a guaranteed income level of $19,874 and a 33 percent tax rate, the break-even income level is $$60,224. All families of four earning less than $60,224 would receive some income benefits.

For people who are now covered by welfare programs, the negative income tax would increase the incentive to work, and that is what proponents of the negative income tax like. However, for people who are too well off to receive welfare but who would become eligible for NIT payments, the negative income tax might create work disincentives. It would provide these families with more income, and they might choose to buy more leisure.

The possibility of disincentive effects has worried both social reformers and legislators, so in the late 1960s the government carried out a number of experiments to estimate the effect of the negative income tax on the supply of labor. Families from a number of U.S. cities were offered negative-income-tax payments in return for allowing social scientists to monitor their behavior. A matched set of families who were not given NIT payments was also observed. The idea was to compare the behavior of the families receiving NIT payments with that of the families who did not receive them. The experiments lasted about a decade and showed pretty clearly that the net effects of the negative income tax on labor supply were quite small.

Even though disincentive effects did not seem to occur to any great extent, the negative income tax has not gained political acceptability. One reason is the high break-even income level. Politicians are not very supportive of programs that may provide income transfers to a family earning significantly more than the poverty income level. Another reason is the transfer of dollars rather than in-kind benefits (food and medical care). Policymakers do not look favorably on the idea of giving a family cash that it can use as it pleases, even though it would make economic sense to do so.

While politicians focus on poverty and government expenditures on programs and support for the poor rise, the poor remain. In a market system, there will always be some people with higher incomes and others with lower incomes. So if those with low incomes are considered poor, there will always be people who are poor in a market economy. Eliminating the difference affects incentives to work, innovate, take risks, acquire education, and so on. Is there an optimal level of income inequality, and can programs be used to minimize some of the negative effects of low income without negatively affecting incentives? These are questions economists attempt to answer. One of the findings with which economists generally agree is that economic growth is a necessary component for reducing poverty. So, economists must determine what leads to economic growth. We will discuss this briefly in the next section.

RECAP

1. Government policies designed to change the distribution of income to one that is more equal involve taking from the rich and giving to the poor—a Robin Hood approach.

2. A tax may be progressive, proportional, or regressive. A progressive tax is one with a marginal tax rate that increases as income rises. A proportional tax is one that rises as income rises, but with the marginal tax rate remaining constant. A regressive tax is one whose marginal tax rate decreases as income increases.

3. Transfer mechanisms include social security, welfare, and unemployment programs.

4. The incentives created by transfer programs may make the problem of poverty worse rather than better.

5. The negative income tax is a proposal to provide transfers, but in a way that minimizes disincentives.

4. Income Distribution Among Nations

Incomes differ greatly from one nation to another as well as within nations. There are "haves" and "have nots" throughout the world—the lowest 90 percent of the population in terms of income has less than 20 percent of the total world income, shown as point *A* in Figure 6. The richest 10 percent of the world's population has more than 80 percent of total world income, the difference between *A* and *B*.

4.a. World Income Distribution

6. Why are incomes unequally distributed among nations?

There is a huge gap in income and wealth between the "haves" and "have-nots" in the world. About 80 percent of the world's population lives in what countries in North America and Europe consider to be poverty. The poorest 10 percent of Americans are better off than two-thirds of the world's population. (The Global Business Insight "Economic Development and Happiness" suggests that the feeling of well-being of a population depends on the level of per capita income but also on freedom.)

Why are some nations rich and others poor? If two countries were equal today, but one's economy was growing faster than the other's, would the two remain equal? Suppose one nation was growing at a rate of 4 percent per year and another nation was growing at a rate of 2 percent per year. How long would it take each of the two countries to double its income? Using the rule of 72, where dividing the growth rate into 72 yields the number of time periods until the item that is growing doubles, we find that an economy with a 4 percent growth rate doubles every 18 years, while one with a 2 percent growth rate doubles every 36 years. Thus, if all nations started out with the same level of income and some grew faster than others, it would not take long before the incomes of different nations were widely unequal.

The answer to why nations have different levels of income is that their economies have grown at different rates. Why have their economies grown at different rates? One reason is that economic growth depends on economic and political systems—the freer the economic and political systems, the greater is the rate of economic growth.

FIGURE 6 | World Lorenz Curve

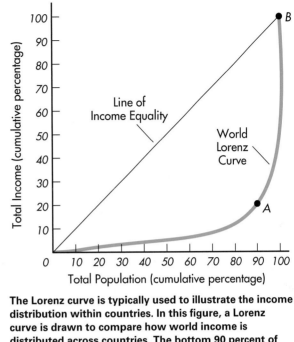

The Lorenz curve is typically used to illustrate the income distribution within countries. In this figure, a Lorenz curve is drawn to compare how world income is distributed across countries. The bottom 90 percent of the world's population, residing in the less developed countries, accounts for 20 percent of the world's income, shown as point *A*. The richest 10 percent of the population, residing in the developed countries, accounts for 80 percent of total income, shown as point *B*. *Source:* Data are from *World Development Report, 1999 and 2000.*

4.b. Foreign Aid

How should the unequal distribution among nations that exists today be dealt with? One approach is welfare—transferring income from the rich countries to the poor countries. Another is to try to increase the growth rates of the poor countries. *Foreign aid* is the name given to programs that transfer income from rich nations to poor nations. The questions about foreign aid include all the questions regarding welfare within the United States—what are the effects on incentives for recipients and for donors, and how much of the aid reaches those who are needy. But foreign aid also involves issues such as whether the aid will spur economic growth. It is possible that the aid will actually hinder growth, because it creates the wrong incentives.

Another approach to the inequality issue that creates positive incentives for economic growth lies in private property rights and title to property. Hernando de Soto, a Peruvian economist, has received a lot of publicity with his study of developing nations. He has suggested that if the institutions of private property in the poorer nations were comparable to those in the industrial nations, rapid economic growth would take place. Poor countries have to reform their political and legal systems to allow poor people to establish clear title to assets, so that they can more easily borrow money against those assets. In Mexico, for instance, the assets for which there are no legal property rights include over 11 million houses, 137 million hectares of land (338.4 million acres), and 6 million unregistered micro-, small-, and medium-

Economic Development and Happiness

A nation's standard of living influences the attitudes of the nation's population toward life in general, although it is not the only factor. Using subjective measures of happiness or satisfaction with life, researchers find that year after year, the Danes, Swiss, Irish, and Dutch feel happier and more satisfied with life than do the French, Greeks, Italians, and Germans. Whether they are German-, French-, or Italian-speaking, the Swiss rank very high on life satisfaction—much higher than their German, French, and Italian neighbors. People in the Scandinavian countries generally are both prosperous and happy. However, the link between national affluence and well-being isn't consistent. Although the developed nations all had higher per capita incomes than the Mexicans, the Mexicans had a higher satisfaction with life than the populations of many of the developed nations. The overall pattern does show that wealthier nations tend to have higher levels of life satisfaction than poorer ones, but income and wealth are not the only factors influencing happiness.

Related to wealth is the type of government under which citizens live. The most prosperous nations have enjoyed stable democratic governments, and there is a link between a history of stable democracy and national well-being. The 13 nations that have maintained democratic institutions continuously since 1920 all enjoy higher life satisfaction levels than do the 11 nations whose democracies developed after World War II.

Source: Bruno Frey and Alois Stutzer, *Happiness and Economics* (Princeton, NJ: Princeton University Press, 2002).

---

sized businesses. About 78 percent of the population of Mexico is involved in that side of the economy. These assets are worth about $315 billion, which is equivalent to 31 times all foreign direct investment in Mexico for all time. No one has title to this property. Thus no one can get a loan using the property as collateral, and no one has the right to sell the property.

Even when legal title is established, it is often difficult to use that title because of the failure of countries to enforce people's ownership of property. In poor nations, the legal system exists for a privileged elite, but it is cumbersome and costly for most of the population. For example, creating a mortgage in Mexico takes a buyer 24 months, working eight hours a day. Foreclosing on a mortgage takes 43 months. Selling a house, if you're among the 78 percent of Mexicans that are poor and you want to do it legally, takes 24 months working eight hours a day. Obtaining legal access for a business—that is to say, setting up a limited liability corporation, or whatever other form allows you to have shareholders—takes 17 months working eight hours a day and 126 contacts with government.

The creation and enforcement of private property rights is a necessary prelude to the functioning of markets, and an economy without markets does not grow very rapidly. Markets do not work when there are no private property rights or when private property rights are not widely available and enforced. As we'll discover in the next chapter, other approaches to enhancing economic growth have been tried. But these policies as a whole have not worked. Poor nations that have not established private property rights remain poor.

1. Income is not distributed equally within individual nations, and different nations do not have the same income.
2. The poor nations are poor at least partly because of their lack of provision and enforcement of private property rights.
3. One approach used to improve the conditions of people in poor nations is foreign aid—a transfer of income from rich nations to poor nations.
4. The incentives created by foreign aid are analogous to the incentives created by welfare systems and so might not be conducive to economic growth.
5. An approach to stimulate economic growth is to provide the population of a country, particularly its poor, with the legal means to establish and maintain private property.

Summary

1. Are incomes distributed equally in the United States?

- The Lorenz curve illustrates the degree of income inequality. *§1.a*
- If the Lorenz curve corresponds with the line of income equality, then incomes are distributed equally. If the Lorenz curve bows down below the line of income equality, then income is distributed in such a way that more people earn low incomes than earn high incomes. *§1.a*
- The Gini coefficient is a measure of the area between the Lorenz curve and the line of equality. The higher the Gini coefficient, the greater is income inequality. *§1.a*

2. How is poverty measured, and does poverty exist in the United States?

- The poverty threshold is a measure of how well basic human needs are being met. *§1.b*
- The income counted in the calculation of poverty statistics is resource earnings and cash transfers. *§1.b.1*

3. Who are the poor?

- Many people fall below the poverty line for a short time only. However, a significant core of people remain in poverty for at least 10 years. *§2.a*
- The incidence of poverty decreases as the economy grows and increases as the economy falls into recession. *§2.a.1*

4. What are the determinants of poverty?

- A lack of education and thus a lack of a full-time or well-paying job are the primary determinants of poverty. *§2.a.1*

5. Do government programs intended to reduce poverty benefit the poor?

- Tax policies that are progressive can reduce the incentives to acquire more income. *§3.c.1, §3.c.2*
- Government programs can reduce individuals' incentives to climb out of poverty. *§3.c.2*
- Subsidies could offset incentives to work or produce. *§3.c.2*

6. Why are incomes unequally distributed among nations?

- As a rule, incomes are distributed more unequally in developing countries than in developed countries. *§4*
- A fundamental reason that standards of living differ among nations is the different growth rates that the economies of these nations have experienced over time. *§4.a*
- Free markets and political freedom lead to economic growth. *§4.a*
- The creation and enforcement of private property rights is a necessity if a nation's economy is to grow. *§4.b*

Key Terms

Lorenz curve *§1.a*	in-kind transfers *§1.b.1*	regressive tax *§3.a*
Gini coefficient *§1.a*	progressive tax *§3.a*	negative income tax (NIT) *§3.d*
cash transfers *§1.b.1*	proportional tax *§3.a*	

Exercises

1. What is a Lorenz curve? What would the curve look like if income were equally distributed? Could the curve ever bow upward above the line of income equality?

2. Why does the health of the economy affect the number of people living in poverty?

3. What would it mean if the poverty income level of the United States were applied to Mexico?

4. What positive arguments can be made for reducing income inequality? What normative arguments are made for reducing income inequality?

5. If one country is growing at a rate of 3 percent per year and another at a rate of 8 percent per year, how long will it take for each to double? What factors might account for the rate at which nations' standards of living grow?

6. Are people who are poor today in the United States likely to be poor for the rest of their lives? Under what conditions is generational poverty likely to exist?

7. Use the following information to plot a Lorenz curve.

Percent of Population	Percent of Income
20	5
40	15
60	35
80	65
100	100

8. If the incidence of poverty decreases during periods when the economy is growing and increases during periods when the economy is in recession, what government policies might be used to reduce poverty most effectively?

9. If the arguments for reducing income inequality and poverty are normative, why rely on the government to reduce the inequality? Why doesn't the private market resolve the problem?

10. How could transfer programs (welfare programs) actually increase the number of people in poverty?

11. What is the difference between in-kind and cash transfers? Which might increase the utility of the recipients the most? Why is there political resistance to the negative income tax?

12. The Gini coefficient for a nation indicates the degree of income inequality within that nation; the Gini coefficient among nations indicates the degree of income inequality among nations. Would you ever expect to have (a) a case in which the Gini coefficient for a nation is smaller than the average of the Gini coefficients for all nations; (b) a case in which the Gini coefficient for income distribution among nations is larger than the average of all nations' Gini coefficients; (c) a case in which the Gini coefficient is zero?

13. Consider the following three solutions offered to get rid of homelessness and discuss whether any of them would solve the problem. First, provide permanent housing for all who are homeless. Second, provide free hospital care for the one-third of the homeless who are mentally ill. Third, provide subsidies for the homeless to purchase homes.

14. What is the relationship between the Gini coefficient and the Lorenz curve? Illustrate your answer using exercise 7.

15. Why would Hernando de Soto's suggestions, if implemented, stimulate economic growth?

ACE

Take the ACE Practice Test for this chapter to review the important concepts and get immediate feedback with answers.

college.hmco.com/economics/students/

Zimbabwe: Income Distribution and Policy

Africa News
May 7, 2003

With the exception of Zimbabwe, which continues to face a sustained decline in output, global output has been rising, save for the temporary recession-propelled setback that started in 2000 and was worsened by the terrorist attacks on the United States on September 11, 2001.

However, accompanied by the increase in global output, there has been an increase in income disparities in both developed and developing countries. Resultantly, one of the most pressing issues facing policy makers today is how to respond to this trend. . . .

Much of the debate about income distribution has centered on wage earnings. For instance, in Zimbabwe an Earnings Survey done by PriceWaterhouseCoopers for the period 1995 and 2000 shows serious disparities between unskilled, skilled and managerial employees.

As a result, the ZCTU has used this analysis as its basis for wage negotiations. At a policy level, the government should look beyond wages if it wants to address the general problem of income inequalities in Zimbabwe.

The distribution of wealth (and, by implication, capital income) is more concentrated than labour income. For instance, in Africa and Latin America, unequal ownership of land has been identified as an important factor in the overall distribution of income. In fact, in recent years, there has been a shift from labour to capital income in many countries.

In transition economies, this shift has been due primarily to the privatisation of state-owned assets, and the government's act of warehousing some of the shares through a trust fund on behalf of the low-income groups is a welcome income redistribution gesture.

Furthermore, pension funds and other financial institutions receive a sizeable portion of capital income, and the share of capital income in total household income typically changes over the life cycle of the individuals in the household.

But is income inequality bad? The following are some of the reasons for addressing income inequalities.

Some societies view equity as a worthy goal because of its moral implications and its link with fairness and social justice. Policies that promote equity can help, directly and indirectly, to reduce poverty.

Another issue is the increase in the awareness about the discrimination suffered by certain groups on the basis of their gender, race, or ethnic origin, which has focused attention on the need to ensure that these groups have access to government services and receive fair treatment in the labour market.

Another factor is that many of today's policies will affect the welfare of future generations, which raises the issue of intergenerational equity.

Another reason why governments are concerned with equity issues is that policies that promote equity can boost social cohesion and reduce political conflict. . . .

Source: Copyright 2003 AllAfrica, Inc.

The article raises several interesting points. The first is that global output has been rising and so has income inequality. The second is that income inequality is relatively less important than wealth inequality. The third point the article makes is that the government has a responsibility for reducing inequality. What should we make of these arguments?

Income inequality does indeed seem to have increased since 1990. One outcome of a market economy is income inequality; those with the most valued resources gain the most income. During periods when economies are growing and more and more countries are embracing a market economy as opposed to a government-run economy, income inequality will widen. A growing economy with growing income inequality does not mean that the rich get richer and the poor get poorer. The poor also get richer; it is just that their income increases may be less than the increases experienced by the rich.

The article notes that wealth is more "concentrated," or more unequally distributed, than "labour income." What does this mean? Labor income is generated by someone only for long as that person works. Wealth can be created by that person, by following generations, and essentially forever, if the wealth can be passed on from generation to generation (inherited). If everyone had the same wealth but different incomes, how long would it take for wealth to be distributed unequally? Wealth is created with income that is saved; if someone's income is not sufficiently high to permit that individual to save, then it is difficult for that person to create wealth. Thus, if incomes are unequally distributed and as a result only the upper 50 percent can save, then fewer will have wealth than have income.

The article suggests that government measures to reduce inequality are necessary because equality is linked to "fairness and social justice." Whether this justification is valid is not within the purview of economics; economists argue that fairness and social justice are in the eye of the beholder, or are normative judgments. Economists attempt to focus on the positive rather than the normative. The article also notes that inequality can increase political conflict and reduce social cohesion. Evidence does not necessarily support this statement, although economists continue to examine the issue of whether "too much" inequality can exist and lead to social upheaval and reduce economic growth. Ongoing research by economists is asking whether "too much" inequality can occur even in a growing economy. They wonder if additional inequality could lead to disincentives for poor to work and perhaps even to revolutions. There are cases where social unrest occurs when inequality is large, but social unrest can also arise under totalitarian governments even when inequality is minor.

The primary point of the article is that inequality of incomes and wealth among and within countries exists and is unlikely to ever disappear. Moreover, the argument that inequality is bad is not necessarily an economic one; some inequality is necessarily the result of a booming economy. If all of a nation's citizens are better off or their standards of living are higher, does it matter whether economic inequality exists? Is someone who is poor in the United States worse or better off than the average citizen in sub-Saharan Africa?

21

World Trade Equilibrium

1. What are the prevailing patterns of trade between countries? What goods are traded?

2. What determines the goods that a nation will export?

3. How are the equilibrium price and the quantity of goods traded determined?

4. What are the sources of comparative advantage?

The United States' once-dominant position as an exporter of color television sets has since been claimed by nations like Japan and Taiwan. What caused this change? Is it because Japan specializes in the export of high-tech equipment? If countries tend to specialize in the export of particular kinds of goods, why does the United States import Heineken beer at the same time it exports Budweiser? This chapter will examine the volume of world trade and the nature of trade linkages between countries. As you saw in Chapter 2, trade occurs because of specialization in production. No single individual or country can produce everything better than anyone else can. The result is specialization of production based on comparative advantage. Remember that comparative advantage is in turn based on relative opportunity costs: A country will specialize in the production of those goods for which its opportunity costs of production are lower than the costs in other countries. Nations then trade what they produce in excess of their own

consumption to acquire other things that they want to consume. In this chapter, we will go a step further and discuss the sources of comparative advantage. We will look at why one country has a comparative advantage in, say, automobile production, while another country has a comparative advantage in wheat production.

The world equilibrium price and quantity traded are derived from individual countries' demand and supply curves. This relationship between the world trade equilibrium and individual country markets will be utilized in the chapter "International Trade Restrictions" to discuss the ways in which countries can interfere with free international trade to achieve their own economic or political goals. ▪

1. An Overview of World Trade _____

?

1. What are the prevailing patterns of trade between countries? What goods are traded?

Trade occurs because it makes people better off. International trade occurs because it makes people better off than they would be if they could consume only domestically produced products. In what sense are they better off? Goods are available at lower prices and with more variety in a world with trade than in a world in which every country consumes only what it produces. Who trades with whom, and what sorts of goods are traded? These are the questions we consider first, before investigating the underlying reasons for trade.

1.a. The Direction of Trade

Table 1 shows patterns of trade between two large groups of countries: the industrial countries and the developing countries. The industrial countries include all of western Europe, Japan, Australia, New Zealand, Canada, and the United States. The developing countries are, essentially, the rest of the world. Table 1 shows the dollar values and percentages of total trade between these groups of countries. The vertical column at the left lists the origin of exports, and the horizontal row at the top lists the destination of imports.

Trade between industrial countries accounts for the majority of international trade.

As Table 1 shows, trade between industrial countries accounts for the bulk of international trade. Trade between industrial countries is a little more than $3.8 trillion in value and amounts to 42 percent of world trade. Exports from industrial countries to developing countries represent 18 percent of total world trade. Exports from developing countries to industrial countries account for 21 percent of total

TABLE 1	The Direction of Trade (in billions of dollars and percentages of world trade)

	Destination	
Origin	Industrial Countries	Developing Countries
Industrial countries	$3,821	$1,597
	42%	18%
Developing countries	$1,926	$1,655
	21%	18%

Source: Table is created from data found in International Monetary Fund, *Direction of Trade Statistics Quarterly,* December 2005.

trade, while exports from developing countries to other developing countries currently represent only 18 percent of international trade.

Table 2 lists the major trading partners of selected countries and the percentage of total exports and imports accounted for by each country's top ten trading partners. For instance, 23 percent of U.S. exports went to Canada, and 9 percent of U.S. imports came from Japan. From a glance at the other countries listed in Table 2, it is clear that the United States is a major trading partner for many nations. This is true because of both the size of the U.S. economy and the nation's relatively high level of income. It is also apparent that Canada and Mexico are very dependent on trade with the United States: 85 percent of Canada's exports and 59 percent of its imports involve the United States, as do 88 percent of Mexico's exports and 55 percent of its imports. The dollar value of trade among the three North American nations is shown in Figure 1.

1.b. What Goods Are Traded?

The volume of trade in petroleum exceeds that of any other good.

Because countries differ in their comparative advantages, they will tend to export different goods. Countries also have different tastes and technological needs, and thus tend to differ in what they will import. Some goods are more widely traded than others, as Table 3 shows. Crude petroleum is the most heavily traded category of goods in the world, accounting for 5.70 percent of the total volume of world trade. Crude petroleum is followed by motor vehicles, transistors and valves, and telecom equipment. The top ten exported products, however, represent

---

TABLE 2   **Major Trading Partners of Selected Countries**

United States				Canada			
Exports		**Imports**		**Exports**		**Imports**	
Canada	23%	Canada	17%	U.S.	85%	U.S.	59%
Mexico	14%	China	14%	Japan	2%	China	7%
Japan	7%	Mexico	10%	U.K.	2%	Japan	4%
U.K.	4%	Japan	9%	China	2%	Mexico	4%
China	4%	Germany	5%	Mexico	1%	U.K.	3%
Germany				**Mexico**			
Exports		**Imports**		**Exports**		**Imports**	
France	10%	France	9%	U.S.	88%	U.S.	55%
U.S.	9%	Netherlands	8%	Canada	2%	Japan	7%
U.K.	8%	Italy	6%	Spain	1%	China	7%
Italy	7%	U.K.	6%	Japan	1%	Germany	3%
Netherlands	6%	U.S.	7%	Germany	1%	Canada	3%
Japan				**United Kingdom**			
Exports		**Imports**		**Exports**		**Imports**	
U.S.	22%	China	21%	U.S.	15%	Germany	13%
China	13%	U.S.	14%	Germany	11%	U.S.	9%
Korea	8%	Korea	5%	France	9%	France	7%
Hong Kong	6%	Indonesia	4%	Ireland	7%	Netherlands	7%
Singapore	3%	Australia	4%	Netherlands	6%	Belgium	5%

Source: Data for all countries from International Monetary Fund, *Direction of Trade Statistics Quarterly,* December 2005.

FIGURE 1 — Merchandise Trade Flows in North America (billions of dollars)

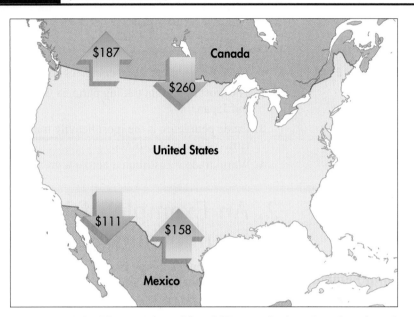

In 2004, the United States exported $187 billion worth of goods to Canada and imported $260 billion of goods from Canada. The same year, U.S. merchandise exports to Mexico were $111 billion, while merchandise imports from Mexico were $158 billion.

TABLE 3 — Top Ten Exported Products (in millions of dollars and percentages of world exports)

Product Category	Value	Percentage of World Trade
Crude petroleum	$338,929	5.70%
Motor vehicles	$302,242	5.08%
Transistors, valves, etc.	$250,430	4.21%
Telecom equipment, parts	$198,729	3.34%
Special transactions	$186,268	3.13%
Data processing equipment	$181,403	3.05%
Petroleum products, refined	$153,311	2.58%
ADP machine parts	$141,754	2.38%
Motor vehicle parts	$138,726	2.33%
Medicinal, pharmaceutical products	$119,158	2.00%

Source: Data from U.N. Conference on Trade and Development, *Handbook of International Trade and Development Statistics, 2003* (TD/STAT.24), p. 156.

only 30 percent of world trade. The remaining 70 percent is distributed among a great variety of products. The importance of petroleum and motor vehicles in international trade should not obscure the fact that international trade involves all sorts of products from all over the world.

?

2. **What determines the goods that a nation will export?**

2. An Example of International Trade Equilibrium

The international economy is very complex. Each country has a unique pattern of trade, in terms both of trading partners and of goods traded. Some countries trade a great deal, and others trade very little. We already know that countries specialize and trade according to comparative advantage, but what are the fundamental determinants of international trade that explain the pattern of comparative advantage?

The answer to this question will in turn provide a better understanding of some basic questions about how international trade functions: What goods will be traded? How much will be traded? What prices will prevail for traded goods?

2.a. Comparative Advantage

Comparative advantage is found by comparing the relative costs of production in each country. We measure the cost of producing a particular good in two countries

Comparative advantage is based on what a country can do relatively better than other countries. This photo shows a man in New Zealand carrying a sheep to be sheared for its wool. New Zealand has a comparative advantage in sheep raising and wool production.

TABLE 4	An Example of Comparative Advantage

	Output per Worker per Day in Either Wheat or Cloth	
	U.S.	India
Wheat	8	4
Cloth	4	3

in terms of opportunity costs—what other goods must be given up in order to produce more of the good in question.

Table 4 presents a hypothetical example of two countries, the United States and India, that both produce two goods, wheat and cloth. The table lists the amounts of each good that can be produced by each worker. This example assumes that labor productivity differences alone determine comparative advantage. In the United States, a worker can produce either 8 units of wheat or 4 units of cloth. In India, a worker can produce 4 units of wheat or 3 units of cloth.

absolute advantage: an advantage derived from one country having a lower absolute input cost of producing a particular good than another country

The United States has an **absolute advantage**—greater productivity—in producing both wheat and cloth. Absolute advantage is determined by comparing the absolute productivity of workers producing each good in different countries. Since one worker can produce more of either good in the United States than in India, the United States is the more efficient producer of both goods.

It might seem that since the United States is the more efficient producer of both goods, there would be no need for it to trade with India. But absolute advantage is not the critical consideration. What matters in determining the benefits of international trade is comparative advantage, as originally discussed in Chapter 2. To find the **comparative advantage**—the lower opportunity cost—we must compare the opportunity cost of producing each good in each country.

comparative advantage: an advantage derived from comparing the opportunity costs of production in two countries

The opportunity cost of producing wheat is what must be given up in cloth using the same resources, like one worker per day. Look again at Table 4 to see the production of wheat and cloth in the two countries. Since one U.S. worker can produce 8 units of wheat or 4 units of cloth, if we take a worker from cloth production and move him to wheat production, we gain 8 units of wheat and lose 4 units of cloth.

The opportunity cost of producing wheat equals $\frac{4}{8}$, or $\frac{1}{2}$, unit of cloth:

$$\frac{\text{Output of cloth given up}}{\text{Output of wheat gained}} = \begin{array}{l}\text{opportunity cost of producing 1 unit of wheat} \\ \text{(in terms of cloth given up)}\end{array}$$
$$4/8 = 1/2$$

Applying the same thinking to India, we find that one worker can produce 4 units of wheat or 3 units of cloth. The opportunity cost of producing 1 unit of wheat in India is $\frac{3}{4}$ unit of cloth.

A comparison of the domestic opportunity costs in each country will reveal which one has the comparative advantage in producing each good. The U.S. opportunity cost of producing 1 unit of wheat is $\frac{1}{2}$ unit of cloth; the Indian opportunity cost is $\frac{3}{4}$ unit of cloth. Because the United States has a lower domestic opportunity cost, it has the comparative advantage in wheat production and will export wheat. Since wheat production costs are lower in the United States, India is better off trading for wheat rather than trying to produce it domestically.

The comparative advantage in cloth is found the same way. Taking a worker in the United States from wheat production and putting her in cloth production, we gain 4 units of cloth but lose 8 units of wheat per day. So the opportunity cost is

$$\frac{\text{Output of wheat given up}}{\text{Output of cloth gained}} = \begin{array}{l}\text{opportunity cost of producing 1 unit of cloth}\\\text{(in terms of wheat given up)}\end{array}$$
$$8/4 = 2$$

In India, moving a worker from wheat to cloth production means that we gain 3 units of cloth but lose 4 units of wheat, so the opportunity cost is ⅔, or 1⅓ units of wheat for 1 unit of cloth. Comparing the U.S. opportunity cost of 2 units of wheat with the Indian opportunity cost of 1⅓ units, we see that India has the comparative advantage in cloth production and will therefore export cloth. In this case, the United States is better off trading for cloth rather than producing it, since India's costs of production are lower.

In international trade, as in other areas of economic decision making, it is opportunity cost that matters—and opportunity costs are reflected in comparative advantage. Absolute advantage is irrelevant, because knowing the absolute number of labor hours required to produce a good does not tell us if we can benefit from trade.

We benefit from trade if we are able to obtain a good from a foreign country by giving up less than we would have to give up to obtain the good at home. Because only opportunity cost can allow us to make such comparisons, international trade proceeds on the basis of comparative advantage.

Countries export goods in which they have a comparative advantage.

2.b. Terms of Trade

On the basis of comparative advantage, India will specialize in cloth production, and the United States will specialize in wheat production. The two countries will then trade with each other to satisfy the domestic demand for both goods. International trade permits greater consumption than would be possible from domestic production alone. Since countries trade when they can obtain a good more cheaply from a foreign producer than they can obtain it at home, international trade allows all traders to consume more. This is evident when we examine the terms of trade.

terms of trade: the amount of an exported good that must be given up to obtain an imported good

The **terms of trade** are the amount of an exported good that must be given up to obtain one unit of an imported good. The Global Business Insight "The Dutch Disease" provides a popular example of a dramatic shift in the terms of trade. As you saw earlier, comparative advantage dictates that the United States will specialize in wheat production and export wheat to India in exchange for Indian cloth. But the amount of wheat that the United States will exchange for a unit of cloth is limited by the domestic tradeoffs. If a unit of cloth can be obtained domestically for 2 units of wheat, the United States will be willing to trade with India only if the terms of trade are less than 2 units of wheat for a unit of cloth. India, in turn, will be willing to trade its cloth for U.S. wheat only if it can receive a better price than its domestic opportunity costs. Since a unit of cloth in India costs 1⅓ units of wheat, India will gain from trade if it can obtain more than 1⅓ units of wheat for its cloth.

The limits of the terms of trade are determined by the opportunity costs in each country:

1 unit of cloth for more than 1⅓ but less than 2 units of wheat

Within this range, the actual terms of trade will be decided by the bargaining power of the two countries. The closer the United States can come to giving up only 1⅓ units of wheat for cloth, the better the terms of trade for the United States. The closer India can come to receiving 2 units of wheat for its cloth, the better the terms of trade for India.

The Dutch Disease

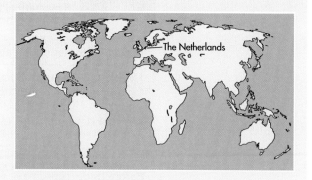

The Netherlands

The terms of trade are the amount of an export that must be given up to obtain a certain quantity of an import. The price of an import will be equal to its price in the foreign country of origin multiplied by the exchange rate (the domestic-currency price of foreign currency). As the exchange rate changes, the terms of trade will change. This can have important consequences for international trade.

A problem can arise when one export industry in an economy is booming relative to others. In the 1970s, for instance, the Netherlands experienced a boom in its natural gas industry. The dramatic energy price increases of the 1970s resulted in large Dutch exports of natural gas. Increased demand for exports from the Netherlands caused the Dutch currency to appreciate, making Dutch goods more expensive for foreign buyers. This situation caused the terms of trade to worsen for the Netherlands. Although the natural gas sector was booming, Dutch

manufacturers were finding it difficult to compete in the world market.

This phenomenon of a boom in one industry causing declines in the rest of the economy is popularly called the Dutch Disease. It is usually associated with dramatic increases in the demand for a primary commodity, and it can afflict any nation experiencing such a boom. For instance, a rapid rise in the demand for coffee could lead to a Dutch Disease problem for Colombia, where a coffee boom would be accompanied by a decline in other sectors of the economy.

Though each country would like to push the other as close to the limits of the terms of trade as possible, any terms within the limits set by domestic opportunity costs will be mutually beneficial. Both countries benefit because they are able to consume goods at a cost that is less than their domestic opportunity costs. To illustrate the *gains from trade,* let us assume that the actual terms of trade are 1 unit of cloth for 1½ units of wheat.

Suppose the United States has 2 workers, one of whom goes to wheat production and the other to cloth production. This would result in U.S. production of 8 units of wheat and 4 units of cloth. Without international trade, the United States can produce and consume 8 units of wheat and 4 units of cloth. If the United States, with its comparative advantage in wheat production, chooses to produce only wheat, it can use both workers in wheat production and produce 16 units. If the terms of trade are 1½ units of wheat per unit of cloth, the United States can keep 8 units of wheat and trade the other 8 for 5⅓ units of cloth (8 divided by 1½). By trading U.S. wheat for Indian cloth, the United States is able to consume more than it could without trade. With no trade and half its labor devoted to each good, the United States could consume 8 units of wheat and 4 units of cloth. After trade, the United States consumes 8 units of wheat and 5⅓ units of cloth. By devoting all its labor hours to wheat production and trading wheat for cloth, the United States gains 1⅓ units of cloth. This is the gain from trade—an increase in consumption, as summarized in Table 5.

The gain from trade is increased consumption.

2.c. Export Supply and Import Demand

The preceding example suggests that countries benefit from specialization and trade. Realistically, however, countries do not completely specialize. Typically, domestic industries satisfy part of the domestic demand for goods that are also

TABLE 5	Hypothetical Example of U.S. Gains from Specialization and Trade

Without International Trade

1 worker in wheat production: produce and consume 8 wheat
1 worker in cloth production: produce and consume 4 cloth

With Specialization and Trade

2 workers in wheat production: produce 16 wheat and consume 8; trade 8 wheat for 5 1/3 cloth
Before trade: consume 8 wheat and 4 cloth
After trade: consume 8 wheat and 5 1/3 cloth; gain 1 1/3 cloth by specialization and trade

imported. To understand how the quantity of goods traded is determined, we must construct demand and supply curves for each country and use them to create export supply and import demand curves.

The proportion of domestic demand for a good that is satisfied by domestic production and the proportion that will be satisfied by imports are determined by the domestic supply and demand curves and the international equilibrium price of a good. The international equilibrium price and quantity may be determined once we know the export supply and import demand curves for each country. These curves are derived from the domestic supply and demand in each country. Figure 2 illustrates the derivation of the export supply and import demand curves.

Figure 2(a) shows the domestic supply and demand curves for the U.S. wheat market. The domestic equilibrium price is $6, and the domestic equilibrium quantity is 200 million bushels. (The domestic no-trade equilibrium price is the price that exists prior to international trade.) A price above $6 will yield a U.S. wheat surplus. For instance, at a price of $9, the U.S. surplus will be 200 million bushels. A price below equilibrium will produce a wheat shortage: At a price of $3, the shortage will be 200 million bushels. The key point here is that the world price of a good may be quite different from the domestic no-trade equilibrium price. And once international trade occurs, the world price will prevail in the domestic economy.

If the world price of wheat is different from a country's domestic no-trade equilibrium price, the country will become an exporter or an importer. For instance, if the world price is above the domestic no-trade equilibrium price, the domestic surplus can be exported to the rest of the world. Figure 2(b) shows the U.S. **export supply curve.** This curve illustrates the U.S. domestic surplus of wheat for prices above the domestic no-trade equilibrium price of $6. At a world price of $9, the United States would supply 200 million bushels of wheat to the rest of the world. The export supply is equal to the domestic surplus. The higher the world price above the domestic no-trade equilibrium, the greater the quantity of wheat exported by the United States.

If the world price of wheat is below the domestic no-trade equilibrium price, the United States will import wheat. The **import demand curve** is the amount of the U.S. shortage at various prices below the no-trade equilibrium. In Figure 2(b), the import demand curve is a downward-sloping line, indicating that the lower the price below the domestic no-trade equilibrium of $6, the greater the quantity of wheat imported by the United States. At a price of $3, the United States will import 200 million bushels.

export supply curve:
a curve showing the relationship between the world price of a good and the amount that a country will export

import demand curve:
a curve showing the relationship between the world price of a good and the amount that a country will import

FIGURE 2   The Import Demand and Export Supply Curves

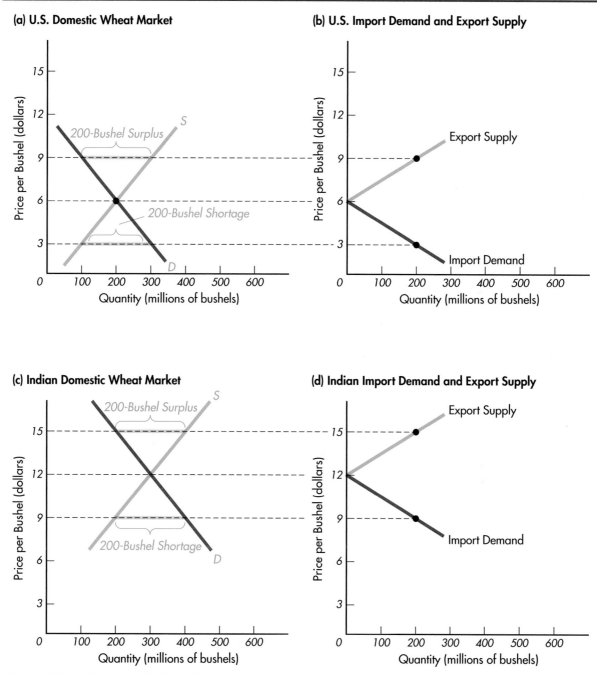

(a) U.S. Domestic Wheat Market

(b) U.S. Import Demand and Export Supply

(c) Indian Domestic Wheat Market

(d) Indian Import Demand and Export Supply

Figures 2(a) and 2(c) show the domestic demand and supply curves for wheat in the United States and India, respectively. The domestic no-trade equilibrium price is $6 in the United States and $12 in India. Any price above the domestic no-trade equilibrium prices will create domestic surpluses, which are reflected in the export supply curves in Figures 2(b) and 2(d). Any price below the domestic no-trade equilibrium prices will create domestic shortages, which are reflected in the import demand curves in Figures 2(b) and 2(d).

The domestic supply and demand curves and the export supply and import demand curves for India appear in Figures 2(c) and (d). The domestic no-trade equilibrium price in India is $12. At this price, India would neither import nor export any wheat because the domestic demand would be satisfied by the domestic supply. The export supply curve for India is shown in Figure 2(d) as an upward-sloping line that measures the amount of the domestic surplus as the price level rises above the domestic no-trade equilibrium price of $12. According to Figure 2(c), if the world price of wheat is $15, the domestic surplus in India is equal to 200 million bushels. The corresponding point on the export supply curve indicates that at a price of $15, 200 million bushels will be exported. The import demand curve for India reflects the domestic shortage at a price below the domestic no-trade equilibrium price. At $9, the domestic shortage is equal to 200 million bushels; the import demand curve indicates that at $9, 200 million bushels will be imported.

2.d. The World Equilibrium Price and Quantity Traded

The international equilibrium price of wheat and the quantity of wheat traded are found by combining the import demand and export supply curves for the United States and India, as in Figure 3. International equilibrium occurs if the quantity of imports demanded by one country is equal to the quantity of exports supplied by the other country. In Figure 3, this equilibrium occurs at the point labeled *e*. At this point, the import demand curve for India indicates that India wants to import 200 million bushels at a price of $9. The export supply curve for the United States indicates that the United States wants to export 200 million bushels at a price of $9. Only at $9 will the quantity of wheat demanded by the importing nation equal the quantity of wheat supplied by the exporting nation. So the equilibrium world price of wheat is $9 and the equilibrium quantity of wheat traded is 200 million bushels.

?

3. How are the equilibrium price and the quantity of goods traded determined?

International equilibrium occurs at the point where the quantity of imports demanded by one country is equal to the quantity of exports supplied by the other country.

FIGURE 3   **International Equilibrium Price and Quantity**

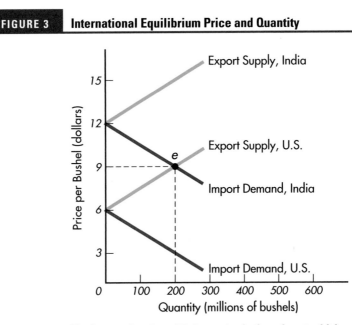

The international equilibrium price is the price at which the export supply curve of the United States intersects the import demand curve of India. At the equilibrium price of $9, the United States will export 200 million bushels to India.